WEEKENDER'S GUIDE
to the
FOUR SEASONS

ROBERT SHOSTECK'S

WEEKENDER'S GUIDE
to the
FOUR SEASONS

Foreword by WILLARD SCOTT

PELICAN PUBLISHING COMPANY
GRETNA 1991

1st printing, August 1969
2nd printing, November 1970
3rd printing, July 1971
4th printing (revised), September 1973
5th printing (revised), March 1975
6th printing (revised), June 1977
7th printing (revised), May 1978
8th printing (revised), August 1979
9th printing, November 1980
10th printing, June 1981
11th printing, November 1981
12th printing (revised), October 1982
13th printing, March 1984
14th printing, February 1986
15th printing (revised), September 1988
16th printing, June 1991

Library of Congress Cataloging-in-Publication Data

Shosteck, Robert, 1910-
    [Weekender's guide to the four seasons]
    Robert Shosteck's weekender's guide to the four
seasons / foreword
by Willard Scott ; [vineyards by David Pursglove].
    —8th ed. p.   cm.
    "Sports and recreation, scenic, historic, and cultural
places and activities within 200 miles of Washington,
Baltimore, and Richmond"
—
    Includes index.
    ISBN 0-88289-701-2
    1. Middle Atlantic States—Description and
travel—Guide-books.
    I. Title. II. Title: Weekender's guide to the four seasons.
F106.S53 1988
917.5'0443—dc19   88-17999
                        CIP

Manufactured in the United States of America

Published by Pelican Publishing Company, Inc.
1101 Monroe Street, Gretna, Louisiana 70053

TABLE OF CONTENTS

Foreword

From the desk of
WILLARD H. SCOTT

Hello Fellow Weekenders! It's your old friend Willard Scott here, and have I got a forecast for you. After hours of grueling research consulting the finest meteorological equipment in the business (the corn on my big toe), I predict 52 weeks of fun and good weather for discovering the best this area has to offer. Flip through the pages of this book and you'll see why I call for a beautiful winter, spring, summer and fall. With the *Weekender's Guide to the Four Seasons* in hand, you'll know why I love this area so much that no matter where I am on Friday, I fly home for the weekend. I learned to swim in Chesapeake Bay and to hike in the Blue Ridge Mountains. I even milked my first cow on a nearby Maryland farm. All in all, I am totally in love with this area. It's got a flavor all its own—for example, did you know that...

> ...you can get a state-subsidized massage in West Virginia?

> ...a bridge across the Catoctin Aqueduct in Maryland is rented for $1 a year?

> ...a wall at Virginia's Stratford Plantation that kept livestock off the mansion's lawn is called the Ha-Ha Wall?

> ...the North Carolina state insect is the honey bee?

> ...a popular park in Virginia Beach, built on the site of a former solid waste disposal facility, is called Mt. Trashmore?

Now that's the kind of history that I like to read! And you'll find more here: skiing, antiquing, polo, jousting, archaeology digs, rafting...

You know that ol' Willard would go just about anywhere for a festival. I plan to keep the *Weekender's Guide* in my back pocket (along with my knife and fork and industrial strength wash 'n dries) so I can keep track of all the crabfests, shoofly pie contests and bull roasts this area has to offer. In this little book you will find places to go and things to do that will help you to reap the benefits of this most beautiful and unique region we call the Mid-Atlantic and I will always call home (collect if possible).

Love,

Willard

HOW TO USE THIS BOOK

Welcome to a world of rolling green hills, long, quiet sandy beaches, country festivals and American history. This is where your hot air balloon departs for a bird's-eye tour of splendid countryside, sailing softly through blue skies. This is also where you join your organized day trip companions, pick up your cross-country skis, mount your bicycle, and find some of the best antiques in the East. If all this isn't quite what you had in mind, read on, because *Weekender's Guide to the Four Seasons* is likely to have what you want: steam engine railroads, pick-your-own-fruit-and-vegetable farms, hunting and fishing, covered bridges, battlefields, sailing, horse events, dog and flower shows, and the charms, history and crafts of out-of-the-way places from Cape May to the mountains of West Virginia and the Outer Banks of North Carolina.

Weekender's Guide to the Four Seasons is designed so that the reader can quickly locate places and pastimes of special interest. Important telephone numbers and addresses necessary for obtaining further information are at your fingertips. The material is organized into four major sections. The first, the Geographic Section, has all or parts of seven states, each a chapter of its own. Under each state there are subsections which specify particular areas, communities, or major parks. The second, the Special Interest Sections, lists sports and pastimes by alphabetical order. They vary in length and detail depending on the nature of the activity and theinformation available. The Special Interest Sections, like the geographic sections, could not of course be all inclusive. They do cover a great variety of places to go and things to do. The entries bring you a wide, representative sampling of ways to enjoy your time. This diversity of choice also describes how entries were selected for the third and fourth sections, the Calendar of Events and the Hotline Numbers. You will discover a great deal more of everything as you set out into the countryside and wander through the locales described here.

The Calendar of Events lists fairs and festivals by month and then by state. Since these festivities are usually held on different days each year, they are arranged by early, middle, and late periods of the month rather than by giving the exact date. The organizers change too, and therefore exact phone numbers and address are not given. The best source of further information is the local or state Tourist Offices or Chambers of Commerce, depending on the size of the event. You will find many of them listed in the Information Sources Index.

You will find that many areas are well worth visiting during the seasons they are not best known for. For example, try cross- country skiing on a snow-covered beach, tennis in summer at a mountain ski resort, or a community festival to shake the cabin fever of a February afternoon.

Some trips, of course, are not for everyone. If you have small children, do not like to walk long distances, or watch your budget carefully, take note of the entries which interest you and call ahead to clarify the distances, costs, facilities, and time involved.

Telephoning ahead is appropriate for anything you would like to do. Volunteers staff many of the places listed and hours and days of operation may vary to fit their schedules. Prices continually change, too, and so only the fact that there is an admission charge is indicated.

Some homes are privately held. Please do not disturb the owners if it is not indicate that visitors are welcome. Many telephone numbers are the home phones of volunteers and club members. Because you may sometimes be calling a home number, particularly for organizational activities, don't call at odd hours; on the other hand, don't give up if there is no answer during the day.

Whenever possible toll-free numbers are listed. Some non-800 numbers are metro lines which means that no area code is needed when dialed from some locations. If you get a recording asking you to dial again, try the number without the area code. (There will be no charge to you for a metro call.) Phone numbers can change as often as prices and hours of operation, so you may have to fall back on Directory Assistance despite efforts to be accurate in this book.

Inns and restaurants are not listed in this edition. There are several fine books on these subjects and not enough space in *Weekender's Guide* to do justice to the many places you will find in the mid-Atlantic region.

Maps, previously included in other editions, were deleted here in the interest of providing readers with more information on the countryside and all it has to offer. It is a good idea to take along a large state map which has all the smaller county areas. You can pick up good maps at the state Tourist Offices listed throughout the book. (They are also referenced in the Information Sources Index.)

Everyone who contributed to the *Weekender's Guide to the Four Seasons* by giving information over the phone and by mail was courteous and helpful. You will meet many kind and interesting people as you travel around and join in the activities listed here.

* * * * * * * * *

Robert Shosteck, author of the previous editions, and originator of the *Weekender's Guide*, died in 1979. He was a gentleman of tireless energy, good humor, and excellent ideas. Mr. Shosteck, a native of Maryland, has left a legacy of pleasure, history, and culture which will continue long into the future.

In this revised and updated edition, editor Susan Cole Doré has maintained the standards he set.

This book is dedicated to Ruth Shosteck

VIRGINIA

ALEXANDRIA AND SOUTH TO QUANTICO

COLONIAL ALEXANDRIA

Alexandria is one of Virginia's oldest and most historic cities. It probably has more original 18th- and early 19th-century buildings standing than any city in America, many of which are used as private residences today. Especially fascinating in the "old town" are the unique and varied doorways.

Alexandria is named after the Scottish merchant John Alexander, who owned much of the land in this city which was established by an act of the Virginia Assembly in 1749. During the American Revolution, Alexandria was the site of a major colonial port.

On the Potomac River just south of Washington, DC and often compared to Georgetown, Old Town Alexandria really has a flavor and Southern charm of its own. A former warehouse district, this waterfront area on the Virginia shore of the Potomac has been renovated during the past two decades and historic buildings and landscaping have been restored to an earlier splendor. To truly appreciate the history of Old Town, wander along the cobblestone streets of Captain's Row and Gentry Row to view the 18th- and 19th-century homes of colonial sea captains and Revolutionary War patriots.

Now the official **Visitors Center**, the **William Ramsay House** was the 1724 home of the city's first postmaster and a city founder. Here, at 221 King Street, you can make tour arrangements for groups and individuals. You can also obtain a restaurant guide and other brochures as well as free parking passes. Open daily, 9:00 a.m. to 5:00 p.m. Closed Thanksgiving, Christmas, and New Year's. Admission free. Telephone: (703) 838-4200.

The **Stabler-Leadbeater Apothecary Shop**, 105-107 S. Fairfax Street, was patronized by Washington and Lee. Early prescription books and original collections of pharmaceutical glass and equipment are exhibited. Open 10:00 a.m. to 4:30 p.m., Monday through Saturday. The shop began extensive renovation in spring 1988. Visitors should call ahead for hours of operation during the renovation. Admission free. Telephone: (703) 836-3713.

Carlyle House is located at 121 North Fairfax Street, between Cameron and King streets, and is rich in history and tradition. In 1755 it was General Braddock's headquarters before the onset of the French and Indian Wars. The house was completed in 1752 by John Carlyle, a Scotch merchant and ship owner, also one of the founders of Alexandria. Carlyle House contains many period furnishings, and an architectural room documenting the original construction of the house and the techniques used in its restoration. Open Monday through Saturday, 10:00 a.m. to 5:00 p.m.; Sunday, noon to 5:00 p.m. Admission charge. Telephone: (703) 549-2997.

Gadsby's Tavern is located at 134 North Royal Street. This famous 18th-century hostelry combines the Coffee House, built in 1770, and the larger City Hotel, added in 1792. It was named for John Gadsby, a famous English innkeeper. A frequent visitor while a young colonial officer, George Washington often took pleasure in the birthnight balls held in his honor in later years, and which today are continued each year on his birthdate. Open Tuesday through Saturday, 10:00 a.m. to 5:00 p.m.; Sunday, 1:00 to 5:00 p.m. Admission charge. Telephone: (703) 838-4242.

The **Torpedo Factory Art Center**, in a renovated building at 105 North Union Street (corner of King Street), houses a myriad of artist studios. You can watch artists working on ceramics, sculpture, jewelry, paintings, and stained glass. All of their work is for sale. The building really was a factory manufacturing torpedoes during two world wars. Open daily, 10:00 a.m. to 5:00 p.m. Closed holidays. Admission free. Telephone: (703) 838-4565.

Alexandria has numerous antique shops, import and specialty shops, and art galleries. A printed list is available from the Alexandria Tourist Council, located in the Ramsay House Visitor Center, 221 King Street, Alexandria, VA 22314. Telephone: (703) 838-4200.

Gentry's Row and Captain's Row, located in the 100-200 blocks of Prince Street, are imposing blocks of houses of important colonial Alexandrians and sea captains. Legend holds that the cobblestone street was paved by Hessian prisoners during the American Revolution. Recent research casts doubt on this story.

Atheneum, 201 Prince Street, is an important example of Greek revival architecture. It was built as a bank in 1850, and is now the gallery of the Northern Virginia Fine Arts Association. Open Tuesday through Saturday, 10:00 a.m. to 4:00 p.m.; Sunday, 1:00 to 4:00 p.m. Closed mid-July through Labor Day. Admission free.

Presbyterian Meeting House, at 321 S. Fairfax Street, was built in 1774. The first Masonic memorial service for Washington was held here. Tomb of the Unknown Soldier of the Revolution is in the churchyard. Open Monday through Saturday, 9:00 a.m. to 4:00 p.m.; Sunday, noon to 5:00 p.m. Admission free. Telephone: (703) 549-6670.

Friendship Fire Company, 107 S. Alfred Street, was organized in 1774. In a collection of early fire-fighting equipment is the little fire engine donated by George Washington in 1775. Irregular hours. Admission charge; children, free.

Boyhood Home of Robert E. Lee is located at 607 Oronoco Street. General Henry "Light-Horse Harry" Lee, of Revolutionary War fame and thrice Governor of Virginia, brought his family here in 1812. Robert E. Lee spent his early years here. The home is furnished with antiques and Lee memorabilia. Guided tours are provided. Open Monday through Saturday, 10:00 a.m. to 4:00 p.m.; Sunday, noon to 4:00 p.m. Closed Thanksgiving and December 15 through February 1, except by appointment. Admission charge.

Christ Church, at 118 N. Washington Street, has a fine Georgian interior and an original chandelier. It was built about 1773; Washington was a vestryman here, and later, Lee was a pewholder. Open Monday through Saturday, 9:00 a.m. to 5:00 p.m.; Sunday, 2:00 p.m. to 4:30 p.m. Admission free. Telephone: (703) 549-1450.

Lee-Fendall House, a Georgian mansion at 614 Oronoco Street, was Lee's boyhood home for nine years. The house was built in 1785 and occupied for many years by General and Mrs. Henry "Light-Horse Harry" Lee. It has been furnished with period pieces, many of them rare antiques. The garden is in a charming early American setting, with old brick walls, boxwood, dogwood, and a huge magnolia. Open Tuesday through Saturday, 10:00 a.m. to 4:00 p.m.; Sundays, 2:00 to 4:30 p.m. Admission charge. Telephone: (703) 548-1789.

The **Lyceum,** 201 S. Washington Street, is housed in a building which was constructed in 1839. The museum interprets Alexandria's history with special exhibitions and events. There is a museum gift shop. Open daily, 9:00 a.m. to 5:00 p.m. Closed Thanksgiving, Christmas, and New Year's. Admission free. Telephone: (703) 838-4994.

George Washington Masonic National Memorial is located on Shooter's Hill, a mile west on King Street from the city center. It is a gift of the Freemasons of the nation in honor of George Washington, who was a Mason. Visitors can see the Masonic Museum, Replica Room of the Alexandria-Washington Lodge, the Shrine and Grottoes Museum. Most impressive are 12 dioramas depicting highlights in the life of Washington. Open daily, 9:00 a.m. to 5:00 p.m. Admission free. Telephone: (703) 683-2007.

Fort Ward Museum and Historic Site is situated at 4301 West Braddock Road between King Street and Seminary Road, just east of Shirley Highway. Included within a 40-acre wooded park, Fort Ward is one of the largest of the Civil War forts constructed for the defense of Washington. Its Northwest Bastion has been accurately reconstructed. It now appears exactly as it did over 100 years ago, with guns mounted, ready to fire through the embrasures. It is by far the best restoration of its kind in the region. The Museum has a splendid display of Civil War items. Open daily, 9:00 a.m. to 5:00 p.m.; Sunday, noon to 5:00 p.m. Admission free.

MOUNT VERNON AREA

Stretching southwestward along the Potomac, the beautiful Memorial Highway is one of four magnificent parkways federally) maintained in Virginia. It leads 17 miles past National Airport and Alexandria to Mount Vernon. The area is also accessible from the Capital Beltway (I-495/95) and from Route 1.

The home of George Washington from 1754 to 1799, **Mount Vernon** is America's most famous historic house. Washington more than doubled the size of the modest house he inherited, which overlooks the Potomac River, and introduced in his home many architectural refinements popular in England at the time. The house is furnished with a combination of period and original Washington pieces. To support the mansion house, he built an extensive village-like group of flanking service buildings, or "dependencies," a dozen of which are open to the public. The gardens remain substantially as they were during Washington's lifetime. The Kitchen Garden is particularly interesting, with its herbs, vegetables, and espaliered fruit and fig trees. Open daily at 9:00 a.m., Mount Vernon closes at 5:00 p.m., from March 1 to October

31, and at 4:00 p.m., from November 1 to February 28. Admission charge. Telephone: (703) 780-2000. There is daily boat service out of Washington, DC April to September.

The **American Horticultural Society**, near Mount Vernon at 7991 E. Boulevard Drive, occupies the 18th-century manor house and the 27-acre estate of Tobias Lear, George Washington's secretary and tutor to his children. The first floor of the manor house is furnished with period furniture and decorations. Visitors may stroll through the formal rose and dahlia gardens and the large areas devoted to annuals and perennials. Gardens and first floor of the manor house are open to the public Monday through Friday, 8:30 a.m. to 5:00 p.m. Admission free. Telephone: (703) 768-5700.

The visitor is urged to visit **George Washington Grist Mill State Park**, on VA 235 three miles from Mount Vernon. The present building is a reconstruction of the mill George Washington built in 1770. He operated it for nearly 30 years, grinding bran and various kinds of flour. In 1799, Washington left the mill to his nephew. Fifty years later it fell into disuse, and was eventually destroyed. Mill open daily, Memorial Day to Labor Day, 10:00 a.m. to 6:00 p.m. The grounds, millrace, and pond are accessible year round. Admission charge. Telephone: (703) 780-3383.

George Washington presented **Woodlawn Plantation** to his ward, Eleanor Parke Custis, and his nephew, Major Lawrence Lewis, after their marriage in 1799. The gift included 2,000 acres of the Mount Vernon estate, a mill, and a distillery. Dr. William Thornton, first architect of the U.S. Capitol, designed the mansion, which was built ca. 1803-1805.

In 1965, the **Pope-Leighey House**, designed by Frank Lloyd Wright, was moved to the grounds. The Georgian mansion and the 1940 Usonian house afford an unusual architectural contrast between early 19th-century plantation life and modest suburban life of the mid-20th century. Woodlawn and the Pope-Leighey House are open daily all year, 9:30 a.m. to 4:30 p.m. Admission charge; special rates for organized groups. Adult combination ticket for both Plantation and House available. Write: Administrator, Woodlawn Plantation, Box 37, Mount Vernon, VA 22121. Telephone: (703) 557-7881.

The "Parish Church of Mount Vernon," **Pohick Church**, completed in 1774, is situated on U.S. 1, 10 miles south of Alexandria. George Washington and George Mason were both members of the vestry. Open daily, 8:00 a.m. to 4:00 p.m. Admission free.

SOUTH TO QUANTICO

Gunston Hall, built 1755-58, was the home of George Mason, author of the Virginia Declaration of Rights. The elaborate carved woodwork was executed by William Buckland. The house has been restored and authentically furnished by the National Society of Colonial Dames of America. The rustic nature trail that circles Mason's deer park contrasts interestingly with the formal 18th-century boxwood gardens. The 556-acre estate includes a restored schoolhouse and kitchen yard.

To reach Gunston Hall take Mount Vernon Memorial Highway and U.S. 1 or I-395/95 to the Lorton-Gunston Hall exit and follow signs. Open daily, 9:30 a.m. to 5:00 p.m. Closed Christmas. Admission charge. Special group rates. Telephone: (703) 550-9220.

The **U.S. Army Engineer Museum** is located at Ft. Belvoir. Follow I-395/95 south to the Belvoir-Newington exit. Exhibits tell the story of the activities of the Engineers in building canals, reservoirs and dams, and their role during times of war. Open Wednesday through Sunday, 8:00 a.m. to 4:30 p.m. Telephone: (703) 664-6104.

The **U.S. Marine Corps Aviation Museum** is at the Marine Corps Base at Quantico. Take I-95 south to Triangle/Quantico exit and follow to base entrance, where directions to museum at Brown Field are available. This museum has exhibits on Marine Corps aviation history, with many old planes on display. Visitors may also tour the base itself, including the officer candidate school, weapons training battalion, and living and dining facilities. Tours given as needed Monday through Friday, 8:00 a.m. to 4:30 p.m. Advance notice preferred. Admission free. Telephone: (703) 640-2741.

Prince William Forest Park is administered by the National Park Service. Located west of I-95 near Triangle, the park has 12,290 wooded acres. Thirty-five miles of trails and fire roads afford access to the wilder regions of the park. Parking areas along park roads provide convenient starting points for many walks. Trails are well maintained.

Pine Grove and Telegraph Road Picnic Grounds, near the main park entrance, are open all year and will accommodate about 1,000 people. Tables, fireplaces, garbage receptacles, water, comfort stations, a playfield, and shelter are provided on a first-come, first-served basis. Self-guiding nature trails begin and end at each picnic ground.

The park's wildlife includes white-tailed deer, red and gray fox, beaver, raccoon, opossum, flying squirrel, gray squirrel, skunk, and woodchuck; also, wild turkey, ruffed grouse, red-tailed hawk, and numerous species of songbirds; and many kinds of fish, reptiles, and amphibians. Only a fe0 years ago, this area was a patchwork of abandoned farms and woodlands, which have since gradually given way to a beautiful forest of 89 known species of trees and shrubs.

The watersheds of the North and South Branches of Quantico Creek lie almost entirely within the park. Erosion by this creek has exposed the ancient granite, schist, and quartzite of the Piedmont. Before 1920, pyrite, containing iron and sulfur, was mined near the confluence of the North and South Branches of Quantico Creek.

A park naturalist is on duty all year to help you enjoy and understand the park's forest and wildlife. He is available for conducted trips, advice on hike routes, illustrated talks, and other programs. In addition, he maintains self-guiding nature trails and exhibits at **Turkey Run Ridge Nature Center.**

Oak Ridge camping area has over 100 sites, with five cabin-camps, each containing a central kitchen and dining hall, warehouse, infirmary, nature lodge, administration building, and sleeping cabins—all for organized groups. Permits are not issued to groups of less than 50 campers. Campers provide own bed linen, blankets, dishes, silver, and cooking utensils. Camping is year round. For permits and information, write: Park Headquarters, Prince William Forest Park, Triangle, VA 22172. Telephone: (703) 221-7181.

NORTHERN VIRGINIA—FAIRFAX COUNTY

This area has several historic points of interest to tourists as well as a number of parks and cultural centers. Among its attractions are Reston, Great Falls Park, and historic buildings in Fairfax and Falls Church. The county also has a network of parks with many recreational facilities. The area is accessible from Washington from the Capital Beltway and by several bridges across the Potomac River.

TURKEY RUN RECREATION AREA

Located just off George Washington Memorial Parkway, this area, under National Park Service jurisdiction, has picnicking facilities and is of special interest to hikers and those interested in natural history. A well-defined trail follows the bank of the Potomac in both directions. The bottomlands are rich in plant life, and are especially attractive in the springtime. Bird students also will find this a rewarding area. Telephone: (703) 442-7557.

Approximately a mile below Turkey Run is the site of an extensive **soapstone quarry**, probably abandoned at least half a century ago. This quarry is located up a steep and narrow ravine, immediately west of Eagle Rock. An inspection reveals cut stone and rusted machinery.

The Claude Moore Colonial Farm is a separate segment of the recreational area, accessible from Beltway exit 13, two miles east on Route 193 to entrance road sign. It is made up of an 18th-century colonial cabin with outbuildings, garden, and livestock. A colonial "family" in costume works the farm, using period equipment, tools, and farming methods.

Visitors are welcome from April through December, Wednesday through Sunday, 10:00 a.m. to 4:30 p.m. Telephone: (703) 442-7557.

Ft. Marcy, a noted Civil War fort which served as part of the defenses of Washington, is located two-and-one-half miles south of the Turkey Run area. Take the George Washington Memorial Parkway to Route 123 south, then one-half mile to Ft. Marcy on the right. A path leads to the fort, one-half mile north of the county line, designated by a road sign.

GREAT FALLS PARK

This park, under management of the National Park Service, receives its name from the impressive cataracts of the Potomac, which plunge wildly over huge boulders and rocks through the mile-long Stephen Mather Gorge. Located north of Beltway exit 13, the park is one of the most important scenic, historic, and recreational areas around Washington. Central features of the park are the locks and trace of the Patowmack Canal. Across the Potomac River is Great Falls, MD and the C&O Canal National Historic Park.

The Patowmack Company was organized under the leadership of George Washington at Alexandria, VA in May 1785. In the first annual report in 1786, the President outlined plans for a route that would bypass the Great Falls by means of a canal, which included a cut blasted out of the palisades on the Virginia shore. A series of locks would enable boats to descend into the river below the cataracts.

In 1793 "Light-Horse Harry" Lee laid out a 43-acre town, named Matildaville. The town had a gristmill, market, sawmill, warehouse, forge, and a stone house for the canal superintendent. Five narrow streets were laid out from the falls to the heights above Difficult Run. Headquarters of the Company and laborers' quarters were located in the town.

The Patowmack Canal scheme was completed in 1802. It was now possible for flat-bottom boats to traverse the Potomac River from Cumberland to Georgetown and Alexandria. Valuable cargoes of flour, corn, whisky, livestock, meats, lumber, and pig iron came into the area from beyond the Alleghenies. On return trips the boats carried manufactured goods for which there was a lively market west of the mountains.

From the very outset the Company had difficulties because of devastating floods and low waters, which interfered with shipping or damaged the canal works. The Company folded and was taken over by the Chesapeake and Ohio Canal Company in 1828. Matildaville was deserted and gradually fell into ruins.

Today one can follow the route of the canal from its beginning, upstream from the falls, a distance of 3,600 feet to the point where it empties into the Potomac River well below the falls. The locks and canal walls were constructed of Seneca sandstone. These are now weathered to a dark salmon red. Some of these blocks bear low relief designs which are thought to be the individual stoneworker's mark.

From Matildaville the path continues through the woods, along the west bank of the canal, and past three locks to the outlet in the Potomac gorge. These locks permitted boats to be lowered over 70 feet into the river. The path goes past Sandy Landing and along the rim of the palisades past Cowhoof Rock promontory. The trail descends precipitously to the mouth of Difficult Run, which is calm and wide, and a rendezvous of local fishermen.

Great Falls Park also has fishing, picnicking and playground facilities, a visitors center with a small museum, and a refreshment stand. Parking charge. Telephone: (703) 759-2915.

Above Great Falls, off Route 193, **Riverbend Park** faces the Potomac River. It offers boating and fishing in the river, here over one-half mile wide and calm. There are picnic facilities and a refreshment stand. One can follow the riverside trail upstream a mile or more. This area is excellent for nature study. There is an Interpretive Center and a Nature Trail. Open 9:00 a.m. to 5:00 p.m. except Tuesdays; noon to 5:00 p.m. Sundays. December through March, open weekends only. Special provisions for the handicapped. Admission free. Telephone: (703) 759-3211.

FAIRFAX COUNTY

From colonial times, **Falls Church** has served as the crossroads between North and South, through which trekked the early pioneers, Braddock's British Army during the French and Indian Wars, and the Union Army enroute to Manassas. It was here that Ranger Mosby's Confederate raiders often harassed the Union forces. Attractions which remain are the celebrated Falls Church, a building dating from 1768, the earthworks of Fort Taylor, the Lynch House (1797), the Wren House (1770), Hollywood (1750), the Mount (1745), Mount Pleasant (1770), and several other fine old estates.

A noted town landmark is the **Falls Church Episcopal Church**, which was erected in 1769. This old church was used as a hospital during the Civil War. The interior was restored to its original Georgian style in 1969. Visitors are welcome.

Washington & Old Dominion Railroad Regional Park follows the former railway right-of-way from Shirlington to Purcellville. It provides 44 miles of hiking and biking trail.

The city of **Fairfax** is noted for its courthouse, dating from 1799. On those courthouse grounds, the scene of some of Confederate Ranger Mosby's exploits, stands a monument to the first Confederate soldier killed in the Civil War.

Bull Run Regional Park, near Centreville, is part of a 5,000-acre area known as the Bull Run—Occoquan Stream Valley, which extends 25 miles along the stream valley on the Fairfax County side of the Occoquan reservoir.

Characterized chiefly for its series of flat, tree-bordered meadows near the meandering Bull Run, it is dotted with picnic tables and shelters. The park offers overnight campsites, two nearby bathhouses with showers, washing machines and dryers, and a camp center stocking limited supplies. Other attractions are a skeet-trap shooting range, a multicircular pool, a playground, and an eight-mile history-nature trail along Bull Run. Two annual hikes are scheduled along this trail, in April and October. Telephone: (703) 631-0550.

Farther downstream southwest of Clifton on the confluence

of Bull Run and the Occoquan is the 100-acre **Bull Run Marina**. From March to mid-November boats are for rent or private ones may be launched from the small boat ramp. Fishing supplies are available from the Marina center. Fishermen need a Virginia fishing license. The park has two parking lots, comfort station, playground, and trails along the edge of the Run. Bull Run Marina may be reached from Route 29-211 or from Braddock Road. Telephone: (703) 631-0549.

Fountainhead Regional Park, off Ox Road (Route 123) on Hampton Road, continues the visitor's tour of the Bull Run-Occoquan Stream Valley. Open March through November, the park offers fishing, boat launches, rowboat rental, "Eager Beaver" cruises, primitive camping, hiking, miniature golf, and picnic facilities. A visitors center provides food, tackle, and bait. Telephone: (703) 250-9124.

Major attractions of **Dranesville District Park**, off Route 193, are its scenic views of the Potomac River and its myriad islands from the riverside trail and the unique hemlock grove, falls, and rapids along Scott's Run. The tract is primarily used as a nature study and hiking area. There are no recreational facilities available.

Vienna's **Freeman's Store and Museum**, built in 1859, was restored in 1976 as a country general store and museum by Historic Vienna, Inc. Over the years it served as a store, Civil War hospital, train depot, post office, and firehouse. Mementos of its varied history are on display, and it offers bargains on items such as penny candies, baskets, brooms, wood toys, and other goods typical of a 19th-century store. The store is on Church Street. Open Saturday, noon to 4:00 p.m.; Sunday, 1:00 to 5:00 p.m. Closed January and February. Telephone: (703) 938-5187. Admission free.

Wolftrap Farm Park, run by the National Park Service, is reached via Route 7, three miles west of I-495 to Trap Road, then left one mile to the park. At performance times there is also access from the Dulles Airport Road.

This 100-acre park includes the Filene Center amphitheatre with musical and theatrical performances throughout the summer. A Children's Theatre offers free activities daily, Monday through Friday. Conducted tours of the Center are also offered. The park has picnic facilities and a nature trail. Telephone: (703) 255-1900.

A recent addition to the many parks in northern Virginia is **Meadowlark Gardens Regional Park**, three miles west of the towers of Tysons Corner, near the Dulles Access Road, along Beulah Road and Meadowlark Road in Vienna. Contact the Northern Virginia Regional Park Authority for more information about the park. Telephone: (703) 352-5900.

Located off Capital Beltway Exit 12, **Dulles International Airport** is one of the world's finest airports. It is built to handle jet traffic, yet to give heretofore unheard-of comfort and convenience to passengers. The terminal, designed by Eero Saarinen, is a masterpiece of architecture and engineering.

Sully Plantation is an important landmark restored by the Fairfax County Park Authority. It is on Route 28 (Sully Road) four miles south of Dulles Airport. Completed in 1795, it was the home of a brother of General "Light-Horse Harry" Lee and uncle of General Robert E. Lee. Richard Bland Lee served as delegate to the Virginia General Assembly and to the First Continental Congress in Philadelphia, was a founder of Phi Beta Kappa, and is generally credited with bringing the nation's capital to the banks of the Potomac. Sully is completely furnished with antiques of the Federal period. In addition to the home, the plantation includes a warehouse, schoolhouse, wine cellar, kitchen, smokehouse, and dairy. Open daily, April through October, 10:00 a.m. to 5:00 p.m. November to April, open weekends only. Guided tours are available, the last one starting at 4:30 p.m. Admission charge. Telephone (703) 437-1794.

At the time **Reston** was built it was America's most advanced and influential "New Town." It is located on 7,400 acres of rolling Fairfax County countryside, 18 miles from Washington, DC. It is accessible via the Capital Beltway (I-495) Exit 11, west on Route 7, left on Route 606.

A multimillion dollar example of a new way to live, Reston is already an established community with townhouses, apartments, single-family homes, industry, recreational, and cultural facilities. Clustered housing is used to preserve open space for lakes, a golf course, riding trails, and other recreational uses. Walkways, separate from roadways, enable children to walk to school and housewives to go shopping without ever crossing a street. The new town's industries make it possible for people to work as well as live in the same community. **Lake Ann Center**, first of seven such neighborhoods, is located at the north end of a man-made 31-acre lake. Its Village Center contains shops, community facilities, and apartments in a striking J-shaped building separated from the lake by a brick-paved plaza and fountain. Townhouses along the lake remind foreign travelers of a European fishing village, with the 15-story apartment tower rising like a church steeple from the quay.

Reston anticipates tremendous population growth. Its prize-winning architecture, original sculpture, and beautiful use of land have attracted visitors from all over the world. For information on walking or motor tours of the town, write to Visitor Center, Reston, VA 22070. Telephone: (703) 471-7030.

Off Route 657, **Frying Pan Park** includes a 1920-era model farm and facilities for fairs and exhibitions, including livestock judging and many horse shows. Conducted interpretive tours are offered around the model working farm. Open daily, 10:00 a.m. to dark. Admission free. Telephone: (703) 437-9101.

Colvin Run Mill with its adjacent miller's house has been restored by the Fairfax County Park Authority. Off Route 743, the mill was established around 1800 by Philip Carper, who is buried in a small graveyard nearby. It was in continuous operation until the summer of 1934.

Before the turn of the century, the mill was a business and social center of the nearby community. Farmers swapped horses or gossip, or discussed crops and politics, while settling accounts or waiting for flour or meal to be ground. Some farmers paid cash, while others paid a "toll" in the form of a small percentage of the flour or meal that went to the miller.

Today one can visit the mill and learn how grain is ground, and also see the miller's house. This two-story brick house stands on the hillside, overlooking the mill. Alongside the road to the house is an ancient white oak, well over a century old, and nearby is the millrace, which carries the water from the millpond to the water wheel. Visitors can also browse in the general store, see the blacksmith shop, and view the exhibits of arts and crafts in the miller's house. Open daily except Tuesday, 10:00 a.m. to 5:00 p.m. January through mid-March, open weekends only. Admission charge.

Dranesville Tavern, a two-story, wood "drover's rest" which dates back to the 1820s, was restored by the Fairfax County Park Authority. The tavern is located on the south side of Route 7 (Leesburg Pike), 10 miles west of Tyson's Corner. It is believed that the original tavern dates back to the 1720s.

The tavern witnessed the transition of the area from remote frontier to developed farms and towns and, in stagecoach days, was a popular stop on the Old Leesburg Turnpike. It served the farmers and tradesmen who moved into the area west of Dranesville and carried on trade with the port of Georgetown and later with Washington.

The restoration recreates a mid-19th-century tavern, with furnished kitchen, dining room, and sleeping quarters. Telephone: (703) 759-2771 or 430-4222.

Lake Fairfax recreational area, eight miles off Capital Beltway Exit 10-W, offers picnicking, swimming, fishing, boating, hiking, and family camping facilities. There is also a playground and a general store where one can purchase supplies. The season is from May to late fall. Rowboats, paddleboats, and canoes are available for rental. There is a carousel excursion boat, miniature golf course, and a miniature railroad for a ride through woods and fields. Entrance charge for out-of-county cars. For reservations and folders, write to Lake Fairfax, 1400 Lake Fairfax Drive, Reston, VA 22090, or telephone: (703) 471-5415. Open 10:00 a.m. to 8:00 p.m., mid-May through Labor Day; picnicking all year.

The historic farmhouse at **Green Spring Farm Park**, built in 1764, is now the home of the Fairfax County Council of the Arts and the Horticultural Center. Here you can see displays and frequent demonstrations by local artists and craftsmen. There is a springhouse on the grounds as well as two ponds with ducks and geese. The park is on Green Spring Road, just north of Little River Turnpike (Route 236). Open Monday, Wednesday, Friday, and Sunday, noon to 4:00 p.m. Park and grounds open daily. Admission free. Telephone: (703) 941-6066.

Facilities at **Burke Lake Park** include picnicking, boating, fishing, camping, golfing, bicycling, hiking, a carousel, playground equipment, and a miniature railroad. It is 12 miles south of Capital Beltway Exit 11 (Route 123). Take a walk on Beaver Cove Nature Trail. Refreshments, boat and bike rentals, and fishing supplies are available at the park concession. Family and group camping is available on a first-come basis. For information and literature, write to the Park Manager, 7315 Ox Road, Fairfax Station, VA 22030. Admission charge for non-county residents.

Lake Accotink Park offers boating, fishing, picnicking, and playground facilities to visitors. There is a refreshment stand and boat rentals. Reach Lake Accotink by taking Exit 5 off the Beltway. Open daily, March through December, dawn to dusk. Telephone: (703) 569-3464.

The 2,000-acre **Pohick Bay Regional Park** offers boating, camping and picnicking facilities, an 18-hole golf course, as well as the state's largest swimming pool. Pohick Bay is about seven miles east of the Capital Beltway off Shirley Highway.

Further information on Virginia parks in the Greater Washington area can be obtained from: the Fairfax County Park Authority, 3701 Pender Drive, Fairfax, VA 22030. Telephone: (703) 941-5000; or the Northern Virginia Regional Park Authority, 5400 Ox Road, Fairfax Station, VA 22039. Telephone: (703) 352-5900.

PIEDMONT REGION

The area, former home to many early American statesmen and presidents, is rich in history and colonial charm. Faithful restorations and frequent historic events promise exciting opportunities to relive the past that is so much a part of Virginia's Piedmont. In the center of one tour, Charlottesville may be reached from Richmond via Route 64. Leesburg, the center of a tour closer to Washington, may be approached from Richmond via Routes 95 and 17. From Washington take Route 66 west for both tours. From the Baltimore Beltway, take Exit 7 to Washington and proceed as above.

UPPER PIEDMONT

A self-conducted circular auto tour of approximately 150 miles offers the visitor a varied view of the Virginia countryside not far from the nation's capital. The suggested tour is from Washington, DC via I-66 to Manassas Battlefield Park and on to Warrenton and the Upper Piedmont Region which lies at the base of the Blue Ridge Mountains. The return route is via "the Hunt Country" and the towns of Upperville, Middleburg, and Leesburg. Depending on the number of sites visited, this circular trip can occupy a full day or a weekend with an overnight stop.

The Manassas area, originally called Tudor Hall, was a sparsely settled region until the Orange and Alexandria Railroad was built in the early 1850s. Because of the importance of the rail junction to the South during the Civil War, two major battles, the First and Second Battles of Manassas (Bull Run), were fought on the rolling farms and woodlands six miles north of the present city. The **Manassas National Battlefield Park** commemorates these historical events.

The first important engagement of the war found

ill-prepared armies of the North and South struggling for control of this strategic railroad junction. The First Battle of Manassas was fought on July 21, 1861, between an impatient Federal army under General McDowell and a Confederate army waiting along Bull Run under generals P. G. T. Beauregard and Joseph E. Johnston. When McDowell's tired and discouraged men began to withdraw late in the afternoon, the retreat at first was orderly. The Warrenton Turnpike (now Routes 29/211) was encumbered with the carriages of congressmen and others who had driven out from Washington to watch the battle. Panic seized many of the soldiers and the retreat back to Washington became a rout. The Confederates were too disorganized to follow up their success. It was at this engagement that General Thomas J. Jackson earned his famous nickname, "Stonewall." An equestrian statue of the famous general can be viewed on the battlefield.

The Second Battle of Manassas, a year later, was fought on August 28-30, 1862. Confederate General Robert E. Lee's Army of Northern Virginia defeated General John Pope's Union Army. This victory provided the incentive for Lee's first invasion of the North.

The Park Visitor Center, near the intersection of I-66 and Route 234, contains a museum, slide program, and a sales counter where books and other literature can be purchased. A three-dimensional map presents the points of interest and the strategies of both battles. A walking tour that starts on the terrace of the visitor center covers the fighting in detail. Grounds open daily, 6:00 a.m. to dark. Visitor Center open daily in summer, 8:30 a.m. to 6:00 p.m.; rest of year, 8:30 a.m. to 5:00 p.m. Visitor Center closed December 25. Admission free. Telephone: (703) 754-7107.

Warrenton is the county seat of Fauquier (pronounced "Faw-kee-er") County, established in 1759 in honor of Lt. Gov. Francis Fauquier on what was then the frontier of English civilization in Virginia. By the time of the Revolution a settlement had grown up, and in 1790 the Court House was built on its present location, a jail was erected, and an academy named in honor of General Warren was founded. During the Civil War it was the center of the almost unbelievable exploits of the "Grey Ghost" of the Confederacy, Colonel John Mosby, and his partisan raiders. Warrenton later became notable for its large horse and cattle farms. In 1888 the Warrenton Hunt was established and in 1900 the Warrenton Horse Show, now nationally famed as the "Hunter

Show of America." The first Virginia Gold Cup Race was run in the spring of 1922; this is a timber race which annually attracts people from all over the United States.

The white-columned building with its spire and clock, known as the **Old Court House**, dominates the ancient crossroads where the town began. From its portico the visitor has one of the finest views in the area. The present building (1893) is a replica of its predecessor (1841) adapted from the original 18th-century Court House. John Marshall was first licensed to practice law on this historic spot, as were many other notable barristers including Samuel Chilton, U.S. Congressman and defender of John Brown.

A few steps behind the Court House on Main Street is the former county jail, a brick and stone building that serves as a museum with an interesting collection of Fauquier County memorabilia. The front portion of the **Old Gaol Museum** dates from 1808 and is now headquarters for the Fauquier Historical Society. The rear structure (c. 1822) is one of few perfectly preserved old jails with its original cells and exercise yard for prisoners. Other points of interest to the tourist may be found in the brochure *A Walking Tour of Warrenton, Virginia*. Write: The Fauquier Historical Society, PO Box 675, Warrenton, VA 22186. Telephone: (703) 347-5525 or 347-1273.

A drive north on Route 17 will bring visitors to Route 50 where a right turn is made to **Upperville**, a small village surrounded by many magnificent estates and horse breeding farms. A stop may be made at **Trinity Episcopal Church.** It was completed in 1960 after five years of careful study and painstaking work by local craftsmen who were assisted by artists and specialists from many parts of the world. The church contains stained-glass windows made in Europe and fine carvings. It is an example of late Norman architecture, built of sandstone quarried in Virginia. Picnic facilities and restrooms. Visitors welcome. Telephone: (703) 592-3343. The public is also invited to visit the church during the annual Stable Tour, which is held at farms in the surrounding countryside in mid-May. The Upperville Colt and Horse Show, "the oldest horseshow in America," takes place annually for a week at the beginning of June.

Eight miles east on Route 50 is **Middleburg** in Loudoun County. The unofficial capital of the "Hunt Country," Middleburg was first known as an overnight stagecoach stop, located midway between Alexandria and Winchester. Today, many visitors are attracted to this picturesque community and its many elegant events. Such activities as the Glenwood Steeplechase and carriage drive in the spring, the Loudoun Junior and Pony Show in June, and in August the Middleburg Wine Festival, combine with Middleburg's unique shops, real estate offices and fine restaurants to make it an interesting place to visit.

Aldie, established in 1810 by Charles Fenton Mercer, figured in the Civil War as the site of some of Ranger Mosby's guerilla activities. **Aldie Mill**, built in 1807 and still retaining its original millstone hoist, fireplace and pegged wooden beams, is no longer operating. Aldie attracts visitors the third weekend in October to its annual Fall Harvest Festival. During this festival you may take tours of the mill and other historic buildings and enjoy a variety of local handmade country crafts. From Aldie, continue eastward on Route 50 to the traffic light at Route 15 and turn left.

LEESBURG AREA

Oak Hill, President Monroe's, home is visible to the west from Route 15 as you drive to Leesburg, just before the Little River crossing. It is Loudoun's most prestigious landmark, and was designed and built circa 1821 under the direction of Monroe's friend, Thomas Jefferson. The home contains many items that were used by President Monroe. Lafayette, in appreciation of Monroe's hospitality in 1825, sent two lovely marble mantels. The famous "Monroe Doctrine" is said to have been written here. Oak Hill is a private residence, not open to the public.

Approximately two miles farther, on Route 15, is the entrance to **Oatlands** just beyond the bridge over Goose Creek. This is a Greek revival mansion built (1803) by George Carter, great-grandson of Robert ("King") Carter. The magnificent gardens contain several of the Oak Hill sandstone slabs which have the footprints of dinosaurs. The home, gardens, and 360 acres of beautiful countryside have been deeded to the National Trust for Historic Preservation. Oatlands hosts many special events such as Loudoun County Day, Spring Point-to-Point races, special exhibits of art and handiwork as well as concerts throughout the season. Open mid-March to late December daily, 10:00 a.m. to 5:00 p.m.; Sunday, 1:00 to 500 p.m. Admission charge. Group rates available.

Write: Administrator, Route 2, Box 352, Leesburg, VA 22075. Telephone: (703) 777-3174.

Two miles beyond Oatlands on the left side of Route 15 is a county landmark, **Mountain Gap School**, one of the oldest one-room schools in Loudoun. It was purchased from the County School Board by the late Wilbur C. Hall, who restored the building to the style of 1885. It is now owned by the National Trust for Historic Preservation and is open to the public. The tiny school sits alone on a spur of the old road between Leesburg and Oatlands, and serves as a reminder of a way of education as it was before the turn of the century.

Rokeby is located east of Route 15, on Route 650. It is a private residence, not open to the public but visible from the road. Rokeby was built about 1754 and has been extensively remodeled. It is of considerable historic significance because the Declaration of Independence, the Constitution, and other federal papers were kept here secretly in a basement vault in August 1814 when the British sacked Washington.

Originally called Georgetown in honor of King George II, **Leesburg** was chartered by the English Crown in 1757 to have 70 one-half acre lots and six streets. Shortly thereafter a bill was introduced to rename Georgetown to Leesburgh (now Leesburg), in honor of Thomas Lee. Leesburg takes you through two centuries of American history with authentic buildings of diverse architecture. The town has been designated as a Historic District by the Virginia Landmarks Commission. Its brick-lined streets abound with antique shops, specialty stores, and a wide variety of restaurants.

At the **Loudoun Museum and Information Center,** 16 West Loudoun Street, there is a wide variety of local artifacts as well as an orientation slide presentation. Next door, in the restored 18th-century log cabin, local craftsmen in period costume demonstrate such forgotten skills as pottery making, weaving, spinning, quilting, and other fine arts. On the third weekend of August, downtown Leesburg serves as the site of August Court Days. This street festival celebrates the opening of the 18th-century judicial court with a wide variety of crafts, entertainment, and displays. A free, illustrated walking tour brochure of Leesburg is available. Telephone: (703) 777-7427.

The Court House, located at the intersection of Routes 7 and 15, was built in 1894-95 on the site of an original brick structure built in 1757. The handsome old elms surrounding the courthouse were witness to many important visitors—

George Washington, James Monroe, John Q. Adams, General Lafayette, and Patrick Henry. Many interesting oil portraits hang on the courthouse walls. The clerk of the court usually will grant permission to visitors to tour the building. Open Monday through Friday, 9:00 a.m. to 5:00 p.m.

Fendall House, an office building at 109 Loudoun Street, was formerly Osburn's Tavern, built about 1795. **Laurel Brigade Inn**, 20 West Market Street, is on Route 7, one-half block off Route 15. It was built on an original lot laid out in 1758. Among famous guests at this historic inn were General Lafayette and President John Q. Adams. During the Civil War the inn served as a hospital. Today the inn is noted for its excellent Southern-style cuisine.

Morven Park, operated by the Westmoreland Davis Memorial Foundation, is located two miles north of Leesburg on Route 698. It is a Greek revival style mansion on a 1,200-acre estate with magnificent boxwoods. It was built in the 1780s by Major Thomas Swann, father of Governor Thomas Swann of Maryland, who died here in 1880. During the Civil War, Confederate troops were based at Morven Park. It was purchased in 1903 by Westmoreland Davis, who later became governor of Virginia. In addition to the magnificent mansion, extensive formal gardens and nature trails, there is a carriage museum in which over 100 horse-drawn vehicles are on display, and the Museum of Hounds and Hunting. Throughout the year many equestrian events are held on the grounds and at the International Equestrian Center. Foremost of these activities is the Fall National Hunt Steeplechase races and the Carriage Drive Competition. Open daily, Memorial Day through Labor Day, 10:00 a.m. to 5:00 p.m.; Sunday, 1:00 to 5:00 p.m.; open weekends after Labor Day until mid-October. Admission charge. Group rates available. Telephone: (703) 777-2414.

Even the most seasoned traveler will succumb to the charm of quaint old Waterford, originally settled by Quakers. To reach **Waterford** go seven miles northwest of Leesburg on Route 698 (old Waterford Road) or three miles north on Routes 7 and 9 and then right two miles on Route 662.

A Friend's Meeting was established in the settlement in 1733, and in 1775 a permanent Meeting House was built. In this building originated what George Washington called the "Loudoun Method of five-year crop rotation." In 1780 the small village received its name from Waterford, Ireland.

The Waterford Foundation is a nonprofit organization

dedicated to fostering early crafts and to restoring the 18th-century mill town to its original state. The Waterford Mill is open from 1:00 to 5:00 p.m. on Saturdays and Sundays from June through October. The Foundation also sponsors the **Waterford Homes Tour and Crafts Exhibit** for three days each October. Waterford homes are open to the public at that time. Artisans and members of craft guilds from Loudoun and adjacent areas offer their products for sale. Demonstrations of handicrafts are staged, and area artists exhibit in the three-day show.

The **American Work Horse Museum**, a nonprofit corporation, is located four miles west of Leesburg, on Route 662, at Paeonian Springs. Dedicated to the role of the work horse in the development of our nation, this museum contains thousands of articles, such as farm implements, harnesses, blacksmith equipment, and veterinary supplies. Open by appointment only. Donations accepted. Write: Dr. H. L. Buckardt, President, Route 1, Box 77, Paeonian Springs, VA 22129. Telephone: (703) 338-6290.

The suggested picturesque tour route home to Baltimore or Washington is back through Leesburg with a short visit at Ball's Bluff Cemetery and a crossing of the Potomac River at White's Ferry.

Ball's Bluff Cemetery is located two miles north of Leesburg off Route 15 Bypass on Route 837. This tiny cemetery, smallest National Cemetery in the U.S., marks the site of the fourth armed engagement of the Civil War. On October 21, 1861 four Union regiments of General Charles Stone's division, under the command of Colonel Edward D. Baker, U.S. Senator and personal friend of President Lincoln, suffered catastrophic losses at the hands of the Confederate forces. At the top of this steep bluff, Col. Baker was killed and over half his men were either killed, wounded or captured during this short engagement. Another casualty of this battle was a young lieutenant of the 20th Massachusetts, O. W. Holmes, who, upon recovering, later became U.S. Supreme Court Justice Oliver Wendell Holmes. The tragedy which occurred here was the result of what has been referred to as "a classic example on how assault troops should not cross a river." The cemetery is open for touring throughout the year and booklets describing the battle are available at the Loudoun Museum and Information Center.

White's Ferry is four miles north of Leesburg off Route 15 on Route 655. The last ferry boat still in operation on the

Potomac is named for a famous Confederate general, Jubal Early. Generals Jeb Stuart and Robert E. Lee crossed the river here with their armies during the Civil War. Beginning around 1833 at what was then known as Conrad's Ferry, passengers and freight were transported across the quarter-mile-wide Potomac River by means of poling a small boat. By 1920 a hay baler engine was used thus allowing two automobiles to cross at the same time. Today the *Gen. Jubal Early* transports up to six cars by a little diesel-powered tug and continues to make its daily crossings. Passengers find quick and easy access to and from the Maryland suburban countryside. Service is offered seven days a week, 6:00 a.m. to 11:00 p.m. (except for unusually high waters). Toll charge.

CULPEPER AND ORANGE COUNTY

Culpeper, about halfway between Washington and Charlottesville on Route 29, figured prominently in both the Revolutionary and Civil wars. Residents of this charming town were among the first to join the cause at Williamsburg in 1777. Ninety years later, it was a sad example of the many towns split by the Civil War—one moment serving the North, another the South.

The **Culpeper Cavalry Museum** at 133 West Davis has exhibits of the largest cavalry battle of the war, the Battle of Brandy Station. Open Monday through Friday, 9:00 a.m. to 4:00 p.m. Admission free. Telephone: (703) 825-8596.

The **Burgandine House**, oldest in Culpeper (ca. 1749), is on South Main Street next to the library. Open to the public by appointment only. No telephone.

The **Roaring Twenties Antique Car Museum**, south of Culpeper near Madison, offers a large collection of antique automobiles. Open by appointment only. Admission charge. Telephone: (703) 948-6290.

Orange County, northeast of Charlottesville, enjoys a national reputation for its outstanding beef and dairy cattle and horse farms. It is also well known for its handsome estates and magnificent gardens. Near Gordonsville, on Route 33 about 15 miles east of Route 29, is **Montebello**, the birthplace of Zachary Taylor. Historians believe the 12th President of the United States was born in a log building which is now a guesthouse on the estate. Montebello is not open to the public, but a roadside marker commemorates the site.

James Madison, fourth President of the United States, made his home at **Montpelier** built in 1760. Open daily, 10:00 a.m. to 4:00 p.m. Admission charge. Telephone: (703) 672-0007. It is located six miles west of Orange, one mile off Route 20.

In Orange proper, the **James Madison Museum**, 129 Caroline Street, presents exhibits on Madison's life from his early youth and education to his death, emphasizing his role in securing religious freedom and later in drafting the Constitution. Reflecting Madison's interest in agrarian reform, the museum also features exhibits tracing the development of agriculture during Madison's life, the beginnings of mechanized farming, and the advances that have taken place since his death. Open March through November, Monday through Friday, 10:00 a.m. to noon; Saturday and Sunday, 1:00 to 4:00 p.m. December through February, Monday to Friday, 10:00 a.m. to noon, 1:00 to 4:00 p.m. only. Closed Thanksgiving, Christmas and New Year's. Admission charge. Telephone: (703) 672-1776.

Six miles east of Orange on Route 20 is a stone marker and bronze tablet in **Leland Memorial Park**. It commemorates the site of a meeting between Madison and the Baptist preacher, Leland, which resulted in the religious freedom clause in the Bill of Rights.

CHARLOTTESVILLE AREA

Charlottesville is distinguished historically not only by the imprint left upon the city and the surrounding area by Thomas Jefferson, but also as the home of President James Monroe and other illustrious Americans.

One of the area's principal attractions is the **University of Virginia**. Founded and designed by Thomas Jefferson, the University of Virginia has developed Charlottesville into one of Virginia's major cultural centers. Begin your tour at the "Academical Village," which is crowned by the **Rotunda**, a white-domed building clearly visible to the right off Main Street. This structure, the last designed by Thomas Jefferson who modeled it after Rome's Pantheon, occupies the northern end of the Lawn, the original college rectangle. Tours begin here year round (except exam time and during school holidays). The Rotunda has some interesting exhibits, and guides will show you the rooms of two of the University's distinguished alumni, Edgar Allen Poe and Woodrow Wilson. Open daily, 9:00 a.m. to 5:00 p.m. Admission free. Visitors may park in Memorial Gym parking lot.

The **Lawn** is a unique feature of the campus. White-columned professors' quarters line either side, along with lodgings for undergraduates. Paralleling the lawn, and 300 feet to the rear of these buildings, are some lodgings for graduate students. The lovely gardens between these homes are enclosed with serpentine brick walls. The University's **Bayly Museum**, on Rugby Road, is open Tuesday through Sunday, 1:00 to 5:00 pm. Admission is free and guide service is available. A map of the entire campus is available in the Rotunda. Telephone: (804) 924-3592. The University is about two miles west of Charlottesville's Downtown Mall on Main Street. The **Downtown Mall** has been restored as a pedestrians-only area, complete with outdoor restaurants, boutiques, and special events.

The **Albemarle County Court House** (1803) is located on Court Square. It is open daily except Sundays and holidays. Across the street is the Albemarle Historical Society Museum in a 19th-century building. Hours vary. Telephone: (804) 296-1492. Admission free. Jefferson's will may be seen in the County Office Building. Nearby, in **Jackson Park**, is the equestrian statue of Stonewall Jackson by Charles Heck.

Monticello, the mountaintop home of President Thomas Jefferson, was designed and constructed by him beginning in 1768. In addition to many unique architectural features, the house contains a number of Jefferson's inventions and possessions. He oversaw every aspect of the furnishing of his house. Nearly all the furniture and other objects at Monticello today were owned by Jefferson or his family, reflecting a lifetime of collecting. The house is equipped with a variety of gadgets, suggested by similar devices that Jefferson had seen on his travels. Contrivances such as the seven-day calendar clock in the entrance hall, the single-acting double doors in the parlor, and the dumbwaiters and revolving serving door in the dining room indicate his love of mechanical ingenuity. If archaeology fascinates you, visit Mulberry Row, where archaeologists are painstakingly uncovering foundations of original buildings. Jefferson's grave is just below the house. The Thomas Jefferson Memorial Foundation has accurately restored the house, gardens, grounds, and central group of buildings situated on the 658-acre estate, 10 minutes from Charlottesville on Route 53. Open March to October, 8:00 a.m. to 5:00 p.m.; November to February, 9:00 a.m. to 4:30 p.m. Closed Christmas Day. Telephone: (804) 295-8181.

Ash Lawn, two miles beyond Monticello on Route 795, is the charming plantation home of President James Monroe.

His friend and neighbor, Thomas Jefferson, participated in the planning of the gardens and house, which was originally called Highlands. Its magnificent boxwood garden is among the loveliest in the state and its ancient trees are particularly outstanding. Numerous special events take place throughout the year including a summer festival, Christmas festivities, a colonial crafts weekend, and other cultural events. Admission charge. Open daily, March through October, 9:00 a.m. to 6:00 p.m.; November through February, 10:00 a.m. to 5:00 p.m. Telephone: (804) 293-9539.

Michie Tavern Museum is a handsomely furnished colonial tavern with an exhibit building offering visitors a striking picture of pre-Revolutionary War life in Virginia. Once the boyhood home of Patrick Henry, it is located en route to Monticello, one mile southeast, on Route 53. Open daily, 9:00 a.m. to 5:00 p.m. Admission charge. The tavern or "ordinary," a converted log slave house used over 200 years ago, serves a colonial buffet from 11:30 a.m. to 3:00 p.m. Closed Christmas and New Year's. Workers available to help handicapped visitors. Telephone: (804) 977-1234.

For more information about the Charlottesville area, contact: The Thomas Jefferson Visitors Bureau, PO Box 161, Route 20 South, Charlottesville, VA 22902. Telephone: (804) 977-1783 or (804) 293-6789. Open daily, November through February, 9:00 a.m. to 5:00 p.m., March through October, 9:00 a.m. to 5:30 p.m., except Christmas, Thanksgiving, and New Year's. An exhibition, "Thomas Jefferson at Monticello," is housed in the Visitors Bureau. Admission free.

Also, Charlottesville-Albemarle Chamber of Commerce, 5th Street N.E. at Market, Charlottesville, VA 22902. Telephone: (804) 295-3141.

LYNCHBURG AREA

About 50 miles southwest of Charlottesville on Route 29 is Lynchburg. Now a city of more than 70,000 people, it dates back to 1757 when John Lynch built a ferryhouse here. A town sprung up on his estate, and Lynch later built the country's first tobacco warehouse. Because Lynchburg served as a supply base for the Confederate Army, it suffered a major battle on June 18, 1864.

The **Lynchburg Museum** in the restored Old Court House at 901 Court Street has exhibits of the city's past. Open daily. Closed Thanksgiving, Christmas Eve, Christmas,

New Year's, and municipal holidays. Admission charge. Children under 12 free when accompanied by adult. Telephone: (804) 847-1459. On Cabell Street is the striking **Point of Honor**, a restored house museum built in 1815 by Dr. George Cabell, Sr., a friend of Patrick Henry. A remarkably sophisticated example of early 19th-century architecture, the house displays an unusual octagon bay facade and finely crafted interior woodwork. Open same hours as the Lynchburg Museum. Admission charge. Telephone: (804) 847-1459.

At Patrick Henry's last home (1794-99) and burial place, **Red Hill**, a restored 18th-century plantation memorializes this American patriot. The Shrine and Museum are five miles east of Brookneal off Route 600, and 35 miles southeast of Lynchburg (follow Route 501). His favorite tree, the oldest osage orange in the United States, still thrives on the grounds. Open November to March, daily, 9:00 a.m. to 4:00 p.m.; March through October, 9:00 a.m. to 5:00 p.m. Closed Thanksgiving, Christmas. Admission charge. Telephone: (804) 376-2044

East of Lynchburg about 20 miles on Virginia Route 24 is **Appomattox Court House National Historical Park**. It is a revered shrine of both armies of the Civil War. A total of 27 buildings and sites have been restored or reconstructed to resemble their appearance in 1865. On April 9 of that year, General Lee surrendered the pitiful remnants of the once mighty Confederate Army of Northern Virginia. General Ulysses S. Grant, through his generous terms, won the enduring respect of the South.

At the 1,320-acre park you may visit the reconstructed **McLean House** where the surrender papers were signed, the **County Jail**, kitchen, guesthouse, and **Clover Hill Tavern**. An interesting event at Appomattox is the living history demonstration where uniformed "soldiers" give first-hand accounts of their impressions and experiences of the final days of the Civil War. The **Court House** serves as Park Museum and headquarters. Open daily. Winter hours, 8:30 a.m. to 5:00 p.m.; summer hours, 9:00 a.m. to 5:30 p.m. Closed Washington's Birthday, Veteran's Day, Thanksgiving, Christmas, and New Year's. Admission charge. On the edge of the park is the little village of **Appomattox**, much of which has been restored. Telephone: (804) 352-8987.

Conveniently located not far from Appomattox Court House, **Holliday Lake State Park** lies deep within the **Buckingham-Appomattox State Forest**. It is a popular place for camping, hiking, swimming, boating, fishing, backpacking, and evening campfire programs. The Visitors Center has exhibits of natural history and area wildlife, along with a slide presentation. Open May 1 to August 31, daily, 6:00 a.m. to 10:00 p.m.; September 1 through December 1, from dawn to dusk. Charges for some activities such as boating and parking. Campgrounds may be reserved through Ticketron. Telephone: (804) 248-6308.

Twin Lakes State Park is located south of Farmville and Rice, about 25 miles east of Appomattox off Route 460. Six cabins overlook the large lake with its white sand beach surrounded by forest. A modern bathhouse, diving tower, parking area, hiking trails, and picnic ground with tables, ovens and shelter provide comfortable facilities for large and small groups. There are facilities for the handicapped, a restaurant, and a small store from which supplies may be purchased. Five miles away off Route 460 is **Sayler's Creek State Battlefield Park**, where half of Lee's Army was captured by General U. S. Grant in the last major battle of the Civil War. The park has interpretive programs and hiking trails. Telephone: (804) 392-3435.

Another state recreation facility is **Bear Creek Lake State Park**, which is located within **Cumberland State Forest**, off Route 60. The Park's 150 acres have facilities for camping, hiking, boating, fishing, swimming, and evening programs.

BLUE RIDGE MOUNTAINS AND SHENANDOAH VALLEY

The two major thoroughfares that traverse the area are I-81 and Skyline Drive. From Richmond, take I-64 west to Waynesboro, then north or south on Skyline Drive; or continue west on I-64 to Staunton, then north on I-81 to Winchester. From Washington take I-66 west to Front Royal or Route 50 west to Winchester and I-81. From Baltimore, I-95 to Washington and proceed as above.

The Valley of Virginia extends southwestward through the state, nestled between the Blue Ridge and the Shenandoah Mountains. It begins at Harpers Ferry, and ends at the Tennessee line, 360 miles away. Shenandoah Valley, its northern and best-known section, is 160 miles long, and 10 to 20 miles wide. This picturesque valley is flanked by wooded ridges, 3,000 to 5,000 feet in elevation. The area is devoted to farming with apple orchards predominant in the northern portion. U.S. Routes 81 and 11 run the length of the Valley. Good roads penetrate the "gaps" which make easy access at six points between Winchester and Lexington.

The tours described in this section begin at Winchester in the north, and proceed southward as far as Natural Bridge and Roanoke. Five or more trips should be planned in order to visit all of the major scenic, historic, and recreational places of interest in the valley.

WINCHESTER AREA

Winchester, at the northern end of the Shenandoah Valley, was once Shawnee Indian camping grounds, to which Pennsylvania Quakers and Germans came to settle in 1732. Thomas Lord Fairfax, proprietor of a five-million acre royal grant, employed George Washington in 1749 to survey lands in what is now Frederick County. During Washington's four years in this area he had his office in a small building at the corner of Cork and Braddock Streets. During the French and Indian War, Winchester was a center of defense against Indian raids. In 1755 Washington was a young Colonel commanding Virginia troops here with headquarters in his old survey office. This building still stands and is open to the public as a museum.

Winchester was a strategic prize of great importance during the Civil War, and the scene of Stonewall Jackson's military exploits. In Confederate hands, it was a serious threat to the National Capital and to the supply lines of federal armies trying to reach Richmond. In the hands of the Union Army, Winchester made Confederate raids and invasion of the north risky; it opened a protected avenue for Union troop movements, south through the Valley, a threat to Lee's main armies. The area was the scene of six battles during the Civil War, and the city itself changed flags 70 times during the four-year conflict.

In Winchester the visitor today will see many other relics of the area's history. Begin the tour at **Hollingsworth Mill House**, the home of the Winchester-Frederick County Visitor Center, 1360 South Pleasant Valley Road, located just off I-81 at exit 80. An 18-minute orientation film gives a historical overview of the area and describes festivals and events. After receiving your information, start your tour next door at Abram's Delight.

Abram's Delight is the oldest home in Winchester, built by Isaac Hollingsworth in 1754. His father, Abraham Hollingsworth, was an early Quaker settler who declared the spot, with its abundant springs, "a delight to behold." He built a log cabin on the property which is typical of the homes of early settlers. The stone house has been restored and furnished and is open daily, April 1 to October 31, 9:00 a.m. to 5:00 p.m. Admission charge.

After visiting Abram's Delight, turn right on Pleasant Valley Road, then left at the next traffic light onto Cork Street. Continue on Cork to the second traffic light and turn onto Cameron Street. At the first traffic light turn right onto Boscowen Street and continue straight for two blocks. Ahead is **Mount Hebron Cemetery**. The ruins to the left of the entrance are the **Old Lutheran Church**, built in 1764. Visitors to the cemetery are welcome. Inside the cemetery, near the Lutheran Church ruins, is the grave of the Revolutionary hero, General Daniel Morgan, who earned his fame as the hero of the Battles of Saratoga and Cowpens. There is also the **Stonewall Cemetery**, where more than 1,000 Confederate soldiers, 829 of whom are unknown, are buried under one large mound.

Passing again the Old Lutheran Church ruins and through the front entrance of Mount Hebron Cemetery, turn right and continue to Woodstock Lane. Proceed right on Woodstock Lane and turn left to Lincoln Street. The **National Cemetery**, established in 1866, is located to the right. Here 4,491 Union soldiers are buried, 2,396 of them unknown.

Continue for one block and turn left again to Piccadilly Street. On the right side of Piccadilly Street is **The Old Stone Presbyterian Church**. Built in 1788, the church has been restored by the First Presbyterian Church of Winchester and is open to the public. Admission free. General Daniel Morgan was a member of this church.

Proceed three blocks, turn right onto Loudoun Street, and continue for four blocks to North Avenue. At this point, turn left for one block and turn left again onto Braddock Street. Watch for a green sign indicating **Stonewall Jackson's Winter Headquarters**. The building itself is set back on the right. Jackson and his staff occupied this home from November 1861 to March 1862 prior to his valley campaign. The headquarters is a memorial to Winchester's role during the Civil War. Open daily, April 1 through October 31, 9:00 a.m. to 5:00 p.m. Admission charge.

Travel south on Braddock Street for two blocks noting the **Handley Library** on the right corner opposite the Post Office. The Library was built with funds left in the will of John Handley, an Irish-born Pennsylvania judge who took a liking to the city. Directly across from the Handley Library is the **Logan House**. Note the huge apple which signifies Virginia's importance in apple production. **General Philip H. Sheridan** used this building as his headquarters in the fall and winter of 1864-65 and from it made his famous ride to Cedar Creek on October 19, 1864, where he turned a Confederate victory into a rout. The building is now the home of the local Order of Elks and is not open to the public.

Continue south on Braddock Street and turn right onto Amherst Street for one-and-a-half blocks. At 226 Amherst Street stands an impressive stone dwelling which was once the **Home of General Daniel Morgan**. The house is now privately owned.

Turn left at the corner of Stewart Street and proceed south on Stewart Street for one block; then turn left on to Boscawen Street for one block. On the left corner directly ahead is the **Christ Episcopal Church**. In the churchyard lie the remains of **Thomas Lord Fairfax**. Visitors are welcome.

Travel one block; then turn right onto Braddock Street, and proceed two blocks south. On the left, at the corner of South Braddock and West Cork Streets, is **George Washington's Office**. George Washington spent considerable time in Winchester during the period 1748-58. He was first employed as a surveyor by Lord Fairfax and used this building as his office and later as headquarters when Virginia troops defended the frontier against the French and the Indians. The museum has an entire room devoted to the Civil War. The remainder of the building houses relics of Winchester's early days. The building is open daily, April 1 through October 31, 9:00 a.m. to 5:00 p.m. Admission charge; children under 12, free.

After touring Washington's Office, proceed east one block on Cork Street to the **Loudoun Street Mall**, Old Town Winchester. There is much to see and do in this two-block pedestrian mall which showcases colonial and 19th-century architecture. **Madigan's Movie Museum**, 16 South Loudoun Street, houses a fine collection of costumes and other movie relics. The costume collection includes those worn by Jessica Lange in *Sweet Dreams*, a movie about country singer and Winchester native Patsy Cline.

Located between Winchester and Strasburg on U.S. 11,

with exits to Interstate 81, **Middletown** is nestled in the heart of the historic Shenandoah Valley. Guests at the elegantly restored **Wayside Inn**, built in 1797, are surrounded by rare antiques as well as delicious food. Telephone: (703) 869-1797. Outdoor attractions are sailboats, ice skating, trap shooting, and fishing. Near the Inn is the **Wayside Theatre**, one of the major summer theatrical groups in Virginia. Telephone: (703) 869-1782.

Belle Grove, about a quarter of a mile south of Middletown, is a one-story structure of hewn limestone, built by Major Isaac Hite, Jr., in 1794. It served as headquarters for General Philip Sheridan during the Civil War, and many interesting historical episodes occurred there. Belle Grove has been restored by the National Trust for Historic Preservation as a working farm and American folk culture center. It is open Monday through Saturday, April through October, 10:00 a.m. to 4:00 p.m.; Sunday, 1:00 to 5:00 p.m. Admission charge. Telephone: (703) 869-2028.

FRONT ROYAL

Front Royal is 16 miles south of Winchester via Route 522. The vast Shenandoah National Park begins at the southern limits of town.

Front Royal was the home of Belle Boyd, the celebrated Confederate spy, and the **Warren Rifles Confederate Museum** is located here at 218 Lee Street. Open April 15 to November 1, 9:00 a.m. to 6:00 p.m., or by appointment the rest of the year. Telephone: (703) 636-6982.

Skyline Caverns features rainbow and brook trout in a cavern stream, a 37-foot waterfall, snow-white flowstone and unique "anthodites," flowerlike calcite formations, among other geological oddities. A coffee shop and gift shop are housed at the entrance of the attractive, rustic lodge. Picnic facilities are available, and there is a miniature railroad. Open daily, except Christmas. Admission charge to caverns; children under seven, free.

A few miles southeast of Front Royal off Route 522 is the **Smithsonian Institution's Conservation and Research Center**, a 3,200-acre annex to Washington, DC's National Zoological Park. The center is not open to the public, but all kinds of animals can frequently be seen from the road. Don't be surprised when you look out your car window and see camels and zebras grazing in the Virginia countryside.

Nestled in the mountains one-half mile north of Strasburg on Route 11 are the 250 wooded acres of **Wayside Wonderland**, where you can swim, picnic, boat, fish, and even scuba dive in the clear lake. On the grounds are **Crystal Caverns** (the first discovered in Virginia); weekend tours are available. Also here is **Fort Hupps Battlefield**, where you can visit the tomb of an unknown Confederate soldier. Outdoor concerts are given during the summer at the Wayside Amphitheatre. The entire park is open Memorial Day to Labor Day, Wednesday to Sunday, 10:00 a.m. to 8:00 p.m. Admission charge. Telephone: (703) 465-5757.

Off Route 81 in Edinburg are the **Shenandoah Vineyards**, where you can join a free winetasting or stroll through the vineyards and winery. Open daily, 10:00 a.m. to 6:00 p.m.; January through February, 10:00 a.m. to 5:00 p.m. Admission free. Telephone: (703) 984-8699.

Basye is a small community perched on the edge of the George Washington National Forest and is the home of one of the larger Virginia ski operations. **Bryce Mountain** is also famous as a summer resort on the western edge of the Shenandoah Valley, located near Orkney Springs, where the Annual Shenandoah Valley Music Festival is held in late July. It is almost due west from Washington, DC and is reached from Mt. Jackson (U.S. Route 11 or I-81) via Virginia Route 263. This mountainous area has an average of 90 inches of snowfall, which, coupled with Bryce's snow-making installation, makes it a popular winter as well as summer resort. Both bus and plane service from Washington are available in the winter season. Telephone: (703) 856-2121.

Sky Chalet mountain resort is located 10 miles west of Mt. Jackson on Route 263. It is noted for fine food and all types of outdoor activities year round. Nearby is Bryce, a short walk by a mountain trail. Telephone: (703) 856-2147.

Shenandoah Caverns are just off Interstate 81, from Exit 68, or U.S. 11, midway between Mt. Jackson and New Market. Shenandoah Caverns' distinction is its sparkling "diamond," glittering masses of flowstone shot with crystals, truly reflecting the name Shenandoah, "Daughter of the Stars." It also features a unique elevator service. Free picnic special rates for groups of 20 or more. Telephone: (703) 477-3115.

At Exit 68 on Interstate 81, you will find **Tuttle & Spice General Store and Free Village Museum**. A vast and unique collection of early Americana items are on display in 10 separate turn-of-the-century shops: toy store, drug store and soda fountain, clothing store, clock, jewelry and lamp shop, tobacco shop, doctor's office and an educational exhibit of American Indian art and artifacts. There is a large gift shop and hundreds of general store items in the main building. Open daily, April through October, 9:00 a.m. to 9:00 p.m. November through March, 9:00 a.m. to 6:00 p.m. Admission free. Telephone: (703) 477-2601.

NEW MARKET TO LURAY

New Market is located at the junction of Routes 81, 11, and 211, in the heart of the Shenandoah Valley, 15 miles west of Luray. Here, where Indian trails crossed, the town was established in 1765 by General John Sevier, who was Governor of Tennessee six times and also U.S. Senator from Tennessee.

The New Market area was the scene of Civil War battles which featured in General Stonewall Jackson's Valley Campaign. Here the young Virginia Military Institute cadets made their famous charge on May 15, 1864. The **New Market Battlefield Park** is located one mile north of the town. The well-preserved 260-acre battlefield park, with its monuments, is visited each year by thousands of students of the Civil War. Visitors can trace the path of the V.M.I. cadets and see the restored, historic Bushong House and its nine dependencies. From the battlefield there are scenic overlooks 200 feet above the Shenandoah River. Each year, on the second Sunday in May, the Battle of New Market is reenacted before crowds of observers.

The impressive **Hall of Valor**, a visitor center and museum, displays exhibits which depict the entire Civil War. In its two-story Virginia Room there are three-dimensional exhibits and a panoramic survey of all the major campaigns of the War. Two award-winning films are also shown. The park is open daily year round, except Christmas, from 9:00 a.m. to 5:00 p.m. Admission charge; group rates available. Telephone: (703) 740-3102.

The **Shenandoah Valley Travel Association Information Center** is open daily, 9:00 a.m. to 5:00 p.m., for free information and literature about tours and points of interest in the Shenandoah Valley. Closed Thanksgiving, Christmas, and New Year's. It is just off Interstate 81, Exit 67. For information write: PO Box 488-WG, New Market, VA 22844. Telephone: (703) 740-3132.

A group of unique American homes exists in Page County.

Built when this area was a part of the frontier of the American colonies, and Indian attack was constantly expected, they contain forts built within their walls. These forts were usually conical, constructed of thick stone and loop-holed, and located in the basements. They were kept supplied with food and usually contained both a fireplace and a tunnel that entered the well above the water level. Sometimes they were built over flowing springs. These fortress-homes remain occupied farm residences, and no effort is made to attract visitors although they are always welcome. If you desire to see one or more of these unusual pioneer homes, for directions write: Page County Chamber of Commerce, 6 East Main Street, Luray, VA 22835.

The **Egypt House** (1735) is the Abraham Strickler home. Located on Route 615, four miles west of Luray, it contains a basement fort and also a fortified room within the fort. **Fort Song**, the C. D. Price Farm (ca. 1733), is south of the town of Stanley on Route 616. It is separated from the house and reached through a tunnel. **Fort Stover** (1790), now a Girl Scout building, has a vaulted cellar. It is four miles north of Luray on Route 660. **Fort Paul Long** (1735) is nine miles west of Luray on Route 615. The cellar fort is built into a hillside under the house. A fort in the **Shirley Home** (ca. 1733) is eight miles west of Luray on Route 762. A well-preserved and strong basement fort may be seen. **Fort Rhodes** (1764) is four miles west of Luray on Route 615. This fort was the scene of an Indian massacre.

Four self-guided, historical, and scenic tours of the Luray area, which feature homes of the early settlers, are available to tourists. Write to the Chamber of Commerce at the above address.

Luray Caverns is one of the largest and most popular caves in the eastern United States and is a major Virginia natural wonder. Special lighting has been installed to enable visitors to photograph the interior of this cavern with any type of camera. Guided tours allow time in the itinerary for those wishing to take pictures. The Great Stalacpipe Organ permits visitors to hear the only organ in the world playing musical selections of concert quality on stone formations.

Another interesting attraction on the grounds of Luray Caverns is the **Car and Carriage Caravan**, a museum which features nearly 100 carts, carriages, and cars in the story of transportation. There is a general admission charge which includes both Caverns and Caravan; children under seven, free. Open daily.

The **Luray Singing Tower** nearby has a 47-bell carillon. Carillon recitals are given on Tuesdays, Thursdays, Saturdays, and Sundays, from mid-March to mid-November.

SHENANDOAH NATIONAL PARK

The 194,596-acre Shenandoah National Park stretches along the crest of the Blue Ridge Mountains from Front Royal south to Waynesboro, VA. It features more than 500 miles of foot trails, 40 kinds of mammals, 200 species of birds, with elevations ranging from 600 to 4,000 feet. About 95 percent of the park area is forested. Set in the heart of the Blue Ridge Mountains of Virginia, its most celebrated features are the succession of panoramas from the crest of the ridge, enabling visitors to view the checkerboard beauty of the Shenandoah Valley.

The **Skyline Drive** ribbons its way through the park for 105 miles, providing 72 overlooks along the way for views of the Piedmont to the east and the Shenandoah River Valley to the west. From Hogback Overlook on a clear day, one may count 11 bends in the river, and see panoramic views of the fertile valley areas where Indian villages once stood. A worthwhile short side trip from Thornton Gap is to Luray, nine miles west. Here one can visit the noted Luray Caverns, which are open the year round.

Shenandoah National Park is open the year round. Occasionally Skyline Drive is closed for short periods during periods of ice and snow. Some visitor facilities such as camping, picnic areas, food, lodging, and service stations are open March through December. Big Meadows campground is open all year, and lodge and cottage accommodations are available from April through October.

Dickey Ridge Visitor Center (Mile 4.6) and **Byrd Visitor Center** (Mile 51) provide general park information, exhibits, orientation films, postcards, maps, backcountry camping permits, and Eagle and Golden Access Passports. Dickey Ridge is open April through October, while Byrd is open daily March through December and on weekends in January and February.

Picnic facilities with tables, fireplaces, water, and toilets are found at Dickey Ridge (Mile 4.6), Pinnacles (Mile 36.7), Big Meadows (Mile 51.2), Lewis Mountain (Mile 57.5), South

River (Mile 62.8), and Loft Mountain (Mile 79.5). Open fires are permitted in fireplaces, but wood is not always available. Visitors are advised to bring their own fuel.

All lodging, food facilities, gift shops, and service stations in the Shenandoah National Park are operated by the ARA Virginia Skyline Company, Inc., PO Box 727, Luray, VA 22835, with whom reservations should be made by visitors desiring overnight lodge, cabin, or hotel accommodations. Telephone: (703) 743-5108 (in Washington, DC area: 293-5350). Listed below are facilities, with opening and closing dates:

Elkwallow Wayside—Counter service, gift shop, and a service station. It is located 24 miles south of North Entrance. Season: late May to late October.

Panorama Restaurant (Thornton Gap)—Coffee shop and counter service; also native craft and gift shop; service station. Located at intersection of Skyline Drive and U.S. Route 211. Open early April through early November.

Skyland Lodge—Accommodations for 450. Facilities include dining room, tap room; native crafts and gift shop; horseback riding; ranger-naturalist hikes and lectures. Located 10 miles south of Panorama. Season: March 30 to November 27.

Big Meadows Wayside & Camp Store—Facilities include grill room, gift shop, camper supplies, and service station. Located nine miles south of Skyland. Season: March 3 to late November.

Big Meadows Campground—Facilities include laundry and showers. Season: March through December. Also see *Camping.*

Big Meadows Lodge—Accommodations for 280. Facilities include dining room, tap room; native crafts and gift shop; horseback riding; ranger-naturalist hikes and lectures. Located one mile off drive from Big Meadows Wayside. Season: mid-May to late October.

Lewis Mountain—Furnished cottages for overnight guests. Outdoor facilities for cooking. Supplies available at nearby Big Meadows. Season: May to October. Also see *Camping.*

Loft Mountain, Wayside—Facilities include campers' store, grill room, gift shop, service station, laundry, showers, ice and wood sales. Located 14 miles south of Swift Run; 25 miles north of Afton. Season: April to mid-October. Also see *Camping.*

Mathews Arm Campground—New camping facility in the northern section at Mile 22.2, two miles north of Elkwallow. Facilities include sites for both tent and trailer camping. Season: May through October.

There are more than 500 miles of trails, including a 95-mile link in the famous Appalachian Trail, which stretches 2,000 miles from Maine to Georgia. Five self-guiding nature trails are available to help visitors learn about the park's natural and cultural history:

Trail Name	Starting Point
Fox Hollow	Mile 4.6
Traces	Mile 22.2
Stony Man	Mile 41.7
Story of the Forest	Mile 51
Deadening Nature	Mile 79.5

Many naturalist-led nature walks and programs are conducted on trails throughout the park. Check program schedules in the "Shenandoah Overlook," at visitor information desks, or on bulletin boards.

Camping in the back country is allowed by permit only. Permits are available at entrance stations, visitor centers, park headquarters, or trailhead self-registration stations. Campers must demonstrate knowledge of park camping regulations.

Shelters—There are seven trailside camping shelters, each sleeping between seven and 11 people, along the Appalachian Trail. These huts are operated by the Potomac Appalachian Trail Club and are intended for use by long distance Appalachian Trail hikers or campers with backcountry permits for three or more days. Campers pay $1 per night for the use of these shelters.

Six locked cabins are located in backcountry areas of the park. These cabins will accommodate as many as 12 people and are fully equipped, except for food. Reservations may be made by contacting the Potomac Appalachian Trail Club, 1718 North Street, Washington, DC 20036. Telephone: (202) 638-5306.

Big Meadows is reached by driving nine miles east from Luray on U.S. 211 to Thornton Gap; then 20 miles south on Skyline Drive to Mile 51.3. Open all year; 14 days maximum stay. There are 255 tent and trailer sites; hot showers, rest rooms with flush toilets, automatic washers and dryers, outdoor cooking facilities, tables, fireplaces, firewood (charge), drinking water, ice, trout fishing in season. Pets allowed under restraint or leash. Obtain food at grocery store or from Big Meadows Wayside.

Lewis Mountain is reached by driving seven miles east from Elkton on U.S. 33 to Swift Run Gap; then eight miles north on Skyline Drive to Mile 57.6. Season is May to October, with 14-day maximum stay. There are 32 tent or trailer sites, rest rooms, flush toilets, garbage disposal cans, outdoor cooking facilities, fireplaces, tables, firewood (charge), drinking water and ice, trout fishing in season. Pets allowed under restraint or on leash. There is also concessionaire-operated riding stables (charge), and a grocery store six miles north at Big Meadows.

There are also camp facilities at **Loft Mountain** and at **Mathews Arm Campground.**

The entrance fee to Shenandoah National Park is $5 per vehicle and $2 per hiker, bicycle, or bus passenger over 12 and under 62 years of age. This fee is good for seven consecutive days. An annual Park Pass is available for $15 per year. Entrance fee is free for holders of the Golden Eagle Passport ($25 per year), Golden Age Passport (free for those over 62), or Golden Access Passport (free if handicapped). The annual Park Pass and all Passports are available at entrance stations or at park headquarters.

For more information, contact: Superintendent, Shenandoah National Park, Route 4, Box 348, Luray, VA 22835. Telephone: (703) 999-2266 or 999-2229.

GEORGE WASHINGTON NATIONAL FOREST

The largest national forest in the eastern United States, this recreational area of more than one million acres lies to either side of the well-known Shenandoah National Park, and is within easy driving distance of the Baltimore-Washington-Richmond areas.

The forest embraces three mountain ranges in western Virginia and part of West Virginia—the Blue Ridge, Massanutten, and Shenandoah Mountains. Visitors come here to enjoy picnicking, camping, fishing, hiking, backpacking, water sports, hunting, and nature study. Many come simply to enjoy the quiet scenic beauty away from the noise, bustle, and pollution of the cities.

For convenience of visitors, there are 13 developed

campgrounds and numerous picnic areas. Many early historic sites are preserved. Of six iron furnaces, two, Elizabeth and Catherine Furnaces, are easily accessible and worthy of a visit. Many hikers visit the remnants of **Signal Knob,** an observation point used by both sides in the Civil War. There is good blueberry picking along the trail in midsummer.

Among spectacular natural phenomena are caves, rock slides, and "lost" rivers. There is **Ramsey's Draft Wilderness,** 10,000 acres of old growth timber including oak, hemlock, and other species spared from the woodman's axe. In the fall, thousands visit the forest to view the spectacular colorful foliage and to avoid the traffic jams in nearby Shenandoah National Park.

Plan your forest trip carefully. Request copies of maps, historic and descriptive booklets, and a list of developed recreational sites, all obtainable from the Forest Supervisor's Office, 210 Federal Building, Harrisonburg, VA 22801. Telephone: (703) 433-2491.

You can get more detailed information about fishing, hiking, food and supply sources, motels, historic sites, etc., by writing the District Ranger's Office in the area you plan to visit.

HARRISONBURG TO LEXINGTON

This is a continuation of the tour of the Valley of Virginia, which began at Winchester. Routes 81 and 11 are the main arteries. Intersecting main east-west roads: Route 33 at Harrisonburg; Route 250 at Staunton; and Route 60 at Lexington.

Harrisonburg is the home of James Madison University and Eastern Mennonite College, and the headquarters of George Washington National Forest.

Massanutten Caverns are located on Route 685, two miles north of Route 33, at Keezletown. Open daily 10:00 a.m. to 6:00 p.m., June 1 to Labor Day; 11:00 a.m. to 5:00 p.m., spring and fall; weekends only, 12:00 p.m. to 5:00 p.m., winter. Admission charge.

Grand Caverns, the first discovered in Virginia, are situated near Grottoes at the junction of Routes 340 and 256. Turn east off Routes 81 or 11 at Weyer's Cave and proceed six miles on Route 256. Open to the public since 1806, Grand Caverns is historic as well as scenic. Stonewall Jackson quartered his troops in the Grand Ballroom, so named because dances had been held there over the years. Its unique shield formations, projecting from the walls, are of special interest. Open in March, weekends only, 9:00 a.m. to 5:00 p.m. Open daily, April through October, 9:00 a.m. to 5:00 p.m. November 1 through February 28, open by reservation to groups of 15 or more. Admission charge; children under six, free. Telephone: (703) 249-5705.

Mount Solon is the locale of the **Natural Chimneys,** seven massive towers of colorful stone which rise majestically for more than 100 feet above their naturally tunneled bases. Formed under an inland sea in the Cambrian Period of the Paleozoic Era at least 500 million years ago, one "Chimney" stands 107 feet high and leans from the perpendicular 13-and-one-half feet, nearly the same as that of the Leaning Tower of Pisa. Admission charge. Open daily, March 20 through November 30, 9:00 a.m. to dark.

To reach Natural Chimneys from Harrisonburg, take Route 42 south, five miles to Route 747; right three miles to Mt. Solon. The park offers camping facilities, including use of water and electricity (limited December through March). There is a camping charge. The park is the home of the oldest continuously held sporting event in the U.S., the annual Jousting Tournament, first held in 1821. There are picnicking facilities, a pool, a camp store, a playground, a gift shop, nature and bicycle trails. Telephone: (703) 350-2510.

Staunton, 24 miles south of Harrisonburg, on Routes 11 and 81, is scenically situated in the heart of a prosperous agricultural, commercial, and educational area. Mary Baldwin College and Stuart Hall are located here. There are a number of self-guided tours offered, including Woodrow Wilson's Birthplace, Skyline Drive, and historical and scenic points of interest. Write to Chamber of Commerce, Box 389, Staunton, VA 24401, for details.

Woodrow Wilson Birthplace is where the 28th president of the United States was born in what was then the Presbyterian Manse at 24 North Coalter Street. The dignity and simplicity of the furnishings and the appealing nursery never fail to charm the visitor to this national shrine. A documentary film on the life of President Wilson is shown. The garden at the rear of the house was restored by the Garden Club of Virginia. Open daily, 9:30 a.m. to 5:30 p.m., closed Sundays in January, February, March, and on Christmas, Thanksgiving, and New Year's Day. Admission charge. Free guide service. Telephone: (703) 885-0897 or 885-3461.

Waynesboro, 11 miles east of Staunton, is an industrial city at the foot of the western slope of the Blue Ridge Mountains, the southern entrance to Shenandoah National Park, and the northern entrance to the Blue Ridge Parkway. It is beautifully located in the rolling plain of the Shenandoah Valley, with rich farm lands surrounding it. The **Clemmer Gardens**, located here, are among the state's finest floral sights.

Swannanoa is near Waynesboro at Afton, atop a mountain at the intersection of U.S. 250, Skyline Drive, and Blue Ridge Parkway. This fabulous marble palace in Italian Renaissance style is filled with works of art and is home of the University of Science and Philosophy. The palace is surrounded by a sculpture garden. Admission charge. Open daily, 8:00 a.m. to 6:00 p.m. during summer months; 9:00 a.m. to 5:00 p.m., winter months.

Waynesboro offers three self-guided tours featuring the Shenandoah Valley and Skyline Drive. Write to Chamber of Commerce, Box 459, Waynesboro, VA 22980, for details.

Lexington is 34 miles south of Staunton, on Routes 11 and 81. This charming old town is the seat of two of Virginia's most distinguished colleges. **Washington and Lee University** was founded in 1749 and later took the name of Washington upon its endowment in 1782 by George Washington. Robert E. Lee served as its president, following the surrender at Appomattox, and at his death in 1870 his name was added. The **Lee Chapel**, in which Robert E. Lee is buried, contains many famous works of art associated with George Washington and Robert E. Lee. Open year round.

The **Virginia Military Institute** was founded in 1839 and is known today as the "West Point of the South." Among its distinguished faculty members was Thomas J. ("Stonewall") Jackson, and it numbers among its alumni the late General George Marshall. A mural depicting the charge of the V.M.I. Cadets at the Battle of New Market and flags of all states are contained in the chapel. Retreat Parade is held each Friday at 4:15 p.m. on the V.M.I. Parade Ground during the school year. The **V.M.I. Museum**, in Jackson Memorial Hall, is open every day, 9:00 a.m. to 5:00 p.m. (Sundays from 2:00 to 5:00 p.m. only.) Guides are available, and admission is free.

The **George C. Marshall Research Museum** is a handsome structure located at the west end of the V.M.I. Parade Ground. The Museum, a memorial to the General of the Armies and World War II's Chief of Staff, houses his personal papers as well as a collection of material relating to the United States military and diplomatic history. The Museum is open to the public daily, from 10:00 a.m. to 5:00 p.m. October 15 through May 15, 9:00 a.m. to 4:00 p.m. Admission fee.

Stonewall Jackson's Home and Museum is open weekdays, 9:00 a.m. to 5:00 p.m.; Sunday, 1:00 to 5:00 p.m. Admission charge. Telephone: (703) 463-2552. Also of note are the **Henry Street Playhouse**, open during summer months; the " **Castle** "; and a number of historic churches and homes, most of which are on self-conducted tour routes. In and around Lexington are many other historic buildings and sites. Among them are **Lawyers Row, Court Square**, and **Goshen Pass**, which leads via the Virginia By Way (Route 39) to Warm Springs and Hot Springs. Write to Department of Visitor Relations, City of Lexington, 107 E. Washington Street, Lexington, VA 24450.

One of America's great natural wonders is 14 miles south of Lexington on Route 11, just off 81, Exits 49 or 50. An arch of stone, created by the action of water over millions of years, **Natural Bridge** stands 215 feet above Cedar Creek, is 90 feet long, and from 50 to 150 feet wide. It was worshipped by the Indians as "The Bridgeod" long before the white man came.

About 1750, a youthful George Washington surveyed the towering stone archway, climbed up its side and cut his initials, which may be seen today. In 1774 Thomas Jefferson bought it and the surrounding 157 acres from King George III of England for 20 shillings.

The grounds are open from 7:00 a.m. until dark. Admission charge. An outdoor pageant, "The Drama of Creation," is reenacted nightly year round under the Bridge. Telephone: (703) 291-2121.

Adjacent to the entrance to Natural Bridge is **Natural Bridge Wax Museum** with a self-guided tour of more than 150 life replicas of folklore and personalities of Natural Bridge and surrounding areas. Open mid-March through November, 9:00 a.m. to 9:00 p.m. Admission charge. Telephone: (703) 291-2426.

Natural Bridge Caverns are open in spring and fall, 10:00 a.m. to 6:00 p.m.; in summer, 9:00 a.m. to 8:00 p.m. Admission charge. Combination Bridge/Caverns tickets available. Group rates. Telephone: (703) 291-2121. **Natural Bridge Zoological Park** is a 25-acre zoo with a five-acre "contact area." It is open April through November. Admission charge. Telephone: (703) 291-2420.

HOT SPRINGS AND WARM SPRINGS

The history of the "Springs of Virginia" is a rich and varied one—and one which reflects the development of social customs and fashions from the earliest days of the nation.

In the late 1700s, the aristocracy of Virginia discovered the pleasures of going up to the Springs in the early summer, and disporting in pleasant company for several months before retiring, as colder weather came on, to the Lowlands again. It was fashionable, in those days, to move from one Spring to another: from the Warm to the Hot, from the Hot to the Sweet, etc. in a group composed of the highest society of the times. Originally valued for medicinal purposes, the Springs became more and more sought after as centers of pleasure and activity, including gambling as well.

Hot Springs, where The Homestead has for more than a century catered to its discriminating clientele, was one of the most prominent of these Springs in Virginia, and has withstood the test of time. The **Homestead** is set within 16,000 Allegheny acres. It reflects a style and grandeur that may still be enjoyed in this day and time.

The Homestead provides a wealth of outlets for your energies: championship golf on three 18-hole courses, tennis on 19 courts, fishing in its own mountain streams, horseback riding, skeet and trap shooting, walks through the Virginia countryside, and two outdoor pools are among its numerous activities and attractions. During the winter season skiing and ice skating are offered.

There is a complete Health Spa at The Homestead, as well as an indoor pool and eight 10-pin bowling alleys. In the evening, dining, dancing, concerts, and movies are a tradition. There is a supervised playground and indoor playroom for children. Telephone: (703) 839-5500 for rates and more information, or write The Homestead, Hot Springs, VA 24445.

The **Warm Springs**, located five miles from The Homestead, were the gateway to the tour of the Springs (which included White Sulphur Springs, now in nearby West Virginia). No properly mannered Virginian would have dreamed of beginning the round at any other point. The approach was from Lexington and the Goshen Pass over what in the present day is now Route 39, the Virginia By-Way.

Life at Warm Springs centered around two covered pools and the sheltered "drinking spring." They have been preserved in their natural, if not their original, condition. The scene is not far from that which greeted the eyes of visitors even before the first Homestead was built at Hot Springs.

And perhaps most interesting of all, the same warm crystal waters fill the pools. Bathers still enjoy them in large numbers. Occasionally the pools are rented for private parties, where some of the old customs, such as floating mint juleps out to the bathers on cork trays, are still observed. There are large numbers who swear by the waters' curative properties, in addition to the many who find in them an opportunity for superlative physical luxury.

ROANOKE VALLEY

Animals were attracted to salt deposits, giving the name, "Big Lick," to the first settlement here. **Roanoke** began as a crossroads from the first movement of Indians, explorers, and settlers. Today Roanoke is the principal city in the Valley.

Scotch-Irish and Germans made their way here from Pennsylvania through the Shenandoah Valley in the 1700s, followed later by English settlers from Eastern Virginia. Salem, the first town in the Valley, was formed in 1802, and Roanoke County was formed from Boteourt County in 1838.

A new era began in 1882 when the Shenandoah Valley Railroad connected with the Norfolk and Western here and the town of Roanoke was formed from Big Lick. It became a boom town, spurred by the coal-hauling railroad and the iron-ore industry. Because of the rapid progress it made after World War II, Roanoke is called "the Star City of the South," symbolized by a 100-foot-high neon star atop nearby Mill Mountain.

Begin your tour of Roanoke with a stop at the **Visitor Information Center**, One Market Square. The visitor center is located on the ground floor of **Center in the Square**, an arts and sciences complex surrounded by Roanoke's historic farmers market. Open Monday through Saturday, 9:00 a.m. to 5:00 p.m.; Sunday, 1:00 p.m. to 5:00 p.m. Telephone: (703) 345-8622.

Roanoke's heritage as a crossroads for transportation and commerce is evident in the **Farmers Market**, where area farmers have sold their produce since the 1870s. At the corner of Campbell Avenue and First Street, S.E., you will find local farmers selling produce throughout most of the year. The market is also the site of a wide variety of restaurants and boutiques.

Visible from the market is Mill Mountain, home of **Mill Mountain Zoo**, which has been in existence since the 1950s. The park exhibits 29 species of exotic and native animals on a 10-acre site. Nestled atop a mountain in the center of the city of Roanoke, the Zoo demonstrates the beauty of nature in many forms. The Zoo is open daily, May 1 through October 31, 10:00 a.m. to 6:00 p.m. Open weekends only, November through December, 10:00 a.m. to 4:30 p.m.

The focal point of the market area is the **Center in the Square**, a restored 1914 warehouse housing three museums, a planetarium, a theater, a tea room, and the Arts Council of the Roanoke Valley.

The **Science Museum of Western Virginia** features changing exhibits about the scientific wonders of the world. The museum offers many programs, activities, and services. The museum's centerpiece is the 140-seat **William B. Hopkins Planetarium**. Open year round, Tuesday through Thursday, 10:00 a.m. to 5:00 p.m.; Friday, 10:00 a.m. to 8:00 p.m.; Saturday, 10:00 a.m. to 5:00 p.m.; Sunday, 1:00 p.m. to 5:00 p.m. Admission charge. Free to members. Telephone: (703) 342-5710.

Also located at Center in the Square is the **Roanoke Valley History Museum**. The heritage of the Roanoke area unfolds before visitors in the galleries and library of the Roanoke Valley Historical Society. Exhibits document Indian life before colonial settlement, the Revolutionary and Civil wars, and Reconstruction. Of special note is the recreation of an 1890 country store and an exhibit of fashions from the 1700s to the 1980s. Open year round, Tuesday through Saturday, 10:00 a.m. to 5:00 p.m.; Sunday, 1:00 p.m. to 5:00 p.m. Closed New Year's, Easter, Thanksgiving, and Christmas. Telephone: (703) 342-5770.

Visitors to the **Roanoke Museum of Fine Arts** will discover two floors of artwork from ancient Egypt, Greece, and Rome through the avant-garde art of the 20th century. Impressive collections of Japanese art and American decorative arts and changing exhibitions of regional, national, and international art are featured at the museum year round. Open Tuesday through Thursday, 10:00 a.m. to 5:00 p.m.; Friday, 10:00 a.m. to 8:00 p.m.; Sunday, 1:00 p.m. to 5:00 p.m.

Closed New Year's, Memorial Day, Independence Day, Labor Day, Thanksgiving, and Christmas. Telephone: (703) 342-5760.

Founded in 1963, **Mill Mountain Theatre** enjoys a permanent home at Center in the Square. The theater provides year-round live professional entertainment in a 440-60 seat Graeco-Roman amphitheater. Reservations can be made at the box office or at any Ticketron location. Telephone: (703) 342-5740 (box office) or (703) 342-5730 (administrative office).

After leaving Center in the Square, travel six blocks west to the **Virginia Museum of Transportation**. Located in a restored railway freight station, the museum actively honors Roanoke's great transportation heritage. There are displays of steam, electric, and diesel locomotives. A walk down the museum's Main Street allows visitors to discover early automotive history. The museum is the permanent home of Expo '86, an exhibit designed and assembled by the United States for the World's Fair in Vancouver, British Columbia. Open year round, Monday through Saturday, 10:00 a.m. to 5:00 p.m.; Sunday, noon to 5:00 p.m. Closed New Year's, Thanksgiving, and Christmas. Admission charge. Telephone: (703) 342-5670.

One of Roanoke's newer historical sites is the **Harrison Heritage and Cultural Center**, located at 523 Harrison Avenue, N.W. The Harrison School building, home of the first high school for blacks in southwest Virginia, now houses the cultural center. The primary focus of the center is the documentation and preservation of black heritage in the Roanoke Valley. Art exhibits, manuscript collections, films, workshops, and dramatic presentations are open to the public. Open June through August, Monday through Friday, 10:00 a.m. to 5:00 p.m. Open the rest of the year, Sunday only, 1:00 p.m. to 5:00 p.m. Admission is free. Telephone: (703) 345-4818.

Also in Salem is **Dixie Caverns**, the only caverns in the Roanoke Valley. Admission charge. There are 96 acres of campsites. Open year round; summer, 9:00 a.m. to 8:00 p.m.; other months, 9:00 a.m. to 5:30 p.m. Telephone: (703) 380-2085.

Smith Mountain Lake, southeast of Roanoke, via Route 122, is the second largest body of fresh water in the state of Virginia. It borders four counties, and is comprised of 20,000 acres of water and 500 miles of shoreline. Fishermen and boaters trek here year round. The fishing is excellent, the lake teeming with bass, trout, and muskies. A state park encompasses 10 miles of shoreline and 1,500 acres of land.

Boat launching areas, hiking trails, and a visitors center are available. Telephone: (804) 721-1203.

FREDERICKSBURG AND THE NORTHERN NECK

The Fredericksburg area is just off I-95 about halfway between Washington and Richmond. No community can claim a closer association with the Washington family than **Fredericksburg**. When George Washington was seven years old, his parents moved to **Ferry Farm**, directly across the Rappahannock River. It is now privately owned and closed to the public, but you can catch glimpses of it during the winter. This is where stories of Washington's youth abound: the cherry tree, throwing a dollar across the river, teaching himself surveying, and riding his father's ferry to school each day. He inherited the farm from his father, and lived here before he moved to Mount Vernon in 1738. Even his early diaries record more than 70 visits to Fredericksburg.

Besides Washington, many other illustrious names contributed to Fredericksburg's niche in the history of our nation, including Thomas Jefferson, James Madison, James Monroe, John Marshall, Patrick Henry, and Admiral John Paul Jones. Commodore Matthew Fontaine Maury, the great naval scientist who plotted the currents of the Atlantic Ocean, conducted much of his work while living in Fredericksburg. Fredericksburg sent six generals into the Continental Army. During the Civil War, it changed hands seven times and was the scene of several battles.

Start your tour at the **Fredericksburg Visitor Center** on 706 Caroline Street. You can watch a free 20-minute film on the history of the city, pick up maps for the walking tour, and get a pass good for free parking throughout Fredericksburg during your visit. Admission to most of the sites in town is free, except for eight historic homes. You can save on admission by purchasing a Hospitality Pass good for five homes. The Visitor Center is open daily, 9:00 a.m. to 5:00 p.m. Summer hours are extended. Admission free. Telephone: (703) 373-1776.

First stop on the walking tour is the **Silver-Smith House**. This 18th-century building on Sophia (pronounced "so-FI-ah") Street is now home of the **Center for Creative Arts**, where local artists display their work. Open Tuesday through Sunday, 10:00 a.m. to 4:00 p.m. Admission free. Continuing down Sophia Street, you will come to the **Old Stone Warehouse**. Historians believe it once served as a tobacco warehouse. Exhibits display artifacts, from 1760 through the Civil War, which have been found in Fredericksburg. Open Sunday, 1:00 p.m. to 4:00 p.m. Admission free. No telephone.

Turn left on Amelia Street and continue one block to Caroline Street, where you will find **Hugh Mercer's Apothecary Shop**. Dr. Mercer operated this shop from 1771 to 1776. His drug store includes a physician's office as well as an office which George Washington occasionally used. You can see such oddities as an apothecary jar decorated from the inside, silverplated pills, and an 18th-century operating room. Mercer served as a brigadier general in the Revolutionary War and was mortally wounded at the Battle of Princeton. Open daily, 9:00 a.m. to 5:00 p.m. (November through March, closes at 4:00 p.m.) Admission charge. Telephone: (703) 373-1569.

At 1306 Caroline Street is the **Rising Sun Tavern**, which was built by Washington's brother Charles about 1760. Here notables like Thomas Jefferson, Patrick Henry, General Hugh Mercer, George Mason, John Marshall, the Lees, and Washington himself did much of the "head" work that preceded the Revolution. The Tavern was an early post office, and stagecoach stop. Refreshments are served at the end of the tour. Open daily 9:00 a.m. to 5:00 p.m. (November through March, closes at 4:00 p.m.) Telephone: (703) 371-1494.

Take a left on Princess Anne Street, passing the **Baptist Church**, built in 1857. Continue to the intersection with William Street, to **City Hall**. Built in 1814, it was the site of a reception for Lafayette in 1824. It served as a market house and as the city's municipal headquarters until 1983. It is now open as the **Fredericksburg Area Museum**, featuring temporary exhibits, permanent exhibits about Fredericksburg's colorful past, and a museum shop. Open daily 9:00 a.m. to 5:00 p.m. Admission charge. Telephone: (703) 371-5668. A block further is **St. George's Episcopal Church and Graveyard**, the third church on this site. Buried in the graveyard are Fredericksburg notables including John Dandridge, father of Martha Washington. St. George's served as the Washington family's church. Open daily, 9:00 a.m. to 5:00 p.m. Telephone: (703) 373-4133.

George Washington was initiated a Mason on November 4, 1752, at the **Masonic Lodge No. 4**, at 900 Princess Anne Street. Inside hangs an original Gilbert Stuart portrait of the country's founding father. Outside is the oldest Masonic

cemetery in America. Admission charge to Lodge. Open
Monday through Saturday, April through October, 9:00 a.m.
to 5:00 p.m.; November through March, 9:00 a.m. to 4:00
p.m. Open Sunday, 1:00 p.m. to 4:00 p.m.

Continue right on George Street, passing the **Presbyterian Church**. Built in 1833, in Greek revival style, it is the
oldest church in Fredericksburg. Clara Barton served here
during the Civil War when it was used as a hospital. Turn
right on Charles Street, passing another **Masonic Cemetery**,
this one dating from 1784. Continue to number 908—the
James Monroe Museum and Memorial Library. The building was used by Monroe as his law office from 1786 to 1789,
and contains furniture he and his wife purchased in Paris,
including the Louis XVI desk on which he signed the Monroe
Doctrine. Reproductions of many of these pieces are now
used in the White House. The library wing has over 15,000
volumes on Monroe's life. Open daily, 9:00 a.m. to 5:00 p.m.
Closed Christmas. Admission charge. Telephone: (703) 373-8426.

Continue down Charles Street, passing the old **Slave
Auction Block**, to **Mary Washington's House**. "All that I
am, I owe to my mother," said George Washington of his
beloved mother Mary. He bought this home and enlarged it
for her. Mary happily spent the last 17 years of her life here.
In 1968, the Garden Club of Virginia restored the gardens,
which remain beautifully maintained. Open daily, 9:00 a.m. to
5:00 p.m. (November through March, closes at 4:00 p.m.)
Admission charge. Telephone: (703) 373-1569.

The **St. James House**, at the corner of Charles and
Fauquier streets, is only open to the public during Historic
Garden Week (the last week in April) and during the first
week in October. The cottage was once owned by George
Washington, and later by James Mercer who had partial
ownership of a Revolutionary War gunnery.

You can continue your tour on foot or by car. The next
stop is three blocks further down Fauquier at the intersection
with Washington Avenue. **Kenmore** was the magnificent tobacco plantation of Colonel Fielding Lewis and his wife,
Betty Washington Lewis, the only sister of George. In a
listing of the 100 most beautiful rooms in America, one of
Kenmore's rooms is included. The home, built in 1752, is
famous for its intricate ornamental ceilings. Tea and fragrant
gingerbread from a Mary Washington recipe are served to
visitors in the colonial kitchen. Open daily, 9:00 a.m. to 5:00

p.m. (November through March, closes at 4:00 p.m.) Admission charge. Telephone: (703) 373-3381.

Three monuments are along Washington Avenue. Near the river is the **Thomas Jefferson Religious Freedom Monument**, commemorating a meeting he attended in 1777 in Fredericksburg to review the laws of Virginia. The results served as the basis for the religious freedom clauses in the Bill of Rights. The **Mary Washington Monument and Grave** were built with donations given by women from all over the country. The **Hugh Mercer Monument** was given to the City of Fredericksburg by the United States in 1906 to honor this colonial doctor. Further down Washington Avenue is the **Confederate Cemetery**, where lie unknown Confederate soldiers from the battles around Fredericksburg.

Elsewhere in the city are other important sites. Near Mary Washington College is the graceful **Brompton**, now the private home of the college's president. It served as Lee's headquarters during the Battle of Fredericksburg. A monument nearby commemorates Richard Kirkland, a man lovingly called by many the "angel of Marye's Heights." A Confederate sergeant from South Carolina, Kirkland asked, and was given permission, to give water to the thirsty and dying Union troops. The powerful monument was designed by the same sculptor, Felix de Weldon, who did the Iwo Jima Memorial in Washington, DC.

South of Route 17 at 224 Washington Street is **Belmont**, the **Melchers Memorial Gallery**. In the midst of a 27-acre estate, the gallery exhibits the works of Gari Melchers and other artists. The home is furnished with fine antiques. Open daily 10:00 a.m. to 5:00 p.m.; Sunday, 1:00 to 4:00 p.m. Admission charge. Telephone: (703) 373-3634.

Fredericksburg and Spotsylvania National Military Park is a historic area west of Fredericksburg, along Route 5, encompassing four Civil War battlefields: Fredericksburg, Chancellorsville, the Wilderness, and Spotsylvania. On December 13, 1862, Union General Burnside's troops crossed the Rappahannock River on pontoon bridges. His attack on Lee's heavily fortified position was a disastrous and bloody failure. West of Fredericksburg were fought the Battles of Chancellorsville, May 1-5, 1863; the Wilderness, May 5-6, 1864; and Spotsylvania Court House, May 8-21, 1864. Throughout the park, you will see miles of trenches and gun pits, the Sunken Road, and Marye's Heights. At Chancellorsville, you may follow the route over which Jackson marched to attack the exposed right flank of Hooker's army. At Guinea Station is the Stonewall Jackson Shrine, the house in which he died. The **Visitor's Center and Museum**, located at Fredericksburg, feature a diorama, an electric map, and collections of arms and photographs and other relics. Route maps to the various battlefields also are available here. The Chancellorsville Visitor's Center is best equipped for handicapped visitors. The park is open daily, 9:00 a.m. to 5:00 p.m. Expanded hours daily during the summer. Closed December 25 and January 1. Admission free. Telephone: (703) 373-4461.

Also a part of the Fredericksburg Battlefield Tour is **Chatham**, a magnificent Georgian mansion built in 1770 and once known for its luxurious gardens and extensive grounds. In 1862-64 when the Confederates utilized the Rappahannock River as their northern frontier, Union armies used this house as headquarters for federal commanders, a communications center, an artillery position, and a field hospital. It was here that Clara Barton and Walt Whitman nursed the wounded. Visitors can see five rooms of the mansion and museum exhibits as well as the grounds and garden. In a cleared vista overlooking Fredericksburg, narrative panels identify landmarks on the city skyline. Open daily, 9:00 a.m. to 5:00 p.m. Closed Christmas and New Year's. Admission free. Telephone: (703) 373-4461.

THE NORTHERN NECK

A popular Rappahannock River resort town and county seat of Essex County, **Tappahannock** was founded as a river port in 1680. Today it is an important crossroads of US 17 and US 360, gateway from Richmond to the historic Northern Neck. Among its famous old colonial dwellings is the **Ritchie House**, on Courthouse Square. Many colonial homes are nearby. An **old customhouse** (closed to the public) is still standing, as well as the first brick courthouse, the **clerk's office**, and the **debtor's prison**, all erected between 1728 and 1750.

Seven miles to the east, across the Rappanannock River, is Warsaw, seat of Richmond County. The **County Courthouse**, on the Green off Wallace Street, was built in 1748. The nearby **Clerk's Office** (1748) is heated by an original open fireplace. Many old colonial records and wills are stored here. Both buildings open Monday through Friday, 9:00 a.m. to 5:00 p.m. Admission free. Telephone: (804) 333-3781.

Two noteworthy points of interest are located near the tip of the Northern Neck of Virginia, east of Warsaw. **Epping Forest**, near Lancaster, is the plantation birthplace of Mary Ball Washington, mother of George Washington. The mansion was built around 1690 and has a beautifully furnished interior of that period. Four original outbuildings still stand: an icehouse, coach house, smokehouse, and laundry house. Not open to the public.

Historic **Christ Church**, nine miles south of Lancaster in Irvington, was built in 1732 by Colonel Robert ("King") Carter, proprietor of the Northern Neck. The church is in the form of a Latin cross, and the interior has the only original high-back pews in the state. Ornate Carter tombs may be seen outside the eastern end of the church. The Reception Center, offering a museum, guided tours, and a slide program, is open April 1 through November 30, Monday to Friday, 10:00 a.m. to 4:00 p.m.; Saturday, 1:00 p.m. to 4:00 p.m.; Sunday, 2:00 p.m. to 5:00 p.m. Closed Christmas. Admission free. Telephone: (804) 438-6855.

Surrounded by broad meadows and commanding a superb view of the Potomac River, **Stratford Hall** remains today as it was when built by Thomas Lee around 1725-30. The Great Mansion sheltered four generations of Lees, including two signers of the Declaration of Independence, Richard Henry Lee and Francis Lightfoot Lee. One of Washington's favorite officers was the dashing "Light Horse Harry" Lee. His son, Robert E. Lee, lived here as a small boy and went on to command the Confederate Army during the Civil War.

In 1929 Stratford Hall was purchased by the Robert E. Lee Memorial Foundation, which carefully restored the Great Mansion and other buildings, while the East Garden with its 18th-century boxwoods was restored by the Garden Club of Virginia according to original plan. Today Stratford Hall is a completely restored, working plantation.

The four massive chimneys on the east and west wings of the Mansion are connected to form tower platforms, a rare architectural feature which makes this handsome structure unlike any other building of its period in Virginia. The Mansion's attractive brick dependencies include the kitchen, wash house, and plantation office. The same type of brick, fired in an adjoining field, was used for the Ha-Ha Wall which kept livestock off the Mansion's lawns and gardens. Today, cattle are again raised on the plantation.

The Old Mill, where cornmeal is still ground, has been

rebuilt on its original foundations. Celebrated also for its ancient beech trees and great forests, the setting of Stratford affords splendid vistas of the Potomac River. Open daily, 9:00 a.m. to 5:00 p.m. Admission charge. Luncheon is served from April through October. Telephone: (804) 493-8038.

The 1,295-acre **Westmoreland State Park** has a water frontage on the Potomac River of 1¼ miles. It is seven miles north of Montross on Route 3.

Visitors to the park can swim at the pool or the beach of sand and shell. Trees fringe the water's edge, merging with a background of picturesque sandstone cliffs. On the beach are a modern bathhouse, parking area, picnic shelters, modern sanitation, and excellent facilities for boating and fishing. A popular pastime is hunting for shark teeth on the beach. Benches located on strategic sites afford gorgeous views of the Potomac River. Located on the cliffs above the beach are 25 housekeeping cabins. The self-guiding nature trail shows how a forest restores itself on abandoned farmland. Evening programs are held two nights a week.

The park has 118 campsites and 24 cabins. Cabin reservations can be made 51 weeks ahead of time, while campsite reservations should be made 90 days in advance. Telephone: (804) 786-2134, or any Ticketron location. A food concessionaire and a restaurant are in the area. Park open Memorial Day through Labor Day, 24 hours a day. Hours vary rest of year; so telephone for information. Nominal parking charge Memorial Day through Labor Day; admission free rest of year. Telephone: (804) 493-8821.

George Washington Birthplace National Monument is on the Potomac River, reached by a two-mile entrance road off Route 3. Here on his father's plantation, Pope's Creek, George Washington was born and spent the first three years of his life.

The **Memorial Mansion** represents a Virginia plantation house of the 18th century. Tradition and surviving houses of the period were used as a basis of its design. It is a house of eight rooms, four downstairs and four in the half-story upstairs, with a central hallway on each floor. The bricks used in its construction were made by hand from clay obtained in a nearby field.

Situated about 50 feet from the Memorial Mansion is **Kitchen-House**, a typical colonial-period frame kitchen built on the traditional site of the old kitchen. It has been furnished to represent a plantation cooking establishment of the period of Washington's youth. In the **Colonial Herb and Flower Garden** are found only those flowers, vines, herbs, and berries that were common to Virginia gardens during that period.

About one mile northwest of the Memorial Mansion, on the banks of Bridges Creek, are the site of the 1664 home of Colonel John Washington and the **Burying Ground** where members of the Washington family are interred.

Across Dancing Marsh are a walking trail and a picnic area that overlooks Pope's Creek. Light refreshments and souvenirs are for sale in the Post Office at the main parking area. Monument open daily, 9:00 a.m. to 5:00 p.m. Closed Christmas and New Year's. Admission free. Telephone: (804) 224-1732.

GREATER RICHMOND AREA AND TIDEWATER

Visitors have been coming to the Tidewater area of Virginia for nearly four centuries. Captain John Smith started a trend when he arrived in 1607, and it's been a popular spot ever since. Richmond, the former capital of the Confederate States of America, is in the center of the Tidewater area. Flowing through the area is the historic James River which provides a stunning backdrop for the plantation country to the southwest.

GREATER RICHMOND AREA

In Hanover County, about 25 miles north of Richmond in Beaverdam, is **Scotchtown**, the home Patrick Henry bought at an auction in 1771. The patriot lived here for seven years while he was a delegate to the First Continental Congress and later as first governor of the independent Commonwealth of Virginia. Scotchtown was built in 1719 and was also the childhood home of Dolley Payne, who married James Madison. The home is now a registered National Historic Landmark. Open, April through October, Monday through Saturday, 10:00 a.m. to 4:30 p.m.; Sunday, 1:30 to 4:30 p.m. Admission charge. Telephone: (804) 227-3500.

The giant **Kings Dominion**, 20 miles north of Richmond and 75 miles south of Washington off I-95's Doswell/Route 30 Exit, is made up of five smaller theme parks: International Street, Old Virginia, Candyapple Grove, Happy Land of Hanna-Barbera, and Safari Village. A simple walk through the gates somehow brings out the kid in everyone, and you will find yourself racing to the 36 rides including five roller coasters (the Grizzly features an 85-foot, spine-tingling drop), a 33-story Eiffel Tower, a restored 1917 wooden carousel, Lost World (a 17-story man-made mountain housing three rides), and a whitewater raft trip. From the park's monorail safari, you can watch tigers, lions, and many other animals in their natural habitat.

Once you have had your fill of rides, you can choose from among 12 shows featuring four hours of entertainment every day. There is a showcase musical stage revue and also a host of country music, clown bands, trained birds and dolphins to entertain visitors. Name performers, such as Loretta Lynn and Christopher Cross, appear at different times of the year in the 7,500-seat Showplace. The summer months also feature a Water Follies Ski Show. There is a variety of restaurants and shops. Overnight facilities include the Kings Quarters Motor Lodge and Kings Hide-A-Way Campground.

Open weekends, from the last weekend of March through May 29, and from Labor Day until the first Sunday in October. Open daily, from the first weekend of June until the end of August. Hours vary, though the park is generally open from 9:30 a.m. until 8:00 p.m. or 10:00 p.m. It is best to call in advance. Admission charge includes all rides, shows, and attractions including the safari monorail ride. Children two and under are free. Two-day and season passes are available. Telephone: (804) 876-5000.

In the **Hanover Court House and Old Jail**, five miles east of I-95's Route 54 Exit, Patrick Henry first made a name for himself with a great speech in the lawsuit, referred to as Parson's Cause, over the question of British control of the New World. Open daily, by appointment only. Telephone: (804) 798-6547. Across the street is the historic **Barksdale Theater**. You can enjoy dinner and theater at reasonable prices inside this pre-Revolutionary tavern which was once operated by the John Sheltons, whose daughter married Patrick Henry. Open Wednesday through Saturday, 6:00 p.m. to 11:00 p.m. Admission free, but there is a charge for dinner and theater. Telephone: (804) 798-6547.

As with much of Virginia, the Tidewater area saw its share of Civil War fighting. The **Richmond National Battle-field Park** encompasses 10 large battlefields (and several smaller ones) all around the Greater Richmond area. It includes some of the most hotly contested land in the Civil War. Here General George B. McClellan's Peninsula Campaign culminated in the Battle of Seven Pines, and the famous Seven Days Battle, which embraced Mechanicsville, Gaines Mill, Savage Station, Frayser's Farm and Malvern Hill. In this area the dashing Confederate cavalry leader, General J. E. B. Stuart, made his famous ride around McClellan. Here, Robert E. Lee assumed command of the Army of Northern Virginia for the first time.

Cold Harbor Battlefield and Cemetery, northeast of the city, is where Grant hurled his men against the Confederates in June 1864. He not only lost the battle, but 7,000 of his men were killed or wounded in 30 minutes. A 97-mile drive will take you on a tour of the fields of combat, the forts and intricate field fortifications, and the historic old houses on the battlefields. Begin at headquarters, where you will see graphic exhibits. At **Fort Harrison**, a museum and a small visitors center provide background and an explanation of what went on within its walls. Other battlefields belonging to the park include the spectacular **Fort Darling** on Drewry's Bluff, where Confederate gunners halted Union efforts to ascend the James River to Richmond; **Beaverdam Creek**, where the Confederates unsuccessfully attacked the Union forces on June 26, 1862; and Gaines Mill.

The **Chimborazo Visitor's Center** in downtown Richmond (3215 E. Broad Street) has a slide program, exhibits, and a museum and its **National Battlefield Information Center** is a good starting point for tours to the surrounding battlefields. Open daily, 9:00 a.m. to 5:00 p.m. Closed Christmas and New Year's. Individual battlefields open daily, dawn to dusk. Admission free. Telephone: (804) 226-1981.

After Appomattox, General Robert E. Lee, "looking for some little, quiet home in the woods," chose **Derwent**, located west of Richmond off Route 60 near Trenholm. The site was far from peaceful as dozens of well-wishers came bearing compliments and opportunities. It was not long before Lee was persuaded to serve as president of Washington College in Lexington (now Washington and Lee University). Derwent is closed to the public but you can admire it from the road.

Off Route 667 near Amelia is **Haw Branch**, an excellent example of Georgian-Federal plantation architecture. The 1745 manor house has tobacco leaf woodwork, original furnishings, an outdoor kitchen, and a museum. Now a Virginia Historic Landmark, Haw Branch is home of the ninth generation of the founder, Colonel Thomas Tabb. The plantation is named for the hawthorne trees that line a nearby stream. Open only to groups of 25 or more, daily, April through

October, 10:00 a.m. to 5:00 p.m. Admission charge. Telephone: (804) 561-2472.

Three other plantations in the area, **Shrum House, Dykeland,** and **Egglestetton,** can only be seen by taking the Flat Creek Plantation Tour (which also visits Haw Branch). It is available only to groups of 25 or more. Open April through October. Telephone Haw Branch for information.

Southwest of Richmond, in the town of Chesterfield, is **Pocahontas State Park,** one of the largest in Virginia. Within its 1,700 acres are three freshwater lakes and a variety of facilities: hiking trails, bridle paths, fishing, horse and boat rentals, playgrounds, camping, cabins, lake swimming, bike paths, a self-guided nature trail, and evening programs. The Visitors' Center has displays on the plant and animal life of the Piedmont region. Telephone: (804) 796-4255.

PETERSBURG

One of Virginia's oldest and most historic cities, Petersburg, located 30 miles south of Richmond (Exit 3 off I-95), received its name from Peter Jones, who opened a trading post with the Indians in 1645. It was here that Cornwallis organized his British troops to prepare for the Yorktown campaign. Petersburg is best known, however, as the site of the largest battleground of the Civil War. The siege of Petersburg, lasting 10 months, was the longest battle of the war. Throughout the city, you will see evidence of its thriving present-day cotton and tobacco trade, foundries, grand old homes, and artistic heritage. Do not miss the restored areas, little shops and restaurants in Old Towne, around Sycamore and Old streets.

The City of Petersburg maintains an **Information Center** at 19 Bollingbrook Street, in the Farmer's Bank. Telephone: (804) 733-2400. Unless otherwise listed, all sites in Petersburg are open Memorial Day through Labor Day, Monday through Saturday, 9:00 a.m. to 7:00 p.m. Open the rest of the year, Monday through Saturday, 9:00 a.m. to 5:00 p.m. Open Sundays, throughout the year, noon to 5:00 p.m. Closed Thanksgiving, Christmas Eve, Christmas Day, and New Year's. Admission free.

You can pick up maps leading you to the start of the self-guided tour. Points of interest near the information center are the **Court House** (1839), **Cockade Alley, Farmers Market** (1876), **Peter Jones Trading Station, Lace Iron Work, Trapezium House** (1817), and two old churches.

Old Blandford Church, built in 1735, has 15 memorial

windows, designed by Louis Tiffany himself, from all Confederate states. Soldiers of six wars rest in adjoining Blandford Cemetery, among them 30,000 Confederates. It was here in 1886 that Memorial Day began.

Centre Hill Mansion, completed in 1823, illustrates the elegant living of both the antebellum and postbellum eras. Later remodeling makes the house museum and its more than 25 rooms an evolution of the Federal, Greek revival, Victorian, and Colonial revival styles. Period wallpaper, textiles, and furnishings recreate the elegance of the 19th century.

Farmers Bank Visitor Center, built in 1817, displays press and plates used to print the Bank's paper currency, examples of currency, and an audio-visual account of 19th-century banking.

At Petersburg, the hard-pressed Confederates withstood a siege lasting from June 15, 1864, to April 2, 1865, with the two armies in almost constant contact. It was the longest siege in American history. **Siege Museum** is housed in the attractive Greek Revival Exchange Building. Its exhibits explore everyday life in Petersburg before the Civil War and during the 10 long months of siege.

Just outside of town, **Petersburg National Battlefield** contains many well-preserved fortifications, trenches, and gun pits. Here occurred the famous Battle of the Crater, in which the Federal Army exploded a huge mine beneath the Confederate fortifications, but failed to penetrate the Confederate lines. A replica of the giant mortar, the *Dictator*, used to shell Petersburg, is in the original location. You may visit Fort Stedman, Battery #5, and the Crater. Audio recordings at sites of interest help visualize the battles. At the **Visitors Center** an audio-visual presentation of the 10-month siege as well as maps, dioramas, photographs, and displays will give more meaning to your trip. Open daily, Memorial Day to Labor Day, 8:00 a.m. to 6:00 p.m. Open rest of the year, 8:00 a.m. to 5:00 p.m. Admission free. Telephone: (804) 732-3531.

Located at 13 Rock Street, the **Petersburg Area Art League** displays works of its 750 members as well as visiting exhibitions. You can watch craftsmen at work, and listen to lectures on photography, ceramics, watercolor, and oil painting. Open Monday through Friday, 10:00 a.m. to 2:00 p.m. Telephone: (804) 861-4611.

At **Fort Lee**, northwest of Petersburg off Route 36, is the **Quartermaster Museum**, which houses a large collection of uniforms, insignia, rations, and flags used by soldiers from the Revolutionary War to the Korean Campaign. The most extensive displays relate to the Civil War. Open Monday through Friday, 8:00 a.m. to 5:00 p.m. Open Saturday, Sunday, and holidays, 11:00 a.m. to 5:00 p.m. Closed Thanksgiving, Christmas, and New Year's. Admission free. Telephone: (804) 734-1854.

HISTORIC JAMES RIVER PLANTATIONS

Virginia was the largest and wealthiest of the British colonies, and remained largely rural for over 300 years. Thanks to the efforts of state and local preservation groups, many of the great homes of Virginia's early years are still standing—restored to their former splendor.

Along both sides of the James River you may visit plantation homes of early leaders, patriots, presidents, and others who set their mark in history. From their wharves, ships departed with tobacco and other farm products, and returned with goods needed by the colonists. The James River was a source of fish, oysters, and other seafood as well as a means of easy communication among the planters. Between Richmond and Williamsburg on Routes 5 and 10, on both sides of the James, markers guide the tourist onto roads leading directly to plantations, gardens, and old churches. Most homes are open year round, though some are only open during Historic Garden Week (last week in April). To get from one side of the James to the other, take the Jamestown-Scotland ferry, or the bridge at Hopewell from Route 5 to Route 10.

On the south bank of the James is the city of Hopewell. It is an outgrowth of the second English settlement in America. **Weston Manor**, off 21st Avenue along the Appomattox River, is a country colonial home dating from about 1735. Restoration has been completed and new furnishings are being added all the time. Open Monday through Friday. Closed January through March. Telephone: (804) 541-2206.

Also in Hopewell is **Appomattox Manor,** at the corner of Cedar Lane and Pecan Avenue. Part of a grant patented in 1632 by Captain Francis Eppes, it is still in the Eppes family. The main section of the house dates from 1763; the dairy kitchen and smokehouse date from 1700. It was headquarters of General Grant from June 1864 to April 1865, when he directed his armies from the present dining room. The home was also used by President Lincoln to direct affairs of the

Federal Union during his stay in City Point in 1865. The manor is not open to the public, but you can drive by it.

Merchant's Hope Church, five miles east of Hopewell, was completed in 1657 and is the oldest Protestant church in America still standing and used as a house of worship. It takes its name from Merchant's Hope Plantation (1635). Its interior was destroyed by Federal troops during the Civil War when it was used as a picket station. The exterior is practically the same as when built and has been declared the "most beautiful Colonial brickwork in America." A legacy left in 1657 includes a "great Bible," still in possession of the church. Open daily, 9:00 a.m. to 5:00 p.m. If the door is locked, you can get the key from the Memorial Gardens superintendent in the house to the left of the church. Telephone: (804) 458-6197.

Brandon Church, 19 miles from Hopewell on Route 10, at Burrowsville, is part of the original Martin's-Brandon Parish founded in 1616. The present building was erected in 1865 to replace earlier churches. The communion silver given to the parish by John Westrope in 1757 is displayed during Historic Garden Week. The doors of the church, which do not have locks, are always open.

Brandon Plantation, designed by Thomas Jefferson, and its gardens extending to the river front are among the loveliest in Virginia. Cultivated since 1614, it may be the longest continuous farming enterprise in the U.S. Turn left at Burrowsville, leaving Route 10 at Brandon Church, and follow marked roads to this vast plantation once owned by John Martin, friend of Captain John Smith, and later by Benjamin Harrison. The estate comprises more than 5,000 acres, planted mostly in small grains and pasture. Admission charge. Gardens open daily, 9:00 a.m. to 5:30 p.m.. House open during Historic Garden Week and otherwise by appointment only. Telephone: (804) 866-8416.

Another 20 miles southeast of Burrowsville along Route 10 is the town of Surry, home of **Smith's Fort Plantation.** Here in 1609, Captain John Smith built a "New Fort" to defend Jamestown directly across the river. Land was given in 1614 by Chief Powhatan to John Rolfe on the occasion of Rolfe's marriage to Pocahontas, daughter of Powhatan. Deep in what was then a hostile wilderness, in 1652, Thomas Warren "did begin to build a fifty-foot brick house." The house was restored in 1935 and furnished with authentic period furniture and furnishings. Open daily, last week of

April through September 30, Wednesday through Saturday, 10:00 a.m. to 5:00 p.m.; Sundays, 1:00 p.m. to 5:00 p.m. Open year round to tour groups by appointment. Telephone: (804) 294-3872.

Drive still further southeast on Route 10 about 10 miles, and you will reach **Chippokes Plantation State Park.** Across the river from Jamestown, Chippokes has been farmed continuously since 1616. The existing house was built about 1854, and has many original furnishings. Its gardens are resplendent with flowering crepe myrtle, azaleas, towering cedars, and gnarled paper mulberry trees. Sheep and cattle graze and soy beans, peanuts and corn are grown on the 1,683-acre plantation, which is operated by the Virginia Division of Parks. The Visitors Center is open daily, Memorial Day through Labor Day, 9:00 a.m. to 5:00 p.m. House tours are offered Wednesday through Sunday, 12:30 p.m. to 4:00 p.m. The park is open year round by reservation to groups of 10 or more. Telephone: (804) 786-2132. Nominal parking charge.

The north bank of the James River is dotted with equally lovely plantations, most of them along Route 5 in Charles City County. **Shirley,** 18 miles east of Richmond, has been the home of the Carter family since 1723. Furnishings include the original family portraits, English silver, superb paneling, and carved walnut stairway. Shirley was the home so often visited by Robert E. Lee, whose mother was Anne Hill Carter. The present owners are the ninth generation to operate the plantation. A complete set of 18th-century buildings form a Queen Anne forecourt. Admission charge. Open daily, 9:00 a.m. to 5:00 p.m. The last tour begins at 4:30 p.m. Closed Christmas. Telephone: (804) 795-2385 (toll-free from Richmond) or (804) 829-5121 (toll-free from Charles City).

Berkeley is one of the most visited and historic of the great James River plantations. It was the site of the first official American Thanksgiving in 1619, the birthplace of President William Henry Harrison, and the ancestral home of President Benjamin Harrison. "Taps" was composed here in 1862. The plantation mansion was built in 1726, and its grounds include terraced boxwood gardens, a restaurant, and gift shop. Admission charge. Open daily, 8:00 a.m. to 5:00 p.m. Telephone: (804) 829-6018.

Westover was built in 1730 by William Byrd II, a founder of Richmond and Petersburg. It is one of the notable plantations between Richmond and Williamsburg, and an outstanding example of Georgian architecture. The grounds and garden are open to the public daily, 9:00 a.m. to 6:00 p.m. House itself is open only during Historic Garden Week. Admission charge. Telephone: (804) 829-2882.

Westover Church was erected in 1737. The families of William Byrd of Westover and two Presidents of the United States, William Henry Harrison and John Tyler, have worshipped in this building. The earlier church of this name was on the Westover estate. In this ancient churchyard was located the oldest recorded tombstone in Virginia. Its inscription, now weathered away, bore the date 1637 in memory of Captain William Perry. Open daily, 9:00 a.m. to 5:00 p.m. Admission charge. Children free. Telephone: (804) 829-2882.

President John Tyler purchased **Sherwood Forest Plantation** in 1842. He doubled the size of the original house, which had been built in 1780 and today is believed to be the longest frame dwelling in the United States. The home is of the Empire period and contains many effects and furnishings of the late president. Two important features are its unusual woodwork and a unique arched ceiling. Since 1845, Sherwood Forest has been the home of the Tyler family. Grounds open daily, 9:00 a.m. to 5:00 p.m.; house open, 9:00 a.m. to 5:00 p.m., but by appointment only. Closed Christmas. Admission charge. Telephone: (804) 829-5377.

Belle Air plantation house, built around 1670, is one of the oldest frame dwellings in America. As the only survivor of its kind in Virginia, it is an important architectural monument. Original heart pine timbers still serve ingeniously as both sturdy structure and interior decorative trim. Plainly visible are huge hand-carved summer beams, expressed sills, intermediate and corner posts, and the finest Jacobean staircase in America. Though elegant for its period, Belle Air reflects the simplicity in which even wealthy pioneer planters lived. It has been restored and beautifully decorated in fabrics and furnishings of the 18th century. Gardens open to the public. First and second floors, smokehouse, laundry kitchen, and herb garden may be visited by groups of 25 or more by appointment only or during Historic Garden Week. Closed December 18 through January 3. Admission charge. Telephone: (804) 829-2431.

EASTERN SHORE

From the Capital Beltway, take Exit 19 (Route 50) to Salisbury, then south on Route 13. From the Baltimore

Beltway, take Exit 4 (Route 3 south), then left on Route 100, right on Route 2, and left on Route 50, continuing as above. From Richmond, follow I-64 south to Norfolk, then take the Chesapeake Bay Bridge-Tunnel to Route 13.

The original name of Virginia's Eastern Shore was "Accomack," an Indian name meaning "across the water place." It is a narrow peninsula between the bay and the ocean, with one through highway, Route 13, running down the middle from Maryland to the bridge-tunnel. The region is noted for its excellent fishing, swimming, boating, and 17th- and 18th-century historic buildings. Visitors can watch thousands of waterfowl feeding or resting in game preserves or see the wild ponies grazing on Chincoteague salt marshes.

The ancient fishing village of **Chincoteague** is reached from Route 13 via Route 175 and a causeway. Close to the Gulf Stream, it is a major fishing port with many sport fishing boats available. At the **Chincoteague Miniature Pony Farm** (201 Maddox Boulevard) you can see the famous small ponies, Falabella miniature horses, and Misty (who has been, alas, stuffed and mounted). Open February to Memorial Day and mid-September through November, daily, noon to 5:00 p.m. Open in summer, daily, 10:00 a.m. to 9:00 pm. Admission charge. Telephone: (804) 336-3066.

The **Oyster Museum** on Beach Road has live exhibits of all kinds of shellfish, including seahorses and clams; also, maritime artifacts and implements of the seafood industry. Open Memorial Day through Labor Day, daily, 11:00 a.m. to 5:00 p.m.; weekends during spring and fall months, 11:00 a.m. to 5:00 p.m. Admission charge. Telephone: (804) 336-6117.

Refuge Waterfowl Museum is at Maddox Boulevard and Beach Road. There are exhibits of boats, weapons, traps, antique decoys, carvings, and art, all relating to the hunting of waterfowl. Open March 1 through May 30 and November 1 through December 20, weekends, 10:00 a.m. to 5:00 p.m. Open Memorial Day through October 31, daily, 10:00 a.m. to 5:00 p.m. Admission charge. Telephone: (804) 336-5800.

A free causeway takes the visitor to **Assateague**, a narrow, 33-mile-long island. To see the wild ponies and three-foot high Sitka deer in the natural habitat, visit the **Chincoteague Wildlife Refuge**, which takes up most of Assateague. It has day-use vacation facilities and a fine beach. Telephone: (804) 336-6122.

Six miles from Chincoteague off Route 13 is the **NASA**

Wallops Visitor Center Flight Facility. Information on self-guided walking tours is available at the Visitor Center, where exhibits commemorate America's space program. Open Thursday through Monday, 10:00 a.m. to 4:00 p.m. Closed Thanksgiving, Christmas, and New Year's. Admission free. Telephone: (804) 824-1344.

Tangier, a get-away-from-it-all island in the middle of the Chesapeake Bay west of Chincoteaque, was chartered by Captain John Smith in 1607. Almost 80 years later, it was settled by John Crockett and his family—and little has changed since. In fact, the town's 850 people still speak with an Elizabethan accent. You will enjoy strolling quaint, carless streets, visiting the crab shanties at the harbor, and filling up on seafood.

The only way to get to Tangier is by boat. If you don't have your own, hop aboard one of the two regular cruise ships serving Tangier. Tangier and Rappahannock Cruises leave from Reedville, VA, at 10:00 a.m., returning at 4:15 p.m., daily, May 1 through the second week in October. Telephone: (804) 333-4656. Tangier Island Cruises leaves from Crisfield, MD, daily, Memorial Day through October 31, departing at 12:30 p.m. and returning at 5:15 p.m.; from November 1 through May 30, Monday through Saturday, departing 12:30 p.m. and returning at 8:00 a.m. the following morning. Telephone: (301) 968-2338 or 425-2631. (See also Special Interest Section, Organized Day Trips.)

Accomac, charming town and county seat, is noted for its many well-preserved federal buildings. The county was formed in 1634, one of the original "shires" of Virginia. Its most famous shrine is the **Debtor's Prison**, built in 1782. In nearby **Makemie Park** stands a monument to Francis Makemie, father of Presbyterianism in America. To him is attributed the Act of Toleration of 1699.

Onancock, founded in 1680, is the site of **Kerr Place**, built in the 1790s and now the local historical society's museum. Open March through December, Tuesday through Saturday, 10:00 a.m. to 4:00 p.m. Telephone: (804) 787-8012. Eight miles south, on Route 718, is **Pungoteague**. The first English-spoken play acted in America, "Ye Beare and Ye Cubb," was performed here in 1665. The third oldest church in the country, established in 1662, stands here. The present structure was built in 1738, replacing an earlier wooden building.

Wachapreague fishing resort is on Route 180, five miles east of Route 13. The fishing season extends from April through October. Among game fish caught in the waters here are croakers, sea bass, white marlin, bluefish, and black drum. Wachapreague also claims the title, "flounder capital of the world."

The **Locustville Academy**, in the town of the same name, is the only survivor of the many schools built during the 1800s. This stately, white-framed building was used between 1859 and 1873.

Nassawadox was established by Quaker dissenters in the mid-1600s. Three miles to the south, just east of Birdsnest, is **Hungar's Church**, built in 1751. It is a rectangular structure of old rose brick in Flemish bond, covered with ivy. Its unique feature is a twin entrance with semicircular brick arches.

Eastville, town and county seat, dating from 1680, has several noteworthy buildings. The ivy-covered **Clerk's Office** was built in 1731. Nearby is the **Debtor's Prison** and the old whipping post. **Christ Church** was built in 1826, and **Taylor Tavern** dates back to pre-Revolutionary days.

Virginia Coast Reserve, near Nassawadox, contains about 35,000 acres of islands and salt marshes that extend to the mouth of Chesapeake Bay. Reserve headquarters are at **Brownsville**, a historic landmark. The area is renowned for large concentrations of shore birds, sea birds, migrating and wintering waterfowl. Visitors come here to see the cormorant, snow goose, egret, heron, ibis, sandpiper, and 10 species of hawk, including the rare falcon. The reserve presently conducts a limited number of natural history field trips and birding expeditions in the spring and fall. Contact reserve headquarters for schedules. Headquarters open daily, 9:00 a.m. to 4:30 p.m. Admission free. Telephone: (804) 442-3049.

East of Oyster is **Wreck Island Natural Area**, an island some seven miles offshore forming a link in the chain of barrier islands separating the Eastern Shore from the Atlantic. Only one-fifth of the island is high ground; the rest is salt marsh interlaced with a maze of pools and creeks. As with all the barrier islands, Wreck is a haven for flora and fauna. It is accessible only by boat from Oyster.

The Eastern Shore of Virginia Tourism Commission is located in Accomac at 1 Courthouse Road, just east of Debtor's Prison. Open Monday through Friday, 9:00 a.m. to 5:00 p.m. Closed holidays. Telephone: (804) 787-2460.

Tourists who wish to link a trip to the Eastern Shores of Maryland and Virginia with a visit to the Norfolk and

Williamsburg areas should take the **Chesapeake Bay Bridge Tunnel**. Consisting of bridges, tunnels, and man-made islands, the 17.6-mile span crosses the lower Chesapeake Bay, connecting the tip of Cape Charles with the southern Virginia mainland. At the Sea Gull Fishing Pier and Snack Bar, located on the island of Thimble Shoal Tunnel (the first tunnel from the south), parking, meals and sandwiches, and bait and fishing tackle are available.

Driving time from shore to shore is 20 to 25 minutes. There is a toll charge. Telephone: (804) 331-2960.

JAMESTOWN—WILLIAMSBURG—YORKTOWN

This historic area can be reached by taking I-64 east from Richmond approximately 50 miles.

More than 350 years of our nation's history are preserved within the span of the 23-mile-long Colonial Parkway linking three of America's greatest shrines—Jamestown, Williamsburg, and Yorktown. The river and woodland parkway moves, as did history itself, from Jamestown, the first permanent English settlement (1607), to Williamsburg, the colonial capital (1699), and from there to Yorktown, where American independence was won (1781). Crucial milestones in American history are crammed into the triangle formed by these three cities. The parkway begins at the Jamestown Visitor Center, passes near the door of the Williamsburg Information Center, and concludes at the Yorktown Visitor Center.

JAMESTOWN

Statues of John Smith and Pocahontas welcome the visitor to the 1,500-acre **Jamestown Island**, operated by the National Park Service. This is the original site where the English landed, May 13, 1607. A tangible reminder of old Jamestown is the ancient tower with its reconstructed church, the location of the first representative legislative assembly in the New World, which met in 1619. For 92 years (1607-1699) Jamestown was the capital city of Virginia. For 13 of those years it constituted the lone English toehold along the Atlantic seaboard.

The first point to visit at Jamestown is the modern **Visitor Center** building just across the footbridge from the parking area. Interpretive theater programs and dioramas of Jamestown activities are constantly shown. In addition, many objects once used by the settlers have been unearthed from ruins and are on display. From the center a walking tour extends over the town site along the old streets and paths to the Church, the statehouse sites, and the ruins of old houses, taverns, and other buildings. The **Old Church Tower** is the only 17th-century ruin standing above ground at Jamestown. Paintings, markers, and recorded messages along the way describe life in the colony. The original landing site and the fort have long since been lost to the river's ebb and flow, but you can see pieces of original pottery and other 17th-century archaeological finds on display at Dale House. Lovely side excursions are the self-guided island loop drives through the wilderness section of the island.

Another road across a sandbar leads to **Glasshouse Point**. An isthmus, which later washed away, existed there in colonial times, when the glasshouse was built in 1608 "in the woods near a mile from James Towne." The present house is a reconstruction, but some of the original ruins are still on the site. You can watch with fascination as craftsmen blow hot glass into bottles and pitchers with the same skill as their colleagues of 350 years ago. Examples of their work are available for purchase.

The Visitor Center and Glasshouse Point are open daily, Memorial Day through Labor Day, 9:00 a.m. to 6:00 p.m. Labor Day through late fall, open to 5:30 p.m. Winter, through May 30, open to 5:00 p.m. The gate to the park opens and closes one-half hour earlier than the Visitor Center. Closed Christmas. Admission charge. Telephone: (804) 898-3400.

Nearby **Jamestown Festival Park** commemorates the first permanent English settlement in the New World in 1607. The Festival Park was built in 1957 by the Commonwealth of Virginia as a reconstruction of that settlement. The **Old Pavilion** dramatizes the heritage transmitted from Great Britain to Jamestown and the **New Pavilion** emphasizes the evolution of our democratic form of government from the first representative assembly held at Jamestown.

At reconstructed **James Fort**, the visitor may climb the ramparts of the palisaded fort with its 17th-century costumed halberdier guides, pose for pictures in the stocks, and visit the thatch and clay houses similar to those in which the first settlers lived. One may watch the changing of the guard, see Chief Powhatan's Lodge, and complete the illusion by clambering aboard three little ships that are full-scale sailing replicas of the *Susan Constant*, *Godspeed*, and *Discovery*. Craftsmen demonstrate pottery, spinning, basketmaking, woodworking, and other colonial handiwork. Seventeenth-century farming methods are also displayed including plots of tobacco and corn.

Added attractions at Jamestown Festival Park are **Mermaid Tavern**, a gift shop, and spacious picnic grounds with running water, soft drink machines, picnic tables, and benches. All exhibits are identified by labels and signs, and the Festival Park provides hostesses and interpreters in the Pavilions and reconstructed sites. Admission charge. Open daily, 9:00 a.m. to 5:00 p.m. Closed Christmas and New Year's. Telephone: (804) 229-1607.

WILLIAMSBURG

Many places around the country call themselves shrines of American democracy, but **Colonial Williamsburg** can accurately claim that title. It was here that such patriots as Thomas Jefferson and Patrick Henry forged ideas into ideals that became the American dream.

Today Williamsburg is restored to resemble its appearance from 1699 to 1780, when it served as capital of Great Britain's largest and most prosperous colony in the New World. During that time, it was the center of activity—political, social, economic, and cultural—in the Old Dominion. A succession of seven royal governors lived in the Palace, the symbol of the power and prestige of the Crown in Virginia. The General Assembly convened and held discussion in the Capitol. Twice a year during the "Publick Times," when the general court was in session and people were in town to conduct business, the town's population doubled and the taverns were crowded. A cross-section of Virginians went up and down Duke of Gloucester Street on foot, on horseback, and in carriages, where today's sightseers can observe various aspects of 18th-century life. Now they come to Williamsburg from all corners of the world not only to view the restored 18th-century city, but also to return home with a renewed appreciation of the precepts, ideals, and traditions upon which our democracy was founded.

Begin your visit at the **Visitor Center**, where an exciting film will make what happened in Williamsburg come alive for you. "Williamsburg—The Story of a Patriot" is shown throughout the day from 8:45 a.m. to 6:00 p.m. Admission charge.

The grounds and shops are open to the public, but to

enter any of the historic buildings you will need an admission ticket which can be purchased at the Visitor Center. The ticket also entitles you to unlimited use of the shuttle buses that circle the entire Historic Area.

Major exhibition buildings in Williamsburg include the **Raleigh Tavern**, a center of social and political life, where one early traveler remarked, "more business has been transacted than on the Exchanges of London or Amsterdam"; the colonial **Capitol**, where Virginia laws were made and her young statesmen trained; **Governor's Palace**; **Magazine and Guardhouse** (1715), from which Lord Dunmore's removal of powder was a signal to revolution; and such unpretentious but inviting homes as **Brush-Everard House** (1717) and **George Wythe House** (ca. 1760). One of the most photographed spots in America is the **Public Gaol**, near the Capitol, with pillories and stocks for debtors and criminals. The **Sir Christopher Wren Building** (1695) is the oldest academic building in America and stands on the campus of the College of William and Mary, the second oldest college in the United States.

Exhibits in the **Archaeological Museum** in the **James Anderson House** display many interesting artifacts dating back to Williamsburg's days as a thriving colonial town. Also of interest is **Bruton Parish Church** (completed in 1715), the court church of the Virginia Colony. Regular services are held in this lovely church which contains the font and communion silver of the Jamestown church. The bell, installed in 1761, has rung for many historic events and may be heard each Sunday. Especially fascinating is the beautiful churchyard which contains a number of early tombstones.

The **Public Hospital** on Francis Street was the first American institution devoted exclusively to the treatment of the mentally ill when it was completed in 1773. Destroyed by fire in 1885, the hospital has been meticulously rebuilt on original foundations after more than 12 years of research. Adjacent to the Public Hospital is the **DeWitt Wallace Decorative Arts Gallery**, a contemporary bi-level museum opened in 1985 and funded by the late DeWitt Wallace, founder of *The Reader's Digest*. The Gallery displays a broad range of English and American decorative arts—furniture, metals, ceramics, glass, paintings, prints, maps, and textiles—dating from about 1600 through 1830. Weary visitors can find respite in the **Lila Acheson Wallace Memorial Garden**, part of the Gallery/Public Hospital complex. This contemporary formal garden, designed by British landscape architect Sir Peter

Shepheard, combines permanent plantings with many seasonal ones and features native materials.

Throughout the Historic Area are 17 restored and reconstructed shops exhibiting more than 30 colonial crafts. They include **Anderson Forge, Boot Shop, Printing Office and Bookbindery, Millinery Shop, Raleigh Bake Shop, Silversmith Shop, Apothecary Shop, Wig Shop, Cabinet Shop, Windmill, Gunsmith,** and **Candle Maker.** Lantern Tours are held several nights each week, headed by a craftsman with a group of 20 lantern-carrying visitors who inspect four shops during a 75-minute tour. Other important exhibition buildings are **Wetherburn's Tavern, James Geddy House and Silversmith Shop,** and shops of the blacksmith, cooper, pewterer, music teacher, harnessmaker, and shinglemaker.

Historic buildings in Colonial Williamsburg are open daily, 9:00 a.m. to 5:00 p.m. The Visitor Center is open daily, 8:30 a.m. to 8:30 p.m. You can write ahead for admission tickets and other information: Colonial Williamsburg, PO Box Drawer C, Williamsburg, VA 23187. Telephone: (804) 229-1000. For room or dinner reservations only, telephone: (800) 447-8679. Many area hotels offer packages including admission tickets. For annual events at Williamsburg, see the Calendar Section.

There are a number of interesting sites nearby operated by the Colonial Williamsburg Foundation. On Francis Street near the Capitol is **Bassett Hall,** the former 18th-century home of Mr. and Mrs. John D. Rockefeller, Jr. The family lovingly restored it during the 1930s and it is handsomely furnished with many of their possessions and artwork. Members of the Rockefeller family stay here on their frequent visits to Virginia, at which time the home is closed to the public. Open daily, March through November, 10:00 a.m. to 5:00 p.m. Open weekends only during winter. Admission charge (tour reservations are requested). Telephone: (804) 229-1000.

Housed in a 19th-century building next to the Williamsburg Inn is the largest collection of American primitive paintings and other objects of folk art in the country. The **Abby Aldrich Rockefeller Folk Art Center** is the gift of Mrs. John D. Rockefeller, Jr., who presented it to Colonial Williamsburg in 1939. Its nine galleries suggest the kind of domestic interiors in which folk art was originally displayed. Open daily, 10:00 a.m. to 6:00 p.m. Closed occasionally throughout the year for exhibition preparation. Admission charge. Telephone: (804) 229-1000, extension 2424.

A one-way, 12-foot-wide historic country road, which leaves Colonial Williamsburg from South England Street, takes you through forests, fields, lush meadows, and green marchlands to **Carter's Grove**, a James River plantation. It contains nearly 700 acres of the original estate. Carter's Grove is being developed as a working plantation, with authentic 18th-century livestock and crops. Future plans call for demonstration of plantation crafts and restoration of all outbuildings.

Built in 1754, the plantation was the home of the influential Burwell family and a meeting place of notable Virginians. The mansion, operated by Colonial Williamsburg Foundation, is considered one of the most beautiful homes in America. It is over 200 feet long and looks over green terraces to the James River. The entrance hall and stair hall are noted for their handsome paneling and carved woodwork, The stable, now an information center, contains exhibit space and a small gift shop. Open daily, March through November, and during the Williamsburg Christmas season, 9:00 a.m. to 5:00 p.m. Telephone: (804) 229-1000.

Within the grounds of Carter's Grove are the remains of the 17th-century **Wolstenholme Towne**. Weather permitting, you can watch archaeologists piecing together clues to this once-thriving village.

Located three miles east of Williamsburg on Route 60, The **Old Country-Busch Gardens** is a 360-acre outdoor family entertainment park featuring seven 17th-century European hamlets with rides, restaurants, and unique shops. You can also enjoy a variety of entertainment including weekend concerts with top celebrities, a family-oriented variety show with acrobats and unicyclists, or a country and western show featuring audience participation. Many of the individual hamlets have entertainment, also, such as the Munich Festhaus and the Italian folk show. You can also attend a Broadway-style musical revue. A special feature of the park is the Loch Ness Monster, a double-loop steel roller coaster with speeds up to 65 m.p.h. From the Rhine boat cruise or from steam-powered trains, you can get a close look at wildlife roaming freely in various parts of the park, including more than 300 native North American and European animals. Baby animals are displayed in a petting zoo, and the Clydesdale horses are stabled in an area called "Heatherdowns." Transportation through the park includes a computer-operated Monorail, a sky-ride, and steam locomotives.

Open weekends spring and fall; daily, from mid-May through Labor Day. Hours vary, so it is best to telephone ahead. Admission charge entitles visitors to all rides, entertainment, and attractions; children under 2, admission free. Parking charge per car. For group rates or further information contact: The Old Country-Busch Gardens, PO Drawer F.C., Williamsburg, VA 23187. Telephone: (804) 253-3350. In the Washington area, telephone: (703) 522-1387; in the Philadelphia area, telephone: (215) 664-3220.

YORKTOWN

Leaving the Colonial Williamsburg Visitor Center, the parkway leads to Yorktown. There are scenic markers and stopping points at strategic spots along the parkway. The large and scenic Ringfield Picnic Area has rest facilities, drinking water, and picnic tables. The road hugs the river-bank for six miles and ends on the bluffs of **Yorktown Battlefield.**

All through the 18th-century, Yorktown was a busy port. The town's "port facilities and good harbor" held a fatal attraction for the British General Cornwallis in the last months of the Revolutionary War. Cornwallis and his British Army were bottled up by George Washington's allied American and French forces and were forced to surrender on October 19, 1781.

The Yorktown Visitor Center and Battlefield are operated by the National Park Service. Climb to the **Siege Line Lookout** where the strategic area of the famous battle will be pointed out by National Park Service historians. The view affords a tremendous sweep of the harbor and toward the Chesapeake Bay where Comte de Grasse with his French fleet held the blockade of the British in Yorktown. Special exhibits at the Yorktown Visitor Center trace the story of the Town of York and events of the decisive three-week siege. On the wall is one of the few graffito murals in the world, created by Hans Gassman, internationally known artist. Among the displays are military tents used by Washington, a partially reconstructed British frigate, bottles, and other artifacts recovered from the river bottom. A number of dioramas depict scenes of the battle. Visitor Center open daily, 8:00 a.m. to 6:00 p.m. Extended hours during the spring and summer; call for details. Closed Christmas Day. Telephone: (804) 898-3400.

Two separate **Loop Drives** leave from the visitor center; one is 12 miles long, the other is eight. Taped narration and recorders are available for rent from the bookstore. Free 35-minute bus tours operate daily, mid-June through Labor Day. You will drive past redoubts, cannons, twisting fortifications, and by **Washington's Headquarters**. Living history demonstrations at **Moore House** enable visitors to partake in the October 19, 1781, British surrender which virtually ended the war. Open daily, Memorial Day through Labor Day, 10:00 a.m. to 5:00 p.m. Spring and fall, open weekends only. Hours vary; call for details. Telephone: (804) 898-3400. Admission free.

Yorktown's famous citizen, Thomas Nelson, Jr., a signer of the Declaration of Independence and wartime governor of Virginia, lived in the early 18th-century Georgian home now called **Nelson House**. Some historians believe that the home served as Cornwallis's headquarters during the siege. Two theatrical presentations dramatize daily colonial life. Open daily, mid-June through Labor Day, 11:00 a.m. to 5:00 p.m. Admission free. Open weekends only in spring and fall. The entire park is open daily, 8:00 a.m. to dusk. Closed Christmas Day. Admission free. Telephone: (804) 898-3400.

The nearby **Yorktown Victory Center**, operated by the Commonwealth of Virginia, opens to visitors the restored village of Yorktown with its 18th-century buildings, artifacts, dioramas, works of art, and replicas of notable documents and objects of the Revolutionary era. A display of 20th-century electronic gadgetry takes you back in time to the sights and sounds of Revolutionary America, from the Boston Tea Party to the final defeat of the British troops by George Washington and the French at Yorktown in 1781. A film and gallery depict these same events. There is a major exhibit of artifacts currently being recovered from Cornwallis's supply ships sunk in the York River, two blocks from the Victory Center. The continuing excavation work is on view to the public. Open daily, January through February, 10:00 a.m. to 5:00 p.m. March through June, 9:00 a.m. to 5:00 p.m. June 15 through August 15, 9:00 a.m. to 7:00 p.m. August through December, 9:00 a.m. to 5:00 p.m. Admission free. Telephone: (804) 229-1607.

NORTH OF HISTORICAL AREA

North of the colonial historic area are a number of places that should interest visitors. **York River State Park**, off

Route 607, has an excellent interpretive program, organized canoe trips on Taskinas Creek, and hikes through the rare and delicate ecological environment that constitutes coastal Virginia. The Visitors Information Center has exhibits, an audiovisual presentation, playground and picnic facilities, and a boat ramp. Park open daily, dawn to dusk. Visitors Center open daily, Memorial Day through Labor Day, 10:00 a.m. to 6:00 p.m. Open during September, weekends only, 10:00 a.m. to 6:00 p.m. Admission free. Telephone: (804) 564-9057.

Mattaponi Indian Reservation is located in King William County, 13 miles west of West Point. It consists of 125 acres, where 23 families of 75 persons live in modern residences. Visitors can use the wooded picnic grounds, spring, and a hard slope into the Mattaponi River that is suitable as a boat ramp. Some boats are available for rental. There is a museum, trading post, and craft shop where pottery is sold. Open daily, 8:00 a.m. to 7:00 p.m. Admission charge. Telephone: (804) 769-2194.

King William County Courthouse, on Route 30 about 18 miles from West Point, was built in 1725 and has been in continuous use since its first occupancy. It is one of the few buildings of that date in the nation which still serves its original purpose today and is a fine example of colonial architecture. The brickwork is Flemish bond. Open Monday through Friday, 8:30 a.m. to 4:30 p.m. Closed national holidays. Admission free. Telephone: (804) 769-2311.

On Route 602 (just off Route 17), **Urbanna** is a mecca for fishing, boating, and crabbing enthusiasts who enjoy sailing and yachting on the Rappahannock and Piankatank rivers and on the Chesapeake Bay. Boat and yacht harbors abound on Urbanna Creek, Fishing Bay, and at Deltaville in Middlesex County, and the area is headquarters for a large crab and oyster fleet. Throughout the season, Urbanna is a popular place for regattas, motorboat and sailing races. Each summer and early fall, local boat owners arrange fishing parties and cruises (especially to Tangier Island), and the town sponsors an Oyster Festival the first weekend in November. Sportsmen also come for the fine quail and duck hunting in the area.

Among historic buildings in Urbanna are the "**Old Tobacco Warehouse**," built circa 1763, now serving as a public library, and the **Old Court House**. Other noted colonial landmarks are **Rosegill**, home of a colonial governor, the **Old**

Tavern (1742), and **Hewick** (1675). The **Custom House** dates from about 1695.

NORFOLK-HAMPTON ROADS AREA

Reach this southeastern part of Virginia from Richmond via I-64 east about 90 miles. From Washington and Baltimore, take I-95 south and proceed as above. The seaports clustered around the mouth of the James River are only about a half hour's drive beyond Williamsburg. The area has long been known as one of the world's finest natural harbors, and is justifiably an important entry in both history and guide books. Hampton Roads has been a major anchorage since colonial times and has extensive harbor facilities and shipyards. The term "Hampton Roads" actually refers to the roadstead or four-mile passageway through which the waters of the James, Nansemond, and Elizabeth rivers pass into Chesapeake Bay. It is often used to designate the harbors and cities that surround the area: Hampton and Newport News on the north shore, and Norfolk and Portsmouth on the south. Route I-64 and its arteries connect the various cities, and its Hampton Roads Bridge-Tunnel (toll charge) has one of the longest vehicular tunnels (nearly one-and-a-half miles) in the United States. This area is approximately 90 miles from Richmond and 200 miles from Washington, DC.

HAMPTON

First stop should be the **Hampton Visitors Center** at Settler's Landing Road and Eaton Street, where you can obtain information on the self-guided driving tour. Open daily, 9:00 a.m. to 5:00 p.m. Closed major holidays. Admission free. Telephone: (804) 727-6108.

Air Power Park, at 413 West Mercury Boulevard, displays vintage jet aircraft. Open daily, 9:00 a.m. to 5:00 p.m. Closed New Year's, Thanksgiving, and Christmas. Admission free. Telephone: (804) 727-6781.

Across from the Air Power Park is the **Syms-Eaton Museum**, depicting the story of Hampton from the first landing of English colonists in 1607 to the present. **Kecoughtan Indian Village** features replicas of lodges and huts of the Indians who first welcomed English settlers to Hampton's shores. Museum and Village open Monday to Friday, 10:00 a.m. to 4:00 p.m.; Saturday and Sunday, 10:00 to 5:00 p.m.

Closed Christmas and New Year's. Facilities for handicapped. Admission free. Telephone: (804) 727-6248.

Old downtown Hampton, around King and Queen streets, will give you the flavor of this 350-year-old city. Stroll along the docks, visit the many fine shops, and (if you time it right) watch the fishing boats and crabbers unloading their catch.

At the corner of Queens Way and High Court Lane is **St. John's Church**. Established in 1610, it is the oldest English-speaking parish in the country. The present church was built in 1728, and the communion silver, prized possession of the parish, is from London (1618). Tours by appointment only. Admission free. Telephone: (804) 722-2567.

The **NASA Visitor Center-Langley Research Center** displays the full range of America's space program. "Hands on" exhibits feature lots of buttons to press and levers to pull, a real treat for children. The center also is loaded with space vehicles, paraphernalia transported to the moon, and satellite equipment. Open Monday through Saturday, 8:30 a.m. to 4:30 p.m.; Sunday noon to 4:30 p.m. Closed Easter, Thanksgiving, Christmas, and New Year's. Admission free. Telephone: (804) 865-2855.

A highlight of your visit to this area is a walking tour of **Fort Monroe** (obtain maps at the Hampton Visitors Center). Forts have occupied this land since 1609, and the present moat-encircled facility remained a Union stronghold throughout the Civil War. It was here at Hampton Roads on March 9, 1862, that the ironclad warships, the *Monitor* and the *Merrimack* (more correctly known as the *Virginia*), engaged in a historic four-hour battle. Located within the old fort's walls is the **Casemate Museum** displaying the cell which held Jefferson Davis prisoner. The ramparts provide panoramic views of the Chesapeake Bay. Open daily, 10:30 a.m. to 5:00 p.m. Closed Thanksgiving, Christmas, and New Year's. Admission free. Telephone: (804) 727-3973.

Other points of interest in the Hampton area include the 11,000-seat **Hampton Roads Coliseum; Buckroe Beach**, a family amusement and recreation area on Chesapeake Bay; **Bluebird Gap Farm**, a livestock zoo for children; **Big Bethel Battlefield**, where the first major land battle of the Civil War was fought on June 10, 1861; **Hampton Institute**, established 1868 and dedicated to the education of freed slaves; and **College Museum**, with an excellent collection of ethnic art.

NEWPORT NEWS

The main thoroughfare in Newport News is Route 143. Just off Jefferson Avenue, you will pass wooded **Deer Run Park**. The park's attractions include nature trails, picnic facilities, a playground, two golf courses, a fishing lake, archery, and 189 campsites. Deer Run Park is the largest city/municipal park east of the Mississippi. Open daily, dawn to dusk. Admission free (there is a charge for campsites). Telephone: (804) 877-5211.

Within the gates of Fort Eustis is the fascinating **U.S. Army Transportation Museum** depicting the extensive history of military transportation. "Nothing happens until something moves" is a military slogan that unfolds here. Exhibits feature overland vehicles, helicopters, fixed-wing aircraft, and rail systems which the Army operated in Europe, North Africa, and the Far East. One of the more unusual displays is the world's only captive "flying saucer." Open daily, 9:00 a.m. to 4:30 p.m. Closed New Year's, Easter, Thanksgiving, and Christmas. Admission free. Facilities for handicapped. Telephone: (804) 878-1109.

From Warwick Boulevard, turn right for a stop at **Virginia Living Museum**, which interprets land, sea, and sky. The natural history exhibits explore the area's unique habitat, while an aquarium has displays of local sea life. The observatory and planetarium are favorites among youngsters, as is the Curiosity Corner stocked with televisions, computers, and other "hands on" exhibits. Open Monday through Saturday, 9:00 a.m. to 5:00 p.m.; Sunday, 1:00 p.m. to 5:00 p.m.; Thursday evening, 7:00 p.m. to 9:00 p.m. Closed Thanksgiving and Christmas. Admission charge. Telephone: (804) 595-1900.

Turn right on Clyde Morris Boulevard for the **Mariner's Museum**, a top area attraction. Here the visitor can see the world's foremost collection of ships, ship models, naval weapons, figure-heads, maritime art, as well as the story of whaling and the history of the Chesapeake Bay. Open Monday through Saturday, 9:00 a.m. to 5:00 p.m.; Sunday, noon o 5:00 p.m. Closed Christmas. Admission charge. Facilities for handicapped. Telephone: (804) 595-0368.

Return to Warwick Boulevard and follow signs into the downtown area. The **War Memorial Museum of Virginia** contains a vast collection of more than 20,000 artifacts tracing

American combat from 1775 to the present: uniforms, weapons, posters, vehicles, and insignia. Open Monday through Saturday, 9:00 a.m. to 5:00 p.m.; Sunday, 1:00 p.m. to 5:00 p.m. Closed Easter, Thanksgiving, Christmas, and New Year's. Nominal admission charge. Telephone: (804) 247-8523.

En route downtown, you will pass the giant **Newport News Shipbuilding and Dry Dock Company**, the world's largest privately owned shipyard. Because of its many top-secret projects, it is closed to the public. You can, however, see some of the facility from the water by taking the harbor cruise (see below).

Continue south past **Christopher Newport Park**. This is a worthwhile stop if you are interested in a stroll through formal gardens or a sweeping view of the waterfront. **Victory Arch**, a short distance beyond, on West Avenue, honors Peninsula servicemen of all wars who marched through the Arch on their way to and from warships.

The best way to get an idea of the size of the giant Hampton Roads harbor area is to take the **Jamestown Island Cruise**, leaving the dock at the corner of 12th Street and Jefferson Avenue. You will follow the same water route sailed in the early 17th century by captains John Smith and Christopher Newport. The comprehensive daily two-hour tour cruises North America's oldest waterway, past Norfolk Naval Base and the water side of Newport News Shipbuilding and Dry Dock Company. There is a full departure schedule which varies with the season. Evening cruises featuring a buffet dinner, music, and dancing and Sunday afternoon cruises are also offered by the cruise line. All cruises have an expert commentator on board. Call ahead for a complete schedule and for reservations. Daily, April through October. Telephone: (804) 245-1553. Toll-free from Williamsburg: (804) 877-6114. (See also Special Interest Section, Organized Day Trips.)

NORFOLK

You can visit the major attractions of Norfolk via a self-guided driving tour, following the blue "Norfolk Tour" signs. Maps and other information are available at the **Norfolk Convention and Visitors Bureau**, 236 E. Plume Street, in the Hampton Roads Maritime Building. Open weekdays, 8:30 a.m. to 5:00 p.m. Telephone: (804) 441-5266. The Ocean View Information Center is in Ocean View (take the fourth "View

St." exit off I-64). Open 9:00 a.m. to 5:00 p.m., Labor Day through June; 9:00 a.m. to 8:00 p.m., June through September. Telephone: (804) 588-0404.

Within walking distance of the main Convention and Visitors Bureau are five sites worthy of a visit. The **MacArthur Memorial** on MacArthur Square serves as the final resting place of General Douglas MacArthur. Located in the completely refurnished Old Court House, it has several galleries of exhibits tracing the career of the illustrious military leader. Visitors are invited to see a film on the general's life and achievements. Open Monday through Saturday, 10:00 a.m. to 5:00 p.m.; Sunday, 11:00 a.m. to 5:00 p.m. Closed Thanksgiving, Christmas, and New Year's. Admission free. Facilities for handicapped. Telephone: (804) 627-2965.

Nearby is **St. Paul's Church,** the only building in Norfolk left standing after the British bombardment of 1776. Today you can still see a cannonball from that battle lodged in the southeast wall. Open Tuesday through Saturday, 10:00 a.m. to 4:00 p.m.; Sunday, 2:00 p.m. to 4:00 p.m., summer only. Admission free. Telephone: (804) 627-4353.

The **Willoughby-Baylor House,** 601 E. Freemason Street, is a brick townhouse built in 1794. The authentic period furnishings were collected according to an inventory made after Captain Willoughby's death in 1800. Just down the street at Number 323 is the **Moses Myers House,** built shortly after the Revolution by Myers, one of America's "merchant princes." It is a classic example of an 18th-century townhouse, and is superbly preserved. About half the furnishings are original. Visitors are guided through the elegant home by costumed hostesses. An adjacent colonial rose garden reflects the tastes of the 18th century. Both homes are open April through December, Tuesday through Saturday, 10:00 a.m. to 5:00 p.m.; Sunday, noon to 5:00 p.m. Open January through March, Tuesday through Saturday, noon to 5:00 p.m. Admission charge; a discount ticket is available for visits to both houses. Still another ticket entitles you to admission to these homes as well as the Adam Thoroughgood House in Virginia Beach. Telephone: (804) 622-1211. All three homes are closed Thanksgiving, Christmas, and New Year's.

If you are intrigued by Norfolk's harbor, you will enjoy a visit to the **Norfolk School of Boat Building,** Pier B at the foot of Brooke Avenue. A maritime cultural center exhibits classic wooden boats under construction in a living museum atmosphere. Open Monday through Friday, 9:00 a.m. to 3:30

p.m. Admission free. Telephone: (804) 627-7266. The self-guided driving tour of Norfolk continues to the **Chrysler Museum**, at the corner of Olney Road and Mowbray Arch. Founded in 1933 as the Norfolk Museum of Arts and Sciences, it was greatly expanded in 1971 when Walter P. Chrysler, Jr., donated his magnificent art collection. The galleries represent many works from 2500 B.C.—Chinese bronzes to major European paintings to the latest in contemporary American art. Its Institute of Glass, acknowledged as one of the most comprehensive collections in the nation, displays thousands of pieces from Tiffany to Sandwich to rare Persian. Open Tuesday through Saturday, 10:00 a.m. to 4:00 p.m.; Sunday, 1:00 p.m. to 5:00 p.m. Closed Thanksgiving, Christmas, and New Year's. Admission free. Facilities for handicapped. Telephone: (804) 622-1211.

An enjoyable diversion is a drive around Colley and Colonial avenues through **Ghent**, a turn-of-the-century residential area undergoing restoration. Next stop is the **Hermitage Foundation Museum** at 7637 North Shore Road. Occupying a wooded estate overlooking Lafayette River, the Tudor mansion has a renowned collection of Oriental and medieval art including wood paneling and bas relief carvings. Open daily, 10:00 a.m. to 5:00 p.m. Sunday, 1:00 p.m. to 5:00 p.m. Admission charge. Telephone: (804) 423-2052.

The **Norfolk Naval Base**, near the junction of Routes 337 and 170, is the world's largest naval base and home port of more than 130 ships of the Atlantic and Mediterranean fleets. Buses leave the tour office at frequent intervals daily, April through October 15, from 10:30 a.m. to 2:30 p.m. Admission charge. You can usually see submarines, aircraft carriers, and destroyers at anchor. Certain ships may be visited on weekends between 1:00 p.m. and 4:00 p.m. Admission free. Telephone: (804) 444-7971 or 444-7955.

On Airport Road, **Norfolk Botanical Gardens** embraces 175 acres of flowers blooming almost year round: azaleas, camellias, dogwood, roses, rhododendron, and many other beauties. Trackless trains and canal boats offer visitors a memorable trip through miles of roadways and waterways. grounds. Open daily, 8:30 a.m. to sunset. Admission charge. Telephone: (804) 441-5385.

Norfolk also boasts the largest zoo in Virginia. **Virginia Zoological Park**, 3500 Granby Street, has modern exhibits of more than 350 animals, and a Public Plant Conservatory with tropical and desert displays. Open daily, 10:00 a.m. to 5:00

p.m. Closed Christmas and New Year's. Admission charge, but from 10:00 to 11:00 a.m. there is free admission every day. Telephone: (804) 441-2706 (recording) or (804) 441-5227.

As in Newport News, there are **harbor tours** offered in Norfolk. Departing from the Waterside Marketplace, the *Carrie B* sails daily, making 1½-hour tours. June through Labor Day, departures are at 10:00 a.m., noon, 2:00 p.m., and 4:00 p.m. The *New Spirit* offers lunch, dinner, and moonlight cruises with entertainment and dancing. April through October. Call for schedules and reservations. Telephone: (804) 625-1368 (recording) or (804) 627-7771.

If you prefer sailing under wind rather than power, you can take a three-hour sailing tour of Norfolk harbor aboard the new, 135-foot topsail schooner *American Rover*. Trips leave daily from The Waterside, Memorial Day through Labor Day, 10:00 a.m. and 6:00 p.m. Special charters are available at other times of the year. Admission charge. Telephone: (804) 627-7245.

PORTSMOUTH AND SUFFOLK

This historic seaport was first explored in 1608. As with the other cities in the area, its past revolves around the sea. A self-guided driving tour will take you to the points of interest. Pick up maps and sightseeing information at the **Portsmouth Visitors Center**, 524 Middle Street Mall. Open Monday through Friday, 9:00 a.m. to 5:00 p.m. (Maps of the driving tour are also available at the Naval Shipyard or the Coast Guard Lightship Museum.)

Start your tour at the waterfront near the foot of High Street. The recently enlarged sea wall, a boardwalk-like area, provides a delightful walk past many of the city's historic spots. The **Portsmouth Naval Shipyard Museum** has an outstanding collection of models of famous naval vessels, relics, trophies, old weapons, flags, and maps. Several exhibits are devoted to the Civil War battle between the *Monitor* and the *Merrimack*. Open Tuesday through Saturday, 10:00 a.m. to 5:00 p.m.; Sunday, 1:00 to 5:00 p.m. Closed Thanksgiving, Christmas, and New Year's. Admission free. Facilities for handicapped. Telephone: (804) 393-8591.

The **Coast Guard Lightship Museum** is located in a retired Coast Guard lightship moored nearby at the foot of London Street. The 101-foot ship, built in 1915, contains all types of Coast Guard equipment and historical exhibits. In its heyday, it served off the coasts of Virginia and Delaware, and in Nantucket Sound. Open Tuesday through Saturday, 10:00 a.m. to 4:45 p.m.; Sunday, 1:00 to 4:45 p.m. Closed Christmas and New Year's. Admission free. Telephone: (804) 393-8741.

The *Carrie B* (see description under "Norfolk") can be boarded in Portsmouth. The 1½-hour trips depart from the foot of Bay Street as follows: June through Labor Day, daily, 10:15 a.m., 12:15 p.m., 2:15 p.m., and 4:15 p.m. No 10:15 departure on Saturday and Sunday. A three-hour evening tour leaves at 6:15 p.m., daily. Admission charge. Telephone: (804) 393-4735.

Hill House, at 221 North Street, is in the heart of the Olde Towne section of the city, noted for its many early 19th-century homes. The house is furnished with original Hill family possessions, and the restored garden features two century-old magnolia trees. Open March through December, Tuesday through Saturday, 2:00 to 5:00 p.m. Nominal admission charge. Telephone: (804) 393-0241.

On nearby Dinwiddie Street is the **Monumental United Methodist Church** (1772), the oldest continuous Methodist congregation in the South. Francis Asbury, the first bishop elected to the Methodist Church in the U.S., once served as pastor here. Open Monday through Friday, 9:00 a.m. to 4:00 p.m.; Sunday, only during services (9:30 a.m. and 11:00 a.m.). Admission free. Telephone: (804) 397-1297.

The **Emanuel A.M.E. Church,** in the 600 block of North Street, is the oldest of its denomination in the area. It had its beginnings in 1775, with a largely slave membership. Benches and gallery rails were handhewn by members. Open Monday through Saturday, 9:00 a.m. to 3:00 p.m.; Sunday, only during services (from 11:00 a.m. to 2:00 p.m.). Admission free. Telephone: (804) 393-2259.

Trinity Episcopal Church, at High and Court streets, was built in 1762. Many Revolutionary War heroes are buried here in the adjoining graveyard. Open by appointment only, Monday through Friday, 9:00 a.m. to 4:00 p.m.; Sunday, only during services (8:00 a.m. and 10:30 a.m.). Telephone: (804) 393-0431.

Two historic homes located in the area are privately owned and not open to the public, but you can drive by and admire them from the street. **Watts House,** at 516 North Street, was built in 1799 by Colonel Dempsey Watts. **Ball House,** 417 Middle Street, was built about 1760, and later served as a barracks during the War of 1812. Lafayette and Andrew Jackson were entertained here.

The huge **Naval Shipyard** takes up four miles of waterfront. Built in 1767, it is the oldest, and largest, in the nation.

About four blocks from the waterfront, at 420 High Street, is the **Portsmouth Museum**. The gallery has monthly shows of ceramics, painting, photography, and dance. Open Tuesday through Saturday, 10:00 a.m. to 5:00 p.m.; Sunday, 1:00 to 5:00 p.m. Admission free. Telephone: (804) 393-8983.

The **Virginia Sports Hall of Fame** (420 High Street) will be of particular interest to sport enthusiasts of all types. Housed in a renovated 19th-century mansion, the Hall honors 70 different sports figures who were either born in Virginia or made their names here. Among those honored are Sam Snead, Arthur Ashe, Jean McLean Davis (world champion horsewoman), and Ace Parker (a football and baseball pro). Open Tuesday through Saturday, 10:00 a.m. to 5:00 p.m.; Sunday, 1:00 to 5:00 p.m. Admission free. Telephone: (804) 397-5273.

Housed with the Portsmouth Museum in the 1846 Court House Building is a spot youngsters will appreciate after long days of sightseeing. Exhibits at the **Portsmouth Children's Museum** are designed to be touched, not just looked at. For children aged 1½ and older, an exhibit called "Magic Eye" displays optics of all sorts: mirrors, lights, optical illusions, etc. Open Tuesday through Saturday, 10:00 a.m. to 5:00 p.m.; Sunday, 1:00 to 5:00 p.m. Nominal admission charge for children; admission free for adults. Telephone: (804) 393-8393.

Portside, a seasonal open-air marketplace at the foot of High Street on the Elizabeth River, features the **Olde Harbour Market**, where a dozen shops offer everything from ice cream and souvenirs to fresh seafood. A water stage features a variety of family-oriented entertainments, and the Visitor Center offers maps and brochures. The Olde Harbour Market is open in April, Monday to Friday, 11:00 a.m. to 2:00 p.m.; Saturday, 11:00 a.m. to 8:00 p.m.; Sunday, 1:00 to 8:00 p.m.; May through September, Monday to Saturday, 11:00 a.m. to 8:00 p.m.; Sunday, 1:00 to 8:00 p.m.; October, Wednesday, Friday and Saturday, 5:00 to 9:00 p.m.

The **Olde Towne Trolley Tour**, a 45-minute guided trolley tour of the Olde Towne historic district, allows visitors a unique way to view more than 50 points of historical interest throughout Portsmouth. Tours depart on the hour. April, weekends only, noon to 4:00 p.m.; May through September, daily, noon to 4:00 p.m.; October, weekends only, noon to 4:00 p.m. Fare charge. Telephone: (804) 623-3222.

The **Suffolk** area is southwest of Portsmouth via Routes 58, 13, or 460. Suffolk dates from 1608, when Captain John Smith sailed and mapped the Nansemond River. A year later a settlement was founded here. Today, Suffolk has a number of claims to fame: it is the world's leading peanut market (home of Planter's Peanuts), and thanks to its 1974 merger with Nansemond County, it is the largest city (430 square miles) in Virginia and the sixth largest in the nation.

The seven freshwater lakes situated to the west and north of the city offer fine fishing year round including bass, pike, crappie, and bream. A city or state fishing license is obtainable from the Clerk of the Court, 441 Market Street. Open Monday through Friday, 9:00 a.m. to 5:00 p.m. Telephone: (804) 934-3111.

Riddick's Folly, a renovated 1839 mansion, is one of the city's most interesting attractions. Located at 510 N. Main Street, it houses a museum and cultural center. The **Chamber of Commerce**, 1001 West Washington Street, can supply additional information to visitors to Suffolk. Open Monday through Friday, 9:00 a.m. to 5:00 p.m. Telephone: (804) 539-2111.

The **Suffolk Museum**, at 118 Bosley Street, features exhibits of fine art and some local history artifacts. Open Tuesday to Saturday, 10:00 a.m. to 5:00 p.m.; Sunday, 1:00 to 5:00 p.m. Admission free. Telephone: (804) 934-3111, ext. 311.

Great Dismal Swamp National Wildlife Refuge is an exciting and unusual area beginning about five miles east of Suffolk, and extending south to the state line. The swamp covers about 600 square miles, and includes many waterways, canals, and Lake Drummond. Cypress and pine forests, heavy moss, coffee-colored water, and a lush growth give this area a unique appearance. The abundant wildlife attracts hunters, fishermen, and naturalists: 207 species of birds, 40 species of trees, and numerous bears, wildcats, foxes, and raccoons. The Boardwalk Trail provides a close look at the ecology. Tours of the refuge are by reservation only. Access into the refuge is by foot or bicycle only; automobiles must be parked at the main gate. Telephone: (804) 986-3705. Headquarters open Monday through Friday, 7:30 a.m. to 4:00 p.m. The refuge itself is open daily, dawn to dusk. Admission free.

VIRGINIA BEACH AREA

The Virginia Beach area is about fifteen miles east of Norfolk, accessible via Routes 58, 60, or 44. If you are traveling from Norfolk via Route 60, you can stop at **Seashore State Park** on Cape Henry. The 2,770-acre park offers a glimpse of almost semitropical lagoons with aged trees gracefully festooned with Spanish moss. The natural dunes area is preserved in its original state with a variety of unusual plant and animal life. Activities include biking, hiking, fishing, sailing, camping, water skiing, nature programs, and tours of the museum. The Visitor Center can provide more information, including an illustrated guide to Bald Cypress Nature Trail. Park open daily, 8:00 a.m. to sunset. Admission free. Telephone: (804) 481-2131.

Cape Henry Cross, to the east of the park in Fort Story Military Reservation, marks the landing site of the first English settlers in America in 1607. They went on to found Jamestown as the first settlement. **Cape Henry Lighthouse,** built in 1791 as an improvement over the inland fires colonists used to build, is the oldest structure of its kind in the United States. Open Memorial Day to Labor Day, 10:00 a.m. to 5:00 p.m. Labor Day through October, 10:00 a.m. to 4:00 p.m. Telephone: (804) 460-1688. Admission free.

Virginia Beach itself is a popular seaside resort with 161 modern motels, hotels, apartments, and cottages to accommodate the large numbers of summer visitors who come here to enjoy the beach, boating, fishing, and other sports. There is also a two-mile biking trail parallel to the Boardwalk, and colorful trolleys you can ride up and down Atlantic Avenue. The **Maritime Historical Museum,** at the corner of 24th and Atlantic in a restored Coast Guard Station, has displays of maritime history, an Information Center, and gift shop. Open Memorial Day through September, Monday through Saturday, 10:00 a.m. to 9:00 p.m.; Sunday, noon to 5:00 p.m. October to Memorial Day, Tuesday to Saturday, 10:00 a.m. to 5:00 p.m.; Sunday, noon to 5:00 p.m. Closed Thanksgiving, Christmas, New Year's Eve, and New Year's Day. Admission charge. Telephone: (804) 422-1587.

The **Virginia Marine Science Museum,** at 717 General Booth Boulevard, houses exhibits which explore the diverse world of Virginia's aquatic habitats. Visitors experience the marine environment of the coastal plains, the Chesapeake Bay, and the deep sea off of the Virginia coast. The museum features a 50,000-gallon aquarium, a deep-sea diving vessel exhibit, and an outdoor boardwalk. Open September 8 through June 21, Monday to Sunday, 9:00 a.m. to 5:00 p.m.; June 22 through September 7, Monday to Saturday, 9:00 a.m. to 9:00 p.m.; Sunday, 9:00 a.m. to 5:00 p.m. Admission charge. Telephone: (804) 425-3474.

The **Adam Thoroughgood House** (4004 Thoroughgood Drive), built around 1680, is an exceptionally well-preserved example of English colonial architecture. The interior has been restored, complete with period furnishings. Costumed guides conduct visitors through the house. Open January through March, Tuesday through Saturday, noon to 5:00 p.m. April through December, Tuesday to Saturday, 10:00 a.m. to 3:00 p.m.; Sunday, noon to 5:00 p.m. Closed Thanksgiving, Christmas, and New Year's. Admission charge. Telephone: (804) 460-0007.

An intact survivor of the 18th century, the **Lynnhaven House** (4401 Wishart Road) is a brick plantation house dating from about 1725. Its Jacobean staircase is one of only two in the state. Open April through October, Tuesday to Sunday, noon to 4:00 p.m. Admission charge. Telephone: (804) 460-1688.

The **Francis Land House** (3131 Virginia Beach Boulevard) is believed to have been built about 1732, and is a fine example of Dutch gambrel roof structure. The City of Virginia Beach saved the house from demolition in 1975 and has undertaken an extensive renovation of the building. Open year round, Wednesday to Saturday, 9:00 a.m. to 5:00 p.m.; Sunday, noon to 5:00 p.m. Telephone: (804) 340-1732.

One of the more remarkable sights in Virginia Beach is **Mt. Trashmore**, a popular park and picnic area built on the site of a former solid waste disposal facility. The 162-acre park, complete with bike trails and soapbox derby ramp, has been lauded here and abroad as a creative solution to a ubiquitous problem.

The **Virginia Beach Information Center**, at the corner of 19th and Pacific Avenue, can provide more information on what to see in this resort, including maps directing you on a self-guided driving tour. They can also help with accommodations. Open daily, 9:00 a.m. to 5:00 p.m. Telephone: (804) 425-7511.

South of Virginia Beach along the coast is an area so unique in its ecology that it is preserved by local, state, and federal governments: **Back Bay National Wildlife Refuge** and **False Cape State Park**. Two chains of sand dunes border the beach and extend almost 70 miles to the south. During the early American colonization period, coastal Indians hunted and fished in this rich environment. Activity reached its peak in the late 1800s when commercial fishing and hunting were at an all-time high. Today the area is preserved, and there is limited swimming, fishing, hunting (waterfowl and deer), hiking, biking, and camping. Certain activities are limited to specific areas, so check first. Open Monday to Friday, 8:00 a.m. to 4:00 p.m., Saturday and Sunday, 9:00 a.m. to 4:00 p.m. Telephone: (804) 721-2412.

MARYLAND

CENTRAL MARYLAND

BALTIMORE COUNTY

The county of Baltimore surrounds the city of Baltimore, but the two are separate political entities. The county extends north to the Pennsylvania state line and encompasses rolling farmlands dotted with scenic horse farms, the suburbs of Baltimore, and 173 miles of Chesapeake Bay shoreline.

Historic sites such as **Towson**, the county seat, and **Reisterstown** give the traveler a picturesque glimpse into the past. In Towson, one can see the **Sheppard-Pratt Hospital Buildings** (c. 1862) on North Charles Street. On the grounds of St. Joseph's Hospital on Osler Drive is a house in which F. Scott Fitzgerald stayed while visiting his wife, Zelda, when she was at Sheppard-Pratt Hospital. Reisterstown on Route 140 was founded in 1758 and still has many well-maintained homes of the Revolutionary War era, and Main Street has a block of shops for antique shoppers.

The **Oella-Benjamin Banneker Site** in Oella on Westchester Avenue between Catonsville and Ellicott City honors the free black American who was commissioned by Thomas Jefferson to help survey and lay out the new capital city of Washington. Benjamin Banneker was born in 1731 near Ellicott City and was a self-educated scientist. The Gilboa Chapel houses the Banneker Memorial obelisk. The chapel is located in the picturesque Historic Register milltown of Oella built on the banks of the Patapsco River. Admission free.

The **Maryland State Police Headquarters**, in Pikesville on Route 140, is housed in a historic structure. It was built as an arsenal after the War of 1812 to protect the route to Washington. After the Civil War, it served as a home for Confederate veterans, and in recent years has served as police headquarters. The building has a venerable exterior appearance. Low brick walls surround the quadrangle, and a fine wrought-iron fence gives the effect of great age.

The **Cloisters Children's Museum of Baltimore City**, on Falls Road South, is housed in a large French Gothic Tudor Revival castle built in 1930. Many of the doorways and doors, however, are original. The castle is located on a 53-acre wooded park with nature trails and is administered by Baltimore City. The museum has exhibits of antiques, medieval furniture, dollhouses, and antique costumes. "Touch and see" exhibits, such as brass rubbings and a music room with instruments created by the staff, are available for children. Performances are given on weekends for children. Telephone hotline for weekly activities: (301) 823-2550. Open year round, Wednesday to Friday, 10:00 a.m. to 4:30 p.m.; weekends, noon to 4:00 p.m. Admission charge. For further information contact: 10440 Falls Road, PO Box 66, Brooklandville, MD 21022. Telephone: (301) 822-2551.

Loch Raven Reservoir Area, built in 1912, is administered by the county and contains a large primeval wooded area surrounding the 10-mile-long reservoir. Deer abound in this protected park and are frequently seen by visitors. The park offers picnicking, hiking, fishing, and boat rentals are available from April through October. Rowboats and small power motor boats are allowed, but no gasoline motors, canoes, or sailboats are permitted. Open year round. Telephone: (301) 252-8755. A skeet range, operated by the Loch Raven Skeet and Trap Club, is open to the public. Skeet range open Tuesday to Sunday, noon to 5:00 p.m. Telephone: (301) 252-3851.

Baltimore City operates the **Pine Ridge Golf Course** in the Loch Raven recreation area. This 18-hole championship course is open to the general public from dawn to dusk, year round except in inclement weather. Telephone: (301) 252-9837.

The **Fire Museum of Maryland**, Beltway Exit 26, displays more than 60 antique fire-fighting vehicles dating from 1822. In addition to the vehicles there is other fire-fighting equipment such as the 1848 telegraph alarm system as well as a photographic exhibit. Open May to October, Sunday, 1:00 to 5:00 p.m. Admission charge. For further information write: Fire Museum of Maryland, Inc., 1301 York Road, Lutherville, MD 21093. Telephone: (301) 321-7500.

Hampton House is one of the largest and most ornate mansions constructed in America during the 1780s. Built by Charles Ridgely, Hampton House was the home of the Ridgely family for 158 years. The family owned the Northampton Ironworks, which supplied cannon and shot to the Continental Army during the Revolutionary War. Almost all of the elegant furnishings are original. The 60-acre park contains 27 buildings, including an overseer's house, slave quarters, stables, and a reconstructed orangerie. The mansion is on the

National Register of Historic Places and is administered by the National Park Service. Thirty-five minute tours of the house are given, with a last tour starting at 4:30 p.m. There is a gift shop and tea room. Luncheon is served from 11:30 a.m. to 3:30 p.m. The mansion is open year round, Monday through Saturday, 11:00 a.m. to 4:30 p.m.; Sunday, 1:00 to 4:30 p.m. The grounds are open Monday. Closed Christmas and New Year's Day. For further information write Site Manager, 535 Hampton Lane, Towson, MD 21204. Telephone: (301) 823-7054.

Gunpowder Falls State Park has several tracts encompassing 16,000 acres. As the Big and Little Gunpowder Rivers approach the Chesapeake Bay, they merge and become one body of water, the Gunpowder River, which flows for eight miles until it meets the waters of the Chesapeake Bay. Gunpowder State Park lies in this stream valley. The "falls" appellation comes from the fact that the two Gunpowder Rivers cross the fall line between the piedmont and tidewater area. The tidewater extends north of I-95 above the point where the two rivers merge. Prosperous mills and factories sprang up along the river's banks during the 18th and 19th centuries, and the sites or remains of some of these institutions may still be seen, although the industry ceased many years ago. Along the Old Post Road, the river enters into Long Calm Ford, one of the famous fording places for colonial travelers en route from Philadelphia to Annapolis.

The main areas are the Hammerman area, a developed area at the mouth of the Gunpowder River, undeveloped central areas along the Little Gunpowder and Big Gunpowder Rivers; and the undeveloped Hereford area astride Route 83 in the northern section of Baltimore County. About 70 miles of hiking trails are located throughout the park. Unsupervised swimming opportunities are available along sections of the river.

Hammerman Area—From the Baltimore Beltway, take Exit 35 to Route 40 East for five miles to Ebenezer Road, right for six miles. This developed area has tidewater fishing and crabbing opportunities, boat launch ramps, a 1,500-foot beach with lifeguard, 500 picnic tables, an archery range, and play fields. Boat and slip rentals are available from March through November.

Central Areas—There are two central areas located between Routes 40 and 147 and between Perry Hall and Kingsville. These areas of the park are undeveloped and offer hiking and informal picnicking opportunities. Small parking facilities and a youth campsite, Camp Cone, are located in these areas.

North Central Railroad Trail—This 7.2-mile gravel trail follows the abandoned bed of the old rail line along the Big Gunpowder River from Ashton north to Monkton. Hikers, horseback riders, and bicyclists can use the trail without competition from motorized vehicles.

The **Jericho Covered Bridge** is east of Route 1, approximately two miles north of Kingsville. The bridge may be reached on Jericho Road off Jerusalem Road or from Joppa Road to West Franklinville Road. This 88-foot, Howe truss bridge was built around 1860. Nearby is the **Jerusalem Mill**, on the banks of the Little Gunpowder adjacent to Jerusalem Road. This mill was constructed in 1772 by David Lee, a Quaker from Bucks County, Pennsylvania. The mill is a unique example of early American architecture and is believed to be the only doubledormed mill in the United States. Behind the mill is a two-story house building, where David Lee manufactured guns during the Revolutionary War.

Hereford Area—The Hereford area is located off I-83 between Hereford and Weisburg. Camp Woods, on Bunker Hill Road, is off Route 45. This is an undeveloped area offering fishing and picnicking with restrooms. A popular summer activity here is "tubing"—coasting down the river on inner tubes. Swimming is at your own risk, although park rangers will give advice as to safe areas. An archery range for hunters and field archers to practice is also available, and there is a youth campsite. The Prettyboy Dam, over 140 feet high, is northwest of the Hereford area. It is owned by Baltimore City, and is an important source of water for the city. Near Prettyboy Dam one may see the remains of the mill of the Clipper Paper Company, built by William Hoffman in 1775, where paper for the use of the Continental Congress was made.

Sweet Air Area—This part of the park features wooded areas, river bottom land and high, open plateaus. The Little Gunpowder River passes through the center of this 1,155-acre preserve.

Permits are required for freshwater fishing; no permits are required for tidewater fishing and crabbing. (See Special Interest section on Hunting and Fishing for permit information.) For campsite permits and other park information write

Park Manager, 10815 Harford Road, Glen Arm, MD 21057. Telephone: (301) 592-2897.

FREDERICK COUNTY

Frederick, the largest Maryland county, is fast becoming an outlying suburb of Washington, although farming is still an important part of the economy. The county ranges from the Piedmont Plateau region in the east and the beginning of the Appalachians in the west. Its many public parks make it a pleasant driving area throughout the year. It is in the Catoctin Mountains that the presidential retreat, Camp David, is located. During World War II and the Vietnam War, chemical and biological weapons research was conducted at Fort Detrick near the city of Frederick. Today, under the U.S. Army Health Services Command, studies on infectious diseases, toxins, and recombinant DNA are conducted there. The Frederick Cancer Research Center of the National Institutes of Health is also located at Fort Detrick.

Frederick County was settled in the early 1700s by German farmers from Pennsylvania, as well as by Scots and English settlers. Both town and county were named in honor of Frederick Calvert, the sixth and last Lord Baltimore. Frederick County was formed in 1748 and, because of its productive iron furnaces, played an important part in both the Revolutionary and Civil wars. From its earliest days, transportation was important as the National Road route cut through the county, and today much of the busy interstate traffic from Baltimore and Washington, DC, passes through it to the west.

Stronghold, a privately owned 3,000-acre park, is reached from Comus off Route 109, right on Route 95. **Sugarloaf Mountain**, a National Landmark, rises to a height of 1,283 feet above sea level and stands out strikingly above the surrounding countryside, about 35 miles from Washington and 25 miles southeast of Frederick. The solitary mountain was named by the early settlers because of its shape, which reminded them of sugar, then commonly stored in a loaf.

En route the motorist passes the old **Comus Inn** on Route 109. This inn serves family-style lunches. An old antique shop is maintained in the adjoining barn.

The arts and crafts shop at the entrance to Stronghold offers a variety of handicraft items as well as small antiques and paintings by local artists. Nearby on the left is a small lake fashioned from a flat field, so natural that it looks like it has always been there. While it is stocked with fish, no fishing is allowed, a precaution to retain the beauty of the pond and surroundings. A winding paved road leads up the mountain for about a mile to a parking area near the top.

Visitors may stop at several lookout points cut out of the natural stands of pine and oak. At First View, the lookout is to the south and east over the rolling farms and woodlands of Montgomery County. The road winds upward to a Second View where one can see the wide Potomac River in the distant south. Here also is a parking facility and two interesting cannons of Revolutionary War days.

Over an acre of level ground at the summit supports a scattered growth of stunted, windblown oaks. On clear days the Bull Run Mountains can be seen far off to the south. The view is unobstructed, since the mountain breaks off into a sheer cliff on both the south and west sides. Those wishing to take a slightly longer hike may follow a 5½-mile logging road which begins a mile and one-half on the road to the east side of the mountain. Unique in this park is a planting of 1,300 chestnut trees grown from irradiated nuts, a part of the research project to save the American chestnut.

Stronghold is open from 9:00 a.m. to sunset every day of the year except December and January. Motorcycles are prohibited; buses are barred on weekends and holidays. Telephone: (301) 869-7846 or (202) 363-7130.

Near Stronghold the visitor may visit the **Lilypons Water Gardens** and fish hatchery. From Stronghold take Ephraim Road to Dickerson, right on Route 28, right on Route 85 two miles, right on Lilypons Road. The aquatic gardens were named in honor of international opera star Lily Pons, who visited here early in the century. The gardens and hatchery are one of the world's largest suppliers of exotic fish and aquatic plants. The aquatic farm offers a beautiful vista of ponds filled with goldfish, water lilies, and lotus. There is a gift shop on the premises where one can buy fish, aquatic plants, and gift items, such as Japanese fish kites and porcelain. Open March through October, Monday through Saturday, 9:00 a.m. to 5:00 p.m.; Sunday, 11:00 a.m. to 5:00 p.m. November through February, 10:00 a.m. to 3:00 p.m. Closed December 24 through January 2. Admission free. Telephone: (301) 874-5133 or 428-0686 (local Washington).

Nearby, on Park Mill Road, the visitor passes Bell's Chapel and the site of the **Amelung Glass Works**, the earliest glass factory in the United States. The beautiful engraved bottles, bowls, and goblets created by John Frederick Amelung between 1784 and 1795 are on exhibit at the Smithsonian Institution in Washington. The Amelung Mansion, listed on the National Register of Historic Places, is a private residence.

Brunswick, originally named Berlin in 1787, may be reached from Frederick on Route 340. Take Routes 17 and 79 into town. The area, bounded by the Potomac River, Central, Park and 10th avenues, and C Street, has been designated a National Historic District. The Chesapeake & Ohio Canal and the Baltimore & Ohio Railroad reached the town about the same time in 1834. However, the influence of the canal displaced that of the railroad for nearly 70 years by providing work for residents and business for warehouses and shopkeepers as barge and packet boat trade increased. It was during the Civil War that the railroad took on a new, more active role. Brunswick's proximity to Washington on a rail line made it an ideal supply depot and guard outpost for the Federal Army. Confederate troops repeatedly sabotaged the railroad and canal properties.

The year 1890 brought the new name and the start of one of our nation's industrial "boomtowns." The B&O Railroad began developing a freight classification yard that by 1907 was one-half mile across, eight miles in length, and contained over 100 miles of track. The expansion eventually wiped out all of old Berlin along the canal, pushing the newly built "Victorian" style homes and businesses upward into the hills overlooking the river.

The **Brunswick Museum** of local history emphasizes the area's role in transportation. It is located at 40 West Potomac Street and has collections of railroad and canal tools, uniforms, documents, and pictures. The third floor of the museum is devoted to a scale model of the railroad system from Brunswick to Washington, DC's Union Station. There are also exhibits of Indian artifacts, Civil War relics, farmers' tools, home furnishings, and utensils. The museum is open April through December, Saturday, 10:00 a.m. to 4:00 p.m.; Sunday, 1:00 to 4:00 p.m. Nominal adult admission fee. Telephone: (301) 834-7100.

The visitor may also see train engines being changed in a 180-degree direction at the **Roundhouse and Turntable.** Steam engines were housed for repair in this 1907 brick roundhouse, but today diesels dominate the scene. The **B&O Railroad station**, built in 1891, still serves passengers. An annual Railroad Days, featuring bus and walking tours, old trains, films and food, is held the first weekend in October. For further information telephone: (301) 834-7100.

Public campgrounds are located one mile east of Lock #30 along the **C&O Canal.** Facilities, open year round, include water, picnic tables, telephones, and vending machines. For camping information telephone: (301) 834-8050.

Point of Rocks is at the intersection of Routes 28 and 15, which crosses the bridge over the Potomac River into Virginia. Point of Rocks is an example of one of the small towns that served the B&O Railroad principally in the late 1800s. The historical highlight of the town is the **B&O Railroad Station,** located just east of town, and which is still used by passengers. The station is listed on the National Register of Historic Places.

Gathland State Park is located one mile west of Burkittsville on Route 17. Gathland was the estate of George Alfred Townsend, war correspondent of the Civil War, who became an important journalist and novelist of the Reconstruction Era. His pen name, Gath, was formed by adding an "H" to his initials and was inspired by a biblical passage: "Tell it not in Gath, publish it not in the streets of Askalon." The 135-acre state park preserves three of Townsend's buildings as well as the unusual monument he had erected in 1896 to honor his fellow war correspondents.

The park affords an excellent view of the scenic Middletown Valley and the surrounding countryside. The South Mountain ridge in this area saw many skirmishes during the Civil War as the Confederates tried to bring the war into the north. The Park Museum displays an interesting assortment of firearms, Indian relics, and Civil War mementos and also contains some of Townsend's writings. The Appalachian Trail traverses the park and passes the base of the Monument. Picnicking is allowed in the park. Picnic sites with tables and fireplaces must be reserved for a small fee. Telephone: (301) 293-2420.

Frederick is noted for its architectural charms as well as its historical associations. The city was founded in 1745 by English and German settlers. In 1765, the first organized community resistance to British rule in the colonies occurred in its Court House Square, when Frederick citizenry burned the Stamp Act in effigy.

Francis Scott Key lived here and the Stars and Stripes flies over his tomb. During the Civil War, the city figured prominently in the Antietam and Gettysburg campaigns. The restored home of Barbara Fritchie, legendary heroine of Whittier's patriotic poem, is here.

Three old covered bridges can be found on country roads off the Old Frederick Road near Lewistown, Graceham, and Thurmont. Also look for brickend barns, a type found along the northern border of Carroll and Frederick counties. Their end walls of brick have decorative designs in the openwork. They date from the late 18th century. For visitor's information on the county, write to the Tourism Council of Frederick County, Inc., 19 East Church Street, Frederick, MD 21701. Telephone: (301) 663-8687.

Monocacy Civil War Battlefield is south of Frederick in the area near the Monocacy River Bridge on I-270. On July 9, 1864, a bloody battle took place here between Union forces under General Lew Wallace and 23,000 Confederate troops under General Jubal Early. The Union forces delayed Early's advance toward Washington for 24 hours, which gave General Grant enough time to reinforce the defenses around Washington. This battle probably prevented the Capital from falling into rebel hands. Several monuments have been erected to commemorate the action that took place on the banks of the Monocacy. Much of the land on which the battle took place is private property and the battlefield site has not yet been developed by the National Park Service. (For further information on the Monocacy site contact the Superintendent of the Antietam Battlefield site in the Washington County section.)

Frederick Historic District, a 33-block area, contains many interesting and historic structures that are well preserved and restored. It is recommended that you park your car at the municipal parking deck on East Church Street near North Market Street and see Frederick on foot. The Tourism Council office is located next door to the parking deck, at 19 East Church Street, where the visitor may pick up detailed information on walking tours, driving tours, and bicycling tours. The council also conducts one-and-a-half-hour guided tours of the city. Some of the historic highlights of Frederick are mentioned below.

On Market Street, near the municipal parking deck, is **Frederick City Hall**. It was here on July 9, 1864, that Confederate General Jubal A. Early demanded and received from the city the sum of $200,000. The banks loyally supported the city authorities who feared the result of a refusal to meet the demand. From here Early proceeded to the Monocacy

River, where his troops were engaged by Union soldiers commanded by General Lew Wallace. It was not until 1951 that final repayment was made to the Frederick banks.

On East Church Street, across from the Tourism Council offices, the county administrative offices are housed in **Winchester Hall.** These stately Greek revival buildings were built in 1843 to house the Frederick Female Seminary, which was later renamed **Hood College** (now located on Rosemont Avenue).

The Evangelical Lutheran Church, 29-31 East Church Street, is opposite Winchester Hall. A log church was first built on this site in 1738 and was replaced in 1752 by the stone rear section of the present church. The twin spires of this Norman Gothic church were added in 1854 and they have been described as the best matched pair of spires in the United States. The five buildings and gardens are open to the public during the day. Telephone: (301) 663-6361.

The Historical Society headquarters and Museum is at 24 East Church Street. This house was built in 1834 by John Loats, who bequeathed it to the Lutheran Church for use as an orphanage. The Loats Orphanage occupied the house from the late 1870s to 1958. It now contains an excellent collection of historical objects of early Frederick. The museum has large collections of lustreware and dolls. The Society library also is a good resource for local historical and genealogical materials. Open March through December, Thursday and Friday, 11:00 a.m. to 4:00 p.m., and Saturday, 9:30 a.m. to 1:30 p.m. Admission free; donations welcome. Telephone: (301) 663-1188.

Court House Square, surrounded by late 18th- and early 19th-century dwellings and law offices, is located at the corner of Church and Court streets. In 1765 it was the scene of the first official repudiation of the hated British Stamp Act. The red brick Court House, erected in 1862, replaced the colonial building destroyed by fire. Busts of Maryland's first governor, Thomas Johnson, and Chief Justice of the United States Supreme Court, Roger Brooke Taney, both members of the Frederick Bar, stand before the Court House.

Behind the Court House at 111 Record Street is the **birthplace of William Tyler Page,** Clerk of the House of Representatives from 1919-29 and author of the "American's Creed." The creed, memorized by thousands of school children is: *I believe in the United States of America as a government of the people, by the people, for the people; whose* *just powers are derived from the consent of the governed; a democracy in a republic; a sovereign nation of many sovereign states; a perfect union, one and inseparable; established upon those principles of freedom, equality, justice, and humanity for which American patriots sacrified their lives and fortunes. I therefore believe it is my duty to my country to love it; to support its constitution; to obey its laws; to respect its flag; and to defend it against all enemies.*

Ramsey House is at 119 Record Street. President Abraham Lincoln visited this house on October 4, 1862, to call on General George L. Hartsuff, who had been wounded in the battle of Antietam. Lincoln spoke in front of this house and again from his special train at the **B&O Railroad depot** on South Market Street.

The **Barbara Fritchie House** and Museum, 154 West Patrick Street, is a restoration of the home and glove shop of John Casper Fritchie and his wife, Barbara. Barbara Fritchie, a devoted Unionist of Civil War days, has been immortalized in the poem by John Greenleaf Whittier with the lines, "'Shoot if you must this old grey head, but spare your country's flag.'" The privately owned museum displays some of Barbara Fritchie's furniture and clothes. Open Monday, Wednesday, Thursday through Saturday, 10:00 a.m. to 4:00 p.m.; Sunday, 1:00 to 4:00 p.m. Admission charge. Telephone: (301) 663-3833.

The **Roger Brooke Taney House** and **Francis Scott Key Museum**, at 123 South Bentz Street near Patrick Street, was built in 1799. This was Taney's farm and summer place during his residence in Frederick, 1801-1823. As Chief Justice of the United States Supreme Court, Taney is well known for the *Dred Scott* decision, which ruled that Congress had no power to prohibit slavery. He also administered the presidential oath to Abraham Lincoln, as well as to six previous presidents at their inaugurations.

The Taney House is furnished with period pieces and the museum contains Taney and Key memorabilia. The building is a fine example of late 18th-century architecture with its slave quarters behind the house. The Francis Scott Key Foundation maintains the buildings and the public is invited to visit by appointment. Contact the Visitors Center at (301) 663-8687 or (301) 663-3540.

Schifferstadt at 1110 Rosemont Avenue near Route 15 is an early German farmhouse, built in 1756, that houses a crafts cooperative. Visitors may view a slide presentation and take a self-guided tour of the three-story, sandstone farm-house, which is considered to be one of the finest examples of early German colonial architecture. The old section of the house is unfurnished in order that visitors may see the construction methods. The farmhouse features two unusual old colonial stoves—a five-plate, cast-iron "jamb" stove and a six-foot squirrel tail oven. The newer section, built in the early 1800s, houses the sales shop, which is filled with the work of regional craftspeople and artists. An upstairs gallery features selected artists monthly, and there are outdoor special events throughout the summer and fall. Open May 1 through December, daily, 10:00 a.m. to 4:00 p.m. Admission free; donations welcome. Telephone: (301) 663-6225.

Rose Hill Children's Museum, at 1611 North Market Street, is a "touch and see" museum for children and adults. The museum, administered by Frederick County, was built in 1767 by Thomas Johnson, Maryland governor and friend of George Washington. The museum features exhibits that children may touch and work with, such as adding stitches to a quilt or popping corn over an open fire. Costumed guides add a colonial flavor to the visit. On the grounds of the 43-acre park are farm and carriage museums, a log cabin, and a working blacksmith. Open April through October, Monday through Saturday, 10:00 a.m. to 4:00 p.m.; Sunday, 1:00 to 4:00 p.m. March, November, and December, open weekends, 1:00 to 4:00 p.m. Admission free. Telephone: (301) 694-1648.

Mountaindale is an out-of-the-way village which lies in the deep, hemlock-clad valley of Fishing Creek, north of Frederick. Make a left turn off Route 15, six miles north of Exit 8, on Mountaindale Road for two miles into the village. The village has been described as an austere community of a bygone era. Almost all the homes are built of squared chestnut logs, chinked with white mortar. It was constructed in the early 1940s by Civilian Conservation Corps youth, who salvaged dead chestnut trees from the nearby mountainside and built this unique village.

Maryland visitors often go to **New Market** seeking bargains. This antiquarian's mecca is located seven miles east of Frederick on Route 144, off Routes 40/70 at the intersection of Route 75. The town, dating back to 1793, has a population of fewer than 500, and thrives on one business—antique shops. Approximately 45 shops line its main street, and tourists make up almost all of its customers. New Market was one of the stops on the National Pike that ran from

Baltimore to Cumberland. Until the end of the horse and buggy age, the town served travelers, providing hotel rooms and food for passengers and the services of wheelwrights and blacksmiths for stagecoaches and six-horse Conestoga wagons. In the 1930s, the first antique shop was opened as a part-time venture and New Market grew to be the "antiques capital of Maryland." (See Special Interest Section on Antiques.)

Catoctin Mountain Zoo, on Route 15, is outside of Thurmont. More than 300 different kinds of animals are on display in a 25-acre wooded setting. This privately owned zoo specializes in breeding rare and endangered species, such as lions, black leopards, Madagascar lemurs, gibbons, and various reptiles. The two-acre Children's Zoo Area has many young animals as well as domesticated farm animals that children may feed and pet. The zoo provides children with cones of food to feed to the animals. The zoo is open daily, April 1 to October 15. During summer months from 9:00 a.m. to 6:00 p.m., spring and fall months, 10:00 a.m. to 5:00 p.m. From Thanksgiving to January 15, daily, 7:00 to 9:00 p.m. Picnic tables are available. Admission charge. Reduced rates for groups. Telephone: (301) 271-7488.

Gambrill State Park, six miles northwest of Frederick off Route 40, attracts visitors interested in hiking, picnicking, camping, fishing, and nature study. Some simply enjoy the drive to the mountain top, with three outlook points on High Knob at the top of Catoctin Mountain. Among attractions are dogwood and wildflowers in spring, and later, mountain laurel and azalea.

Take the self-guided Lost Chestnut Nature Trail to become acquainted with the plant and animal life of the area. During the summer, nature walks and campfire programs are scheduled. There are 35 family camping areas with showers, laundry tubs, and hot water. Enjoy dinner at Dandee's, at the base of the mountain, near the park entrance. The park is open year round, summer, 8:00 a.m. to 9:30 p.m.; fall, winter, spring, the park closes at sunset. For information, write Park Manager, 8602 Gambrill Park Road, Frederick, MD 21701. Telephone: (301) 473-8360.

To reach **Catoctin Furnace**, which is located near Cunningham Falls State Park, go north on Route 15 from Frederick, past Lewistown, and right on Route 806 approximately one mile. Catoctin Furnace District, a National Register historic landmark, is jointly administered by the Maryland and U.S. Park Services. Built in 1774 by Thomas Johnson, first governor of Maryland, it continued in operation until 1905. Iron ore was extracted from nearby iron ore banks, lime was brought in from the Frederick area, and charcoal, the other ingredient in iron production, was made in the nearby hollows from the plentiful supply of hardwoods. The furnace had been in operation only a few years when it was called upon to supply cannon ball, armor plate, and other materials to the Continental Army. During the Civil War the furnace produced plates for the ironclad ship *Monitor*. Over the years it produced stoves, kitchen ironware, and other iron products for which there was a demand.

Today, one can stroll around the partly restored furnace that dates from 1857, see the ruins of the once elegant superintendent's residence, the workers' stone cottages along the road, and visit the general store. Antiques, arts and crafts, and many turn-of-the-century products are sold here. Admission free. For information, contact Cunningham Falls State Park, Thurmont, MD 21788. Telephone: (301) 271-7574.

Cunningham Falls State Park, in the beautiful Catoctin Mountains, is named for a scenic 78-foot-drop cascade that extends over a 220-foot area of Big Hunting Creek. The 5,000-acre park has two developed areas—**Manor Area**, which may be reached from Route 15, 15 miles north of Frederick, and the **William Houck Area**, which is located off Route 77 west of Thurmont.

Park facilities include a 43-acre stocked lake, picnicking and camping areas, and hiking trails. Trails lead to scenic mountain overlooks such as Cat Rock and Bobs Hill. Visitors may swim, boat, and fish in Hunting Creek Lake, which has two sandy beaches and a bathhouse nearby. During the winter snowshoeing and cross-country skiing are permitted.

The park is open year round. Campgrounds open mid-April through October with showers, toilets, tables, and fireplaces provided. Trout fishing is permitted year round, except for a one-month period that varies annually. Contact park superintendent for fishing regulations. Admission charge. For further information, contact Park Superintendent, Route 3, Box 132, Thurmont, MD 21788. Telephone: (301) 271-7574.

Catoctin Mountain Park, operated by the National Park Service, adjoins Cunningham Falls State Park and is 65 miles from Washington and 55 miles from Baltimore. It is west of Thurmont, bounded by Route 81 on the north and Route 77 on the south. The Visitor's Center is located on Route 77 at Park Central Road. **Camp David**, the mountain retreat of presidents, is located here. Most of the park (except for the Camp David area) is open to the public for recreational uses year round. Interpretive services offered during the summer months include guided walks, lectures, and campfire programs. Whiskey making is demonstrated at the **Blue Blazes Whiskey Still**, a Prohibition-era still that was relocated to the park. Family camping is available in the Owens Creek Campground from mid-April through October. There are 52 sites with a central comfort station. Fee charged for sites. The park also offers bridle trails, a five-mile scenic drive on Park Central Road, self-guided nature trails, and picnicking areas. In the fall there are orientation lectures on compass use and woodslore. In the winter, ski-touring lectures are given. For further information, contact Park Superintendent, Thurmont, MD 21788. Telephone: (301) 663-9330.

Two old churches in **Thurmont** are of more than passing interest. **Apples Church**, built in 1826, is one of the oldest in Frederick County. Consisting of one room with a high pulpit, this church features a gun corner where worshippers stacked their guns in case of an unexpected Indian attack. An Indian graveyard is nearby. To reach the church, go one mile out Main Street, then left on Apples Church Road. Open to public during services. The **Moravian Church** is accessible via Route 77 east from Thurmont, then to Graceham. This 18th-century church still has an active congregation. It is open to the public.

Frederick County maintains three lovely covered bridges, which are still in use. Although the original trusses are in place, they have been reinforced with concrete piers and steel beam supports. The **Utica Bridge** (c. 1850) is the largest of the three bridges. It spans Fishing Creek for 100 feet, with a 17.5-foot roadway, and its original Burr arch and trusses are still in place. The Utica bridge was originally over the Monocacy River, but was moved to Fishing Creek when half of the bridge was destroyed in the 1889 Johnstown Flood. It was during this flood that most of the 52 covered bridges in Maryland were destroyed. **Loys Station Covered Bridge**, on Old Frederick Road, off U.S. 77, has a 90-foot span and a 12.5-foot wide roadway. This multiple Kingpost truss bridge was originally constructed in 1850. The county maintains a park and picnicking facilities near the bridge. The **Roddy Road Covered Bridge** is the smallest covered bridge in Maryland and is of the single Kingpost truss type. It is 40 feet long, spans Owen's Creek, and was built around 1856. The bridge is surrounded by a 17-acre natural area.

Eight miles north of Thurmont on Route 15 is the **Grotto of Lourdes Replica** and the campus of **Mount St. Mary's College**. The Grotto is the first national Catholic shrine in the United States and is located on the mountainside above the campus of Mount St. Mary's College. The setting is highlighted by the statue of the Virgin Mary, which contains a carillon. This is a replica of the famed Grotto of Lourdes in France. Stations of the cross are found along the winding garden path from the statue to the Grotto itself. Mount St. Mary's College, founded in 1808, is the second oldest Roman Catholic College in the United States. The Grotto is open daily, dawn to dusk. Telephone: (301) 447-6122.

The **St. Elizabeth Seton Shrines**, located on Route 15 in Emmitsburg, commemorate the life of Mother Elizabeth Ann Seton (1774-1821), who, in 1975, became the first native-born American to be canonized by the Catholic Church. On the beautiful grounds are located the Stone House (c. 1770), the White House (c. 1810), and the Seton Shrine Chapel in St. Joseph's Provincial House. Mother Seton and her companions opened the first Catholic parochial school in the United States at the "White House" in Emmitsburg. A visitors center and gift shop are located on the grounds. Open daily, 10:00 a.m. to 5:00 p.m. Admission free. For information contact, Director, 333 South Seton Avenue, Emmitsburg, MD 21727. Telephone: (301) 447-6606.

CARROLL COUNTY

This county, named for Charles Carroll of Carrollton, is located in north central Maryland and borders the Mason-Dixon Line. It is rich in beautiful scenery and prosperous farms, and offers many historic attractions. Carroll County is part of the Piedmont Plateau and the county seat at Westminster is 56 miles northwest of Washington and 31 miles northwest of Baltimore. The county was first settled in 1723 by English and Scotch-Irish families from the Baltimore and Annapolis areas. In the mid-18th century German, Swiss, and Scotch-Irish settlers from Pennsylvania moved to the county.

Some prominent Carroll County natives have been Francis Scott Key and Revolutionary War hero Mordecai Gist. Another Carroll County native was Jacob R. Thomas of Union

Bridge, who in 1809 invented a harvester and reaping machine. The invention was later perfected and marketed by Obed Hussey and his cousin, Cyrus McCormick.

Agriculture remains an important aspect of the economy of Carroll County. Brick-end barns are a local architectural feature that the visitor to Carroll and Frederick counties may observe. The side walls of the barns were made of brick with designs fashioned by leaving out some of the brick in order to provide ventilation.

Your first stop in Carroll County should be **Westminster.** Parking is available on Main Street between 206 and 210 East Main Street and at the public parking lot near the Courthouse on Court Street. Tourist information may be obtained from the Carroll County Tourism Department at 210 East Main Street, Westminster, MD 21157. Telephone: (301) 848-4500. The office is open year round, Monday to Saturday, 9:00 a.m. to 5:00 p.m.; Sunday, 10:00 a.m. to 2:00 p.m. Closed on Thanksgiving, Christmas, and New Year's.

The **Shellman House** and the **Kimmey House,** next door, 206-210 East Main Street, are the chief attractions of Westminster. Shellman House, a substantial home built in 1807, is headquarters of the county historical society. A gazebo and a restored 19th-century garden are behind Shellman House. The society maintains a collection of about 150 examples of early 19th-century dolls, a unique collection of American flags, maps and fans, and the hobnail glass collection of the late Mrs. H. L. Mencken. The basement rooms have an exceptional collection of tools and implements used before the machine age. Telephone: (301) 848-6494 or 848-9531.

The **Postal Museum** in Historical House commemorates establishment of the first county-wide R.F.D. in the United States. In 1899 the postmaster at Westminster, E. W. Shriver, drew up a plan for rural free delivery and persuaded the Post Office Department to adopt it. Philatelists will find special interest in this unique exhibit. The museum is open daily, 1:00 to 4:00 p.m., except Monday and holidays. Admission free. Telephone: (301) 848-6494.

The **County Courthouse** (1838), still in use, is on Court Street, one block off Main Street. It is a Greek revival building with a two-story portico. The former **Main Court Inn,** at the intersection of Main and Court streets, is now occupied by stores. In bygone days its nearby courtyard was a stagecoach depot. Beneath the building were cells in which slaves were confined while awaiting sale.

Western Maryland College, on West Main Street, was founded as a private academy in 1860 and reorganized in 1867 as a college. It was the first co-education college south of the Mason-Dixon Line.

The **Union Mills Homestead**, built in 1797, is located on Route 97, seven miles north of Westminster. The rambling clapboard farm home and grist mill overlook picturesque Pipe Creek. At various times it served as an inn, stagecoach office, post office, schoolhouse, and magistrate's office. The old mill alongside Pipe Creek has been restored to operating condition and visitors may purchase grain produced by the mill. The Homestead today is a museum of 18th- and early 19th-century Americana. Its 23 rooms are filled with the furnishings and household articles used by the six generations of the Shriver family, who lived here. The visitor will see the old postmaster's desk, a ballroom, kitchen, guest room, and dining room; also collections of toys, business documents, and family heirlooms.

The Homestead, mill, and giftshop are open May, September, and October, weekends only, 10:00 a.m. to 5:00 p.m. Admission charge. For further information contact Union Mills Foundation, 3311 Littlestown Pike, Westminster, MD 21157. Telephone: (301) 848-2288.

The **Carroll County Farm Museum** is located one mile south of Westminster on Center Street, off Route 140. The basic buildings include an 1852 farm home and barn which ranks among Maryland's best examples of Civil War period construction. Eight rooms are furnished with late 19th-century period furniture. Costumed guides escort visitors through the main house. There are many outbuildings, such as a springhouse, smokehouse, blacksmith shop, and wagon shed, all surrounded by 140 acres of rural farmland. A genuine log cabin moved from another location serves as an entrance point.

An abundance of early farm life memorabilia is displayed throughout the museum complex. Included are early model reapers, threshing machines, furrow and shovel plows, harnesses, oxen yokes, carriages, wagons, and other horse-drawn equipment. Also featured is one of the first rural carrier wagons to deliver mail in Carroll County. Blacksmithing, broom making, butter making, quilting, spinning, woodworking, threshing, pottery items, and musical instruments are among the impressive exhibits.

The Farm Museum and gift shop are open Saturdays,

Sundays, and holidays, noon until 5:00 p.m., late April to late October and on holidays. Open weekdays during July and August, 10:00 a.m. to 4:00 p.m. Closed on Mondays. Group tours by appointment. Admission charge. Picnic tables are available for visitors. Address inquiries to Curator, Carroll County Farm Museum, 500 South Center Street, Westminster, MD 21157. Telephone: (301) 848-7775.

The old community of **Taneytown** is on Route 97, eight miles east of Emmitsburg. A land patent was given to Raphael Taney of St. Mary's County in 1754. The first deeds were taken out in 1762. The town was noted for its Revolutionary War musket works.

Terra Rubra, the birthplace of Francis Scott Key, is four miles south of Taneytown off Route 194, 1⅓ miles on Keysville-Bruceville Road. The land patent, given to Key's grandfather, was named for the red color of the soil. The first house, built in 1770, was destroyed by a storm in 1850 and then replaced by the present brick structure. A monument was erected honoring Key in 1915. The house is privately owned and is not open to the public.

In Union Bridge on Route 75 at 41 Main Street is the **Western Maryland Railway Historical Society Museum**. It contains artifacts of the Western Maryland Railroad and numerous other railroad memorabilia, such as one of the first pay phones, an old telegraph set, and HO models. This red brick building with white marble keystones, built in 1902, was saved from demolition and has been completely restored. Open April through December, Wednesday to Saturday, 11:00 a.m. to 4:00 p.m.; Sunday, noon to 5:00 p.m. Closed major holidays. Tours may be arranged during the week by appointment. Telephone: (301) 868-5849.

A short distance from Keymar, on the Bruceville Road, is the sleepy village of **Bruceville**, which virtually died when the highway was rerouted. Most of its old stone houses were once occupied by workers in a nearby grist mill and fertilizer plant. The single street of Bruceville overlooks the Monocacy River. This "ghost town" should be a delight for antiquarians and for photographers.

From nearby Middleburg the route is east on Route 77 six miles to **Uniontown**, then right three miles on Route 84 to **New Windsor**. The village of Uniontown has been listed on the National Register of Historic Places and is a typical small Carroll County town of more than 100 years ago. At New Windsor the **Brethren Service Center** trains dedicated young people as social workers who, under various denominational auspices, seek to alleviate illiteracy, poverty, and poor health conditions in areas both in the United States and abroad. Of special interest to tourists is the **International Gift Shop**. Here one can purchase products of native craftsmen from countries all over the world. Products which meet the Service Center Council's standards are sold for the benefit of the producers. Over 10,000 visitors come here annually to see and buy handwoven textile products; wood, stone, and metal crafts; paintings; and sculpture. All are sold at very reasonable prices.

Continue south on Route 84, two miles to Marston; then on Route 407 to Route 27. A Historical Society roadside sign points to the site of the first Methodist meetinghouse in America. The **John Evans House**, built in 1764, stands in a field alongside a country road. A stone rectangle nearby marks the site of the first Methodist church, built by a congregation organized by Robert Strawbridge, a pioneer Methodist minister.

MONTGOMERY COUNTY

Most of this county's attractions are within a 30- or 40-minute drive from Washington and an additional 40 minutes from the Baltimore area. Scattered through the county are a number of regional and state parks, each with a variety of recreational facilities and nature centers offering educational nature programs. On a one-day trip the motorist can visit the scenic and historic places in the Potomac Valley or enjoy the vistas from Sugarloaf Mountain in Frederick County. Off to the northeast is the area of historic sites in the Olney, Brookeville, and Sandy Spring triangle.

Glen Echo National Park, off Capital Beltway Exit 40, was a Chautauqua meeting ground in the late 19th century. It was turned into a popular amusement park which continued until 1968. An important feature of the present park is an active art center and gallery. Local artists rent space in the center and conduct classes and demonstrations; the gallery exhibits and sells the creations of the resident and teaching artists. The gallery is open year round, Tuesday to Saturday, noon to 5:00 p.m.

A children's adventure theater offers theatrical and puppet performances on a year-round basis. In the summer, children can ride on the old Glen Echo amusement park carousel and adults can attend free outdoor concerts. Small admission charge for carousel. Picnic areas are on a first-come, first-served basis. No camping facilities are available. Call for program hours. Telephone: (301) 492-6282.

Clara Barton National Historic Site is near Glen Echo at 5801 Oxford Road. This unique, 38-room Victorian house was the home of Clara Barton, founder of the American Red Cross, and headquarters of that organization from 1897 to 1904. Miss Barton was a humanitarian known for her relief work during and after the Civil War and for her support of black and women's rights. She moved to Glen Echo in 1897 and lived there until her death in 1912.

The house was patterned after the Red Cross Relief Hotel erected in Johnstown, PA, after the flood of 1889. The architectural style of the interior of the present building follows the style of that hotel. The house is not a typical home and, in fact, Clara Barton broke many Victorian decorating rules. The central hall rises up three stories with galleries from which one can peer over the balustrades. Although the Park Service refutes the allusion, many have noted the resemblance to a Mississippi River sternwheeler.

Clara Barton built a utilitarian home and warehouse for her work. Her housekeeping was extremely casual for the times. The wooden paneling was selected because it was cheaper than the plaster used in upper-class homes and even cheaper than the wallpaper used in middle-class homes. She even had muslin wall coverings, normally used as a base for wallpaper.

The Park Service continues to restore the house and the tour given by the Service gives a fascinating insight into an unusual woman. Special programs are usually given twice a month. Open daily, 10:00 a.m. to 5:00 p.m. Reservations are requested for groups of 10 or more. Telephone: (301) 492-6245. Admission free.

The **Cabin John Regional Park**, maintained by the Maryland National Capital Park and Planning Commission, has two areas—the Park and the Nature Center. Both are off Capital Beltway Exit 36.

The park offers a variety of attractions for all ages—picnic tables, camping sites, nature trails, and an ice skating rink. A marked nature trail, maintained by the Potomac Appalachian Trail Club, starts north of the park and winds along Cabin John Creek to the Potomac River. Approximately four miles of the trail are in the park itself. Noah's Ark, a

petting zoo of farm animals and poultry, is a popular feature
with children. A miniature railroad offers a one-mile ride
through woods and fields. On the playground, children will
delight in scrambling over a pumpkin coach and a play fort,
Fort Cabin John, in addition to slides and climbing areas.

There are seven primitive campsites. Use is limited to
residents of Montgomery County. No hookups are available.
Permit office telephone: (301) 299-4555. Small fee charged.

The **Locust Grove Nature Center** is located on Democracy Boulevard. Directions: take Old Georgetown Road north
from the Capital Beltway to Democracy Boulevard, past
Montgomery Mall to park entrance. Nine tennis courts and
four handball courts are situated near the nature center. The
center offers nature programs and a small collection of live
animals, such as snakes, turtles and spiders, are on display.
The nature programs offered by the center are listed in local
newspapers and local libraries. Reservations are requested
for lectures by the center's naturalist. The center is open
Tuesday through Friday, 9:00 a.m. to 5:00 p.m. Telephone:
(301) 365-2530.

The **National Institutes of Health** is the principal medical research arm of the federal government, whose mission is
to improve the health of the nation by increasing our understanding of the processes underlying human health and by
acquiring new knowledge to help prevent, detect, diagnose,
and treat disease. NIH is located on a 300-acre campus in
Bethesda. Most NIH divisions maintain their own laboratory
and clinical research programs. Well over 2,600 research
projects are in progress at all times on the Bethesda site,
making NIH one of the largest research centers in the world.
The NIH **National Library of Medicine** is the world's largest reference center devoted to a single subject. Currently,
the Library's collection includes 2,500,000 items. As one of its
services, the Library produces and publishes the *Index Medicus*,
an indispensable reference journal for investigators and practitioners throughout the world. The Library has also pioneered
in the use of such technology as automated retrieval, computer-
assisted publishing, and communications satellites, to make
its resources available to scientists and practitioners all across
the nation.

The NIH Visitors' Center is open daily, Monday through
Friday, 10:00 a.m. to 4:00 p.m. Featured are health films and
videotapes, exhibits, and a model laboratory. There is a

scheduled tour of the Library at 1:00 p.m. each weekday. Telephone: (301) 496-1776.

The **Bethesda National Naval Medical Center**, the president's official hospital, is located across Wisconsin Avenue. The medical center serves the medical needs of Navy personnel and their dependents. The center also conducts cancer research in association with the NIH Cancer Institute.

The **Beall-Dawson House and Doctors' Museum**, 103 West Montgomery Avenue, Rockville, MD, is headquarters of the Montgomery County Historical Society. The house was built in 1815 by Upton Beall, the second clerk of the Montgomery County Court. Constructed of red brick with a main section and a wing, it is a fine example of the Federal style of architecture. There are extensive grounds with many box bushes.

The interior is beautifully designed in the neo-classic style of Robert Adam, with a wide entrance hall and staircase. It is furnished with pieces from the period 1815-60. The drawing room, with its lovely Adam mantel, is furnished with many pieces of pre-1890 furniture such as a Duncan Phyfe sofa, Sheraton Empire chairs, early Victorian chairs, lamps, and bric-a-brac. The dining room is furnished in the Empire style with a formal banquet table. A collection of china and glassware is on display. There are interesting portraits and pictures pertaining to Montgomery County and Maryland history.

The Society has a collection of period clothes which is on display from time to time. The house is open Tuesday through Saturday, noon to 4:00 p.m., the first Sunday of each month, 2:00 to 5:00 p.m. During the summer the house is open by appointment. Admission charge; children under 12 free. Telephone: (301) 762-1492.

Wheaton Regional Park offers a variety of recreational opportunities that appeal to young and old. Near the main entrance is **Old MacDonald's Farm**, with miniature farm buildings housing all types of livestock and poultry. Visitors see many chicks, ducklings, piglets, and lambs during spring and summer. Nearby is a large playground and picnic area, restrooms, and snack bar.

A short distance away is the main depot of the **Scenic Railroad**, a one-mile miniature line that skirts the lake and choo-choos through the woods. Nominal fee charged. Near the railroad is a renovated antique carousel. The lake is well stocked with fish, and visitors are welcome to try their skill with rod and reel. The park offers bike and bridle trails, with bike rentals and a riding stable.

The **Brookside Nature Center** is located off Glenallen Avenue, at the north end of the park. It can be reached by a foot trail from the **Old MacDonald's Farm** area. One can also reach the small museum and nature trail by returning to Georgia Avenue, turning right, then right again on Randolph Road, to sign (about one block) indicating entrance to park. Follow this road about a half-mile to nature center. A naturalist is generally on duty during the week to conduct groups on nature walks or in special programs. Open Tuesday to Saturday, 9:00 a.m. to 5:00 p.m.; Sunday, 1:00 to 5:00 p.m. Telephone: (301) 946-9071.

Ten primitive camping sites are available to Prince George's and Montgomery County residents. A small fee is charged. Telephone: (301) 946-7033.

Brookside Gardens, adjacent to the Nature Center, includes 50 acres of public gardens with two conservatories, a rose garden, an azalea garden, a Japanese tea house, and an herb garden. There is also a horticulture reference library, which is aimed at the home gardener. Admission free. The gardens are open year round, 9:00 a.m. to sunset, except Christmas Day. The greenhouse is open daily, 9:00 a.m. to 5:00 p.m. Lectures and tours are offered by the staff; two-week advance notice is requested for weekday lectures. Telephone: (301) 949-8230. To reach the park complex, take Beltway Exit 31 north on Georgia Avenue.

The **National Capital Trolley Museum** is in Wheaton on Bonifant Road. The museum features operating U.S. and European trolley cars. Following a two-mile round-trip ride through Northwest Branch Regional Park, visitors may view a film presentation and a picture exhibit in the visitors center. The museum is a nonprofit organization run by volunteers. Open weekends, Memorial Day, July 4, and Labor Day, noon to 5:00 p.m. During July and August, also open on Wednesday, noon to 4:00 p.m. Admission free. Nominal charge for trolley rides. Telephone: (301) 384-9797.

Rock Creek Regional Park/Meadowside Nature Center can be reached via Beltway Exit 31 north.

Among recreational facilities in this park are a picnic area, playgrounds, an archery range, boat rental, hiking trails, a horse trail, and a boat ride on Needwood Lake aboard the *Needwood Queen*, replica of a 19th-century Mississippi sternwheeler. Rowboats, sailboats canoes, and pedalboats may be rented from May to September, Tuesday through Sunday, 10:00 a.m. to 7:00 p.m. Telephone: (301) 948-5053. Fishing is good in the stocked lake, and visitors may buy supplies in the bait and tackle shop. Maryland fishing permits are required and may be purchased in the shop. There are also a Visitor's Center and a snack bar that serves sandwiches and refreshments. No camping sites are available.

The **Meadowside Nature Center** offers natural and cultural history programs throughout the year, Tuesday through Sunday. The park is open from 8:00 a.m. to sundown. Telephone: (301) 924-4141.

The visitor can take a historic tour of the **Olney, Brookeville, Sandy Spring Area**, affording an opportunity to see many historic sites and homes, some dating from the early 19th century. The area was first settled by Quakers in Sandy Spring, which is the oldest ongoing community in Montgomery County. Start the tour off Capital Beltway Exit 31 north.

St. John's Episcopal Church, located to the left of the intersection of Georgia Avenue and Route 108, was built in 1842 and is the oldest Episcopal church in continuous use in the county. The early-American white stucco building has been renovated twice—in 1910 when the Dutch bell tower was added and again in 1980 with a new transept that doubled the size of the church. **Olney House**, known as "Little Olney" by local residents, is located across the intersection on the right. Little Olney is a large white house dating from the early 19th century and now contains a group of small shops. St. John's and Little Olney are the two remaining buildings from the original community.

The suggested tour from Olney is north on Route 97 (Georgia Avenue), two miles to Brookeville, right on Brighton Road to Brighton, right on Route 650 (New Hampshire Avenue) to Ashton, right on Route 108 (Sandy Spring Road) to Sandy Spring, continue on Route 108 to return to Georgia Avenue.

Much of the route from Olney to Brookeville is still rural and gives one a glimpse of the county's charming rural landscape, mainly pasture land, corn fields, and woodland plots.

The **Brookeville Academy**, an old stone building that served as a school from 1815 until 1900, is on the right. There are a score or more of old homes, amid stately trees and well-kept gardens that recall the Brookeville of yesteryear. These homes are located to the left and right of the post office. By making a right turn onto Brighton Road, one comes to the **Caleb Bentley Home.**

When the British captured Washington in August 1814, President Madison took refuge at the Bentley home after his flight from Washington. It was then the home of the postmaster, Caleb Bentley. This handsome structure, dating from 1779, is a private residence, but may be viewed from the road on the right.

The narrow, winding road to **Brighton** passes through picturesque farmland and over a rickety one-way bridge spanning a small stream. Brighton is marked by a small Episcopal chapel, **St. Luke's.** Located next to St. Luke's is the last grange hall in Montgomery County, which is now used by the Sandy Spring Players. **Brighton Dam** and **Triadelphia Lake,** with fishing, boating, and picnicking facilities, are less than a mile to the east.

The route to **Sandy Spring** is to the right, past the village of Brinklow, and at Ashton turn right for the short trip to that old Quaker village.

Turn left down Meetinghouse Road to the red brick **Friends' Meeting** built in 1817. One can peer in the windows (some are original 19th-century panes) to note the stark simplicity of the interior. Century-old trees ring the meetinghouse and the turnaround in front, and several early 19th-century homes surround the meetinghouse to give one a glimpse into the past. There is historical evidence of a 1753 frame structure predating the present meetinghouse, although the Friends emigrated to Sandy Spring from Anne Arundel County in the early 18th century. Behind the meetinghouse is a graveyard which contains unmarked graves from the early period of the Meeting. The earliest Friends did not place gravestones in their cemeteries because of their beliefs, although this practice gave way so that the first marked stones appeared in the 1850s.

Most of the Patuxent River Valley, from Rocky Gorge Dam above Laurel to Route 97 above Sunshine, is under the jurisdiction of the Washington Suburban Sanitary Commission, and called **Patuxent River Recreational Areas.** The two large reservoirs along this river are a major source of water for the suburban Washington area. The Commission has set aside seven recreational areas for public use for fishing, boating, picnicking, hunting, and horseback riding.

The recreation areas are open during daylight hours. Boating and fishing activities are allowed from March to December. Picnicking is permitted from April to October. The specific Patuxent River Recreation Areas include **Brighton Dam** (with its lovely Azalea Gardens), **Green's Bridge Fishing Area, Triadelphia Lake Picnic and Fishing Area, Pigtail Branch Fishing Area, Brown's Bridge Fishing Area, T. Howard Duckett Reservoir** (Rocky Gorge), and **Scott's Cove.**

Reservoir-use permits are issued by the Commission. The permits cover all activities—fishing, boating, boat mooring, hunting, and horseback riding. For hunting and fishing, state permits, in addition to the WSSC permits, are necessary. Hunting is limited to shotguns and bow and arrows and is permitted in designated areas along Triadelphia Lake.

Brighton Dam Information Office is open daily for permit purchases, 8:00 a.m. to 8:00 p.m. Telephone: (301) 774-9124.

Washington Suburban Sanitary Commission Headquarters: 4017 Hamilton Street, Hyattsville, Maryland, across from Magruder Park. Licenses may be obtained at the cashier's window. Hours: 8:15 a.m. to 5:00 p.m., Monday through Friday. Telephone: (301) 699-4172.

Except for the 500-acre, developed Clopper area, **Seneca Creek State Park** in Gaithersburg has a rustic, wild atmosphere in its 5,000 acres. One can follow streamside trails, which afford an opportunity to observe abundant and varied wildlife and to enjoy the scenic beauty of this primitive area. Wild ducks and muskrats in the creek, and deer, squirrel, wild turkey, quail, rabbit, and woodchuck may be seen in the forests and meadows. Wild flowers are abundant along the woodland trails, especially in spring and early summer. A visitors center is located at the entrance to the park where summer programs are offered. No admission is charged for visitors center.

The Clopper developed area includes a 90-acre, man-made lake, 250 family picnic sites, softball field and flat grass areas for games, hiking and biking trails, and five large rental shelters. There is a boat rental concession during the summer from Memorial Day to Labor Day where canoes, paddle, sail, and row boats are available. During May and September the boat concession is open only on weekends. The concession is closed during the winter, but visitors may bring their own lightweight boats. No boat trailers may be brought in, except by handicapped persons. A pontoon craft plys the lake with a guide giving a 45-minute interpretive lecture. A nominal fee is charged. The rides begin at 1:30 p.m., 3:00 p.m., and 4:30 p.m. Group tours may be arranged.

During the winter, the park offers cross-country skiing and ice skating on the pond. No camping facilities are available.

The park is open from 8:00 a.m. to sunset, Memorial Day to Labor Day; 10:00 a.m. to sunset during fall and winter. Telephone: (301) 924-2127.

The old **Saint Rose Catholic Church** stands at the intersection of Clopper and Game Preserve Roads near the Seneca Creek State Park entrance. The congregation dates back to 1834, when the Clopper family donated the land to the church. The present frame structure was erected in 1884 after a fire destroyed the first church. The walkway contains some of the brick from the original structure.

Following Clopper Road, make a left turn on Route 118, then left on Black Rock Road to see the stone shell remains of the once-prosperous **Blackrock Mill** built in 1815. The mill was powered by a single overshot waterwheel and operated into the 1920s with its two large millstones for grinding grain and a vertical saw to cut lumber. It is now part of Seneca Creek State Park and will be restored in the future.

Located in upper Montgomery County, **Poolesville** was first settled in 1793 by John Poole when he built a log house and operated a small store from it. The town grew in the early 1800s, as farming developed in the area, and the C&O Canal and cross-river ferries opened up. Poolesville was an important staging area during the Civil War because the Confederate troops attempted to cross the Potomac there to gain access to Washington. Federal troops were stationed in Poolesville from 1861 through 1865.

Historic Poolesville, with many 19th-century homes preserved, is worthy of a visit. A visitor may take a one-half mile self-guided tour of the 20 buildings in the historic district. Call the Poolesville town hall for a free brochure describing the buildings. Telephone: (301) 428-8927.

C&O CANAL NATIONAL HISTORICAL PARK

One of the most popular weekend escapes for city folks is the 184.5 miles of the Chesapeake and Ohio Canal, paralleling the Potomac River from Washington, DC, to Cumberland, MD. The Canal and its towpath make an enjoyable spot for a picnic, an afternoon bike or hiking trip, or even a more ambitious field trip exploring the ecology, geology, and culture of the towns along its banks. The canal was an engineering feat when it was first built, and today it is no less a marvel.

As early as 1753, George Washington envisioned a waterway connecting the Ohio Valley and the Chesapeake Bay. Three decades later, a start was made on his ambitious plan when he and other like-minded Virginia gentlemen chartered the Patowmack Company. Plans were made to cut "skirting" canals around five falls along the Virginia side of the river at what is now Great Falls National Park. Though Washington resigned from the company in 1789 when he became the first U.S. president, his interest in the project never lessened. The skirting canals were finally completed in 1802, two years after his death, although the rest of the plan was never carried out.

Merchants still dreamed of a completed canal across the Alleghenies providing a more economic means of transportation. Expanding the Patowmack Company's canal was the only answer. Construction of what was known as the Chesapeake and Ohio Canal began on July 4, 1828, when President John Quincy Adams removed the first spadeful of dirt of what was dubbed the "magnificent ditch." As if to predict the eventual fate of the canal, that same day construction was begun in Baltimore of the Baltimore & Ohio Railroad. The race for the west across the Alleghenies was on.

Problems plagued the C&O Canal Company from the beginning. Supplies were scarce, excavation much more difficult than imagined, and skilled labor virtually unavailable. To complicate matters, a feud developed between the Canal Company and the B&O Railroad to obtain land rights. Because the bluffs come so close to the river, there was often room for only one right-of-way. The canal company fought a bitter court battle, and finally reached Cumberland, MD, in 1850—eight years after the railroad had arrived. By then it was an accepted fact of life that trains were faster and less expensive than canal travel. Regrettably, plans to continue the canal to Pittsburgh were finally dropped.

Although the canal never achieved the economic success George Washington had dreamed of, for 75 years the completed portion of the canal saw active traffic along its waters. Mules walking along the towpath pulled barges at the rate of four miles per hour. The 184.5 miles of the canal consisted of 74 lift locks which raised barges from sea level at Georgetown to 605 feet at Cumberland. Eleven stone aqueducts carried the canal over major Potomac tributaries, and seven dams supplied water for the canal. There were also a number of waste weirs to control the water level, hundreds of culverts to carry roads and streams under the canal, a 3,118-foot tunnel to take it under a mountain, and a variety of stop locks, river locks, bridges, section houses, and lock houses.

In 1889, an enormous flood swept the Potomac Valley, leaving the canal in ruin. It was rebuilt and used until 1924 when another flood seriously harmed the already financially troubled canal company. It was again damaged by Hurricane Agnes in 1972, and has undergone extensive repairs in recent years. Since 1971, the canal has been a national park.

The following are some of the more popular spots along the canal starting from its mouth at the Potomac River in Georgetown.

Milemarker 0: Tidewater Lock (Washington, DC)

This is the point where barges entered from the Potomac River or ended their long trip down the canal. You can still see the remains of four arched stone bridges that once crossed the waterway. From here to Seneca (23 miles), the canal is restored to resemble its appearance in the 19th century. A Visitor Center located in the Foundry Mall (between Thomas Jefferson and 30th streets in Washington, DC) can supply maps and other information. Many of the organized barge trips start from this point. Open Wednesday through Saturday, 10:30 a.m. to 6:30 p.m. Admission free. Telephone: (202) 472-6685.

5.0: Brookmont (Maryland)

It was near here, just beyond Lift Lock 6, that the directors of the C&O Canal Company staged their impressive ground-breaking ceremony. On July 4, 1828, President John Quincy Adams pushed his shovel into the ground and hit a tree root, but undaunted, launched the canal with a speech that compared it to the Pyramids of Egypt and the Colossus of Rhodes. Today Lift Lock 5 has parking facilities as well as an overhead footbridge from Brookmont to its picnic facilities. It is a short walk beyond Lift Lock 6 and its lockkeeper house to this historic spot. A "skirting canal," around Little Falls, enters from the Potomac River. It is marked with slalom gates where some of the area's finest kayakers may be seen on practice runs.

10.0: Carderock (Maryland)

This area has picnic facilities, playfields, rest rooms, and excellent scenic views of the Potomac Valley from the rocky cliffs. The nimble-footed can enjoy rock climbing, or hiking along the river or the Chesapeake and Ohio Canal towpath.

14.0: Great Falls (Maryland)

One of the Washington area's most important scenic attractions is Great Falls of the Potomac. Here the river roars through a rocky cataract, dropping over 50 feet to the narrow Stephen Mather Gorge, flanked on either side by 200-foot palisades. The **Great Falls Tavern Museum** is devoted to the history of the C&O Canal. Built between 1828 and 1831, the Tavern was once a popular resort for Washingtonians. The park offers interpretative programs, historic and nature walks, and special events throughout the year. The "Canal Clipper" barge operates from here. Visitor Center and museum open daily, 9:00 a.m. to 5:00 p.m. Admission free. Telephone: (301) 299-3613. One can also inspect the old canal locks and stone locktender's houses. There is a picnic area beside the canal and a snack stand nearby. Nature exhibits are set up during the summer months. Rental bicycles and boats are available at the concession on the canal above the museum. Visitors can walk or bike up the towpath or go on the canal via rowboat or canoe. The area saw much gold mining activity in the late 19th century, and you can visit the old Ford and Maryland mines.

Those interested in walking or rock climbing will find **Bear Island** and the towpath adjacent to Widewater attractive locales. **Billygoat Trail**, marked by blue-painted tree blazes, traverses Bear Island (no longer an island) from the Great Falls area, back to the canal at the lower end of Widewater. This three-mile hike will take two hours or longer, depending on the stamina and agility of the hiker. Note: The river is extremely dangerous at this point, and visitors are advised to heed Park Service warnings.

16.5: Swain's Lock (Maryland)

This is a good place for picnicking, boating and fishing, and ice skating on the canal in winter. Boat rentals, refreshments, and bait are available at the locktender's house. Visitors can explore the rugged, rural beauty of the canal and river in boats, or hike in either direction along the old towpath. This is also an excellent area for bird study. At Locks 21 and 22, there are old lockkeepers' houses still standing.

19.6: Pennyfield Lock (Maryland)

On the site of Lock 22, this area offers picnicking and group camping facilities, and is another prime area for bird watching. A state game refuge, where one can observe waterfowl as well as songbirds, is located between the canal and river, beginning a half-mile above the lock on the far side of Muddy Branch.

22.8: Seneca (Maryland)

This is a popular boating and fishing area, both in Seneca Creek and in the Potomac River. The river is broad and quiet here with its waters impounded by a long dam downstream. There is a large picnic area, and food and refreshments are available. A special attraction is the old 114-foot, three-arched stone aqueduct carrying the canal over Seneca Creek. It is one of 11 masonry aqueducts along the canal.

A half-mile upstream are the ruins of the Seneca sandstone quarry, which supplied cut stone for many of Washington's public buildings. The extensive marsh alongside the canal once served as a turnaround basin for canal boats. Today it is an important bird study area.

35.5: White's Ferry (Maryland)

This privately operated recreational area has been a ferry crossing since 1833. Confederate General Jubal Early crossed the Potomac near here when he made his attack on Washington in 1864. A flat-bottomed **cable ferry** still crosses the river here, operating from 6:00 a.m. to 11:00 p.m., dependent on water conditions. Toll charge for automobiles. Telephone: (301) 349-5200.

Other facilities include boat rentals and moorings, fishing, water skiing, biking, and hiking. You can purchase bait, and a stand sells food and refreshments. Opposite the towpath are the ruins of a warehouse-granary. Its chutes poured grain directly into the holds of canal boats for transport to Washington.

37.8: Marble Quarry (Maryland)

Stone from Marble Quarry, located 1½ miles below Wood's Lock, was used for the beautiful columns of Statuary Hall in the U.S. Capitol. The area will lure fishermen; just below an electric generating plant, the water is quite warm and teeming with fish. The next lock, Wood's, was built in 1831 of red sandstone.

42.2: Monocacy Aqueduct (Maryland)

This aqueduct, built between 1829 and 1833, is the longest on the canal. Stone for the seven-span, 560-foot structure was quarried at nearby Sugarloaf Mountain. The atmosphere is very much as it was in the days when mule-drawn barges moved up and down the canal. Facilities include a boat ramp, parking lot, and picnic tables.

48.2: Point of Rocks (Maryland)

Here centered the court battle between the C&O Canal Company and the B&O Railroad over the rights to the narrow strip of land bordering the river. Facilities include a free boat ramp and parking. Telephones and snacks are available nearby.

55.0: Brunswick (Maryland)

This small town served as an important Potomac crossing during the Civil War. In 1890, when railroad yards were built here, the town grew rapidly (see complete listing in Frederick County section above). A number of stores are located near the towpath, along with a free boat ramp and parking.

58.0: Weverton (Maryland)

This canal town was founded in 1835 by Casper W. Wever, who built the first bridge at Harpers Ferry.

60.7: Harpers Ferry (West Virginia)

Between Weverton, MD, and the bridge at U.S. 340 at Sandy Hook, the towpath joins the Appalachian Trail leading from Maryland into Virginia. The Shenandoah River Lock was used by canal boats to descend to the river and then cross over to Harpers Ferry. Maryland Heights is perched directly above the lock and can be reached via a marked footpath. (See the complete listing for Harpers Ferry in the West Virginia section.)

69.4: Antietam Creek Aqueduct (Maryland)

Completed in 1835, this 140-foot aqueduct has three unequal arches. At the Ranger Station you can obtain information on the site. A year-round tent campground is available, with free parking. Telephone: (301) 739-4200. Antietam Ironwork and Furnace, just a short walk away, supplied cannon balls during the Revolutionary War. Also nearby is Antietam National Battlefield Site, which can be reached via Harpers Ferry Road (see listing in Washington County section below).

99.3: Williamsport (Maryland)

George Washington once considered this town as a possible site for the nation's capital. It blossomed as a canal town after 1835 when the first barges came through. The Williamsport Town Park is on the riverfront between Lock 44 and the Conococheague Creek Aqueduct, a 210-foot three-arch span.

108.6 to 109.2: Four Locks (Maryland)

Instead of following the river at this point, the canal

avoids a five-mile loop by cutting across Praether's Neck. Four locks within this one-mile shortcut give the stretch its name. At mile marker 109 there is a picnic area and boat ramp. There is a Ranger Station on the site.

112.4: Big Pool (Maryland)

This natural depression in the right-of-way was filled with water and used as part of the canal. Its width made it an excellent turning point for boats. Fort Frederick State Park is nearby (see complete listing in Washington County section.)

124.0: Hancock (Maryland)

Named for James Hancock, a Revolutionary soldier who operated a ferry, this town grew in 1839 with the early canal traffic. The Park Service facilities include a museum and Visitor Center. Open daily, 8:30 a.m. to 4:30 p.m. Admission free. Telephone: (301) 678-5463. A path near Tonoloway Creek leads to a town park.

140.9: Fifteen Mile Creek Aqueduct

From here it is a short walk to Little Orleans, a German settlement of the late 19th century. The churchyard of St. Patrick's has some old graves of many of the Irish immigrants who worked on the canal. There is a picnic area along the towpath.

155.2 to 155.8: Paw Paw Tunnel (Maryland)

The river takes a six-mile bend at the point, and to avoid following it, the C&O Canal Company cut across the valley and through a mountain. The 3,118-foot tunnel was built between 1836 and 1850, and is lined with four to seven layers of brick. It is possible to walk or bicycle through the dimly lit tunnel during most months of the year. A marked nature trail for hikers goes over the tunnel offering a scenic view. Across the Potomac River bridge is the town of Paw Paw, West Virginia.

175.5: North Branch (Maryland)

A canal boat replica is moored beside Lock 75 and features a furnished captain's cabin. A log cabin lock house completes the historical setting. Each year on the last full weekend in August, the C&O Canal Boat Festival takes place here, featuring arts, crafts, and special exhibits.

184.5: Cumberland (Maryland)

Here the canal came to an end at a loading basin known as Shantytown. Dam No. 8 was destroyed when a modern flood control facility was built in the 1930s. There is access to Cumberland from the towpath. The town was built on the site of Caiuctuc, an old Shawnee town. It has a historic district and a small park, dedicated to the C&O Canal. (See the complete listing for Cumberland in the Allegany County section below.)

Because of the amount of territory the C&O Canal traverses, there is a wide variety of recreational activities available for visitors.

You can relive the olden days on the canal by taking a relaxing trip on a replica of a 19th-century mule-drawn **barge**. The *Canal Clipper* is moored just below Great Falls Tavern, making frequent voyages up the canal. Trips start by "locking through" Lock 20, and during the 1½-hour excursion Park Service interpreters bring to life the exciting days through music and living history. Trips operate Wednesday through Sunday, five trips a day. Charters are available. Admission charge. Telephone: (301) 299-2026 or 299-3613.

Another canal barge, *The Georgetown*, leaves from the Georgetown Visitor Center (between 30th and Thomas Jefferson streets), mid-April through mid-October, Wednesday through Sunday. Telephone: (202) 472-4376.

A replica of a dry dock canal barge, 92 feet long by 14½ feet wide, is on display in North Branch, MD. This bicentennial-gift to America was built by Navy Seabees and coordinated by a local group of enthusiastic citizens. You can take a tour through the mule stable, the hay house, and the captain's cabin.

For the most part the towpath is very good for **bicycling**. The elevated trail, originally 12 feet wide, is built mainly on earth and crushed stone, a good walking surface for the mules that pulled the barges. The towpath is generally unobstructed and follows the entire length of the canal. It can become slippery for several days after a strong rain and may occasionally be washed out or even flooded. Cyclists are advised to carry tools and materials to repair broken chains or spokes and flat tires. Four popular day trips along the towpath are from Great Falls Tavern to Georgetown (14 miles), from Fifteen Mile Creek to Paw Paw Tunnel (15 miles), from Dam 4 to Lock 33 (24 miles), and from Dam 4 to Harpers Ferry (25 miles). There is access by motor vehicle to either end of these areas. Bikes can be rented at the following locations along the towpath:

Mile	Location
0.0	Jack's Boats, Washington, DC (202) 337-9642
0.5	Harry Thompson Boat Center, Washington, DC (202) 333-9711

3.1	Fletcher's Boat House, Washington, DC (202) 244-0461
16.6	Swain's Lock, MD (301) 299-9006
60.0	River and Trail Outfitters, Sandy Hook, MD (301) 834-9950
77.0	Barron's Store, Snyders Landing, MD (weekends only), (301) 432-5255 or 432-8594
112.4	Fort Frederick State Park, MD (Big Pool only), (301) 842-2504

For more information, trail maps, and detour information, contact park headquarters.

Camping throughout the park is restricted to designated areas. "Hiker-Biker" overnight campsites for tents are spaced approximately every five miles along the canal from Carderock to Cumberland. Campsites are allocated on a first-come, first-served basis, except for Marsden Tract which must be reserved by calling (301) 299-3613. For specific information on campsite facilities, contact park headquarters.

Canoeing on the canal is a relaxing pastime, especially between Georgetown (mile marker 0) and Violets Lock near Seneca (mile marker 21). Portages are necessary around each lock. Upstream from Violets Lock, only a few stretches of the canal are deep enough for canoeing; they include Big Pool, Little Pool, and a 4.5-mile section from Town Creek to Oldtown.

Canoes can be rented at most of the locations listed above for bicycles.

Hiking along the towpath can be made-to-order; there is no such thing as getting lost, and you can walk as long as you feel like it and simply turn around. There are also many trails leading off the towpath. Maps of the entire route along the canal can be obtained from the park headquarters. In 1954, Supreme Court Justice William O. Douglas took Washington newspaper editors on a hike that made history. By the time the long walk from Cumberland to Georgetown was over, he had won the necessary support for preserving the C&O Canal. Each spring the C&O Canal Association leads the public on a shortened hike. Admission free. Telephone (301) 739-4200.

Five Boy Scout Councils in the area have worked with park rangers to develop the C&O Canal Historic Trail. A trail guide, *184 Miles of Adventure*, highlights historic and geological features along the route, and can be a handy companion for hikers. The guide is available from any Boy Scout Council.

orseback riding is permitted on the towpath from Seneca to Cumberland. Horses must be kept 100 feet away from picnic areas and campgrounds, and large groups must make camping arrangements with private landowners.

During the winter months when the canal freezes over, park rangers test the thickness of the ice. If it is safe, they allow **ice skating** on the somewhat bumpy but exhilarating surface. Telephone: (301) 299-3613.

For more information on the C&O Canal National Historical Park, contact the Park Superintendent, PO Box 4, Sharpsburg, MD 21782. Telephone: (301) 739-4200. For specific information on the portion from Georgetown to Seneca, telephone (301) 299-3613.

HOWARD COUNTY

Howard County, in the western corridor between Baltimore and Washington, DC, is a rural area although its eastern portion has become a suburb of both cities. There are several historic towns in Howard County such as Ellicott City, Elkridge, and Savage that provide a pleasant visit for the weekend traveler.

John Smith is said to have explored the Patapsco River near the location of **Elkridge**, which is the oldest settlement in the county. Elkridge, originally named Elk Ridge Landing in colonial times, was settled early in the 18th century by tobacco farmers who were attracted to the area's rich soil and the accessibility of the Patapsco River. By 1746 the settlement rivaled Annapolis as a port and commercial center. Ships sailed from Elk Ridge Landing for the markets in England loaded with hogsheads of tobacco, iron ore, lumber, and flour from the Ellicott mills.

Ellicott City, south of Baltimore near the intersection of Routes 29 and 144, is a truly unique town. It is nestled between two gorges, the narrow Tiber Creek and the rocky valley into which the Patapsco River flows. Many of the old houses, built of a dark local granite, seem to be wedged into the rocky hillside. A number of old buildings on Main Street actually straddle Tiber Creek.

The town was founded by three Quaker brothers from Bucks County, PA—Joseph, John, and Andrew Ellicott. They helped revolutionize the economy of Maryland by persuading farmers to grow wheat instead of tobacco and by introducing fertilizer. Ellicott City developed around Ellicott's grist and flour mill, established in 1772 on the east bank of the river, and grew with the building of the Cumberland Road and the coming of the B&O Railroad in 1830. The site of the mill is now a modern flour-milling operation. In the 1970s the company producing Washington Self-Rising Flour moved its mill here. The stone ruin adjacent to the mill was the home of George Ellicott, son of one of the original founders. It was built in 1789 and is the only reminder of the original Ellicott family.

The visitor who enters the town from Route 29 (Columbia Pike) sees a series of stone houses, making up **Tongue Row**. Built by the widow Ann Tongue in the 1840s, these quaint, handsome structures house a variety of interesting shops, with a passageway leading to more shops and gardens on a lower level, convenient to the parking lot behind the post office. There are three other parking areas—the Fire Station lot on Ellicott Mills Drive, and two Old Court House lots which may be reached off Main Street via Court Avenue and Park Avenue.

The **Ellicott City B&O Railroad Station Museum** is located at the east end of Main Street. The Ellicott City station was the first terminus to be built outside Baltimore. It was on the Ellicott City-Baltimore route that the famous race between the steam engine "Tom Thumb" and a horse-drawn carriage occurred in 1830. The horse won the race because of a mechanical failure on the "Tom Thumb." The museum offers a tour of the 1831 stone building, a multimedia presentation of the history of railroading as it began in America, and a 45-foot model of the railroad in the Patapsco Valley from Baltimore to Ellicott City as it was in the 1870s. Open April through December, Wednesday to Saturday, 11:00 a.m. to 4:00 p.m.; Sunday, noon to 5:00 p.m.; January through March, Saturday, 11:00 a.m. to 4:00 p.m.; Sunday, noon to 5:00 p.m. Admission charge. A 1927 restored caboose is available for birthday parties. Telephone: (301) 461-1944.

The first stone building on Main Street, west of the bridge near the railroad museum, is the **Patapsco Hotel**, now an apartment building. The former **Townhall**, two doors west of the hotel, is a five-story building with a series of cellars dug out of the rocky hillside behind each of four stories. Visiting shoppers will not want to miss the many restaurants and shops on Main Street. The **Old Country Store** offers everything from old-fashioned penny candy to rare pieces of expensive furniture.

A short distance up the steep Old Columbia Pike (Route 29 cut-off) is the cemetery in which many of the Ellicotts are buried. Beyond the cemetery, a private lane leads to the **Friends Meeting House**, a plain stone structure erected in 1799 and now a private home not open to the public.

On Church Road, at the top of the highest point overlooking Ellicott City, are the ruins of the **Patapsco Female Institute**, built in 1837. Only the stone walls remain of this once-magnificent Greek revival structure, which was a finishing school for young women. The old **Court House** faces Court Avenue on Capitoline Hill. It is a Classic revival granite building. The British cannon on the lawn, captured at the Battle of Bladensburg, was one of the few trophies that fell into American hands during the War of 1812.

For an Ellicott City walking tour brochure and further Howard County information, contact the Howard County Tourist Information Center at 3430 Courthouse Drive, Ellicott City, MD 21043. Telephone: (301) 730-7817.

Enchanted Forest may be reached from the Baltimore Beltway via Exit 15, nine miles west on Route 40; or from Washington on Route 29 to Route 40 west for two miles. This is a privately operated children's amusement park with nursery rhyme character rides. Children may pet a variety of tame animals. Catered birthday parties in the Gingerbread House are available. Open daily, May 15 to Labor Day week, then weekends until end of October; also from Easter weekend until May 15. Admission charge, plus ride fares. Contact: 10040 Baltimore National Pike, Ellicott City, MD 21043. Telephone: (301) 465-0707.

Stillridge Herb Farm is on Route 99 in Woodstock, three miles from Route 29, north of I-70. The nine-acre farm welcomes visitors for an informal tour of the greenhouse and of the decorative, working gardens. Its stock is restricted to culinary herbs, and medicinal herbs are not grown. A three-and-a-half-hour lecture, tour, and tea is offered for groups of up to 50 persons (individuals may arrange to join a group). The program begins at 10:30 a.m. with a tour of the gardens and greenhouse, tea at 11:00 a.m., followed by a lecture and a sampling of foods at 12:30. The program generally ends at 2:00 p.m. The staff will give advice on herb gardening, and there is a gift shop that sells live plants, herbal arrangements, and potpourris. Open Monday through Saturday, 9:00

a.m. to 4:00 p.m. Admission free; charge for lecture and tea program. For further information write: Stillridge Herb Farm, 10370 Route 99, Woodstock, MD 21163. Telephone: (301) 465-8348.

The little village of **Savage** is tucked away between two busy highways, I-95 and Route 1, and is equidistant from Baltimore and Washington. Savage was a hub of textile activity in the 19th century. The mills, developed by John Savage of Philadelphia in 1816, operated constantly from 1816 to 1945.

In their heyday, the mills manufactured cotton duck that was made into sails for the clipper ships that sailed from nearby Baltimore harbor. One of the first hydro-electric generating plants was constructed on this site in 1918. The mill provided electricity for the village, as well as providing other services, such as a company store, for which the workers were paid in scrip currency printed by the company. **Historic Savage Mill**, a 166-year-old cotton mill, has been renovated into a marketplace featuring more than 50 specialty and antique shops, artists' studios, and galleries. Throughout the mill historical panels and museum displays describe mill life and the technology of the weaving industry. The mill's Foundry Street Studio houses a colony of artists and craftsmen. Sculptors, painters, woodcarvers, and potters welcome guests into their studios to see works in progress and to discuss aspects of the finished pieces. The artists' work is exhibited and is for sale. Savage Mill is open 362 days a year. Monday to Saturday, 10:00 a.m. to 5:30 p.m.; Sunday, noon to 5:30 p.m. Telephone: (800) 367-6687 (toll free outside Maryland) or (301) 792-2820.

The **Bollman iron truss bridge** spans the Little Patuxent River nearby and is now a foot bridge from which the visitor may view the lovely, tranquil scene provided by the ruins of the old boiler building extending over the stream. The Bollman railroad bridge, moved from nearby Route 1 in 1865, is the only one of its kind still in existence and was used until 1955. Across the stream, a footpath leads to another scenic view of the mill complex.

In the village of Savage the visitor may still see the white cottages built for the mill workers, and at the corner of Baltimore and Foundry streets is a privately owned stone building that houses the county library. Called **Carroll Baldwin Hall**, the building and the small park behind it are early examples of community planning by the industrialists who ran the town.

The 13,000-acre **Patapsco Valley State Park** includes both sides of the Patapsco River from US 1 westward to the Liberty Dam on North Branch, and Sykesville on the South Branch of the river. The park is divided into seven recreational areas, at points of greatest scenic beauty and suitability for public use. All areas have picnic tables, fireplaces, shelters, parking space, and sanitary facilities. Except for special campsites in the Hollofield area, pets are not allowed in the park.

Avalon Area (Howard County) is accessible from US Route 1 from South Street. Facilities include two lighted pavilions, a large playfield, and a softball field. The **Thomas Viaduct**, built around 1833-35, may be seen with its eight stone arches, measuring 58 feet high. They support the 612-foot-long railroad bridge, the oldest of its kind in use. The bridge was built nearly 60 feet high in order to allow sailing ships to pass under it.

Glen Artney Area (Baltimore County) is directly across the river from Avalon and can be reached by the same routes. It is developed for picnicking and accommodates about 60 persons, and has water and flush toilet facilities.

Orange Grove Area (Howard County) can be reached from Elkridge via US Route 1 on South Street. This area is one-and-a-half miles along a scenic route from the Avalon area and is the historic site of the old **Gambrill Grist Mill**, the ruins of which may be seen on the banks of the river. Also at this location is the famous **Swinging Bridge**. A walk over this swaying foot span is a must for all park visitors. The bridge is 200 feet across and is approximately 45 feet above the river. Five miles of wooded trails are also available for bird watchers and nature lovers. During Hurricane Agnes, in 1972, the Avalon and Orange Grove areas, including the Swinging Bridge, were washed away but have been reconstructed.

Hilton Avenue Area (Baltimore County) is accessible, at the lower end of Hilton Avenue, off South Rolling Road in Catonsville. It is the most heavily forested section of the park. In the spring, dogwood glades make this area an especially picturesque scene. Facilities include 24 Class-A campsites with showers and toilets. A youth camping site is also available for groups. At the **Patapsco Valley History Center** maps and exhibits are featured.

Hollofield (Howard County), off US Route 40, is three miles west from Exit 15 of the Baltimore Beltway. The dominant feature here is a scenic overlook, 367 feet above the river, which affords an excellent view of the Patapsco River Gorge. The area is lighted at night. The Hollofield area also features a large pavilion and two lighted shelters with a large covered barbecue pit nearby. Other facilities include 60 improved campsites serviced by a sanitary building equipped with hot and cold water, showers, and laundry tubs. There are also 15 campsites in an auxiliary area for campers with pets.

Pickall Area (Baltimore County) is reached from the Baltimore Beltway on Johnnycake Road. This area features a one-mile physical fitness trail among large oaks, hickories, and stately tulip poplars. Facilities include 11 large shelters for groups.

McKeldin Recreation Area (Carroll County) is accessible via Marriottsville Road northeast of Marriottsville Post Office. There are eight shelters and three large pavilions. A special camping area for large groups is also available. One of the dominant features of this area is the overlook to Liberty Dam, a Baltimore water supply reservoir.

There are 20 miles of nature trails in Patapsco State Park. Picnic and camping areas are patrolled by uniformed park rangers who will assist patrons in locating reserved facilities. Year-round programs, such as night hikes, astronomy hikes, and campfire activities, are scheduled. Published calendars may be obtained from park offices. Campsites are closed from November 1 to the second week in April. Admission charge on weekends and holidays from April to September. For reservations or information write: Park Superintendent, Patapsco State Park, 1100 Hilton Avenue, MD 21228. Telephone: (301) 747-6602.

Columbia is a planned city embracing over 15,000 acres. About one-fifth of the area has been set aside for parks, lakes, woodlands, and other recreational purposes. It consists of planned villages grouped around a shopping mall, between Baltimore and Washington off Route 29.

The visitor may obtain information about Columbia at the **Exhibit Center** off Little Patuxent Parkway on Wincopin Circle. Columbia offers many recreational facilities, most of which are open to visitors. Among these, in season, are boating on the downtown lake, outdoor skating on two lakes, indoor ice skating and swimming, horseback riding, golfing on two courses, hiking, and a shooting preserve. Cultural activities include music, theater, and art. The Merriweather Post Pavilion of Music, in a beautiful woodland setting, draws topflight summertime entertainment. For more information about Columbia, contact the Columbia Exhibit and Information Center, 10215 Wincopin Circle, Columbia, MD 21044. Open Monday through Friday, 8:30 a.m. to 5:00 p.m.; weekends, 10:30 a.m. to 5:00 p.m. Telephone: (301) 992-6060.

At **Cider Mill Farm** visitors see apple cider and butter made from mid-September through early April. There are free samples of hot or cold cider. During the apple season in the fall special events, such as pony rides, storytelling, and crafts demonstrations, are scheduled. Shop for homemade apple pie, breads, cakes, jelly, and honey. Baked goods are sold only on weekend mornings. Open daily, September to December 24, December 26 to April, Friday, Saturday and Sunday, 10:00 a.m. to dark. Admission free. For group tours contact the farm at 5012 Landing Road, Elkridge, MD 21227. Telephone: (301) 788-9595.

WESTERN MARYLAND

GARRETT COUNTY

Garrett County, the westernmost area of Maryland, lies within the Alleghany plateau and contains the highest point in the state—Backbone Mountain, 3,340 feet. It is the only county in Maryland where the rivers do not flow entirely eastward into the Potomac. From the crest of Backbone Mountain, the waters flow northward toward the Ohio and Mississippi rivers. The Youghiogheny River, which has been designated a Wild and Scenic River, begins in Garrett. Seventy percent of the county is forest area. Garrett County was created in 1872 and was named for John W. Garrett, president of the Baltimore and Ohio Railroad, who had done much to further the development of the area.

Begin your tour of Garrett County in Grantsville. The **Casselman Hotel** (c. 1824) was built to serve the travelers on the National Road. Many of the early features of the building have been preserved. One of the three dining rooms was originally used during the stagecoach days and diners may see the original fireplace where food was prepared. The building has been in continuous use for more than 150 years and is still serving as a hotel. The hotel is listed on the

National Register of Historic Places. The restaurant is open year round. Located on Main Street (Route 40) in Grantsville. Telephone: (301) 895-5055.

Casselman Bridge State Park is probably the smallest state park in Maryland. When it was built in 1813 the stone bridge was the longest single span bridge (80 feet) in the United States. It was built to link Cumberland, Maryland, to Wheeling, West Virginia, on the National Pike (Route 40). It was in use until 1933 and has been designated a National Historic Landmark. The bridge is located one mile east of Grantsville on Route 40. Its five-acre park has picnicking facilities.

Nearby in the shadow of the stone bridge is **Penn Alps,** a remodeled log stagecoach stop that serves as a restaurant and crafts shop. The main building was constructed in 1818 and diners will see the stones of the huge fireplace that date back to the days when stagecoach travelers used the Cumberland Road to Wheeling. Another relocated log stage-coach stop (c. 1818) serves as a demonstration center for spinners, weavers, potters, a bird carver, a blacksmith, and a Tiffany stained-glass craftsman. The crafts shop also sells the handiwork of local craftsmen. The demonstration center is open Monday through Saturday, 8:00 a.m. to 8:00 p.m.; Sunday, 11:00 a.m. to 2:00 p.m. Telephone: (301) 895-5985.

Braddock's Trail, built by British General Edward Braddock's army in 1755, was an improvement of the old Indian route, Nemacolin Trail. The trail was a major route west until it was abandoned in the 19th century with the construction of the National Road (Route 40). The trail can be seen at Little Meadows, one of Braddock's most important encampments and a site used by George Washington. It is four miles east of Grantsville on the north side of Route 40.

Nearby are **Savage River State Forest** and **New Germany State Park,** off Route 48 (the National Freeway) via Exit 22 or Exit 24 on Lower New Germany Road. Savage River State Forest is the largest Maryland state forest and it has two sections. Two state parks, **New Germany State Park** and **Big Run State Park,** are located in the larger eastern portion of the forest. The forest contains a 450-acre reservoir with limited boating use; no motorized boats are allowed. The damming of the Savage River has enabled control of a 5½-mile whitewater canoeing course where competitions are held. (See also Special Interest Section on Canoeing). In other non-wilderness areas, the forest offers a 26-mile snowmobile trail, 50 miles of moderately difficult hiking ,trails and 26 designated primitive camping sites. Although no fee is charged, permits are required for the campsites, which are on a first-come, first-served basis. Permits and directions to the sites may be obtained at the office near the New Germany State Park entrance. The office is open year round, Monday through Thursday, 8:00 a.m. to 4:30 p.m.; Friday, 8:00 a.m. to 8:30 p.m.; Saturday and Sunday, 9:00 a.m to 5:30 p.m. On weekends park rangers will direct visitors. Telephone: (301) 895-5759.

New Germany State Park is located on the site of a once-prosperous milling center. The 13-acre lake was formed by damming the river in operation of the mills. New Germany is a large cross-country ski center (see Special Interest Section on Skiing). It has camping, hiking, picnicking, trailer camping, boating, fishing, and swimming facilities, as well as a playground, food concession, toilets, and showers. Eleven cabins are completely furnished. The lake is stocked with game fish. Numerous hiking trails take one through the old hemlock grove and along Poplar Lick Run. The summer cabin rentals are handled in Annapolis (see Herrington Manor State Park entry). During the winter the Park Manager takes reservations for the cabins. Camping facilities are available May to Labor Day. Camping charge; weekend day-use park charge. For reservations and information write to Park Superintendent, Grantsville, MD 21536. Telephone: (301) 895-5453.

Big Run State Park lies wholly within the Savage River State Forest, near its northern border. Big Run attracts the backpacker and canoeist who seek the peace and quiet of the backwoods. There is excellent fishing, notably for bass and trout. Many visitors come here to walk the 16-mile Savage Trail, which follows the ridge from near Route 40 southward to the Savage River Dam. Camping sites are available with toilets and drinking water. The park is open year round. Admission free. Campsite charge. For information, write Park Manager, Route 2, Box 63, Grantsville, MD 21536. Telephone: (301) 895-5453.

To drive to **Deep Creek Lake** from Oakland and the south, take Route 219 10 miles to lake. From Cumberland and the east, take Route 40/48 to Keiper's Ridge, south on 219 to park signs. Deep Creek Lake is the largest freshwater lake in Maryland. It is 12 miles in length with a shoreline of 65 miles covering nearly 3,900 acres. A wide variety of activities abound, including boating, water skiing, fishing, swimming, hiking, picnicking, sailing, downhill and cross-country skiing, snowmobiling, and skating. There are a number of campgrounds in the area. Motels, cottages, and condominiums also dot the shoreline. Some provide dock facilities, sandy beaches, and swimming areas.

Built in 1925 by the Youghiogheny Electric Company, the lake was purchased by the Pennsylvania Electric Company in 1942. It is now leased to the Maryland Inland Fish and Game Commission for the nominal fee of one dollar a year. The state park is located on the northeastern section of the lake with four hiking trails, snowmobile trails, swimming, boating, and 112 campsites (no hookups, but showers are available). Interpretive summer programs are given by the park staff. Reservations are advised for weekend use of camp sites. Small charge for camp sites. Park admission charge on weekends. Telephone: (301) 334-1948.

Potomac State Forest (via Route 40 west from Cumberland to Grantsville and south on Route 495), is suggestive of the Rocky Mountains. Its many peaks and ridges are about 3,000 feet in elevation. The ridge called Backbone Mountain is located here and an eastern "continental divide" occurs causing waters from the western slopes to flow toward the Mississippi River. You can enjoy hiking, camping, fishing, and hunting in season, and snowmobiling in winter. There are 35 primitive campsites available without hookups or showers, although most sites have spring drinking water. Deer, small game, grouse, and turkey lure the hunter. Many abandoned coal mines may be seen in and near the forest. Admission free; small charge for camping sites. Telephone: (301) 334-2038.

Oakland, the county seat, sits on a plateau of 2,650 feet above sea level. Oakland is located on Route 219, which can be reached from Routes 40 and 48 via Hagerstown and Cumberland or from the south in West Virginia on Route 219 or Route 81 to Route 50. The coming of the railroad at the end of the 19th century encouraged development of the Deer Park/Oakland area. It was known for its clean air and beautiful scenery and had a Chautauqua meeting ground.

The **Garrett County Historical Museum**, located on Center Street, is devoted to county-related historical and cultural events. The museum displays artifacts from the Civil War, and a collection relating to Thomas Edison on loan from the Edison Fund. The museum also has many items from the grand old hotels—Glades, Oakland, Deer Park, and Mountain

Lake Park hotels—from the Victorian era. None of these frame structures have survived. The museum is open June through August, Monday to Friday, 10:00 a.m. to 4:00 p.m. Telephone: (301) 334-3226 or 387-9171.

One block away at the corner of Liberty and Second streets is the **B&O Railroad Station** (c. 1884). The station is a picturesque remainder of the 19th-century resort community. This Queen Anne-style building is composed of incised brick and has a round tower with a conical roof and arched windows. The station has been placed on the National Register of Historic Places. Across the street one can visit **St. Matthew's Episcopal Church**, the church of the presidents. The church was attended during their summer vacations by presidents Grant, Harrison, and Cleveland. This handsome building was built in 1868 by John Garrett as a memorial to his brother, Henry, and has been restored by the St. Matthew's congregation. It is open to the public.

Swallow Falls State Park and **Herrington Manor State Park** are both located in **Garrett State Forest** in the southwestern end of the state, three miles east of West Virginia. Both parks offer picnicking areas and interpretive programs during the summer season. For reservations and information about both parks contact Park Superintendent, Herrington Manor State Park, Route 5, Box 122, Oakland, MD 21550, or telephone: (301) 334-9180. Swallow Falls Park may be reached from Oakland—take Liberty Street (Route 20) northwest nine miles. From the north, take Route 48, Exit 14 to Route 219 south.

Probably the most beautiful site in the county, the 51-foot **Muddy Creek Falls** is the longest in the state. **Swallow Falls State Park** is a scenic paradise of rushing water and towering trees, cliffs and narrow gorges and misty glens. Maryland's last virgin forest is found in the park with giant pines and hemlocks that rise more than 100 feet. Muddy Creek Falls is located near the confluence of Muddy Creek and the Youghiogheny River. Hiking trails along the Youghiogheny skirt the rapids and one trail features a swinging bridge across Muddy Creek above the falls. The park was the site of summer vacation camps in 1918 and 1921 of Henry Ford, Thomas Edison, and Harvey Firestone. The park has 64 campsites near a washhouse with running water, laundry tubs, showers, and toilets. Campsites are closed from the last day of deer season to May 1.

Herrington Manor State Park surrounds a 53-acre lake

with housekeeping cabins. Forest plantations around the lake, representing Maryland state reforestation practices, may be seen via easily accessible trails in the 365-acre park. Twenty cabins may be rented from the second week in June through the second week in September for two-week periods. A limited number of cabins are available during the winter. Call park office for reservations. Telephone: (301) 334-9180. Swimming, boating, and fishing are allowed on the lake. Only electric motors of one horsepower or less are permitted. During the winter the park offers five miles of cross-country skiing trails. Reservations for the cabins are accepted after December 1 for the following season and are awarded by lot. Write to Park Superintendent, RFD No. 5, Box 122, Oakland, MD 21550.

Reach **Cranesville Swamp** via Liberty Street (Route 20) approximately 10 miles out of Oakland. Make a left turn after Paul's Wood House onto a dirt road and after traveling on this road for approximately a half-mile make a right turn onto another dirt road. After traveling on this road approximately a half-mile you will see a large stone marker. At this marker there is a path where you may walk to the swamp.

The Cranesville Swamp, bridging the Maryland-West Virginia border, is a rare pocket of sub-Arctic swamp surviving from the Ice Age. The swamp has been designated a National Natural Landmark and is owned and administered by The Nature Conservancy, a nonprofit private organization. The boreal bog preserves a rare assemblage of plant life that is typical of colder Canadian climates. The preserve presently covers 313 acres of swamp land and is the southernmost tamarack forest in the United States. There is no resident naturalist on the site, but the Herrington Manor State Park rangers will assist visitors in getting to the swamp. Admission free. Telephone: (301) 334-9180. The Nature Conservancy periodically conducts guided tours for its members. Contact the Maryland chapter of The Nature Conservancy, 35 Wisconsin Circle, Chevy Chase, MD 20015. Telephone: (301) 656-8673.

ALLEGANY COUNTY

Allegany County was formed in 1789, and its first settlers in the mid-18th century were English. Later immigrants came from Scotland, Wales, Ireland, and Germany. Unlike other sections of Maryland, Allegany is not an agricultural area. During the 19th century, bituminous coal and iron ore mining and the glass-making industry developed. Those industries declined in the 20th century and there has been high unemployment although modern industrial companies moved into the county. Allegany County is located in the heart of the Allegany plateau with elevations ranging from 2,850 feet near Frostburg to Cumberland's 620 feet.

The **Green Ridge State Forest** is bounded on the east by the seven great bends in the Potomac River and is accessible from Route 40, six miles west of Piney Grove. Chief attractions are rugged scenery, 92 primitive campsites, hiking, hunting, and fishing facilities. Four streams in the forest are stocked with fish.

A large portion of the forest is made up of 10-acre lots, which were sold to individuals with the intention of planting apple orchards. The developer went bankrupt and the lots were sold for taxes. In 1930, the state began buying up the lots to form the State Forest.

Other unique features include **Old Stone Furnace** at Chimney Hollow and the 3,080-mile-long **Paw Paw Tunnel**, part of the historic C&O Canal. The forest also features large plantations of red, white, and Scotch pine. Nearby are **Sideling Hill Wildlife Management Area, Belle Grove Game Farm,** and **Billmeyer Game Refuge.** For information, contact Park Manager, Star Route, Flintstone, MD 21530. Telephone: (301) 478-2991.

Rocky Gap State Park is near Flintstone, west of Green Ridge, about seven miles east of Cumberland. Rocky Gap lies in an area of impressive scenic beauty. Rugged mountains surround it, and a splendid mile-long gorge, descending to Rocky Gap Run, displays sheer cliffs, rock slides, and dense forests. The road which bisects the day-use area was once the first wagon road westward through this vicinity, in use long before the National Pike was developed. Known as the "Old Hancock Road," its construction was authorized by the Maryland Assembly in 1791. The 243-acre, man-made lake has two bathing beaches, modern bathhouses, drinking fountains, and boating and food concessions. Picnic areas have charcoal grills. Visitors may enjoy swimming, boating, nature study, fishing, or hiking on the park's winding trails. The campground consists of 278 wooded campsites with washhouses and hot showers. Interpretative programs such as films, nature study hikes, and crafts exhibits are scheduled year round in the park. For information, write Park Manager, Route 1, Box 90, Flintstone, MD 21530. Telephone: (301) 777-2138.

Cumberland, once known as Wills Creek, took its present name from Fort Cumberland, located here during the French and Indian Wars. It was the western terminus of the Chesapeake and Ohio Canal (see C&O Canal National Historical Park section above), and the starting point of the historic National Road, first federally funded highway in the U.S., which helped open to settlement the area west of the Alleghenies. To reach Cumberland from Hagerstown, take Route 70 to Hancock, then Routes 40 and 48.

Enroute to Cumberland from Hancock, the motorist crosses five mountains. A stop can be made at each overlook for a scene of grandeur and beauty. The mountain views, from east to west, are: Sideling Hill (1,600 feet), Town Hill (1,600 feet), Green Ridge (1,575 feet), Polish Mountain (1,340 feet), and Martin's Mountain (1,695 feet).

Cumberland offers visitors a walking tour of its historic places. One can also take a motor tour of the area to visit points within several miles of the city. Maps and directions may be obtained free of charge from the Allegany County tourism office on Baltimore Street at Green Street.

Leave your car on any parking lot off Baltimore Street, the city's main street, which is now a pedestrian mall complete with four mini-parks with fountains, flowers, trees, and benches where people enjoy eating lunch amidst the handsome turn-of-the-century commercial buildings. Walking west across the bridge over **Wills Creek** and up the hill you enter the beautiful and historic **Washington Street District**. Up to the 600 block it is listed on the National Register of Historic Places. At the beginning of the street you will see **Emmanuel Episcopal Church** (c. 1848), built on the site of **Fort Cumberland** (1753). The Fort Cumberland tunnels under the church are open for touring during Allegany County's official Heritage Days Festival the second weekend of June. They were used to obtain water from Wills Creek, as an escape route, and for storage of ammunition. Washington Street traverses the oldest and finest residential area in the city. As you climb the hill, the **First Presbyterian Church** is on the right. Beyond, where the street levels off, is the **Allegany County Library** (c. 1849), once an academy. Directly across the street is the impressive **Allegany County Court House** (c. 1893). This **Prospect Square** area was the parade ground for Fort Cumberland, during its occupancy by General Braddock and his aide, George Washington. The first fort was built on this site in 1750 and was the scene of Washington's first military command in 1754, during the French and Indian Wars. It was here also that Washington, in 1794, made his last military appearance in a review of troops called out to suppress the Whiskey Rebellion.

A block farther up the street is **St. Paul's Lutheran Church** (c. 1958). Its history goes back to 1795 when a log church was built on this site. On Fayette Street, behind St. Paul's, is **St. Peter and Paul Church** and **Monastery**. The monastery, built in 1849 by the Redemptorists, was taken over by the Carmelites in 1866. Cross the street and proceed to **History House** (c. 1867), at 218 Washington Street. This old home is headquarters of the Allegany County Historical Society. Many interesting exhibits of the early history of the area can be seen here. At 108 Washington Street is the old **Walsh Home** built in 1866, now occupied by the Board of Education, and the birthplace of Bishop James Walsh, a missionary in China imprisoned for many years by the Chinese Communists. This historic district maintains a uniformity of architectural quality that is tied together by the tree-shaded street where coal and rail barons in another era lived in ornate mansions, many of which are now restored.

One block to the left of Washington Street is Greene Street, where **Riverside Park** and **George Washington's Headquarters** (c. 1755) are located. This building was used by Washington during the French and Indian Wars and again during the Whiskey Rebellion. Also in the park is the **Thomas Cresap Monument**, erected to the memory of a noted pioneer and patriot. In the **Oldtown** area in 1740, Cresap built the first home and fort (now open to the public) and laid out the first trail to lands west of the Alleghenies. Opposite the approach to the bridge, on the Masonic Temple grounds, is the starting point of the **Old Cumberland Road** (also known as Braddock Road) to the west. Across the Potomac River is the terminus of the famous **Chesapeake and Ohio Canal**, opened in 1850.

For an interesting 16-mile circuit drive, take Route 220 south, out Greene Street to the "Dingle Circle," left to Gephart Drive, and right to the Ridgedale Reservoir. This high point affords an excellent view of Cumberland.

A few miles farther down Route 220 south is **Cresaptown**, named for sons of the Cresap pioneer settler family. Turn right on Route 53, a picturesque road which leads to Route 40. Just west of the intersection of Routes 53 and 40 is the restored **Old Toll House**, erected in 1833, the first toll house on the Old Cumberland Road.

On the western outskirts of the city you will pass through the famous **"Narrows."** The "Narrows" is a natural 1,000-foot breach in Wills Mountain. Known as the "Gateway to the West," this transportation route played an important part in the development of the west. The picturesque gap in the Allegheny Mountains has been designated a Natural Landmark. The Narrows also boasts a "Lover's Leap" legend—an Indian princess and her lover, an English trapper, are said to have leaped to their deaths from here.

A detour off Route 40 on Route 220 north will bring you to Nave's Crossroads. Turn right for a short distance to the Route 40 east direction. At this area sits Colonial Manor Motor Lodge, originally known as **Turkey Flight Manor.** It is the oldest brick house in the Cumberland area, built in 1758. Soldiers were hospitalized here during the Civil War.

To drive to Frostburg from Cumberland, take Route 48 to Exits 33 or 34 to Route 40 west. Frostburg began with the log home Meshach Frost built for his bride in 1812. When the National Road brought stagecoach service, their home became an inn, **Highland Hall.** During the 1840s Frostburg became a commercial mining, brick, and lumber center. These industries declined during the late 19th and early 20th century. Today, Frostburg's biggest employer is Frostburg State College.

The town retains many of its old historic homes, which may be seen on a walking tour of Main Street. A map and description of the homes may be obtained from the Allegany County Tourism office in Cumberland. Some of the homes date from the National Road days, as well as from the Civil War and Victorian eras. A few examples of interesting buildings in Frostburg are:

Frost Mansion, built of local brick in 1846. After Mrs. Meshach Frost died in 1876, the Frost heirs added six rooms and a mansard roof and turned the farmhouse into a summer hotel, where many important people from Baltimore and Washington were guests.

The **Methodist Church** has occupied the same site longer than any other congregation in town. A stone church, built in 1835, was replaced in 1855 by a frame building; the present church dates from 1870. Stained-glass windows memorialize many of the town's earliest citizens.

Fisher building is noteworthy for its glazed brick facade. Andrew Ramsay, of Mt. Savage, found a process for baking and glazing brick in a single firing, and won a prize at the St. Louis Fair for his product. But he was an eccentric who refused to share his secret, which died with him.

WASHINGTON COUNTY

Washington County lies in the Hagerstown Valley between two ridges. This valley is a continuation of the Shenandoah Valley of Virginia. The Appalachian Trail runs along the entire eastern boundary of the county. The early 18th-century settlements in Washington County began as frontier outposts. In 1756, the Maryland General Assembly authorized the construction of Fort Frederick to provide a base for British military operations and protection for local homesteaders against the Indians, who were allied with the French. In 1776 the county was founded and named for General George Washington. During the Civil War, Washington County was the scene of several significant and bloody battles—South Mountain, Harpers Ferry, and Antietam.

Antietam National Battlefield, in Sharpsburg where Routes 35 and 65 meet, is the site of the bloodiest single-day battle in the Civil War. It remains much as it was before that September day in 1862. Battlefield tour roads now wind through and around peaceful farms and pastures.

The battle on September 27, 1862, greatly altered the course of the Civil War, although neither side gained the upper hand at Antietam. General George B. McClellan and the Federal forces prevented the Confederates under General Robert E. Lee from carrying the war effectively into the North and caused Great Britain to postpone recognition of the Confederate government. Of almost equal importance was the long-awaited opportunity given President Lincoln to issue the Emancipation Proclamation. Five days after the Federal victory, Lincoln issued his preliminary proclamation which warned the South that, on January 1, 1863, he would declare free all slaves in territory still in rebellion against the United States. Henceforth, the war would have a dual purpose: to preserve the Union and to end slavery.

At the Visitor's Center exhibits and an explanatory slide show tell the story of the campaign. Pick up a map and directions for a self-guided tour of the battlefield. The battlefield site contains a national cemetery of Federal soldiers from the Civil War and some from later wars. The remains of Confederate soldiers are scattered in private cemeteries in the area. In 1869 the state of Maryland attempted to identify and record the remains of the Confederate soldiers, and the resulting publication is available for study in the Antietam resource library. The library contains 900 publications, as well as folders and monographs. The library is open by appointment to researchers and to relatives of Antietam battle veterans. Open Monday through Friday, 8:30 a.m. to 5:00 p.m. The Antietam National Battlefield Site and Cemetery, administered by the National Park Service, is open May 30 to Labor Day, daily, 8:00 a.m. to 6:00 p.m.; during winter, daily, 8:30 a.m. to 5:00 p.m. Admission charge. Telephone: (301) 432-5124.

Burnside Bridge, over Antietam Creek, is probably the most famous of the Washington County bridges. It figured prominently in the Battle of Antietam for it was where a few hundred Georgia riflemen held off four Federal divisions for hours, changing the outcome of the battle. This beautiful three-arch, 12-foot-wide bridge was built in 1836.

The stone bridges in Washington County date from the 1820s and 1830s, the road and bridge building period of the National Road project. The stone bridges are a result of the pride that Marylanders, and particularly natives of Washington County, displayed in building bridges to endure. The Scotch, German, and Irish immigrants to the area were skilled stonemasons, and the native limestone was an ideal building material. When the Secretary of War suggested building covered wooden bridges as a cost-cutting measure, Maryland refused to comply and continued to use stone in Washington County. An illustrated brochure of the 28 stone bridges in the county may be obtained from Washington County Tourism Division, Court House Annex, Hagerstown, MD 21740. Telephone: (301) 791-3130.

Greenbrier State Park, on Route 40, 10 miles east of Hagerstown, is located on South Mountain near the scene of several Civil War engagements. The area was first settled in 1754 and was the scene of Indian raids during the French and Indian Wars. Local furnaces furnished the iron for cannons during the Revolutionary War. The Appalachian Trail, an attraction for hikers and campers, passes through the park. A 42-acre lake, fed by forest springs, is used for bathing and fishing. The park offers hiking trails, picnicking, boating facilities, and 328 campsites. The campsites have showers and are available on a first-come, first-served basis. No pets are allowed in the park. The park is open during daylight hours. Admission charged during summer. Telephone: (301) 791-4767.

Washington Monument State Park is off Alternate Route 40, two miles southeast of Boonsboro.

Originally constructed in 1827, this rugged stone tower was the first memorial dedicated to George Washington. It was built on the summit of South Mountain by citizens of nearby Boonsboro from materials picked up at the site. Three states are visible from the top of the Monument—Maryland, Virginia, and West Virginia—as well as such historical sites as Antietam, Harpers Ferry, and Winchester.

The park museum highlights the historic interest of the region, with displays of firearms, Indian relics, and Civil War mementos. The famous Appalachian Trail winds through the park and past the base of the Monument. The Cumberland Valley is a flyway for migratory birds, and an annual count of migrating hawks and eagles is made at the Monument by ornithologists.

There are two picnic sites with a large playfield between them. Available are about 100 picnic tables, 35 fireplaces, six shelters, hot and cold water, and toilets. There are also 15 campsites adjacent to water and sanitary conveniences.

The park has set aside one camping site for youth groups. The park is open 8:00 a.m. to 9:30 p.m. in the summer. The camp grounds are closed during winter. Admission free for park; charge for campsites. For further information contact Park Superintendent, Route 1, Box 147, Middletown, MD 21769. Telephone: (301) 432-8065.

Crystal Grottoes Caverns are located near Boonsboro, west on Route 34. An underground limestone cavern of beauty and enchantment, Crystal Grottoes contains corridors of jeweled stalactites and stalagmites of unusual design and formation. A 40-minute guided tour was developed by the owner, who is a geology professor, and it is limited to small groups of approximately 15. The cavern was discovered in 1940 in the course of excavating a rock quarry. A sheltered pavilion is available for picnicking. Open March through November, daily, 9:00 a.m. to 6:00 p.m.; December through February, weekends, 11:00 a.m. to 5:00 p.m., weekdays by reservation. Admission charge. Telephone: (301) 432-6336.

Also in Boonsboro is the **Scoper House Museum**, which

contains Civil War memorabilia and Indian artifacts. The museum is on Main Street and can be identified by the five cannons sitting on the front yard. Open May to September, Sunday, 1:00 to 5:00 p.m. Admission charge. Telephone: (301) 432-6969.

Fort Frederick State Park is off I-70's Big Pool Exit; the park entrance is two miles on Route 56. Fort Frederick is a beautifully preserved, historic fort erected in the 1750s during the French and Indian Wars. Fort Frederick and a chain of smaller forts protected the Maryland frontier. A classic fort of that period, it was designed by skilled military engineers. The massive stone walls provided protection for hundreds of settlers. It served as a barracks for captured British and Hessian troops during the American Revolution, and figured as an outpost in the Civil War.

The C&O Canal runs through the southern end of the park. A museum on the grounds displays relics found at Fort Frederick. The park has camping, fishing, picnicking, hiking, and boating facilities. There are 28 primitive campsites, and permits are issued on a first-come, first-served basis. Permits may be obtained from the Park Superintendent, PO Box 177, Big Pool, MD 21711. Telephone: (301) 842-2155.

Hagerstown, the seat of Washington County, is at the junction of interstates 70 and 81. It was in 1739 that Jonathan Hager, a German immigrant, settled on his first tract of land, "Hager's Fancy." Hager's original homestead, built over natural springs to provide a water supply safe from Indian attack, survives.

Today, Hagerstown is a modern industrial city in the Allegheny foothills that reflects the artistic skill of Hagerstown's 18th-century German, Scotch, and Irish stonemasons. The city offers many points of interest for visitors to see, and the Washington County Tourism Division, located at Summit Avenue, provides a map and descriptions of the sites. A few of the most prominent are: The **Zion Reformed Church**, at Potomac and Church streets, was originally built in 1774, but extensive renovations were made to the stone structure in the 19th century. It is the oldest building in the city. Jonathan Hager (1719-75), founder of Hagerstown, is buried in the graveyard behind the church.

The **Miller House**, a typical townhouse of the late Federal period (built early 1820s) and the **Valley Store Museum** are at 135 West Washington Street. The Miller House is headquarters of the Washington County Historical Society.

The elegant interior is noteworthy for its original hanging stairway rising in a graceful curve to the third floor and for its spacious, high-ceilinged drawing rooms. On exhibit are period furniture pieces; a collection of early photographs, papers, and artifacts of the C&O Canal and of the Civil War; a doll and antique clock collection; and Hagerstown's first fire engine and first taxi. The Valley Store Museum is a display of a typical country store of the 1860-1915 era and contains fixtures and merchandise from Washington County stores. Open Wednesday through Friday, 1:00 to 4:00 p.m.; Saturday and Sunday, 2:00 to 5:00 p.m. The Society maintains a genealogy library which is open Monday, 9:00 a.m. to 4:00 p.m. Telephone: (301) 797-8782.

Hager House and Museum, the home of Jonathan Hager, was built in 1739-40 and is located at 19 Key Street near the City Park. The house was originally one-and-a-half stories high. Built as a fort home and a fur trading post, the Germanic floor plan spans two springs of water. Hager wanted to assure fresh water within his stronghold, in case of Indian attacks. He used the basement as a blacksmith shop and the upper floors for living quarters. Restored in 1953, today it is owned by the City of Hagerstown and furnished by the Washington County Historical Society. Open to the public, April to October, Tuesday through Saturday, 10:00 a.m. to 4:00 p.m.; Sunday, 2:00 to 5:00 p.m. Admission charge. Telephone: (301) 739-8393.

Of special interest to visitors is the national award-winning City Park, noted for its beautiful design. The **Washington Museum of Fine Arts**, located at the lakeside in City Park, contains a notable collection of sculpture, paintings, and graphic arts, including examples of works of foremost artists of America and Europe. Open Tuesday through Saturday, 10:00 a.m. to 5:00 p.m.; Sunday, 1:00 to 6:00 p.m. Donation. Telephone: (301) 739-5727.

The **Rose Hill Cemetery** is located on Memorial Boulevard and Potomac Street. Located within Rose Hill is a five-acre section called Washington Cemetery, dedicated to the Confederate soldiers who died in the battles of Antietam and South Mountain. The cemetery was the result of the work of Henry Kyd Douglas, a Hagerstown native and the youngest officer on General Stonewall Jackson's staff. Feeling the injustice of the neglect of Southern Civil War dead, Douglas gathered the remains of many Confederate soldiers from the local countryside. Washington Cemetery is a flat, grassy area with a plaque listing the names of the known dead buried there. To the east is the **Thomas Kennedy Monument,** which marks the grave of the noted merchant-lawyer who spent almost two decades fighting for the passage of the "Jew Bill," which would grant Jews the same civil rights enjoyed by all other citizens. Kennedy won his fight in 1826. The shaft was erected in 1919 by prominent Maryland Jews.

The **Maryland Theatre,** near the city's Public Square, was designed by a famous New York theater architect, Thomas W. Lamb. Maryland Theatre was constructed in 1915 in neoclassical style and has flawless acoustic qualities. Slated for demolition after a 1974 fire destroyed the theater's lobby, the building was purchased by a concerned citizen who formed a committee to preserve and restore this architectural work of art. Today it is a reminder of more romantic times and provides a home for the Maryland Theatre Orchestra and is the scene of a full calendar of events.

Williamsport, an old town on the historic Chesapeake and Ohio Canal, is southwest of Hagerstown on Route 11 at the intersection of Route 68. The town was laid out in 1786 by Gen. O. H. Williams, for whom it is named. It supports a brick kiln and limestone quarry. West of town is the old Conococheague Creek Bridge. The Chesapeake and Ohio Canal crosses the creek by means of a long stone aqueduct.

UPPER CHESAPEAKE

HARFORD AND CECIL COUNTIES

This tour of historic and scenic places in **Harford** and **Cecil counties** is along Route 40 to Elkton and back to the Washington-Baltimore area via several state roads and Route 1. Round trip from Washington is approximately 195 miles. The trip can be extended into the northern portion of Delaware, notably Wilmington and New Castle, or into southeastern Pennsylvania. Harford County, lying between Pennsylvania and the Chesapeake Bay, was established in 1773 and named for Henry Harford, the son of the last Lord Baltimore. The county boasts 38.9 miles of Chesapeake Bay shoreline and ranges from the coastal plain area at sea level to 750 feet in the Piedmont Plateau.

Ladew Topiary Gardens are famous for topiary sculptures. The garden is approximately 14 miles north of Baltimore on Route 146, from Exit 27 of the Baltimore Beltway. The 22 acres contain life-size figures of many types of birds and beasts, and sculptured hedges that reflect the versatile artistry of Harvey Ladew. Flowers bloom throughout the growing season, including roses, azaleas, dogwood, hydrangea, and irises. The large white clapboard house contains a museum displaying a collection of English antiques, fox hunting memorabilia, a library, and a gift shop. The garden is open mid-April through October, Tuesday through Friday, 10:00 a.m. to 4:00 p.m.; Saturday and Sunday, noon to 5:00 p.m. The house is open Wednesday, Saturday, and Sunday. Group tours by appointment year round. The house has a Christmas Open House the first Friday, Saturday, and Sunday of December. Admission charge. For further information write: 3535 Jarrettsville Pike, Monkton, MD 21131. Telephone: (301) 557-9466.

Rocks State Park is off Route 24, eight miles northwest of Bel Air, which is on Route 1. It can also be reached via Route 147 from Baltimore. Turn left onto Route 1, at Benson, and left on Route 24 at the next intersection. This area is an imposing scenic site, with lofty and rugged rock formations separated by the deep valley of Deer Creek. A trail leads from the park headquarters and from the picnic area to the famous King and Queen Seats, 94 feet high. The cliffs overlooking the valley below are 190 feet high. An old iron mill, established early in the 19th century, once stood in the area. The power for the water wheel came from Deer Creek. Pig iron from this mill was used in building the Civil War warship *Monitor*.

The park offers picnicking, canoeing, and hiking facilities year round. For further information write: Park Manager, 3318 Rocks Chrome Hill Road, Jarrettsville, MD 21084. Telephone: (301) 557-7994.

Susquehanna State Park is just north of Havre de Grace, off Route 155, accessible from Routes 40 and 95. The area of the park was settled more than 200 years ago, and many early structures built by the first settlers may be visited. The park publishes a self-guided walking tour brochure of a historic trail that includes restored canal and mill structures. The imposing four-story **Rock Run Grist Mill** was built in 1794 and has been restored to operating condition. Visitors receive a package of meal as a souvenir of their visit. The mill operates in summer, weekends and holidays, 2:00 to 4:00 p.m. Other sights include the mill race and pond, the miller's house (not open to the public), the carriage barn, a springhouse, and the manor house.

The **Jersey Toll House**, near the mill, was originally built as a residence for the tollkeeper of the Rock Run covered bridge, which was the first bridge built over the turbulent Susquehanna River. This bridge was destroyed in 1854. The tollkeeper's house is furnished with period antiques and early Americana. Open Memorial Day to Labor Day, weekends and holidays, 10:00 a.m. to 6:00 p.m.

The 2,200-acre park has facilities for picnicking, boating, hiking, fishing, horseback riding, and camping. A nature trail will interest students of natural history. The shad run in April, in addition to the pike, perch and bass, makes this one of the best fishing grounds in the state. The park is open year round. The camping area is open May through October. Admission free; charge for campsites. For further information write: Park Superintendent, 801 Stafford Road, Havre de Grace, MD 21078. Telephone: (301) 939-0643.

Steppingstone Museum, administered by a nonprofit organization, is also located in Susquehanna State Park on the bluffs above the river. It is an outdoor agricultural museum devoted to preservation and demonstration of the rural arts and crafts of the 1880-1910 period. An 18th-century stone farmhouse is furnished with period furniture and outlying buildings contain a replica of a country store and a cooper shop, woodworking shop and leather shop. Open May to early October, Saturday and Sunday, 1:00 to 5:00 p.m. Admission charge. For further information write: Park Manager, 461 Quaker Bottom Road, Havre de Grace, MD 21078. Telephone: (301) 939-2299.

Students of military history will find the **Army Ordnance Museum** of interest. It is readily accessible from Routes 95 and 40, east of the town of Aberdeen, which is northeast about 30 miles from the center of Baltimore. Along Maryland Boulevard, leading to the museum, is a two-mile-long display of tanks and self-propelled artillery. Visitors can also see guns, tanks, and other weapons used in all wars to World War II and the Vietnam War, including captured German and Viet Cong weapons. The U.S. Army Ordnance Museum has the most complete collection of weapons in the world and is a resource for students at the Army Ordnance Center and school.

The museum, covering 20 acres, originated around 1918 when the Army convened a commission to study the use of weapons in World War I. In order to make the technical evaluations the commission utilized the Aberdeen Proving Ground facilities. The museum also operates a small gift shop. Open Tuesday through Friday, noon to 4:45 p.m.; weekends, 10:00 a.m. to 3:45 p.m. Admission free. For further information write: Army Ordnance Museum, Aberdeen Proving Ground, MD 21005. Telephone: (301) 278-3602.

The historic town of **Havre de Grace** calls itself the "water sports capital of the upper Chesapeake Bay." It derives its name from an incident in 1782 when a Frenchman in the entourage of the Marquis de Lafayette exclaimed upon seeing the Susquehanna shoreline, "Ah, c'est Le Havre—Le . Havre de Grace!"

Havre de Grace, located off Route 40 and I-95 on the southern banks of the Susquehanna River, is a delightful old town that has been designated a National Historic District. It was settled in 1658 and has many historic ties as it lies on the Old Post Road between Philadelphia and Williamsburg. In addition to the many large, historic houses, there are such interesting shops to visit as **Bomboy's** homemade candy shop on Market Street and the **Sail Maker's Loft** on North St. John Street. The **Rodgers House** at 226 N. Washington Street was the home of Colonel John Rodgers, commander of a militia company during the Revolutionary War. The house has been restored and a restaurant serving luncheon and dinner (closed Monday) occupies the first floor. At the corner of Pennington and Union streets stands **Seneca Mansion**, built in 1869 by Stephen J. Seneca. It is a very ornate Victorian house with a proliferation of copper-covered turrets, bay windows, dormers, and porches.

The **Susquehanna Museum** on Conesteo Street is housed in the old lockhouse of the **Susquehanna and Tidewater Canal**. The canal began operations in 1840 and mule-driven barges transported boats of 150-ton capacity 45 miles through a system of 29 locks from Havre de Grace to Wrightsville, PA. The lockhouse served as the home and office of the lockmaster and is decorated with 1840-75 period furniture. Open June through August, Sunday, 1:00 to 5:00 p.m. Telephone: (301) 939-1800.

The **Concord Point Lighthouse** is located at the south end of town, where the Susquehanna River empties into the Chesapeake Bay. It was built in 1827 and is one of the oldest lighthouses on the East Coast. The lightkeeper's former home, an 18th-century structure, is across the road from the light. It was once a stagecoach station and an inn. The lighthouse is open June to October, Sunday, 1:00 to 5:00 p.m.; and by appointment. Admission free. Telephone: (301) 939-1800. A walking tour brochure of the city may be obtained from the Chamber of Commerce, PO Box 339, Havre de Grace, MD 21708. Telephone: (301) 939-3303.

Cecil County is in the upper northeast corner of the state. Our tour begins in **Perryville**.

The three-story **Rodgers Tavern** is located on West Main Street about one mile off Route 40, at the north side of the toll bridge over the Susquehanna River. It served as a stopping place for travelers on the Post Road who were waiting for the ferry. It was built in 1666. The tavern was operated by Col. John Rodgers, who fought under General George Washington during the Revolutionary War. His son, also named John, was a naval hero of the War of 1812. It has been verified that the tavern was patronized by such illustrious persons as Martha and George Washington, Thomas Jefferson, James Madison, and the Marquis de Lafayette. Open May through October, second Sunday of each month, 2:00 to 4:00 p.m. Telephone: (301) 442-1772.

Principio Furnace is located two miles east of Perryville on Route 7. The original works were built before 1719, the first in the British colonies. Later, they supplied cannon balls and cannons for the Revolution. During the War of 1812, the furnace was destroyed by the British. In 1836, a new furnace was in operation, and continued in business until 1886. The ruins of the furnace, on private property, may be seen from the road. The scenery around the area is very beautiful. Principio Creek follows a winding course through the primeval, wooded valley.

Elk Neck State Park is located at the northern end of Chesapeake Bay, at the tip of the narrow peninsula between the Elk and Northeast rivers. It is on Route 279, nine miles south of the town of North East. Its varied topography—heavily wooded bluffs, marshes and beaches—offers unusual opportunities for nature walks and observation of wildlife. The park is a wildlife sanctuary and visitors may see white-tailed deer and other woodland animals. Bird watchers will also enjoy the spring and autumn migrations of waterfowl as the park is located on the Atlantic flyway. The park offers swimming, camping, boating, fishing, crabbing, and picnicking opportunities. A concession supplies food and refreshments. Fully furnished housekeeping cabins are available from spring to fall. Reservations for summer rentals must be arranged by writing the Annapolis office. There are four boat launch ramps and a boat rental concession where boaters may also purchase gasoline. The park offers year-round camping, and there are areas set aside for youth groups and for pet owners. For further information and reservations contact Park Superintendent, 4395 Turkey Point Road, North East, MD 21901. Telephone: (301) 287-5333.

The historic tree, **Richards Oak**, is located on Route 1 at Richardsmere, one-and-a-half miles west of Rising Sun, close to the highway. A roadside marker tells the story. General Lafayette, en route with his army to Yorktown, camped under this tree on April 12, 1781. The venerable oak is estimated to be about 500 years old. It is 80 feet high, with a 115-foot branch spread, and its trunk is 24 feet around.

Gilpin Covered Bridge is north of North East, near the town of Bay View. It is easily accessible from Routes 95 or 40, 1.5 miles north on Route 272. The bridge crosses North East Creek and is a 119-foot, Burr truss bridge built around 1860.

The **West Nottingham Academy** campus is near the town of Colora. From Rising Sun drive west on Route 273, about one mile, to Route 276, turn left for two miles to Firetower Road, then right to the school. The academy was founded in 1744 by the Reverend Samuel Finley, who later became president of the College of New Jersey (now Princeton University). Finley was an Irish-Presbyterian minister who preached at revivals known as "the Great Awakening." The school, the second oldest continuously operating boarding school in the United States, is now a non-sectarian school. Its distinguished graduates include two signers of the Declaration of Independence—Richard Stockton of New Jersey and Benjamin Rush of Pennsylvania. The campus is extremely attractive with its complex of old buildings and an unusual variety of different types of trees. Most of the buildings date from the 19th century, but portions of the headmaster's house are said to predate the school and may date from as early as 1688.

St. Mary Anne's Episcopal Church, located at 315 S. Main Street in North East on Route 272, was built in 1742. The churchyard contains the graves of a number of Indian converts. The church has a Dutch gambrel roof and an unusual bell tower. The original Bible and communion silver were gifts from Queen Anne, who had actively supported the original St. Mary's parish. The church was renamed in her honor. The church welcomes visitors; inquire at the rectory. Telephone: (301) 287-5522.

The **Brick Meeting House** (East Nottingham Friends Society) in Calvert, at the junction of Routes 272 and 273, was built in two stages, in 1724 and 1751. It was used as a hospital during the Revolutionary War. In defiance of society principles, several members joined the Revolution and were read out of the society. It is the oldest house of worship in Cecil County. An original log meetinghouse was built in 1709.

Rock Presbyterian Church, which dates from 1761, is on Route 273, a mile west of Fair Hill, near the bridge over Little Elk Creek. The church is in a very picturesque locale, against a steep, rocky hillside. A small stone building across the road was used as a school in colonial days. Schoolhouses were uncommon in the 18th century and this is a historically important building. The schoolhouse is now used by the church for Sunday school classes.

The **Old Bohemia Mission**, or St. Francis Xavier Church, is off Route 282 two miles north of Warwick. Founded in 1704, it was one of the earliest Catholic churches in the colonies. The present church dates from 1792. During the 18th century, the Jesuits developed a mission which included a self-supporting plantation. Graduates of the school operated by the Jesuits included John Carroll, the first U.S. Catholic bishop, and Charles Carroll, signer of the Declaration of Independence. Many early church relics and old farm equipment are exhibited in the rectory museum and a farm building nearby. The church does not have an active congregation, but is still used for special occasions and is served by the pastor of St. Joseph's Church in Middletown, Delaware. The Old Bohemia Society maintains the church. Open third Sunday in April, May, September, and October, at 4:00 p.m. For further information write: Old Bohemia Historical Society, PO Box 61, Warwick, MD 21912.

Elkton is on Route 40, 51 miles from Baltimore. The **Cecil County Library** and the **Historical Society of Cecil County** are housed in a beautiful 19th-century house. The society has restored the original basement kitchen, a country store exhibit, an early firehouse, and a log cabin schoolhouse. The museum, which may be seen by appointment, includes a collection of Indian artifacts. The society offices are open Monday and Thursday, noon to 4:00 p.m. Admission free. For further information write: Historical Society of Cecil County,

135 East Main Street, Elkton, MD 21921. Telephone: (301) 398-0914.

Hollingsworth Tavern, W. Main Street, near Bridge Street, dates from colonial times. A striking event in its history was that George Washington and his adversary, Lord Howe, both stopped there within a two-day period during August of 1777. There are several other historic buildings in Elkton. Inquire at the Library or the Cecil County Office of Planning and Economic Development regarding the location and history of these sites. Telephone: (301) 398-0200, ext. 144.

An interesting short side trip is along a rural road from Elkton to the old port of entry, **Head of Elk,** just south of town. In colonial days ships from overseas put in at this port, and it was here that troops from the south came ashore during the Revolutionary War.

Chesapeake City, five miles south of Elkton on Route 213, is the western terminus of the Chesapeake and Delaware Canal. The 14-mile canal, which connects the Chesapeake Bay with the Delaware River, is administered by the U.S. Corps of Engineers. Picnicking areas are located along the canal, where visitors can observe a variety of ocean-going ships as well as smaller pleasure craft.

South Chesapeake City, one of the few remaining canal towns in the United States, has been listed as a National Historic District. The 38-foot **C&D Canal Waterwheel,** built in 1837, has been preserved in the **Old Lock Pump House,** located at Second Street and Bethel Road. The wooden wheel, equipped with buckets, was used to raise the water level of the canal above the locks. The water was lifted from Back Creek and dumped into the canal at a rate of 1,200,000 gallons an hour. Two steam engines, which may still be seen in a stone house, provided the power. In 1910 the Corps enlarged the canal and removed the locks, making the canal a free-flowing waterway. The pumphouse has been turned into a museum with exhibits on the development of the Chesapeake and Delaware Canal and there are two working models, one with the locks. Open Monday through Saturday, 10:00 a.m. to 4:15 p.m.; Sunday, 10:00 a.m. to 6:00 p.m. Admission free. Telephone: (301) 885-5621.

Charlestown, located on the Northeast River on Route 267 off of Route 40, was created by an act of the Maryland General Assembly in 1742 to provide a shipping port at the head of the Chesapeake Bay. Its port activity and position along the Philadelphia-Williamsburg Post Road contributed to a busy town during the mid-18th century. However, with the predominance of Baltimore as the Chesapake shipping port and the removal of the county seat in the 1780s to Elkton, Charlestown was bypassed. Many citizens moved away and some even dismantled their homes and rebuilt them in Baltimore.

During the Revolutionary War, Charlestown was an important supply area. Because it was on the post road, the town served as a stagecoach stop. At that time, Charlestown had 10 taverns located within a four-block area. Today, on Market Street, visitors may see **Tory House, Red Lyon Tavern, Indian Queen Tavern,** and the **Brick Mansion,** all of which were taverns at one time.

Colonial Charlestown, Inc. is located in the **Tory House** on Market Street. This green frame house was built in 1810 on the foundations of an earlier building. The house was believed to have been confiscated by the state from a loyalist after the Revolutionary War. The basement of the tavern housed the kitchen and dining room for the patrons and it had a separate entrance. It has been restored, complete with tables and utensils. Visitors may tour the upper floors where a small museum is located. The communal sleeping room may also be seen, although it is used today for community activities. Open May through September, first and third Sundays, 2:00 to 4:00 p.m. and by appointment. Admission free. Telephone: (301) 287-8793.

Also located within a block on Market Street are Indian Queen Tavern and Red Lyon Tavern, both built around 1755. The Indian Queen is owned by the Maryland Historic Trust, while the Red Lyon is privately owned. The Brick Mansion, also on Market Street, is one of the oldest buildings in town and is privately owned. While it was operated as a tavern, George Washington is said to have stopped here.

The **Paca House,** on Market Street, was the home of John Paca, father of William Paca, signer of the Declaration of Independence. The frame section of the house is partly of log construction and is the oldest section, while the newer stone section was added later in 1750.

The **Colonial Wharf,** authorized by the General Assembly in 1742, was built of heavy logs and stone ship ballast and extended 300 feet out into the river. During the Revolutionary War Charlestown was a supply depot for the Continental Army and a massive stone warehouse stored grains near the wharf. The stone wharf may still be seen and today is used by small pleasure craft.

Mt. Harmon Plantation, on Grove Neck Road in Earleville, is an 18th-century tobacco plantation located on the banks of the Sassafras River. The house is furnished with period American and English antiques and is complemented by a formal boxwood garden. There is a tobacco prize house on the grounds. Open April through October, Tuesday and Thursday, 10:00 a.m. to 3:00 p.m.; Sunday, 1:00 to 4:00 p.m. Admission charge. Telephone: (301) 275-2721.

KENT COUNTY

Kent County was established in 1642 and at that time encompassed the whole of the Maryland section of the Eastern Shore. **Chestertown,** the county seat, rivals Annapolis for its preservation of 18th-century buildings and was known for its lavish and extravagant life-style, which reached its height in the decade before the Revolutionary War. However, the independent and egalitarian spirit of the Eastern Shore character was observed by an Englishman who remarked "that the inferior order of people pay but little external respect to those who occupy superior station."

This town is the foremost historic attraction of the northern Eastern Shore. The spirit of the 18th century lives in this well-kept community, with its many buildings which date back to the 1700s. Chestertown was founded in 1698 and has served as the Kent County seat since 1706. This aura of the past pervades **Town Square** with its cast-iron fountain, old lamps, and colonial-style store fronts. Chestertown is the home of **Washington College,** the only college having a direct association with George Washington. Chartered in 1782, it is the nation's tenth oldest institution of higher learning.

A combined walking and motor tour is suggested, beginning at Front and Cannon streets. A detailed walking tour brochure may be obtained from the Kent County Chamber of Commerce, 400 High Street, Chestertown, MD 21620. Telephone: (301) 778-0416. The **Hynson-Ringgold House** is rich in historical and architectural interest. The rear section dates from 1735, while the front was designed by the noted English architect William Buckland and built in 1771. The mansion, surrounded by a walled garden, is now the home of the president of Washington College.

The **Customs House**, at Front and High streets, dates from the 1730s. It was the center of the rich trade with the sugar plantations of the British West Indies in colonial days. Near this site, on May 23, 1774, irate citizens boarded the brigantine *William Geddes* and threw the detested tea into the Chester River. In this way the citizenry expressed their anger over passage of the "Intolerable Acts" by the British Parliament.

Widehall, at 101 Water Street, is an elaborate merchant's house built about 1770. This beautiful Georgian home was built by Thomas Smythe, head of Maryland's government from 1774 until 1776. Most of the town's historic buildings are on or near Water Street. Six other Water Street structures, at numbers 103, 107, 109, 110, 115, and 201, were 18th-century merchants' homes.

Turn left on Maple Avenue, and left on Queen Street. The **Nicholson House**, at 111, was built in 1788 by Captain John Nicholson of the Continental Navy. The houses at 102 and 105 Queen Street date back to the early 1700s. Across the street in Church Alley is the only local example of a Philadelphia town house. It is the **Geddes-Piper House**, a three-and-one-half story home which was once owned by William Geddes, the port's customs collector, of Chestertown Tea Party fame. The house serves as the headquarters of the Kent County Historical Society. Admission charge. Open May through October, Saturday and Sunday, 1:00 to 4:00 p.m.

A right on High Street will lead to the **White Swan Tavern** (c. 1733) at 231. The tavern has been restored to appear as it would have looked in 1795. Five rooms are available for overnight guests and a tea room is open year round, daily, 3:00 to 5:00 p.m. Tours are conducted at 2:00 p.m. Reservations advised. Telephone: (301) 778-2300. The **Masonic Building** is at Park Row and Lawyer's Row. At the corner of Cross Street is **Emmanuel P.E. Church**, erected in 1768. Its rector, Rev. Dr. William Smith, was the founder of Washington College. The nearby **Court House** dates from 1860.

Around the corner to the left, on Mill Street (numbers 101-103), is a three-sectioned **"telescope" house**, the last of its kind in the area. One section was once a tavern. The gardens in the rear are a notable feature of this landmark. At 107 Mill Street is a small dormered tradesman's house (c. 1750s).

Continue west on High Street past 411 and 414, both

mid-18th-century homes. At 532 High Street is the **"Rock of Ages" House**, built entirely of stone. It is believed that the stone was brought over as ship's ballast by Captain Palmer, who erected the house.

The final stop at **Washington College** is to the right on College Avenue to Campus Avenue, a short drive. Here the visitor can see Middle, East, and West Halls, which date from 1845. They replace an earlier structure, built between 1783-88 and destroyed by fire in 1827.

George Washington was one of the college's first governors and took part in a meeting at which the building's design was determined and a fund-raising lottery approved. Today the visitor, strolling about the campus, will note buildings in many styles of architecture, including the very modern.

A side trip to **Rock Hall** from Chestertown on Route 20 west will bring the traveler past **St. Paul's Church** at the intersection of Routes 20 and 21. St. Paul's was established in 1692, and the present edifice was built in 1711. It is one of the oldest Episcopal churches in Maryland. The church is surrounded by old oak trees, some about 400 years old. Tallulah Bankhead, the actress, is buried in St. Paul's graveyard. The church is open to the public during daylight hours.

Rock Hall, on Route 20, is a charming colonial town memorable for a historic trip by Col. Tench Tilghman, aide to Gen. Washington. He stopped off at Rock Hall on his way from Yorktown to Philadelphia, carrying the news to the Continental Congress of Cornwallis's surrender. When Tilghman arrived at an inn to rest and change horses, he shouted, "A horse for the Congress! Cornwallis is taken!" Today, Rock Hall is a fishing center serving areas as far away as New England with fresh Bay seafood. On Main Street, the **Rock Hall Museum** is located in the Municipal Building. The museum has a collection of miniature Chesapeake Bay workboats, old photographs of Delaware River and Chesapeake Bay passenger ships, and fishing equipment. Open year round, Friday through Sunday, 2:00 to 4:00 p.m. Telephone: (301) 778-1399. Be sure to take the waterfront walk at the deep sea port to view the fishing fleet and pleasure craft. And enjoy the seafood restaurants.

Eastern Neck National Wildlife Refuge, located eight miles south of Rock Hall on Route 445, teems with wildlife, especially deer, waterfowl, and small game. Explore along automobile and walking trails, or take the Boardwalk Trail across a marsh to an observation platform. There are various game animals along the Wildlife Trail. This 2,285-acre island refuge has an undeveloped 400-acre section open to nature-lovers and photographers on foot. Open year round, dawn to dusk. Headquarters building open Monday through Friday, 7:30 a.m. to 4:00 p.m. Admission free. Telephone: (301) 639-7056. A nearby boat rental concession offers you a chance to fish or crab. No license is needed, but there is a county fee for boat trailer parking.

North, on Route 213, are the historic towns of **Galena** and **Georgetown.** The latter was once a busy port of entry, and a popular stop on the post road between Annapolis and Philadelphia. During the War of 1812 the town was almost totally destroyed by a landing party from Admiral Cockburn's fleet. The **Kitty Knight House** was spared when Kitty prevailed on the Admiral to save the house, because a bedridden old lady lived there. This old home is now a country inn. Telephone: (301) 648-5155. Today Georgetown is a busy yachting center.

UPPER EASTERN SHORE

A tour of this area, composed of Kent, Caroline, and Queen Anne's counties, acquaints the visitor with several historic small towns—Centreville, Church Hill, Chestertown, and Georgetown. The Eastern Shore route is recommended as a leisurely alternative route for travel to the Wilmington-Philadelphia area. It has the virtue of uncongested highways and rural scenery.

Kent Island, in Queen Anne's County, is the gateway to the Eastern Shore from the west. The island was settled by Virginians in 1631 and claims its antiquity in friendly rivalry disputes with St. Mary's, which was established in 1634 by Lord Baltimore's settlers. William Claiborne, Virginia secretary of state, established an Indian trading post on Kent Island and his claim led to armed encounters with Maryland officials who were determined to retain their legal hold on the Eastern Shore.

Kent Island today is the eastern terminus of the William Preston Lane Jr. Memorial Bridge, commonly known as the **Bay Bridge**. The twin spans of the bridge are 43 miles long and 186.5 feet high above mean water. An excellent view of the bridge may be enjoyed from a small fishing pier and parking lot area in **Matapeake State Park**. It is on Route 8, just south of the bridge from Route 50.

The traveler may wish to continue south on Route 8 to the **Kentmorr Harbor Marina** and, in season, while eating at the marina restaurant, observe the great variety of ships, including the oyster and clam fleets. Telephone: (301) 643-4700. Visitors may pick up tourist information at Stevensville, the junction of Routes 50/301 and Thompson Creek Road. The motorist, traveling eastward on Route 50 across the island, is afforded a wonderful view of the Kent Island Narrows as he leaves via a working drawbridge.

Wye Mills, on the Queen Anne's and Talbot county line on Route 50, is a picturesque village. The visitor may see an authentic replica of a colonial school as well as a church and mill. Nearby **Wye Plantation** was the summer home of William Paca, a signer of the Declaration of Independence. The original plantation mansion was demolished, but William Paca's grave site is marked. The plantation site is now used as a conference center.

The 400-year-old white oak, known as the **Wye Oak**, is preserved in the 21-acre state park near the village. With a height of 95 feet and a 165-foot spread, it is believed to be the largest of its species in the United States. Its circumference exceeds 37 feet. The tree is Maryland's official state tree. A quaint early American schoolroom is displayed in a small building near the Wye Oak.

Wye Church, a small brick structure, was consecrated on October 18, 1721. It was built on the foundations of an earlier church. Among interesting features are the high box pews, the hanging pulpit, the west gallery bearing the Royal Arms of England, and the original 1737 communion service in silver. Tours, mid-April through November, Tuesday, Saturday, and Sunday, 10:00 a.m. to 3:00 p.m. Nearby are Wye Vestry House and Parish House, which were built in 1948-58 to appear as they would have in the early 18th century. Telephone: (301) 827-8853.

Old Wye Mill stands on land which was patented in 1664. The mill itself was built in 1721. Flour for Washington's troops at Valley Forge was produced here. The owner of the mill, Colonel William Hemsley, received an open-ended contract from the Continental Congress to provision the army during the Revolutionary War. The mill is presently owned by the Society for the Preservation of Maryland Antiquities and is open to the public. Flour and water-ground cornmeal may be purchased. Open March through December, Saturday and

Sunday, 11:00 a.m. to 4:00 p.m. Telephone: (301) 827-6909 or 438-3747.

The **Tuckahoe State Park,** embracing the meandering Tuckahoe Creek stream valley, affords visitors a chance to fish, canoe, and hike. It is reached by traveling east on Route 50 to Route 404, east to Queen Anne, left on Route 480, then follow signs to park entrance. Campers will find Tuckahoe State Park a convenient base for short trips to Annapolis, Easton, St. Michaels, and Chestertown.

The park has 71 improved campsites as well as picnicking and hiking facilities. A 20-acre lake offers boating and fishing opportunities. A boating concession rents rowboats. **Adkins Arboretum,** a 500-acre arboretum developed in a natural wooded setting, is open from May to September. The highlight of a trip here is the opportunity to inspect the largest overcup oak in the nation, a 235-year-old tree with a height of 118 feet and a spread of 120 feet. For further information, write Park Manager, Route 1, Box 23, Queen Anne, MD 21657. Telephone: (301) 634-2810.

Centreville, the county seat of Queen Anne's County, is on Route 213 off of Route 301. The chief attraction here is the attractive 18th-century town green with the **Court House** (1792), which residents claim is the oldest county courthouse in continuous use in Maryland. A statue of Queen Anne, dedicated by Princess Anne in 1977, stands on the square. On the southern side of the square, a row of 19th- and early 20th-century houses make up **Lawyer's Row.**

On Commerce Street the visitor will see **Wright's Chance,** the Queen Anne's County Historical Society headquarters, and **Tucker House,** the society's museum. Both houses date from the late 18th century and are representative Eastern Shore plantation homes. Wright's Chance is furnished with Chippendale and Hepplewhite pieces. Tucker House is the repository for county and state historical information. Open May to October, Friday, 11:00 a.m. to 4:00 p.m. Nominal admission charge for each house. For further information write: Queen Anne's County Historical Society, 124 South Commerce Street, Centreville, MD 21617.

Church Hill is eight miles north of the county seat. It is named for **St. Luke's Episcopal Church,** which dates from 1732. This is an impressive church, with gambrel roof, arched windows, and Flemish bond brick walls. Inside, on either side of the chancel, hang two tablets, one the Lord's Prayer, the other the Ten Commandments—said to be gifts of Queen

Anne. The church is open to the public during daylight hours. **The Academy**, on the church grounds, served as an elementary school in the early 19th century before the days of public education. This small brick building dates from 1817, and is still used by St. Luke's.

Caroline County is the only Eastern Shore county with no bay or ocean shoreline, although the Choptank River is navigable up to Denton. On the east it borders Delaware and on the west Talbot County. On the north and south are Queen Anne's and Dorchester counties, from which it was created in 1773. The county was named in honor of the sister of the sixth Lord Baltimore. She was also the wife of Governor Eden, the last colonial governor of Maryland. The county prides itself on its agricultural production and claims it is the leading Maryland county in the production of vegetables for marketing and processing, and among the top three in the United States. For further information write: Caroline County Commissioners, PO Box 207, Denton, MD 21629.

On the Delaware-Maryland state line at Marydel the visitor will see a **Mason-Dixon Crownstone**, which was erected in 1765. Crownstones were placed every 100 miles on the line and few have survived. The Marydel crownstone is an elaborately carved English limestone post bearing Lord Baltimore's coat of arms on the Maryland side and William Penn's on the Delaware side.

South on Routes 311 and 313, the traveler reaches Denton, the county seat. Denton is noted for its vegetable canneries and light industries. From spring through fall the **Caroline County Farmers Market** sells home-baked goods and fresh vegetables grown by local farmers. Open Friday, 11:00 a.m. to 3:00 p.m.

Two miles south of Denton on Route 404 is the 100-acre **Martinak State Park**. This park has facilities for picnicking, camping, boating, fishing, and walking paths. There are 60 improved camping sites. The wreck of a **pungy**, a type of Chesapeake Bay sailing vessel no longer used, is on display in the park. The pungy (pronounced "punk") was larger than the skipjack and was used for carrying cargo. A cabin museum contains memorabilia of George Martinak, who donated the land for the park. Campsites open from April 1 to November 1. Day use facilities open year round, 8:00 a.m. to 4:30 p.m. For cabin rental and other information write Park Manager, Deep Shore Road, Denton, MD 21629. Telephone: (301) 479-1619.

On Route 16, the motorist traveling south reaches the town of **Choptank** on the Choptank River. The Choptank River is one of the longest rivers on the Eastern Shore and is navigable up to Denton. The county operates the **Choptank-towne Marina** that has 70 boat slips for rent and two boat launch ramps.

East on Route 318 is **Federalsburg**. The town is located on the Marshyhope Creek, a tributary of the Nanticoke River, and has a marina within the town limits. The marina is designed for small cruisers and outboards and has 23 boat slips, a launch ramp, and fishing pier. There are restaurants and shopping for both motorists and boaters. North of Federalsburg, off Route 306, the municipally owned, six-acre **Chambers Lake** offers bass, pickerel, and sunfish fishing.

TALBOT COUNTY

Talbot County has 602 miles of waterfront. The extensive shoreline, believed to be the longest of any county in the country, is a result of the many tidal rivers and creeks that intersperse the land mass. The county has several historic towns—St. Michaels, Oxford, and Easton—which have old buildings and also many picturesque maritime locales where the visitor can observe and participate in fishing and oystering activities. Oxford is known as a yachting port and the area is one of the oldest settlements in the state. In addition to the English settlers, French Acadians from Canada settled in this area leaving a slight French influence.

Easton is 12 miles south of Wye Mills on Route 50. It is the county seat of Talbot County, and dates its origin from a Quaker meetinghouse built in the 1680s. A dozen places of historic interest can be seen on a walking tour of about one mile. A walking tour and map brochure may be obtained from the Talbot County Chamber of Commerce, PO Box 1366, Easton, MD 21601. Telephone: (301) 822-4606. Guided walking tours are conducted by the Historical Society.

The **Talbot County Court House** stands on Washington Street between Dover and Federal streets. The original building (1712) was replaced in 1794, and again enlarged and remodeled in 1958. It was on these grounds on May 24, 1774, that the "Talbot Resolves" were adopted. The sentiments of the resolves were later incorporated into the Declaration of Independence. Nearby is the headquarters and museum of the **Talbot County Historical Society**. A public parking lot is adjacent to the main building at 25 South Washington Street, which was built in the 1790s. Number 29 is a Federal-style townhouse, dating from 1804-10, with a garden in the rear. In addition, the society complex houses a three-room gallery that exhibits rotating collections and there is a museum shop. Open year round, Monday through Saturday, 10:00 a.m. to 4:00 p.m.; Sunday, 1:00 to 4:00 p.m. Closed Sundays, January through March. Closed major holidays. Walking tours available with reservations. Admission and tour charges. For further information write: PO Box 964, Easton, MD 21601. Telephone: (301) 822-0773.

At 106 South Street is the **Academy of Arts**, housed in a 19th-century primary school. The exhibits of the academy range from the visual arts to dance and music performances. Film and concert series are presented throughout the year. Visitors can see works of local artists as well as the permanent art collection. Open year round, Monday through Friday, 10:00 a.m. to 4:00 p.m.; Saturday, 1:00 to 4:00 p.m. Admission free. Telephone: (301) 822-0455.

Turn left on Talbot Lane to South Lane, then to **Talbot County Women's Club**. The wing of this house dates from 1793. The brick section dates from 1843 and is an example of the early Federal period. Continue on Talbot Lane to Dover Street, left to Harrison Street. The **Bullitt House**, one of Easton's most beautiful homes, was built in 1790.

Turn left on Goldsboro to Washington Street. On the right, at the corner, is a 150-year-old building formerly the **Frame Hotel**, now an office building. Across the street at 119 is the **Smith House**, built in 1803. The building served as both the home of Thomas P. Smith and the office of the newspaper from which the Easton *Star-Democrat* grew. The Chesapeake Bay Yacht Club now occupies the building.

The **Brick Hotel** at Washington and Federal streets, once Easton's leading hotel, was the scene of important civic events and balls. The facade has been altered from its original appearance and now the building houses offices.

Near the south edge of town, on Washington Street beyond Brookletts Avenue, is the **Third Haven Meeting House**, built in 1682. It is believed to be the oldest frame church building in America still in use. Built at the headwaters of the Tred Avon River, worshippers came by boat to attend services. William Penn preached here. Visitors may inquire at the residence on the grounds regarding visiting the building. Usually open from 9:00 a.m. to 5:00 p.m. Telephone: (301) 822-0293.

No Corner for the Devil, a hexagonal structure also known as Union Church, is located three miles south of Easton on Route 50. The wide angles were devised, so a story goes, "to give the Devil no corner on which to sit to hatch evil." The ruins of **White Marsh Church** are about two miles beyond, to the left on Route 50. The churchyard contains the grave of Robert Morris, father of the Revolutionary War financier. A local society maintains the graveyard.

St. Michaels, a picturesque old seaport, is near Easton on Route 33. The town was settled in the 1670s and during the colonial period was an important port and shipbuilding center. The Baltimore clipper ship is said to have been conceived here.

The chief attraction in St. Michaels is the **Chesapeake Bay Maritime Museum** on Maritime Street. It is devoted entirely to preserving the crafts, way of life, heritage, and traditions of Chesapeake Bay. The 18-acre complex includes the **Hooper Strait Lighthouse**, an aquarium, a waterfowl and decoy exhibit, a collection of 60 Chesapeake Bay sailing craft and a comprehensive maritime library. Open May through October, daily, 10:00 a.m. to 5:00 p.m.; April, November, and December, daily, 10:00 a.m. to 4:00 p.m.; January, February, and March, Saturday, Sunday, and holidays, 10:00 a.m. to 4:00 p.m. or by appointment for groups. Admission charge. Telephone: (301) 745-2916.

There are a half-dozen other very old homes that one can see on a stroll down the six blocks of the village. Its shipyards are still active and fishermen and other watermen still use its harbor daily. The visitor may dine at **Longfellow's Restaurant** and enjoy the harbor scene. The restaurant serves lunch and dinner throughout the year. Telephone: (301) 745-2624.

Visitors to St. Michaels may take a cruise aboard the *Patriot* on the Miles River, St. Michaels harbor, and past many historic homes and plantations. Trips begin at 11:00 a.m., 1:00 and 3:00 p.m., Tuesday through Sunday, from Memorial Day to Labor Day. Weekend trips are scheduled from May 1 to Memorial Day and from Labor Day to mid-October. Fare charge. Telephone: (301) 822-6201 (Baltimore phone exchange). **The Inn**, at Talbot and Mulberry streets, was built in 1817 and has an overhanging porch typical of the inns of the period. The **Cannon-Ball House**, at the north end of the Green, has an interesting story about its connection with the War of 1812. A cannonball from a British warship hit the chimney of this house and rolled down the attic stairway, endangering the lives of occupants.

St. Mary's Square Museum is located in two old buildings on the Green. The main building is a log house built in the late 1600s or early 1700s, while the square frame building is at least 100 years younger. The frame house is called a "teetotal" building because it is an absolute square. The explanation and history of the term is not known. The museum exhibits include St. Michaels' memorabilia such as old household items, furniture, and photographs. Open May through October, Saturday and Sunday, 10:00 a.m. to 5:00 p.m. Nominal admission charge. Telephone: (301) 745-9561.

Tilghman Island lies at the end of Route 33, 22 miles from Easton. The island is connected to the mainland by a drawbridge, which is accessible year round. The island is an important seafood center in the county, with fleets active in winter and in summer. Visitors may charter fishing boats, tour the oyster processing plants, and accompany a working skipjack. The 23-vessel skipjack fleet, the last working sailing ships on the bay, works out of Tilghman Island.

The fishing charters accept parties of up to six persons, including novice fishermen who will be given instruction by the crew. In November, tourists may be picked up at 5:00 a.m. by skipjack captains, be served breakfast and lunch aboard, see oystermen at work, and be returned to shore at 3:00 p.m.

Oxford existed as a port of entry as early as 1694. Today Oxford is important in boatbuilding and is the home of watermen whose livelihood is harvesting oysters, crabs, clams, and fish. It is a charming residential town.

In the Oxford Cemetery, near the entrance to town, stands the **Tench Tilghman Monument**, erected in honor of the Revolutionary War hero. On entering town, the first stop is the **Oxford Town Museum**. Open Saturday and Sunday, 2:00 to 5:00 p.m., and at other times by appointment. Telephone: (301) 226-5122.

In the next block on the left side is the **Academy House**, built in 1848, and once officers' quarters of the Maryland Military Academy. Across the street is the **Barnaby House**, built in the 1770s. The **Grapevine House**, not far from The Strand, is recognized by the grapevine in the front yard. The vine was brought here from the Isle of Jersey in 1810 by a sea captain. It still bears fruit.

The **Robert Morris Inn,** on the corner of The Strand and Morris Street, was built about 1710. The house was the home of Robert Morris, Sr., the father of the man who became known as the Philadelphia financier of the Revolutionary War. The original house has been expanded, although the original ornate staircase can be seen in the inn. Telephone: (301) 226-5111.

The **Tred Avon Ferry,** connecting Oxford with Bellevue, leaves from a pier near the Robert Morris Inn. It was started in 1760 and is one of the oldest private ferry crossings in the United States. Currently, the ferry is powered by diesel engines and can accommodate cars, buses, and foot passengers. The ferry operates year round. Fare charged. Telephone: (301) 226-5408.

Byeberry, facing Town Creek, is one of the oldest houses in the area. Records show it existed in 1695. It can be reached from the end of Tilghman Street.

Visitors should not miss the Oxford boatyards on both sides of Town Creek, or the **Sail Loft.** Here sails used by traditional Bay craft are made. Visitors are welcome to the loft, which is open weekdays from 8:00 a.m. to 4:00 p.m.

SOUTHERN EASTERN SHORE

DORCHESTER COUNTY

Dorchester County, established in 1669, is very much bound to the seafood industry, but also possesses some of Maryland's most productive agricultural lands. Crops such as soybeans, barley, corn, wheat, pickling cucumbers, and tomatoes are produced for packing plants and for fresh consumption. Detailed tourist information and self-directed walking tours of Cambridge, East New Market, and Vienna may be obtained from the Dorchester County Department of Tourism, PO Box 307, Cambridge, MD 21613. Telephone: (301) 228-3234. The chamber is located on the east end of town at the corner of Route 50 (Sunburst Highway) and Maryland Avenue.

The **Cambridge** area of Dorchester County is bounded by the broad Choptank River and Chesapeake Bay, and is known as the "Sportsmen's Paradise." The area beckons visitors interested in fishing, boating, swimming, water skiing, and crabbing. Hunting (deer and waterfowl) also is popular in this area. Visitors wishing to learn more of the past will find scores of homes and churches dating back 200 years or more. Cambridge was established in 1686; other nearby communities are even older. There are a number of antique shops in the area, and Cambridge has many good restaurants.

Two-and-a-half blocks left on Maryland Avenue is the **Meredith House**, the home of the **Dorchester County Historical Society**. This fine mansion, built in 1760, contains exhibits related to Dorchester County and includes a Governor's Room honoring six Maryland governors who were born in Dorchester County. The **Neild Museum** houses social history exhibits such as the county's maritime and industrial development and Indian artifacts. Also on exhibit are an original 1834 McCormick reaper and an 18th-century smokehouse. On the grounds of the museum is a typical 18th-century formal garden. Open Thursday and Friday, 10:00 a.m. to 4:00 p.m. Admission charge. Telephone: (301) 228-7953. Continue across the bridge to the historic High Street to begin a walking tour of Cambridge.

This tour of historic Cambridge on foot is less than one mile. The walking tour extends from the **County Court House** at High Street and Court Lane to the **Long Wharf** on the Choptank River. The present Court House was completed in 1852 on the site of the original 1687 building.

Diagonally across the street is the **Christ P.E. Church**, a 19th-century edifice on the site of the first church, built in 1693. Notable Revolutionary War soldiers and other war heroes and statesmen are buried in the adjoining graveyard. Many old gravestones have dates in the 1600s. At the north end of the brick wall around the cemetery, on High Street, is the former **office of Josiah Bayly**, tenth Attorney General of Maryland, and adjoining it is his old home, both dating from the 1790s. Most of the nearby houses on High Street, from the Court House to the River, were constructed in the 1700s.

Long Wharf, at the foot of High Street, was the site of the old steamboat wharf. A city park with picnic tables and a public boat basin are now located here. One can see the **Roosevelt Memorial, war memorials, Cambridge Yacht Club** and Basin. The Clayton Sea Food processing plant is on the right. The Todd Sea Food processing plant is nearby, along Cambridge Creek.

Your tour of Cambridge should include a drive along Water Street and Hambrooks Avenue and Boulevard. Begin on Water Street where it joins High Street at the Yacht Club. **Glasgow**, a large brick house painted white, dates from 1760. The **Annie Oakley House**, near the end of Hambrooks Boulevard, and **Hambrooks**, built about 1803, are two other notable mansions in this area of palatial homes. Annie Oakley and her husband built their house in 1913 after touring the world with the Wild West Show and deciding Cambridge was the most delightful place to live.

Located at 210 Talbot Avenue, the **Brannock Maritime Museum** houses collections of marine artifacts which illuminate the rich heritage of the Chesapeake Bay. The museum library features a growing collection of books, magazines, pamphlets, diaries, and letters documenting the history of the Cambridge area. Open by appointment. Telephone: (301) 228-6938.

The **Dorchester Heritage Museum** is located a few miles west of Cambridge on Horn Point Road, off Route 343. Four areas of county historical significance are highlighted in the Heritage Room, the Watermen Room, Aviation Hall, and Archaeology Room. Located on the Horn Point property of the University of Maryland, the museum is a working museum for local school children who are involved in construction of exhibits and in archaeological digs. Open Saturday and Sunday, 1:00 to 4:30 p.m. Admission free. Telephone: (301) 228-4924 or 228-6172.

The University of Maryland's **Horn Point Environmental Laboratories** are best known for their research on oysters and the blue crab, one of Maryland's major resources with an annual harvest value of about $7,000,000. The laboratories also conduct research to develop new seafood products and new processing methods. Informal self-tours of the laboratories are available. Open year round, Monday through Friday, 8:30 a.m. to 4:30 p.m. Call ahead for guided tours. Telephone: (301) 228-8200.

A few miles west on Route 343, at Lloyds, the motorist will see the **Spocott Windmill** and its 1775 miller's house. In 1850, John Radcliffe reconstructed a post windmill mentioned in historical records. This structure was destroyed by the blizzard of 1888. The millstones, the interior stairs, and some of the timbers were saved and were used in 1971 to reconstruct the windmill, which is still used occasionally to grind grain. Open Sunday and Monday, 8:00 a.m. to 4:00 p.m. Admission free. Telephone: (301) 228-7090.

From Cambridge, the circular trip back to Wye Mills and

Route 50—via Taylor's Island, Blackwater Wildlife Refuge, and Martinak State Park—is 85 miles.

Take Route 16 southwest of Cambridge to Church Creek area. **Old Trinity Church**, built about 1675, has been restored. Many notables, including members of the Carroll family, are buried in the churchyard. Anna Ella Carroll, who contributed to the Tennessee Campaign strategy planning for Abraham Lincoln, is buried here. The miller's grave is marked with old millstones. There are many old houses in this area, and the **Old Baptist Meeting House**, at Woolford, is a landmark. Also known as the Old Woolford Mace Burying Ground, the meetinghouse stands unused. The cemetery, with gravestones dating back to the late 1600s, may be visited.

Continue 10 miles to **Taylor's Island**. Here, near Mulberry Grove, is the first schoolhouse built in Dorchester County. The **LeCompte House**, erected in 1710, was used as a Methodist meetinghouse until the chapel was built. The **Old Brick Church**, also Methodist, dates from 1787.

On Green Briar Road, east of Seward, one can see a marker identifying the site where **Harriet Tubman** lived and worked as a slave. Harriet Tubman is known for her work in freeing 300 slaves through the Underground Railroad. Continuing on Green Briar Road, turn right to Bestpitch Ferry Road, south one mile to **Bazel Church** where Harriet Tubman worshipped.

Three miles farther, at Bucktown, the motorist sees **Yarmouth** or White House, built in 1735. Continue left to Airey and US 50, where a one-mile jog to the right brings you to Route 16, and then to **East New Market**, settled in 1660. The East part of the name was added in 1827 to distinguish this town from the "New Markets" in Western Maryland and Virginia.

On Main Street are five old buildings noted for their architecture: **House of Hinges, Manning House, Edmondson House, Collins House,** and **Smith Cottage**. Several are more than 200 years old. Traveling toward the town of Secretary, the tourist passes **Maurice Hall** and **Friendship Hall**, which is a fine two-and-a-half-story brick structure, circa 1740, with pilasters on the front and two oval windows in the pediment of the west gable end. Friendship Hall is noted especially for the original raised paneling, cornices, mantels, and floors throughout the house, plus the lovely gardens and boxwood surrounding it. At Secretary (left on

Route 14) is **My Lady Sewall's Manor**, erected in 1662 for Lord Sewall, Secretary of the Province of Maryland. It is now property of the Catholic Church.

The **Blackwater National Wildlife Refuge** is located on Ken Wallace Road off of Route 335, south of Cambridge. The 14,253-acre refuge is a wintering place for a great variety of waterfowl and other bird species. At the Visitor's Center tours can be planned and guides are available.

In the late fall many large flocks of Canada geese and ducks can be observed on the refuge. The official bird list shows that 240 different species of birds have been observed and approximately 150,000 ducks winter in the area. Dozens of species nest here in the spring and early summer. Two short hiking trails and a 4.5-mile wildlife drive are open from dawn to dusk throughout the year.

The Visitor's Center offers interpretive films and exhibits. Open Monday to Friday, 7:30 a.m. to 4:00 p.m.; Saturday and Sunday, 9:00 a.m. to 5:00 p.m. Admission free. Telephone: (301) 228-2677.

WICOMICO COUNTY

Wicomico County and its county seat, Salisbury, are nestled in the heart of the famous Eastern Shore, where opportunities for boating, fishing, bathing, and hunting abound. Many historic and scenic places beckon the visitor interested in reliving American history. Although the county was only created in 1867 from Somerset and Worcester counties, the city of Salisbury was chartered in 1732. All through the area the sightseer can visit picturesque waterfront towns and villages, where there are oystering, crabbing, and fishing boats alongside the piers. The Eastern Shore's large poultry industry is centered here.

A driving tour of approximately 40 miles around the Salisbury area takes about two hours to complete. It covers historical points of interest and a cable ferry. Begin at the town of **Delmar**, seven miles north of Salisbury. It is situated on US 13 and Maryland Route 54, the dividing line between Maryland and Delaware. On the right, just before you cross the railroad tracks, is the original **High Ball**, one of the earliest of railroad signals which has been restored to its original condition.

Continue west on Maryland 54 about seven miles, following the tour signs to the double crownstone marker of the

Mason-Dixon Line. This marker, dating from 1768, has the coat of arms of Lord Baltimore on the Maryland side and that of William Penn on the Delaware side. It is located on the north side of the road and is well marked.

Continue west on Maryland 467, approximately 1.5 miles, and turn left into a lane leading to **Double Mills Pond.** The mill operates by water power and is used to grind corn into meal. During the week when they are grinding, the miller will be very glad to take you on a tour of the mill.

From Double Mills, continue west on Route 54, crossing US 50 to Mardela Springs. On the left is **"Spring House."** This is an old health spa of the early 1800s. When you leave here, backtrack to the junction of US 50 and Route 54. Turn right onto US 50 and continue approximately 4.5 miles. On your left is the old **Spring Hill Church**, which was built in the 1700s and is one of the early Episcopal churches of the area.

Leaving Spring Hill Church, take Route 347 for 5.5 miles, passing through Hebron to Quantico. After Quantico, about a mile-and-a-half farther, is the junction of 347 and 349. Cross the highway and turn south onto Route 352. After about 4.5 miles turn left to old **Green Hill Church.** This church was built in 1782 from bricks and material shipped over from England. It has the original box pews, winecup, pulpit, and brick floor.

Upon leaving Green Hill Church, continue south on Route 352. At the intersection, turn left to the town of Whitehaven. Here you cross over the Wicomico River on the Whitehaven or **Lower Ferry** and follow the tour signs to Allen Road. Turn right to US 13, then left eight miles to the Salisbury city limits.

On the campus of Salisbury State College, **The North American Wildfowl Art Museum,** located in Holloway Hall, has the world's largest collection of bird carvings. The 2,300 pieces date back to 1870. The museum presents an 18-minute, audio-visual show with a setting of the Eastern Shore marshlands. Because bird carving is Maryland's official pastime, the museum sponsors an annual wildfowl art exhibit as well as a bird carving competition in the spring. Open year round, Tuesday to Saturday, 10:00 a.m. to 5:00 p.m.; Sunday, 1:00 to 5:00 p.m. Admission charge, children under 12 free. Telephone: (301) 742-4988.

Poplar Hill Mansion, at 117 Elizabeth Street in the Newtown Historic District, was built in 1805 and is the oldest house in Salisbury. It features pilasters in the main entrance, Palladian windows, outstanding cornice work, the original floors, and some of the original windows. The large mansion is furnished with 18th- and 19th-century furniture. Open year round, Sunday, 1:00 to 4:00 p.m., and by appointment. Telephone: (301) 749-1776.

The **City Hall Museum and Cultural Center**, at 110 East Church Street, is in a Queen Anne-style building, built in 1896. It has two galleries that exhibit traveling and local multi-media collections. Other exhibits include county and Eastern Shore historical and archaeological artifacts and a Fibers Room of historical textile displays. Open year round, Tuesday to Saturday, 10:00 a.m. to 2:00 p.m. Admission free. Telephone: (301) 546-9007.

The **Salisbury Zoological Park**, on South Park Drive in the City Park, is one of the finest small zoos in the country. The park emphasizes a natural setting for the 350 animals. While the zoo concentrates on waterfowl species, it also has some rare animals. Open year round, Memorial Day to Labor Day, 8:00 a.m. to 7:30 p.m., September to May, 8:00 a.m. to 4:30 p.m. Admission free. Telephone: (301) 548-3188.

WORCESTER COUNTY

Worcester County is the easternmost county in Maryland and is the only one facing the Atlantic Ocean. Although the county is known today for the beaches at Ocean City and on Assateague Island, the county seat, Snow Hill, was a thriving colonial commercial center. Snow Hill, on the Pocomoke River, was once a main port and a tobacco inspection station. Tobacco, grain, and livestock were shipped to English and West Indian ports until Baltimore overshadowed the Eastern Shore ports.

Snow Hill, county seat of Worcester County, was founded in 1642. It is on Route 12, 18 miles south of Salisbury, and is located six miles from the Sinepuxent Bay and is on the Pocomoke River. As a result of the navigability of the Pocomoke from the Chesapeake Bay, Snow Hill was made a royal port in 1694 and was a thriving shipping port until Baltimore eclipsed all the Maryland port towns. Snow Hill, which is relatively flat and generally snowfree, was named for a London suburb and retains a quiet, brick-sidewalked, tree-lined atmosphere with homes dating from the 18th century. The older houses are frame, with large outside chimneys, separate kitchens, and often with colonnades. Some have second-story galleries. A walking tour brochure may be obtained from the Julia A. Purnell Museum.

The **Julia A. Purnell Museum**, on Market Street, is housed in a small, white frame building that was built as a Catholic church in 1891. The museum contains a unique collection of Americana—tools for tobacco processing, for crop farming, and for household chores. The exhibits range from Indian artifacts to Victorian era costumes and furnishings. Workshops, craft classes, and clinics are held by the museum. A shop offering the work of local craftsmen is also open during museum hours. Open Monday to Friday, 10:00 a.m. to 5:00 p.m.; Saturday and Sunday, 1:00 to 5:00 p.m. Admission charge, school children free. Telephone: (301) 632-0515.

The **Mt. Zion One-Room Schoolhouse** has been restored and is complete with tin lunch pails, recitation bench, double slates, and a school bell. Open by appointment. Telephone: (301) 632-0515.

The genealogical records and other historical data of the **Worcester County Historical Society** are located at the public library. The library also exhibits rotating collections which make it worthy of visiting. For further information telephone: (301) 632-2600.

All Hallows Episcopal Church, at Market and Church streets, was constructed in 1748 at a cost of 120,000 pounds of tobacco. Gifts from Queen Anne to the church included a Bible dated "London, 1701," and a bell, hanging in the churchyard. An unusual feature of the church is the 15-foot-high windows. The stained glass of the windows dates from 1890 and replaced the original clear glass. The church is open to the public.

Cruises aboard *Tillie the Tug*, will take the visitor on a one-hour tour of the Pocomoke River. The tug is a made-to-order vessel that gives daily cruises, from April through October. The tug may be chartered by groups for longer cruises. Bus tours of the area surrounding Snow Hill may also be arranged. Both tours are operated by Snow Hill Tours, Inc. Telephone: (301) 632-2650.

Four miles northwest of Snow Hill off Route 12 on Old Furnace Road, the visitor may see **Nassawango Furnace**, the remains of a significant iron ore smelting enterprise, started in 1832. For 15 years iron ore was taken from the nearby swamp and smelted into iron bars. The operation was then recognized as an unprofitable one, and the works were abandoned. People moved away; the town fell into decay and disappeared through the years. The 30-foot furnace tower has been repaired and excavation has disclosed the dam, spillway, and foundations of homes. The **Furnacetown Museum** on the grounds includes weaving and dyeing shops and a blacksmith shop. Demonstrations are given periodically. A gift shop is also open to visitors. Open April to November, Tuesday to Saturday, 11:00 a.m. to 5:00 p.m.; Sunday, noon to 5:00 p.m. Nominal admission charge, children under 12 free. For further information write: Furnacetown Museum, PO Box 111, Snow Hill, MD 21863. Telephone: (301) 632-2032.

Nearby, between Furnace Road and Red House Road, the visitor may see a primeval bald cypress-gum swamp at the **Nassawango Creek—E. Stanton Adkins Preserve.** The Nature Conservancy owns 154 acres of wilderness that is home to swamp species of deer, otter, nesting wood duck, and many reptiles.

Pocomoke River State Park is located within the Pocomoke State Forest and has two separate areas, the Shad Landing and Milburn Landing areas. The park, and the adjacent forest, are a paradise for nature enthusiasts. Roads and trails through the area provide access to a region typical of a Deep South swamp, as well as upland loblolly pine stands. The combination of swamp and upland makes for a great variety in plant and animal life. During the Civil War era, the swamps of this area provided hiding places for runaway slaves and for Southern sympathizers.

Bird watchers and hunters are attracted here because of the great variety and abundance of bird life. Pocomoke is said to support a greater number of bird species than any other Atlantic inland area. The fishing in Pocomoke River State Park requires no license because the Pocomoke River is considered tidal waters up to Snow Hill. Hunting is allowed in the State Forest area. Interpretive programs are offered during the summer at both Shad Landing and Milburn Landing. Activities include nature walks, evening campfire talks, canoe and fishing trips, and junior park ranger programs.

The **Shad Landing Area** is located 3.5 miles south of Snow Hill, on Route 113. It borders the Pocomoke River and Corkers Creek. The waterways, winding through a cypress swamp, remind one of the Florida Everglades. Facilities include picnicking, tenting and camp trailer areas, a swimming pool, showers, marina, and commissary. The river offers good bass fishing, and boating facilities are available. Bike, canoe, and rowboat rentals are available. A "fish for fun" pond is available for young people. The young anglers are encouraged to return the fish to the pond. No pets allowed in this area.

Also south of Snow Hill, **Milburn Landing Area** is accessible from Route 364 (seven miles northeast of Pocomoke City). It is also situated on the north bank of the Pocomoke River. A picnic area, playfields, campsites, water, laundry, and toilet facilities are provided.

Assateague is a barrier island, a narrow strip of land extending 33 miles, from the Ocean City inlet to the Virginia end of the peninsula. At its southern tip, the Virginia island of Chincoteague is located on the Chincoteague Bay side of Assateague. The island is divided into different areas administered by the Maryland and U.S. Park Services and the U.S. Fish and Wildlife Service. The Maryland section, reached from Route 50 via Route 611, contains Assateague State Park and the U.S. Assateague Island National Seashore.

The island once extended from Virginia to Delaware, but in a 1933 storm, an inlet was cut through at Ocean City. The island varies in width from one-third of a mile to about one mile. The low sand dunes are constantly changing because of storms and the normal action of tides, waves, and winds.

The island affords swimming and bird-watching opportunities at an unspoiled, quiet beach. The park is very popular in the summer; its gently sloping sand beach is considered one of the finest on the East Coast. U.S. and state conservation efforts have built up a 14-foot-high sand dune to enhance the protective nature of the barrier island. Bird watchers come in fall to observe the flocks of waterfowl in Sinepuxent Bay and its shallow tributaries.

Assateague State Park encompasses a two-mile strip at the northern tip of the island. The beach is divided into separate areas for swimming, surfing, and surf fishing. A one-mile Oceanic Trail is available for self-guided walks. During the summer the park offers body surfing demonstrations, salt marsh walks, nature discussions, and awards weekly surf fishing certificates for the largest fish caught in six categories. The campsites are open year round, although the washhouses are closed from November to Easter. For further information write: State Park Manager, Route 2, Box 293, Berlin, MD 21811. Telephone: (301) 641-2120, TTY for deaf (800) 492-5662.

The **Assateague Island National Seashore**, administered by the U.S. National Park Service, is composed of two sections, the area north of the state park and the area south of the state park to the Virginia state line. Camping, swimming, bay canoeing, crabbing, fishing, and hiking opportunities are available in the National Seashore area. Oversand vehicles are also allowed on a 14-mile stretch of beach. Permits are required for both oversand vehicle use and for camping. The park is open year round; oceanside campsites are open from April through September; bayside campsites are open year round. Admission free; campsite charge. Visitor Center open daily, 8:30 a.m. to 5:00 p.m. For further information write: National Park Service, Route 2, Box 294, Berlin, MD 21811. Telephone: (301) 641-1441.

Ocean City is a noted seaside resort which attracts thousands of summer visitors, drawn to its 10-mile, broad beach and three-mile boardwalk. Opportunities for deep-sea fishing are available on charter party boats. Ocean City has scores of motels, guest cottages and hotels, and fine restaurants to accommodate visitors, especially during the summer months. The convention hall holds year-round trade shows and entertainment, including bluegrass, rock, and country bands. It is 29 miles east of Salisbury on Route 50.

Although Ocean City is known for its summer beach activities, the resort is open all year. With the development of large condominium complexes, the owners from metropolitan areas utilize their properties in the off season. As a result, September and Christmas are active periods. Many restaurants remain open all year, and there is entertainment such as the monthly big band dances from October to April. The uncrowded beaches are a marvelous area from which to observe the autumn flight of wildfowl. For further information on hotel accommodations and activities, contact Ocean City Visitor's Bureau, PO Box 116, Ocean City, MD 21842. Telephone: (301) 289-8181.

The **Ocean City Life Saving Station Museum**, at South Boardwalk and the Inlet, was a life saving station built by the U.S. Treasury Department and used to house the U.S. Life Saving Service crew. It was used from 1878 to 1962. Today the museum houses Ocean City historical memorabilia. Exhibits include doll house models of the resort's old hotels, shipwreck artifacts, saltwater aquariums, and hand-carved decoys. A museum shop sells brass, doll house furniture, and books. Open June through September, 11:00 am. to 10:00

p.m.; winter, Saturday and Sunday, noon to 4:00 p.m.; May and October, daily, 11:00 a.m. to 4:00 p.m. Admission charge. Telephone: (301) 289-4991.

Four miles west of Ocean City, on Route 50, the **Ocean Downs Race Track** offers harness racing from May to September. Telephone: (301) 641-0680. Bus trips of the surrounding Worcester County area are also offered by Snow Hill Tours, Inc. Telephone: (301) 632-2650.

SOMERSET COUNTY

Somerset County is the southernmost Maryland county on the Eastern Shore and was established in 1666. The Somerset area was a religious haven for dissident Virginians and also was the area in great dispute between Lord Baltimore and the royal colony of Virginia.

Princess Anne, the county seat, is 12 miles south of Salisbury on Route 13. This town, laid out in 1733, was named in honor of Anne, daughter of King George II. A walking tour brochure and other information may be obtained from Somerset County Tourism, PO Box 243, Princess Anne, MD 21853. Telephone: (301) 651-2968.

There are several historic buildings worthy of a visit. The **Teackle Mansion,** now headquarters of Old Princess Anne Days, Inc. and the Somerset County Historical Society, is a Georgian-style home built in 1801. It is furnished with period furniture and contains historical exhibits. George A. Townsend, author of the famous 19th-century novel *The Entailed Hat,* used the mansion as the setting for the home of the novel's heroine. The house is at the end of Prince William Street. Open year round, Sunday, 2:00 to 4:00 p.m. Admission charge. Telephone: 651-2968. The **Washington Hotel,** in the center of town, dates from the 1740s and has operated as an inn since 1797. Nearby is the new Princess Anne Motel, which was constructed in an old style in keeping with the colonial period of the town.

St. Andrew's Episcopal Church, on Church Street, was built in 1770 and reconstructed twice. One of its treasures is the communion silver dating from 1717. **Manokin Presbyterian Church** (1765) is located on Somerset Avenue, north of the bridge. The tower was added in 1888. Presbyterian meetings have been held on this site since 1672, and its congregation was organized in 1686. Both churches are open to the public.

The **Rehobeth Church** at Rehobeth, erected in 1705, was built under the direction of Francis Mackemie, the founder of Presbyterianism in America. It is still in use and always open to visitors. It is south of Princess Anne on Route 13, then right on Route 667, five miles to Rehobeth on Route 406. The ruins of **Coventry Episcopal Church**, built in 1740, are across the road.

Eastern Shore Early Americana Museum, located at Hudsons Court on Route 667, is housed in a huge three-story, converted poultry house. Its exhibits are devoted to rural Americana, some dating to 1750. The **Country Store** is a 19th-century replica general store with many original items still in their original packaging. Open year round, Thursday to Sunday, 10:00 a.m. to 5:00 p.m., or by appointment. Admission charge. Telephone: (301) 623-8324.

The motorist who wishes to take side trips to get a glimpse of secluded villages and beautiful scenery can visit **Deal Island** at the west end of Route 363 from Princess Anne or four small villages on Route 361 further south. Deal Island is connected to the mainland by bridge and has two quaint fishing villages—Deal Island and Wenona. The island is an ideal place to observe the maritime activities on Tangier Sound. Wenona is the home port of a portion of the last remaining skipjack fleet. In Deal Island village is the grave of Joshua Thomas, the evangelical minister who converted many bay islanders to Methodism and who resisted the British invaders during the War of 1812.

Returning to Route 13, the motorist may take the second side trip to the small communities of **Manokin, Upper Fairmont, Rumbley,** and **Frenchtown**. These villages are south from Princess Anne on Routes 13 and 413, west on Route 363. Upper Fairmont is located on a peninsula between the Manokin and Big Annemessex rivers. The community is a cluster of predominantly Victorian homes and several churches, served by a single old-time country store. The **Fairmont Academy**, in Upper Fairmont, was founded in 1839 and was in continuous use as a school until 1968. Several rooms have been set up to reflect classrooms of bygone days, and it is also used for community activities. Open by appointment. Write: Fairmont Academy Historical Association, Upper Fairmont, MD 21867.

Crisfield, terminus of Route 413, derives its livelihood from oysters, crabs, and fish. It is the self-styled "Sea Food Capital." Scores of boats come and go, bringing tons of marine edibles from every direction. The lower waterfront part of town gives Crisfield its character. Many structures are built on oyster shells deposited over the decades on marshland. Here one finds the seafood processing plants, marine railways, and piers. Crisfield also manufactures oyster tongs, knives, dredges, muskrat traps, and packing cases. It has skilled craftsmen who make sails and duck decoys. Visits to these unusual shops usually can be arranged. Crisfield has two motels, but local residents also offer bed and breakfast accommodations. For further information contact the Crisfield Area Chamber of Commerce, Somers Cove at 7th Street, PO Box 292, Crisfield, MD 21817. Telephone: (301) 968-2500.

The **Crisfield Historical Museum**, one block from the city wharf, has exhibits of early Indian inhabitants, maritime history of Somerset County, and prominent county residents, such as Governor J. Millard Tawes. Open Monday through Saturday, 10:30 a.m. to noon and 1:30 to 5:00 p.m. Admission free, donations welcome. Telephone: (301) 968-2390.

Crisfield is the mainland port from which visitors can take ferries and cruises to **Smith Island** and also to Tangier Island in Virginia (see also Virginia section).

Smith Island in reality is a group of about four large islands, including the one designated as Martin National Wildlife Refuge. The islands straddle the Maryland-Virginia State Line, although the three villages of Smith Island are in the Maryland section. The Martin Wildlife refuge is, for the most part, closed to the public because of the fragile nature of the waterfowl population inhabiting the island. Even scientific studies have disturbed the heron rookeries there.

Smith Island is Maryland's only inhabited island accessible exclusively by boat. Comprised of three separate villages, Ewell, Tylerton, and Rhodes Point, Smith Island lies in the Chesapeake Bay 12 miles west of Crisfield. When Capt. John Smith explored the Chesapeake Bay in 1608, he gave this island his name. Captain Smith wrote in his log, "Heaven and earth seemed never to have agreed better for man's commodious and delightful habitation."

The direct descendants of the original settlers from England and Cornwall in 1657 inhabit Smith Island, a quiet, peaceful land. Most of its citizens derive their livelihood from the unpredictable waters of the Chesapeake.

Year-round ferries, *Captain Jason* and *Island Belle II*, leave daily from Crisfield. There are cruises aboard the

Captain Tyler including lunch and a bus tour of the island. The *Captain Tyler* operates Memorial Day to September, daily, at 12:30 p.m. returning at 5:15 p.m. Telephone: (301) 425-2771. Passenger ferries to Tangier Island also leave from the City Dock. Telephone: (301) 425-2631 and (301) 968-2338. (See also Special Interest Section, Organized Day Trips.)

Janes Island State Park is located at the mouth of Crisfield Harbor, two miles north of Crisfield on Route 358. The park is composed of two topographically separate areas: a small developed portion on the mainland, known as the Hodson Area, which may be reached by automobile, and an island area of several thousand acres, entirely separated from the mainland by the Annemessex Canal, and bordered by waters of the Big and Little Annemessex rivers and the Tangier Sound. The island portion of the park is accessible only by boat.

The mainland portion of the park has camping and picnic areas, sanitary facilities, and a boat launching ramp. The island portion offers swimming, crabbing, fishing, camping, and picnicking. The miles of shoreline and marsh areas and the inland ponds abound in waterfowl and birds. For further information write: Park Superintendent, Route 2, Box 40, Crisfield, MD 21817. Telephone: (301) 968-1565.

SOUTHERN MARYLAND

ANNE ARUNDEL COUNTY

The Anne Arundel County area was settled by Puritans from Virginia and the county was created in 1650. The provincial capital was moved from St. Mary's City because of its inaccessibility to Arundell Towne, which was renamed Annapolis in 1695. Annapolis was convenient both for English ships and as a meeting place for tobacco planters and politicians. In 1699, an observer noted that there were "fourty dwelling houses" in Annapolis. A French traveler described the elegant society of Annapolis in 1781, noting that "a French hair dresser is a man of importance among . . . the fine women" and it was said he commanded "a thousand crowns a year salary."

Anne Arundel County, bordering on the western shore of the Chesapeake Bay, has 437 miles of shoreline and is a mecca for sailing and boating enthusiasts who moor their craft at the many deepwater piers of the Severn, South, Rhode, and

West rivers. The northwestern portion of the county, however, is largely suburban for it is situated in the Baltimore-Washington corridor. Also located in this area is the Baltimore-Washington International Airport and its airport-train terminal, the first of its kind, and **Laurel Race Course**, famous for "The Washington International," a major race held in November for thoroughbred horses from around the world.

Annapolis is a charming but bustling small city with activities to satisfy many different tastes. The city is the capital of the state, the home of the **U.S. Naval Academy**, and a base for many sailing and boating activities. It is also on the busy ocean shipping route from Hampton Roads in Virginia to Baltimore and is near the western approach to the **Chesapeake Bay Bridge**, which connects the Eastern and Western Shores of the state.

In planning a trip to Annapolis, one should set aside an entire day in order to enjoy the sights of the city on foot in a leisurely manner. Free parking is available at the Naval Academy Stadium parking lot, Rowe Boulevard and Taylor Street. A shuttle takes visitors to the center of the city. For Academy visitors there is free parking available near Halsey Field House. Municipal parking is also available for a nominal charge at the City Parking Garage on Main Street between Green and Conduit streets.

It is well worthwhile for visitors to consider a guided walking tour. **Historic Annapolis, Inc.** and **Three Centuries Tours of Annapolis** offer walking tours of the city and give informative lectures of 90 minutes to two hours. Historic Annapolis, located in the Old Treasury (c. 1745) building, State Circle, is a nonprofit historic preservation organization. It owns the Paca House and offers preservation and educational programs, as well as colonial restoration advice to building renovators. Telephone: (301) 267-8149. Three Centuries Tours conducts prearranged tours, such as the two-hour "Early Bird" walking tour and a "Colonial Life" tour for young people, as well as group tours by arrangement. All Three Centuries tour guides wear period costumes. Three Centuries is located at 48 Maryland Avenue. Telephone: (301) 263-5401.

Town Crier offers pedicab tours of Annapolis. For tour schedules contact the company at 3 Church Circle, Suite 100, Annapolis, MD 21401. Telephone: (301) 268-0239 or 263-7330.

For those wishing to discover Annapolis on their own, the best information available is in the booklet "Rambling Thru Annapolis," available at the Annapolis Public Information and Tourism Office, 160 Duke of Gloucester Street ((301) 263-7940) and at many shops throughout town.

A good place to start a tour of Annapolis is the **Victualling Warehouse Museum**, at 77 Main Street. The museum has a small maritime exhibit and a scale model of the waterfront as it appeared in 1751. The scale model and an interpretive lecture from the Museum staff provide the visitor with a historical and architectural understanding of the city. Historic Annapolis, Inc. tours leave from the museum, which is open daily, 11:00 a.m. to 4:30 p.m. Nominal admission charge. Telephone: (301) 268-5576.

Highlights which will be seen on a walk through the area include the **State House**, capitol of Maryland and the oldest in continuous legislative use in the country. At the capitol there are free guided tours. Open year round, daily, 9:00 a.m. to 5:00 p.m. Nearby is the **Governor's Mansion** on School Street, which may be viewed en route to **St. John's College** campus, which is bordered by St. John's Street and College Avenue. This four-year, liberal arts college, third oldest in the United States, was chartered in 1784, but traces its beginnings to King William School that opened in 1696. On the campus grounds are the famous **Liberty Tree**, a 400-year-old tulip poplar, and **McDowell Hall** (c. 1740). A walk down King George Street offers views of **Ogle Hall** (U.S. Naval Academy Alumni House, c. 1739), the **Chase-Lloyd House** (c. 1769), and the **Hammond-Harwood House** (c. 1774). The Chase-Lloyd House was one of the first three-story townhouses built in Annapolis. It is now a home for the elderly, but is open to the public year round, daily except Wednesday and Sunday, 2:00 to 4:00 p.m. Admission charge. The Hammond-Harwood House, an outstanding example of Georgian colonial architecture located at 19 Maryland Avenue, is a beautifully furnished museum of decorative arts. Open April through October, Tuesday to Saturday, 10:00 a.m. to 5:00 p.m.; Sunday, 2:00 to 5:00 p.m.; November through March, Tuesday to Saturday, 10:00 a.m. to 4:00 p.m.; Sunday, 1:00 to 4:00 p.m. Admission charge.

At this point you may enter the **U.S. Naval Academy** through Gate #3 to visit the **Museum**, the beautiful **Chapel**, and **Bancroft Hall Dormitory**. The Chapel contains the **crypt of John Paul Jones**, whose body was transferred in 1905 from an abandoned cemetery in Paris where he had died in 1792. Visitors may see the **Bancroft Hall Memorial Hall** collection of Naval memorabilia and a sample "Midshipman room." Academy buildings are open to the public Monday through Saturday, 9:00 a.m. to 4:50 p.m.; Sunday, 11:00 a.m. to 4:50 p.m. Naval Academy tours leave from Ricketts Hall inside Gate #1 each half-hour during the summer and hourly in the winter, Monday through Saturday, 9:00 a.m. to 5:00 p.m.; Sunday, noon to 5 p.m. Tour charge. Advance tour arrangements may be made through Tour Guide Service, PO Box 1527, Annapolis, MD 21401. Telephone: (301) 263-6933.

A walk from the Naval Academy grounds through Gate #3 on King George Street will bring the visitor to the **William Paca House** (c. 1765) and **Garden**. This elegant Georgian mansion, home of Declaration of Independence signer and three-term Maryland governor, has been authentically restored. The reconstructed garden features a Chinese-trellis bridge, domed pavilion, and fish-shaped pond. Visitors may enter the garden at 1 Martin Street or through the House at 186 Prince George Street. House and garden open year round, Tuesday through Saturday, 10:00 a.m. to 4:00 p.m.; Sunday, noon to 4:00 p.m. The garden is also open Monday, 10:00 a.m. to 4:00 p.m. Admission charge for combined garden and house admission or separately. Telephone: (301) 267-6656 or 269-0601.

Near Paca House, on East and Prince George streets, stands **Brice House**, a magnificent 18th-century mansion (not open to the public). Left on Prince George Street to Randall Street will bring you to the Market Space and inner harbor area. Here in the picturesque **City Market House**, built in 1858, oysters and clams are shucked and can be eaten on the half-shell. Carry-out food, fresh produce, bakery goods, and desserts are also available and several landscaped areas are ideal for sitting, eating, and people watching. Annapolis also offers formal dining ranging from seafood to continental restaurants.

One can stroll along the waterfront to see an occasional skipjack oyster boat or a clamboat, as well as the many yachts that tie up at **City Dock**. A further walk (or drive) is past the Hilton Inn and Annapolis Yacht Club across Spa Creek to Eastport, the sailing center of the Chesapeake Bay. This is a picturesque locale for photographers.

Visitors may also take cruises on several vessels—a 40-minute guided tour of the bay on the *Harbor Queen* and a 40-minute guided tour of the tidewater areas on the *Miss Anne*, as well as an all-day cruise to St. Michaels on the *Annapolitan II*. A 90-minute tour of the Severn River and

Chesapeake Bay to Thomas Point Light House on the *Rebecca Forbush* takes visitors on a different route. The cruises are operated by Chesapeake Marine Tours on the City Dock, from mid-May to early October. For fare information and schedules, telephone: (301) 268-7600.

Another beautiful outdoor spot in Annapolis is the **Helen Avalynne Tawes Garden** at 580 Taylor Avenue. This award-winning botanical garden features representations of Maryland's natural resources. Open Monday to Friday, sunrise to sunset. Admission free. Telephone: (301) 269-3656.

Across the South River from Annapolis, by boat or by Route 252, is the **London Town Publik House** (c. 1760), which served as a stopping place for travelers who used the Annapolis-Londontown ferry on their way between Williamsburg and Philadelphia. The Publik House is the only remnant of the once-prosperous tobacco inspection town of the 18th century, which was eclipsed by Annapolis when it became the state capital. The Publik House is furnished with mid-18th century antiques and is surrounded by eight acres of gardens. A relocated log tobacco barn is open to the public and a portion of the garden is devoted to crops and plants grown in the 19th century. During the summer, demonstration programs are offered. Open Tuesday through Saturday, 10:00 a.m. to 4:00 p.m.; Sunday, noon to 4:00 p.m. Closed Monday and months of January and February. Admission charge. Telephone: (301) 956-4900.

Sandy Point State Park is located, on US 50-301, about eight miles east of Annapolis, in view of the Chesapeake Bay Bridge. This 680-acre park is famous for its sandy bathing beaches, surf fishing, bird watching, and view of large ocean-going vessels on their way to and from Baltimore. The park is located on the Atlantic Flyway, the migratory route of eastern birds, and autumn finds bird-lovers enjoying the splendid spectacle provided by the profusion of wild geese and ducks overhead. The **Sandy Point Farmhouse**, an early 19th-century building, is centrally located in the park. It has been placed on the National Register of Historic Places. The park has picnicking facilities, toilets and showers, a playground, boat rentals, and a food-refreshment stand. Although there are no family camping sites, there is a section reserved for youth groups. The park is open year round for day use activities. From May 15 to September 30 the park is open 24 hours a day to provide access to the Bay for fishing and boat launching. For further information contact Park Superintendent, 800

Revell Highway, Annapolis, MD 21401. Telephone: (301) 757-1841.

CALVERT COUNTY

Calvert County is almost completely surrounded by water—on the east by the Chesapeake Bay and on the west by the Patuxent River. Calvert Cliffs, famous for its Miocene Age fossil deposits, form the bay coastline for 30 miles from Chesapeake Beach to Solomons Island. In 1608 when he first explored the bay, Captain John Smith described these cliffs. From June to September Calvert County beaches are popular for their gradual sloping sandy bottoms, light wave action, and warm salt water.

There is a small municipal beach at **North Beach** with a narrow 300-foot beach with an unnetted swimming area and no guard service. Open from June to August. Admission free. Telephone: (301) 535-1600.

Breezy Point may be reached from Chesapeake Beach on Route 261 south to Breezy Point Road. There is a half-mile sandy beach with netted swimming area for protection from sea nettles, a bathhouse, playground, picnic tables, marina, boat ramps, and fishing pier. Rental cottages and group picnic facilities are available. Open daily. Admission charge. Telephone: (301) 257-2561.

The **Chesapeake Beach Railway Museum** on Route 261 features exhibits on the resort town that was constructed in the 1890s. The Chesapeake Beach Railway Company ran between Washington, DC, and Chesapeake Beach from 1900 to 1935. The museum is housed in the restored railway station. Open Saturday and Sunday, 1:00 to 4:00 p.m. Closed November through April. Admission free; donations welcome. Telephone: (301) 855-6472 or 855-7770.

Historic **Lower Marlboro** can be reached from Route 4 by turning right on Route 523 and going approximately four miles. It is one of the oldest towns in Maryland and was an important port until the Patuxent River silted over. One can browse through this settlement, once a British port, which saw the building of one of Maryland's oldest schools, the Marlboro Academy; the early establishment of a ferry service; and later, a steamboat wharf. Several 18th-century homes are still a part of the community.

Return on Route 262 to where Routes 2 and 4 join, at Sunderland. At the junction is **All Saints Church**, founded in

1692 and rebuilt in 1774 with Flemish bond brick walls. The baptismal font and paneling were brought from England in 1735.

Prince Frederick has been the seat of Calvert County since 1723. From Prince Frederick continue south on Route 2/4 to the **Battle Creek Cypress Swamp Sanctuary**, on Gray's Road off Route 506. This 100-acre Nature Conservancy preserve contains one of the last remaining sites where bald cypress is to be found occurring naturally in the state of Maryland, and it is one of the northernmost significant stands of bald cypress in the United States. Although cypress was once widespread in the Chesapeake Bay region, it is now reduced to the Pocomoke River on the Eastern Shore of Maryland, Battle Creek, and a few scattered small occurrences. Just why the cypress stand at Battle Creek has survived is not fully understood. The cypress in the swamp are up to four feet in diameter and 100 feet high. The wet habitat formed by periodic flooding creates an important breeding area for several species of salamanders and tree frogs. A quarter-mile boardwalk trail provides easy access to the most interesting part of the swamp. The Nature Center features exhibits and natural history lectures. Open April through September, Tuesday through Saturday, 10:00 a.m. to 5:00 p.m.; Sunday, 1:00 to 5:00 p.m.; October through March, to 4:30 p.m. Special tours and earlier visiting hours may be arranged. Admission free. Telephone: (301) 535-5327.

On Route 264 it is one-half mile to **Christ P.E. Church**. Although the present building dates from 1769, the original structure was built in 1672. There is a one-room schoolhouse on the grounds and a unique garden of biblical plants. Route 264 continues four miles to **Broomes Island**, a small community of oystermen and fishermen. From September to March you can see working oyster boats.

The Visitors Center, high on an observation platform, affords a view of the **Calvert Cliffs Nuclear Power Plant** and the majestic Chesapeake Bay. The Nuclear Power Plant is off Route 4, eight miles south of Port Republic. Look for a sign. A 100-year-old barn has been converted to a museum, with many archaeological and agricultural displays. Ruins of a 17th-century plantation home are nearby. No visitors are allowed inside the Nuclear Power Plant, but there is an audio-visual tour. An operating miniature reactor and interpretive exhibits describe the nuclear generation cycle. Open year round, daily, 9:00 a.m. to 5:00 p.m. Admission free. Telephone: (301) 234-7484.

Calvert Cliffs State Park offers extensive hiking and nature trails, many beautiful picnic areas, and a youth camping area. The unique feature of this park is its miles of cliffs, rising in places to 100 feet, containing visible beds of fossils, some estimated to be 15 to 20 million years old. Fossils of more than 600 species of mollusks and fish can be found here. Note that digging in the cliffs is dangerous and prohibited. Open June through September, daily, noon to sunset; May to June, and October, Wednesday to Sunday, 10:00 a.m. to 6:00 p.m.; closed November through February. Admission free. Telephone: (301) 888-1622.

Middleham Chapel, the oldest cruciform-designed church in Maryland, is on Route 24 at Lusby. Near the present building (1748) lie many gravestones from the early 1700s. A memorial plaque to the Parrans, an old Maryland family, is dated 1729.

The **Cove Point Light Station** is located on a two-acre lot at the end of Route 497, which intersects with Route 2/4, two miles below Lusby. This 51-foot structure is the oldest brick tower lighthouse in the Chesapeake Bay area. The Coast Guard lighthouse has been in continuous use from 1828 to the present. Until 1877 the lights were fueled by whale, coal, and lard oils. There is an excellent view from the top of the lighthouse. Open March through September, Tuesday to Wednesday and Friday to Sunday, 8:00 to 11:00 a.m. and 1:00 to 4:00 p.m. Admission free. Telephone: (301) 326-3254.

The tiny town of **Solomons** is almost completely surrounded by water. It lies between the Chesapeake Bay and the mouth of the Patuxent River, which is two miles wide at this point.

Located at the southern tip of Calvert County, at Solomons, the **Calvert Marine Museum and Lighthouse** is devoted to local maritime history, fossils of the Calvert Cliffs, and the marine life of nearby Chesapeake Bay and its tidal waters. The museum may be reached on Route 2 or by boat.

The visitor can see artifacts, exhibits, and documents in the Maritime History, Aquatic, and Waterman's Rooms; stroll through the small craft shed; and visit the woodcarver's shop, marine art gallery, and exhibits on area marine life and fossil remains. There is also a Ship's Store that offers local handicrafts, fossil jewelry, prints, and watercolors for sale. The Drum Point Lighthouse was moved six miles to its present location and restored and furnished in an early 1900s style.

Built in 1883, it is a cottage lighthouse with screw-type piles. The museum and lighthouse are open May through October, Monday through Saturday, 10:00 a.m. to 5:00 p.m.; Sunday, noon to 5:00 p.m. Open November through April, Monday through Friday, 10:00 a.m. to 4:30 p.m.; weekends, noon to 4:30 p.m. Admission free. The museum also offers cruises of the Patuxent River estuary on a chunk-built, log canoe, the *William B. Tennison*. This boat, converted from a sailboat to a powerboat, is the oldest licensed passenger-carrying vessel on the Chesapeake Bay and is described as an oyster buy-boat of the bugeye class. The *William Tennison* operates one-hour cruises, May through October, Wednesday through Sunday, 2:00 to 3:00 p.m. Fare charge. Telephone: (301) 326-2042.

PRINCE GEORGE'S COUNTY

The eastern Washington suburbs of Prince George's County offers tour opportunities at government facilities such as the USDA Beltsville Agricultural Research Center, Andrews Air Force Base, and the National Aeronautics and Space Administration's Goddard Space Flight Center. The county, however, also has a long and varied history which can still be seen in the rural tobacco-growing regions in the southern portion of the county and in its many historical mansions.

The county was created in 1696, and it was named in honor of Prince George of Denmark, husband of Princess Anne (Queen of England from 1702-14). At the time, Prince George's included all the western portion of the state and it was not until 1748 that the present boundaries were fixed. Much of Washington, DC, was originally part of Prince George's. Another historical event was the invasion of Washington in 1814, when the British troops marched through Prince George's from the Chesapeake Bay to burn the capital city. The county government is very active in attempting to preserve historical sites and many new sites are being restored and made available for public use

The **Montpelier Mansion**, owned by the Maryland National Capital Park and Planning Commission, was constructed in the 1770s or 1780s, and is an excellent example of Georgian architecture. Officially designated as a Registered National Historic Landmark by the United States Department of Interior, the Mansion contains 22 rooms, 10 fireplaces, and seven baths. Many of the rooms have impressive decorative features: columns, plaster scrolls and entablature, ornamental fireplaces and mantels. The wings of the Mansion have an unusual semi-octagonal design. A permanent exhibit is on display on the history of Montpelier.

The visitor to Montpelier may inspect the Mansion as well as the magnificent boxwood gardens and a variety of stately trees, including an unusual triple flowering dogwood. The Mansion is one mile west on Route 197 from the Baltimore-Washington Parkway.

Tours are given Sundays, noon to 4:00 p.m., March through December. Special tours may be arranged at other times, as well as private luncheons and receptions. Telephone: (301) 779-2011. Admission charge; school groups free.

The **Montpelier Cultural Arts Center**, located on the grounds of the Mansion, houses three art galleries. Exhibits of local artists and craftsmen are on display. The public is welcome any day except holidays, 10:00 a.m. to 5:00 p.m. Telephone: (301) 490-2329, 953-1993, or 953-1994.

Beltsville Agricultural Research Center of the U.S. Department of Agriculture covers 7,200 acres of land 15 miles north of Washington. A substantial amount of the agricultural research carried out in the United States is performed here. The Center includes 50 laboratories, 36 greenhouses, and hundreds of barns for animals and poultry. More than 3,000 experimental animals and thousands of fowl make up the testing population.

In the late 1930s, the Center developed the Beltsville small white turkey to provide the American people with a small turkey that would fit into a refrigerator and could be eaten at one sitting by a small family.

The **National Agricultural Library**, the world's largest life sciences library, is also open to the public. The library was founded in 1862 at the request of Abraham Lincoln and has a collection of 1.5 million volumes, including rare books dating back to the 15th century. The library also subscribes to 23,000 serial publications. Guided and self-guided tours are offered. Monday through Friday, from 8:00 a.m. to 4:30 p.m. Center telephone: (301) 344-2483, Library telephone: 344-3937.

While all labs and barns are closed on weekends, visitors may drive through the Center and view the livestock from the highway. Powder Mill Road is the main road through the Center. It runs for about seven miles to the Patuxent Wildlife Research Center, which is only open to scientists. To reach the Beltsville Center from the Capital Beltway, take Exit 25 north on Route 1 for 1.5 miles.

In order to visit the **Goddard Space Flight Center** from the Capital Beltway (I-95/495), take Exit 22A, then left on Route 193, left on Soil Conservation Road to "Visitors Entrance" sign.

The Goddard Space Flight Center, one of the largest research and development facilities of the National Aeronautics and Space Administration, is responsible for scientific and environmental satellites, tracking, and communications. The Center is named in honor of Robert H. Goddard, recognized as the "father of American rocketry." Visitors will see the collection of spacecraft and flight articles, as well as exhibits about America's Space Flight Program in the NASA/Goddard Visitor's Center and Museum. Open Wednesday through Sunday, 10:00 a.m. to 4:00 p.m., except Thanksgiving, Christmas, and New Year's. Model rocket launches first and second Sunday of each month. Admission free. Refreshments and souvenirs may be purchased. Telephone: (301) 344-8981.

College Park is the largest of the five **University of Maryland** campuses and is the main campus where its president resides. The University was chartered in 1856 and offers many activities that are open to the public. Only a few of them are mentioned below. Please call (301) 454-3311 for further information.

The Dairy Science Department sells its dairy products through the Turner Lab **Dairy Sales Store** between Campus Drive and Knox Road on the west side of Route 1. Ice cream made by the students is sold by the cone or in bulk. The store also sells milk, eggs from University poultry, as well as a small selection of sandwiches and drinks. The store is open Monday through Friday, 8:00 a.m. to 5:00 p.m. Telephone: (301) 454-4521.

The **Astronomy Observatory** is open to the public on the 5th and 20th of each month. The staff gives a lecture beginning at 8:00 p.m.; 9:00 p.m. during Daylight Savings Time. Weather permitting, the audience may look through the telescopes; the largest is 20 inches in diameter. From University Boulevard, right on Metzerott Road, pass Central Administration Building to Observatory on left. Advance reservations requested for large groups. Telephone: (301) 454-3460.

The **Art Gallery** offers between six and eight exhibitions of national and international artists during the academic year.

The gallery has a permanent collection of 20th-century American prints and paintings and some African art. Open only during academic year, Monday through Friday, 10:00 a.m. to 4:00 p.m.; Wednesday, 10:00 a.m. to 9:00 p.m.; Sunday and Saturday, 1:00 p.m. to 5:00 p.m. Telephone: (301) 454-2763. From Route 1, take Campus Drive west, past Cole Field House to large parking lot (Lot 1), left to end of parking lot. The Gallery is in the Art-Sociology Building next to the Tawes Theatre.

The **Wind Tunnel** is one of the largest in the eastern United States and performs aerodynamic testing of airplanes, trucks, automobiles, ships, garbage cans, and many other items. The public is welcome from Monday through Friday, 8:00 a.m. to 4:00 p.m., but is requested to make advance reservations. Telephone: (301) 454-2413. From Route 1, take Campus Drive west, make first right onto Stadium Drive; the wind tunnel is in the first building on the right.

Originally built for Governor Samuel Ogle, the 18th-century mansion **Belair** belongs to the town of Bowie. The visitor can stroll around the grounds and note the architectural features of this ornate structure, erected in 1746, and the 20 varieties of trees on the grounds of the Mansion. The wings were added about 1900. Governor Ogle was interested in race horses and brought to this country the original thoroughbreds from which have descended much of the stock which has made Maryland famous in American horse-racing history. The Mansion is currently being restored and is open to the public only on the second Sunday of each month.

Belair can be reached from the Capital Beltway (I-95/495) via Exit 19, Route 50 to Route 197, left to Route 450, and on to Tulip Grove Road.

The **Belair Stables Museum**, located on Belair Drive and Tulip Grove Road, preserves the stables owned by William B. Woodward in its heyday. These stables produced two triple crown winners, Gallant Fox in 1930 and Omaha in 1935, as well as Nashua who won two of the triple crown races in 1954. The museum has a carriage room, a tack room, and collections of photographs, racing silks, and farm tools on exhibit. Open May, June, September, and October, Sunday, 1:00 to 4:00 p.m., and by appointment. Admission free. Telephone: (301) 262-6200.

Robert M. Watkins Regional Park is approached from the Capital Beltway (I-95/495), Exit 15, east on Route 214

(Central Avenue), three miles to Enterprise Road, right to park entrance.

This 438-acre regional park centrally located in Prince George's County is owned and operated by the Maryland National Capital Park and Planning Commission. A variety of both active and passive recreational facilities is designed to keep every member of the family occupied.

An 85-year-old carousel and a miniature train ride that chugs through the wooded countryside of the park are in operation daily throughout the summer months. A nominal fee is charged for both.

In addition to these attractions, there are over more than 200 picnic tables located conveniently near an extensive children's playground area, plus group picnic areas. Senior citizen and handicapped picnic areas may be reserved. Adjacent to the train ride and near the playground is a snack bar. Football, baseball, and softball fields are available, plus eight tennis courts. In the athletic field area is an administration-Visitors Center Building that houses shower and locker rooms. During the summer months free concerts in the park are held in the evenings. The park also hosts the "Festival of Lights" each December.

Thirty-four first-come, first-served campsites are available. Two group sites (10 persons or more) are available on a reserved basis. Campers may use tennis courts, showers, and toilets. There is a $5.00 charge for out-of-county residents on weekends. Open all year. Reservations and information telephone: (301) 249-6200.

The **Watkins Nature Culture Center** is open all year, Tuesday through Saturday, 9:00 a.m. to 4:00 p.m.; Sunday, 11:00 a.m. to 4:00 p.m. Closed Mondays and holidays. The Center offers exhibits and nature lectures. Telephone: (301) 249-6202.

Upper Marlboro is accessible from Baltimore via Routes 3 and 301. From the Capital Beltway (I-95) take Exit 11 to Route 4 nine miles to the town of Upper Marlboro.

Founded in 1706, the town was named for the Duke of Marlborough. It is the seat of Prince George's County and has been an important tobacco center since its founding. Tobacco auctions are held during an eight-week period from mid-March to May, Monday through Thursday, 9:00 a.m. to 1:00 p.m. Tourists are always welcome at the auction warehouses in Upper Marlboro, La Plata, Hughesville, and Waldorf.

Call Maryland Tobacco Authority for further information. Telephone: (301) 782-4594.

A walk or drive through Upper Marlboro affords the visitor the opportunity to see many early homes spanning the period from before the 18th century to the Victorian era.

Three blocks off the main street, near the new public school, is a small graveyard on what was once the Beane property. Located here is the **tomb of Dr. William Beane and his wife,** who were lifelong residents of the town. Dr. Beane's arrest by the British in 1814 caused Francis Scott Key to protest to the British admiral on his flagship in Baltimore harbor. During the subsequent bombardment of Fort McHenry, Key was inspired to compose our national anthem.

Among other historical attractions is **Trinity Church,** founded in 1810 by Thomas Claggett, who in 1802 became the first person to be consecrated a bishop in America. The present brick edifice dates from 1846. Trinity is on Church Street, just off Main Street near the courthouse. Nearby is a large marker commemorating the site of the **birthplace of John Carroll,** first bishop and archbishop of the Catholic Church in the United States.

The **Prince George's Equestrian Center,** at 5600 Water Street in Upper Marlboro, is a training facility for licensed thoroughbred trainers and home base for horse shows, antique car shows, dog shows, camper rallies, and concerts. Telephone: (301) 952-4740.

One can combine a tour of Upper Marlboro with a visit to several unique Episcopalian churches which date back 150 years or more. Most of them are located in western and southern Prince George's County.

St. Barnabas Church can he reached from the Washington area via Capital Beltway Exit 15, Route 214, and right on Church Road for two miles (near the village of Leeland). This brick edifice, dating from 1773, was a replacement for the church built in 1710. The parish itself was founded in 1704 or possibly earlier. The first brick church, which replaced an earlier wooden chapel, was begun in 1708.

A painting over the altar, *The Last Supper* (1722), is the work of Gustavus Hesselius, a noted Swedish artist who painted in America from 1711 to 1775. It was the first commissioned religious painting in the American colonies. The parish communion vessels are dated 1714. The building is

not open except during services or by special arrangement.
Telephone: (301) 249-9671.

St. Thomas at Croom is accessible via Route 301, to
Route 382 to Croom Road, then left to Croom. The church is
on a hilltop at the edge of the village. The church was built in
1732, with a bell tower added in 1888 honoring Bishop Claggett.
The parish itself was founded in 1674. Interior features
include traditional box pews, a balcony, and stained-glass
windows. The edifice is surrounded by venerable oaks and an
old graveyard bearing some famous Maryland names: Calvert,
Bowie, Oden, and Carr. Telephone: (301) 248-4290.

St. Paul's at Baden is reached from Route 301, south on
Route 381, and then left six miles to Baden. This church,
founded in 1689, was also served by Rev. Claggett from 1780
to 1786. The present building dates from 1733. A sundial was
added on the front wall in 1753. The church is cruciform and
constructed of very old brick. The interior has plain pews and
a balcony; the one memorial window is in Bishop Claggett's
honor. A very old model pipe organ is adjacent to the choir
room.

St. John's at Broad Creek is on Livingston Road near
Silesia. Return to Capital Beltway toward Virginia, take Exit
3 onto Route 210 past Oxon Hill Road, bear right on Livingston
to church on right. An air of antiquity surrounds this church,
erected in 1732. George Washington is said to have worshipped at Broad Creek Church because it was accessible by
boat when his own church was snowed in. It has a number of
lovely stained-glass windows. The church bell is hung from a
heavy log frame in the churchyard.

A mile south on Riverview Road is **Harmony Hall**, built
by the same builder as St. John's Church.

Andrews Air Force Base is situated just outside the
Capital Beltway (I-95/495) between Routes 4 and 5. From the
Beltway take Exit 9, and follow signs to the base.

The "Aerial Gateway to Official Washington" is the airport for the president and important government officials as
well as foreign dignitaries. Drop-in, one-hour guided tours
are available June 1 to September 1, Tuesday and Thursday,
10:00 a.m. Telephone; (301) 981-4511. For groups of 10 or
more and during the winter, two weeks' notice and a written
request are necessary. Tours vary according to interests of
the group, and may include visits to the control tower,
aircraft, a parachute loft, the presidential plane, and the
weather station. Admission free.

Wild World is a family recreation and entertainment park, with reserve and water attractions and amusement park rides. In the summer, visitors should bring bathing suits to enjoy the water rides (locker rooms and showers are provided). To get to Wild World from the Capital Beltway (I-95/495), take Exit 15A, Route 214 East (Central Avenue). From Baltimore, take Route 3 to Route 301 South to Route 214 West.

Other thrills include the Whirling Wild Fling, the Flip Flopper Sky Escaper, a wrap-around Cinema 180, and a roller coaster. The less venturesome may enjoy the arcade games, magic and puppet shows, or gift shopping. A full-fare cafeteria, and picnic grounds for box lunches or party catering, are provided. (No food may be brought into the park.)

Wild World is open daily, 10:00 a.m. to 10:00 p.m., from Memorial Day until Labor Day; open weekends only, May and September. Admission charge; most rides included in admission. For further information write: 13710 Central Avenue, PO Box 1610, Mitchellville, MD 20716. Telephone: (301) 249-1500.

The world-renowned **Paul E. Garber Preservation, Restoration and Storage Facility**, also known as the **Silver Hill Museum,** houses the Smithsonian Institution's reserve collection of air and space craft. More than 150 aircraft are stored at the Facility, with approximately 90 on display, in addition to numerous spacecraft, engines, propellers, and other flight-related objects. There are about 100 World War II German and Japanese airplanes that have been restored as well as a few World War I German aircraft. The Facility is named in honor of Paul Garber, head curator of the Air and Space Museum, who was one of the Air Mail Service pilots in the early 1920s. From the Capital Beltway (I-495/95) take Silver Hill exit (Route 5 north), follow Route 5 for one mile to St. Barnabas Road (Route 414), continue on St. Barnabas Road a half-mile to Facility.

The public will see the behind-the-scene activities of the staff who are restoring and repairing the Smithsonian Air and Space Museum collection. Guided tours may be arranged, Monday through Friday, 10:00 a.m., and Saturday and Sunday, 10:00 a.m. and 1:00 p.m. Reservations must be made at least two weeks in advance. Telephone: (202) 357-1400. Admission free. Individuals or groups of up to 40 persons will be accepted for the tour, which lasts between two and three hours. Special tours for handicapped visitors are available upon request. There is no heating or air conditioning in the six hangar buildings, so visitors are advised to dress appropriately.

A private, nonprofit corporation offering vocational training and sheltered work experience for mentally retarded and other handicapped adults, the **Melwood Horticultural Training Center** is a pioneer in horticultural therapy. Its Plant Shop, open 9:00 a.m. to 5:00 p.m., Monday to Friday and 10:00 a.m. to 5:00 p.m. on Saturday, sells plants, macrame hangings and wooden planter boxes, and picnic tables handmade by trainees. Tours of the facility can be arranged on request. For information, write Melwood Center, 5606 Dower House Road, Upper Marlboro, MD 20780. Telephone: (301) 599-8000. From Capital Beltway (I-95/495) take Exit 11, Route 4 (Marlboro Pike) to third traffic light. Right on Dower House Road, one-half mile. Center is on left.

The **Mary Surratt House** is approached from the Capital Beltway, Exit 7, Route 5 four miles to Clinton. Built in 1852, this wood-frame house served as a tavern and meeting place for the community of Surrattsville (now called Clinton), as well as the home of the John Surratt family. It is recognized as being significant in U.S. history because of the controversy surrounding the assassination of President Lincoln in 1865.

The widow Mary Surratt was implicated in the assassination plot against Abraham Lincoln because the assassin John Wilkes Booth was known to have visited her boarding house in Washington, DC. He also used Surratt House in southern Prince George's County as a resupply point in his escape after the assassination of Lincoln on the evening of April 14, 1865. Mary Surratt and three others were convicted for complicity in the assassination and were hanged on July 7, 1865. She was the first woman to be hanged by order of the U.S. government. The citizens of the Clinton area have continued to believe in the innocence of Mary Surratt and as a result formed a committee to restore the Surratt House.

The house is open to the public and tours are conducted by costumed docents on Thursday and Friday, 11:00 a.m. to 3:00 p.m., and Saturday and Sunday, from noon to 4:00 p.m. Closed January and February. Group tours by reservation on Wednesday. Admission charge. Telephone: (301) 868-1121.

To reach **Louise F. Cosca Regional Park** and its **Clearwater Nature Center** from the Capital Beltway (I-95/495) take Exit 11, Route 5 to Clinton. This 500-acre park in southern Prince George's County is owned and maintained by the Maryland National Capital Park and Planning Commission. The Nature Center staff offers a varied natural history program. Highlights of the park include the 14-acre artificial Lake Clinton, where fishing and boating equipment can be rented; an extensive children's play area featuring a pioneer camp; nearly 200 picnic tables; nine picnic shelters; plus baseball and softball fields. An adjacent fieldhouse is located near the 10 public tennis courts and athletic area. Twenty-four campsites are available on a first-come, first-served basis with showers, water, and electricity hookups; and more than three miles of nature trails weave their way throughout the park. A tram train ride, in operation during the summer months, and weekends at other times (weather permitting), gives park visitors the opportunity to take a leisurely park tour, sit-down fashion.

The wooded park is bisected by Butler's Branch, a main waterway draining into Piscataway Creek. The nature trails, and the path along the electrical power line right-of-way, affords an opportunity for the study of the rich and diverse natural history of the area.

Admission free for Prince George's and Montgomery county residents. There is a charge for out-of-county residents on weekends and holidays. A small fee is charged for all camping hookups. Telephone for Nature Center: (301) 297-4575; for Park Permit Office: (301) 699-2415.

The **National Colonial Farm Museum** is a cooperative project of the Accokeek Foundation and the National Park Service. It is an operating example of a middle-class, 18th-century, Tidewater tobacco plantation. The farm is planted with various crops and orchards grown there in colonial times, and is stocked with sheep, hogs, cattle, horses, and poultry. Every effort is made to introduce varieties and breeds of the colonial period. Farming methods and implements of the mid-18th century are used by the costumed staff.

The farm buildings are re-creations of typical structures on a colonial plantation. One authentic colonial tobacco barn is being restored. Many of the buildings are open to the public. From the Capital Beltway (I-95) take Exit 3A south to Accokeek.

The farm is open daily, except Monday, 10:00 a.m. to 5:00 p.m. Special group tours may be arranged, and special demonstrations are given during the weekends. Write to the National Colonial Farm Museum, 3400 Bryan Point Road,

Accokeek, MD 20607, or telephone: (301) 283-2113. Admission charge, free for children under 12.

Oxon Hill Farm is accessible from Capital Beltway (I-95/ 495) Exit 3A, Indian Head Highway (Route 210) off Oxon Hill Road. This demonstration farm for children is like many farms found in the Maryland and Virginia countryside around Washington at the end of the 19th century. Much of the farm work here is done just as it was then—the family cow is milked by hand and the horse team earns its keep by plowing the fields and hauling wagonloads of corn, wheat, oats, and other things. Special demonstrations are given throughout the year. Open daily, year round, 8:00 a.m. to 5:00 p.m. Admission free. Mailing address: National Capital Parks East, 1900 Anacostia Drive, SE, Washington, DC 20020. Telephone: (301) 839-1177.

Fort Washington Military Historical Park is reached from Capital Beltway (I-95/495) Exit 3A, south on Indian Head Highway (Route 210). Fort Washington, under jurisdiction of the National Park Service, is a notable example of an early 19th-century coastal defense. It is on the same site as the earliest fort erected for the defense of the nation's capital. It was begun late in 1814, as a replacement for the first fort, destroyed during the War of 1812. The new fort was built between 1814 and 1824.

Little altered since it was rebuilt, it is an enclosed masonry fortification, entered by a drawbridge across the dry moat at the main entrance. Two half-bastions overlook the river above and below the fort. At three levels—water battery, casemate positions, and ramparts—guns could deliver heavy fire on an enemy fleet in the river.

On the parade ground visitors can see the officers' quarters and the soldiers' barracks. Near each is a magazine and guardroom. During the Civil War, Union troops manned the fort, but it was never attacked. One can spend a good part of a day, and walk about three miles, if interested, in touring the old fort and the eight batteries which surround it on the Potomac side and along Piscataway Creek.

Free tours of the fort are conducted by the park historian on request, Monday through Saturday. Scheduled tours are given on Sunday, 1:00 p.m. and 3:00 p.m., by park rangers and volunteers in civil war costumes. Tours for groups at other times can be arranged by writing or telephoning the park ranger. Picnic areas are available in various parts of the park. A small souvenir shop sells military memorabilia and literature. The fort and park are open year round, daily, 8:30 a.m. to 5:00 p.m. Mailing address: Ft. Washington Park, National Capital Parks East, 1900 Anacostia Drive, SE, Washington, DC 20020. Telephone: (301) 292-2112.

Another attraction in Prince George's County is the **Merkle Wildlife Sanctuary and Visitor Center**. Located on the Patuxent River in the southern part of the county, it was established in 1932 by Edgar Merkle as a breeding and nesting ground for Canada geese. The Merkles sold the land to the Maryland Department of Natural Resources in 1970, with the understanding that the 1,600-acre tract would be maintained as a sanctuary for Canada geese.

The Visitor Center offers scheduled interpretive nature programs during the week, and special programs on weekends. Some of the programs require payment of a nominal fee, and all require reservations.

The sanctuary is open daily, year round, 8:00 a.m. to 5:00 p.m. The Visitor Center is open from 10:00 a.m. to 4:00 p.m., Tuesday through Saturday (hours subject to change). Admission free. For information write: 1170 Fenno Road, Upper Marlboro, MD 20772. Telephone: (301) 888-1410.

For additional information about Prince George's County contact: Prince George's Travel Promotion Council, 6600 Kenilworth Avenue, Riverdale, MD 20737. Telephone: (301) 927-0700; Maryland National Capital Park and Planning Commission, History Division, 4811 Riverdale Road, Riverdale, MD 20737. Telephone: (301) 779-2011.

CHARLES COUNTY

Charles County, with its southwestern shoreline facing Virginia across the Potomac River, was long considered a frontier area and has had ties with Virginia throughout its history. Roads were bad and river transport was more reliable in sailing craft. Several sailboats were developed on the river, such as the bugeye, a sophisticated version of the Indian log canoe, and the "Black Nancy" and the Potomac River dory-boat, flat-bottom boats with sails that were used for oyster tonging, crab dredging, and fishing.

The post road between Philadelphia and Williamsburg ran through Charles County and the necessity for ferrying passengers across the Potomac River fostered close communication with Virginia. During the Civil War, there were many Southern sympathizers among the slave-owning tobacco planters

in Charles County. Tobacco growing was the most important livelihood for county residents and continues to be a
significant part of the economy. Each spring tobacco auctions
are held in La Plata, Hughesville, and Waldorf. The county
remains rural with many small towns.

A tour of Charles County may be made in one day,
covering the historic sites with a stop to eat at one of the
"crab houses" at Popes Creek on the Potomac River. The tour
can begin at Smallwood State Park and at Doncaster State
Forest.

Smallwood State Park is located four miles west of
Mason Springs on the Mattawoman Creek, which empties
into the Potomac River. Route 224, which leads to the park,
may be reached via Route 225 from either Routes 210 or 301.
This 450-acre area is centered around the manor house of
Revolutionary War hero General William Smallwood, who
also served as governor of Maryland from 1785 to 1788. The
general is buried on the slope below his house, which has
been restored and furnished with 18th-century period furniture. During the summer, demonstrations are given of candle
dipping, cooking, and other 18th-century domestic activities.
The manor house is open from Memorial Day through Labor
Day, Saturday and Sunday, noon to 5:00 p.m. and by appointment during the rest of the year.

Picnicking facilities are available for visitors to the park,
and there is a self-guided hiking tour of the manor grounds.
The park also has six boat launching ramps at Sweden Point
with a paved parking lot. The ramps are available for use only
during the summer. There is also a boat concession for
boaters and fishermen and a snack bar. The park is open year
round, daily, 8:00 a.m. to sunset. For further information
contact Park Manager, Route 1, Box 64, Marbury, MD 20658.
Telephone: (301) 743-7613.

Doncaster Demonstration Forest is reached via Routes
210 or 301 to Ironsides, and Route 6, three miles west to the
forest entrance. It is primarily a demonstration forest for
promoting timber management practices and has several
experimental pine plantations. It contains a variety of trees,
including poplars, gums, oaks, and pines. The state works
with the Charles County forester in assisting county residents to improve their timber properties.

This 1,500-acre forest offers hiking, picnicking, and hunting opportunities. There are also approximately 10 miles of
bridle trails for owners who bring their own horses. It is a

sanctuary for many species of game animals and birds. For information write to Forest Superintendent, Route 1, Box 425, Indianhead, MD 20640. Telephone: (301) 934-2282.

Old Durham Episcopal Church is located one mile south of Ironsides on Route 425. The original log church was built in 1692 and was one of the original Anglican parishes created in southern Maryland. (Although the Maryland proprietorship was the personal domain of Catholic Lord Baltimore, the Anglicans were able to persuade the government to establish official Church of England parishes with government perquisites.) The present brick building was begun in 1732 and subsequently has been enlarged many times. An ancient sundial near the front gate and graves dating from 1695 make this old church an interesting stop for the tourist. It is open to the public by request. Telephone: (301) 743-7468.

On Route 6, south of Doncaster Demonstration Forest, is the **Nanjemoy Baptist Church**, which is one of the oldest continuously active Baptist churches in Maryland. In 1790 four Baptist men fled from religious persecution in Virginia to Charles County and established the Nanjemoy church in 1791.

Return to Route 6 east to **Port Tobacco**, originally a Potopaco Indian village where Captain John Smith stopped and Jesuit Father White taught Indian children. In colonial days it was a busy port, with wharves, warehouses, a custom house, hotels, churches, and inns. It also was the county seat until replaced by La Plata. A springhouse containing the original town well occupies the middle of the square. The nearby part of the river on which the town depended for its commerce has been long since silted up. The old **Court House**, and a number of 18th- century houses, were restored around Court House Square. The original courthouse was built in 1719, destroyed in 1808, and rebuilt in 1819. The second courthouse was destroyed in 1892 and in 1973 there was a reconstruction of the 1819 building. The first floor is a display of the 1819 courthouse and a museum, containing colonial artifacts unearthed during excavation of the site, is located on the second floor. The courthouse and museum are open June through August, Wednesday to Saturday, 10:00 a.m. to 4:00 p.m.; Sunday, noon to 4:00 p.m. September through May, weekends only, noon to 4:00 p.m. Admission charge, children under 10 free. Telephone: (301) 934-4313.

Turn right on Route 427 to **Chapel Point**. Two historic

religious sites, **St. Ignatius Church** and **St. Thomas Manor,**
stand on a hilltop overlooking the Potomac and Port Tobacco
rivers. The Catholic parish dates from 1662, though the
present building was erected in 1798. St. Ignatius is one of
the oldest continuously active Roman Catholic churches in
the United States. The beautiful interior of the church is
dominated by 18th-century architecture. The manor, built in
1741, is occupied by the Jesuits and is not open to visitors.
From Chapel Point, the idyllic view of the two rivers is one
never to be forgotten.

Continue east on Route 427 to Bel Alton, right on Route
301, two miles, then south to **Popes Creek** for a gourmet crab
luncheon or dinner in one of the "crab houses" for which this
tiny community is noted. Guests may watch the steaming of
the hard-shell crabs. The crab houses are built on piles over
the Potomac River, with plenty of windows to provide a good
view of the broad river. Return to Route 301, continue south
to Route 234 where, at Allen's Fresh, there is a popular
fishing place in early spring. Two miles further south on
Route 301 at Newburg, turn left on Route 257 to **Wayside
Church,** an original parish of Maryland, dating from 1692.
The present brick church dates from the early 18th century,
and there are tall cedars and ancient gravestones in the
adjacent burial ground.

The route is back to 301, north to **La Plata,** the county
seat. La Plata is one of four towns in which loose leaf tobacco
auctions are held Monday through Thursday, from mid-March
to the first week in May, 9:00 a.m. to 1:00 p.m. Buyers from
all the great tobacco companies buy millions of pounds of
tobacco leaf at these sales. Tourists are always welcome.

West of La Plata off Route 225, on Mitchell Road one
mile from the Port Tobacco Court House, is **Mt. Carmel
Convent,** the first Carmelite convent in America. Two original structures of the convent—believed to have been the
receiving parlor and living quarters—date from 1790. The
chapel, open to the public, and the new convent buildings are
located beyond the original buildings. There is a small gift
shop of handcrafted items. The historic buildings are open to
the public May to October, daily, 8:00 a.m. to 4:00 p.m. By
appointment in winter. For further information contact the
convent, Route 4, Box 4035A, La Plata, MD 20646. Telephone: (301) 934-1654.

The visitor may visit the **Dr. Samuel A. Mudd Home
Museum,** which may be reached by traveling north from La

Plata on Route 301 to Waldorf, right on Route 5, left on Route 382, right on Route 232 in Malcolm. After shooting President Lincoln on April 14, 1865, actor John Wilkes Booth escaped from Washington to the home of Dr. Mudd who treated him. Dr. Mudd was charged with conspiracy in the assassination and was convicted and imprisoned but was pardoned in 1869. The house has been restored by the Mudd Society. Open weekends, noon to 4:00 p.m. Admission charge. Telephone: (301) 645-3295.

North of Waldorf is **Cedarville State Forest**, which can be reached from Route 30 via the Cedarville Road.

This park has facilities for picnicking, fishing, hiking, and camping including 130 campsites with toilets, showers, laundry tubs, and fireplaces. There are also 14 miles of marked foot trails and many springs in the park.

The headwaters of the **Zekiah Swamp** is located in the area and rare plants such as the sundew and carnivorous pitcher plant may be observed. A wide variety of wildlife may also be seen, including the bald eagle. The swamp, which empties into the Wicomico River to the south, is an important ecological feature of the southern Maryland peninsula and played an important part in the Civil War when the swamp was used by Southern sympathizers for clandestine activities. Cedarville also has an extensive growth of mature holly trees. The visitors center is open June through September, Saturday, Sunday, and holidays, 11:00 a.m. to 6:00 p.m. The park is open year round, weekdays, 8:00 a.m. to sunset; weekends, 9:00 a.m. to sunset. For further information contact Park Manager, Route 4, Box 106A, Brandywine, MD 20613. Telephone: (301) 888-1638 or 888-1622 (local call to Washington).

ST. MARY'S COUNTY

The first English-speaking Catholic settlers, under Governor Leonard Calvert, landed at St. Clement's Island in the Potomac River to found the colony of Maryland. The first colonists who arrived on the *Ark* and *Dove* numbered two Jesuit priests, a lay brother, and 140 men. After celebrating mass at St. Clement's on March 25, 1634, and resupplying, the settlers moved to their permanent settlement on the banks of St. Mary's River and established the capital of the Maryland colony there. St. Mary's is thus the oldest official county in the state.

St. Mary's County is located at the southern tip on the western shore and may be reached from Charles County on Route 5, from Calvert County on Route 2/4 crossing at Solomons over the Governor Johnson Bridge to Route 235, and from Virginia over the Governor Nice Bridge (toll) on Route 301 to Route 234.

The St. Mary's County Chamber of Commerce Information Center is located in the center of Mechanicsville on Route 5, south of Charlotte Hall. Visitors may get information on St. Mary's as well as on the neighboring counties of Calvert and Charles. Open daily, 9:00 a.m. to 5:00 p.m. Contact: Chamber of Commerce, Route 5, Box 41-A, Mechanicsville, MD 20659. Telephone: (301) 884-5555.

A popular **Farmers Market** is located on Route 5 at Charlotte Hall. It is open Wednesdays and Saturdays throughout the year. Here tourists will find real bargains in the flea market, produce stalls, the Amish food and produce stands, and in the antique and used household goods shops. Hours are from 7:00 a.m. to 5:00 p.m.

Many Amish farmers have settled in the area south of Charlotte Hall. A trip through the picturesque countryside reminds one of the Lancaster, PA, area without the traffic. A suggested trip is along Route 236 from New Market to Budd's Creek.

Sotterley, built in 1717, is an outstanding Georgian-style mansion. (Turn left off Route 235 at Hollywood.) It exemplifies the colonial plantation way of life. In one of the most beautiful settings in the state, it commands a sweeping view of the Patuxent River. The estate is a working colonial plantation. Open daily, June through September, 11:00 a.m. to 5:00 p.m. Open by appointment months of April, May, October, and November. Admission charge. Telephone: (301) 373-2280.

In Leonardtown, on Route 5, one can view **Tudor Hall**, near the Court House. This 1756 Georgian mansion overlooks Breton Bay. The mansion features a hanging staircase and a captain's walk.

St. Mary's County "Old" Jail Museum is now the headquarters for the St. Mary's Historical Society. The museum exhibits artifacts relating to the county. One of the rooms is furnished as a woman's jail cell as it would have appeared in 1857, when the jail was built, and another is furnished as a physician's office as it appeared in the early 20th century. Open Tuesday through Saturday, 10:00 a.m. to 4:00 p.m.

Piney Point is four miles south of Valley Lee on Route 5.

The first summer White House—during Monroe's term—was in this locality. The chief attraction here is the **Lundeberg School of Seamanship**, a U.S. Merchant Marine training school. It has a floating schoolhouse, and various types of log canoes, schooners, skipjacks, and daysailers. The yacht *Manitou*, a yawl used by the late President Kennedy for summer cruises, is moored here. The research library contains more than 8,000 volumes on maritime history, including some 18th-century manuscripts. Open first Sunday of every month, 9:00 a.m. to 5:00 p.m. Admission free. Telephone: (301) 994-0010.

In Lexington Park, on Route 235, is the **Naval Air Test and Evaluation Museum**. This private museum explains the experimental work at the nearby Patuxent Naval Air Test Center. Aircraft, such as the RASC Vigilante, the A7 Corsair II, and the World War II Loon, are on display outside the museum. Inside exhibits include a photographic survey of naval air history, the technological development of computers, wind tunnel models, and aircraft carrier testing equipment. Open year round, Tuesday through Saturday, 11:00 a.m. to 5:00 p.m.; Sunday, noon to 5:00 p.m. Admission free. Telephone: (301) 863-7418.

Maryland was established in 1634 when the first settlers started a permanent settlement on the banks of St. Mary's River and called it **St. Mary's City**. Here, in 1649, the Assembly decreed religious toleration for the first time in America. At the entrance to the town is a monument commemorating the Act. Today St. Mary's City is a small, unincorporated rural town with St. Mary's College located there.

The state has developed an 800-acre park, an outdoor museum called **Historic St. Mary's City**, that is a reconstruction of the 17th-century town. Archaeological excavations of the colonial site are in progress and may be observed by the public. A replica of Maryland's **State House of 1676**, which served as the Capitol until 1694, has been reconstructed on the site. This two-story Jacobean structure contains historic exhibits. Open last weekend in March through November, Wednesday to Sunday, 10:00 a.m. to 5:00 p.m. The Visitor Center is open daily, year round, 10:00 a.m. to 5:00 p.m. Open all holidays except Thanksgiving, Christmas, and New Year's. Telephone: (301) 862-1634 or 862-1666.

"The Maryland Dove," a representation of one of the ships that transported Maryland's first settlers, is moored before the State House. The *Dove* was the smaller of the two ships that brought the settlers from England in 1634. Although there is no exact description of the *Dove*, the replica is the same type and approximate size as the original. The present *Dove* was designed by William A. Baker and was built by James Richardson, who employed methods and tools used in the 17th century.

The **Godiah Spray Plantation**, a working 17th-century tobacco plantation, has also been reconstructed on its site. Further plans call for an inn and maritime exhibit complex to be built.

Nearby is **Trinity Church**, erected in 1829 with bricks taken from ruins of the original State House. The **Leonard Calvert Monument**, in the churchyard, marks the site where the colonists first assembled in 1634 to establish a government for the colony.

Chancellor's Point Nature Trail and **Natural History Center** is at the mouth of St. Mary's River. It is reached via Route 5 and south on Rosecroft Road. Here you can walk along a mile-long loop trail that traverses an area with the same fauna and flora the settlers found here more than 300 years ago. The beach is rich in all sorts of fossils washed down from the cliffs. The trail is open during daylight hours. Parking available.

St. Ignatius Church, at St. Inigoes on Villa Road, off Route 5, dates from 1785 and is on the site of the original church, built in 1641. Its boxwood hedges, more than 300 years old, are a notable feature of the setting. The church is open to visitors daily, 9:00 a.m. to 4:00 p.m.

Point Lookout State Park on Route 5, is at the tip of St. Mary's County, where the Potomac River empties into the Chesapeake Bay. During the Civil War, more than 20,000 Confederate prisoners were held under appalling conditions at Camp Hoffman, which stood on this site. Today, at Scotland, MD, one mile north of the park, one can visit the monument commemorating the Confederate soldiers. It is the only federal memorial to Confederate soldiers. The Visitor's Center offers interpretive lectures on the Civil War historical background of Point Lookout as well as natural history lectures.

The state park offers facilities for swimming, picnicking, oystering, fishing, boating, and camping, and there are three miles of bathing beach. There are 147 campsites, including 27 that have full hookup facilities. Rental boats are available for those wishing to take advantage of one of the best fishing and crabbing spots in Maryland. Hiking and biking trails are located in the park and there is a bicycle rental concession. Open year round, daily, 8:00 a.m. to sunset. Campsites are open from April to October. Further information on facilities and fees is available from Park Superintendent, Scotland, MD 20687. Telephone: (301) 872-5688.

To reach **St. Clement's Island** the visitor must go to Colton's Point and take a boat to the island where Lord Baltimore's first settlers landed in Maryland. To reach Colton's Point, go south on Route 5, west and south on Route 242 to end of road. From Virginia, take the Governor Nice Bridge (toll) on Route 301 to Route 234, right at Route 242 to the end of the road.

The **St. Clement's Island Interpretive Center-Potomac River Museum** at Colton's Point overlooks St. Clement's Island. The museum exhibits depict the history of man in this area from the days of the original Indians. Included are exhibits of Indian and colonial artifacts unearthed nearby. Other exhibits concern the activities and lives of the farmers and watermen of the region. Open Monday through Friday, 9:00 a.m. to 4:00 p.m.; Saturday and Sunday, 12:30 to 4:30 p.m. Summer, open Monday to Friday, noon to 4:00 p.m. Closed Christmas, New Year's, and Easter. Donation.

On the island of **St. Clement's** a 40-foot cross marks the first landing and celebration of the mass in Maryland. Although inhabited at one time, today the 40-acre island is uninhabited. Each year the island is the site of the Blessing of the Fleet on the last Sunday in September. Boat trips to the island may be arranged by appointment. The state-owned island has picnicking facilities with drinking water. Boat captains conduct a guided tour or visitors may take their own self-guided tour. For further information contact museum curator, Colton's Point, MD 20606. Telephone: (301) 769-2222.

DELAWARE

This second smallest state in the Union is called the "Diamond State" because of its value as a state and its position in history compared with its size. Delaware is also called the "First State" because it was the first to ratify the Constitution. It was claimed by Henry Hudson for the Dutch in 1609, but in 1638 the Dutch formed a joint venture with the Swedes. Fort Christina is a monument to the first major Swedish settlement. In 1664 the area was seized by the British and incorporated in the lands held by the Duke of York, and then, in 1682, it was given to William Penn. In 1704 the three counties of Delaware established a separate legislature, but remained technically under the control of the Governor of Pennsylvania until the colony became a state in 1776.

The state has an excellent system of natural waterways which have helped the development of its economy. The 14-mile **Chesapeake and Delaware Canal** connects the upper Chesapeake Bay with the Delaware River. The actual excavation and construction, begun in 1804, were delayed and not completed until 1829. Originally the canal had four locks. It has been both deepened and widened several times in its history, and is now an open waterway. Although the canal faced competition from the railroads as early as 1832, almost as soon as it opened, it was a major economic and social phenomenon in the life of the state. Showboats brought entertainment; floating stores sold goods and carried the informal news of the day. During World War II the canal was used as an alternate route for vessels in order to avoid German submarines which patrolled the Atlantic from Virginia to the Delaware capes. Delaware City now contains the only lock left from the old canal. There and in other towns you can walk along the edge of the canal as it exists today. The only other landmark of the original canal is the old stone pumphouse in Chesapeake City, Maryland. From Delaware City it is possible to visit **Fort Delaware State Park** located on Pea Patch Island, in the Delaware River. The fort, built in 1859, served as a prison for Confederate soldiers in the Civil War. Visitors can inspect the old fort and tour the museum. Open end of April through September. Admission charge. Ferryboats leave Delaware City Saturdays, Sundays, and holidays, 11:00 a.m. to 6:00 p.m. Telephone: (302) 834-7941. Delaware City is on Route 79, two miles east of Route 13, and 10 miles south of New Castle.

There are numerous, well-maintained historic and cultural sites in Delaware. Of particular note is the first stone positioned by the surveyors of the Mason-Dixon line at the extreme southwest corner of the state (it is literally a corner) off Route 54. The state also boasts numerous state parks and wildlife refuges, of which, for purposes of space, only a cross-section is listed in the following pages.

The Dutch were the first to establish a settlement in 1631 near present-day Lewes. They were followed by the English in the 1660s. Visitors can see monuments, museums, and buildings devoted to these pioneer settlers.

Christ Church at Broad Creek, three miles east of Laurel near the southwest corner of the state, was erected in 1771. It is a fine example of early church architecture. Guides are available during summer months on Sundays, 1:00 to 4:00 p.m. Continue east on Route 24, then east on Route 26 to Dagsboro. Here a stop can be made at **Prince George's Chapel**, built in 1757. Part of the original pine interior can still be seen. Admission free. Telephone (Zwaanendael Museum): (302) 645-9418. Continuing east on Route 26 the traveler passes the **Blackwater Presbyterian Church**, one mile west of Clarksville. Organized in 1667, the present edifice was built 1767.

DELAWARE SHORE

In Lewes one should visit the **Zwaanendael Museum**, erected in 1931 to commemorate the first settlement by the Dutch in 1631. Exhibits include a model of the first settlement, a small whaling display, antique household goods, glassware, old newspapers, and a sea captain's chest washed ashore after a wreck. Open Tuesday through Saturday, 10:00 a.m. to 4:30 p.m.; Sunday, 1:30 to 4:30 p.m. Admission free. Telephone: (302) 645-9418.

Memorial Park, facing Lewes-Rehoboth Canal, commemorates the bombardment and defense of Lewes in the

War of 1812. The **DeVries Monument** marks the site of the first Dutch landing. Many old homes and churches are preserved in Lewes. Among them are the Episcopal, Presbyterian, and Methodist churches.

The **Lewes Historical Complex** is located at Third and Shipcarpenter streets. The complex includes the **Thompson Country Store**, which dates from 1800 and still has the original lights, shelves, and cabinets, as well as the old Post Office counter. Other museums in the complex include the **Ellegood and Blacksmith Shops**, the **Plank House** (ca. 1700), the **Rabbit's Ferry Gallery** (18th century), and the **Burton-Ingram House** (ca. 1800). The Lewes Historical Society also owns the **Coast Guard Boathouse** and the **"Overfalls" Lightship**, located at the foot of Shipcarpenter Street. The museums are open from July 1 through September 15, Tuesday to Friday, 10:00 a.m. to 3:00 p.m.; Saturday, 10:00 a.m. to 12:30 p.m. The museum gift shops are open all day on Saturday. Self-guided tours are offered during the season and guided tours are available at 10:30 a.m. on Thursday, Friday, and Saturday. Admission charge. Telephone: (302) 645-0458.

Operated by the Lewes Historical Society, the **Marine Museum**, located in the "Cannonball House" on Front Street, still has a cannonball stuck in its foundation from British attacks. The museum has an impressive and interesting collection of nautical artifacts including treasure chests, figureheads, ship models, etc. Telephone: (302) 645-0458.

There are several interesting annual events in Lewes. A Christmas Fair and House Tour are held every year on the first Saturday of December. A Craft Fair is held in mid-July. For information write: The Lewes Historical Society, Third and Shipcarpenter Streets, Lewes, DE 19958. An excellent Antiques Flea Market is held yearly on the first Saturday in August. Information for both visitors and dealers, telephone: (302) 645-9673.

Historic **Fenwick Island Light** is actually over the state line in Delaware, eight miles north of Ocean City, MD. At the foot of the tall white tower is a marker for the Trans-Peninsula Line, the south boundary between Maryland and Delaware.

Bethany Beach, six miles farther, is one of Delaware's many excellent summer resorts. As he travels north on Route 1, the tourist has an additional choice of **Delaware Seashore State Park, Dewey Beach, Rehoboth Beach**, and **Cape Henlopen State Park**. All offer ocean bathing, surf fishing, and picnicking. Five miles beyond Rehoboth, turn right from Route 1 to Route 9 to reach Lewes and Cape Henlopen State Park.

Cape Henlopen State Park occupies a sandy hook with ocean and bay views on three sides. Excellent recreation facilities are available, including tennis courts, basketball courts, a baseball field, and a nine-hole frisbee golf course. A picnic area as well as a camping area for tents and self-contained units (no hookups) are available. There is a pier for crabbing and fishing. Special areas have been designated for ocean swimming and surf fishing. The state park is of interest because of its rare plants and waterfowl. Canada and snow geese pass through on migration routes, and there are numerous terns. Porpoises are often viewed offshore. Lilies, beach plums, and cranberry bogs, as well as the natural habitats of many wild animals, can be seen from two carefully marked nature trails. Admission charge. For further information write: Park Superintendent, 42 Cape Henlopen Drive, Lewes, DE 19958. Telephone: (302) 645-8983. Camping information: (302) 645-2103.

The 8,817-acre **Prime Hook National Wildlife Refuge** is less than 10 miles beyond the Park. Its marshes, freshwater ponds, brush, and upland attract over more than 260 species of birds and about 25 kinds of mammals and reptiles. Migratory waterfowl populations reach their peak from October to December. In summer the visitor can enjoy hiking, fishing, canoeing, and nature study. Two wildlife trails traverse several habitats, and 15 miles of waterways are open to canoeists. The hunting of deer, waterfowl, and upland game is permitted in season by special regulations. For further information, write: Refuge Manager, RD 1, Box 195, Milton, DE 19968. Telephone: (302) 684-8419.

Return to Route 1, continuing north to Milford, north on Route 113 to Frederica. **Barratt's Chapel**, built in 1780, is called the "Cradle of Methodism in America." Here the first sacrament of communion was administered by Methodist clergymen. Visitors are welcome to the chapel and adjoining museum. Open Saturday and Sunday, 1:30 p.m. to 4:30 p.m. Other times by appointment. Telephone: (302) 335-5544, or if no answer (302) 335-5669. Tours can sometimes be arranged the same day.

John Dickinson Mansion is five miles north of Frederica, east on Kitts-Hummock Road. It is the home of the "Penman of the Revolution." Dickinson drafted, among many papers, the 1778 Articles of Confederation. His home is a fine example of 18th-century plantation architecture, and has interesting furnishings. Open Tuesday through Saturday, 10:00 a.m. to 4:30 p.m.; Sunday, 1:30 to 4:30 p.m. Closed Mondays. Admission free.

The **Camden Friends Meeting House** (1805), west of Route 13 on Camden Wyoming Avenue in nearby Camden, is open to the public and still in use. For information write: Route 2, Box 194B, Camden, DE 19934. Telephone: (302) 697-6910.

DOVER AREA

Continue into Dover, the state capital, via Route 113-A, stopping at **The Green**, in the center of the city. Be sure to visit the **Old State House**, constructed in 1792. It is in excellent condition. Open Tuesday through Saturday, 10:00 a.m. to 4:30 p.m.; Sunday, 1:30 to 4:30 p.m. Closed Mondays. A visitors center behind the Old State House has extensive information and an audio-visual presentation on sites in the area. Open Monday to Saturday, 8:30 a.m. to 4:30 p.m.; Sunday, 1:30 to 4:30 p.m. Telephone: (302) 736-4266.

On Legislative Avenue is **Legislative Hall**, which houses the General Assembly, and the **Hall of Records**. Preserved here is the original royal grant from Charles II to the Duke of York (1682). Open Monday through Friday, 8:00 a.m. to 4:30 p.m. The Research Room of the Hall of Records contains a great deal of interesting material including genealogical records. Open Tuesday through Friday, 8:30 a.m. to 4:15 p.m.; Saturday, 8:00 a.m. to 12:30 p.m., and 1:00 to 3:45 p.m. Telephone: (302) 736-5318.

Governor's House, built in 1790, is still used as the Governor's Mansion. It was a stopping point of the "underground railroad" in pre-Civil War days. Open Saturday, 2:30 to 4:30 p.m. Closed holidays and holiday weekends. Admission free.

Delaware State Museum, on Governor's Avenue, contains exhibits dealing with the 300-year history of the state. Models of Victor Talking Machines are exhibited in Johnson Building (Building No. 3). E. R. Johnson, founder of the company, was a Delaware native. Building No. 2 is a museum of early Delaware trades. Tools and partially recreated work areas for a blacksmith, a cobbler, a printer, and a druggist can be seen, as well as tools and products of other trades. Building No. 1 houses a collection of 18th-century Delaware furniture, as well as a shipbuilding exhibit containing ship-wright's tools, sailing ship models, and the wheelhouse of an old ferry. Shipbuilding was a major industry in this state at one time. Open Tuesday through Saturday, 10:00 a.m. to 4:30 p.m.; Sunday, 1:30 to 4:30 p.m. Closed Monday. Admission free. Telephone: (302) 736-4266.

Christ Church, built in 1734, is at Water and South streets. There is a monument to Caesar Rodney, signer of the Declaration of Independence, in the churchyard.

A suggested **tour route** to other points of interest in Dover begins at the **Friends Meetinghouse** at Fourth and West streets. Go east to Market Street, and north to Sixth, to **Old Town Hall**. Proceed east to **Old Swede's Church** at Seventh and Church, and then east into **Fort Christina State Park**. Go north on Locust to Eleventh Street, left to Market Street to **Free Library** at corner of Tenth Street. Continue on Eleventh Street and on Pennsylvania Avenue to Union Street, turning right to Lovering Avenue, site of Delaware Academy of Medicine.

Delaware Academy of Medicine, located at Lovering Avenue and Union Street, has the largest medical library in the state as well as an interesting collection of early medical and dental instruments. The building (1816) originally housed the bank of Delaware. It was disassembled brick by brick and rebuilt in its present location in 1930. Open Monday through Friday, 8:30 a.m. to 4:30 p.m. Telephone: (302) 656-1629.

The Octagonal Schoolhouse (1836) was one of the earliest one-room schools established under the Delaware Free School Act of 1829. Located at Cowgill Corner, east of Dover on Route 9 between Leipsic and Little Creek. The school's thick stone walls are covered with whitewashed stucco. Its eight-sided shape was considered to use interior space and light more efficiently than the usual rectangular school. The schoolhouse functioned as District No. 12 in Kent County until 1930 when it was turned into a community center. Currently closed for renovation; visitors should inquire about hours. Telephone: (305) 736-4266.

Several historic sites in the **Smyrna Area** are worthy of visitation. Further information can be obtained from the Delaware Tourist Bureau, Wilmington. Toll-free telephone: (800) 282-8667 (in Delaware); (800) 441-8846 (outside the state).

The **Allee House**, a mid-18th-century Delaware plantation house, was built by a Huguenot family in 1753. It is a fine example of the Queen Anne style, with interesting architectural details including an original kitchen fireplace with lugpole and trammel. Open Saturdays and Sundays from 2:00 to 5:00 p.m. This home is located on Dutch Neck Road, two and a half miles north of Leipsic off Route 9. Telephone: (302) 736-4266 (for group tours).

Island Field Archaeological Museum (part of the Delaware State Museum) is built over a carefully excavated prehistoric cemetery occupied by aboriginal Indians more than 1,200 years ago. The items uncovered at the burial site have been left in place as found. Exhibits and slide shows around the perimeter show other artifacts from this area (and from Delaware as a whole) and trace the history of man from Paleo man (from 10,000 to 8,000 B.C.) through Woodland man (from 1,000 B.C. to 1,700 A.D.). The first anthropological finds in this area were made by roadbuilders in 1928. The cemetery was found in 1967.

Bombay Hook National Wildlife Refuge is a very popular location for studying waterfowl and animal life. It includes over 12,000 acres of tidal marsh and 1,200 acres of freshwater ponds. The combination of swamp, upland, tidal marsh, and thicket provides diversity of habitat, accounting for 260 bird species observed here, as well as 34 species of mammals and 31 kinds of reptiles and amphibians. You can take the tour route, walk the nature trails, or climb up the observation towers in order to see waterfowl and wildlife. Tours, trail walks, outdoor classroom studies, movies, and slide shows are offered with advance reservations. For more information write: Refuge Manager, RD 1, Box 147, Smyrna, DE 19977. Telephone: (302) 653-9345.

WILMINGTON AREA

New Castle dates back to 1651 when Fort Casimir was built here under order of Governor Stuyvesant of New Amsterdam. The English gained control from the Dutch in 1664 when the town received its present name.

Many historic points surround **The Green**, formerly the Public Square, between Delaware and Market streets at Third Street. The **Old Court House** (1732) was Delaware's colonial capitol and county seat for many years. Now a museum, it features several portraits of signers of the Declaration of Independence as well as changing exhibits. Open Tuesday through Saturday, 10:00 a.m. to 4:30 p.m.; Sunday, 1:30 to 4:30 p.m. Admission free. Telephone: (302) 323-4453.

Town Hall (1832) and **Market Place** (1682) are at Second and Delaware streets. The **New Castle and Frenchtown Railroad Ticket Office** (1832) is at Battery Park. It was one of America's oldest railroads. A section of track is nearby. The exteriors of these sites and of the **New Castle Academy** (opened in 1798, on the Green, as a public school) can be viewed on a walking tour.

Amstel House (1730), at Fourth and Delaware streets, is now a museum. Displayed are colonial arts, handicrafts, and furnishings. Open Tuesday through Saturday, 11:00 a.m. to 4:00 p.m.; Sunday, 1:00 to 4:00 p.m. Closed November to April. Admission charge. Telephone: (302) 328-8215.

Old Presbyterian Church (1707), at 25 E. Second Street, was originally a Dutch church, built in 1657. This is believed to be the oldest Presbyterian church in the United States. Open daily, 10:00 a.m. to 5:00 p.m. Admission free.

Dutch House, 32 East Third Street, is one of the oldest houses in the state, and dates from the late 17th century. Open Tuesday through Sunday, 11:00 a.m. to 4:00 p.m. Closed November to April. Nominal admission charge. Telephone: (302) 328-8215.

The **George Read II House** on the Strand is a fine example of late Georgian/early Federal architecture. It was built between 1797 and 1804. It has been restored under the auspices of the Historical Society of Delaware. Open March through December, Tuesday through Saturday, 10:00 a.m. to 4:00 p.m.; Sunday, noon to 4:00 p.m. January and February, open weekends and during the week by appointment. Admission charge. Telephone: (302) 322-8411. The Historic Society also sponsors walking tours through the New Castle Historic District which cover the development of the town since 1650. Arrangements may be made at Read House. Charge for the tour or combined Read House and walking tour ticket.

The town of New Castle occasionally hosts special events, chief among them an annual "Day in Old New Castle" on the third Saturday of May. Twenty private houses and some lovely old gardens are opened to the public at this time. Residents wear colonial costume. There is a single admission charge to all the events. For information write: "A Day in Old New Castle," Box 166, New Castle, DE 19720.

Wilmington is seven miles north of New Castle, via Route 9. Several historic landmarks in the city are worthy of visits. **Old Swede's Church**, at Seventh and Church streets, was built in 1698. It is open from noon to 4:00 p.m., Monday through Saturday. Guide service is available. Groups should make reservations. Telephone: (302) 652-5629. **Fort Christina Monument** is located in a small park at the foot of Seventh Street close to Old Swede's Church. **Old Town Hall** (1798), facing Market Street Mall, was built on land given by John Dickinson, signer of the Declaration of Independence. Inside there are exhibits of 18th- and 19th-century decorative arts, antique toys, restored jail cells, and changing exhibits on the history of Delaware. Open Tuesday through Friday, noon to 4:00 p.m.; Saturday, 10:00 a.m. to 4:00 p.m. Admission free. **Old Friends Meeting House**, built in 1816, is nearby at Fourth and West streets.

Across the Mall is **Willingtown Square**, a group of restored 18th-century homes which can be viewed from the outside. The Historical Society of Delaware has its offices here. The Eclectic Depot, an excellent museum gift shop, is also located in this block. Open Tuesday through Friday, 11:00 a.m. to 3:00 p.m. Telephone: (302) 655-7161. Nearby is the **Grand Opera House** (1871), now Delaware Center for Performing Arts. It has a striking cast-iron facade.

Tourists interested in art may wish to see the permanent collection at the **Delaware Art Museum**, 2301 Kentmere Parkway. The museum possesses several major collections, including the largest collection of English Pre-Raphaelite paintings and decorative arts in the United States, 19th- and 20th-century American painting collections, and important works by Howard Pyle and other well-known illustrators. Changing exhibits are also featured. The museum contains a library, a sales and rental gallery, and a museum store. Open Tuesday, 10:00 a.m. to 9:00 p.m.; Wednesday to Saturday, 10:00 a.m. to 5:00 p.m.; Sunday, noon to 5:00 p.m. Admission free. Telephone: (302) 571-9590.

The Library, 505 Market Street Mall, is well worth a visit. It contains excellent material on the history of Delaware and the Middle Atlantic area from colonial times to the present day, as well as unique material on genealogy and local history. There is an emphasis on political, legal, economic, and social history, including books, manuscripts, pamphlets (including some from the famous "pamphleteers" of the American Revolution), ledgers, maps, charts, sketches, deeds, wills, reports, "broadsides" (early printed political posters), photographs, and newspaper collections, including the printed and private papers of Delaware families. Open Monday, 1:00 to 9:00 p.m.; Tuesday through Friday, 9:00 a.m. to 5:00 p.m. Telephone: (302) 655-7161.

Ashland Covered Bridge is on Route 82 in the village of Ashland (in the northwestern part of the state near the Pennsylvania border). The bridge is a 52-foot Town lattice bridge, built around 1870. It is about a half-hour drive from Wilmington.

The Henry Francis Dupont Winterthur Museum is a major attraction in the Wilmington area. It is on Route 52, five miles west of the city. It contains more than 100 period rooms reflecting the American domestic scene between 1640 and 1840. The *New York Times* described the collection as being so fine that "no other collection comes even close in matching its range, its richness, and its quality." South Wing is open without appointment. Open Tuesday through Saturday, 10:00 a.m. to 4:00 p.m.; Sunday, noon to 4:00 p.m. Admission charge. Special events and tours, such as Winterthur in Autumn, Yuletide at Winterthur, Open House, Winterthur in Spring, the Steeplechase, and Country Fair, are scheduled throughout the year. Reservations needed for some tours and events. Telephone: (302) 656-8591.

The Winterthur Gardens, a major accomplishment in themselves, boast unusual flowers from all over the world interspersed with stands of trees, winding brooks, and broad vistas. Garden tours are self-guided unless the visitor chooses a tram tour, available mid-April through mid-November, for an extra charge. Open year round, Tuesday through Saturday, 9:00 a.m. to 5:00 p.m.; Sunday, noon to 5:00 p.m. Admission charge. Breakfast, lunch, and snacks are served in the Pavilion. Light lunches are available from the Gallery Beverage Bar. Winterthur continues to make a significant effort to be accessible to visitors with special needs. There are elevators. Wheelchairs can be provided or accommodated. Sign language interpretation is available when telephone arrangements are made in advance. Telephone: (302) 428-1411 (for hearing impaired information).

Delaware Museum of Natural History, five miles west of Wilmington at Greenville on Route 52, features exhibits in natural settings. Of special interest are Hall of Mammals, Hall of Birds with a 27-pound egg of the extinct Elephant Bird, and Hall of Shells, which includes a section of Australia's Great Barrier Reef. Open Monday through Saturday, 9:30 a.m. to 4:30 p.m.; Sunday, noon to 5:00 p.m. Admission charge. A nature film is shown Wednesday through Saturday each hour on the half-hour from 10:30 a.m. to 3:00 p.m., and on Sunday at 1:00 p.m. and at 3:00 p.m. The Discovery Room, where children can participate in a hands-on approach to science and learning, is open to school groups by reservation during the week. On Sundays it is open to all children after each film showing. Telephone: (302) 658-9111.

The Hagley Museum, the original du Pont mills, estate, and gardens, is located on a 238-acre site on Brandywine Creek. The museum grounds are three miles north of Wilmington via Routes 52 and 141. This is a National Historic Landmark. You may visit the museum buildings and take a bus ride along the Brandywine. Open daily, April through December, 9:30 a.m. to 4:30 p.m. January through March, Monday through Friday, one tour daily at 1:30 p.m.; weekends, 9:30 a.m. to 4:30 p.m. Admission charge. Telephone: (302) 658-2401.

Eleutherian Mills, the Georgian residence built by E. I. du Pont in 1803 overlooking his powder yards, and the First Office of the Du Pont Company, are open the same hours as The Hagley Museum (1837). There is Lammot du Pont's Workshop, and a Barn containing a sight-and-sound Cooper (keg maker) Shop plus displays of 19th-century vehicles, farm implements, and weathervanes. There is also an excellent library of business and economic history. For the daily weekday tour January through March, call for tour times. Visitors must board a bus at The Hagley Museum for the trip to this area. No extra admission charge. Telephone: (302) 658-2400.

Nemours Mansion, named for the original du Pont residence in northern France, was built by Alfred I. duPont. An adapted version of a Louis XVI French chateau, it was completed in 1910. The mansion contains 77 rooms. Many of them with their fine rugs, tapestries, art, and furniture can be viewed by the public. One-third of a mile of French-style gardens surround the house. Visitors must be over 16 years of age and must join a tour. Tours are offered May through November, Tuesdays through Saturdays, 9:00 a.m., 11:00 a.m., 1:00 p.m., 3:00 p.m.; Sundays, 11:00 a.m., 1:00 p.m., 3:00 p.m. Admission charge. For reservations or information write: Reservations Office, PO Box 109, Wilmington, DE 19899. Telephone: (302) 651-6912.

Rockwood, a country estate built in the 1850s three miles north of Wilmington at 610 Shipley Road, is a fine example of rural Gothic architecture. Furnishings range from the 18th century to the Victorian period, reflecting ways of life of five generations of one family. Open Tuesday through Saturday, 11:00 a.m. to 4:00 p.m. (last tour begins at 3:00

p.m.). There is a gift shop and garden tours are also available. Telephone: (302) 571-7776.

For a change in scenery, the tourist may find attractive a ride on the **Wilmington and Western Railroad,** an old steam rail line which chugs through scenic Red Clay Valley. The depot is on Route 41, four miles west of Wilmington. A lay-over is permitted at the Mt. Cuba picnic grounds. Open May through October, Sunday at noon, 1:15 p.m., 2:00 p.m., and 3:45 p.m. June through September, Saturday, noon, 1:15 p.m., and 3:45 p.m. Admission charge. The **Wilmington and Western Flea Market,** the largest open-air bazaar in Delaware, is on the grounds of Greenbank station. Open April through November, weekends only, dawn until dusk. Telephone: (302) 998-1930.

A return via Route 301 and Chesapeake Bay Bridge presents an opportunity to visit several historic shrines in the Odessa-Middletown area approximately 25 miles south of Wilmington.

In Odessa there are three houses, constituting a branch of Winterthur, which deserve special attention. **Corbit-Sharp House** (1774) is a beautiful example of Georgian colonial architecture. It now contains numerous fine antiques from the state of Delaware, as well as original furnishings belonging to the Corbit family. A formal garden and herb garden adjoin the mansion. Another Georgian home is the **Wilson-Warner House** (1740), also a museum, furnished in period furniture and antiquities. The third of the museum trio is **Brick Hotel Gallery** (1822). The building served as a hotel and tavern for over a century before being used as a private residence. It is now an art gallery containing period furniture, American silver, and the Sewell C. Biggs collection of 18th- and 19th-century American paintings. Telephone: (302) 378-4069. Admission charge for each site. (Discount on combined ticket for all three sites.) The hours listed also apply to all three sites. Open Tuesday through Saturday, 10:00 a.m. to 4:30 p.m.; Sunday, 1:00 to 4:30 p.m. Closed Mondays, Christmas Eve, Christmas, New Year's, Thanksgiving, and the Fourth of July.

Old Drawyers Presbyterian Church is a brick structure erected in 1773 on the site of an earlier church. This historic shrine has an adjoining graveyard and beautiful grounds.

The **Appoquinimink Friends Meeting House** in Odessa is only 20 feet square, probably the smallest brick house of worship in the country. This church, built in 1785, is still used each week. **Old Union Methodist Church,** four miles south of Odessa on Route 13, was built in 1847. **St. Anne's Episcopal Church** on East Green Street, a mile south of Middletown on Route 897, is dated 1768. It has original box pews and a Palladian window, as well as a classic example of a wineglass pulpit with clerk's desk, lectern, and pulpit in three tiers. The church grounds contain lovely boxwood and numerous colonial graves near a 300-year-old William Penn Oak, one of the few in the country. Telephone: (302) 378-2401.

The **Welsh Tract Baptist Church,** a few miles south of Newark, Delaware, at Cooch's Bridge on Route 72, was founded in the early 1700s by Welsh settlers. The brick church, built in 1746, bears marks of cannonballs used in a skirmish between Washington's and Cornwallis's troops in 1777.

Lums Pond State Park contains the largest inland lake in the state, built many decades ago to supply water for the locks of the Chesapeake and Delaware Canal. The park is accessible from the Washington area and Baltimore via I-95 to Elkton, north on Route 40, south on Route 301. You may want to spend some time here enjoying the many outdoor activities, while planning short excursions to any of the historic-cultural sites within an hour's drive.

Among summer activities, which extend from Memorial Day to Labor Day, are: hiking, fishing, camping, canoeing, sailing, power boating, swimming, and rowing. There are pleasant horse trails, and horses can be rented from a private stable near the park. Athletic facilities include those for baseball, basketball, volleyball, tennis, shuffleboard, lacrosse, and soccer. Nature study and evening programs are offered during summer months. Observe a beaver colony at work as you walk along the Beaver Pond Nature Trail. You also can dig for marine fossils in old canal soil. Admission charge. For further information, write: Park Manager, PO Box 56, Kirkwood, DE 19708. Telephone: (302) 368-6989.

PENNSYLVANIA

The Keystone State was settled first by the Swedes and Dutch, and then by the British. William Penn landed at Chester, DE, at the head of a band of Quakers and friends, more than 300 years ago, in 1682. He had accepted, in the New World, the largest grant of land ever given to a British subject (in payment of a debt owed by the Crown to his family). By 1700 the areas presently known as Philadelphia, and Bucks, Chester, Delaware, and Montgomery counties, had been settled.

The city of Philadelphia, which served as the state capital until the end of the 1700s, has played an illustrious role in the history of the nation. In addition to hosting the First Continental Congress at which the Declaration of Independence was written and adopted, and providing the lion's share of financial backing for the Revolution, the city served as the new nation's first capital from 1775 to 1789, and (after surrendering its position to New York for one year) again, from 1790 to 1800. During the Civil War it threw in its lot with the North. Early in its history it became a vital shipping center. During and after World War I it became a major industrial city. We know it today as a city important in manufacturing and commerce, as well as one of the richest historical sites in the country.

In the southeastern Pennsylvania counties near Philadelphia there is much to see that is unique to each of the many national, cultural, and religious groups that settled here. William Penn considered religious freedom the pivotal one, and Pennsylvania boasts a particularly large and varied trove of very lovely churches. Almost everything one might wish to see, from world-famous Longwood Gardens to a number of the oldest houses, stores, inns, museums, and places of work in the country, can be visited. Here, too, are some of the nation's loveliest residential areas, most fashionable shopping streets, most creative artists' colonies, best nightclubs, and the single largest civic park (Philadelphia's Fairmount Park) in the world.

As we travel westward into the state one of the major sites is Valley Forge. Here Washington's army encamped from December 13, 1777, to June 19, 1778, having crossed from New Jersey to avoid the British and regroup during a hard winter. Approximately 11,000 strong, the Continental Army spent a bitter, under-clothed and under-fed winter. Many soldiers did not even have boots. The suffering was overwhelming, so terrible in fact, that Washington almost decided to abandon the cause. It is impossible to visit here and not be moved by the sacrifices which helped to purchase our freedom.

Even farther west we come to the famous Pennsylvania Dutch country, famous for delicious food, beautiful farms, magnificent examples of trades and handicrafts, and distinctive, immaculate houses. The word *Dutch* actually was a mispronunciation of the word *Deutsch*, meaning "German," but the usage has survived.

The unique architecture of each barn in Montgomery County, the art shows of Bucks County, the marvelous antique shops, the hostelries which have catered to travelers for two centuries, are only a few of the discoveries to be made in Pennsylvania.

PHILADELPHIA

Philadelphia, "Cradle of Liberty" and birthplace of our nation, deserves a place on every weekender's itinerary. This city and surrounding counties north, south, and west of the city offer a panorama of historic landmarks, 20th-century architecture, picturesque countryside, and beautiful homes, gardens, and parks.

Begin your tour of the city with a visit to **Independence National Historical Park**, under jurisdiction of the National Park Service. This park area includes some 40 historical sites located between Front and Seventh streets, and Pine and Market from Second to Sixth streets. A walk of about two miles which begins and ends at or near Independence Hall passes most of these Independence Park sites here in the heart of Philadelphia. Most of them are open to the public. All sites in the park that are accessible to tourists are open during the same hours. Information for all (and a walking

tour map) can be obtained at the Independence Park Visitors
Center on Third Street near Chestnut, as well as at some of
the other sites. A few of the more important landmarks are
mentioned immediately below. The walking tour described
here includes some sites outside of the official boundaries of
the park. Open 9:00 a.m. to 5:00 p.m., daily, Labor Day to
Memorial Day (all sites). Open 9:00 a.m. to 6:00 p.m., daily,
Memorial Day to Labor Day. Admission free (all sites). Telephone: (215) 597-8974 or 627-1776 (24-hour recording). **Independence Hall** enjoys a gracious setting on a broad green
mall. As you step inside the front door, you imagine the
Revolutionary War patriots in the Assembly Room signing
the Declaration of Independence, or debating the provisions
of the Constitution. Special tours, just for this building,
depart every 15 minutes from the east wing. In front of
Independence Hall, across Chestnut Street, is **Liberty Bell
Pavilion**, home of the famed Liberty Bell. Read the words
cast deep into the metal around the top: "Proclaim Liberty
Throughout All the Land Unto All the Inhabitants Thereof."
It was this bell's deep voice that summoned the people of
Philadelphia to the first public reading of the Declaration of
Independence on that hot eighth of July 1776. A recorded
voice tells the history of the bell.

Adjoining Independence Hall is **Congress Hall**, a bus-
tling place from 1790 to 1800, when Philadelphia was the
national capital and both houses met in this building. Here
Washington was inaugurated for his second term. Behind the
Hall, to the south, is **Independence Mall**. On summer evenings, a historical Sound and Light presentation, "A Nation is
Born," is given here. Around the corner on Fifth Street is the
Old Custom House, later Second U.S. Bank, built in 1824.
This building, a fine example of Greek revival architecture,
houses an exhibit of old Philadelphia furnishings, and a
portrait gallery of Revolutionary War patriots.

The **Fire Museum** is located at 147 North Second Street
at Quarry Street. The museum depicts 300 years of fire-
fighting history, authentic examples of equipment, tools, and
fire fighters' regalia. Open Tuesday through Sunday, 9:00
a.m. to 5:00 p.m. Admission free. Telephone: (215) 923-1438.

Go to Arch Street and turn right until you reach the
Betsy Ross House, 239 Arch Street. This tiny brick residence with the Stars and Stripes flying in front is where
(according to tradition) Ross lived and made the first American flag with its circle of 13 stars. The house has been

restored and furnished with authentic pieces from the Revolutionary period. In addition to the Flag Room there is a room where the Ross family is supposed to have had its upholstery shop. Open 9:00 a.m. to 5:00 p.m., daily. Late April through late October, 9:00 a.m to 6:00 p.m. Tours are self-guided. Admission free. Telephone: (215) 627-5343. Continue to Fourth Street to the **Arch Street Friends Meeting House** on the left. This structure, which dates from 1804, is the oldest Quaker meetinghouse in Philadelphia. Open Monday through Saturday, 10:00 a.m. to 4:00 p.m. Admission free. Telephone: (215) 627-2667. At the corner of Fifth Street is the **Christ Church Burial Ground**. Seven signers of the Declaration of Independence are buried here.

On the Mall (at Eighth and Spruce streets), visit the **National Museum of American Jewish History** and **Mikveh Israel Chapel**; in the adjacent graveyard, see the graves of Rebecca Gratz, Haym Solomon (a patriot and financial backer of the American Revolution), and other Jewish patriots. This is the oldest Jewish congregation in Philadelphia, founded in 1740. Telephone: (215) 923-3811.

On Second Street between Market and Arch streets stands one of America's most beautiful religious buildings, **Christ Church**, completed in 1754. (The congregation was founded in 1695.) There, row upon row, are the straight-backed pews where George Washington, John Adams, Benjamin Franklin, and many other patriots worshipped. It has one of North America's oldest Palladian windows and a notable wine glass pulpit, as well as the font where William Penn was baptized.

Between Third and Fourth streets is **Franklin Court**, dedicated to the life of Ben Franklin. Open daily, 9:00 a.m. to 5:00 p.m. Across the street on Chestnut is the **Marine Corps Memorial Museum**. Open daily, 9:00 a.m. to 5:00 p.m. Next door at 320 Chestnut Street is **Carpenter's Hall** (although located physically in the park, this is privately owned by the Carpenters Association), site of the meeting of the First Continental Congress, held September 1774, where Washington, Patrick Henry, and others denounced British colonial policies. The museum itself is devoted to 18th-century building procedures and the early decades of the Carpenter Company itself (formed by a group of master builder-designers who banded together to protect their trade and assist each other in times of need). Open Tuesday through Sunday, 10:00 a.m. to 4:00 p.m. Closed Mondays. January through February,

Wednesday to Sunday, 10:00 a.m. to 4:00 p.m. Admission free. Telephone: (215) 925-0167.

Hill-Physick-Keith House, at 321 South Fourth Street, was the home of Philip Syng Physick, father of American surgery. Open Tuesday through Saturday, 10:00 a.m. to 4:00 p.m.; Sunday, 1:00 to 4:00 p.m. Closed holidays except the Fourth of July and Labor Day. Closed for special functions. Admission charge.

At the corner of Walnut and Fourth streets is the **Todd House** (1776). Early in its history it was the home of Dolley Payne Todd before she married James Madison, fourth president of the United States. Telephone: (215) 597-8975. Guided tours of Todd House and neighboring **Bishop White House** can be arranged by going to the Visitors Center at Third and Chestnut streets as early as possible on the day you wish to take the tour (or, even better, the preceding day as all tours tend to be fully booked by noon). Tours are held approximately every hour on the hour, beginning at 10:00 a.m. Only 10 people are allowed on each tour. (The tours sometimes go to Todd House only.) These are the only two sites in Independence National Historical Park which have tours handled in this manner.

Across Walnut Street at 321 Willings Alley is **St. Joseph's Church,** first built in 1733, and the oldest Catholic church in Philadelphia. The church is not part of the park itself, but is open to the public. Open 7:00 a.m. to 6:00 p.m., daily. Admission free. Telephone: (215) 923-1733. Across, at the corner of Third Street, is Bishop White House, home of the "Father of the American Protestant Episcopal Church." At Third and Chestnut streets is the **First Bank of the United States** (built in 1795), oldest bank building in the nation. This is a private bank library, not open to the public. Only the outside can be viewed by the tourist.

Nearby, toward Fourth Street, the visitor passes the **Pemberton House,** home of the Army-Navy Museum. At the corner of Third and Walnut streets, on the left, is the old Philadelphia Stock Exchange, built in 1832. In the middle of the next block is **Powel House,** the home of Samuel Powel, first mayor of Philadelphia. It was built in 1765. (This is not part of the National Park, but is maintained by the Landmark Society.) Open Monday through Saturday, 10:00 a.m. to 4:00 p.m.; Sunday, 1:00 to 4:00 p.m. Admission charge. Telephone: (215) 627-0364.

Just beyond Market, on Second Street, is **Christ Church,**

erected in 1727. Washington, Adams, Franklin, Morris, Lafayette, and many members of the Continental Congress worshipped here.

Thaddeus Kosciusko House (1775), at Third and Pine streets, contains exhibits which detail the owner's contribution to the American Revolution. Open daily, 9:00 a.m. to 5:00 p.m. Telephone: (215) 597-7132. **Perelman Antique Toy Museum**, in Abercrombie House (1758), at 268-270 South Second Street, contains approximately 3,000 American toys dating from 1820. Some are animated. Admission charge. Telephone: (215) 922-1070.

As mentioned above, there are about 20 other sites belonging to Independence National Historical Park, which can be visited by the tourist (although a few only from the exterior). The hours and information number for all are listed at the beginning of this description.

A superb collection of ship models, paintings, and marine lore may be seen at the **Philadelphia Maritime Museum**, located at 251 South 18th Street. Open Monday through Saturday, 10:00 a.m. to 5:00 p.m.; Sunday, 1:00 to 5:00 p.m. Admission charge. Telephone: (215) 925-5439.

Elsewhere in the city is **Penn's Landing**, Philadelphia's urban waterfront where Philadelphia founder William Penn landed his ship in 1682. Majestic sailing vessels, unique floating restaurants, museums, and landscaped gardens offer visitors a recreational paradise.

Of interest is the *Gazela of Philadelphia*, an old Portuguese square rigger docked on the Delaware River at Penn's Landing. Open daily, noon to 5:00 p.m. Admission charge. Telephone: (215) 923-9030.

The *USS Olympia*, the flagship of Admiral Dewey at the Battle of Manila Bay in the Spanish-American War, and *USS Becuna*, a Guppy Class World War II submarine, are also docked at Penn's Landing and may be visited. Aboard you can see the big guns, the torpedo tubes, and the Admiral's quarters. Open daily, 10:00 a.m. to 4:30 p.m. Closed Christmas and New Year's. Admission charge (one charge for both ships). Telephone: (215) 922-1898.

The **Port of History Museum**, at Delaware Avenue and Walnut Street, features frequently changing exhibits, international arts and crafts, and presentations of dance, music, and theater. Open Wednesday to Sunday, 10:00 a.m. to 4:30 p.m. Admission charge. Telephone: (215) 925-3804.

Philadelphia's new look is **Penn Center, Centre Square,**

and **Dilworth Plaza**, an ultramodern city-within-a-city. Here, Claes Oldenburg's 45-foot-high "Clothespin" sculpture stands before 40-story buildings gleaming in aluminum, enamel, and stainless steel. Penn Center, Centre Square, and Dilworth Plaza begin at **City Hall** (the world's largest municipal building) and reach westward toward the Schuylkill River along the John F. Kennedy Boulevard, a broad avenue reminiscent of Europe. Tree-dotted esplanades run between the buildings and, below street level, a concourse houses smart shops and restaurants. Across the way stands City Hall. It towers 548 feet above the intersection of Broad and Market streets, and is topped by a 37-foot statue of William Penn. A circular observation platform at the base of the statue gives visitors a full circle of spectacular views.

For shopping, there's Philadelphia's **Gallery Malls I and II**, more than 250 indoor stores in the heart of downtown. In the city's renovated Society Hill area is **Head House Square** and **Newmarket**, an architectural wonderland of unique glass boutiques. The area has become a prototype for urban restoration projects across the United States.

You can spend days visiting museums and galleries in the Philadelphia area. Some of the major ones are described below.

Visitors can delight in the **Philadelphia Museum of Art**, at 26th Street and Benjamin Franklin Parkway, with its priceless collections of paintings by American and European masters. Lovers of antiques will enjoy visiting the period rooms and exhibits of oriental rugs and objets d'art. Open Wednesday through Sunday, 10:00 a.m. to 5:00 p.m. Admission charge. Telephone: (215) 763-8100 or 787-5450 for group tours. **The Rodin Museum**, which contains the largest collection of sculptures by Auguste Rodin outside Paris, is located at Benjamin Franklin Parkway at 22nd Street. It is administered by the Philadelphia Museum of Art. Open Tuesday through Sunday, 10:00 a.m. to 5:00 p.m. Donations suggested. Telephone: (215) 787-5476.

University Museum of Archeology/Anthropology (of the University of Pennsylvania), 33rd and Spruce streets, is a "museum of man" with important archaeological and anthropological collections pertaining to ancient and primitive cultures around the world. Major Egyptian, Mesopotamian, Mayan and Meso-American, North and South American, Polynesian, Chinese, and African exhibits, to name just a few, are housed here. In addition special exhibits, cultural events, weekend films, etc., are scheduled for adults and children. Open Tuesday through Saturday, 10:00 a.m. to 4:30 p.m.; Sunday, 1:00 to 5:00 p.m. Closed on summer Sundays. Telephone: (215) 898-4000.

The **Please Touch Museum for Children**, at 210 North 21st Street, was the first museum in the United States for children ages seven and younger. Children are introduced to the museum experience with a variety of cultural, art, and science exhibits. The Childlife Center, a permanent exhibit focusing on the history of childhood in the Delaware Valley, offers an opportunity for children to understand their contributions to society. Open Tuesday to Saturday, 10:00 a.m. to 4:30 p.m.; Sunday, 12:30 to 4:30 p.m. Admission charge. Telephone: (215) 963-0666 or 963-0667.

On Fifth Street (at Arch Street) is the **U.S. Mint**. Free tours, showing the production of U.S. coins, are offered. Open Monday through Friday, 9:00 a.m. to 4:30 pm.; Saturday and Sunday in summer, 9:30 a.m. to 4:30 p.m.

At 15 South Seventh Street is the **Atwater Kent Museum**. The museum, the first home of the Franklin Institute, displays rare prints, paintings, models, and memorabilia reflecting the social and cultural history of Philadelphia. The museum features both permanent and rotating exhibits. Among the items in the permanent collection are photographs of Hog Island (the largest shipyard in the world prior to World War I), a complete collection of the photographic plates of Eadweard Muybridge (one of the pioneers in motion study), a history of Philadelphia through maps, a history of the first 200 years of Philadelphia, a William Penn exhibit, and a history of the city's police and fire departments and other municipal services. Open Tuesday through Saturday, 9:30 a.m. to 5:00 p.m. Admission free. Telephone: (215) 922-3031.

The **Afro-American Historical and Cultural Museum**, at Seventh and Arch streets, opened in 1976. Exhibits trace black history from its African heritage, through the Revolutionary and Civil wars, and up to the present day. Another gallery is devoted to art and photographs by black artists. Open Tuesday through Saturday, 10:00 a.m. to 5:00 p.m.; Sunday, noon to 6:00 p.m. Admission charge. Telephone: (215) 574-0380.

For both adults and children the oldest natural history museum in the United States is a must. Here at the **Academy of Natural Sciences Museum** with its great African Hall, exhibits include Egyptian mummies, giant dinosaurs, **rare** animals, an African cave, minerals, gems, and a live animal show. A permanent exhibit, "Discovering Dinosaurs," features more than a dozen dinosaur specimens, including a huge Tyrannosaurus Rex, as well as many hands-on displays. Open daily, 10:00 a.m. to 4:00 p.m. Admission charge. Closed Thanksgiving, Christmas, and New Year's. For children there is a special museum room called *The Outside-In*, where they can see and touch live animals. Open Monday through Friday, 10:00 a.m. to 4:00 p.m.; weekends, 10:00 a.m. to 5:00 p.m. Telephone (for the entire museum): (215) 299-1000.

The **Franklin Institute Science Museum** is a city museum that interprets scientific facts in simple and dramatic form. Displays, many operated by push buttons, cover astronomy, atomic energy, chemistry, electric communications, and the graphic arts. It is located at 20th Street and Benjamin Franklin Parkway. Also at Franklin Institute is the famous **Fels Planetarium**, where the universe unfolds before your eyes. Open Monday through Saturday, 10:00 a.m. to 5:00 p.m.; Sunday, noon to 5:00 p.m. Admission charge (for the institute). Nominal admission charge (in addition for the planetarium). Telephone: (215) 448-1200 or 564-3375 (recording).

Graff House, on the southwest corner of Seventh and Market, is a reconstruction of the house where Jefferson wrote the Declaration of Independence.

Visit the **Mummers Museum**, at Second Street and Washington Avenue, to see flamboyant exhibits highlighting the historical tradition of the Philadelphia Mummers Parade. The costume displays are accompanied by videotapes of the parades. Open Tuesday to Saturday, 9:30 a.m. to 5:00 p.m.; Sunday, noon to 5:00 p.m. Admission charge. Telephone: (215) 336-3050.

For the gourmet or gourmand there is a delightful open-air Italian market which extends from Ninth and Christian to Ninth and Wharton streets. The booths are set up beginning at dawn, and are laden with fruit and vegetables, meat and fish, homemade pastries, and imported cheeses and oils. Some handicrafts are displayed in the section near Federal Street. Open Tuesday through Friday, 8:00 a.m. to 5:00 p.m.; Saturday, 7:00 a.m. to 5:00 p.m. Telephone: (215) 929-5792.

On the Delaware River in southwest Philadelphia **Old Fort Mifflin**, called the "Alamo of the Revolutionary War," has been restored and is open to visitors. It is located on Old Fort Mifflin Road, at the end of Island Road, beyond the airport. Militia musters and patriotic activities are scheduled from time to time. Open weekends, 11:00 a.m. to 5:00 p.m. Nominal admission charge. Telephone: (215) 365-5194.

Fairmount Park System comprises more than 8,000 acres of rolling countryside, flower gardens, woods, sparkling streams, a bicycle path, and a hundred miles of bridle paths. This is the largest civic park in the world. Winding through the park is the Schuylkill River, edged with hundred-year-old boat clubs and dotted with sailboats and the fragile rowing shells of college and club crews. The park contains 23 historical houses, once the country homes of early Philadelphians. Eight of the most interesting houses have been restored and are open to the public. They are: Cedar Grove, Laurel Hill, Lemon Hill, Mount Pleasant, Solitude, Strawberry Mansion, Sweetbriar, and Woodford. A Japanese house with garden, and a cabin lived in by General Grant in the last days of the Civil War, can also be seen. Hours houses are open vary. It is best to telephone in advance for information on this as well as on available bus tours. Admission charge. Combination house tour tickets available. Telephone: (215) 686-2176.

You can attend one of the "Under the Stars" free summer concerts at **Fredric R. Mann Music Center**, other shows at **Robin Hood Dell East**, or see a summer performance at the **John B. Kelly Playhouse** in the park. The **Zoological Garden**, also in the park, is the oldest zoo in the United States, housing more than 1,600 birds, animals, and reptiles. Open daily, hours vary; call for specifics. Closed Thanksgiving, Christmas Eve, Christmas Day, and New Year's. Admission charge. Telephone: (215) 243-1100.

On the far side of the Schuylkill River in Germantown there are two places of interest not very far from each other. **Deshler-Morris House** (1772), 5442 Germantown Avenue, was used by George Washington from 1793 to 1794. It has been restored and furnished in period. Open April through December, Tuesday to Sunday, 1:00 to 4:00 p.m. Closed legal holidays. Telephone: (215) 596-1748.

Beyond is **Cliveden** (1763-67), which was built as the country residence of Chief Justice Benjamin Chew, a lawyer, jurist, and political figure from Philadelphia. Shortly after it was completed it was the scene of a battle between the Continental Army under Washington, and British troops who had taken the house. The grounds still show the marks of fighting. The Chew family lived here for another 200 years before the house was turned into a museum. The library contains 200,000 pages of Chew family papers. Throughout the house there are examples of some of the finest 18th- and 19th-century furniture built in Philadelphia, as well as family portraits, and Chinese porcelain made specifically for the Chews. Open April through December, Tuesday to Saturday, 10:00 a.m. to 4:00 p.m. Telephone: (215) 848-1777.

To plan visits to Philadelphia, write to the Philadelphia Convention and Visitors Bureau, Three Penn Center Plaza, 19102. Telephone: (215) 636-3319.

CHESTER AND DELAWARE COUNTIES

From Baltimore it is approximately 65 miles, via Exit 32 of I-695 and north on Route 1, to West Grove, the first stop on a tour of Chester and Delaware counties. The initial point of interest on Route 1 is the **Red Rose Inn**, near West Grove in Jennersville. This inn, founded in 1740, has served travelers for more than 235 years. Each year, at a public ceremony on the first Saturday after Labor Day, a rent of one red rose is duly paid by the inn owners to a descendant of William Penn in accordance with the original deed. Open Monday through Thursday, 11:30 a.m. to 9:00 p.m.; Friday and Saturday, 11:30 a.m. to 10:00 p.m.; Sunday, 11:30 a.m. to 2:00 p.m. and 4:00 to 8:00 p.m. Telephone: (215) 869-3003.

The adjacent **Star Rose Gardens** are a beautiful sight from July through October. Visitors can either walk or drive through the grounds. Across the highway from Red Rose Inn is the old **Fanlight House**, now an antique shop. Its formal sunken gardens and boxwood hedges are worthy of a visit. Continue north for three miles on Route 796 and then right on Route 926 to Route 841 and left half a mile to **Primitive Hall and Library**, a noted example of early county architecture. A mile beyond is a long wooden fence which marks the beginning of part of the noted **King Ranch**. This 12,000-acre tract is used to fatten 6,000 steers, which are shipped from Texas each year, about May 1. They graze approximately six months before being marketed.

Return to Route 926 east to intersection with Route 82 then south to Route 1 and **Kennett Square**, the birthplace and center of America's mushroom-growing industry. Today there are 450 growers in the Chester County area. Numerous gift shops sell mushrooms and mushroom-motif objects, and at the T&P Mushroom Center and others, the grower himself may wait on you.

Longwood Gardens, two miles east of Kennett Square,

is one of the nation's outstanding horticultural displays. Four acres are under glass in greenhouses, and more than 350 acres comprise waterfalls, display gardens, and fountains. Visitors may stroll through the flower, rock, herb, and vegetable gardens. One of the notable areas is the Italian Water Garden. Open daily, 9:00 a.m. to 5:00 p.m. Colored fountain displays from mid-June through August at 9:15 p.m. Admission charge. Telephone: (215) 388-6741.

Brandywine River Museum, housed in a Civil War-period grist mill, is a study and display center for the tradition of Brandywine art, especially the work of Howard Pyle, his students, and the members of the Wyeth family. The museum is located on Route 1, just east of Chadds Ford, at intersection of Route 100. Write to the museum: Box 141, Chadds Ford, PA 19317, regarding current exhibits. Open daily, 9:30 a.m. to 4:30 p.m. Admission charge. Telephone: (215) 388-7601.

Nearby, also on Route 1, is **Barnes Brinton House** (1714), restored and furnished as an early 18th-century tavern. Open Memorial Day to Labor Day, Thursday and Friday, noon to 5:00 p.m.; weekends, 10:00 a.m. to 5:00 p.m. Open rest of year by appointment. Colonial craft exhibitions during open hours on weekends. Admission charge. Telephone: (215) 388-7376.

John Chad House (1724), home of the farmer, Brandywine River ferryman, and tavern keeper who founded Chadds Ford, is located on Route 100, one-quarter mile north of US Route 1. It has been furnished in early 18th-century style. Beehive-oven bread-baking exhibitions are held during weekend open hours. Open Memorial Day to Labor Day, Thursday and Friday, noon to 5:00 p.m.; weekends, 10:00 a.m. to 5:00 p.m. Open fall, winter, and spring by appointment. Admission charge. Telephone: (215) 388-7376.

The **Christian C. Sanderson Museum** is located near the Brandywine River Museum, on Route 100 near Route 1. It includes a collection of early Wyeth family art, many mementos of the Battle of Brandywine, a collection of presidential autographs, exhibits of Indian artifacts, and all sorts of Americana that belonged to the Sanderson family. The Barn Shops and Chadds Ford Inn are adjacent. Open weekends, 1:00 to 4:30 p.m. Write the Museum: Chadds Ford, PA 19317. Telephone: (215) 388-6345.

Brandywine Battlefield State Historical Park is located one mile west of Chadds Ford. The battle, fought on

September 11, 1777, resulted in the British capture of Phila-delphia, at that time the U.S. capital. The headquarters of General Washington and Marquis de Lafayette were located here and may be visited. Open daily (except Monday), June through September, 9:00 a.m. to 8:00 p.m.; October through May, open weekdays (except Monday), 9:00 a.m. to 5:00 p.m.; Saturday, Sunday, holidays, noon to 5:00 p.m. Telephone: (215) 459-3342.

At Painter's Crossroads, turn left two miles on Route 202 for a stop at **Brinton House**, erected in 1704, and ancient **Penn Oak**, a 300-year-old tree with a 21-foot diameter. It is one mile west of Dilworthtown on Brinton Bridge Road. Cornwallis used this tree as a gallows to hang American spies at the time of the Battle of Brandywine.

Continue north on Route 202 to **West Chester** and the **Chester County Historical Society Museum** located at 225 North High Street. It offers exhibits on local history, begin-ning with colonial times. There are furnished period rooms, and collections of silver, glass, china, pewter, and needlework. Open Tuesday and Thursday to Saturday, 10:00 a.m. to 4:00 p.m.; Wednesday, 1:00 to 8:00 p.m.; Sunday, noon to 4:00 p.m. Admission charge. Telephone: (215) 692-4800.

Among historic homes of interest to tourists are **David Townsend House**, 225 North Matlack Street. Open May through October, Tuesday, Thursday, and Saturday, 1:00 to 4:00 p.m. Open at other times by appointment. Admission charge. Also of interest are the **First Presbyterian Church**, the **Old Bank, High Street Friends Meeting**, and **Channing Way House**. Obtain information on location and hours from the Tourist Bureau. The campus of **West Chester State College** is also here, and one may wish to drive through the grounds en route to other points of interest.

Return to Route 1 and continue to Middletown Road, turn left, two miles to Forge Road and **Tyler Arboretum** (right to Painter Road). This noted arboretum has hundreds of species of trees and shrubs, all labeled, from many parts of the world. An unusual feature is the Garden for the Blind, containing plants, bulbs, and herbs selected for fragrance and distinctive texture. Labels are duplicated in braille. Open May through October, 8:00 a.m. to 8:00 p.m.; November through April, 8:00 a.m. to 7:00 p.m. Admission charge. Telephone: (215) 566-5431.

The **Franklin Mint**, the world's largest private mint, is located on Route 1, south of Media, and five miles north of

Chester. The museum contains collections of porcelain, furniture, crystal, medallions, bronze and pewter sculpture. Special demonstrations of such arts as watercolors and porcelain painting techniques are held periodically in the museum. Open Tuesday through Saturday, 9:30 a.m. to 4:30 p.m.; Sunday, 1:00 to 4:30 p.m. Closed Christmas, New Year's, Easter, and Thanksgiving. Admission free. Telephone: (215) 459-6168; (215) 459-6168.

The route is south on Route 352, to Chester, with a stop at Upland, to inspect the **Caleb Pusey House** (1693), oldest English-built house in Pennsylvania. Turn right on Upland Avenue soon after entering city limits of Chester. Caleb Pusey was a friend and business associate of William Penn and operated the first grist mill in the colony. The Pusey House is part of the Landingford Plantation, which includes the Log House, the Mill, the Barn, and mill houses. A nearby schoolhouse built about 1849 has been acquired and is being developed as a museum in which hundreds of artifacts, unearthed in the area, will be displayed. The house is open Tuesday through Sunday, 1:00 to 5:00 p.m. Admission charge.

Old **St. Paul's Churchyard**, on Third Street between Market and Welsh streets, is the oldest Swedish burial place in the United States. A marble shaft marks the grave of John Morton, signer of the Declaration of Independence. The **Penn Memorial Landing Stone** marks the spot where William Penn first set foot on his colony, October 28, 1682. It is located at Front and Penn streets.

The Delaware County Historical Society historical library, containing local records, documents, newspapers, genealogical material, etc., is located at Wolfgram Memorial Library, Widener University, Chester, PA 19013. Open Monday through Friday, 10:00 a.m. to 3:00 p.m.; first Sunday of each month, 1:00 to 5:00 p.m. Admission charge. Telephone: (215) 874-6444. The **Old Court House**, built for Governor William Penn in 1724, is the oldest building in the U.S. in continuous use. It is located at Fifth and Market streets and can be viewed from the outside only.

Deshong Memorial Arts Gallery, at 11th and Avenue of States, displays a noteworthy collection of late 19th-century European art and Asian art objects. Open Tuesday through Saturday, 10:00 a.m. to 4:00 p.m. Admission free. Telephone: (215) 499-4474. **Taylor Memorial Arboretum**, 10 Ridley Drive, offers guided tours through its grounds. Noted for its collection of heather, camellias, and ornamentals. Open Monday through Saturday, 8:00 a.m. to 4:30 p.m. Admission free. Telephone: (215) 876-2649.

From Chester the route is east on 291 to **Governor Printz Park** and **Morton Homestead**, both historic shrines of New Sweden. These historic places, built by Swedish settlers before Pennsylvania's founding as an English colony, are administered by the state Historical and Museum Commission. Turn right on Wanamaker Avenue to enter **Governor Printz Park**. In 1643, Johan Printz, Royal Governor of New Sweden, built his capital on Tinicum Island in the Delaware River. This structure and others were destroyed by fire. The remains of the capital, the first permanent European settlement in Pennsylvania established by Swedish and Finnish colonists, and Indian relics may be seen today by visitors. The park is open weekdays, 8:00 a.m. to 5:00 p.m.; Sundays, 1:00 to 5:00 p.m. Telephone: (215) 521-9360. About a mile north of the park, on the banks of Darby Creek, stands **Morton Homestead**. It is easily reached via Route 420. This log and stone structure was built in 1654 by the great-grandfather of John Morton, member of the Continental Congress and signer of the Declaration of Independence. Tradition has it that Morton was born here in 1725. Open Tuesday through Saturday, 9:00 a.m. to 5:00 p.m.; Sunday, noon to 5:00 p.m.

Continue north on Route 420 to Route 13, then turn right to Darby. On Main Street above 10th is the **Darby Friends' Meeting House**. The original structure was built in 1684. This one, the third on the site, was erected in 1805.

In order to reach Philadelphia, continue on Route 13 into the city and go down Market Street to City Hall. If you do not wish to tour Philadelphia on this trip, return via Routes 13 and 95 to the Baltimore-Washington area.

BUCKS COUNTY

Bucks County, adjoining Philadelphia on the north, is steeped in early American history. The area is noted for its scenery, artists, and lovely old inns.

For a tour of Lower Bucks County of approximately 65 miles, leave Philadelphia on Bristol Pike (1675). In Cornwell Heights, right at the city line is the **Red Lion Inn** (1730), still in operation. Delegates to the First Continental Congress stopped here. Telephone: (215) 788-3153. Two miles east, at Cornwells Avenue, is **Vandegrift Burying Ground** (1776).

Bristol, founded in 1681, has several historic buildings.

King George II Inn (formerly **Delaware House**), dating from 1765, is one of the nation's oldest inns in continuous operation as an inn. In the course of its history the inn (located at 102 Radcliffe Street) has had four presidents of the United States as guests. Telephone: (215) 788-5536. **Friends Meeting House**, Market and Wood streets, was established in 1704. Nearby is the old **St. James Episcopal Church** and cemetery. Telephone: (215) 788-2228.

Go north on Radcliffe Street, to No. 610, the Victorian home of the late Joseph R. Grundy, manufacturer and U.S. senator. Now called the **Margaret R. Grundy Museum**, the house is a fine example of Victorian architecture. It has been furnished with antiques which belonged to the Grundy family. Open Monday through Friday, 1:00 to 4:00 p.m.; Saturday, 1:00 to 3:00 p.m. Closed Saturdays in July and August. Group tours by appointment. Admission free. Telephone: (215) 788-9432. Attached to the museum by underground passage is a library. An interesting building in itself, the library was constructed underground with one wall of windows facing the river.

Every year on the third Saturday of October, an Historic Bristol Day is held featuring tours of all these historic buildings as well as a number of privately owned old houses opened especially for the occasion. Telephone: (215) 788-3443. Walking tours of the old market town on the waterfront are held on the first Friday of every month, June through September, at 7:00 p.m. The tour begins at Bristol Wharf on Mill Street at Radcliffe Street.

Pennsbury Manor is the great house built by William Penn in 1683, 26 miles from Philadelphia. The manor, on the outskirts of Morrisville, is on Pennsbury Manor Road, just off Bordentown Road, about one mile outside Tullytown. Pennsbury Manor, deserted and neglected by 1800, was completely restored in the 1940s on the basis of historical and archaeological research. Tourists may visit the manor house, back house, brewhouse, stables, plantation office and gardens, and see exhibits of archaeological artifacts. Guided tours are available. Special events and activities are scheduled from time to time. Open Tuesday through Saturday, 9:00 a.m. to 5:00 p.m.; Sunday, noon to 5:00 p.m. The last tour begins at 3:30 p.m. Closed Mondays and most state holidays. Open Memorial Day, Fourth of July, and Labor Day. Admission charge. Telephone: (215) 946-0400.

Fallsington is a colonial village built around the **Friends**

Meeting House in which William Penn worshipped. Although the original meetinghouse is no longer standing, three meetinghouses built in 1728, 1789, and 1841 still are and can be viewed from the exterior. The last is still in use by the Friends. The original meetinghouse was built in 1690. It is located three miles southwest of Trenton, only a few miles from the intersection of Route 1 and Tyburn Road.

Homes have been restored to original condition by a nonprofit organization. The **Burges-Lippincott House** is a fine example of 18th-century colonial architecture, and the **Stagecoach Tavern** has been restored as an 18th-century stage stop. Altogether, more than 25 pre-Revolutionary War buildings are clustered around Meetinghouse Square. The **Schoolmaster's House** (1757) provides a gateway to the square. The **Moon-Williamson House**, one section of which shows evidence of Swedish occupancy, is believed to be the oldest structure in the village. Tours are conducted at 1:15 and 2:30 p.m. and include an audio-visual presentation. Open March 15 to November 15, Wednesday through Sunday, 1:00 to 5:00 p.m. Group tours can be arranged. Admission charge. A walking tour map is available from Historic Fallsington, 4 Yardley Avenue, Fallsington, PA 19054, for a nominal charge. Telephone: (215) 295-6567.

Proceed west out of Yardley on Route 332 to **Newtown**, one of Bucks County's most beautiful and picturesque colonial towns. More than three dozen colonial buildings have been preserved. The **Brick Hotel** has been serving three meals a day continuously since 1740. In the lobby is a mural depicting a colonial scene, painted by well-known artist Edward Hicks. Arrangements can be made to take a tour of the building between 9:00 a.m. and 5:00 p.m. Telephone: (215) 968-9971. The **Newtown Presbyterian Church** was erected in 1769, replacing an earlier structure. **Court Inn**, on Court Street, headquarters of the Newtown Historic Association, was a noted tavern built in 1733. It is open on Sunday, from 2:00 to 4:00 p.m. A free brochure, *Walking Tour of Newtown*, is available.

The **Hicks House**, 122 Penn Street, was the home of the noted colonial painter. **Temperance House** (1722), 5 South State Street, was named for a sign painted by Edward Hicks. **Bird-in-Hand House**, built in 1690, is the oldest frame building in the state. It served as an Army clothing depot during the Revolution. This house, now a private home, derives its

name from a Hicks sign of Franklin's famous adage: "A bird i
the hand is worth two in the bush."

Go south on Route 413 to **Langhorne**, which also has
some pre-Revolutionary War homes. Another **Hicks House**,
Bellevue and Maple avenues, was built by Edward Hicks'
grandfather. The **Richardson House** (1737), across the street,
was once a general store. It is now a community center. The
Friends Meeting, on Maple Avenue, was built in 1731.

Go west on Route 213 to **Playwicki County Park**. This
park is a mecca for bird watchers, botanists, and fishermen.
Two old stone-arched railroad bridges are favorite subjects of
artists and camera fans. Continue on Route 213 to Feasterville.
The **Buck Hotel**, at junction of Route 532, was opened in
1735. It achieved fame as a meeting place of politicians.
Return to Philadelphia via Route 532, or east on State Street
to Route 1.

For another tour take Route 532 from Philadelphia about
15 miles to **Washington Crossing**. This national shrine, now
a state park, is noted for the 22-foot, famed painting of
Leutze's *Washington Crossing the Delaware*, which is housed
in a memorial building. This is an exact copy by Robert B.
Williams, a noted artist of Washington, DC. Narration and
music accompany the exhibit. Visitors can stand at the point
of embarkation from which General Washington and his 2,400
men boarded boats on Christmas night, 1776. Their dramatic
crossing marked the turning point of the American Revolution. Admission free. Among other places of interest in the
park are the **Thompson-Neely House**, furnished with pre-
Revolutionary pieces; the **Old Ferry Inn**, a restored hostelry;
and the **Taylor House**.

The **grist mill**, built about 1740, provided meal and flour
for Continental troops. A nearby cemetery has unmarked
headstones for the graves of some of America's first unknown
soldiers. Nominal admission fee. Groups may rent picnic
pavilions. Buildings open daily, year round, Monday to Saturday, 9:00 a.m. to 5:00 p.m.; Sunday, noon to 5:00 p.m. Telephone: (215) 493-4076.

Bowman's Hill State Wildflower Preserve is located in
the upper part of the park. This preserve is best visited
during the spring and summer months. More than 800 species
of plants can be seen in natural habitats along 15 nature
trails. Guided tours are available. Open daily, 8:30 a.m. to
sundown. Admission free. Telephone: (215) 862-2924.

A detour to the **Vansant Covered Bridge** may be of

interest. Take Aquetong Road past Thompson Memorial Church, then left on Covered Bridge Road.

The main route is north to the **New Hope** area. This town is an internationally known artists' center, with many galleries and frequent art shows. It is also replete with points of historic interest, and has many antique and gift shops, fine restaurants, and unusual specialty shops.

New Hope (northwest of Washington Crossing on Route 32) dates from the 19th century, and has a number of interesting areas including a Historic District. The **New Hope Town Hall** dates from 1790 and is open to visitors during regular business hours. At 29 North Main Street is the **Old Franklin Print Shop**. Open Monday through Saturday, 10:00 a.m. to 5:00 p.m.; Sunday, 1:00 to 5:00 p.m. Admission charge. A number of older buildings can be viewed from the outside, such as the **New Hope Library** on Ferry Street, which is in a converted church, and the **Bucks County Gazette Office** on Bridge Street. Many old homes have been converted into shops: **Vansant House** on Mechanic Street (probably the oldest house in New Hope), **Coryell Mansion**, and **Flood House** (both on South Main Street).

Leisurely sightseeing trips are offered on the historic **Delaware Canal** on mule-drawn barges. Trips leave from South Main Street, daily, April through Labor Day; weekend trips during spring and fall. Fare charge. Telephone: (215) 862-2842.

For an interesting 10-mile side trip, go north on Route 32 along the old canal to **Center Bridge**, a town popularized by artist E. W. Redfield, whose stone home is at the left of the bridge. At Lumberville is the noted **"Hard Times Tavern,"** now a private home. From Cuttalossa Road, turn left past **Solebury School**, built in 1755. In **Lahaska**, off Route 263, there are many fine antique shops. A charming shopping area, **Peddler's Village** is made up of about 46 boutiques scattered about a village green. They specialize in arts and crafts and imported wares. As you continue west on Route 202, you will pass the **Buckingham Friends Meeting**, built in 1768 and used as a hospital during the Revolution (open to special tours only).

Bucks County Playhouse is now a summer theater. It was originally the Parry Mills, destroyed by fire in 1790 and rebuilt. There are regular performances from April through mid-October, and special performances throughout the rest of the year. Admission charge. Telephone: (215) 862-2041. The nearby **Parry Barn** is maintained by New Hope Historical Society, which sponsors frequent art exhibits. The **Logan Inn**, on Cannon Square, has been in operation since 1732. Telephone: (215) 862-5134.

Doylestown is farther west on Route 202. **The Mercer Museum**, built by the late Dr. Henry Mercer in 1916, houses a vast collection of tools, machines, and artifacts used prior to the age of steam. The library, with its enormous number of books and manuscripts, is a gold mine for historical researchers and genealogists. Original paintings by Edward Hicks, Jonathan and William Trego, and other famous artists are on display; also folk art, crafts, and ceramics. Open year round, Monday through Saturday, 10:00 a.m. to 5:00 p.m.; Sunday, 1:00 to 5:00 p.m. Admission charge. Telephone: (215) 345-0210.

Fonthill, on East Court Street, houses a collection of paintings, antiques, and the Mercer tiles which were made on the premises. Tour reservations are suggested. Open daily, 10:00 a.m. to 3:30 p.m. Admission charge. Telephone: (215) 348-9461. Nearby is the **Moravian Tileworks**, a working pottery, where tiles for the State Capitol buildings were made. Tours available. Open daily, 10:00 a.m. to 5:00 p.m. Admission charge. Telephone: (215) 345-6722.

From Doylestown the direct route to Philadelphia is south on Route 611. One may also visit other historic sites in **Wrightstown** which would add a few miles to the tour. Go east on Route 202 to Buckingham and right on Route 413 to Wrightstown. The **Octagonal Schoolhouse** (1802) is on Swamp Road, off Route 232. Also on Route 232 is **Old Anchor Inn** (1724), oldest public house in continuous operation in Bucks County. Telephone: (215) 598-7469.

Wrightstown is the site of the **Walking Purchase Monument**, on the Friends Meeting House grounds. It recalls the "walk" planned by Thomas Penn, whereby the land over which a man could walk in a day and a half could be purchased from the Indians. Three men started at sunrise, September 1737, and practically ran 100 miles, thus gaining 500,000 acres of the Indians' best land for a trifle. For additional information write: The Wrightstown Historical Commission, PO Box 500, Wycombe, PA 18946.

South of Wrightstown, in Tyler State Park, is the **Twining Ford Covered Bridge**, over Neshaminy Creek. It is built of hemlock, 181 feet long, the longest in the county. Telephone (for state park): (215) 968-2021. Return to Route 232 and head south into Philadelphia.

For an 80-mile extension to Upper Bucks County continue on Route 611 and turn right on Pt. Pleasant Road, to River Road along the Delaware River. The **Delaware Canal,** opened in 1830 and operated for a century, lies between the highway and river.

A splendid panoramic view of **Tohickon Creek Valley** is your reward for ascending **Boileau Rock,** a 200-foot cliff at Horseshoe Bend. Nearby, off Dark Hollow Road, are **Loux** and **Cabin Run Covered Bridges.** Proceed north on Route 32 to Tinicum Creek. The **Erwinna Covered Bridge** is a short distance to the left.

Tinicum County Park, up Route 32 a half mile, includes the old John Stover residence. An annual art festival is held in the restored Stover barn. Telephone: (215) 294-9320.

Ralph Stover State Park is located in central Bucks County, two miles off Route 32. It provides tourist cabins and facilities for hiking, fishing, swimming, nature study, and athletics. There is a mile-long trail to High Rocks, a scenic outlook point. For further information, write Park Manager, Box 209-L, R.R. 1, Pipersville, PA 18947. Telephone: (215) 982-5560.

The **Uhlerstown Covered Bridge,** over the Delaware Canal, is unique with its windows in midspan. Proceed to Upper Black Eddy, and turn left into **Ringing Rocks Park.** Rocks in this three-and-a-half-acre field of boulders, fragments of Triassic diabase, produce bell-like sounds when hit with a hammer. Nearby is an attractive waterfall. Return to Route 32 for a brief stop at **Indian Rock Hotel,** an early American inn still in service. The profile of an Indian head can be seen at the base of the palisades.

A short distance west on Route 212 leads to **Durham.** Here are ruins of **Durham Furnace,** built in 1727. It produced chains, cannonballs, and small shot for the Continental Army. Just west of the furnace is the house of **George Taylor,** a signer of the Declaration of Independence and officer of the furnace company. About one and a half miles from Durham, on Route 212, is **Haupt's Mill Covered Bridge,** over Durham Creek. Ruins of an old mill are nearby. On Route 412, 0.4 miles west of Springtown, is the **Indian Walk Monument,** the midday stop of the group of men who made the "Walking Purchase" of 1737. **Pleasant Valley,** on Route 212, is a very old settlement with many old homes.

Continue to **Quakertown,** seven miles south. This town's claim to fame rests on the legend that the Liberty Bell was hidden here in September 1777, after the British occupied Philadelphia. The bell was then kept in Allentown while the British occupied the capital of the young nation. The **Red Lion Inn** (1748) is decorated in a lovely blend of colonial and Victorian styles, and functions as an inn today. The original **Friends' Meeting House** was founded in 1730; the current one dates from 1862.

The **Burgess-Foulke Museum,** administered by the Quakertown Historical Society, is open summer weekends and by appointment. The nearby **Country Store Museum** is well worth seeing. Open Monday through Saturday, 9:00 a.m. to 5:00 p.m. Closed Sundays and holidays. Telephone (for information on all these sites): (215) 536-3499. Walking tours, either self-guided or by appointment, are also available.

Turn south on Route 313, to Route 563. To the left are three parks, **Weisel, Nockamixon,** and **Lake Towhee.** The entrance to Lake Towhee Park is from Old Bethlehem Road. This park offers boating, fishing, camping, ice skating, nature study trails, and bird watching. Visitors may have the experience of wild mallards, black ducks, and Canada geese approaching them as they picnic. Posted nature trails have been developed in this park, with "walk books" available to interested visitors. The **Elephant Hotel** is an early tavern at the edge of Nockamixon State Park.

Return to Route 313, turning south (left) to Route 113. To the left is **Irish Meeting House Cemetery** (1725). **Deep Run Mennonite Church,** on Deep Run Road, was established in the early 18th century. Return to Dublin, and Route 313. Of special interest to those of the Roman Catholic faith is the **National Shrine of Our Lady of Czestochowa.** To reach the shrine, turn right on Ferry Road. The shrine houses a reproduction of the famous Black Madonna icon in the Shrine of Jasna Gora, Poland, which is believed to be more than 1,600 years old. Telephone: (215) 345-0600. Return to Route 313 and go south on Route 611 into Philadelphia.

NORTHWEST OF PHILADELPHIA

The area northwest of Philadelphia is rich in historic sites connected with colonial America and the Revolutionary War period. Outstanding is **Valley Forge National Military Park,** one of the shrines of our war for independence. It is located on the Schuylkill River, between King of Prussia and

Phoenixville on Route 23, near Exit 24 of the Pennsylvania Turnpike and accessible from Philadelphia via the Schuylkill Expressway, Route 76. Washington's army was encamped here from December 19, 1777, until June 19, 1778. The 3,000-acre park comprises the major portion of the area occupied by the Continental Army. Begin your tour at the park Visitor Center located at the junction of Route 23 and North Gulf Road.

Visitors can walk through **Washington's Headquarters**, the building in which he lived and conferred with such notables as Lafayette, Knox, Wayne, Greene, Hamilton, and von Steuben. Varnum's Quarters are sometimes open to the public but check first at the Visitor's Center. Throughout the park are log huts, replicas of the quarters which housed Washington's soldiers during the bitter winter of 1777-78. Visitors may also see restored fortifications, redoubts, and numerous monuments. Special activities are planned throughout the year. Four special dates are celebrated annually: December 19, the day the Revolutionary army encamped here; the weekend nearest to the official observation of George Washington's birthday; May 6, the date of the American Alliance with France; and June 19, the day the army marched out. Troop musters are held periodically. Bus tours featuring a taped narration are available during the summer months, and on a limited basis in the fall. Bikes can be rented during the summer months and on fall weekends. New activities and programs are planned frequently. It is best to check with the park for specific, timely information. The hours specified below apply to the Visitor's Center and Washington's Headquarters. Open daily during summer, 8:30 a.m. to 6:00 p.m. Labor Day to Memorial Day, 8:30 a.m. to 5:00 p.m. Closed Christmas Day. Admission free. Telephone: (215) 783-7700.

A privately owned **museum of war memorabilia** operated by The Valley Forge Historical Society is located on Route 23, about two miles west of King of Prussia. The museum contains personal possessions of George and Martha Washington, as well as rifles and other items used in the Revolution itself. Open Monday through Saturday, 9:30 a.m. to 4:30 p.m.; Sunday, 1:00 to 4:30 p.m. Closed Christmas Day. Admission charge. Telephone: (215) 783-0535. **Washington Memorial Chapel**, built in memory of George Washington, is nearby on Route 23, adjacent to Valley Forge park. Sunday services honor a different state of the Union each week. The Washington Memorial National Carillon, which has 58 bells, is used for recitals by guest carilloneurs from the United States and Europe. Souvenirs and homemade edibles are available at the Cabin Shop behind the chapel. Open Monday through Friday, 8:00 a.m. to 5:00 p.m.; Saturday, 8:00 a.m. to 5:30 p.m.; Sunday, 8:00 a.m. to 6:00 p.m. Admission free. Telephone: (215) 783-0120.

Mill Grove was the first home in America of John James Audubon, the noted artist and naturalist. Audubon lived here from 1804 to 1806, and gained his first impressions of American birds and animals from trips into the nearby woods and fields. His art studio and taxidermy room have been restored in the mansion's attic. The interior decorations, collections of Audubon lithographs, and exhibits are notable memorials of his achievements. To reach Mill Grove from Valley Forge, go north on Route 363, across Schuylkill River, and left on Audubon Road. From the Pennsylvania Turnpike, take Exit 24.

The 130-acre **Wildlife Sanctuary** at Mill Grove includes six miles of trails where visitors may observe wildlife, particularly the many species of birds attracted to the area. About 51 species nest in the sanctuary. Approximately 174 species pass through on migration routes. Mill Grove is open Tuesday through Saturday, 10:00 a.m. to 4:00 p.m.; Sunday, 1:00 to 4:00 p.m. The sanctuary is open 7:00 a.m. to dusk, Tuesday through Sunday. Both Mill Grove and the Audubon Sanctuary are closed on Monday. Admission free. Telephone: (215) 666-5593.

Old Norrington Tavern is located north of Mill Grove, on Ridge Pike at Trooper (Norristown), and reached via Route 363. This is the site of Jacob D. Custer's clock shop.

Rittenhouse Farm, on the Germantown Pike near Norristown, was the home of David Rittenhouse, colonial scientist, astronomer, and instrument maker. Here he built the first telescope in America. The original house, now surrounded by other buildings, is currently in use as the Valley Forge Hospital. **Norriton Presbyterian Church**, on Germantown Pike at Fairview Village, was once part of Rittenhouse Farm. This church was organized in the late 1600s, and was used as a hospital during the Revolution. In its graveyard are buried 28 soldiers of the Continental Army and many ancestors of Mary Todd Lincoln. Telephone: (215) 539-5599.

Morgan Log House (1695) was built by Daniel Boone's grandparents. It is the only house of this style in the United States today. Located in Towamencin Township above Gwynedd, on Weikel Road, one block west of Route 363 (Valley Forge Road). The house is furnished in the style of the early 1700s and can be viewed at any time by appointment. Open end of April through end of November, 1:00 to 5:00 p.m. Admission charge. Telephone: (215) 368-2480.

Perkiomen Bridge, on Route 422 at Collegeville, is one of the oldest bridges still in use in the United States. It was built in 1799 at a cost of $20,000 with funds raised through a lottery. The **Perkiomen Bridge Hotel**, still operating as a hotel today, was built in 1701. The public rooms are decorated in part according to the period, and are open 11:00 a.m. to midnight. Telephone: (215) 489-9511. **Augustine Lutheran Church** at Trappe, on Route 422, is the oldest unchanged Lutheran church in America. It was built in 1743 under the direction of Dr. M. M. Muhlenberg, noted theologian. He is buried in the churchyard. Telephone: (215) 489-2686.

The **Peter Wentz Farmstead**, at Center Point (Worcester), is located on Route 73 near Route 363 intersection. Here General Washington established headquarters before and after the historic battle of Germantown. The house, which dates from 1758, has been restored and furnished according to the year 1777. The barn, which houses Durham cattle, Dorset sheep, and old gray geese, is also open to the public. Open Tuesday through Saturday, 10:00 a.m. to 4:00 p.m.; Sunday, 1:00 to 4:00 p.m. Closed Mondays except Memorial Day and Labor Day. Closed Christmas and Thanksgiving. Admission free. Telephone: (215) 584-5104. Also at Center Point on Route 73 is the **Ironmaster's House and Blacksmith Museum**. Unusual tools and a working forge recreate the period in state history when iron played a major role. Visitors see old trivets, banks, kitchen utensils, door stops, etc., as well as displays which chronicle the history of iron in Pennsylvania. There is also a small gift shop. Open by appointment. Admission free. Telephone: (215) 584-4441.

Dawesfield, on Lewis Lane in Ambler, served as Washington's headquarters in the fall of 1777. It was the scene of the court martial of General Anthony Wayne, when he was acquitted of guilt for the Paoli massacre. It is accessible from Route 73 near Ambler.

Hope Lodge, at the intersection of Bethlehem Pike (old Route 309) and 73 in Whitemarsh, was built in 1721 by Samuel Morris. During the Revolutionary War it was used as a hospital. It is an architectural masterpiece in the finest Georgian tradition. The interior is very impressive, with large fireplaces, classical pilasters and pediments, arched doorways, and exquisite 18th- and 19th-century furnishings. There is a notable collection of Chinese export porcelain, and the paintings in the house include portraits by Thomas Sully and Jacob Zicholtz. Open Tuesday through Saturday, 9:00 a.m. to 5:00 p.m.; Sunday, noon to 5:00 p.m. Open Memorial Day, Fourth of July, and Labor Day. Closed Mondays and other major holidays. Admission charge. Telephone: (215) 646-1595.

The **Abington Art Center** is located at 515 Meetinghouse Road, in Jenkintown. The art center is housed in the more interesting parts of the Lessing J. Rosenwald estate and its art-deco style art gallery (one room of which has been recreated at the Library of Congress) dates from 1939. Now one of the largest fine arts centers in Pennsylvania, Abington Center features changing fine arts exhibits from the United States and abroad. In addition to its regular fine arts, dance, and crafts curricula, the center holds weekend films, lectures, and workshops. Open Labor Day to Memorial Day, Monday through Saturday, 9:00 a.m. to 5:00 p.m. For summer hours and special events, contact the center. Admission to gallery, free. Charges for some tours and events, as well as for classes. Telephone: (215) 887-4882.

Abington Friends Meeting, on Greenwood Avenue in Jenkintown, has existed as a Quaker meetinghouse since 1697. Here, Benjamin Lay, in 1737, published his book against slavery.

Bryn Athyn Cathedral, on Route 232 at Bryn Athyn, is a Swedenborgian Center noted for its distinctive 14th-century Gothic and 12th-century Romanesque architecture. Open Monday through Saturday, 9:00 a.m. to noon. Conducted tours are offered daily except Thursday and Saturday, between 2:00 and 5:00 p.m. Telephone: (215) 947-0266. **Curtis Arboretum**, at Greenwood Avenue and Church Road in Wyncote, Cheltenham Township, offers an opportunity for a stroll through a 45-acre parklike area with hundreds of species of labeled trees and shrubs. The arboretum is accessible via Route 73, east of the intersection with Route 152. Admission free. Open daily, 6:00 a.m. to 8:00 p.m. Telephone: (215) 884-7675.

Beth Sholom Synagogue, in Elkins Park, is the only synagogue ever designed by Frank Lloyd Wright, the distinguished architect. This modern house of worship is open to visitors by appointment only, and can be reached via Routes 611 or 73. Admission free. Telephone: (215) 887-1342.

The Buten Museum of Wedgwood, 246 North Bowman Avenue, Merion, houses the famous collection of more than 10,500 pieces of antique and modern Wedgwood ceramics. The museum is a stately turn-of-the-century mansion in the heart of the community. Once the residence of pianist Josef Hoffmann, the museum has three rooms normally open to the public. A selection of objects from the enormous Wedgwood collection (dating from 1759) is displayed throughout these rooms. The music room is paneled in walnut from Steinway, the famous maker of pianos. The house also boasts fine wrought ironwork. Use of the library is by appointment. Among its treasures are Josiah Wedgwood's letters, a collection of Wedgwood catalogues from 1773 to the present, as well as histories of ceramics and classical antiques. Open Monday through Friday, 2:00 to 4:00 p.m. Admission charge. Telephone: (215) 664-6601.

Barnes Art Foundation, 300 Latchs Lane, in Merion, contains a notable collection of Impressionist art. More than 1,000 paintings hang in this appropriately French mansion. Among the artists represented are: Cezanne, Picasso, Matisse, and Renoir, as well as Titian, El Greco, and Tintoretto. Open Friday and Saturday, 9:30 a.m. to 4:30 p.m.; Sunday, 1:00 to 4:30 p.m. Limited admissions, so advance reservations are desirable. Admission charge. Telephone: (215) 667-0290.

Old Gulph Schoolhouse, Matsonford Road, Upper Merion, was built circa 1696. It served as a rural schoolhouse but is now used for religious education. **Hanging Rock**, at Montgomery Avenue at Gulph Mills, has an unusual rock formation protruding over the highway. It is said that Washington's engineers shaped it.

Merion Meeting House, on Montgomery Avenue in Merion, was originally a log structure, replaced by a stone building in 1695. William Penn, founder of the Commonwealth, preached here. It is still used as a place of worship by the Quakers.

Old Roberts School in Upper Merion, built in 1848, is fully restored as a period schoolhouse. It has a small basement museum, and stands in front of the modern Roberts School.

Pottsgrove Mansion, a state-administered historic site, is located on Route 422 at the west edge of Pottstown. Built in the 1750s by John Potts, the noted ironmaster, it is distinguished for its fine architectural features and elegant furnishings, especially its Philadelphia Chippendale furniture. The mansion is surrounded by beautifully landscaped grounds, and an 18th-century flower and herb garden. Open Tuesday through Saturday, 9:00 a.m. to 5:00 p.m.; Sunday, 1:00 to 5:00 p.m. During winter, 10:00 a.m. to 4:30 p.m.; Sunday, 1:00 to 4:30 p.m. Admission charge. Telephone: (215) 326-4014.

Northwest of Schwenksville, off Route 29, is **Green Lane Reservoir**. This 814-acre lake is well stocked with game fish. Fishing is free for those under 16 years of age.

Nature study enthusiasts may be interested in visiting some of the areas described below. There is **Morris Arboretum**, at Chestnut Hill in West Philadelphia off Route 422, a 175-acre collection of 3,500 native and exotic trees and shrubs. Special gardens include an English park, an oak alley, an azalea meadow, a swan pond, a Japanese garden, and a rose garden. No cars are allowed inside the arboretum. Tours are available Saturday and Sunday at 2:00 p.m. Open daily, 9:00 a.m. to 5:00 p.m.; open Thursday, June through August, 9:00 a.m. to 8:00 p.m. Closed Christmas Day. Admission charge. Telephone: (215) 242-3399. **Schuylkill Valley Nature Center**, in Roxborough, also in West Philadelphia, has nature trails, including one for the handicapped. **Swiss Pines**, at Malvern, west of the Pennsylvania Turnpike and Route 29, offers picturesque outdoor Japanese and Polynesian gardens, a large rhododendron display, and several ponds with wildfowl. **Zoo America, 1776**, in the Elmwood Park Zoo, Norristown, displays animals in their 1776 environment. Described earlier in this section is the **Audubon Wildlife Sanctuary**, with its six miles of marked trails, and **Longwood Gardens**.

READING-BERKS AREA

The Reading-Berks area offers visitors a wide array of activities and historical sites such as the Daniel Boone Homestead, Hopewell Village, the Crystal Cave, and the Conrad Weiser Homestead. As the "factory outlet capital of the U.S.A.," Reading draws smart shoppers from all over the country. Visitors to the area may also enjoy Pennsylvania Dutch meals and roam through any of its six picturesque farmers' markets.

READING AND VICINITY

The first tour begins at Morgantown where Routes 10 and 23 intersect. To begin, go east on Route 23 to Warwick;

then continue north on the road to Birdsboro. **Hopewell Village** is located about six miles south of Birdsboro on Route 345.

Hopewell Village National Historic Site, administered by the National Park Service, is one of the oldest ironworks in the country. Life in Hopewell Village, from its origin during the Revolutionary decade to the last iron production over a century later, was dominated by the constant operation of its massive furnace. The furnace was established in 1770 to supply cast iron for Mark Bird's three forges in Birdsboro. A village grew up around the furnace, consisting of the families of more than 65 workmen. The furnace prospered, supplying pig iron for forges and red-hot iron for stoves, pots, and kettles. Hopewell's prosperity peaked in the mid-1830s, except for a brief boom during the Civil War. In 1883, the furnace "blew out" for the last time.

Today, visitors, with the help of Park Service information and maps, can tour the village. It is recommended that visitors first stop at the visitors center for an informative orientation. On a fascinating walking tour, visitors can see a coaling shed, anthracite furnace, charcoal hearth, water wheel, and blast machinery. During July and August "villagers" dress in period costumes and display village trades and crafts. Open May through September, daily, 9:00 a.m. to 6:00 p.m.; October through April, daily, 9:00 a.m. to 5:00 p.m. Admission free.

French Creek State Park adjoins Hopewell Village. The park has three lakes available for swimming, boating, and fishing. For the hiker, there are seven marked trail routes accessible from the camping area. For information and literature, write Park Manager, R.D. #1, Box 448, Elverson, PA 19520. Telephone: (215) 582-1514.

The tour continues north through Birdsboro and Baumstown less than a mile to the **Daniel Boone Homestead**, where Daniel Boone was born in 1734. The homestead is now a museum depicting country life of 18th-century Pennsylvania. Near the restored house are a blacksmith shop, smokehouse, and barn. The homestead area is a state sanctuary for deer, raccoon, pheasants, quail, and other wildlife. A nearby lake offers public fishing. Open May through September, Tuesday to Saturday, 8.30 a.m. to 5:00 p.m.; Sunday, noon to 5:00 p.m. Closed Monday. October through April, Tuesday through Saturday, 9:00 a.m. to 4:30 p.m.; Sunday, noon to

5:00 p.m. Closed Monday. Admission charge; children under 12, free.

Return to Baumstown and go four miles east on Route 422 to Douglassville. The **Mary Merritt Doll Museum** in Douglassville has a display of more than 1,500 dolls—toys, miniatures, and antiques—some dating from the early 1700s. There are also miniature period rooms, furnished dollhouses, and a full-size replica of a mid-19th-century Philadelphia toy shop. Open Monday through Saturday, 10:00 a.m. to 5:00 p.m.; weekends, 1:00 to 5:00 p.m. Admission charge.

Adjacent is **Merritt's Americana Museum of the Pennsylvania Dutch Country**. Here one can see rooms furnished with early Pennsylvania furniture, Stiegel glass, and cigar store Indians. There is a very large collection of iron and metal ware of all periods. The thousands of articles are well arranged to give the visitor a bird's-eye view of the whole panorama of 18th- and 19th- century life in America. Hours same as for doll museum. Admission to the doll museum covers the Americana Museum.

To get to the **Boyertown Museum of Antique Vehicles** take Route 662 north to Yellow House, then east six miles to Boyertown. The museum features a collection of about 80 vehicles dating from 1763 to 1950. Open Tuesday to Friday, 8:00 a.m. to 4:00 p.m.; weekends, 10:00 a.m. to 2:00 p.m. Admission free. The Duryea Day Antique and Classic Automobile Meet is held annually at the museum the Saturday before Labor Day (rain or shine). Return to Reading via Route 562, a distance of 16 miles.

One of Reading's main tourist attractions is the **Pagoda**, located atop Mt. Penn (1,200 ft.). The pagoda is listed in the National Register of Historic Places. Visitors are afforded a wide view of the surrounding countryside from the Observation Tower. The pagoda is open daily during the winter, noon to 8:00 p.m.; summer, 11:00 a.m. to 9:00 p.m. Nominal admission charge. Reading's **Fairgrounds Market**, located on 5th Street Highway in Reading, features typical Pennsylvania Dutch foods; there are 100 different stalls. The market is open Thursday and Friday, 8:00 a.m. to 9:00 p.m.; Saturday, 8:00 a.m. to 5:00 p.m.

The **Reading Public Museum and Art Gallery**, 500 Museum Road, has an unusual collection of art from the Early American and Hudson River schools, and Pennsylvania German folk art. The museum and **Botanical Gardens** are open to the public, October through May, Monday through

Friday, 9:00 a.m. to 5:00 p.m.; Saturday, 9:00 a.m. to noon; Sunday, 2:00 to 5:00 p.m. From June through September hours are Monday through Friday, 9:00 a.m. to 4:00 p.m.; Sunday, 2:00 to 5:00 p.m. Closed Saturday. Admission free. Adjacent to the museum is the **Planetarium**. Shows contain a unique blend of theater arts, music, and the science of astronomy. The show may be viewed during the winter months, Wednesday and Thursday, 7:30 p.m.; Sunday, two shows at 2:00 p.m. and 3:00 p.m Summer hours, daily shows also at 1:00 p.m.; closed Saturday and Sunday. Admission charge.

The **Historical Society of Berks County** is located at 940 Centre Avenue (PA Route 61), Reading. The museum is open October through May, Tuesday to Saturday, 9:00 a.m. to 4:00 p.m., and Sunday, 2:00 to 5:00 p.m. Admission charge.

Other places of interest in and about the City of Reading include: **Angelica Park**, a 45-acre regional park south of Reading offering boating, fishing, picnicking, and sports facilities; **Antietam Lake**, part of the City of Reading water supply, offering fishing and picnicking; **Callowhill Historical District**, where many fine residences, churches, and commercial buildings are now preserved around Penn Square and along North and South Fifth Street as examples of Federal and Victorian period architecture; **City Park and Firemen's Bandshell**, a 33-acre park, also known as Penn's Commons, where music and cultural events are regularly scheduled throughout the summer; **Lake Ontelaunee** bird sanctuary, located east of Route 61 and north of Reading, near Leesport; and **Penn Square**, located at the center of downtown Reading. This historic square once contained public market houses. The square now hosts many cultural, social, and commercial festivities throughout the year.

Reading is famous as the outlet shopping mecca of the eastern region of the United States. In town, there are several outlets where shoppers can buy an assortment of merchandise, especially clothing, shoes, linen, leather goods, power tools, and outdoor furniture at bargain prices. For information about the outlets, contact the Pennsylvania Dutch Travel Association or contact the Reading Outlet Center and Mart, 801 North Ninth Street, Reading, PA 19604. Telephone: (215) 373-5495.

St. Peter's Village, south of Reading, was owned by the Knauer family in 1731. Now under new management, it has been restored to its original appearance, as the center of a former quarrying operation.

Visitors can see the general store, post office, bread and pretzel bakery, barber shop, cigar factory, creamery, boarding house, and dwellings. The Inn at St. Peter's has dining facilities for visitors. Craft shops and bake shops are also open to visitors. Carriage and sleigh rides are available in season. The village is located on Route 23, 10 miles east of the Morgantown Exit of the Pennsylvania Turnpike and four miles west of Bucktown on Route 100. Open year round, weekdays (except Monday), 10:30 a.m. to 5:00 p.m.; Saturday, 11:00 a.m. to 6:00 p.m.; Sunday, noon to 6:00 p.m.

NORTHERN BERKS COUNTY

To begin the second tour, take Route 222 north to Kutztown. The **Farmer's Market**, open Saturdays, has more than 1,000 stands offering a wide choice of local products. Also on Saturdays in Kutztown is the **Renninger's No. 2 Antique Flea Market**, located on Noble Street one mile south of town. Open 9:00 a.m. to 5:00 p.m.

A worthwhile detour is the **Crystal Cave**, on Crystal Cave Road (Route 3), two miles west of Kutztown. Crystal Cave has been a tourist attraction ever since it was discovered in 1871. The cave has exquisite stalactite and stalagmite formations, enhanced by artificial lighting. Guides present an informative slide show explaining the history of cave formation. The cave is situated in a 125-acre park that includes picnic areas, hiking trails, and facilities for other family activities. Open February through May and Labor Day through October, daily, 9:00 a.m. to 5:00 p.m., weekends to 6:00 p.m.; Memorial Day through Labor Day, daily, 9:00 a.m. to 6:00 p.m., weekends to 7:00 p.m.; in November, Friday, Saturday, Sunday only, 9:00 a.m. to 5:00 p.m. Closed December and January.

Continue west from the caves to Route 143, north to Lenhartsville for a visit to the **One-Room Schoolhouse** and museum. The schoolhouse is part of a complex of exhibits reflecting the "Fireplace Era" and the "Woodstove Era." The complex is operated by the Pennsylvania Dutch Folk Culture Society. Visitors to the site can view a one-room schoolhouse, log house, folklife museum, farm equipment building, house of fashions, and the genealogical library. Open May through October, Saturday, 10:00 a.m. to 5:00 p.m.; Sunday, 1:00 to 5:00 p.m. Nominal admission charge. While in Lenhartsville, visit the **Blue Rocks** off Route 143. This natural wonder consists of an ice age fossil stretching a mile long and covering 15 acres. A ride on the "Blue Rock Special" carries the visitor on a mile-long sightseeing trip across the rocks. A guide explains their origin. Blue Rocks offers camping, hiking, and picnicking facilities as well as refreshments and supplies. Open daily, 9:00 a.m. to 5:00 p.m. Admission charge.

There are two old covered bridges in the Lenhartsville area. Inquire locally for directions.

Continue north on Route 143 to Kempton. In Kempton, off old Route 22, is the **Pennsylvania Dutch Farm Museum**. At the museum a display of farm and home antiques can be seen; the items are primarily from the Berks County region. Open May through October, weekends only, 11:00 a.m. to 6:00 p.m. Admission charge; children under 12, free.

The little town of Kempton is also the headquarters for the **Wanamaker, Kempton and South Scenic Rail Road** steam engines and passenger cars. The trains take the Hawk Mountain Line, a scenic meandering route through woods and along the banks of Maiden Creek to the small town of Wanamaker and back to Kempton. At the Wanamaker end of the tour there is a shop that sells antiques and a trackside picnic grove with lovely nature trails. The W.K.&S. operates April through October, weekends, 1:00 to 5:00 p.m. Fare charge. Telephone: (215) 756-6469.

Return to Lenhartsville, turning west on old Route 22, going through Hamburg to Shartlesville. Just outside Shartlesville is **Roadside America**, billed as "the World's Greatest Indoor Miniature Village." A total of 67 scenes make up this miniature panorama. Open July through Labor Day, weekdays, 9:00 a.m. to 6:30 p.m.; weekends, to 7:00 p.m.; September through June, weekdays, 10:00 a.m. to 5:00 p.m., weekends, to 6:00 p.m. Admission charge.

While in Shartlesville, visit **Tecumseh's Frontier Trading Post and Museum**, a reconstruction of an 18th-century frontier fort built originally to protect the early Pennsylvania Dutch settlers from Indian raids during the French and Indian Wars. There is also an Indian village in the rear of the fort. Open June 1 through August 30, daily, 9:00 a.m. to 9:00 p.m.; rest of the year, daily, 10:00 a.m. to 5:00 p.m. Admission free. Telephone: (215) 488-6622.

Turn left on Route 183 to **Christmas Village** at Bernville. This enterprise offers an unusual collection of Christmas gifts, decorations and ceramics, and a special Christmas display which is set up on Labor Day and remains until the end of the year. Visitors can walk through the House and Village. Open October, weekends, 7:30 to 9:30 p.m.; November 1 to Thanksgiving, Friday to Sunday, 5:30 to 9:30 p.m. Thanksgiving to January 1, Monday to Friday, 6:00 to 9:00 p.m.; weekends, 5:00 to 10:00 p.m. Admission charge. Telephone: (215) 488-1110.

From Bernville, travel to Womelsdorf to visit the **Conrad Weiser Historic Park**. The simple stone house built by Weiser in 1729 (enlarged in 1751) is set in a beautiful wooded area. Conrad Weiser, a German immigrant, spent the winter of 1712-13 as the adopted son of Chief Quaynant of the Iroquois Indians. Weiser's knowledge of the Indians made him an adept negotiator. Weiser was instrumental in establishing Indian policy in the area and in keeping Pennsylvania free from Indian disturbances until the French and Indian War.

The house is now a museum and memorial to one of Pennsylvania's earliest peacekeepers. Open year round, Tuesday through Saturday, 8:30 a.m to 5:00 p.m.; Sunday, noon to 5:00 p.m. Closed Monday. Nominal admission charge; children under 12, free. Telephone: (215) 589-2934.

For additional information on Berks County, contact the Reading-Berks Pennsylvania Dutch Travel Association, 3045 North Fifth Street, Reading Plaza North, Reading, PA 19605. Telephone: (215) 921-0646. Also the monthly publication *Reading Magazine*, available at newsstands in the Reading area, is an excellent source on local current events, concerts, festivals, and sports events in the Reading-Berks area.

LANCASTER AREA

Lancaster and the surrounding Pennsylvania Dutch country comprise one of the nation's major tourist attractions. The city of Lancaster is located approximately 106 and 67 miles northeast of Washington, DC, and Baltimore respectively. It is at the intersection of Routes 222, 283, and 30. One of America's oldest inland cities, Lancaster has many historic buildings in its downtown area, as well as the oldest continuously operating farmers' in the United States. This city was the nation's capital for one day, September 27, 1777; it was the state capital from 1799 to 1812.

Visitors come to Lancaster County to visit the farms, homes, and workshops of the "plain people," members of the Amish, Mennonite, and Brethren religious sects. The Amish are of special interest because their dress and rejection of "worldly" devices has remained unchanged for more than 300 years. They cling to the horse and buggy and reject the use of all electric-powered devices and modern plumbing.

Tourists come here to sample local delicacies, such as shoofly pie, and partake of meals served in the Pennsylvania Dutch style. It is advisable to make advance reservations for motel rooms, especially during the summer season. Visitors also will find it advantageous to stop first at the **Visitors Information Center,** located at the Greenfield Road Exit off Route 30, for a brief orientation including exhibits, color movies, and maps. Three days or longer should be spent in order to see all of the major attractions of the area. Suggested in this guide are five tours, each approximately one-half day's duration. The first covers historic Lancaster. It is followed by four motor tours, north, east, south, and west of the city.

The walking tour begins on Penn Square. Facing King Street is **Old City Hall,** built in 1795. Nearby, in Center Square, is the **Central Market,** where many types of farm delicacies are sold by Amish and Mennonite farmers. The market is open from 6:00 a.m. to 3:30 p.m. every Tuesday and Friday. Proceed across Penn Square, south on Queen Street to the **Montgomery House** (1804), and on to Vine Street. To the left is the **Lancaster County Art Center,** built about 1825.

Continue east on Vine turning left on Duke Street. To the right is **Trinity Lutheran Church,** built in the 1760s. Diagonally across to the left, at the corner of King Street, is the **Court House,** erected in 1852. East on King Street are four 18th-century buildings: **DeMuth Tobacco Shop** (1770), the oldest tobacconist in the United States; **DeMuth House,** once the home of the noted artist, Charles DeMuth; a private home at 122 East King Street, **Bowsman House** (1762), with a carved angel's head under the eaves; and the **Sign of Ship House** (1761).

Return to Duke Street, then north to the **Muhlenberg House,** the former Trinity Lutheran parsonage. Beyond the intersection, on the right, is the **schoolhouse of the First Reformed Church** (1760). At Orange Street is **St. James Episcopal Church,** founded in 1744. This present building was erected in 1820.

Proceed east on Orange Street to the middle of the block beyond Lime Street. On the left is the **home of Christopher Marshall,** noted diarist of the Revolutionary War era. Near the corner is the fine Georgian home of Lancaster's first mayor, John Passmore. Turn back on Orange Street; on the left, past Duke Street, is the **First Reformed Church.** The present building was erected in 1852 on the site of an 18th-century edifice. Turn right on reaching Prince Street, to the **home of Andrew Ellicott,** built in 1780. Ellicott was America's first native-born city planner. South on Prince Street, at the corner of King, is the **Fulton Opera House,** America's oldest living theater (1852), named in honor of inventor Robert Fulton. Turn left to return to the start of the walking tour.

There are several other points of interest in Lancaster, conveniently reached by automobile. At the corner of College Avenue is the **North Museum and Planetarium of Franklin and Marshall College.** The museum, featuring exhibits on science and natural history, is open Wednesday to Saturday (Sunday during the summer months), 9:00 a.m. to 5:00 p.m. The planetarium is open Saturday and Sunday with two shows each day at 2:00 p.m. and 3:00 p.m. Admission is free. During the week the planetarium can be visited by appointment.

Go west on Buchanan Avenue, past Buchanan Park, then left on President Avenue, and across Marietta Avenue to **Lancaster County Historical Society** at No. 230 on the right. It is open Monday to Saturday, 1:00 to 5:00 p.m. There are interesting exhibits on local history. Admission is free.

Around the corner on Marietta Avenue is **Wheatland,** a Greek revival mansion built in 1828, owned by James Buchanan (15th president of the United States) from 1848 until his death in 1868. The mansion, used by Buchanan in 1856 as his presidential campaign headquarters, has been restored to its mid-19th-century appearance. Period rooms contain outstanding collections of American Empire and Victorian decorative arts, many of which belonged to Buchanan. Tours of the 17-room house and grounds are conducted by guides wearing costumes appropriate to the 19th century. Open April 1 through November 30, 10:00 a.m. to 4:15 p.m. Open in December for candlelight tours; check for specific dates. Telephone: (717) 392-8721. Admission charge. The return route to the city center is east on Marietta Avenue.

The tour can be extended to include a visit to Rock Ford Plantation and to **Hammond's Pretzel Bakery.** The bakery is two blocks east on Marietta to West End Avenue and right six blocks to No. 718. It is open 7:00 a.m. to 5:00 p.m., weekdays; 8:00 a.m. to noon on Saturdays.

Continue south on West End Avenue and into Hershey

Avenue to Route 222. Turn left on Queen Street for three blocks to Chesapeake Street, right to Duke Street, and across the Conestoga River Bridge. Turn right along the river drive for about one-half mile to **Rock Ford Plantation**, located in Lancaster County Park. This is the restored 1792 estate of Edward Hand, Adjutant General during the Revolution and a member of the Continental Congress. It is an authentic example of refined country living in the late 18th century. Visitors can also see the **Kauffman Collection** of American pewter and utensils. Open April 1 through November 30, Tuesday through Saturday, 10:00 a.m. to 4:00 p.m.; Sunday, noon to 4:00 p.m. Admission charge. Special evening candle tours are conducted several times each year. Telephone: (717) 392-7223.

NORTH OF LANCASTER

This circuit tour encompasses Route 272 (Oregon Pike) to Ephrata, Route 322 to Brickerville, left on Route 501 to Lititz, right on Route 772 to Manheim, and return via Route 72. The distance is approximately 38 miles.

First stop is the **Landis Valley Museum**. This museum complex includes a farm home, barns, a one-room schoolhouse, and many outbuildings. On display are thousands of items reflecting rural life, culture, and the economy in the 18th and 19th centuries including a large collection of farm implements and vehicles, and tools of various rural crafts. Open weekdays (except Mondays), 9:00 a.m. to 5:00 p.m.; Sundays, 1:00 to 4:30 p.m. Admission charge. Children under 11, free.

Continue north two miles to second intersection on right. Turn in here, going less than a mile to a picturesque **covered bridge** across Conestoga Creek. Return to Route 222, and continue north to intersection of Route 322 at Ephrata.

Visitors may go on a conducted tour of the medieval-like **Ephrata Cloister** of monastic Seventh-Day Baptists who settled here in 1720. The society, which once numbered more than 300 members, dwindled and was finally disbanded in 1929. A visit to the Cloister reveals a unique and amazing expression of the religious fervor which was an outstanding characteristic of early Pennsylvania.

Charity, always a part of the Cloister way of life, was nobly demonstrated during the Revolution when some 500 wounded soldiers from the Battle of Brandywine were brought here in September 1777 to be nursed by the members. The buildings on Mt. Zion (the hill to the west), which served as a hospital, had to be burned following their occupation in order to arrest the spread of camp fever. A monument in the Mt. Zion Cemetery marks the graves of many soldiers who died here.

The surviving buildings, extensively restored, include the Saal (chapel), Saron (sisters' house), Almonry (alms and bake house), Beissel's log house, a householders' cabin, three cottages, and the 1837 Academy. Bethania (brothers' house), which stood nearby, was razed around 1910. In addition to self-disciplines, the celibate orders engaged in printing, illuminated calligraphy, singing and composing music, spinning, weaving, and papermaking. These crafts are demonstrated during a pre-performance tour of the buildings.

From July until Labor Day on Saturdays and several Sundays, visitors can see an evening musical drama, "The Vorspiel," which depicts everyday life in the Cloister in the late 1700s. The musical drama begins at 9:00 p.m. Reservations required. Included in the price of the show is a tour of the Cloister beginning at 6:30 p.m. The Cloister may also be visited every day except Monday. Visiting hours during daylight saving time: weekdays, 9:00 a.m. to 5:00 p.m.; Sundays, noon to 5:00 p.m. Admission charge.

Other attractions in Ephrata include the **Green Dragon Farmer's Market.** The market, located approximately eight miles north of Ephrata, is open from 10:00 a.m. to 10:00 p.m. every Friday. The **Cloister Country Store** and a **covered bridge** near Reamstown are four miles north on Route 22.

The tour route is west from Ephrata on Route 322 to Brickerville, then south on Route 501, past the **Speedwell Forge Fishing Lake.** Stop off in Brickerville to stroll over the grounds of **Elizabeth Furnace** (1763), where Baron Stiegel operated the finest glassworks in the colonies.

Continue on Route 501 to Lititz. The **Lititz Historical Foundation** is located in the Mueller House at 137 East Main Street where guides depict the way of life in 18th-century Lititz. Open Wednesday, Thursday, Friday, and Saturday, from Memorial Day to Labor Day. Nearby is the old Lititz **Moravian Church** and **Linden Hall,** one of the oldest girls' schools in the country, founded in 1745.

The **Sturgis Pretzel Bakery,** 219 East Main Street in Lititz, is believed to be America's earliest such firm. At the bakery, pretzels are hand-shaped and baked in century-old ovens. Tours offered weekdays, April through October.

Continue west for five miles on Route 772 and you will arrive in Manheim. The town was founded by Baron Stiegel, who was noted for his famous glass products. The remains of his home are on Main Street. The **Manheim Historical Society**, located in the Missimer-Weil House, Charlotte and High streets, is a museum of early American antiques and Stiegel glass. It also has an Old Country Store shop. Open daily, 10:00 a.m. to 4:00 p.m.; Sunday, 1:00 to 4:00 p.m. At the **Old Rose Church** a rent of "one red rose" was paid to Stiegel's heirs annually on the second Sunday in June.

Three **covered bridges** are located south of Manheim, each crossing Chickies Creek. Ask for directions locally.

The tour continues south on Route 128 toward Lancaster. **Rutt's Country Market** is at Mechanicsville, one mile to the right, off Route 72, and **S. C. Weaver's Meat Market** is on the main road, in East Petersburg. Two miles south of East Petersburg, at the village of McGovernville, is another covered bridge.

EAST OF LANCASTER

This circuit tour is east out of Lancaster returning via Route 772 and Hempstead Road, a distance of about 33 miles. Take Route 340 and then Route 30, east out of Lancaster. On the left, past Bridgeport, is the **Price and Keemer Pottery** (open weekdays only). Several other craft outlets are also located in Bridgeport. The **Amish Homestead**, on the right, is an authentic, 71-acre Amish farm, actually occupied and farmed by an Amish family. It is open daily, March through November; weekends only during the winter. Tours are conducted through the house and all farm buildings. Admission charge. For additional information telephone: (717) 392-0832. Nearby, **The Lancaster County Heritage Wax Museum** is open all year. This museum presents life-size figures that recreate momentous events in Lancaster's history. Admission charge.

Nearby, on the right, is the **Mennonite Information Center**, where visitors can secure authentic information on this religious sect. On the north side of Route 30 is a children's attraction, **Dutch Wonderland**. The magic land of make-believe recreates favorite storybook characters and scenes in a 34-acre village behind a replica of a medieval castle. One can ride miniature trains, a stern-wheel boat, and some old automobiles. Open daily, June 1 to September 15; weekends at other times, weather permitting. Admission charge.

Next along the route is the **Amish Farm and House,** where visitors may go on a conducted tour through 10 rooms of this 1805 home and farm. Ten farm buildings, livestock, and poultry are included in the tour. On the grounds there is also an old covered bridge, a museum, and blacksmith shop. Open daily during the summer months, 8:30 a.m. to 8:00 p.m. Other months, 8:30 a.m. to 4:00 p.m. Admission charge.

The **Mill-Bridge Village** is east on Ronks Road, one-eighth mile to the covered bridge at Soudersburg. On the grounds, a grist and cider mill powered by a 16-foot water wheel can be seen. Visitors may observe Amish and Mennonites at work in the blacksmith, carriage, or woodshops, or engaged in toleware art, spinning, or candlemaking. Visitors can camp at the village. Telephone: (717) 687-8181.

Two miles beyond Soudersburg is the **Jacob and Jane Zook Hex Shop,** located on Route 30, Paradise, PA 17562. Jacob Zook was a 12th generation Dutchman and an authority on Pennsylvania Dutch folk art, especially Hex signs. Make a left turn on the next paved road, leading to Intercourse, at junction of Routes 772 and 340. Pass a covered bridge en route. There are several interesting shops in this village. Less than a mile east on Route 340 is the **Plain and Fancy Farm**. The farm is mostly noted for its restaurant, which serves Pennsylvania Dutch food in the family style. Visitors can take an Amish buggy ride on the farm. Open year round, except Sundays, weather permitting. Admission charge. Telephone: (717) 768-8281.

In Bird-In-Hand visit the **Old Village Store**, an authentic 19th-century store, with a pot belly stove. Open daily, except January and February. Admission free.

The **Mascot Roller Mill** is passed en route. At Monterey make a sharp left turn to **Heller's Church**, an old country church. Bear left to Route 340 towards Lancaster.

A side trip of interest to some is a visit to **The Ford New Holland Machine Company.** For information, telephone: (717) 354-1100. To reach the plant, turn right at Heller's Station to Route 23, then east six miles to New Holland. Free tours begin at the Visitor Center.

Mid-18th-century pioneers of the Jewish faith are buried in **Shaarai Shomayim Cemetery**, established in 1747, on the outskirts of Lancaster. Joseph Simon, trader, landholder, and businessman, who came to Lancaster in 1740, is buried here. He was a founder of the Union Fire Co., Lancaster Library Co., a Conawago Canal Commissioner, and supplier to the Continental Army.

Dutch Land Tours, located in Bird-In-Hand, offers a four-hour and a two-hour farm tour of Lancaster and Amish areas. Tours leave from the **Bird-In-Hand Farmers Market,** located at Route 340 and Maple Avenue. For more information on tours write to: Box 265, Bird-In-Hand, PA 17505. Telephone: (717) 392-8622.

SOUTH OF LANCASTER

This circuit tour begins on Route 222, south to Penn Hill. Backtrack to Route 372, and east to Route 896, then north by various roads to Lancaster. The distance is 58 miles.

Follow Route 222, to junction with Route 741, en route passing the **Hans Herr House,** oldest area landmark, built in 1719 by the first Swiss German Mennonites. Guided tours. Open Monday through Saturday, 9:00 a.m. to 4:00 p.m.; closed Sunday. Admission charge. Continue to Lime Valley. Two covered bridges to the east cross Pequa Creek. New Providence is the home of the Lime Valley Roller Mill, as well as a lime kiln and the Old Conowingo Ore Mill.

Continue on Route 222 through Quarryville to the **Robert Fulton Birthplace,** near Bethel, now a national shrine and museum owned by the state. Two miles beyond is the **Penn Hill Meeting House,** a Quaker landmark.

Retrace your steps to Quarryville, turning right on Route 372. Four miles to the east is **Middle Octorara Presbyterian Church,** erected in 1754. Continue to **Green Tree Inn** (1763), where Route 896 intersects. This was the home of Robert Fulton's parents. The route is left on Route 896 three miles, then left two miles to **Sides Cider Mill.** A paved road to the left leads to **Keen's Old Stone Mill House.** Turn around and continue north four miles to Strasburg.

Park your car and enjoy a ride on the **Strasburg Railroad,** America's oldest operating short-line railroad. The hour-long round trip to Paradise and return traverses picturesque Amish countryside. The line was chartered in 1832 and the equipment in use dates from the late 19th century. At the depot one can board an assortment of old railroad cars. Trips are scheduled several times daily from May through the end of October. Weekends only during the winter months. Admission charge. Telephone: (717) 687-7522.

East of Strasburg on Route 741 is the **Choo Choo Barn**. Here one sees, in miniature, scenes from daily life in the Pennsylvania Dutch country. Open daily in summer; weekends remainder of year. Admission charge. On the same track is the **Toy Train Museum**, on Paradise Lane in Strasburg. The museum is open daily in the summer. Admission charge. Telephone: (717) 687-8976.

Continue west on Route 741 to the **Eagle Americana Shop and Gun Museum**. On display is a fine collection of Pennsylvania and Kentucky rifles, as well as weapons from crossbows through World War II rifles. The museum, housed in a stone mill built in 1740, also displays collections of early glass, china, brass, tin, iron, and Indian items. Open daily, mid-April to October. Admission charge.

Continue on Route 741, past Lampeter one mile, turning right to the **Meylin Gunsmith Shop**. A Swiss gunsmith built a forge here in 1719 and began making rifles. He produced the first rifle bore gun made in the colonies. This Lancaster rifle became known as the "Kentucky rifle" when Daniel Boone and other frontiersmen carried it into Kentucky Territory. Visitors can see the original store, shop, and displays of rifles. Return to Lancaster, approximately four miles north.

WEST OF LANCASTER

This circuit tour goes west on Route 230 to Elizabethtown, south on Routes 743 and 441, and east on Route 30. Distance is 45 miles.

Begin on Route 222 north, turn left on Route 230 for six miles to an optional detour to the right to a covered bridge on the Mechanicsville Road. Continue on Route 230 to Mt. Joy. Here one can tour the **A. Bubes Brewery and Catacombs** located in the Central Hotel at 102 North Market Street. At this pre-Civil War brewery, equipment used for processing and storing beer can be viewed daily, May through October, 9:00 a.m. to 5:00 p.m. Lunch is served daily at the Central Hotel.

The **Masonic Home**, with its noted formal gardens, is located here. Turn south on Route 743, one mile east on Route 230. Travel four miles on Route 743, turning left to **Donegal Presbyterian Church**. In 1777, the entire congregation gathered under a large oak tree (still standing) and "bore witness" to their support of General Washington.

Proceed right on the road to Chickies, located on the Susquehanna River. The **Circle Creek Farm** in Chickies offers unique lodging and meals in timber tepees. Reservations must be made in advance; write to: R.D. 1, Columbia, PA. Telephone: (717) 426-1234. The **Chickies Rock Observation Site** is a promontory that affords a sweeping view of the great river valley. Continue on Route 441 into Columbia at the Route 30 intersection. The **First National Bank Museum** is located here at Second and Locust streets. The 1814 bank is one of the country's only restored banks in its original setting. The colonial architecture, especially the original unsupported staircase, is very interesting. The museum features exhibits depicting the history of banks in the area. Tours of the museum are by appointment only. Telephone: (717) 684-2521.

For additional information on Lancaster County, contact the Pennsylvania Dutch Visitors Bureau, 501 Greenfield Road, Lancaster, PA 17601. Telephone: (717) 299-8901.

LEBANON AREA

This part of the Pennsylvania Dutch country was settled largely by German immigrants, beginning in the early 1700s. The city of Lebanon was founded in 1750. Reach it by taking I-83 north to Harrisburg, then go east on Routes 322 and 422.

First stop is the **Lebanon County Historical Society Museum**, at 924 Cumberland Street. Here the visitor can see exhibits that reflect more than 200 years of history of the area. The house itself belonged to a well-known Revolutionary War doctor, the Reverend Doctor William Henry Stoy. The building later served as Lebanon's first county courthouse. The museum includes recreated rooms with original equipment for a railroad watchbox, drug store, physician's office, Victorian parlor, children's toyroom, colonial kitchen, schoolhouse, clothing store, barbershop, and a weaver's establishment. There is an excellent museum shop open the same hours as the museum. Open Monday, 1:00 to 4:30 p.m. and 7:00 to 9:00 p.m.; open Wednesday, Friday, and Saturday, 1:00 to 4:30 p.m. Closed holiday weekends. Groups are asked to make appointments. Admission free. Telephone: (717) 272-1473.

The **Dutch Market** is located near 9th and Cumberland

streets. Everything offered in the market stalls is homemade by the Pennsylvania Dutch farm folk. Visitors will delight in the fresh produce, unusual baked goods and preserves, as well as prepared meat products, especially the famous Lebanon bologna. Open Friday, 3:00 to 8:00 p.m., and Saturday, 6:00 a.m. to 2:00 p.m. Admission free. Telephone: (717) 272-9227.

Two blocks from the market is Willow Street, noted for two old churches. **Salem Lutheran Church**, at the corner of 8th Street, was built circa 1735. Telephone: (717) 272-6151. **Tabor Reformed Church**, at the corner of 10th Street, dates from 1762. Telephone: (717) 273-4222.

Proceed north to Maple Street and turn left; proceed three miles on Route 72 to Tunnel Hill Road. The oldest transportation tunnel in the United States, the **Union Canal Tunnel**, was cut through a mountain in 1827, and used from 1832 to 1885.

Middle Creek Wildlife Area, 10 miles southeast of Lebanon near Newmanstown, is a 5,000-acre wildlife management area. The reserve contains waterfowl and wild and farm animals which can be viewed on self-guided vehicle and hiking tours. Picnicking, fishing, boating, and in-season hunting are the featured activities. A visitors center and a museum containing mounted exhibits of all wildlife native to Pennsylvania are located here. Open March through November, Tuesday through Saturday, 9:00 a.m. to 5:00 p.m.; Sunday, noon to 5:00 p.m. Closed Mondays. The area itself is open all year. For information write: Manager, Middle Creek Wildlife Area, Newmanstown RD 1, Newmanstown, PA 17088. Telephone: (717) 733-1512.

Tulpehocken Manor Plantation (1769), on Route 422, three miles east of Lebanon, was the home of Captain Michael Ley. George Washington visited here several times. The plantation is privately owned. Hours vary. Telephone: (717) 866-4926. **Zeller's Fort** is an 18th-century Indian fort, off Route 419 near Newmanstown. Open all year for tours by appointment. Telephone: (215) 589-4301. Donations.

Several plants where Lebanon bologna is made are located nearby. Visitors are shown how the sausage is prepared, and are taken through the smokehouses where the meat is aged and seasoned. (For additional information see the Special Interest Section, Industrial Tours.)

The area's most notable historical monument is **Cornwall Furnace**, five miles south of Lebanon on Route 72, then left a mile on Route 501. In Cornwall follow signs to this unique, well-preserved iron furnace depicting the beginnings of Pennsylvania's iron and steel industry. It is administered by the state as an important historical site. Peter Grubb began mining the rich iron ore banks along Furnace Creek in the 1730s. In 1742 he established a furnace at the present site, which continued in operation until 1883. The ore mines remained in operation until 1972. The sturdy stone miners' houses built over a century ago are still standing.

Cornwall Furnace played an important role in the production of cannons and other military equipment during the Revolution. Washington and Lafayette are said to have visited here during their encampment at Valley Forge to observe the casting of cannons. Hessian prisoners were used as laborers at the furnace. The visitor today can see all the equipment and buildings used in the production of iron and the casting of iron products—the charging platform, furnace and casting room, as well as the interesting blowing equipment. A steam engine dating from 1856 is on display, and there is a collection of 19th-century horse-drawn vehicles in a former blacksmith's shop. Open Tuesday through Saturday, 9:00 a.m. to 5:00 p.m.; Sunday, noon to 5:00 p.m. Tours are self-guided. Admission charge. Telephone: (717) 272-9711.

From Cornwall, one can go west on Route 117 two miles to Mt. Gretna, or east on Route 419 through Pennsylvania Dutch farmlands to Schaefferstown. **Mt. Gretna** is a 100-year-old resort community with 6,000 acres of wooded parklands, lovely Victorian cottages, boating and swimming on Lake Conewago, golf, and an excellent summer theater (Gretna Productions, Inc.), which is one of the oldest in the country. There are also well-known summer music festivals: Jazz at Gretna and Music at Gretna (chamber concerts). Telephone: (717) 964-3627 (theater); (717) 964-3836 (jazz and chamber music); (717) 964-3058 (general information). Plan your overnight stay elsewhere as there are no hotels or motels within the community.

Historic **Schaefferstown** lies east of Lebanon on Route 501. The area has many lovely old stone houses, farmhouses, and churches with unique architectural details. The major site of interest here is the **Alexander Schaeffer Homestead**, with its 1736 Swiss-type bank house and bank barn. Here you can see assorted 18th-century furnishings, artifacts, and farm equipment. Artists, craftsmen, folklorists, and farmers gather on special festival weekends in the summer and fall to share knowledge about local folklore, arts, and crafts. In the village center, two blocks east of the homestead, is a small museum which contains exhibits on spinning wheels, quilts, 18th- and 19th-century cookware, and the culture of tobacco. It is also the site of the first municipal waterworks in America, built in 1750. Open Memorial Day to Labor Day by appointment. Admission free for homestead and village museum. Admission charge for festivals. Telephone: (717) 949-2244; (717) 949-3685; (717) 949-3552.

Established in 1753, **Michter's Distillery**, west of Schaefferstown off Route 419, is the oldest operating distillery in the United States. Visitors can go on conducted tours of the plant and see how 50 barrels of whiskey are produced daily by the old-fashioned pot still method. (See the Special Interest Section, Industrial Tours.)

From Schaefferstown, go north on Route 501 to Myerstown. The **Tulpehocken Lutheran Chnrch**, three miles east of town, dates from approximately the early 19th century. The church was formed in 1744. Telephone: (717) 866-5190.

YORK COUNTY

York, first capital of the United States, is located within two hours' drive of Gettysburg, Lancaster, Harrisburg, and Hershey. York County offers a host of outdoor activities year round; the county is fortunate to have within its boundaries three state parks. Other York County attractions include farmers' markets, brick-end barns, outlet stores, and several Revolutionary sites.

In the following section, three different motor tours, each covering 60 miles, are outlined. Before getting in your car, a walking tour of historical downtown York is suggested. A detailed walking tour map and guide can be obtained from the **Visitors and Tourist Bureau**, located at 1 Marketway East, PO Box 1229, York 17405. Open daily, 8:00 a.m. to 5:00 p.m. Telephone: (717) 848-4000. Some of the sites visited on the tour are described below.

The **Museum and Library of the Historical Society of York County**, at 250 East Market Street, features a comprehensive picture of daily life in 18th-century York County. The contents of the museum include a life-size village square display. The Society's library contains nearly 15,000 volumes and extensive genealogical holdings (including the histories of more than 1,200 regional families). Museum open, Monday through Saturday, 9:00 a.m. to 5:00 p.m.; Sunday, 1:00 to 4:00 p.m. Library open, Monday to Saturday, 9:00 a.m. to 5:00 p.m. Closed Sunday. Nominal admission charge. Telephone: (717) 848-1587.

The **Bonham House**, located at 152 East Market Street, reflects the life and times of the Bonham family during the late 19th century. The rooms are arranged to display different styles and fashions from the red Victorian parlor to the Federal dining room. Also exhibited are the genre paintings of Horace Bonham which have been cited as excellent examples of 19th-century American art. Open Tuesday through Saturday, 10:00 a.m. to 4:00 p.m.; Sunday, 1:00 to 5:00 p.m. Closed Sundays, January through March. Nominal admission charge. Telephone: (717) 845-2422.

Next visit the **York County Colonial Court House**, a full-size reconstruction of the courthouse where the Articles of Confederation were adopted in 1776. The courthouse is located at the intersection of West Market Street and Pershing Avenue. Open weekdays, 9:00 a.m. to 4:30 p.m.; weekends, 1:00 to 4:30 p.m. Admission charge. Telephone: (717) 846-1977.

Nearby, on Philadelphia Street, is the **Central Market House**. Here county farmers sell their produce Tuesday and Thursday, 7:30 a.m. to 4:30 p.m. and Saturday, 6:30 a.m. to 4:30 p.m. Should you wish to visit other markets in the area, there is the **Farmer's Market** at West Market and Penn streets. This picturesque market is open Tuesdays, Fridays, and Saturdays, 6:00 a.m. to 3:30 p.m. **Eastern Market**, on Memory Lane, is open Fridays, 1:00 to 10:00 p.m.

The **Quaker Meeting House** at 135 West Philadelphia Street, built in 1766, is used for regular service. To the right, on Beaver Street, is **St. John's Episcopal Church**. The present structure includes part of the original brick church built in 1765. The bell, presented to the congregation by Queen Caroline of Denmark, can be seen in the vestibule. Regular services are held on Sundays, 7:30 p.m. and 10:00 p.m.

To the south of the church, at 157 West Market Street, are three historical buildings currently maintained by the York County Historical Society: the **Golden Plough Tavern**, the **General Gates House**, and the **Barnett Bobb Log House**. The Golden Plough Tavern, distinguished by its half-timber construction, is believed to have been built in 1741. Architectural historians note that the construction of the Plough reflects the medieval character of the Black Forest in the

18th century, making the structure an anachronism then and now. The tavern also is home to a fine collection of studied furnishings reflecting the William and Mary period. The General Gates House (ca. 1751) was rented by General Gates while he was in York. The house was the site of the famous, but unsuccessful, campaign to replace General Washington with Gates as the head of the Continental Army. It is authentically furnished with fine pieces spanning the country styles of Chippendale and Queen Anne. The Barnett Bobb Log House, which more than 150 years old, is typical of houses built by early German settlers in the York area. The Golden Plough Tavern, General Gates House, and Barnett Bobb Log House are open, Monday through Saturday, 10:00 a.m. to 4:00 p.m.; Sunday, 1:00 to 4:00 p.m. Admission charge covers the three restorations. Telephone: (717) 848-1587.

Close by, at 757 West Market Street, is the **Fire Museum**. Here you will see a restored turn-of-the-century firehouse and a collection of old equipment from all 72 fire companies in York County (some dating back to pre-Revolutionary days). Open April through November, Saturdays and the second Sunday of each month, noon to 4:00 p.m. Admission free. Telephone: (717) 843-0464.

Nearby, visitors can relax at **Penn Common**, a park that was set aside in the original Penn grant. The Common, located on College Avenue, was used as a military campsite in both the Revolutionary War and War of 1812.

While in York, visitors may be interested in visiting some unique sites outside of the historical section of town. Physical culture fans may wish to visit the **Weight-Lifting Hall of Fame and Museum** of antique lifting equipment, located at 56 North Ridge Avenue, under the auspices of York Barbell Company. Also located here is the Bob Hoffman **Softball Hall of Fame**. Open Monday through Saturday, 10:00 a.m. to 4:00 p.m. Admission free. Telephone: (717) 767-6481.

The **Rodney C. Gott Harley-Davidson Motorcycle Museum** is a favorite of motorcycle enthusiasts. Motorcycles from 1903 to the present are on display in the museum. Tours of the museum are offered Monday through Saturday, 10:00 a.m. to 3:30 p.m. on the hour. Admission free. Telephone: (717) 848-1177.

Factory outlet shopping is big business in the York area. Two of the most popular outlets are the **Danskin Factory Outlet** for women's and children's fashions and the **Pfaltzgraff**

Pottery Outlet. York boasts of various outlets handling the following items: candles, nuts and candies, children's clothing, shoes, women's fashions, wicker products, Indian jewelry, plastercraft, jeans, macrame, paperback books, handcrafted leather goods, handbags and belts, raincoats, jackets, pewterex products, metalware, furniture, fabrics, pottery, glassware, luggage, lamps, hosiery, cookies, cashmere sweaters, lingerie, men's and boy's clothing, toys, baby needs, and bedding.

The following three motor tours cover major points of interest in York County.

YORK—HANOVER AREA

To begin, take Route 30 west out of York for approximately 15 miles to Route 194 south. The **Hanover Shoe Farms** are located on Route 194, approximately three miles south of Hanover. The farm is the largest in the world devoted to the breeding of harness race horses.

Retrace your route to Hanover and turn left on High Street (Route 116) to McSherrytown. Drive through town, take the second road to the right, and turn left at the dead end to view **Conewago Chapel.** The chapel, high on the hillside, cannot be missed from a distance. The Conewago Chapel is significant for many reasons. It was the first Catholic Mission in Pennsylvania, established in 1730. The present structure, built in 1787, replaced the original log chapel constructed in 1741. The chapel is also the first parish church in America dedicated to the Sacred Heart of Jesus. In recent years the church was elevated to the eminence of a Minor Basilica by Pope John XXIII; there are only a half dozen churches in the United States which have been bestowed such an honor. Along with the church's exquisite Georgian architecture, visitors can see beautiful 19th-century murals by Austrian painters. Open daily. Admission free.

After leaving the chapel, you may want to visit the delightful town of New Oxford, on Route 30 west. The town is full of antique stores. Close by is the **Little Red School House,** an authentic recreation of a schoolhouse of the 1860s. Open daily. Admission free. (Ask for directions in New Oxford.)

You will find the 3,320-acre **Codorus State Park** two miles off Route 216, three miles east of Hanover, and only three miles north of the Maryland line. It boasts one of the largest outdoor swimming pools in the nation, plus a five-mile-long lake for swimming, boating, and fishing. In summer, visitors can enjoy hiking, nature study, camping, horse-back riding, fishing, canoeing, sailing, powerboating, and evening programs. In winter, there is ice skating and tobogganing. For information and literature, write Park Manager, R.D. #3, Hanover, PA 17331. Telephone: (717) 637-2816.

Continue east on Route 30. Two miles beyond Thomasville tourists may wish to inspect the large stone quarry. The tour ends in York, three miles to the east.

YORK—WELLSVILLE—LEWISBERRY

Leave York via Bull Road until you reach Route 921. Turn right on 921 and right again on the first road. You will cross **Bentzel's Mill Covered Bridge** and pass the old mill. Return to Route 921, and go south two miles to Dover and continue on Route 74 to Rossville. Go west at Rossville one mile to Wellsville and turn right. Proceed about a mile to the **Warrington Quaker Meeting House**, erected in 1769 and still periodically used. Nearby, the visitor can inspect an old **brick-end barn**. This type of barn was commonly built in the 1700s in Pennsylvania. The brick ends have openings, necessary for ventilation, in various patterns such as trees and birds.

Just past Rossville east on Route 177 is **Gifford Pinchot State Park**. Conveniently located between York and Harrisburg, off I-83, this 2,338-acre park offers year-round recreation. There is hiking, camping, nature study, fishing, canoeing, sailing, boating, and lake swimming. Winter activities include skiing and ice skating, and the 1,300-foot toboggan chute is a real thriller. For information, write Park Manager, R.D. #2, Lewisberry, PA 17339. Telephone: (717) 432-5011.

From Wellsville, about four miles west on Route 74, is **Round Top**, a noted ski resort. Continue east on Route 177, from Wellsville toward Lewisberry, and take a right on Route 382 before town. By taking this detour you will be able to view the **Redland Quaker Meeting House**, built in 1811. The road east of Lewisberry is paved with brick, one of the few remaining roads of this type. Continue on Route 382 and turn left on Route 111 (not the expressway). Go north to Route 262 and take a right to **River View**. From this high vantage point, you will have a spectacular view of the Susquehanna River. Continue on Route 382 until York Haven; then take Routes 181 and 92 to Mt. Wolf. Turn left to Starview and follow the signs to **Codorus Furnace**, a Revolution-era smelting furnace which was originally owned by Pennsylvania's signer of the Declaration of Independence, Col. James Smith. The furnace is situated along a creek surrounded by rolling hills and is an ideal picnic spot.

Take the road left through Highmount and to Route 30; then turn right for the return trip to York. About a mile beyond Hallam, off Route 462, is the **Shoe House**, a unique three-story residence in the shape of a shoe. The house features an ice-cream smorgasbord. Open during the summer months, daily, 9:00 a.m. to 5:00 p.m.; winter months, weekends only. Admission charge.

YORK TO INDIAN STEPS MUSEUM

From York, go east on Prospect Street (Route 124) approximately eight miles, turn left, and then go three miles to **Samuel S. Lewis State Park**. The 71-acre park is open for day use only. For information telephone: (717) 432-5011. From the top of **Mt. Pisgah** (more than 1,000 feet above sea level) the visitor can see the broad expanse of York County, the multiple-arch concrete bridge over the Susquehanna River, and parts of Lancaster County across the river.

A worthwhile stop before Samuel S. Lewis Park is the **Wills School** in Delray, on Route 124, six miles from York. This school, built in 1875, was in use until 1955. All of the original furnishings—desk, organ, blackboards, water cooler, pot-bellied stove, and wall decorations—can be seen. Mannikins garbed in period clothing add a touch of realism to the school. A venerable white oak, one of the largest and oldest in the area, stands behind the school.

After leaving the park, follow the signs to Long Level, along Route 624 which is exceptionally scenic. At **Long Level** the traveler can inspect the ruins of the old Susquehanna Canal. At Craley, follow Route 124 to York Furnace, and signs to **Indian Steps Museum**. Dedicated to the American Indian, this museum displays great quantities of relics of the Susquehannock and other Indians who lived along the "long winding river." The exhibits are arranged in seven rooms in the old mansion which houses the collection. The museum is open April through October, Tuesday through Saturday, 11:00 a.m. to 4:00 p.m.; Sunday, 11:00 a.m. to 6:00 p.m.; closed Monday. Admission free. About 200 feet from the museum stands the oldest and largest female holly tree found in this latitude, a 65-foot high specimen.

HARRISBURG AND HERSHEY

The major attractions in the Harrisburg-Hershey area are the public buildings and museums in the Capitol Hill area of Harrisburg and the many attractions that comprise "Chocolate Town, U.S.A." Harrisburg is approximately 115 miles northeast of Washington, DC, and 75 miles north of Baltimore. Hershey is 12 miles east of Harrisburg on Route 322.

HARRISBURG

Harrisburg, capital city of the Keystone State since 1812, is famed for its picturesque "front steps" leading down to the broad Susquehanna River. The city has many beautiful parkways and gardens and numerous old homes.

In the middle of the city, between North and Walnut streets, towers the 272-foot **State Capitol** building, of Italian Renaissance style, with a dome patterned after that of St. Peter's in Rome. At the entrance to the Capitol are 27 dynamic granite figures, sculptured by a Pennsylvanian, George Grey Barnard. The Rotunda, the Legislative Chambers, and the Governor's Suite are lavish with mahogany, marble, statuary, and paintings. The corridor floors contain more than 400 mosaics which were designed and executed by Henry Mercer of Doylestown. Free conducted tours of the Capitol are available to visitors. Tours are offered Monday through Friday, 9:00 a.m. to 4:00 p.m. The cafeteria in the Capitol building is open to the public.

The **Governors Mansion**, located on North Second Street, is open to visitors, May through mid-October, Tuesdays and Thursdays, 10:00 a.m. to 2:00 p.m. Admission free.

Directly north of the Capitol, on Third Street between North and Forster streets, is the **State Museum of Pennsylvania**. The main portion of the museum is the William Penn Memorial Hall. This impressive three-storied hall is dominated by an 18-foot stylized bronze statue of Penn created by the Pennsylvania sculptress, Janet de Coux. Exhibitions of works from the permanent Pennsylvania Collection of Fine Arts, along with changing art shows, are on display in the Fine Arts Galleries on the ground floor of the Museum. As many as 10 or 12 major exhibitions of historic and contemporary arts and crafts are presented annually, along with several small or special showings. In addition, the museum has exhibits on the decorative arts and history of the state; displays of fine furniture, glassware, pottery, pewter and other materials, a transportation exhibit in the Hall of Industry and Technology, a Hall of Anthropology, a Gallery of Military History, and a Planetarium. The museum is open in summer, Tuesday through Saturday, 9:00 a.m. to 5:00 p.m.; Sunday, noon to 5:00 p.m.; in winter, Tuesday through Saturday, 10:00 a.m. to 4:30 p.m.; Sunday, noon to 4:30 p.m. Admission free. For more information and schedules on Planetarium shows and other special museum programs, telephone: (717) 787-4978.

To the north of the museum stands the **tower of the Archives Building**. Its 21 levels contain extensive collections of official public records, historical manuscripts, and microfilms for research and writing on the history of Pennsylvania from William Penn's time down to the present. The public entrance to the Search Room of the Archives Building is off Third Street through the ornamental gates and the west garden court. Visiting researchers may ask at the Search Room for the documentary materials they need, and may use the desks and other facilities of the room for their work. Open Tuesday through Friday, 9:00 a.m. to 5:00 p.m. Closed weekends.

Across from the Capitol, at the intersection of Third and Walnut streets, is the Strawberry Square Shopping Mall. On the third floor of the mall is the **Museum of Scientific Discovery**. Exhibits display the wonders of physics, electronics, astronomy, and more. The museum's exhibits are "hands on," allowing the visitor to participate. Although the museum is a favorite of children, most of the exhibits are geared to mature audiences. Open Tuesday through Saturday, 10:00 a.m. to 6:00 p.m.; Sunday, noon to 5:00 p.m. Closed on Monday. Admission charge. Children under three free. Telephone: (717) 233-7969.

West of Capitol Hill on Front Street, the gaily colored mansions of the Commonwealth's statesmen, reposing in the shadow of giant oaks and elms, look out on the glittering river beyond. In the middle of the river is lovely **City Island Park**, with a bathing beach, baseball stadium, recreated 19th-century village, and facilities for motorboating, canoeing, sailing, and fishing.

John Harris Mansion, 219 South Front Street, is the home of the **Dauphin County Historical Society**. The mansion was built in 1766 by Harrisburg's founder and has since been "Victorianized." The museum specializes in 19th-century

Victorian decorative arts. Researchers may be interested in the Society's archives, which date from 1750 to the present. Open Monday through Friday, noon to 4:00 p.m. Closed weekends. Nominal admission charge.

Fort Hunter Mansion Museum (1814) is a 19th-century Federal style mansion located on the site of what once was an old French and Indian War fort. From Harrisburg it is approximately six miles north via Front Street. On the mansion tour, which lasts one hour, visitors can see exhibits of antique furniture, costumes, pewter, glass, and toys. Open May through October 15 and December 1 to 23, Tuesday through Sunday, 10:00 a.m. to 4:30 p.m. Admission charge. Children under six free.

There are several other interesting sites in the Harrisburg vicinity. At the northern end of the city, the **Pennsylvania Farm Show Building**, with 13 acres under one continuous roof, is the site of the annual Pennsylvania Farm Show, held annually in mid-January. The exhibition is the largest of its kind in the world.

The now quite-famous **Three Mile Island Visitor Center**, located off Route 441 south, 10 miles outside of Harrisburg in Middletown, is open daily. The visitors center offers exhibits as well as an informative film on nuclear power production. The center is open daily, 10:00 a.m. to 5:00 p.m. A drive-around plant tour, lasting about one hour, is offered daily, Monday through Friday, 9:30 a.m. and 1:30 p.m., Tuesday and Thursday, 6:30 p.m.; weekends, 9:00 a.m. In-plant tours lasting three hours are only offered for groups of eight or more (yes, it's safe!). Arrangements must be made in advance. Telephone: (717) 948-8829. Admission free.

From Routes 15 and 11, 30 miles north of Harrisburg, travelers can take a 15-minute ride across the Susquehanna River on the old **Millersburg Ferry**. Landings are at Liverpool and Millersburg, and the ferry is operated daily from dawn to dusk. Nominal fare. The **Millersburg Ferryboat Campsites** are open in the summer for camping. Telephone: (717) 444-3200.

HERSHEY

Hershey, with its wide variety of tourist attractions, is built around the world's largest chocolate factory. This community and showplace was created by Milton S. Hershey, more than 60 years ago. He founded the **Hershey Chocolate Company** on a site near his birthplace, and proceeded to build the greatest chocolate business in the world. By the early 1920s "Chocolate Town, U.S.A." had established itself as one of the most unique places to visit. The streetlights are shaped like kisses (some chocolate and others foil wrapped). Street names, such as Cocoa Street and Chocolate Avenue, won't allow you to forget where you are. The ambience of the town is sweetened by the scent of chocolate. "Chocolate Town, U.S.A." is just two hours from the Washington Beltway.

Chocolate World replaced the Hershey chocolate plant tours in the early 1970s. At Chocolate World, a good place to begin your tour of Hershey, you can take a ride through the chocolate processing procedure—from the tropical plantations to the processing of chocolate at the plant. After the ride, you can visit the tropical garden where cocoa, banana, and palm trees grow. At Chocolate World, "chocoholics" will enjoy the wide variety of bizarre chocolate items for sale. Open Memorial Day through Labor Day, daily, 9:00 a.m. to 6:45 p.m. Thereafter, daily, 9:00 a.m. to 4:00 p.m. Admission free.

A visit to the **Hershey Museum of American Life** will take you back through the lives of the earliest explorers on this continent. Other displays include the dress and artifacts of North American Indians, Stiegel glassware in great variety, the famous Apostolic Clock, Conestoga Wagons, a rare gun collection, models of Pennsylvania canal boats, and antique automobiles. Open Memorial Day through Labor Day, 9:00 a.m. to 6:00 p.m.; Labor Day through Memorial Day, 10:00 a.m. to 5:00 p.m. Admission charge.

The Hershey Gardens and Arboretum, together covering 23 acres with more than 100,000 tulips, roses, and chrysanthemum plants, constitute the grounds of the Hotel Hershey. The gardens originated in 1936, when Milton Hershey was asked to contribute one million dollars to a National Rosarium in Washington, but instead decided to beautify his own community. The gardens contain a holly collection with 80 different varieties and more than 400 varieties of roses. Open April and May, daily, 9:00 a.m. to 5:00 p.m.; June through August, daily, 9:00 a.m. to 7:00 p.m. Admission charge.

Hotel Hershey, where you may wish to stay or to dine, is a noteworthy example of the Spanish style of the 1930s. Hershey's four golf courses, 54 holes in all, have been the scene of P.G.A. and other national tournaments. The Juvenile Course is specially designed for children.

Hersheypark, founded in 1906, has been recognized as

one of America's top theme parks. It is comprised of seven theme areas, including ZooAmerica, a 10-acre complex featuring plants and animals representing five natural regions throughout North America; a 17th-century English village; an 18th-century German town; a 19th-century Pennsylvania Dutch settlement; a petting zoo; a contemporary area featuring a 330-foot-high Kissing Tower and Twin Turnpike rides. There is live entertainment in five theaters and the 37 amusement rides include three roller coasters and 14 rides just for children. Open mid-May through mid-September, 10:30 a.m. to 10:00 p.m.

For group rates and group picnic planning, telephone: (717) 534-3916. For up-to-the-minute information about hours and entertainment, telephone: (717) 534-3900. Admission charge. Children under four free.

Hersheypark Arena seats 7,300 spectators for concerts, plays, ice shows, hockey games, and other sports. There is public ice skating in season. Telephone: (717) 534-3911.

The **Pennsylvania State Police Academy** is located at the north edge of Hershey, on Air Park Road near Route 743. It offers guided tours of its criminology exhibits, the academy, and the stables. Tours, Monday through Friday, 10:00 a.m. to noon and 12:30 to 2:30 p.m. Admission free.

Founders Hall of Milton Hershey School is located south of the center of Hershey on Route 322. The school was founded in 1909 by Milton Hershey to provide a good education and life-style for "social" orphan boys. The visitors area at Founders Hall is worth a visit to see the film on the founding of Hershey and exhibits on the history of the school. Film shown six times daily, 9:30 a.m. to 2:30 p.m. Open weekdays, 9:00 a.m. to 4:00 p.m.; weekends, 10:00 a.m. to 4:00 p.m. Admission free.

In the Hershey area there are several other attractions (not chocolate coated) worth a visit. **Dan-D-Village**, located three miles north of Hershey off Route 39W, is a Pennsylvania Dutch barn containing an unusual antique furniture collection, an outlet for Pennsylvania furniture and pottery, and period exhibits including a display of animated antique German dolls. Open daily, Monday to Saturday, 10:00 a.m. to 5:00 p.m.; Sunday, noon to 5:00 p.m. Admission free.

Also three miles outside of Hershey, but to the west, is **Indian Echo Caverns**, off Route 322. The caverns were opened in 1783, and they contain beautiful displays of stalactite and stalagmite formations. The caverns are always 52 degrees, so carry a sweater! Open Memorial Day through Labor bay, daily, 9:00 a.m. to 6:00 p.m.; April, May, September, and October, daily, 10:00 a.m. to 4:00 p.m.; March and November, weekends only. Admission charge.

SOUTH CENTRAL PENNSYLVANIA

CHAMBERSBURG AREA

The Chambersburg area, 24 miles west of Gettysburg on Route 30, has a number of historic points of interest including memorials to the abolitionist John Brown, the birthplace of President James Buchanan, and Thaddeus Stevens' blacksmith shop and iron furnace. In addition, one can visit churches, covered bridges, and state parks in the area.

If you plan to visit the birthplace of our 15th president, turn off at Greencastle, on Route 16, which leads to Mercersburg, 11 miles to the west. At Greencastle, see **Martin's Mill Covered Bridge** and the **Enoch Brown Park**, a memorial to a schoolmaster and his pupils, massacred in 1764. The **Brown's Mill School**, state-maintained, is an old one-room school in which early residents were educated. It is open afternoons, Thursday through Sunday and by appointment.

Greencastle is noted for its many large colonies of purple martins which make their homes in boxes provided by the municipality. The birds are "at home" from March until early August. At **Mercersburg**, the restored log cabin in which President Buchanan was born can be seen at the Mercersburg Academy amidst the Gothic-style buildings. Turn on Route 416, which leads to Route 30 and into Chambersburg, a distance of 16 miles.

Chambersburg was laid out in 1763 on the site of Chambers Fort, one of 13 such forts in the area. The town grew, especially after the railroad arrived in 1837. A serious setback, however, occurred in 1864, when raiding Confederates burned the town, destroying 537 buildings. A monument in **Memorial Square** recalls this episode. The unusual fountain seen in Memorial Square was made in France for the Philadelphia Exposition of 1876. It was purchased and moved to its present site in 1877, serving as a memorial to local men who fought in the Union Army.

North of Memorial Square, near North Main and King streets, is **Falling Spring Presbyterian Church**, established in 1739. Here a rose-rent ceremony takes place each year, in which a church elder pays the rent, one red rose, to a descendent of Benjamin Chambers. Behind the church lie buried many early pioneers, as well as Indians, who once lived in the area. Two other churches make annual rose payments to descendents of Benjamin Chambers. They are the First Evangelical Lutheran and Zion United Church of Christ. Also, in Chambersburg, a few blocks out Philadelphia Avenue, is **Wilson College**, a private women's college founded in 1869.

Rocky Spring Presbyterian Church, founded in 1738, is a picturesque structure located a few miles northwest of the city. The church was constructed without a chimney so that smoke from the stoves would not attract the attention of Indians. Instead, the smoke was directed to the attic where it filtered through the cracks inconspicuously.

Caledonia State Park is located 11 miles east of Chambersburg, on Route 30. The park includes the **Thaddeus Stevens Blacksmith Shop Museum**. Here one can inspect the iron furnace developed by Stevens, who was a noted abolitionist and advocate of free schooling of children by the state. The park has facilities for swimming, picnicking, camping, hiking, fishing, and golfing. Both the park and the blacksmith museum are open only during summer months. The **Graeffenburg Inn**, located in the park, has been operating for more than 150 years. The **Totem Pole Playhouse**, at Caledonia on Route 30, offers productions year round. Telephone: (717) 352-2161 for park, 352-2164 for playhouse.

Cowan's Gap State Park is located off Route 75, 18 miles from Chambersburg. It is nestled high in the Tuscarora Mountains. The lake in the park is a very popular fishing spot; there are also boating, swimming, and picnicking facilities. Winter sports include skiing and ice skating. Rental cabins and tent-camping sites are available. For reservations and information telephone: (717) 485-3948.

For additional information about the Chambersburg area contact: Greater Chambersburg Chamber of Commerce, 75 South Second Street, Chambersburg, PA 17201. Telephone: (717) 264-7101.

Franklin County Tourist Council, 175 East Queen Street, Chambersburg, PA 17201. Telephone: (717) 263-8282.

GETTYSBURG

Gettysburg is the site of the greatest battle of the Civil War, July 1-3, 1863. The battlefield is now a **National Mili-**

tary Park administered by the National Park Service. Nearly 35 miles of park roads lead to various monuments, memorials, and landmarks such as Little Round Top and Cemetery Ridge.

The Battle of Gettysburg, one of the most important and hotly contested battles of the Civil War, resulted in 51,000 casualties, making it the war's bloodiest battle. At Gettysburg the Federal Army of the Potomac, under General Meade, met the invading Confederate Army.

On the third day, after a heavy two-hour artillery barrage, Confederate forces advanced in the face of deadly fire that shattered their ranks and spelled disaster for the Confederate Army. They retreated on the evening of July 4, ending the last major offensive of Lee's army and presaging the war's outcome.

On November 19, 1863, President Lincoln dedicated Soldier's National Cemetery on the battlefield, as he delivered his most famous speech, the Gettysburg Address.

The park is open year round. The **Visitor Center** is located just south of the city at the intersection of Routes 15 and 134. Here tourists can see an accurate and instructional orientation program as well as many exhibits created by the National Park Service.

Licensed guides conduct visitors on a complete two-hour tour of the park. A fee is charged per car or per chartered bus. If you wish to tour the battlefield at your own pace, however, you can do so easily with the help of the map and text of the park brochure available at the Visitor Center. A one-hour walking tour leading to **Meade's Headquarters** and the **High Water Mark** is also delineated in the brochure.

For a fee, you can also tour the battlefield in an air-conditioned bus, and hear Raymond Massey and a cast of actors recreate "The Battle of Gettysburg." The main bus terminal is at the Gettysburg Tour Center on Baltimore Street.

The **Gettysburg Cyclorama**, a panoramic painting of the climax of Pickett's charge, by the French artist Paul Philippoteaux, is in the Visitor Center. There is a small admission charge to see this artistic spectacle (children free), unless the visitor holds a current Federal Recreation Area Entrance Permit. Also at the Cyclorama is an electric map of the battlefield and a large collection of Civil War relics.

Erected near the site of Lincoln's Gettysburg Address is

a 307-foot **National Tower.** For a panoramic view of Gettysburg and the battlefield, ascend to the top by elevator. Admission charge.

The **Battle Theatre,** opposite the Visitor's Center, offers a film and diorama, "America at Gettysburg." Admission charge.

There are also about 15 commercially operated tourist attractions in the surrounding area. They include wax museums, dioramas, collections of Civil War relics, and a fantasyland for youngsters.

Soldier's National Museum includes dioramas of 10 major battles of the Civil War. This exhibit is located near the intersection of Routes 140 and 15. Admission charge.

Located at the Gettysburg Tour Center is **Old Gettysburg Village,** with craft shops, a country store, and several specialty shops. Summer hours: 10:00 a.m. to 10:00 p.m. Closed during the winter. Admission free.

Lincoln Room Museum, in a building on Lincoln Square, exhibits the room where Lincoln spent the night before delivering the Gettysburg Address. A recording recreates the delivery of the famous speech. Summer hours: 9:00 a.m. to 7:00 p.m. Admission charge.

Hall of Presidents and First Ladies is next to the National Cemetery on Baltimore Street. It is a display of life-size wax: figures with authentic reproductions of First Ladies' gowns. Admission charge.

Jenny Wade House and Olde Town, also on Baltimore Street, tells the story of Gettysburg's heroine in an authentic setting. Summer hours: 8:00 a.m. to 9:00 p.m. Winter: 8:00 a.m. to 5:00 p.m. Admission charge.

National Civil War Wax Museum is an audio-visual presentation of the Civil War with 200 life-size figures in 36 scenes. It is located on Route 15, six blocks south of town. Admission charge.

General Lee's Headquarters, on Route 30, now houses a collection of Civil War relics. Admission free.

There is a live presentation at **A. Lincoln's Place Theatre,** 777 Baltimore Street south from Lincoln Square. Daily performances. Palm Sunday through October. Admission charge.

Another attraction on Baltimore Street is the **Farnsworth House and Garret Museum.** Guides dressed as Civil War soldiers conduct tours of the house and museum, which feature authentic Civil War letters, photographs, artifacts, and weapons. During the summer season, open daily, 1:00 to

3:00 p.m.; 8:00 p.m., tour of Garret Museum only. Telephone: (717) 334-8838.

The **Lincoln Train Museum,** on Steinwehr Avenue, offers seven dioramas on the role of trains in the Civil War; also a collection of more than 1,000 model trains. Open March 1 through November 1. Admission charge.

Also on Steinwehr Avenue, visitors can view a multimedia show entitled *The Conflict.* Through music and slides the history of the Civil War is retold. The program lasts 45 minutes and begins every hour from 10:00 a.m. to 10:00 p.m. For additional information, telephone: (717) 334-8003.

On the **Gettysburg Railroad,** you can take a 16-mile round-trip ride to Biglerville on old coaches pulled by steam locomotive. On occasion, a 50-mile round trip is offered to Mount Holly Springs. Trains for the short trip leave the station on North Washington Street in Gettysburg on weekends only from June 1 through October 31. For schedules and fares telephone: (717) 334-6932.

Two nearby attractions of interest to children are the **Gettysburg Game Park** and **Gettysburg Miniature Horse Farm.** The former is located in Fairfield, nine miles southwest of Gettysburg on Route 116. Many of the animals are domesticated and can be fed and petted. It is open daily, 10:00 a.m. to dark, April to December. Admission charge. The miniature horse farm is off Route 30, west of Gettysburg. Turn left at Knoxlyn Road, about three miles from the city. At the farm you can see miniature thoroughbreds, Appaloosas, and draft horses. Many of these full-grown miniature horses weigh only 50 pounds. Visitors can take pony, sulky, and wagon rides, the latter with miniature vehicles. The farm is open daily, 10:00 a.m. to dusk, Memorial Day through September. For hours during the winter telephone: (717) 334-7259.

Also near Gettysburg is **Mister Ed's Elephant Museum,** on Route 30, 12 miles out of town. One man's personal collection of more than 4,000 elephant figures forms a unique attraction. Telephone: (717) 352-3792.

For the visitor to Gettysburg, **The Eisenhower Farm** is within easy reach only by bus. Buses leave the Visitor Center every 15 minutes, 9:00 a.m. to 4:15 p.m. Nominal fare. The farm is the place where President Dwight David Eisenhower lived out his final years with his wife, Mamie. The renovated neo-Georgian home, the cattle barn, and the putting green, situated amid 500 acres of corn adjacent to the battlefield, are among its special features.

A motor tour covering some of Adams County's historic and scenic sites is outlined below. The tour, which starts and ends in Gettysburg, covers some 36 miles around the city. It includes many of the county's famous orchards.

The tour begins at the **Gettysburg Travel Council Office**, on Carlisle Street (Business Route 15 North). The tourist office is housed in the old **Western Maryland Railroad Station** (1858), one of many historic buildings in Gettysburg. Drive south along Carlisle Street to what is now known as **Lincoln Square**. From the square, turn right onto Route 30 West (Chambersburg Street). As you enter the square, on your left, notice the **Wills House**, which is now the Lincoln Room Museum (see description above). As you continue along Chambersburg Street, **Christ Lutheran Church** (1863) will be on the left about one-half block beyond the square.

Continue west on Chambersburg Street for three blocks to the second traffic light. Keep in the left lane and continue straight ahead on Springs Avenue, where there are the first of a series of signs designating the "Scenic Valley Tour." At the intersection of Springs Avenue and Route 30 West is a monument commemorating the young men of Gettysburg who joined together in defense of Pennsylvania when the Confederate invasion began in June 1863. On Springs Avenue you will climb **Seminary Ridge**, at the top of which is the **Gettysburg Lutheran Theological Seminary** (1826). Signs indicate the turn left to West Confederate Avenue and into **Gettysburg National Military Park** (see description above). Scenic Tour signs guide you through the military sites in the park.

After a visit to the park, follow the tour signs and take a right turn onto Waterworks Road and pass the entrance road to the **Eisenhower Farm**. The farm is not open to the public, except for organized bus tours, but you may be able to see some Angus cattle grazing in the pasture. As you continue straight ahead you will cross Marsh Creek via **Sauk's Covered Bridge**. This 150-year-old bridge has "lattice-work" siding, a unique form of bridge construction.

The Township after crossing Marsh Creek is called "Freedom." The title is appropriate in that the whole area was once part of the **Manor of Maske**, a 43,500-acre plantation of the Proprietors of Pennsylvania (the William Penn family). In this area the Mason-Dixon Survey was undertaken between 1763 and 1767 in order to settle the boundary dispute between Maryland and Pennsylvania. There still remain in place a very few of the famous stone markers which traced the final **Mason-Dixon Line**. The tour route intersects Route 116, which was the old "Hagerstown Road" out of Gettysburg. The road was used by Lee's troops as they retreated south in 1863.

When the route you are following ends at a stop sign, turn left toward **Orrtanna**. The orchards through which you will be traveling extend for miles and miles. You cannot miss the roadside camps set up to house migrant laborers. At the intersection you will see the **Knouse Food Cooperative** which handles millions of apples, cherries, and other fruit produced in the area. Turn right at the intersection, cross the railroad tracks, and continue straight ahead up to the summit of **Mt. Newman**. You will arrive at the **Church of St. Ignatius Loyola**, built in 1816 by the Jesuits from Conewago Chapel (see York County section for description of the chapel). The church, along with its graveyard, is worth a visit. From St. Ignatius Church, continue down the hill to the intersection with Route 234. This stretch of road provides a panoramic view of the Buchanan Valley. At the intersection, turn right onto Route 234 to Biglerville. Beyond **Camp Nawaka**, along Route 234, the road runs through what is known as **The Narrows** with **Conewago Creek** on your right. The Conewago is noted for its scenic beauty and its excellent trout. Hence, the Narrows is a favorite picnic spot.

As you approach Arendtsville, the **South Mountain Fairgrounds** are on your left. In addition to the annual fair in September, the grounds are headquarters for the Apple Blossom and Apple Harvest celebrations held each year in the county (see calendar of events). In Arendtsville, you will pass two churches, **Trinity Lutheran** and **Zion United Church of Christ**, both of which have congregations dating back to about 1804. Just before you enter Biglerville, note on your left the sign pointing to the **Fruit Research Laboratory**, indicative of the importance of fruit cultivation in the county.

Biglerville, once known as Middletown, was plotted in 1817 and now calls itself the "Apple Capital of the U.S.A." At the traffic light in Biglerville, turn onto Route 34 toward Gettysburg. One-fourth of a mile along the road to Mummasburg (the turnoff is approximately three miles south of Biglerville) is **Russell's Tavern**, which was Washington's stopping place one night in 1794, as he returned from quelling the so-called "Whiskey Rebellion." Washington actually did sleep in the tavern. Continue south on Route 34 seven miles to Gettysburg. As you come over **Keckler's Hill** into Gettysburg, you might like to imagine how Confederate General Jubal Early felt as he traveled over this hill with his troops in 1863. Route 34 becomes Carlisle Street as it enters the Borough of Gettysburg.

For additional information about Gettysburg contact: The Gettysburg Travel Council Information Center, 35 Carlisle Street, Gettysburg, PA 17325. Telephone: (717) 334-6274.

CARLISLE AREA

The year 1720 marks the coming of the white man to the Cumberland Valley, where Carlisle is now located. The town, nestled in the Cumberland Mountains 29 miles north of Gettysburg, is off the main tourist track yet worth a visit.

The earliest settler in the valley was an Indian trader, James Le Tort, who arrived at Great Beaver Pond, two miles south of Carlisle. In the decade following 1720, Scotch-Irish settlers began arriving in considerable numbers.

Carlisle, named for Carlisle, England, was laid out in 1751. Like its namesake, the town is bound by streets North, South, East, and West. The intervening streets, Louther, High, and Pomfret, running east and west, and Bedford, Hanover, and Pitt, running north and south, were all named for streets in Carlisle, England.

The **First Presbyterian Church** (1757), and **Dickinson College**, chartered in 1783, are among Carlisle's interesting institutions. The courtroom on the second floor of the **Old Court House** is a classic example of early courtrooms. Carlisle was the home of Molly Pitcher, famed heroine of the Battle of Monmouth, and several monuments have been erected to her memory in the "Old Graveyard."

Other historical buildings include the **County Jail** (1854), noted for its Roman architecture, the **Duncan-Stiles house** (1815), and the **Ephraim Blaine House** (1749). For more information and details on an interesting walking tour, stop at or write to the Greater Carlisle Area Chamber of Commerce, 212 North Hanover Street, Carlisle, PA 17013. Telephone: (717) 243-4515.

The **Cumberland County Historical Society** was founded in 1874 to gather and publish facts of regional history. The society maintains a library and museum which are open to the public, Monday, 7:00 to 9:00 p.m.; Tuesday through Friday, 1:00 to 4:00 p.m. The library has newspapers dating back to 1785. Among attractions in the museum are the oldest American-made printing press in existence, the finest collection of Schimmel and Mountz woodcarvings in Pennsylvania, a notable collection of early mechanical banks, iron products of 18th-century forges, photos of Jim Thorpe and other great Carlisle Indian School athletes, and products of Cumberland County artisans and manufacturers. Telephone: (717) 249-7610.

The **Village of Colonial Peddlers**, located in a picturesque setting along Letort Creek in Carlisle, has several antique, craft, and Americana shops all in the "Spirit of 1776." Shops open Monday through Saturday, 10:00 a.m. to 5:00 p.m.; Sundays and holidays, 1:00 to 5:00 p.m.

The **Carlisle Barracks**, the second oldest military post in the United States, currently houses the Army War College. There are several interesting sites worth visiting on the base. The **Omar N. Bradley Museum**, which houses General Bradley's collection of more than 200,000 books, 30,000 volumes of periodicals, a huge collection of personal papers, and military memorabilia, is open to the public Monday, 8:00 to noon; Wednesday and Friday, 1:00 to 4:00 p.m. Admission free. **The Hessian Powder Magazine** (1777) was used in Revolutionary days, 1777-89, as a munitions post. Hessian prisoners were brought here from Trenton. Open May through September, Saturday and Sunday, 1:00 to 4:00 p.m. Admission free. **The Military History Institute** houses the largest collection of materials related to U.S. army history dating from the French and Indian War to the present. Open Monday through Friday, 8:00 a.m. to 4:30 p.m. Admission free. Telephone: (717) 245-3434.

Eight miles west of Carlisle, in Newville on Route 641, is **Laughlin Mill** (1763), a classic example of a mill village of the 18th century. Just west of Newville, near State Game Land, a sign directs the visitor to the **Thompson Covered Bridge**, built in 1853. Five miles south of Carlisle on Route 34 is the **Antique Bike Museum** with a collection of bicycles from 1830 to the present era. Admission free.

A Broadway theater in a rural setting, **Allenberry Playhouse**, on Route 174 at Boiling Springs five miles east of Carlisle, is open April to November. Telephone (717) 258-3211 for program information and reservations.

To the east of Carlisle at 5103 Carlisle Pike, Mechanicsburg,

is the **Great Factory Store**, a factory discount outlet of
nationally advertised brands.

An interesting scenic return route is via Route 81, west
to Centerville, then south on Route 233, which passes through
Pine Grove Furnace State Park and Mount Alto State Park,
then through Waynesboro and into Hagerstown. **Mount Alto
State Park** is a lovely, out-of-the-way place for picnicking.
The 24-acre park with a creek running through it is located
approximately 20 miles north of Hagerstown.

NEW JERSEY

For the visitor, South Jersey offers a wide range of attractions, from historic sites and unspoiled **Pine Barrens** to the dazzling night life of Atlantic City. The area divides readily into four tourist regions: the southern half of the **Delaware River Region**, which stretches up along the river from Salem in the south to Camden; **Cape May**; the **Shore**, which includes **Atlantic City**; and the **Delaware Bay Area**.

South Jersey has a number of fine state forests and parks. Visitors are reminded that New Jersey state law prohibits pets and alcoholic beverages inside these areas. Fishing licenses are required for all freshwater fishing. (This includes fishing above the freshwater point on the Delaware River and other rivers that empty into the ocean.) No licenses are required for saltwater fishing, although it is normally prohibited on bathing beaches during the day when lifeguards are on duty. Additional information on licenses and fishing areas can be obtained from the New Jersey Division of Fish, Game, and Wildlife, 363 Pennington Avenue, Trenton, NJ 08625. Telephone: (609) 292-9450. Permits for overnight camping must be obtained from park managers.

New Jersey is notable for historic sites relating to the colonial period, the Revolution, and even the Civil War. General Washington based his operations here because the dense forests hid more than 80 illegal iron foundries which could produce essential guns and cannons. One of the major causes of the Revolution was the desire of the colonists to be allowed to manufacture their own goods. According to British law all raw materials had to be exported to Britain and the finished products then imported at high prices. General Washington had to judge carefully which of the local residents were sympathetic to his cause and could be trusted to lead his men safely through the wooded countryside. At that time, only about one-third of the colonists supported the Revolution; another third, Tories, supported the British Crown, although many did not fight and after the war emigrated to

Canada and the West Indies; the final third were indifferent. New Jersey has a large number of excellent historical societies and other groups. Today the societies are responsible for preserving many sites, and they often publish or distribute information on them.

PINE BARRENS

The New Jersey Pine Barrens extend through more than one million acres in the southern part of the state. Scientists say that this land was at the bottom of the sea many thousands of years ago. Today most of it is a densely wooded wilderness area often resembling a jungle. Marshy grassland, cedar groves, and lakes abound. Water is plentiful here, but the dry, sandy soil left during the glacial meltings of the last ice age makes the pine forests highly flammable and only fitfully hospitable to many delicate forms of plant life.

This part of New Jersey, largely because of the Pine Barrens, is sparsely inhabited. The absence of good dark earth, and the capricious appearance of rivulets, ponds, and bogs with water always near the surface but rarely reliable in one place, led the colonists who first settled South Jersey to avoid the Pine Barrens. The word "Barrens" reflects their assessment of its potential for farming.

The Barrens, however, teem with more tolerant species of plants and wildlife. Sand dunes which would do credit to a beach or a desert alternate with pine, oak, and cedar, as well as with cranberry bogs. An enormous variety of flowers and about 20 species of orchids grow wild. Several hundred different kinds of birds either nest here or pass through on migration routes. There are deer and foxes as well as smaller animals like raccoons. In short, there is a great deal to interest both the tourist and the professional naturalist.

This sprawling, almost primeval forest enfolds numerous historic sites and extends through many of the southern New Jersey state parks mentioned in this section, among them Wharton, Green Bank, Bass River, and Lebanon.

There are two organizations based in the Washington, DC, area which occasionally sponsor tours of the Pine Barrens. These tours are usually formed in direct response to the number of people who have indicated an interest. They are conducted by Dr. Stanwyn G. Shetler, a curator of the Botany Department at the National Museum of Natural History, who explains the fascinating ecology, wildlife, and plant life of the area. Participants are normally asked to bring their own lunches, water canteens, binoculars, and cameras. The tours are usually one day long, but a two-day tour which includes both the Barrens and the birds at Cape May is sometimes arranged. People interested in this tour should contact one of the following organizations. The Audubon Naturalist Society of the Central Atlantic States, Inc. (not a part of the National Audubon Society), 8940 Jones Mill Road, Chevy Chase, MD 20815. Telephone: (301) 652-9188. The Smithsonian Resident Associates Program, The Smithsonian Institution, Washington, DC 20560. Telephone: (202) 357-3137.

A large part of the 100,000 acres of **Wharton State Forest** belongs to the Pine Barrens and is of interest primarily to campers who like wilderness areas. There are picnic areas, cabins, and campgrounds. Four rivers of varying sizes flow through the park: the Mullica River, the Batsto River, the Branch Wading River, and the East Oswego Branch. Swimming (including one-day use), boating, and fishing are permitted at Atsion Lake. Fishing is also allowed in the river and tidewater areas. The Batona Trail is open to hikers for 47 miles. (Visitors are reminded that licenses are required for all freshwater fishing.) The irregularly shaped park is so large— it extends from five miles west of the Garden State Parkway halfway across the state, and is about 15 miles deep from Batsto in the south to one of its northernmost points—that it can be reached by numerous routes. The southeastern corner of the forest is called Green Bank State Forest. It, too, is an undeveloped area. Open chiefly for hiking and picnicking, Green Bank is managed as part of Wharton. For information write to the Wharton Superintendent, Batsto RD 4, Hammonton, NJ 08037. Telephone: (609) 561-0024.

From the town of Greenbank, on Route 542, it is approximately four miles to the 200-acre **Batsto Historic Area**, located in Wharton State Park. Guided tours are offered through the Batsto Village Restoration. This ironworks produced military equipment of great value to the cause of the American Revolution. The restoration includes the sawmill, furnace, blacksmith shop, grist mill, farm buildings, store, workmen's houses, mansion, and Batsto Nature Area. Guided tours are available for the mansion, the Nature Area, and some of the other sites. Craft demonstrations of candle making, weaving, seatweaving, pottery making, and wood carving are given on varying days of the week and on weekends. There are nearby facilities for swimming, boating, fishing, and picnicking. Open Memorial Day to Labor Day, 10:00 a.m. to 6:00 p.m. Open Labor Day to Memorial Day, 11:00 a.m. to 5:00 p.m. Closed Thanksgiving, Christmas, and New Year's. Nominal admission charge for the mansion, some tours, and parking during the summer months. It is recommended that anyone interested in a particular craft demonstration telephone to check the schedule. Telephone: (609) 561-3262.

Continue east on Route 542 to Route 9, and turn south eight miles to **Smithville**. This is a restoration of an 18th- and 19th-century New Jersey village. Stroll along the main street and peer in the windows of these charming old buildings. Among the many buildings are a grist mill, furnished homes, craft shops, and a chapel. Thirty or more old-fashioned shops offer visitors all types of arts, crafts, and souvenirs. Three excellent restaurants are a major attraction. Admission free. Open daily except Christmas Day. For information telephone the Smithville Inn: (609) 652-7775.

CAMDEN AND HADDONFIELD

Upon entering New Jersey via the Delaware Memorial Bridge, go north on Route 551 to **Swedesboro**. The **Moravian Church** at Oldman's Creek, three miles south of town, was built between 1786 and 1789. It is the oldest Moravian church in South Jersey. **Trinity Episcopal (Old Swede's) Church** is on King's Highway, in town. Built in 1784, it is a fine example of church architecture of its period. It is open for worship and also by appointment. Telephone: (609) 467-1227.

Bridgeport is six miles to the left on Route 322. One can visit the **Schorn Log Cabin**, two miles east of town. This 17th-century cabin was built by Swedish settlers, and was used by slaves fleeing the South as a stopping-off point. Take Routes 295 and 534 to **Woodbury**.

The **Hunter-Lawrence House**, 58 North Broad Street, is headquarters of the Gloucester County Historical Society. It was the home of the Reverend Andrew Hunter, chaplain with Washington at Valley Forge, and of Captain James Lawrence of "Don't give up the ship" fame. Its museum displays 18th-century weapons, costumes, furniture, coins and manuscripts, and a collection of Indian relics. Open Wednesday and Friday, 1:00 to 4:00 p.m., and by appointment. Telephone: (609) 845-4771. The **Woodbury Friends' Meeting House**, on North

Broad Street, was built in 1715, and can be visited by appointment. Telephone: (609) 845-5080 or 848-8900.

Red Bank Battlefield Park is along the Delaware River, west of town. It was here, in October 1777, that 400 colonial troops defeated 1,200 Hessian soldiers who were British mercenaries. This victory, and that at Saratoga, caused the French to enter the Revolutionary War, and thus helped turn the tide for a patriot victory. The fortifications were built to protect Philadelphia from British forces. Open daily, 9:00 a.m. to dusk. Admission free. Telephone: (609) 853-5120.

The **Ann Whitall Mansion** is located at 100 Hessian Avenue in the nearby town of National Park. Built in 1748, this home was in the midst of the engagement at Red Bank. Many cannonballs are still embedded in its walls. The home, which contains original furnishings, served as a temporary hospital after the battle. Open daily, 9:00 a.m. to 4:00 p.m. Admission free.

Camden, eight miles to the north via Route 30, was the home of poet **Walt Whitman**. His home at 330 Mickle Street contains original furnishings and Whitman memorabilia. Open Wednesday through Friday, 9:00 a.m. to noon and 1:00 to 6:00 p.m. Open Saturday, 10:00 a.m. to noon and 1:00 to 6:00 p.m. Open Sunday, 1:00 to 6:00 p.m. Admission free. Telephone: (609) 964-5383.

Whitman Poetry Center, a center for the fine and performing arts, is located at Second and Cooper in Camden. It houses a poetry library and a gallery which hosts paintings, sculpture, and photography exhibits. On weekends, and sometimes during the week, there are concerts and plays. No admission charge for library and exhibits. Admission charge for performances. Library and gallery open daily, 9:00 a.m. to 4:00 p.m. Open evenings for performances. (Gallery shows may be viewed at intermission.) Telephone: (609) 757-7276.

Campbell Museum houses an exceptional collection of elegant food-service utensils, tureens, bowls, platters, and silver gathered from various parts of the world and dating from 500 B.C. to the present. The collection, begun in 1966 by the Campbell Soup Company, includes silver from 13 countries, and ceramic objects gathered from 19 lands. The tureen collection is probably one of the most valuable in the United States. Many examples originally graced the tables of royal families of Europe.

The museum is located in Camden, on Campbell Place, south of Federal Street. Open Monday through Friday, 9:00

a.m. to 4:30 p.m. Admission free. Guided tours may be arranged in advance. A film is shown with tours. Check with guide. Telephone: (609) 342-6439.

Haddonfield, six miles east on Route 561, is the locale of many historic houses and the noted **Indian King Tavern**, which was prominent in New Jersey history. Located at 233 East King's Highway, it was the meeting place of the legislature which in 1777 proclaimed New Jersey's independence from Britain. Open Wednesday through Friday, 9:00 to 11:30 a.m. and 1:00 to 5:30 p.m. Open Saturday, 10:00 to 11:30 a.m. and 1:00 to 5:30 p.m. Open Sunday, 1:00 to 5:30 p.m. Admission free. Telephone: (609) 429-6792.

Most of the historic houses and buildings are within an area of a few blocks and are easily visited on a walking tour. Unless otherwise indicated they are privately owned and can be viewed only from the outside. Begin at **Borough Hall** on King's Highway There is an all-day parking lot located in the rear. To the left of Borough Hall is **Glover House**, built in 1816. Across the street to the right are several brick houses dating from the 1830s. Indian King Tavern (described above) is next, at 233 King's Highway. In the next block, at 255 is the **Hedry-Pennypacker Home**, and the **Alexander House** at the corner of Grove Street. There are four historical buildings to the right on Potter Street. The **Old Pottery**, at No. 50, dates from 1805. Return to the highway and cross over. The **Haddon Fortnightly Club House** (1857) has a balcony and stage. It is still used as a private clubhouse.

Number 300 King's Highway was built in 1738. **Greenfield Hall**, at 343, is the home of the Historical Society of Haddonfield. Hours vary. It is safest to telephone first. Telephone: (609) 429-7375. Next door, the **Hip Roof House** dates from 1742. Restoration of the outside and part of the inside has been completed. The restored part of the interior can be viewed during hours when the Historical Society is open. At the corner of Hopkins Lane to the right is a **double house** (Nos. 438 and 444), erected in 1790. Return via Hopkins Lane past **Pope John Library** (just beyond Grove Street) on right and **Friends Meeting House** at Lake and Wood streets. A number of Hessian soldiers are buried in this Quaker cemetery. **Friends School**, built in 1789, is at the corner of Haddon Avenue. It still serves as a school. Several old houses can be seen on Haddon Avenue. **Haddonfield Public Library** is also here. The current building dates from 1917, but the library itself dates from 1803 and is one of the oldest in the state. It began as a private library which was open to the public. Telephone: (609) 429-1304. Turn right on Clement Street, to the **Tanyard House** at 38 Tanner Street, built in 1739.

Return to King's Highway, turn right, and cross the railroad tracks. The **Willis-Stretch Home**, at No. 8, is famous for its boxwood garden. Return to the starting point and go left a half block on Haddon Avenue to **Haddon Fire Company No. 1**. It has a small museum housing antique fire-fighting vehicles and equipment. The original fire company was organized in 1764, and there have been three successive buildings on this site. Open daily, 10:00 a.m. to 4:00 p.m. Admission free. Telephone: (609) 429-2400.

DELAWARE RIVER REGION

This region can be reached by taking I-95 north to the Delaware Memorial Bridge.

Salem is four miles to the southeast of the Delaware Memorial Bridge on Routes 45 and 49. This town was settled by Quakers in 1675. The **Friends Meetinghouse**, built in 1772, has excellent examples of old Wistarburg glass. It is on East Market Street and is still used for services. **The Friends Burying Ground**, a couple of blocks away on West Broadway, is the site of the famous 500-year-old **Old Salem Oak**, under which Salem's founder, John Fenwick, made his peaceful treaty with the Leni-Lenape Indians. **Fort Mott**, three miles north, was built during the Civil War. Now a state park, its fortifications and tunnels are of interest to the tourist. Nearby more than 2,400 Confederate prisoners of war, and 300 Union soldiers, are buried at Finn's Point National Cemetery on the banks of the Delaware River. The Confederates had been interned at Fort Delaware on Pea Patch Island, called by many "The Andersonville of the North." Fort Mott has fishing, boating, and picnicking facilities. The **Delaware River Bridge** is six miles north of the park.

The Alexander Grant House, at 79-83 Market Street, built in 1721, is now a museum and home of the Salem County Historical Society. The Grant House contains period furnishings, including fine collections of china, Wistarburg glass, and old dolls. The octagon-shaped John Jones Law Office, built about 1735 and reported to be the first brick law office in the 13 colonies, was recently moved to its present site behind

Alexander Grant House. A barn at the same site contains carriages, a large collection of 18th- and 19th-century farm implements, and Indian artifacts. All three buildings can be viewed at the same time. Open Tuesday through Friday, noon to 4:00 p.m. Open also by appointment. Admission charge. Telephone: (609) 935-5004.

There are numerous other historic buildings in Salem which can be viewed by appointment with the Historical Society. A one-day **Open House Tour** is held the last Saturday in April on odd-numbered years. Lunch is served at one of the churches. Admission charge.

Dotting the countryside surrounding Salem City are more than 60 18th-century homes, churches, and meetinghouses. Many of them have on their walls the most outstanding glazed brick designs found in America. Additional information can be obtained from the Salem County Historical Society, and at the Chamber of Commerce, 92 Market Street, Salem, NJ 08079. Chamber of Commerce telephone: (609) 935-7510.

ATLANTIC CITY AND SHORE AREA

To reach this popular area, follow I-95 north to the Delaware Memorial Bridge, then take Route 40 east to the shore.

Atlantic City, the major New Jersey seaside resort, is noted for its popular Convention Hall, for its annual Miss America pageant in September, its six-mile Boardwalk, and its many recreational facilities and amusements, including the major resort hotels. Among the available activities are sailing, deep- sea fishing, boat and bus sightseeing, horseback riding, tennis, racquetball, squash, biking on the Boardwalk, surfing, swimming, and several amusement piers. Garden Pier has an arts center; Central Pier has a Sky Tower as well as helicopter charter flights and sightseeing. Several other major piers—the Steel Pier, Steeplechase Pier, and Million Dollar Pier—are undergoing extensive remodeling and rebuilding. When completed they will include luxury shops, restaurants, and entertainment.

Atlantic City is a year-round resort with 450 motels, hotels, and guesthouses, as well as a great many restaurants. Advance reservations are suggested for accommodations during the summer months.

The course of the famous Boardwalk can be traveled by almost everyone. There are trams and jitneys as well as motorized wheelchairs for the handicapped.

There are several other points of interest in the Atlantic City area. The **Renault Winery**, Bremen Avenue, Egg Harbor City, has 1,400 acres including vineyards, wine cellars, a glass museum, and a hospitality center where one can enjoy wine tasting. Open Monday through Saturday, 10:00 a.m. to 5:00 p.m.; Sunday, noon to 5:00 p.m. Guided tours. Admission charge. Telephone: (609) 965-2111.

There is always a flower show at the **Fischer Greenhouses**. Here 150,000 African violets are produced annually. Open daily, 9:00 a.m. to 5:00 p.m. Telephone: (609) 927-3399. Greenhouses are located on Oak Avenue in Linwood. This town is off Route 9, less than a half hour south of Atlantic City.

The **Atlantic City Race Course**, at McKey City Circle in McKey City, is less than a half hour west of the city off Routes 40-322. Races are held from late May through early September. Telephone: (609) 641-2190.

Gardner's Basin, at the north end of North New Hampshire Avenue and the bay in Atlantic City, features the tall ship *Young America*, antique boat exhibits, a small local species aquarium, a waterfront park, seasonal musical concerts, and a seafood restaurant. Admission charge. Telephone: (609) 348-2880.

Proceed south 10 miles on Route 9 to Somers Point. The **Somers Mansion**, built in 1720-30, has been restored as closely as possible to the way it looked when the Somers family lived in it, more than 250 years ago. Open Wednesday through Friday, 9:00 a.m. to noon and 1:00 to 5:00 p.m.; Saturday, 10:00 a.m. to noon and 1:00 to 6:00 p.m. Closed Thanksgiving, Christmas, and New Year's. Admission free. Telephone: (609) 927-2212.

Across the street from the Mansion is the **Atlantic County Historical Society Library and Museum**, which contains exhibits on the history of the area. Open Wednesday through Saturday from 10:00 a.m. to noon and from 1:00 to 4:00 p.m. Admission free. Telephone: (609) 927-5218.

Both the Mansion and Library/Museum are operated by the Atlantic County Historical Society. The Society recommends that sizable groups make appointments for tours. If there is no answer at one site during "open" hours, use the telephone number for the other site, as a tour is probably in progress.

At present there are nine major casino resort hotels, and several others are planned or under construction. These offer visitors the opportunity to play baccarat, slot machines, craps, roulette, blackjack, and big six. Video blackjack and poker are also available. There is a great variety of entertainment including cabaret, nightclub, and dinner shows featuring major show-business personalities. These resorts offer health clubs as well as restaurants, bars, and boutiques.

Bass River State Forest, a short distance north of Atlantic City, is bisected by the Garden State Parkway. It can be reached by driving north on I-95, east on Route 40, north on Routes 575 and 9 to New Gretna. It also is convenient to several popular seashore resorts.

During summer months you can enjoy hiking, horseback riding trails, fishing, canoeing, sailing, boating, swimming, and camping. The Absegami Natural Area is known for interesting nature walks through pine and oak woods and a white cedar bog. From the state forest you may take short trips to nearby points of interest, such as Batsto Village in Wharton State Forest, Renault Winery, Smithville, and Atlantic City. For information, write to Forest Manager, New Gretna, NJ 08224. Telephone: (609) 296-1114.

Bass River also administers **Penn State Park**, a few miles away. Leave the Garden State Parkway at Exit 52, New Gretna. Turn right immediately after leaving the parkway and go one mile to a fork. Bear left at the fork (the right fork goes to Bass River State Forest itself), and bear right at each of the following two forks. Turn right on Route 563 and go about three or four miles. After passing Mick's Canoe Rental, take the first paved road on the right and continue about one mile to Lake Oswego. This is a real wilderness area. Fishing and canoeing are allowed on the lake. Swimming is not allowed because there is no lifeguard. There are a few picnic tables.

Located about 10 miles northwest of Atlantic City, the **Edwin B. Forsythe National Wildlife Refuge's Brigantine Division** has approximately 24,000 acres of saltmarsh, open waterways, and woodlands. The refuge itself is by Oceanville (not in the city of Brigantine), approximately two miles south of Smithville on Route 9. To reach Refuge Headquarters, take Great Creek Road west off Route 9 approximately one-quarter mile. As many as 100,000 migratory waterfowl stop off here in the early spring and late fall to feed and rest. More than 275 bird species have been observed.

Take the Wildlife Drive around the West Pool and East Pool, where you can observe the wildlife. Ascend the observation tower for a panoramic view. You can walk the half-mile Leeds Eco-Trail. Have an insect repellent handy if you plan a summer visit. For literature, maps, and a calendar of wildlife events, write to Refuge Manager, PO Box 72, Oceanville, NJ 08231. Telephone: (609) 652-1665.

The best route to **Lebanon State Forest** is by entering north on the New Jersey Turnpike and east on Route 70. The forest is one mile east of the junction of Routes 70 and 72 at Four Mile Circle. Within this recreational area of the famous pine barrens in Central New Jersey there are large Atlantic white cedar swamps and open bogs. In summer you can enjoy hiking, fishing, and swimming. There are 93 family campsites available, as well as riding trails if you bring your own horse. For information write to Lebanon State Forest, PO Box 215, New Lisbon, NJ 08064. Telephone: (609) 726-1191.

Also plan to visit nearby points of interest, especially the cranberry and blueberry plantations around Whitesbog, or the Batsto restoration in Wharton State Forest (see Pine Barrens section). At Brown's Mill are the ruins of Hanover Furnace (1791-1864).

OCEAN CITY—WILDWOOD—CAPE MAY

The ocean resorts are accessible via I-95 north to the Delaware Memorial Bridge and east on Route 40 to Routes 55 and 47. They can also be reached by ferry from Lewes, Delaware, to Cape May.

The Cape May County Chamber of Commerce operates two information centers. The **Seaville Information Center,** in the service area of the Garden State Parkway at mile post 18 near the Sea Isle City Exit, is open April through October, 9:00 a.m. to 5:00 p.m.; November through March, 10:00 a.m. to 4:00 p.m. The **Cape May Courthouse Information Center,** reached via Exit 11 from the Garden State Parkway, is open daily, Easter through October 31, 9:00 a.m. to 5:00 p.m.; November through March, Monday to Friday, 9:00 a.m. to 4:30 p.m.

Ocean City lies on an eight-mile-long island, between the ocean and the Intercoastal Waterway. Visitors can choose among 100 hotels and motels, and from about 250 guest-houses, furnished apartments, and condominiums. Among its attractions are its two-and-a-half-mile Boardwalk, saltwater fishing, crabbing, boating, sailing, bicycling, and water skiing. Other outdoor activities include tennis, golf, softball, shuffle-board, and surfing.

The **Ocean City Historical Museum** is located at 409 Wesley Avenue. Visitors can see a fully furnished 19th-century Ocean City home. Other displays deal with the social history of the area between 1890 and 1910, and with the Indian life before the coming of the white man. There are ship models and other nautical memorabilia in the Sindia Room. Open June 15 through September 15, Monday through Saturday, 10:00 a.m. to 4:00 p.m. Open September 15 through June 15, Tuesday through Saturday, 1:00 p.m. to 4:00 p.m. Admission free. Guided tours are available. Telephone: (609) 399-1801. The **Wreck of the Sindia,** located at 16th Street and the beach, is listed as a historic site by the State of New Jersey. Salvage operations on the cargo of the ship (which was wrecked September 15, 1901) are currently underway.

The U.S. Coast Guard Station Great Egg, on the La-goon, at 101 North Point Road, Ocean City, provides tours of its installation including the Coast Guard boats and its com-munications center. Open daily, 8:00 a.m. to 4:00 p.m. Tele-phone: (609) 399-0119.

Many fine resorts dot the coastline from Ocean City to Cape May along Ocean Drive. Among these are **Strathmere, Sea Isle City, Avalon, Stone Harbor,** and the **Wildwoods.** There are many motels and guesthouses to accommodate visitors. The fisherman has a choice of deep-sea fishing on daily charter boats, surf casting, and pier fishing. No licenses are required. Fishing is not permitted on bathing beaches while lifeguards are on duty, which is usually approximately 9:00 a.m. to 6:00 p.m. during June, July, and August. The **Stone Harbor Bird Sanctuary** is a nesting ground for thou-sands of waterfowl, chiefly egrets and herons. The sanctuary is located on Third Avenue in the southern part of the town of Stone Harbor.

Wildwood is a popular summer resort with a fine beach and three-mile boardwalk. Ocean fishing from party boats is very popular here. There are shops and restaurants galore, as well as five amusement piers and a water ride park. **Holly Beach Station**, in downtown Wildwood, is a beautifully land-scaped 12-block mall which is lighted at night.

A few miles to the south are the Cape May City and Cape May Point resorts. There are a beach promenade and many stately 19th- century homes. **Cape May** has long been known as the "summer home of the Presidents." Brochures listing addresses of the numerous historic houses and inns, as well as special events like antique shows, band concerts, and dances, are readily available at hotels, motels, and shops.

There are a number of interesting shopping areas, among them the **Victorian Shopping Mall** on Washington Street and a variety of **Beachfront** shops. A small tour trolley travels along streets which are tree-shaded by day and illuminated by gaslights in the evening. A number of excellent marinas are at hand for those who want to sail, fish, or take a ride on a motorboat or cabin cruiser. The beaches are well supplied with lifeguards.

One of the major attractions, of which there are many at Cape May, is the **Emlen Physick Estate**. This 16-room mansion (1881) designed by the famous 19th-century architect Frank Furness—is used today as a museum of Victorian toys, costumes, artifacts, and the **Balsberg** book collection. **The Cape May County Art League** has its headquarters in the **Carriage House**, which predates the mansion itself. A small barn behind the Carriage House contains a collection of 19th-century tools. Other buildings on the nine-acre estate are used by artists and craftsmen for classes and craft demonstrations during the summer months. **The Mid-Atlantic Center for the Arts** (MAC) has its office at Hill House on the estate. MAC is responsible for operating the estate as a community and cultural center. MAC also sponsors numerous tours of the area. Two major events are a Christmas tour of decorated private houses (held on the Saturday between Christmas and New Year's), and a Columbus Day Victorian Week (in October), which includes a house tour as well as many other tours and events. Admission charge. For information on tours and events write to: MAC, Box 164, Cape May, NJ 08204. Telephone: (609) 884-5404. For information on arts and crafts, classes and demonstrations, write to the Cape May County Art League, Box 596, Cape May, NJ 08204. Telephone: (609) 884-8628.

There are several Coast Guard stations and a **Training Center** that may be of interest to visitors. This area has served as a naval base since the American Revolution when the Continental Navy used it. During the War of 1812 the British captured it briefly. Through the beginning of the 19th century, pirates took refuge in the many sheltered coastal inlets. Since the middle of the First World War the Cape May area has been used either by the U.S. Navy or by the Coast Guard as a base and training facility, for both sea and air operations. Admission free. Training Center telephone: (609) 884-8451.

Fisherman's Wharf, at Schellenger's Landing, is a local landmark. Dozens of commercial fishing boats come and go from 12 large docks. The daily catch is often 100,000 pounds.

Cape May Bird Observatory is on the shore of Lily Lake, at 707 East Lake Drive, Cape May Point. Its sand dunes, marshes, and holly woods attract many of the approximately 400 species of birds which frequent Cape May County (the largest number of species reported in any county outside Florida and southern California). The Observatory holds an annual hawk watch from mid-August to mid-November. Eighty-nine thousand hawks, a national record for this kind of watch, were recorded in 1981. The observatory has a gift shop and ornithological library. Open daily, mid-August through late October, 9:00 a.m. to 5:00 p.m. Open November to mid-August, frequently but not on a regular basis, 9:00 a.m. to 5:00 p.m. Telephone: (609) 884-2736.

Many old homes and churches can be seen along Route 9, on a drive north toward the town of Cape May Courthouse. The **Cold Spring Presbyterian Church** was established in 1714. The **Friends Meeting House**, built in 1716, is still in use. It is located in Seaville on Route 9. The **Capt. George Hildreth House**, at Cold Spring, was built in the mid-1800s. Behind this house is a restored group of houses and other buildings named **Cold Spring Village**. There are craft shops and a restaurant which is located in the former Grange Hall. Open from the end of May through September. Telephone: (609) 884-1810.

The museum of the local historical society is located at the John Holmes House, in **Cape May Courthouse**. It contains displays of Indian relics, antique furniture and utensils, whaling equipment, ship models, old china, and glassware. Open mid-June through mid-September, Monday through Saturday, 10:00 a.m. to 4:00 p.m. Open mid-September through end of December, Tuesday through Saturday, 10:00 a.m. to 4:00 p.m. Closed January, February, and March. Open April through mid-June, Tuesday through Saturday, 10:00 a.m. to 4:00 p.m.

The *Atlantus*, a sunken concrete ship, may be seen at

Cape May Point at the foot of Sunset Boulevard. It was one
of three experimental concrete ships built during World War
I in an attempt to overcome the wartime steel shortage. It
was blown aground in a storm in 1926. **Cape May Lighthouse**
is also located at Cape May Point. The current lighthouse was
built in 1859, but there has been a light here since 1744. It is
operated by the Mid-Atlantic Center for the Arts. Admission
charge. Telephone: (609) 884-5404.

The **Bennett Bog** is a wildlife sanctuary with rare and
unusual forms of plant life. It is on Shunpike, south of
Tabernacle Road, in Erma. This town is three miles north of
Cape May, west of Route 9.

The route to **Belleplain State Forest** is north into New
Jersey, southeast on Route 49, south on Route 47, and east on
550 for about eight miles. This forest beckons the visitor
looking for a change from ocean beach vacations. You will find
a quiet rural atmosphere with lots of room to roam and two
lakes that offer all kinds of diversions. In summer you can
find hiking, fishing, camping, swimming, boating, sailing, and
playground and athletic activities. Pets and alcoholic beverages, however, are prohibited in New Jersey state parks. For
information, write Forest Manager, Box 450, Woodbine, NJ
08270. Telephone: (609) 861-2404.

Many ocean beaches and Cape May are about a half-hour
away. Also nearby are Stone Harbor Bird Sanctuary and
Bennett Bog at Erma.

DELAWARE BAY AREA

This area can be reached by taking I-95 north to the
Delaware Memorial Bridge, then going southeast on Route
49. The route of this tour is a continuation of the preceding
trip. The tourist can stop at a number of points of interest en
route from the Cape May area to the Delaware River Bridge.
North on Route 83 (or Routes 50 and 47) one may stop off at
Belleplain State Forest, between Belleplain and Woodbine.
Here the visitor may stroll through a nature study area, or
go fishing, swimming, or boating on Lake Nummy.

Wheaton Village, 15 miles to the northwest, is a restored 19th-century glass town. Located at 10th and G streets
in Millville, it can be reached via Routes 47 and 49. It is
approximately one hour's drive from Cape May as well as
from Philadelphia and from the Delaware Memorial Bridge.

The village contains a replica of an 1888 glass factory, a museum of American glass, a craft demonstration building, a general store, an 1876 one-room schoolhouse, and an agricultural center which houses a pictorial exhibit of 19th- and early 20th-century farming methods and farm implements dating from the 1800s. The village contains several gift shops and boasts its own small train. Open daily, 10:00 a.m. to 5:00 p.m. Closed Thanksgiving, Christmas, New Year's, and Easter Sunday. Hours may vary somewhat in winter. Admission charge. Telephone: (609) 825-6800.

Cumberland County's Liberty Bell, which tolled freedom's cry on July 7, 1776, is one of only three Liberty Bells in America and the only one in New Jersey. It can be seen in the lobby of the courthouse in Bridgeton.

Greenwich is a very old village on the Cohansey River, six miles west of Bridgeton. A monument in the square commemorates the burning of a cargo of taxed tea in its harbor in 1774 by men disguised as Indians.

Gibbon House (1730), on Ye Greate Street, is the headquarters of the Cumberland County Historical Society. The house is furnished in the style of the period and is notable, among other things, for a fine old kitchen with a nine-foot fireplace. It also contains a museum with collections of 19th-century children's toys, samplers, Ware chairs, antique lighting devices, and glass. A major item here is the figurehead of the *Ship John*, which sank in Delaware Bay in 1797. It was carved by William Rush, one of the foremost figurehead artists of his day. Open Tuesday through Saturday, noon to 4:00 p.m.; Sunday, 2:00 to 5:00 p.m. Closed mid-December to early April. Admission charge and guided tours during the week. Nominal admission charge and no guided tours on weekends. Telephone: (609) 455-4055.

There is a **Genealogical Library at Pirate House**, a few hundred yards farther down Ye Greate Street. Open Wednesday, 1:00 to 4:00 p.m.; Sunday, 2:00 to 5:00 p.m. Telephone: (609) 455-8580.

The town also hosts an annual Christmas in Greenwich, in mid-December. There are caroling and other festivities at the beautifully decorated Market Square, a Swedish ceremony at the Presbyterian Church, a harpist and freshly baked gingerbread men at Gibbon House, and special exhibits and entertainment through the town. Further information can be obtained from the Historical Society.

Returning to Route 49 via Othello and Shiloh, go north

five miles to Peck's Corner, then left to the **Hancock House** at Hancock's Bridge. This house, built in 1734 by Judge William Hancock and his wife Sarah, has blue-glazed header bricks. During the American Revolution this house, closest to the bridge, was used as a barracks. It is the only house in the state of New Jersey in which a wholesale massacre occurred. On March 21, 1778, a party of patriots was killed here by the British under Major Simcoe. In 1932, in memory of these men, the house was turned into a shrine. The house contains a large collection of antiques which, while not original, are representative of styles common to the period. Open Tuesday to Saturday, 10:00 a.m. to 5:00 p.m.; Sunday, 2:00 to 5:00 p.m. Nominal admission charge. Adjacent is a cedar plank house built by the Swedes more than 200 years ago.

Parvin State Park, which centers around a lake on a branch of the Maurice River, is about halfway between the Delaware Memorial Bridge and Atlantic City, off Route 40. It is easily reached via I-95 to Delaware Memorial Bridge, east on Route 40, and south on Route 553. A special feature is a nature trail through a unique botanical area where swamp flowers not often seen elsewhere may be observed. The park offers fishing, hiking, camping, swimming, boating, playground activities, and evening hikes, lectures, and slide shows. The park often serves as a convenient base for short trips to nearby attractions, such as Ft. Mott park, Wheaton Village, and the Cape May resort area. For information, write Parvin State Park, RD No. 1, Box 374, Elmer, NJ 08318. Telephone: (609) 692-7039.

WEST VIRGINIA

HARPERS FERRY AND EASTERN GATEWAY

Harpers Ferry was founded in 1733 by Peter Stephens when he set up a ferry service at the confluence of the Shenandoah and Potomac rivers. In 1747 Robert Harper took over the ferry service and later built a mill. After President George Washington recommended to Congress that a national armory be built at Harpers Ferry, construction of the arms factory began in 1796. By the 1830s, both the C&O Canal and B&O Railroad reached Harpers Ferry, making it an important transportation center.

Harpers Ferry is particularly notable in American history for John Brown's Raid, a prelude to the Civil War. On October 16, 1859, Brown and 22 followers seized the U.S. Arsenal in an attempt to liberate the slaves and set up a black stronghold in the nearby mountains. It was also the scene of several Civil War engagements and was occupied by both Union and Confederate forces. Prior to the Battle of Antietam, it was captured by General "Stonewall" Jackson in 1862. This is an area of unusual scenic beauty, where the Potomac and Shenandoah rivers have carved a passage through the Appalachian Mountains. Today one can visit mid-19th-century buildings, as well as an old cemetery, museums, and the noted Jefferson Rock. The historic district of the town, **Harpers Ferry Historical Park**, is administered by the U.S. Park Service.

The Visitor's Center in the **Stagecoach Inn** (1826), on Shenandoah Street, offers an audio-visual program and interesting exhibits. Visitors may pick up self-guiding tour brochures and information on conducted tours. Park historical buildings are open year round, and in the summer costumed docents are available for lectures and explanations. Open year round, 8:00 a.m. to 5:00 p.m. Admission free. For information and free brochure write: Superintendent, Box 65, Harpers Ferry, WV 25425. Telephone: (304) 535-6371. The **Master Armorer's House**, nearby, built in 1858, is a museum on the history of gun making. **John Brown's Fort**, located at

Shenandoah and Potomac streets, was the fire-engine house where Brown made his last stand on October 18, 1859. Across Shenandoah Street, the visitors complex includes a John Brown Museum, two theaters, and a social history exhibit of 19th-century Harpers Ferry. A gift and book store is located in this complex.

Stone Steps, carved in the natural rock, lead uphill from High Street to the **Harper House** (1775-82), built by Robert Harper. It is the oldest surviving structure in Harpers Ferry and is furnished in mid-19th-century style. Further up a steep trail to the left is **Jefferson Rock**, a huge balanced boulder from which Thomas Jefferson, in 1783, viewed the confluence of the Shenandoah and Potomac rivers. He described the view as "one of the most stupendous scenes in nature," and said the view was "worth a voyage across the Atlantic." A path continues from the rock to Morrell House (c. 1858), on Filmore Street. This was the paymaster's house and later was one of the buildings of Storer College.

Another park trail leads from Jefferson Rock across the bridge over the Shenandoah River and ascends **Loudoun Heights**, where it joins the **Appalachian Trail**. A three-mile circuit hike follows the latter trail eastward to the point where it descends to Route 340 and back to the starting point.

Another three-mile hike leads to the stone fort ruins on **Maryland Heights**. To reach this blue-blazed trail, drive east on Route 340 to the far side of the Potomac River Bridge; turn onto the old road that parallels the railroad and canal. About 200 yards beyond Sandy Hook you will see the Maryland Heights parking area on the right. The three-and-a-half-hour hike begins at the stone steps at the parking area and ascends steeply to the overlook cliff. From the almost bare ridge one can get a spectacular view up the Shenandoah and the Potomac valleys. The descending trail leads to the **Chesapeake and Ohio Canal**, about a half-mile above the railroad bridge to Harpers Ferry.

In the private area of Harpers Ferry, the visitor will find many restaurants and shops in which to browse. On High Street the visitor can visit the **John Brown Wax Museum,** which recreates the John Brown story. Open April to December, 9:00 a.m. to 5:00 p.m.; February and March, Saturday and Sunday, 10:00 am. to 5:00 p.m. Admission charge. Telephone: (304) 535-6342. The **West Virginia Information Center,** on Route 340, is open year round, daily, 9:00 a.m. to 5:00

p.m. Telephone: (304) 535-2482. The **Appalachian Trail Conference**, located on Washington Street, is the headquarters for the volunteer groups who maintain the trail. The conference office has a library and slide display and offers guidebooks and maps for sale. Open Monday to Friday, 9:00 a.m. to 5:00 p.m. Telephone: (304) 535-6331.

A few miles west of Harpers Ferry on Route 340 is **Charles Town**, where in the evenings horse racing fans can watch thoroughbreds race at a modern and well-lighted track.

Harewood, three miles west of town on Route 51, was the home of Colonel Samuel Washington, brother of George Washington. This Georgian mansion was built in 1768-70, and on the grounds are Colonel Washington's office and a family graveyard.

The Jefferson County Courthouse (1836), in the center of Charles Town at the corner of Washington and George streets, was the scene of John Brown's trial in 1859 before the outbreak of the Civil War. The courtroom in which John Brown was tried has been preserved and may be viewed. Open year round, Monday through Thursday, 9:00 a.m. to 5:00 p.m.; Friday, 9:00 a.m. to 7:00 p.m. Closed holidays. Admission free. Telephone: (304) 725-9761.

Also at the corner of George and Washington streets is the **Charles Town Post Office**. It was Charles Town Postmaster William Wilson who started the first Rural Free Delivery in the country, in 1896. Open year round, Monday to Friday, 8:30 a.m. to 5:00 p.m.

The **Jefferson County Museum**, one block east of the courthouse, at 200 East Washington Street, contains John Brown memorabilia, including the wagon which carried John Brown to the place of his execution. There is also a collection of old guns and rifles and other Jefferson County-related items. Open April to November, Monday to Saturday, 10:00 a.m. to 4:00 p.m. Admission free, donations accepted. Telephone: (304) 725-8628.

North on Routes 9 and 48 takes the visitor to **Shepherdstown** (1762), one of the oldest towns in West Virginia. Here were established West Virginia's first newspaper, first post office, and the first church west of the Blue Ridge. The area bounded by Mill, Rocky, Duke, and Washington streets has been designated a National Historic District.

At the north end of Mill Street stands the **James Rumsey Monument**, overlooking the Potomac River. The monument commemorates James Rumsey's first public demonstration of a steam-powered boat in 1787.

Eight miles west of Shepherdstown on Route 45 is **Martinsburg**. This city was founded by General Adam Stephen, who served in both the French and Indian and Revolutionary wars. He was also a member of the Virginia Legislature. The **General Adam Stephen House**, at 309 East John Street, is a limestone building situated on a hill overlooking Tuscarora Creek at the edge of the city. It has been restored with furnishings of the 1750-1820 era. A log cabin, smokehouse, and other outbuildings have also been restored on the three-acre estate. Open April through October, Saturday and Sunday, 2:00 to 5:00 p.m., or by appointment. Telephone: (304) 267-4434.

Within a two-block area are several other interesting buildings. A showplace of Martinsburg is **Boydville**, built in 1812 and home to some of the city's most distinguished citizens. The house at 601 South Queen Street is shaded by venerable trees and bordered by high boxwood hedges. The grave and monument to General Adam Stephen is in one corner of this property. Martinsburg was the birthplace of Belle Boyd, noted Confederate spy, and the scene of one of her most notable exploits. The **Old Stone Jail**, built in 1795, is a stone building that has served as a jail, hospital, and nurses' residence.

The **Boarman House**, on Public Square, is one of the oldest in the city, built between 1778 and 1792, and later operated as a tavern. The **Market House**, at Queen and Burke streets, well over a century old, was used as a market and housed municipal offices for many decades. On King Street is the **Tuscarora Presbyterian Church**, which was built in 1802. The church was established by Scotch-Irish settlers in 1740. Wooden pegs on which pioneers hung their guns during services can be seen in the vestibule.

Berkeley Springs State Park is on Route 9 about 25 miles west of Martinsburg or may be reached from I-70 on Route 522 south from Hancock, MD. The seven-acre state park is located in the center of the town and offers Roman baths, massages, dry heat or steam cabinets, and a swimming pool. The mineral water of the springs has no sulphur content and is quite clear. These springs, famous for reputed curative properties, were given to the colony by Lord Fairfax and were used regularly by George Washington. The town was established as a health spa in 1776.

Open year round, Saturday through Thursday, 10:00 a.m. to 6:00 p.m.; also Friday, April through October, 10:00 a.m. to 9:00 p.m.; Friday, November through March, 10:00 a.m. to 7:00 p.m. Reservations necessary. For further information write: Berkeley Springs Sanitorium, Berkeley Springs, WV 25411. Telephone: (304) 258-2711.

The 6,115-acre **Cacapon State Park** is south of Berkeley Springs on Route 522. It offers a variety of facilities, including a large stone lodge where meals and overnight or weekly accommodations are available. There is swimming, fishing, boating, hiking, golfing, tennis, and horseback riding. No camping facilities. Rental cabins also are available. Open year round. For further information contact Cacapon State Park, Berkeley Springs, WV 25411. Telephone: (304) 258-1022.

POTOMAC HIGHLANDS

Northeastern West Virginia is one of the few places east of the Mississippi that is still a primeval wilderness area. Good roads provide easy access to stately forests, scenic overlooks, streams, and lakes in the highlands. National and state forests provide campsites, roadside parks, scenic overlooks, and hundreds of miles of hiking trails. This part of West Virginia also provides rock climbing, hunting and fishing opportunities, ski slopes, and has much to offer the bird lover, botanist, and the history-minded visitor. The adventuresome will be attracted to the 262 known caves and the 24 whitewater streams located in the highlands area. For further information contact: Potomac Highland Convention and Visitors Bureau, Elkins, WV 26241. Telephone: (304) 636-8400.

There are many old houses in and near Romney, whose town charter dates from 1762. The **Mytinger House**, on Gravel Lane, is the oldest building in town—more than 200 years old. It consists of a log kitchen, dwelling, and clerk of court's office. Other houses are of considerable architectural interest and date back to the mid-1700s.

The **Fort Ashby** Indian Fort and Museum is located north of Romney near the junction of Routes 28 and 46. Erected in 1755, it is the only remaining fort of the 69 directed to be built by Colonel George Washington as a defense against the Indians and the French. Open by appointment. Admission free. Telephone: (304) 298-3319 or 298-3255.

Washington had surveyed this area as a young man for

Lord Fairfax, whose six-million-acre grant extended to what is now the Maryland-West Virginia Line. The **Fairfax Stone** marking the state line as a result of a U.S. Supreme Court decision is located north of Thomas off Route 219. The present stone is one mile north of the original 1746 stone.

In this area is **Ice Mountain**, on the North River, three miles east of Slanesville on Route 29. Cold blasts of air come out of rock crevices even on the hottest summer days and ice is found 18 inches below the surface on the southern end of the mountain. The old **Iron Furnace**, east of Romney on Route 45 near Bloomery, is built of cut stone blocks. It produced military items for the Confederate army during the Civil War.

The central feature of the 133-acre **Cathedral State Park** is the majestic stand of ancient hardwoods and hemlocks, the only remaining virgin hardwood forests in West Virginia. This forest has been designated a Natural Landmark by the U.S. Department of Interior. It mirrors the American wilderness before the white settlement of the continent. Here you can see the state's largest hemlock, 21 feet in circumference and 90 feet high. The area is accessible from the east on Route 50, just beyond the southwest corner of the state of Maryland, near Aurora and the intersection of Routes 50 and 24. In summer you can enjoy hiking and picnicking in this day-use park. Admission free. Telephone: (304) 735-3771.

Petersburg, on Route 220, is accessible from Front Royal (75 miles), and is known as the "Trout Capital" of the state. Here the fisherman finds in abundance the rainbow, brown, brook, and golden trout, the latter unique to West Virginia. Bass fishing is tops in the South Branch of the Potomac. Hunting also is popular in the area, and portions of two national forests are open to hunting in season.

Country Store Museum, built with 100-year-old logs, is stocked with a wide variety of general-store merchandise of 80 to 100 years ago. This store-museum is located one-fourth mile north of Petersburg on Route 42. Open June, Saturday and Sunday, 10:00 a.m. to 4:30 p.m; July and August, Tuesday to Sunday, 10:00 a.m. to 4:30 p.m. Telephone: (304) 257-4026.

The **Petersburg Fish Hatchery** is located south of Petersburg off Route 220 and may be visited daily during daylight hours. The hatchery raises rainbow and golden trout for stocking of state streams. The streams are stocked in the fall and spring and, depending on the season, the visitor will see the different life phases of the trout from eggs to adult size. Admission free. Telephone: (304) 257-4014.

The **Smoke Hole Caverns** are located on Route 28, eight miles south of Petersburg. They contain the longest "ribbon" stalactite in the world. The name derives from the fact that the Seneca Indians used the cavern to smoke their meat. Open year round. Admission charge. Telephone: (304) 257-4442.

The eastern slope of **Saddle Mountain**, a geologic feature in the shape of a saddle, was the birthplace of Nancy Hanks, mother of Abraham Lincoln. It is accessible from Route 50 near Antioch, west of Romney. The visitor can see a stone marker showing the location of her cabin.

Lost River State Park is 3,712 acres large and located about 23 miles south of Wardensville, off Route 259, four miles west of Mathias. From the east, take I-66 to I-81, west to Strasburg, north on Route 55 to Wardensville. Among recreational facilities available are hiking trails, bridle paths, outdoor games, playground equipment, a swimming pool, and picnic tables. The park has vacation cabins and a restaurant. This sulphur springs area belonged to the Lee family of Virginia and was used by them as a summer resort in the early 19th century. A cabin built by "Light Horse Harry" Lee of Revolutionary War fame is in the park and may be visited. The park derives its name from the Lost River, which vanishes beneath mountains several times. About four miles south of Wardensville the river flows under Sandy Ridge and emerges on the north side of the mountain, where it is called Cacapon River. Telephone: (304) 897-5372.

Blackwater Falls State Park, a 1,688-acre park located within the northern boundaries of the Monongahela National Forest, is on Route 32, four miles southwest of Davis. It is accessible from Romney via Routes 50 and 93. The scenic falls are 65 feet high, and the gorge is about 500 feet deep. The Blackwater River winds down the canyon in a series of rapids and cascades with drops of 1,350 feet in 10 miles. A 200-step stairway leads from the parking area to the foot of the falls. Tent and trailer facilities, rental cabins, and a 55-room lodge are available. Visitors can enjoy swimming, boating, horseback riding, fishing, hiking, picnicking, winter sports, and use of playground facilities. There is a restaurant and refreshment service. Open year round. Admission free. Telephone: (304) 259-5216.

Canaan Valley State Park is a four-season resort south of Blackwater Falls State Park on Route 32. It is situated in a mountain valley, 3,000 feet above sea level. Surrounding peaks rise to 4,200 feet or more, providing spectacular rugged scenery. The park offers fully equipped cabins and a 250-room lodge, as well as campsites year round. There is an 18-hole golf course, a nature center, hiking and nature trails, swimming, fishing, tennis, and evening programs. In winter there is skiing and ice skating (see also Special Interest Section, Downhill Skiing). Telephone: (304) 866-4121.

Monongahela National Forest, an 851,000-acre recreation area located in the Allegheny Mountains near the eastern border of West Virginia, is accessible via Route 50, west to Route 220, then south past Petersburg to the forest boundary. The state's highest peak, **Spruce Knob** (4,862 feet in elevation), ascends from this mountainous forest, and nearby are **Seneca Rocks**, whose towering walls rise dramatically almost 1,000 feet above the forest below. Within the forest are many unique areas of special interest.

There are excellent opportunities for picnicking, fishing, hiking, boating, and whitewater canoeing. Since wild game finds the forest a sanctuary, you may get a glimpse of bear, deer, beaver, turkey, or grouse. There are 21 campgrounds, 850 miles of hiking trails, and 40 recreation sites in the forest.

Within this national forest are also state parks such as the Blackwater Falls State Park, Calvin Price State Forest, skiing resorts such as Snowshoe and Canaan Valley (see also Special Interest Section, Downhill Skiing), and the Cass Scenic Railroad (see also Special Interest Section, Railroads).

For further information contact the Forest Supervisor, Monongahela National Forest, Elkins, WV 26241. Telephone: (304) 636-1800; or the district rangers at Bartow, Marlinton, Parsons, Petersburg, Richwood, and White Sulphur Springs; or the West Virginia Division of Parks and Recreation, 1800 Washington Street East, Charleston, WV 25305.

The **Dolly Sods Wilderness** may be seen from the Dolly Sods scenic overlook off Route 28 on Route 19. The overlook sits on a plateau from which the visitor can see an open vista of the cranberry and blueberry bogs of the wilderness area. There are few facilities available, but this is an area for the hiker and camper who seeks the beauty and tranquillity of a remote area. Visitors may get information from the **Spruce Knob/Seneca Rocks Visitor Center** on Route 28. Telephone: (304) 567-2827 or 257-4488.

The **Gaudineer** scenic area within the Monongahela National Forest, located north of Route 250/92 between

Huttonsville and Bartow, has a stand of uncut virgin spruce. There is a picnic area for day use.

The **National Radio Astronomy Observatory**, at Green Bank on Route 92, is a national research center for a consortium of nine universities. The scientists at the observatory study the universe through radio waves. The observatory presents a one-hour tour that includes a movie and a bus trip of the complex, which has six telescopes ranging from 40 feet to 300 feet. Open Memorial Day through Labor Day. Check with the observatory for changing hours. Admission free. Telephone: (304) 456-2011.

The **Cass Scenic Railroad State Park** is an 855-acre complex that includes trips on the mountain railroad (see Special Interest Section, Railroads), wildlife and historical museums, a country store, and a restaurant. Picnicking and hiking facilities are available. Cass is located off Route 28/92 south of Bartow. Open Memorial Day to Labor Day, Tuesday to Sunday, and September to October, Saturday and Sunday, 9:00 a.m. to 5:00 p.m. Telephone: (304) 456-4300.

The **Cranberry Mountain Visitor Center**, located in a scenic mountain spot of the Monongahela National Forest (on Route 39, west of Route 219 at Mill Point), offers interpretive programs on the **Cranberry Glades**, the **Falls of Hills Creek**, the **Cranberry Backcountry**, and the **Highland Scenic Highway**. The visitors center has an exhibit hall, auditorium, restroom facilities, nature trails, and limited picnicking outside the center. Open May 1 through May 31, weekends only; Memorial Day to Labor Day, daily, 9:00 a.m. to 5:00 p.m.; September and October, weekends, 9:00 a.m. to 5:00 p.m. Admission free. For further information contact: U.S. Forest Service, Box 110, Richwood, WV 26261. Telephone: (304) 653-4826.

The 750-acre **Cranberry Glades Botanical Area** is two miles from the Cranberry Mountain Visitor Center. One can take a self-guided tour on a half-mile boardwalk to see the plants that are unusual so far south and are more native to the northern areas of Wisconsin and Canada.

Bordering on the glades, the **Cranberry Backcountry** is a northern hardwood area. This large area encompasses 53,000 acres of the forest and has 75 miles of hiking trails within it.

The 23-mile **Highland Scenic Highway** proceeds north from the Cranberry Mountain Visitor Center through the Cranberry Back Country with many overlook and picnicking areas along the way. The highway ends at Route 219 near Marlinton.

The three **Falls of the Hills Creek**, further west on Route 39 from the Cranberry Mountain Visitor Center, is a beautiful scenic area with a very fragile ecosystem. A very steep three-quarter-mile trail takes the hiker 250 feet down a narrow ravine. The lower falls are the longest, 63 feet in height. The trail has stops along the way and the hiker will see the unusual layering consisting of three layers of sandstone and three of shale. It is the geologic formation, unique to this spot, that caused the erosion creating the falls.

Leaving the Monongahela National Forest, the **Pearl S. Buck Birthplace** museum is located in Hillsboro on Route 219. Pearl Buck was born in her grandparents' home in 1892. Mrs. Buck won both the Pulitzer and Nobel prizes for literature. Open May to November, Monday to Saturday, 9:00 a.m. to 5:00 p.m.: Sunday, 1:00 to 5:00 p.m. Admission charge. Telephone: (304) 653-4430.

Droop Mountain Battlefield has been partly restored and visitors may visit its small museum containing Civil War artifacts. This 288-acre park is on Route 219, five miles south of Hillsboro. The battle took place on November 6, 1863, and was the largest Civil War engagement in West Virginia. The park offers hiking trails, a playground, and picnic tables. Open daily, 7:30 a.m. to 5:00 p.m. Admission free. Telephone: (304) 653-4254.

Approximately 25 miles farther north off Route 219, near Slatyfork, is **Snowshoe**. It is an all-season resort at the top of Cheat Mountain, known as a mecca for skiers. (See Special Interest Section, Downhill Skiing.) Its summer programs offer tennis, hiking, horseback riding, and a Junior Sports camp. There are also conference facilities, restaurants, and a variety of accommodations. Telephone: (304) 799-6600.

Beyond Elkins, where Routes 219 and 250 divide as they continue northward, is the longest two-lane covered bridge still in use on a federal highway. Built in 1852, **Philippi Covered Bridge** spans the Tygart Valley River and was used by the armies of both the North and South. Philippi, 25 miles west of Elkins on Route 250, was the site of the first land battle of the Civil War.

NEW RIVER AREA

The southeastern section of West Virginia offers visitors a diverse choice of activities ranging from a stay at an historically renowned mineral springs spa, the Greenbrier, to roughing it on a whitewater raft trip down the New and Gauley rivers. The visitor to West Virginia may wish to see a coal mine or visit one of the many glass factories (see Special Interest Section, Industrial Tours, for the Beckley Exhibition Coal Mine and glass factories).

The Greenbrier, a luxury hotel with 700 rooms and a complex of shops, is situated within a 6,500-acre tract on Route 60, just off of I-64 at White Sulphur Springs. The resort was established in 1778, when Virginians escaped the hot, sultry summers of the Tidewater to take advantage of the mountain air and curative powers of the mineral waters. The Greenbrier is one of the three remaining mineral springs resorts that were so popular in the 18th and 19th centuries. (The others are Berkeley Springs, West Virginia, and The Homestead at Hot Springs, Virginia.)

The hotel has a complete year-round sports program including an 18-hole championship golf course, riding stables, skeet and trap shooting, swimming, biking, ice skating and skiing, and hiking and jogging trails. Indoor facilities include shopping, theaters, and heated pools, as well as sulphur baths, saunas, and whirlpools. The resort has a dining room, two restaurants, and a nightclub. Telephone: (304) 536-1110; (800) 624-6070.

Lewisburg is a tranquil agricultural community that is the third oldest town in the state. The town was founded in 1782 and was named in honor of General Andrew Lewis. The **Fort Savannah Inn**, on North Jefferson Street, is part of an original fort from which General Lewis in 1774 mustered troops to Point Pleasant, near the confluence of the Kanawha and Ohio rivers. Lewis and his troops defeated the Shawnee Indians under Chief Cornstalk in what has been considered to be the first battle of the Revolutionary War. The inn offers lodging and meals. Telephone: (304) 645-3055. Across the street is the **Andrew Lewis Park**, where troops and cattle assembled prior to the battle at Point Pleasant.

On Church Street, the **Old Stone Church**, built in 1796, is still in use. This restored Presbyterian church has a slave gallery and an adjoining cemetery where Civil War soldiers are buried.

The **Lost World Caverns** are located one-and-a-half miles north of Lewisburg on Fairview Road. This private cavern features a cave 1,000 feet long and 75 feet wide with several waterfalls and many terraced stalagmites. Open year round, 9:00 a.m. to 7:00 p.m. Admission charge. Telephone: (304) 645-6677.

The 3,600-acre **Babcock State Park** features waterfalls, rugged scenery, and an operating grist mill. It is located at Clifftop on Route 41, off Route 60. Facilities include rental cabins, campsites, a swimming pool, boating, and fishing. There are more than 20 miles of trails, including the "Island in the Sky" trail where hikers must squeeze through a crevice and a cave. The **Glade Creek Grist Mill** is an operating mill that was reconstructed from old mill parts from around the state. The mill provides cornmeal and buckwheat flour which park visitors may purchase. Open late April through the fourth Monday in October, 9:00 a.m. to 5:00 p.m. Telephone: (304) 438-5662.

Bluestone Lake is an 1,800-acre lake created by the damming of the New River near Hinton on Routes 20 and 3. The lake is the center of a recreation area that includes the Bluestone and Pipestem state parks and five camping and fishing areas. Geologists consider the New River to be the oldest river in the world, originating millions of years ago. The **Bluestone Dam** is a concrete gravity dam that closes a 2,048-foot gap between mountains and rises 165 feet above the stream bed; tailwaters below the dam challenge fishing and canoe buffs. The U.S. Corps of Engineers offers tours of the dam, June through August, Wednesday and Thursday, 1:30 p.m.; Saturday and Sunday, 2:00 p.m. Telephone: (304) 466-1234.

Bluestone State Park and **Pipestem State Park** offer rental cabins, campsites, hiking, golf course, boating, fishing, and water-skiing opportunities. In the winter, cross- country skiing trails are open at Pipestem. For further information telephone: Bluestone State Park, (304) 466-1922; or Pipestem State Park, (304) 466-1800.

The **Big Bend Tunnels** and **John Henry Statue** are located on Route 3 near Talcott. A statue of John Henry, the "steel-driving" man, stands in a small overlook. Legend says Henry worked on the Chesapeake and Ohio Railroad tunnels in 1873 and that he died after competing with a steam-powered drill in an attempt to prove he could work faster than a machine. Visitors can get a glimpse of the twin tunnels, 6,500-feet long, in the distance.

Hawks Nest State Park is a 256-acre park which features a lodge built on the rim of the canyon near the **New**

River Gorge Bridge, and is off Route 60 near Ansted. The park offers boating, fishing, picnicking, and hiking opportunities. An aerial tram carries visitors from the lodge to a marina in the gorge below, providing a wide view of the New River and surrounding mountains. Fare charge for the tram. **Hawks Nest State Park Museum** is perched on the mountain above the park and contains early firearms, unusual West Virginia historical pieces, and displays of Indian and pioneer life and the production of coal and lumber. Open April through October, daily, 9:00 a.m. to 5:00 p.m. Admission free. Telephone: (304) 658-5212, (800) 642-9058 (West Virginia), and (800) 624-8632 (out of state).

On Route 19 between Hico and Fayetteville, the **New River Gorge Bridge** rises 876 feet above the river. This bridge is the highest span east of the Mississippi River and is the longest four-lane, steel arch bridge in the world. It is 3,030 feet long.

NORTH CAROLINA

Kitty Hawk... Cape Hatteras... Albemarle Sound. The northeastern corner of North Carolina evokes images of a diverse vacation land that offers something for everyone: sun-lovers, history buffs, gourmets, sailors, even hang gliders.

The history of the "Tar Heel State" dates back to the very beginnings of the country. Colonists settled in this area as early as the 16th century, and you can visit the towns and cities where they left their mark. The area is also famous for its water sports. No matter where you are in northeastern North Carolina, you are never far from a cove, swamp, bay, or the ocean itself. And where there is water, there is seafood. You will enjoy stopping at the many little restaurants and diners by the side of the road—all one-of-a-kind establishments serving seafood just barely out of the water.

ALBEMARLE SOUND

Often called the "Cradle of American History," Albemarle dates back to the 16th century. King Charles II deeded the land to eight Lord Proprietors, one of whom was George Monck, Duke of Albemarle. In 1665, the colony's first representative assembly met in this region. Two years later, the colony's first organized resistance to British authority, Culpeper's Rebellion, took place here.

This area also boasts the state's first school (in Pasquotank County, 1705), first church building (near Edenton, about 1705), and the oldest still-standing church (St. Thomas, in Bath, 1734).

Throughout the region, you will see brown and yellow signs directing you along the Historic Albemarle self-guided driving tour. It will take you to towns in the area, and from there you can take the individual tours offered by the sites themselves. A map of the route is available from Historic Albemarle Tour, Inc., PO Box 759, Edenton, NC 27932.

Telephone: (919) 482-7325. To reach the Albemarle Sound area, from Richmond take I-64 southeast to Portsmouth, then Route 17 south. From Washington and Baltimore take I-95 south to Richmond and proceed as above.

Just over the North Carolina-Virginia border in Camden County is **Dismal Swamp State Park**. This swamp and bog wilderness has no visitors' facilities and is simply set aside as a natural area. One of the few remaining stands of Atlantic white cedar grow in the park. There is no road access, but you can enter in canoes via the Dismal Swamp Canal, the oldest canal in America still in service. Admission free. No telephone.

Cypress swamps and massive gum trees dominate **Merchant's Millpond State Park** (off Route 158 in Gates County). The 1,800 acres are largely undeveloped, although there are facilities for hiking and canoeing. Excellent fishing is available in Millpond for largemouth bass, crappie, catfish, chain pickerel, and shad. Overnight group canoe trips can be arranged with the park superintendent. Nature trails and picnicking facilities also are offered. Open daily at 8:00 a.m.; closing hours vary. Admission free. Telephone: (919) 357-1191.

On Route 17 is the Pasquotank County seat of **Elizabeth City**. A 30-block area in the heart of the city is included in the National Register of Historic Places. The district is architecturally distinguished by Greek revival, Queen Anne, and colonial revival houses, a charming Victorian courthouse, and many antebellum commercial buildings. **Christ Episcopal Church** has 18 beautifully matched stained-glass windows. Built around 1906, the **Federal Building** is one of the finest neoclassical revival structures in the state. The **Elizabeth City Chamber of Commerce** (502 East Ehringhaus) has brochures and maps of the Historic District. Open Monday through Friday, 9:00 a.m. to 5:00 p.m. Closed holidays. Admission free. Telephone: (919) 335-4365.

The area's history is well explained at Elizabeth City's **Museum of the Albemarle**. There are exhibits of regional history, geography, religion, and economy. The museum also covers history of the Coast Guard, which has the world's largest aircraft repair and supply center for Coast Guard aircraft. In addition to exhibits, the museum offers lectures, "touch talks," and slide programs. Open Tuesday through Saturday, 9:00 a.m. to 5:00 p.m.; Sunday, 2:00 to 5:00 p.m. Closed New Year's, Martin Luther King's Birthday, Good Friday, Memorial Day, July 4, Labor Day, Veteran's Day,

Thanksgiving, and Christmas. Admission free. Telephone: (919) 335-1453.

If you like crafts, visit **Watermark Crafts** in Elizabeth City's old train station (109 Hughes Boulevard). More than 300 crafts are made on the premises by members of the Watermark Association of Artisans, including pottery, decoys, quilts, wood working, baskets, copper tooling, and caning. Open Monday through Saturday, 10:00 a.m. to 5:00 p.m. Admission free. Telephone: (919) 335-1434.

Visitors entering **Hertford** will cross a unique, S-shaped bridge. The town celebrated its Bicentennial in 1958, and many of the homes date to the 18th and 19th centuries, especially those along Front, Church, Grubb, Market, and Dobb streets. The **Newbold-White House**, on Harvey Point Road, built about 1685, was an early meeting place of the proprietary government of North Carolina. Thought to be the oldest standing brick structure in the state, it has been restored to its original condition by the townspeople. Open Tuesday through Saturday, 10:00 a.m. to 4:30 p.m.; Sunday, 1:30 to 4:30 p.m. Admission charge. Telephone: (919) 426-7567.

Hertford is the seat of Perquimans County, and the **County Courthouse**, on Church Street, is worth a visit. Built between 1823 and 1825 in a simplified Federal style, it has been enlarged over the years to double its original size. The oldest part is the two-story front section. There are no organized tours, but visitors may view the building during business hours, Monday through Friday, 8:30 a.m. to 5:00 p.m. Admission free. Telephone: (919) 426-5676.

The Perquimans Chamber of Commerce, in the Municipal Building (114 West Grubb Street), can answer visitors' questions and provide flyers on the town. The Chamber of Commerce also has a walking tour featuring historic homes and buildings. Open Monday, Tuesday, Thursday, and Friday, 9:00 a.m. to 5:00 p.m.; Wednesday and Saturday, 9:00 a.m. to noon. Admission free. Telephone: (919) 426-5657.

Continuing southwest on Route 17, the road leads to Chowan County. The fertile lands of the Chowan River brought settlers to this area as early as 1658. They planned the town of **Edenton** in 1712, and 10 years later it was incorporated as the first capital of the province of North Carolina. The town served as a prosperous port in the 18th and early 19th centuries. This commercial activity rapidly turned Edenton into a center of learning, taste, and political activity within the colony. Many noted American patriots lived here including

Joseph Hewes, a Revolutionary War leader and signer of the Declaration of Independence; Samuel Johnston, a governor of North Carolina; and James Iredell, Supreme Court justice and speaker of the General Assembly. Even the infamous pirate Blackbeard sailed from Edenton's port. Throughout the Revolutionary War, Edenton exporters defied British blockades by sending supplies to Washington's army and the besieged northern colonies. The ladies of Edenton did their part to aid the war effort. On October 25, 1774, 51 local women decided to join their Boston peers in protest of the British tax on tea. They signed a resolution supporting the acts of the rebellious provincial Congress. Led by Penelope Barker, the women poured their tea for the last time, and agreed not to buy more until the tea tax was abolished by Parliament.

Today, three centuries of homes, a waterfront setting on Albemarle Sound, and resplendent gardens make any route through town a delight. Start your tour at the **Barker House Visitor Center** at the far end of South Broad Street. Built in 1782, it was once home of Thomas Barker, colonial agent in England, and his wife Penelope of Edenton Tea Party fame. The Center has an orientation slide show and offers guided tours to four historic buildings. Maps are available for self-guided walking tours along the National Recreation Trail to see the exteriors of 28 sites in the Historic District. Visitor Center open Monday through Saturday, 10:00 a.m. to 4:30 p.m.; Sunday, 2:00 to 5:00 p.m. Closed Easter, Thanksgiving, December 24 to 26, and New Year's. Admission free; charge for tours. Telephone: (919) 482-3663 or 482-2637.

Besides the Barker house, other buildings on the guided tour are the Iredell House, St. Paul's Episcopal Church, the Cupola House, and the Chowan County Courthouse. Built around 1773, the **Iredell House** was the home of James Iredell, a British subject who came to America in 1768 as deputy collector for the Port of Roanoke. He was later named attorney general of North Carolina and then appointed to the first U.S. Supreme Court. The house is listed on the National Register of Historic Places, and now has a museum of late 18th- and early 19th-century furnishings as well as a charming one-room schoolhouse and other dependencies on the grounds.

St. Paul's Episcopal Church is just what you think of when you imagine a colonial brick church. In fact, it has been called an "ideal in village church architecture." Begun in 1736 and completed some 30 years later, it still has an active congregation and is listed on the National Register of Historic Places. Buried in the churchyard are colonial governors Charles Eden, Thomas Pollock, and Henderson Walker.

The **Cupola House**, a National Historic Landmark, is named for the small cupola rising above the roof which enabled sea captains to observe ships entering the bay. Built about 1725, it has rare Jacobean features such as large chimneys, decorative finials, and a second-story overhang. Part of the downstairs woodwork was sold to the Brooklyn Museum of Fine Arts, but has been carefully reproduced. You can even trace your finger over 150-year-old signatures scratched in the wavy glass window panes. The herb garden in back and the formal garden in front have been restored according to a 1769 map.

In the heart of the Historic District, the village green is framed by the **Chowan County Courthouse**, a fine example of Georgian architecture and a National Historic Landmark. Built in 1767, it has been in continuous use for more than 200 years. A beautifully paneled room above the courtroom served as a ballroom for dancing, classes, and public festivities, and as a banquet room during the visit of President James Monroe in 1819.

Also around the village green are the **Bond House**, built around 1805 for Joseph Blount Skinner; the **East Custom House**; a monument to Joseph Hewes, signer of the Declaration of Independence; three Revolutionary War cannons; and a bronze teapot commemorating the Edenton Tea Party.

Each spring in odd-numbered years, the Edenton Woman's Club Pilgrimage allows visitors to tour many town and countryside homes and buildings not normally open to the public. Telephone: (919) 482-3663 or 482-2637.

Cross Albemarle Sound, the largest freshwater sound in the world, on Route 37, then turn left on Route 64 into Creswell. Just south of town is the splendid 19th-century coastal plantation estate, **Somerset Place**. The Greek revival mansion was built about 1830 by Josiah Collins, who had come to America from Somerset, England. This merchant and prominent citizen of nearby Edenton worked long and hard to open up the swampy lands around Lake Scuppernong (now called Lake Phelps). His son, Josiah, Jr., also a successful merchant, manufacturer, and planter, joined him in business. The plantation grew, and about 1830 the mansion was built. The farm continued prospering until the time of the

Civil War, which drove Josiah III from his home, ruined the magnificent estate, scattered the servants, and sent his sons into battle. His widow and sons attempted to revive the enterprise to no avail, and were finally forced to sell the plantation. Restoration work began in 1951 and still continues on the beautifully preserved mansion and outbuildings. The authentic restoration was accomplished through extensive documentary and archaeological research which has exposed the remains of slave buildings, a hospital and chapel, an overseer's house, original brick walks, and the completely detailed formal garden layout. Open November 1 through March 31, Tuesday to Saturday, 9:00 a.m. to 5:00 p.m.; Sunday, 1:00 to 5:00 p.m. April 1 through October 31, Monday to Saturday, 9:00 a.m. to 5:00 p.m.; Sunday, 1:00 to 5:00 p.m. Admission free. Telephone: (919) 797-4560.

Somerset Place is within the boundaries of **Pettigrew State Park**, named for Confederate General James F. Pettigrew. The park also includes parts of the old Pettigrew and Bonarva plantations and the 16,600 acres of Lake Phelps. Lined with magnificent cypress trees, the spring-fed lake is an angler's paradise with largemouth bass, yellow perch, and various types of panfish. Wind conditions make it an ideal spot for sailing, and facilities include a boat ramp. Birders enjoy Pettigrew's reputation as a wintering area for the Canada goose and several species of duck. There are also tent and trailer campsites and picnic grounds. Admission free. Open daily at 8:00 a.m., closing hours vary. Telephone: (919) 797-4475.

About 18 miles south of Plymouth off Highway 45 is **Pungo National Wildlife Refuge**. The 12,000 acres are similar in terrain to Great Dismal Swamp, and in fact it is sometimes considered the southern end of the swamp. Pungo Lake makes up almost one-fourth of the refuge, and is a good spot to watch wintering birds such as swans, geese, and shallow-water ducks. There are no organized activities for visitors. Open daily, dawn to dusk. Admission free. Contact Mattamuskeet Refuge Manager for information.

Continuing south of Highway 45, then left on Route 264, you will come to **Mattamuskeet National Wildlife Refuge**, also popular among bird watchers. As many as 20,000 whistling swans winter here during December and January, along with 20,000 Canada geese and close to 80,000 ducks. You can also spot southern bald and golden eagles, and during other times of the year, osprey, herons, and egrets. There is a walking trail, dikes along the marsh area (for foot traffic only), and a causeway over Lake Mattamuskeet, the largest natural lake in the state. Fishing is permitted from March through September, and a managed duck hunt is held annually, usually in early December. There is no visitors center, but you can pick up brochures and other information at the Refuge Office, just off Route 264. Office open Monday through Friday, 7:30 a.m. to 4:00 p.m. Refuge itself open daily, dawn to dusk. Admission free. Telephone: (919) 926-4021.

Still another refuge is south of Route 264 on Pamlico Sound. **Swanquarter Wildlife Refuge** has limited access via a marked gravel road. The bird watching is minor compared to Mattamuskeet because the marsh areas are inaccessible, but there is a fishing pier available on the sound. The waterfowl season corresponds to the state season; contact the Refuge Manager at Mattamuskeet for details. Swanquarter Refuge open daily, dawn to dusk. Admission free.

You can continue north on Route 264 through the farms and swamplands of Hyde and Dare counties, crossing the Intracoastal Waterway to Nags Head, or take the ferry boat leaving Swanquarter for Ocracoke Island. The toll ferries take two and a half hours to cross Pamlico Sound, and leave Swanquarter daily at 9:30 a.m. and 4:00 p.m. If you are coming from the opposite direction, ferries leave Ocracoke at 6:30 a.m. and 12:30 p.m. Reservations are advisable. Telephone: (919) 926-1111 (if departing from Swanquarter) or (919) 928-3841 (if departing from Ocracoke).

OUTER BANKS

The famous Outer Banks of North Carolina are favorite spots for those who abhor crowded beaches with wall-to-wall condominiums. About the nearest the Outer Banks comes to this type of resort is Nags Head, which can still be relatively uncrowded. The further south you go along this 120-mile stretch of sand dune islands, the less crowded they become. It is entirely possible to be the only one on a beautiful beach in Hatteras—even on a holiday weekend. If you want night life, you can find it; if your tastes run more to quaint fishing villages, you will also be kept happily occupied.

The geography of the Outer Banks is rather unique, owing its landscape to storms, winds, and waves. Many geologists believe the ever-changing sand dunes are slowly moving towards the mainland. The inlets and sound have always had a strong maritime activity, and many of the residents have kept the "high tide" accent and customs of their 17th-century forefathers. The area is also noted for its superlative fishing.

To reach the Outer Banks from Richmond, take I-64 southeast to the "168—South" Exit, and continue to the junction with Route 158, proceeding east. From Baltimore and Washington, take I-95 south to Richmond, then proceed as above.

Driving south on Route 158, you will cross a bridge over Currituck Sound onto Bodie (pronounced "body") Island, giving you your first glimpse of the Outer Banks sand dunes. On your right is the **Outer Banks Chamber of Commerce Welcome Center**, which can provide you with a host of sightseeing information including maps, lodging and restaurant listings, and brochures. Open daily, 9:00 a.m. to 5:00 p.m. Closed Thanksgiving, and from Christmas through New Year's. Write: Box 90-CC, Kitty Hawk, NC 27949. Telephone: (919) 441-8144.

Continuing south on Route 158, you will see looming in the distance the **Wright Brothers National Memorial** commemorating Orville and Wilbur's historic powered-aircraft flight on December 17, 1903. The actual location of the flight is about 300 yards from the monument, marked by a large pylon. Nearby are reconstructions of their launching apparatus, the hangar, and their living quarters. At the Visitors Center, the Wright brothers' story is told through exhibits and full-scale reproductions of their 1902 glider and 1903 flying machine. Open daily, 9:00 a.m. to 5:00 p.m., with extended hours in the summer. Closed Christmas. Admission free. Telephone: (919) 441-7430.

If the Wright brothers inspire you to take flight yourself, you can try hang gliding in **Jockey's Ridge State Park**. Its 100-foot-high sand dune is the largest on the east coast (beginners start on the lower slopes). Even if you don't hang glide, the exhilarating view from atop the dune is well worth the climb. Open daily, 8:00 a.m. to dusk; June through August, 8:00 a.m. to 9:00 p.m. Admission free. Telephone: (919) 441-7132.

Nags Head is a popular resort with excellent beaches and facilities for fishing. Local legend says the town's name stems from an old practice of tying lanterns to ponies' necks at night and walking them along the beach. Ship captains would spot the swinging lights, and thinking they were boats at anchor, would run their own ships aground where waiting pirates would seize the cargo.

Today's natives treat visitors with more respect, and in fact welcome them with open arms. Along the beach are hundreds of hotels, motels, and cottages. There is a local height restriction of three stories, so you will not find glaring concrete highrises to spoil the atmosphere. Besides swimming, there are outfitters who can assist you with sailing, windsurfing, jet skiing, and even diving to local shipwrecks. Up and down Route 158 you will find the usual assortment of miniature golf courses, amusement parks, surf slides, and roller rinks. There is even a 35-foot replica of a 19th-century windmill which grinds grain.

South of Nags Head at Whalebone Junction, take a right on US 64-264 to Manteo on **Roanoke Island**. Four miles west of town is **Fort Raleigh National Historic Site**, the scene of the first English colonizing attempt (1585-86) within the limits of the present-day United States. Originally built in 1585, the now-restored fort lends an understanding to Sir Walter Raleigh's attempt to start an English colony in America. The small earthworks structure was built by the colonists as a defense against possible attack. Signs along the historic area trail explain more about the colony, and a granite stone memorializes Virginia Dare, the first English child born in the New World. The colony was not to last, however, and the complete disappearance of the settlers remains a mystery to this day. At the Visitors Center, a 10-minute film speculates on the cause of the disappearance, and artifacts and a diorama of the town add to the intrigue. You can also see a model of the type of ship in which the settlers sailed. The story of the settlement is portrayed throughout the summer in the 2,000-seat Waterside Theatre. A mixture of song, dance, sudden Indian attacks, and a tender love story, "The Lost Colony" will fuel your imagination as you try to answer the questions that have puzzled historians for centuries. Performances mid-June through end of August, Monday through Saturday, at 8:30 p.m. Admission charge. Telephone: (919) 473-3414 (for ticket information during summer only), or (919) 473-2127 (business office). The park itself is open 24 hours a day; Visitors Center open daily, 9:00 a.m. to 5:00 p.m. with extended summer hours. Closed Christmas. Admission free. Telephone: (919) 473-2117.

Another memorial to the Elizabethan men and women sent by Sir Walter Raleigh, the **Elizabethan Gardens** are an imaginative concept of 16th-century English gardens. The formal and informal plantings include an herb garden, the Queen's Rose Garden, the Mount, and antique garden ornaments. Herbs and wildflowers are at their peak in May and June, and the gardens are even popular in the winter months. Open daily, 9:00 a.m. to 5:00 p.m. Admission charge; children under 12, free. Telephone: (919) 473-3234.

Also on Roanoke Island is the **North Carolina Aquarium**, offering a self-guided tour through displays depicting many aspects of local marine life: waterfowl, sharks, whaling, fishing, and barrier island ecosystems. "Touch tables" let youngsters hold starfish, sea urchins, hermits crabs, and other sea critters. There are also daily films, frequent workshops, and special programs ranging from arts and crafts to seafood cookery. Open Monday through Friday, 9:00 a.m. to 5:00 pm. Weekend hours vary during peak seasons. Admission free. Telephone: (919) 473-3493.

Retrace your steps across Route 64-264 to Bodie Island, and turn right onto Route 12 at Whalebone, the northern end of **Cape Hatteras National Seashore**. Its 45 square miles makes it the largest stretch of undeveloped seashore on the Atlantic Coast. You can drive the length of the park on Highway 12, a relatively narrow paved road with soft shoulders. The various islands are connected by bridges and ferry boats, and the road passes through a number of quaint villages (not part of the park) reflecting the unique culture of the region. A stop at **Whalebone Junction Information Center** can provide you with a map of the entire park and information on campsites and park programs. Open daily, Memorial Day through Labor Day, 8:00 a.m. to early evening. Admission free. No telephone.

At nearby **Coquina Beach**, visitors will get a good idea of why this coast is often called the "Graveyard of the Atlantic." A combination of strong ocean currents, a narrow channel, treacherous shoals, and frequent storms have been responsible for more than 1,500 shipwrecks in the past 400 years. Remains of one such tragedy is accessible to visitors at Coquina Beach: the remains of the four-masted *Laura A Barnes*, stranded on a sandbar of Bodie Island in 1921, is now displayed on the beach itself.

Three lighthouses within the National Seashore have guided seafarers through the treacherous waters for centuries. The **Bodie Island Lighthouse** can be seen just opposite

Coquina; it is closed to the public. (The other lighthouses are described below.)

At the tip of the island, the **Oregon Inlet Fishing Center** has one of the largest fleets of sport fishing boats on the mid-Atlantic Coast. You can arrange charters for inshore and offshore fishing trips to these justly famous, bountiful waters. In abundance are flounder, bluefish, marlin, dolphin fish, striped bass, tuna, and wahoo. Telephone: (919) 441-6301. Park facilities at the inlet include a public boat launching ramp, a restaurant, and a camp store.

Cross Oregon Inlet by bridge onto Hatteras Island, where you'll enter **Pea Island National Wildlife Refuge**, the winter home of the Greater Snow Goose and dozens of other species of birds. About five miles south of the Oregon Inlet Bridge are refuge observation platforms offering excellent views of wildlife, the ocean, and even shipwrecks along the shore. Beaches are open to the public. Beware of strong rip tides and littoral currents; walk, do not drive, across the barrier dunes to sand beaches. The refuge does not have a visitors center, but there is a refuge office. Open daily, 8:00 a.m. to 4:30 p.m. Admission free. Telephone: (919) 987-2394.

Continuing south, you will find nothing but untouched beaches, dunes, and occasional villages such as Rodanthe (with the Chicamacomico Lifesaving Station, which presents reenactments of lifesaving operations), Waves, Salvo (which has the country's second smallest post office), and Avon. Another **Visitors Center** is located at Cape Hatteras, the "elbow" of the island where it turns west. Here is the often-photographed, black-and-white striped **Cape Hatteras Lighthouse**. The 208-foot structure, tallest lighthouse in the United States, was built in 1870, and still warns ships off treacherous Diamond Shoals. When the lighthouse was built, the shoreline was more than 1,500 feet away, but constant erosion has brought the Atlantic to within 70 feet of its base. The "Save Cape Hatteras Lighthouse Campaign" is working to preserve the structure, and guides in the Visitors Center will tell you how you can become a "Keeper of the Light." Cape Hatteras Lighthouse is currently closed to the public. Cape Hatteras Visitors Center open 9:00 a.m. to 5:00 p.m. Admission free. Telephone: (919) 995-5209 or (919) 995-4474.

You can continue south on Highway 12 past more beaches and fishing areas, past the towns of Frisco and Hatteras, to the tip of the island. A free ferry takes cars across the Hatteras inlet to **Ocracoke Island**. Service is during daylight hours, every 40 minutes in the summer, and every hour in the winter. Telephone: (919) 986-2353. About 10 miles beyond the ferry docks is a platform over the marshland which enables you to see the small Ocracoke ponies, the remnants of a once larger herd. At the far end of the island, the tiny village of Ocracoke, in its isolation, has retained much of its early charm. The houses in this fishing village have pleasant yards with giant, moss-covered oaks and yaupon trees. In the early 1700s, the pirate Blackbeard sold his booty here. He and his crew were killed at Teach's Hole in 1718. As with the other villages along the Outer Banks, Ocracoke is a fishing haven. A Park Service **Visitors Center** near the harbor has nature displays and organized activities such as walks through the forests, lessons in riding the waves on "boogie" boards, and trips wading through the saltmarshes on the bay side of the island. Visitors Center open daily, May through September, 9:00 a.m. to 5:00 p.m. Admission free. Telephone: (919) 928-4531.

Four British soldiers, killed off the coast during World War II, are buried in the **British Cemetery** in Ocracoke; as part of the American Bicentennial celebration, the land in this tiny graveyard was officially declared British soil.

There is also a lighthouse in Ocracoke, a pleasant walk from the Visitors Center. It is closed to the public, however.

Throughout Cape Hatteras National Seashore, camping is permitted only in designated areas; campsites are at Oregon Inlet, Salvo, Cape Hatteras, Frisco, and Ocracoke. There are also a number of commercial campgrounds in the area.

For more information write: Cape Hatteras National Seashore, Route 1, Box 675, Manteo, NC 27954. Telephone: (919) 473-2111.

SPECIAL INTEREST SECTIONS

═══════ **ANTIQUES AND AUCTIONS** ═══════

Antique collecting in the mid-Atlantic states is an exciting and varied experience because the range of quality collectibles is broad and because so much is available. Excellent examples of furnishings, art, utensils, maritime objects, glass, fittings, farm implements, toys, handcrafts, quilts, and fixtures are bought and sold in heavy trading throughout the region. Objects vary from English and Early American 16th and 17th century to Colonial, Appalachian, early 20th century, and Depression. Fine examples and good buys of many periods can still be found at flea markets and garage sales by astute and lucky collectors. For the shopper who would like information or guidance, there is an abundance of stores. The following listing represents only a portion of all the antique shops to be found in the area covered in *Weekender's Guide*. Also included are some auctioneers for those folks who enjoy the thrill of bidding (or just watching). Some shops may operate only during the summer season.

The pleasure of ownership can be a great feeling. However, whether you are a knowledgeable collector or you have just started, it is fitting to offer the traditional advice: "Caveat emptor!" ("Let the buyer beware.")

DELAWARE

BRIDGEVILLE
Tull's Carriage House, Market Street

CENTERVILLE
The Collector, 5716 Kennett Pike

DELAWARE CITY
Dragon Run Antiques, 213 Clinton

DOVER
Flamm Antiques, Route 13, N. DuPont Highway
James M. Kilvington Antiques, 126 Ross Street

Meeting House Square Antiques, 305 S. Governor's Avenue
Old Dover Antiques, 666 S. DuPont Highway
Old Sleigh Antiques, 2151 S. DuPont Highway
Elaine Owen, Route 13, N. DuPont Highway
Roberts Antique Lamps, 2035 S. DuPont Highway
The Stable Shoppes, 809 N. State Street

ELSMERE
Merrill's Antiques, 100 Northern Avenue

GEORGETOWN
Brick Barn Antiques, Routes 18 & 9
Candlelightantiques, 406 N. DuPont Highway
Edwin L. & Oleta Smith Antiques and Gadgets, 422 Race
  Street

GREENWOOD
Ruth Mervine, Route 36
Royal Antiques, Route 13

HOCKESSIN
Antique Imports, Old Lancaster Pike

LAUREL
Culver's Antiques, Route 9
Five Points Antiques Shop, Route 13
The Golden Door, 214 E. Market Street
Jackson's Antiques, Fifth & Spruce
Val's Antiques, 304 Fourth Street

LEWES
Marvel Gallery, 138 Second Street

LINCOLN
Wilson's Auctions, Route 113

MIDDLETOWN
Middle of Town Antiques Shop, Broad & Main
G. W. Thomas Antiques, Route 13

MILTON
York's Homestead Antique Shoppe, Route 9

NEWARK
Billie's Flea Barn, Route 40
Corner Cupboard, 140 E. Cleveland Avenue
Iron Hill Auction, 1115 Elkton

NEW CASTLE
  Becky's Antique Shop, DuPont Highway
  Jackson-Mitchell, Inc., Third & Delaware Streets
  Quality House, 124 Delaware Street
  Sebul's Auction, Route 13, Tybout's Corner

OCEAN VIEW
  Antique City, Route 26
  Iron Age Antiques, Central Avenue & Daily Street

ODESSA
  Locust Run Antiques, Fifth & Osborne

REHOBOTH BEACH
  Dinner Bell Inn Antiques Barn, 2 Christian Street
  The Hudson House Antiques, Route 1 & Benson Street; also on
    Airport Road

SEAFORD
  Blue Hen Farm Antiques, Road 541
  McCallister's Antique Shop, Route 13 North
  Wells Antiques, 900 Concord

SELBYVILLE
  Seaport Antique Village, Route 54

SMYRNA
  A&M White House Antiques, Route 13
  A Bit of the Past, 1652 S. DuPont Highway
  Eileen C. Gant Antiques, Route 13, DuPont Highway
  Peacock Plume, Inc., N. DuPont Highway
  Sayers, 19 S. Main

WEST MILFORD
  Harper Antiques, Route 14

WILMINGTON
  The Antique Shop, 1707 Chestnut
  Bonnie's Antiques, 2000 Newport Gap Pike
  Brandywine Antiques, 2116 N. Market Street
  Cooper's Antiques, 2015 Limestone Road
  The Corner Shoppe, 1200 Newport Gap Pike
  1818 Antiques, 1818 Marsh Road; also 402 Delaware Avenue
  Greenwood Book Shop, 110 W. Ninth Street
  Sally King Antiques & Gifts, 1701 N. Lincoln
  Samuel S. Kirshner, 808 W. 22nd Street
  Rudnick & Mata Auction Associates, 1908 N. Broom
  David Stockwell, Inc., 3701 Kennett Pike

MARYLAND

ANNAPOLIS

Anne Arundel Antiques, 306 Monterey
Antiquarians of Annapolis, 250 Prince George Street
David and Linda Arman, 3 Church Circle
Church Circle Antiques, 3 Church Circle
Gingerbread Shop, 29 Maryland Avenue
The Lion Mark, 25 Maryland Avenue
Ron Snyder Antiques, 1809 McGuckian Street
Treasure Chest, 47 Maryland Avenue

BALTIMORE

Baltimoretown Antiques and Collectibles, 1719 E. Lombard
   Street
W. Berry & Son, 222 W. Read Street
E. J. Canton, 2107 Town Hill Road
Charles Village Shop, 414 E. 31st Street
Dickeyville Antiques, 2412 Pickwick Road
The Dusty Attic, 9411 Harford Road
Harris Auction Gallery, 875 N. Howard Street
Imperial Half Bushel, 831 N. Howard Street
Amos Judd & Son, 843 N. Howard Street
Thelma Judkins, 841 N. Howard Street
The London Shop, 1500 Bolton Street
Maidstone, 1810 Frederick Road
Margolet Antiques, 833 N. Howard Street
Peacock & Parrett Antiques, 5718 Greenspring Avenue
The J. S. Pearson Co., 16 W. Hamilton Street
Ruth Rogers, 895 N. Howard Street
Nancy Scott Antiques, 7625 Bellona Avenue
Myrtle Seidel Antiques, 1015 N. Charles Street
E. A. Shaw Antiques, 857 N. Howard Street
Think N Things Antiques, 1330 Smith Avenue
Weber's Farm Antiques, 2526 Proctor Lane
Wilson's Ltd., 14 W. Franklin Street

BETHESDA

"All of Us Americans" Folk Art, 5530 Pembroke Road
Jane Alper Antiques, 5309 Edgemoor Lane
Antiques by Wallace, Inc., 4912 Cordell Avenue
Wm. Blair Ltd., 4839 Del Ray Avenue
The Brass Lion Antiques, 4910 Cordell Avenue
Sarah Eveleth & Ben Summerford Associates, 4918 Del Ray
   Avenue
Fleur-De-Lis Antiques, 7921 Norfolk Avenue
Mark Keshishian & Sons, 6930 Wisconsin Avenue
Law-Ford House Antiques, 7921 Norfolk Avenue

Montrose Galleries, 7800 Wisconsin Avenue
O'Rourke Ltd., 7950 Norfolk Avenue
Prints and Prose Antiques, 5315 Westpath Way
Quill and Brush, 7649 Old Georgetown Road
Walter Reed Antique Shop, 8118 Woodmont Avenue
M. Wang Gallery, 8010 Norfolk Avenue

BOWIE
Treasure House Antiques, 13010 Ninth Street

BRADDOCK HEIGHTS
Grandaddy's Antique Shop, Route 40

BUCKEYSTOWN
Buckeys Antiques Village, Route 85

CAMBRIDGE
Cambridgetowne Antiques, 411 Muse Street
Cloverdale Antiques, Route 50 E.

CHESAPEAKE CITY
Blue Max Antiques, Bohemia Avenue

CHESTERTOWN
Big Dipper Inc., 851 High Street
River Country Antiques, Route 213, Kings Town

CHEVY CHASE
Mendelsohn Galleries, 6826 Wisconsin Avenue
Webster Fine Art Inc., 4007 Bradley Lane

CHEWSVILLE
Robert E. Shobe Antiques, Old Forge Farm, Old Forge & Clopper Roads

CHURCHVILLE
Hatt-in-Hand Antiques, 3100 Aldino Road

CLINTON
Beltway Antique Exchange, 5810 Kirby Road

COCKEYSVILLE
Bill Bentley's Antique Show Mart, 10854 York Road

COLLEGE PARK
Alvin's Attic, 5001 Greenbelt Road
Gaslight Lane Antiques, 5000 Berwyn Road
Len's Country Barn Antiques, 9929 Rhode Island Avenue

DAMASCUS
    Bea's Antiques, 24140 Ridge Road

DUNKIRK
    Penwick Square, Route 4

ELLICOTT CITY
    Antique Peddler, 43 E. Patrick Street
    Attic Treasures, 24 E. Church Street
    Colonial Jewelers, 9 W. Patrick Street
    Ellicott's Country Store, 8180 Main Street
    Fogle Auction Gallery, 5305 Jefferson Pike
    Franklin Rappold, Inc., 53 E. Patrick Street
    Gaslight Antiques, 118 E. Church Street
    The Wagon Wheel Antiques, 8061 Tiber Alley

FUNKSTOWN
    Funkstown Antique Mart, 6 N. West Side Avenue
    Hudson House Galleries, Inc., 32 E. Baltimore Street
    Ruth's Antique Shop, Inc., 41 E. Baltimore Street

GAITHERSBURG
    Antique Gallery of Gaithersburg, 19366 Montgomery Village
      Avenue
    Craft Shop, 405 S. Frederick Avenue
    Doris Frohnsdorff, 19300 Meadridge Place

GALESVILLE
    Pink Domain Antiques, 970 Main Street

HIGHLAND
    Pine Hill Antiques, 13960 Waynewight Road, Route 108
    Yankee Trader, Routes 108 & 216

HOLLYWOOD
    Sotterley Mansion, Route 245

HUDSONS CORNER
    Eastern Shore Early Americana Museum

HYATTSVILLE
    The Antique Underground, 3500 E. West Highway

KEEDYSVILLE
    Frederick B. Hanson Country Antiques at Pry Mill, RD 1

KENSINGTON
    Adaire Antiques & Objets d'Art, 3750 Howard Avenue

Antiques and Uniques, 3750 Howard Avenue
Antiques Anonymous, 10421 Fawcett Street
Anna Feng Antiques, 3758 Howard Avenue
Koryo Antiques, 10419 Fawcett Street
Kramer & Scott, Inc., 3774 Howard Avenue
Rice's Antiques, 4208 Howard Avenue
Second Chance Antiques, 3740 Howard Avenue
This N That Antiques, 4216 Howard Avenue

KEYMAR
The Looking Glass Antiques, 950 Francis Scott Key Highway

KINGSVILLE
Pete's Pekins, 7818 Bradshaw Road

LAUREL
Antique Market, Washington Boulevard
Laurel Antique Shop, 99 Main Street
Sadler's General Store, 420 Main Street
Colonel James Auction Galleries, 13718 Baltimore Boulevard

LAYTONSVILLE
The Gate House Antiques, 21125 Burnham Road
Stools 'N Things Antiques, 5405 Riggs Road
Yesteryear Farms Antique Village, 7420 Hawkins Creamery
Road

LIBERTYTOWN
Liberty Antiques, Main Street

LUTHERVILLE
R. T. Powers, 914 Jamieson
The Wood Butcher Ltd., 506 Seminary Avenue

MOUNT RAINIER
Markley Used Furniture, 2207 Varnum Street

NEW MARKET
Coach House Antiques, 43 Main Street
Comus Antiques, 1 N. Federal Street
Country Squire Antiques, 4 W. Main Street
Federal House, 13 W. Main Street
Cynthia Fehr, 51 W. Main Street
The Klackers, 108 W. Main Street
The Old Silver Shop Metz Country Store, 26 W. Main Street
Peace and Plenty Antiques, 32 Main Street
Thomas' Antiques, 60 W. Main Street

OCEAN CITY
Dragon Retreat, 117 72nd Street
Moffett Cottage Antiques, 8006 Coastal Highway

OLNEY
Antiques at the Horse Fair, 16810 Georgia Avenue
The Briar's Antiques, 4121 Briars Road
Carl's Antiques, 16650 Georgia Avenue

OXFORD
The Flea Market, Morris Street

PHOENIX
Maryland Miniatures, 3907 Eland Road

POCOMOKE
Jerry E. Tiller, Route 1

POTOMAC
John Hanson Antiques, 9812 Falls Road
Norma & William Wangel, 11058 Seven Hills Lane
The Willow Tree, 11905 Devilwood Drive

RANDALLSTOWN
Gloria C. Speert, 9802 Southall Road

REISTERSTOWN
Nettie Penn Antiques, 234 N. Main Street

RHODESDALE
Cloverdale Antiques, Route 1, Cloverdale Road

RISING SUN
Hunter's Sale Barn, Route 276

RIVERDALE
Treasure Hunt, 4704 Riverdale Road

ROCKVILLE
The Loft, 1050 First Street
Roger's Auction Gallery, 12101 Nebel Street

ROYAL OAK
Oak Creek Sales, Route 329

ST. MICHAELS
Nina Ayres Lanham, The Old Inn, Talbot & Mulberry Streets

SALISBURY
>Holly Ridge Antiques, Morris Leonard Road
>The Rocking Horse, 412 Lincoln Avenue

SAVAGE
>The Antique Gallery Ltd., Savage Industrial Center
>Cele's Old Mill Antiques & Interiors, Savage Industrial Center

SILVER HILL
>Iron Gate Antiques, Howard Johnson's Motor Lodge, 3131
>Branch Avenue

SILVER SPRING
>Breezewood Farms Antiques, Blair Street
>Four Winds Antiques, 2405 Norbeck Road
>Marisa Antiques, 1411 Highland Drive
>Nouveau Architectural Display, 9521 Georgia Avenue

STEVENSON
>Heirloom Jewels, Stevenson Village Center

STEVENSVILLE
>Old Schoolhouse Antiques

TANEYTOWN
>Carousel Antiques, 202 E. Baltimore Street
>The Krogh's Nest, 54 W. Baltimore Street

TRAPPE
>Ferry Boat Antique Mart, Route 50

UNION BRIDGE
>Red's Antiques, Route 75

UNIONTOWN
>The Woodwards, 3443 Uniontown Road

WALKERSVILLE
>Creative Corner, 1 W. Federal Street

WESTMINSTER
>Westminster Antiques, Taylorsville Road

WHITE MARSH
>Foley's Antiques, 10807 Railroad Avenue

WOODSBORO
>Circuit Rider Shop, Route 550

NEW JERSEY

ATLANTIC CITY
Princeton Antiques, 2917 Atlantic Avenue

BEACH HAVEN
Wizard of Odds, Culber Avenue & Long Beach Boulevard

CAPE MAY
Antiques et al, 605 Hughes Street
The Victorian Look, 654 Hughes Street

COLLINGSWOOD
Anthony C. Schmidt Fine Arts, 112 E. Linden Avenue

ELMER
Elmer Auction, Broad Street

ENGLISHTOWN
Englishtown Auction Sales, 90 Wilson Avenue

HADDONFIELD
Sanski Art Center, 50 Tanner Street

HAINSPORT
J. R. Ianni Antiques, Route 38

MAURICETOWN
Wagon Wheel Antiques, High Street

MONROEVILLE
Bragdon's Auctions

MOORESTOWN
Auld Lang Syne, 111 E. Main Street
Grand Junction Antiques, 101 Chestnut Avenue

MOUNT LAUREL
Crown & Feather Antiques, 163 E. Moorestown, Centerton Road

MULLICA HILL
Anthony & Ellen Barrett Antiques, S. Main Street
Eagle's Nest Antiques, 38 S. Main Street
King's Row, 44 N. Main Street
Robert and Ann Schumann Antiques, 74 N. Main Street

OCEAN CITY
The Suttons Antiques, 1741 Asbury Avenue

PLEASANTVILLE
Joseph Rubinfine, RFD 1

REPAUPO
S & S Auction, Repaupo Road

SMITHVILLE
Captain's Chest Antiques, 1478 New York Road

VINCENTOWN
Barthold's Antiques, 166 Main Street
Moore's Place Antiques, Route 205
Pump House Antiques, Newbold Road

WEST BERLIN
Bertolino Galleries, 406 Harrison Avenue

WEST CREEK
Peaceable Kingdom, Route 9

WOODSTOWN
Yellow Barn Antiques, Route 40

NORTH CAROLINA

EDENTON
Colonial Cottage Antiques, Morgan Bark, Highway 17 S.
Edenton Antiques and Upholstery, Highway 17 S.
Edenton Floral Company and Antiques, 202 S. Broad Street
Granny's Attic Antiques, Highway 17 N.
Queen's Quest, Inc., 112 Water Street

PENNSYLVANIA

ABBOTSTOWN
Henny Penny Antiques, 186 Route 30 W.
Wallace's Antiques, 320 W. King Street

ABINGTON
Abington Antique Shop, 1165 Old York Road

ADAMSTOWN/DENVER
Tex Johnson Antiques, 40 Willow Street

AVONDALE
The Carpenter's Tool Chest, 401 Pennsylvania Avenue, Route
41

BALLY
  Thomas L. Banks Antiques, Route 100

BIRD-IN-HAND
  House of Antiques, 2643 Old Philadelphia Pike

BLUE BELL
  Judy and Alan Goffman Fine Art, 402 Wood Drive
  Martin Auctioneers, (717) 354-7006

BRADDOCK
  J. Roy's Antiques, 903 Braddock Avenue

BRISTOL
  C & C Auctions, 216 Mill Street

BRYN MAWR
  Antique Barn, 508 Bryn Mawr Avenue
  Bryn Mawr Antiques, 1027-1029 Lancaster Avenue
  Steven Butler Antiques, 1201 Lancaster Avenue
  Robert David Antiques, 724 Lancaster Avenue
  Hayestock House, 19 N. Merion Avenue
  Harvey Wedeen Antiques, 1024 Lancaster Avenue

BUCKINGHAM
  Brown Brothers Gallery, Route 413
  Edna's Antique Shoppe, General Greene Inn, Routes 263 & 413

CAMPBELLTOWN
  Stauffer House Antiques, Highway 322

CAMP HILL
  Fu-Ming-Fair, 483 N. 25th Street
  House of Curios, 2106 Market Street

CARLISLE
  Boots Corner, 324 W. Willow
  Olde Bedford Shoppes, 40-44 Bedford Street
  Elizabeth Schiffman, 551 S. Hanover Street

CARVERSVILLE
  Hobby Horse Antiques, Saw Mill Road

CHADDS FORD
  Brandywine Valley Antiques, Route 1

CHALFONT
  Guthrie & Larson Antiques, 2 Butler Avenue

CHAMBERSBURG
Yesteryear Antiques, 518 E. King Street

COATESVILLE
Don Howe, Inc., 360 Harmony Street

COLLEGEVILLE
Early American Antiques, 1646 Main Street

COLLINGDALE
McMenamin's Auction, Macade Boulevard & Chester Pike

CONSHOHOCKEN
The Spring Mill Antique Shop, Barren Hill & River Roads, Spring Mill
Zetles Antiques, RFD 1, Spring Mill

COOPERSBURG
Robert & Lori Snyder, Limesport Pike, RD 3

COVENTRYVILLE
Coventry Antiques, RD 2, Olde Route 23

DOWNINGTOWN
Philip H. Bradley Co. Antiques, E. Lancaster Avenue, Route 30

DOYLESTOWN
Heritage Antiques, 69 E. Oakland Avenue
Robertson & Thornton, Route 202

ELVERSON
Stallfort Antiques, RD 1, Grove Road

FLEETWOOD
Palmer & Virginia Smeltz, Route 662 N.

FORT WASHINGTON
The Meetinghouse Antiques, 509 Bethlehem Pike

FURLONG
Franklin's Antiques, Route 263, York Road

GARDENVILLE
Durham Cabinet Shop, Route 413

GETTYSBURG
American Print Gallery, 219 Steinwehr Avenue

Knorrwood Antiques, 227 N. Washington Street
The Maples Antiques, 207 E. Middle Street
Nannie's World, 15 Seminary Ridge
Red Schoolhouse, Route 2

GREEN LANE
Colonial House Antiques, Routes 63 & 29
Ironmaster's Mansion Antiques, Gravel Pike, Route 29

HAMBURG
Jon Ahrens Antiques, 211 Fawn Court
Chris A. Machmer Antiques, 604-610 S. Sixth Street
Thomas's Antiques, 5 N. Fourth Street

HANOVER
By Chance Antiques & Gifts, 429 Baltimore Street

HARRISBURG
Ditlow's Antique Shed, 5103 Jonestown Road
Fox Chase Antiques, Fox Chase Road
Richard Marden, 3829 Club Drive

HAVERFORD
McClees Galleries, 343 W. Lancaster Avenue
Jackie Sidford, 520 Lancaster Avenue

INTERCOURSE
Willowdale Antiques, 101 E. Street Road

JOHNSTOWN
Gallagher & Co., 736 Railroad Street

KENNETT SQUARE
Clifton Mill Shoppes, 162 Old Kennett Road, Clifton Mill
Kennett Auction, Inc., Cedar Croft Road
Willowdale Antiques, 101 E. Street Road

KING OF PRUSSIA
W. Graham Arader III, 1000 Boxwood Court

KUTZTOWN
Robert Burkhardt, Route 1, Monterey
Greenwich Mills, Route 737 N.

LAHASKA
Alba Ltd., Route 202
1821 House, Route 202
Lahaska Antiques Courte, Route 202

Lippencott Antiques, Route 202
Oriental Gallery, Street Road & Route 202
Peddler's Village, Route 202 & Street Road
Howard Szmolko, Mechanicsville Road

LANCASTER

Buchters Antiques, 6 Pilgrim Drive
Fulton Market Auction, 607 Plum Street
Heather Valley Antiques, 1072 Centerville Road
Frederick A. Heinitsh, 723 N. Duke Street
Clarence Hinden Jr. Antiques, 2475 Lincoln Highway E.
Rutt's Antiques, 2180 Old Philadelphia Pike

LANSDOWNE

Clements & Sons Auction, 11 S. Lansdowne Avenue

LEBANON

Ebersole's Auction Barn, 1800 Thompson Avenue
Kleinfelters Auction, 105 Chapel Street

LEDERACH

Jean W. Clemmer, Hickory Tree Farm, Route 113

LENHARTSVILLE

Ahrens Antiques, RD 1
Hex Barn Antiques, Route 22

LEWISTOWN

Theresa Redmond Culbertson, RD 5
Smithers Antiques, 24 Chestnut Street

MANHEIM

Conestoga Auction Co., Graystone Road
Gerald & Miriam Noll, Route 7
William & Carol Warfel Antiques, 58 Snyder Street

MARIETTA

Hovey & Evelyn Gleason, 114 E. Market Street
Harry B. Hartman Antiques, 452 E. Front Street
The Secret Cupboard, 234 E. Market Street
White Swan Tavern Antiques, 14 E. Front Street

McCONNELSBURG

Campbell's Antiques, 121 Lincoln Way W.

MECHANICSBURG

American Antiques, 3336 Durham Road, Route 413
White Barn Antiques, RD 1, Trindle Road

MENDENHALL
Sally Borton Antiques, Village of Fairville, Kennett Pike, Route 52
Mendenhall Antiques, Kennett Pike, Route 52

MERTZTOWN
Hilltop House, Clay Road

MORRISVILLE
Helen Murphy, 525 Jefferson Avenue

NAZARETH
Old Red School House, Cherry Hill

NEW BRITAIN
Bucks County Cabinet Shop, 134 Iron Hill Road
The Rockafellow's Antiques, 609 E. Butler Avenue

NEW HOPE
The Antiquary, 40 W. Ferry Street
Colonial Arms Antiques, 441 York Road
The Corner, 8 N. Main Street
Country Antiques at the Church, Route 202 & Upper Mountain Road
Crown and Eagle Antiques, Route 202
The Golden Griffens, 15 W. Mechanic Street
Ochre House, 4 Walton Drive
Olde Hope Antiques, Route 202
The Pink House Antiques, Route 179, W. Bridge Street
Poole Antiques, Ingham Road
Francis J. Purcell II, Route 2
Queripel Interiors, 93 W. Bridge Street
Manford J. Robinson, 4 Walton Drive
Ronley at Limeport, Star Route, River Road
Sheffield House, Route 202
Joseph Stanley, 181 W. Bridge Street
Miriam Young, Route 202

NEW OXFORD
A Touch of Antiquity, Route 30 E.

NEWTOWN
The Hanging Lamp, 140 N. State Street
Ren's Antiques, 14 S. State Street
The Village Smithy, 149 N. State Street

NEWTOWN SQUARE
Vito Angelucci Antiques, Route 252

NORRISTOWN
Allen Antiques, RD 3

OLEY
Ralph & Kathryn Heist, RD 2

PARADISE
White Elephant Antiques & Gifts, Route 30

PERKIOMENVILLE
John Jeremicz, Jr., Route 29

PIPERSVILLE
Courthouse Antiques, Route 611

PLEASANT VALLEY
Bowers Antiques, Route 212

POINT PLEASANT
River Run Antiques, River Road, Route 32

POTTSTOWN
Penn Wick, Ridge Road, RD 4
The Sampler Antique Shop, Laurelwood Road, RD Star Route

QUAKERTOWN
Russell E. Hill Antiques, 1465 N.W. End Boulevard
Webber's Antiques, Thatcher Road, Route 3

RAHNS
James Gallery, Routes 29 & 113

READING
Antietam Antiques, 3100 St. Lawrence Avenue
Barry B. Dobinsky Antiques, 1229 Oley Street
Little Deer Antiques, 1400 Commonwealth Boulevard
Moseley's Antiques & Curios, 859 Acacia Avenue, Riverview
    Park
Orth Auction, 418 Morgantown Road
Pennypacker Auction Centre, 1540 New Holland Road, Kenhorst
Arlene & Quentin Sternberg, RD 2
Emily S. Troutman, 325 N. Sixth Street

REINHOLDS
B & S Antiques, Route 897 & Mechanic Street

RIEGELSVILLE
Little House Antiques, 250 Linden Lane

SHIPPENSBURG
Eschenmann's Antiques, 216 Ridge Avenue

SPRING CITY
Richard Wright Antiques, 807 Schuylkill Road, Route 724

THOMASVILLE
Helen's Antiques, Route 30

TOPTON
Stump Antiques, 214 Barclay Street

VILLANOVA
Diana H. Bittel Antiques, 1829 Old Gulph Road

WERNERSVILLE
Marilyn J. Kowalski, Grandview Road, RD 3

WEST CHESTER
Dale E. Hunt, 20 Ellis Lane

YARDLEY
Geraldine Lipman Antiques, 5 Byron Lane
Meyer Trading Co., Afton Avenue & Delaware Canal
C. L. Prickett Antiques, Stony Hill Road

YORK
Paul Ettline's Antiques, 3790 E. Market Street
Kennedy's Antiques, 4290 W. Market Street
Joseph Kindig, 325 Market Street
Yellow Bird Cage Antiques, 11 S. Beaver Street

VIRGINIA

ALEXANDRIA
Anchorage House, 603 Queen Street
Antony-Bradley Gallery, 8904 Bridgehaven Court
Apothecary Shop, 105 S. Fairfax Street
C & M Antiques, 311 Cameron Street
Camelot Collection, 106 N. St. Asaph Street
Canal Company of Olde Towne, 800 N. Fairfax Street
Carousel Antiques, 907 King Street
Carriage House Antiques, 122A S. Royal St., Old Town
Cavalier Antiques, 400 Prince Street
A Collector's Shop, 222 1/2 S. Washington Street
Coopermann's, 102 S. Alfred Street
Eileen's Antiques, 311 S. Washington Street
Falquier & Harned Ltd., The Atrium, 277 S. Washington Street

Betty Gaines Antiques, 222 S. Washington Street
Liros Gallery, Inc., 628 N. Washington Street
The Living Room Antiques, 1305 King Street
Monument Antiques, 1636 King Street
Shirley Myers Antiques, 311 Cameron Street
Odds & Ends Shoppe, 1511 Mt. Vernon Avenue
The Pineapple, 311 Cameron Street
Presidential Coin & Antique Co., 6204 Little River Turnpike
Glenn C. Randall Fine Antiques & Works of Art, 229 N. Royal
    Street
Silverman Galleries, 110 1/2 N. St. Asaph Street
Sleigh Bell Antiques and Collectibles, 2014 Mt. Vernon Avenue
A Thieves Market, 7704 Richmond Highway
The Two Harolds Antiques, 103 N. Alfred Street

ARLINGTON
A. Adcock Yankee Peddler Antiques, 1108 N. Irving Street
Crystal Cage, 554 23rd Street S.
A Cupboard Antique Shops, 2645 N. Pershing Drive, 3157
    Wilson Boulevard, and 106 Wayne Street
Petticoat Lane Interiors & Accessories, 4522 Lee Highway
Serendipity Antiques, 2901 Columbia Pike

BARBOURSVILLE
Antiques at Burlington, Burlington Farm, Route 20

BEDFORD
Peggy's Antiques, 804 E. Main Street

BERRYVILLE
Talio Antiques, US 340

CENTREVILLE
First Impressions, 13809 Lee Highway
International Antiques, 13826 Lee Highway

CHARLOTTESVILLE
The Balogh Gallery, 1018 W. Main Street
Caldonia, 1205 W. Main Street
Bernard M. Caperton Antiques, 1113 W. Main Street
Cochran's Mill Antiques, 435 E. Rio Road
Salem M. Eways, Inc., 1417 N. Emmet Street
Paula Lewis Court Square, 216 Fourth Street N.E.
1740 House Antiques, Route 250 W.
South Street Antiques, 100 South Street W., The Warehouse
The Windmill Antiques, 1020 W. Main Street
Ann Woods Ltd., 1211 W. Main Street

CHESAPEAKE
Violet's Antiques, 3008 S. Military Highway

EMPORIA
The Crowned Leopard, 418 S. Main

FAIRFAX
Cannon Ridge Antiques, 12716 Lee Highway

FALLS CHURCH
Americana Antique and Art Gallery, 3118 Patrick Henry Drive
Country Peddler Antiques, 418 S. Washington
Daube's Old Brick House, 2814 Graham Road
Martin Antiques, 706 S. Washington

FORT DEFIANCE
Dean Wilson Antiques, I-81

FREDERICKSBURG
Ruth Bonanno Antiques, 619 Caroline Street
Camelot Mews, 802 Sophia Street
Kendall's Antiques, Route 3
The Virginians, 1501 Caroline Street

GAINESVILLE
Barter Post, Routes 29 & 211

GLEN ALLEN
Wigwam Reservation, Highway 1

GLOUCESTER
Trophy Room Antiques, Route 17

GRAFTON
Heritage Hut Antiques and Country Store, Route 17

GREAT FALLS
Village Gallery Antiques, 718 Walker Road

HAMPTON
Pembroke Antiques, 2538 W. Pembroke Avenue
Peninsula Antique Mall, 2041 W. Pembroke Avenue

HANOVER
The Old Store Antiques, Route 301

IRVINGTON
Ship and Sea Nautical Antiques, Route 3

LEESBURG
Antique Center of Leesburg, King Street, Route 15

LORTON
Pohick Antique & Craft Center, 9304 Richmond Highway

LOUISA
Glenburnie Farm Antiques, Route 613

LYNCHBURG
Jackson's Antiques, 2627 Old Forest Road
Little Shop at Plain Dealing, Wiggington Road
Timbrook Antiques, 9223 Timberlake Road
Wards Road Bargain Shop, 4439 Wards Road

MANASSAS
Law's Antique Center, 7217 Centreville Road
Law's Auction & Antiques, 7209 Centreville Road

McLEAN
Beauport Antiques, 6816 Elm
Evans Farm Inn Country Store, 1696 Chain Bridge Road

MECHANICSVILLE
W. D. Brumble Antiques, 6363 Chamberlayne Road
Governor's Antiques, 6240 Meadow Bridge Road
The Millstone, Route 301

MIDDLEBURG
Middleburg Antiques Center, Route 50 W.
Powder Horn Antiques, 200 W. Washington Street
The Sporting Gallery, 101 Washington Street

MIDLOTHIAN
Gates Antiques Ltd., 12700 Old Buckingham Road

MILLWOOD
The Old Mill Antiques Shop, Routes 255 & 723

NATURAL BRIDGE
Antiques by Bradford, Highway 130

NEW CHURCH
Worcester House Antiques, US 13

NEWPORT NEWS
The Antique Cupboard, 205 W. Mercury Boulevard
Brill's Antique Shop, 10527 Jefferson Avenue

Cottage Antiques, 5111 W. Mercury Boulevard
Fine Arts Shop, 10178 Warwick Boulevard
Gammon's, 12436 Warwick Boulevard
James River Antique Mall, 9906 Jefferson Avenue
Plantiques, 10377 Warwick Boulevard
Riverside Antiques, 9601 Warwick Boulevard
Ricki Skloff Interiors, 10355 Warwick Boulevard
Village Antiques, 10221 Warwick Boulevard

NORFOLK
American Antique Importers, 242 W. 21st Street
Auslew Gallery, 101 Granby Street
Colonial Antiques, 119 W. Little Creek Road
D. I. Deutsch, 124 College Place
Family Tree Antiques, 420 W. Bute Street
Nautical Antiques, 6150 Virginia Beach Boulevard
Scope Antiques, 111 Virginia Beach Boulevard
Durwood Zedd Auction Co., 122 W. 21st Street

PORTSMOUTH
Desks Inc., 800 Crawford Street
Mt. Vernon Antique Shop, 258 Mt. Vernon Avenue

PURCELLVILLE
Cochran's Antiques, 10th Street

RICHMOND
America Hurrah Antiques, 405 Libbie Avenue
Anne's Antiques, 6725 Midlothian Turnpike
Antiques Warehouse, 1310 E. Cary Street
Bradley's Antiques, 103 E. Main Street
Chandler's Antique Shop, E. Williamsburg Road
Goodwill Industries, Inc., 809 W. Broad Street & 607 McGuire
   Center
Gresham's Country Store, 6725 Midlothian Pike
Hampton House, 5720 Grove Avenue
M. Kambourian Sons, 13 W. Grace Street
Chas. Navis Antiques, 5605 Grove Avenue
Reese Antiques, 207 E. Main Street
Richmond Art Co., Inc., 101 E. Grace Street
Shamberger's, Inc., 5208 Brook Road
Tudor Gallery, 5115 Cary Street Road
Westhampton Antiques, 5716 Patterson Avenue

ROANOKE
Carriage House Antiques, Highway 220 S.
Jezebel's, 7726 Williamson Road N.W.
Mike's Trading Post, 1805 Orange Avenue N.W.

Paraphernalia, Inc., 107 Market Square S.E.
Southern Traders F.M., 3361 Melrose Avenue N.W.
24th Street Antiques, 12 24th Street N.W.
The Virginia Galleries, 1402 Grandin Road S.W.
Webb's Antiques, 3906 Garst Mill Road S.W.
Woodard-West Ltd., 2223 Crystal Spring Avenue S.W.

RUTHER GLEN
Boone's Antiques, Highway 207 E.
Rebel Hill Antiques, Route 1

SALEM
Furniture Mart, 211 College Avenue, S. Salem
Humble Home Antiques, 2229 Main Street, W. Salem
Twine Hollow Auctions, 44 Industrial Circle

STAUNTON
AAA Antiques, Route 250 E.
Mint Spring Antiques, Route 2

STEPHENS CITY
The Whitneys, Lime Kiln Road

SUFFOLK
Shorty's Antiques & Produce, 107 E. Pinner

THORNBURG
Eastern Antique Mart, Route 1
Eastern Sales & Auction Co., Route 3

UPPERVILLE
The Golden Horse Shoe, Route 50

VIENNA
Bird-In-The-Cage Antiques, 130 Maple Avenue, E. Vienna
Joann Reisler, 360 Glyndon Street N.E.
Vienna Antique Center, 318 Maple Avenue
Village Antiques, 120 Lawyers Road

VIRGINIA BEACH
Angela of London, 4507 Holly Road
Bay Bridge Antiques, 4516 Shore Drive
The Iron Gate, 3600 Atlantic Avenue
Newel Post Antique Gallery, 2973 Virginia Beach Boulevard
Princess Anne Antiques, 2325 Virginia Beach Boulevard

WILLIAMSBURG
Alley Antiques, 423 Prince George Street

The Bookpress, 420 Prince George Street
Schwan's Antiques, Route 5
Shaia Oriental Rugs, Duke of Gloucester Street
TK Oriental Art & Antiques, 1784 Jamestown Road
Ricks Wilson Ltd., 400 Duke of Gloucester Street, Merchants
Square

YORKTOWN
The Swan Tavern Antiques, 104 Main Street

WEST VIRGINIA

BERKELEY SPRINGS
Arwood's Antiques, Route 522 S.
Tom H. Seely, Winchester Road

CHARLES TOWN
Rinaldi's Antiques, Jefferson Terrace

HARPERS FERRY
Belle-Haus Antiques, 1200 Washington Street
Jason's Antiques, 1307 Washington Street
Mary Longsworth Antiques, 1141 Washington Street
My Father's Workshop, 1163 Washington Street
The Old Shop Antiques, 1195 Washington Street
Red Bull, 1335 Washington Street
Stone House Antiques, Potomac Street
Washington Street Antiques, 1080 Washington Street
The Yankee Doodle Shop, 1328 Washington Street

SHEPHERDSTOWN
Barber's Bazaar, 116 W. German Street
Matthews and Shank, 115 E. German Street

ARCHAEOLOGY

If you are an amateur archaeologist, or if you have always wanted to get down on all fours at a "dig," you'll find plenty of opportunities to get the dirt of eons past under your fingernails. The mid-Atlantic area abounds with archaeological treasures, but many sites are being threatened by parking lots, convention centers, and condominium developments.

To keep pace with urban sprawl and to rescue archaeological artifacts before they are forever bulldozed from view, each state has an archaeologist on staff who is, among other tasks, responsible for organizing digs. Often they race against time, bulldozers, and limited resources to rescue priceless treasures, so volunteers are usually welcomed with open arms. Some projects are done in conjunction with government programs such as the National Historic Preservation Act and the National Register Program, which require states to "accommodate" the public—a bureaucratic word that means "use volunteers."

Volunteers have helped at a prehistoric Indian site in Parkersburg, West Virginia, where a Japanese steel plant was about to be built. Amateur archaeologists in Wilmington, Delaware, surveyed along South Wilmington Boulevard and found artifacts dating to the early 18th century. In Alexandria, Virginia, volunteers at the Archaeology Research Center dig on land once occupied by 18th- and 19th-century families. And an ongoing project along Maryland's Calvert Cliff has unearthed a number of prehistoric fossils.

Most state archaeology offices maintain lists of willing volunteers. When a project surfaces, they call those on the list to give them an opportunity to help. You can contact these offices in your state to sign up:

Delaware: Alice Guerrant
                   Bureau of Archaeology and
                   Historic Preservation
                   No. 15, The Green
                   Dover, DE 19903
                   (302) 736-5685

Maryland: Maureen Kavanagh
                   Maryland Geological Survey
                   2300 North St. Paul Street
                   Baltimore, MD 21218
                   (301) 554-5500

                   Louise Akerson
                   Baltimore Center for Urban Archeology
                   802 E. Lombard Street
                   Baltimore, MD 21202
                   (301) 396-3156

                   Beth Cole
                   Maryland Historical Trust
                   21 State Circle
                   Annapolis, MD 21401
                   (301) 974-2438

Wayne Clark
Jefferson-Patterson Park and Museum
Route 2, Box 50A
St. Leonard, MD 20685
(301) 586-0050

New Jersey: Lorraine E. Williams, State Archaeologist
New Jersey State Museum
205 W. State Street
Trenton, NJ 08625
(609) 292-8594

North Carolina: Stephen R. Claggett, Chief Archaeologist
Division of Archives and History
Department of Cultural Resources
109 E. Jones Street
Raleigh, NC 27611
(919) 733-7342

Friends of North Carolina Archeology
(contact at the above address)

Pennsylvania: Stephen G. Warfel, Division of Archeology
State Museum of Pennsylvania
PO Box 1026
Harrisburg, PA 17120
(717) 787-4978

Virginia: Catherine Slusser, State Archeologist
Virginia Historic Landmarks Commission
221 Governors Street
Richmond, VA 23219
(804) 786-3143

Alexandria Archaeology Research Center
PO Box 178
City Hall
Alexandria, VA 22314
(703) 750-6200

Fairfax County Archaeology Survey
Office of Comprehensive Planning
4100 Chain Bridge Road
Fairfax, VA 22030
(703) 642-5807

West Virginia: Jeffrey R. Graybill
Blennerhassett Historical Park Commission
PO Box 283
Parkersburg, WV 26101
(304) 428-3000

Each state also has an archaeology society of amateurs and professionals. Chapters sponsor local digs—good opportunities to learn more about archaeology. Contact your state society for the chapter nearest you:

Delaware: Archaeological Society of Delaware
                         PO Box 801
                         Wilmington, DE 19899

Maryland: Maryland Archaeology Society
                         (contact Maryland Geological Survey
                         at above address)

New Jersey: Archaeological Society of New Jersey
                         Herbert Kraft
                         Seton Hall University

                         Department of Anthropology
                         South Orange, NJ 07079
                         (201) 761-9543

North Carolina: Archaeological Society of North Carolina
                         c/o Vincent Steponaitis, Executive Secretary
                         Research Laboratories of Anthropology
                         University of North Carolina
                         Chapel Hill, NC 27514
                         (919) 962-6574

Pennsylvania: Society for Pennsylvania Archaeology
                         c/o State Museum of Pennsylvania
                         PO Box 1026
                         Harrisburg, PA 17120
                         (717) 787-4978

Virginia: Virginia Archaeology Society
                         (contact Virginia Historic Landmarks
                         Commission at above address)

West Virginia: West Virginia Archaeology Society
                         (contact Blennerhassett Historical Park
                         Commission at above address)

Local universities often need volunteers to help with their work. For example, Catholic University in Washington, DC, operates Thunderbird site in Front Royal, Virginia, and Salisbury (Maryland) State College works on the original St. Mary's colony settlement.

Veteran volunteers advise wearing old clothes and shoes, a hat, and work gloves. At the end of your day of fieldwork you can expect to be hot, tired, and no doubt caked with dirt.

Battlefields 355

But you'll have the satisfaction of having made a vital contribution to man's knowledge of his past.

If you do not fancy getting down on all fours in dirt, many museums need volunteers to help sort and identify artifacts. These can include museums specializing not only in prehistoric memorabilia, but "newer" artifacts as well. The Alexandria Archaeology Research Center, for example, frequently needs volunteers to sort through papers pertaining to Virginia's colonial history, mark maps, and give talks to visitors and school groups.

BATTLEFIELDS

Weekender's Guide to the Four Seasons includes Valley Forge, Yorktown, and other areas associated with many of the scenes of important battles of the Revolutionary War. It also covers much of the territory that was at the heart of the Civil War from the site of its first major land battle, Manassas, to the quiet village, Appomattox, where the war came to a close four years later.

Many locales in the mid-Atlantic states were involved in both wars. Battlefield locations listed here are, for the most part, those set aside by federal and state governments. A few private homes or sites of particular interest to the visitor are also included.

BIKING

The bicycle is rightly considered one of the higher forms of elementary technology. Easy to store, transport, and maneuver, as well as inexpensive to operate, it is especially attractive in this time of limited energy supplies. It was developed in Europe and introduced into this country in approximately 1875.

According to the *Encyclopedia Britannica*, the idea that such a machine could be built occurred to people long ago. Representations of a two-wheeled version with no pedals occur in the art left behind by the Babylonians, the Egyptians, and the residents of Pompeii. This kind of bicycle was built every so often in the centuries that followed; but, major progress was made in 1839 when the Scotchman Kirkpatrick Macmillan built one with pedals. Soon there were other developments. Tandem bicycles which would seat two were built, and are still used today. Efforts to build tricycles resulted in inventions which made possible the automobile. This was particularly true of the hub brake and the differential (which, by allowing the two back wheels to rotate at different speeds, made it possible to go around a curve). The modern lightweight 10-speed touring bicycle is a distinct improvement, making touring vastly easier and racing much more fun.

This section contains information on some national organizations, touring and racing clubs, as well as names of sources where route maps and tour information can be obtained.

MAJOR BICYCLE ORGANIZATIONS AND CLUBS

There are several national and regional biking organizations which deserve special mention because of the wide range of services they provide.

The League of American Wheelmen (L.A.W), founded in 1880, is a national organization of bicyclists and bicycle clubs. L.A.W. promotes safe touring, club riding, family riding, and commuting. It is the only cycling organization with a full-time lobbyist and legislative affairs program. In addition, the League publishes information on more than 500 biking events, nationwide, every year. Members receive a directory of members and services, and have access to extensive information on routes, accommodations, points of interest, laws, and L.A.W. Hospitality Homes where League members may stay overnight. The League provides biking courses and course materials through its affiliates, and will provide assistance in starting a bicycle club. Reasonable fee. League of American Wheelmen, Suite 209, 6707 Whitestone Road, Baltimore, MD 21207. Telephone: (301) 944-3399.

The **United States Cycling Federation**, a national amateur bicycle racing organization, provides information on racing procedures, routes, and events, nationwide. United States Cycling Federation, PO Box 669, Wall Street Station, New York, NY 10005. Reasonable membership fee.

Bikecentennial, Inc., develops intra- and interstate bicycle trail systems, sponsors extended trips along these trails, and provides appropriate maps and guidebooks. The Virginia section of the coast-to-coast TransAmerica Trail and a Virginia loop trail beginning and ending in Washington, DC, lie within the mid-Atlantic region. Bikecentennial, Inc., PO Box 8308, Missoula, MT 59807. Telephone: (406) 721-1776. Reasonable membership fee.

Washington Area Bicyclist Association (WABA), is a nonprofit citizen's association devoted to "getting a better deal for the bicyclist." WABA promotes safer cycling throughout the area; publishes a bimonthly newsletter; coordinates a legal service to protect cyclists' rights; provides a pedal pool of biking routes, tips, maps, general biking information, lobbying efforts, testifying, and surveys; and serves as a clearinghouse for bicycle commuting information. Reasonable membership fee. Washington Area Bicyclist Association, 530 Seventh Street S.E., Washington, DC 20003. Telephone: (202) 544-5349.

American Youth Hostels (AYH), Potomac Area Council, sponsors weekend trips year round, an extended summer-trips program through the United States and Canada, and promotes the establishment of hosteling clubs which receive organizational support from the Council. AYH also provides extensive reference and resource material for trip planning and research, including bike routes and maps and backpacking and canoeing information. The Potomac Council will provide information and addresses on all member hostels and area councils. Reasonable membership fee. American Youth Hostels, Potomac Area Council, 1332 Eye Street N.W., Washington, DC 20036. Telephone: (202) 783-6161 or 783-4943.

STATE AND LOCAL BICYCLE ORGANIZATIONS, CLUBS, AND ROUTE INFORMATION CONTACTS

DELAWARE

Delaware Friends of Bikecology   (Touring)
2 Barley Mill Drive, Greenville, DE 19807

MARYLAND

HOTLINE: (301) 333-1663
   "Bicycling Maryland Highways," Maryland State Highway Administration, Monday through Friday, 8:15 a.m. to 4:15 p.m. (After hours requests for return calls will be recorded.)

Baltimore Bicycling Club, Inc.   (Touring)
PO Box 5906, Baltimore, MD 21208   (301) 486-7422

Bicycle Matters
Metropolitan Washington Council of Governments, 1875 Eye Street N.W., Suite 200, Washington, DC 20003   (202) 223-6800

Chesapeake Bicycle Tours   (Commercial)
PO Box 345, Westminster, MD 21157   (301) 876-2721
   Provides several summertime tours along part of the 600 miles of shoreline in Talbot and Kent counties, for both novices and experienced bicyclists, originating in either Easton or Tilghman Island on Maryland's Eastern Shore. Reservations four weeks in advance. Tours include both scheduled and optional activities. Fee.

Chesapeake Wheelmen Bicycle Racing Club, Inc.   (Racing)
PO Box 11354, Baltimore, MD 21239   (301) 296-4236

Country Cycling Tours   (Commercial)
140 W. 83rd Street, New York, NY 10024   (212) 874-5151
   Conducts tours of Maryland's Eastern Shore.

Hearthside C.O.B.R.A.   (Racing)
15 Churchville Road, Belair, MD 21014   (301) 893-1000

Open Road Bicycle Tours, Ltd.   (Commercial)
601 Summit Drive, Haymarket, VA 22069   (703) 754-4152

Offers country inn bicycling vacations for singles and families in Talbot, Kent, Anne Arundel, and Frederick counties.

Oxon Hill Bicycle and Trail Club   (Touring)
PO Box 18081, Oxon Hill, MD 20745

NEW JERSEY

Jersey Shore Touring Society   (Touring)
PO Box 8581
Red Bank, NJ 07701   (201) 747-8206

South Jersey Wheelmen   (Touring)
PO Box 2705, Vineland, NJ 08360   (609) 327-1336

The Summit Cycling Club   (Touring)
217 South Davis Avenue, Audubon, NJ 08106   (609) 547-3848

PENNSYLVANIA

Center City Touring Club   (Touring)
630 South Fourth Street, Philadelphia, PA 19147   (215) 922-1283

Hanover Cyclers
c/o C. E. Stough, 240-C Messersmith Road—RD#10, York, PA 17404

Lancaster Bicycle Club
PO Box 535, Lancaster, PA 17604

Pennsylvania Bicycle Club   (Touring)
PO Box 27535, Philadelphia, PA 19118   (215) 233-5626

Philadelphia Bicycle Coalition   (Advocacy)
PO Box 8194, Philadelphia, PA 19104   (215) 387-9242

VIRGINIA

Bike Virginia, Inc.   (Commercial)
PO Box 203, Williamsburg, VA 23187   (804) 229-4620
Provides several established weekend tours (including accommodations) through scenic and historic areas of Virginia, for a set fee. Also offers day trips of a similar nature, for a set fee, which include lunch. Family and group rates are available.

Blacksburg Bicycle Club   (Touring)
c/o The Unicycle, 1702 South Main Street, Blacksburg, VA 24060

Capital Community Cyclists   (Touring)
Box 12423, Richmond, VA 23421

Emporia Bicycle Club   (Touring)
PO Box 631, Emporia, VA 23847

Hill City Wheelmen   (Touring)
c/o Bike's Unlimited, PO Box 4344, Lynchburg, VA 24502

Peninsula Bicycling Association
PO Box 5639, Parkview Station, Newport News, VA 23605

Richmond Area Bicycling Association, Inc.   (Touring)
409-H North Hamilton Street, Richmond, VA 23221

Tidewater Bicycle Association   (Touring)
PO Box 12254, Norfolk, VA 23502

WEST VIRGINIA

Blackwater Bikes
PO Box 190, Davis, WV 26260   (304) 259-5286

Elk River Touring Center
Slatyfork, WV 26291   (304) 572-3771

Harrison County Biking
2216 Goff Avenue, Clarksburg, WV 26301   (304) 622-8081

Mountain State Wheelers   (Touring)
Box 8161, South Charleston, WV 25303   (304) 345-4136

WASHINGTON, DC, METROPOLITAN AREA

HOTLINE: (202) HEY-BIKE
    "Washington Area Biking Information": Bike Hotline, PO Box
208, College Park, MD 20740.

Potomac Pedalers Touring Club, Inc.   (Touring)
PO Box 23601, L'Enfant Plaza Station,
Washington, DC 20026   (202) 363-TOUR

ADDITIONAL SOURCES OF ROUTE INFORMATION
AND MAPS

Baltimore Regional Planning Council   (301) 554-5629
2225 North Charles Street, Baltimore, MD 21218
    Preferred route map of the greater Baltimore area, including:

routes suitable for bicycle use, problem intersections, and hills; detailed cyclist's view of the Baltimore street system; and long distance loops in central Maryland. Available at Baltimore-area bicycle shops. Small fee for maps.

Bikecentennial, Inc.   (406) 721-1776
PO Box 8308, Missoula, MT 59807
   Transamerica Trail (from Astoria, OR to Yorktown, VA), Appalachian Section (the 500 miles of the Transamerica trail from Breaks Interstate Park near the Kentucky-Virginia border to Yorktown near the Chesapeake Bay), and Virginia Loop maps. Reasonable fee for maps.

Chesapeake and Ohio Canal National Historical Park
PO Box #4, Sharpsburg, MD 21782   (301) 443-0024,
                                (301) 678-5463, or (301) 722-8226
   Provides map and information on the 185-mile Chesapeake and Ohio Canal Towpath. Free.

Maryland State Highway Administration Map Distribution Section
2323 West Joppa Road, Brooklandville, MD 21022
   Statewide, county, municipality, or area maps. Small fee for maps. A complete list of maps is also available. Free.

Montgomery County Office of Planning and Project Development
c/o Bikeways and Trails Coordinator,
101 Monroe Street, Rockville, MD 20850   (301) 251-2177
   "Bicycling Routes in Lower Montgomery County," a map of bicycle facilities and preferred bicycle roads in the more urbanized parts of the county. Free.

National Park Service, Mid-Atlantic Regional Office
143 South Third Street, Philadelphia, PA 19106   (215) 597-7018
   Information and maps for bicycle routes and trails in the national parks of the Mid-Atlantic states. Free.

North Carolina Department of Transportation   (919) 733-2804
State Bicycle Coordinator, Bicycle Program, PO Box 25201, Raleigh, NC 27611
Statewide maps, "Mountains to the Sea." No charge.

Northern Virginia Regional Park Authority (NVRPA)(703) 352-5900
5400 Ox Road, Fairfax Station, VA 22039
   Maps and information on northern Virginia trails such as the Mount Vernon Parkway.

Public Works Planning   (703) 558-2941
Department of Public Works, Room 221,

1400 North Courthouse Road,
Arlington, VA 22201
    Maps of Arlington County. Free.

Tourism Council of Frederick County   (301) 663-8687
19 East Church Street, Frederick, MD 21701
    Maps of four scenic bicycle tours in the Frederick area. Reasonable charge for maps.

Virginia Department of Highways and Transportation (804) 786-2964
Richard C. Lockwood, State Bicycle Coordinator, 1401 East Broad Street, Richmond, VA 23219
    County road maps. Small fee for maps.

Virginia State Division of Tourism   (804) 786-4484
202 North Ninth Street, Suite 500, Richmond, VA 23219
    Information on biking in Virginia state parks, and national parks in the state of Virginia (such as the Shenandoah National Park bicycling routes for the Blue Ridge Parkway and Skyline Drive), as well as Eastern Shore trails at the Chincoteague Wildlife Refuge and on Assateague Island. (Virginia has a number of excellent routes.) Small fee for maps.

Visitors Center, Colonial Williamsburg   (804) 229-1000
Colonial Parkway, Williamsburg, VA 23185
    Map of historic triangle bicycle tour to Yorktown, Jamestown, and Williamsburg, as well as four loops in the same area (Williamsburg to Waller Mill Park and York River State Park; Williamsburg to Yorktown; Williamsburg to Jamestown Island and Park; Williamsburg to Carter Grove). Free.

Washington Area Bicyclist Association   (202) 393-2555
1332 Eye Street, N.W., Suite 441, Washington, DC 20005
    "Greater Washington Bicycle Atlas," provides maps and information on selected bicycle touring trips in Pennsylvania, Maryland, and Virginia. Available at Washington-area bicycle shops or from the Association. Reasonable fee for maps.

Wilmapco   (302) 737-6205
Suite 101, Stockton Building, University Office Plaza, Newark, DE 19720
    Map of preferred bicycle routes on the Eastern Shore of Maryland; north and north central Delaware; southwestern New Jersey. Small fee for maps.

▬▬▬▬▬▬ BIRDING ▬▬▬▬▬▬

    The birding associations and birdwalks listed in this section are only a partial listing of all the groups and activities available from Cape May to Cape Hatteras. Birding, like many other pastimes, is primarily volunteer-oriented. Therefore a wealth of information may not be readily available from a few obvious sources. The associations listed below will give you a good start on learning about birding if you are new to the subject or new to the area. The weekend sections of your local newspapers should also be helpful in identifying other associations and outings.

Local birdwalks are usually free of charge and open to everyone. Some longer trips may be on a membership-only basis, but inquire first. The cruises and pelagic trips listed below are open to everyone, although costs vary.

BIRDING ASSOCIATIONS

Audubon Naturalist Society of the Middle Atlantic States
8940 Jones Mill Road, Chevy Chase, MD 20815   (301) 652-9188

Carolina Bird Club, Inc., PO Box 1220, Tryon, NC 28782
    Newsletter: Mr. Clyde Smith, Jr.   (919) 781-2637
    2615 Wells Avenue, Raleigh, NC 27608

Delmarva Ornithological Society
PO Box 4247, Greenville, DE 19807
    Publications: Dr. Lloyd L. Falk
    123 Bette Road, Lynnfield, Wilmington, DE 19803

Maryland Ornithological Society   (301) 377-8462
Cylburn Mansion, 4915 Greenspring Avenue
Baltimore, MD 21209
    Publications: Mr. Chandler S. Robbins (301) 776-4880, ext. 281
    Patuxent Wildlife Research Center, Laurel, MD 20810

New Jersey Audubon Society   (201) 891-1211
790 Ewing Avenue, Franklin Lakes, NJ 07417
    Cape May Bird Observatory
    Peter J. Dunne, Dir.   (609) 884-2736

Potomac Valley Audubon Society   (304) 725-6423
201 River Road Avon Bend, Charles Town, WV 25414

Southern Maryland Audubon Society   (301) 535-5327
Battlecreek/Cypress Swamp Nature Center
c/o Courthouse
Prince Frederick, MD 20678

Virginia Society of Ornithology   (804) 625-6082
c/o Robert L. Ake, Pres.

615 Carolina Avenue, Norfolk, VA 23503
    Publications: Mr. Frederick R. Scott
    115 Kennondate Lane, Richmond, VA 23226

BIRD WALKS—DC AREA

Great Falls, MD   (301) 299-3613
    Two walks monthly along the C&O Canal, led by volunteer.
Two- hour morning walk preceded by 20-minute slide show.

Great Falls, VA   (703) 759-2915
Visitors Center, Great Falls Park
    A few walks a month, on weekends, led by volunteer ornitholo-
gists.

Rock Creek Park Nature Center   (202) 426-6829
5200 Glover Road, N.W., Washington, DC 20015
    Birding walks during fall and winter and migratory periods.

CRUISES AND PELAGIC TRIPS

Baltimore Canyon Pelagic Cruises   (301) 854-6262
PO Box 9423, Washington, DC 20016
    Ron Naveen runs private all-day cruises from Ocean City, NJ
(sunrise to sunset). There are 26 trips a year on Saturdays.

Outer Banks Pelagic Cruises   (202) 363-8994
4114 Fessenden Street, N.W., Washington, DC 20016
    Paul G. DuMont, Jr., runs private 10-hour cruises from Hatteras
Village on the Outer Banks of NC in mid-August and on Labor Day,
Columbus Day, and Memorial Day.

Virginia Barrier Island Cruises   (804) 442-3049
The Nature Conservancy, Virginia Coast Reserve-Brownsville,
Nassawadox, VA 23413
    All-day cruises are offered along the Virginia Barrier Islands
from May 1 to mid-October. Boat carries six persons and can be
chartered by groups. TNC claims it is possible to see as many as 175
species in one day.

CAMPING

Within the states covered by *Weekender's Guide to the
Four Seasons* hundreds of thousands of acres of mountain,
woodland, and shore are open to public use. Shenandoah
National Park in Virginia draws large crowds, but Jefferson,
Monongahela, and George Washington national forests com-
prise even larger portions of these lands. Found throughout

this book, however, are many smaller parks and forests that are open to the public for camping. Their varying facilities range from primitive campsites reached only on foot to areas approachable from main automobile routes that offer full trailer hookups and such amenities as laundry tubs, showers, and flush toilets.

The Camping Index indicates those areas mentioned in the book where camping is permitted. It will enable the reader to refer in the geographical section to the appropriate descriptive text of interest and to set the camping facilities offered in the context of other attractions. An address to write to and an information telephone number are usually provided.

366   Canoeing

CANOEING

Canoeing involves using the various paddle strokes and the current to navigate around obstructions like rocks and overhanging limbs. Broad, deep rivers with swift currents, extremely shallow or rocky streams, or rivers in flood stage are not appropriate for inexperienced canoers. For safety, canoers should always go in pairs. State laws normally require that individual flotation devices be worn.

Information on fluctuations in water currents and levels

can be obtained by calling the National Weather Service at (202) 899-3210, after 11:00 a.m., for a daily tape recording of river stages in most of Maryland, Virginia, and West Virginia. This data can then be correlated with minimum and maximum levels for a given river. Known maximums and minimums for rivers in the mid-Atlantic region can usually be obtained from local outfitters, or by writing for the U.S. Geological Survey's monthly *National Water Conditions* which compares existing water levels to established norms. Write to Hydrologic Information Unit, Mail Stop 420, Reston, VA 22092. Telephone: (703) 860-6867. Information on many rivers can be obtained from river guidebooks. Among other services, the American Canoe Association, Inc., provides a complete list of canoeing titles. Write to PO Box 248, Lorton, VA 22079. (Membership fee.) Telephone: (703) 550-7523.

The canoeing season is from March through most of November. Winter canoeing (because of the dangers of hypothermia in case of upset) is for experienced canoers. Whitewater canoeing also requires certain specific skills. They can be learned in courses or by accompanying experienced canoeists. For information on courses and other aspects of canoeing write to: Canoe Cruisers Association, PO Box 572, Arlington, VA 22216, or, American Rivers Conservation Council, 323 Pennsylvania Avenue S.E., Washington, DC 20003.

Tidewater administrations, as well as State Forest and Park Services, are also good sources of canoeing information. In New Jersey, for example, there are numerous possible canoe trips through the rivers and lakes of the Pine Barrens. Most of the major launches are in or near state parks. (Some are privately owned.) Canoes can usually be rented in the parks or at outfitters nearby. The parks in southern New Jersey are described in the section on that geographic area. In Pennsylvania, write to the Department of Environmental Resources, Pennsylvania Scenic Rivers Program, PO Box 1467, Harrisburg, PA 17120. Telephone: (717) 787-6816. Information for Assateague Island can be obtained from Assateague Island National Seashore, Route 2, Box 294, Berlin, MD 21811. Telephone: (301) 641-1441. Another good data source is the Tourism Council of the Upper Chesapeake, PO Box 66, Centreville, MD 21617. Telephone: (301) 758-2300. Or contact the Maryland Department of Natural Resources, Park and Wildlife Service, Tawes State Office Building, Annapolis, MD 21401. Telephone: (301) 269-3195. Many canoe outfitters also handle kayaks, including giving lessons.

CANOE ORGANIZATIONS

Canoe Cruisers Association, PO Box 572, Arlington, VA 22216
Canoe U, PO Box 6055, Suffolk, VA 23433
Coastal Canoeists, PO Box 566, Richmond, VA 23204
Greater Baltimore Canoe Club, PO Box 591, Ellicott City, MD 21043
Monocacy Canoe Club, Box 271, Route 5, Frederick, MD 21710

CANOE OUTFITTERS

Outfitters	River	Telephone
Adventure Tours, Inc.	Delaware River	(717) 223-0505
Barron's Store	Potomac River	(301) 432-5255
		(301) 432-8594
Blue Ridge Outfitters	Shenandoah,	(304) 725-3444
	Potomac, Tygart	(800) 554-2560
Chamberlain Canoes	Delaware Water Gap National Recreation Area	(717) 421-0180
Doe Hollow Canoe Rentals	Delaware River	(215) 498-5103
Downriver Canoe Co.	Shenandoah River	(703) 635-5526
Eagle's Nest Outfitters	North Fork, South Branch of Potomac	(304) 257-2393
Hudson Bay	Potomac River	(301) 948-2474
James River Experiences, Ltd.	James River	(804) 794-3493
Kittatiny Canoes, Inc.	Delaware River	(717) 828-2338
Louis Matacia	Potomac River	(703) 560-8993
New River Canoe Livery	Gauley, New Rivers; in spring: Walkers, Wolf Creeks	(703) 626-7189
New River Dories	New River	(304) 465-0855
NRCL Galax Outpost	New River	(703) 236-7576
Old Field Canoe Rentals	South Branch of Potomac	(304) 538-2874
Point Pleasant Canoe	Delaware River	(215) 297-8400
		(717) 588-6776
River & Trail Outfitters	Potomac, Shenandoah & tributaries	(301) 695-5177
Shenandoah River Outfitters, Inc.	Shenandoah River	(703) 743-4159
Springriver Outfitters	Potomac River	(301) 881-5696
Swain's	Potomac River	(301) 299-9006
340 Outfitters, Inc.	Shenandoah River	(703) 635-5440
Trans-Montane Outfitters Ltd.	Cheat "Narrows," Dry Fork River	(304) 259-5117
White's Ferry	Potomac River	(301) 349-5200

National Association of Canoe Liveries and Outfitters
221 North La Salle Street
Chicago, IL 60601   (312) 346-1600
This organization provides information on locating outfitters.

CAVERNS

Caverns hold a subtle fascination for many people; they provide an opportunity to see a part of our earth that sunlight does not touch, a netherworld where water flows and life has a toehold in total darkness. Throughout the area covered by *Weekender's Guide* are underground caverns or caves, major attractions that charge admission fees and that are usually open year round. The greatest number of them are concentrated in the Shenandoah Valley of Virginia. Most of these caverns maintain year-round temperatures in the low 50s (bring a sweater), are now well lighted artificially, and have hour-long guided tours through the subterranean wonderlands of stalactites, stalagmites, and shimmering rock formations. Nearly all of them have gift shops, restaurants, and picnic grounds nearby.

MARYLAND
Crystal Grottoes Caverns, MD—142

PENNSYLVANIA
Crystal Cave, PA—251
Indian Echo Caverns, PA—275

VIRGINIA
Crystal Caverns, VA—32
Dixie Caverns, VA—46
Grand Caverns, VA—39
Luray Caverns, VA—34
Massanutten Caverns, VA—39
Natural Bridge Caverns, VA—42
Shenandoah Caverns, VA—32
Skyline Caverns, VA—31

WEST VIRGINIA
Lost World Caverns, WV—313
Smoke Hole Caverns, WV—309

COVERED BRIDGES

Covered bridges are curious yet picturesque reminders of a previous age. One often speculates fleetingly about the endurance of the structures when seeing them from a nearby highway. These bridges are fast disappearing, but some are being carefully preserved by devoted individuals who cherish these relics of the past. Some 19th-century covered bridges survive and some new covered bridges are still being constructed. The tourist may see covered bridges throughout the mid-Atlantic states. The Philippi Covered Bridge, the longest two-lane covered bridge still in use on a federal highway, is located at Philippi on Route 250 in West Virginia, 27 miles east of Clarksburg.

The Society for the Preservation of Covered Bridges keeps track of the bridges and catalogues them in a "World Guide to Covered Bridges." The World Guide lists 231 bridges in Pennsylvania, six in Maryland, two in Delaware, nine in Virginia, one in New Jersey, and six in North Carolina.

The wooden covered bridge of the 19th century is an American phenomenon, although similar bridges are found throughout the world. However, the Europeans generally built their bridges of stone because of the scarcity of wood. In the United States, with its abundant forests, the wooden bridge was the cheapest type to build. Once the principle of the truss was utilized for bridge building, bridges spanning the many rivers from Maine to Georgia were built.

In the United States the bridge-building boom was a result of ingenious carpenters and craftsmen who capitalized on their knowledge of building barn support systems. In 1792, Timothy Palmer built a two-arch truss bridge over the Merrimac River. Subsequently, bridges were covered to protect the trusses from the extremes of weather. Wood can survive being submerged in water, but it is the alternate wetting and drying that will quickly destroy the wooden trusses. In 1806, Palmer built his patented arch-truss bridge 550 feet over the Schuylkill River and then covered it. It was a two-lane bridge and lasted for 70 years until it was destroyed by fire. Bridges soon not only had roofs, but also side walls. The enclosure of the bridges protected the trusses, provided a reassuring covering for horses and cows, and served as signboards advertising messages such as "Dr. Parker's Indian Oil for Ills of Man and Beast" and religious messages such as "The wages of sin is death [sic]."

Bridges are formally described by the truss system used. A truss is a triangular support; a triangle can not be distorted, only broken. Various improvements were added to the basic truss to strengthen the supports. The following is a list of diagrams and descriptions of the main types of trusses one will find in the Middle Atlantic areas covered in *Weekender's Guide to the Four Seasons*.

Kingpost truss

Queenpost

Multiple kingpost

Burr arch-truss

Town lattice truss

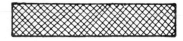

Long and Howe trusses (Howe truss substituted wrought-iron verticals)

With the coming of the railroad, wooden bridges proved inadequate because, under too much tension, the joints were pulled apart. For further information write: The Society for the Preservation of Covered Bridges, Richard Capwell, Treasurer, 526 Power Road, Pawtucket, RI 02860.

Some of the covered bridges have been described in the geographic sections of the *Weekender's Guide*.

Conestoga Creek Covered Bridge, PA—256
Erwinna Covered Bridge, PA—240
Gilpin Covered Bridge, MD—150
Haupt's Mill Covered Bridge, PA—240
Jericho Covered Bridge, MD—91
Loux Covered Bridge, PA—240
Loys Station Covered Bridge, MD—102
Martin's Mill Covered Bridge, PA—276
McGovernville Covered Bridge, PA—258
Mechanicsville covered bridge, PA—261
Paradise covered bridge, PA—259
Pequa Creek covered bridges, PA—260
Philippi Covered Bridge, WV—312
Reamstown Covered Bridge, PA—257
Roddy Road Covered Bridge, MD—102
Sauk's Covered Bridge, PA—281
Soudersburg Covered Bridge, PA—259
Thompson Covered Bridge, PA—284
Twining Ford Covered Bridge, PA—239
Uhlerstown Covered Bridge, PA—240
Utica Covered Bridge, MD—102
Vansant Covered Bridge, PA—237

▬▬▬▬ CROSS-COUNTRY SKIING ▬▬▬▬

Cross-country skiing is enjoying a great increase in popularity in the mid-Atlantic region. The flat and rolling contours of Virginia, Washington, DC, West Virginia, New Jersey, Maryland, and Pennsylvania offer an appetizing variety of terrain for the novice to expert skier. This is a sport which is easy to take up—all you need are skis, boots, poles, and a snow-covered area.

The following is a listing of many places within 200 miles of Washington and Baltimore where good skiing can be found. Rental equipment, food, and lodging are usually also available. Recreational and day skiers should also check with local golf courses and regional parks for ski possibilities close to home. Areas which are not specifically designated for skiing, such as biking and bridle trails, logging and fire roads, and the rare but exquisite snow-covered beach, can make fine ski areas.

Many of the locations listed, with the exception of private resort trails, are often left unplowed. Many trails in parks and forests are not marked. Skiers are well advised to obtain maps, including topographical maps from the U.S. Geological Survey, before leaving home for large park and wilderness areas since park offices keep irregular hours during winter months and may be closed when you arrive. If you plan to ski in a wilderness area, it is a good idea to inform local authorities or friends of your plans and destination. Weather and snow conditions can make or break a holiday— be sure to check the reports before taking off. The following numbers may be useful:

- Washington metropolitan area weather, hourly reports: (202) 936-1212.
- Western Maryland and northern Virginia mountain area two-day forecast: (202) 899-3240.
- Maryland Department of Natural Resources recording (includes ski conditions for New Germany and Herrington Manor): (301) 768-0895.
- West Virginia full ski reports and transfers to major ski resorts: (800) 225-5982.

Several clubs and organizations sponsor trips and races. Check the weekend section of your local newspaper or call state and county parks or local ski equipment outfitters.

These organizations and outfitters provide planned ski tour packages which include instruction and rentals; day and weekend tours are available.

- Fairfax County Park Authority, VA: (703) 941-5000. Organized trips offered through Wakefield Recreation Center.
- Montgomery County Recreation Department, MD: (301) 495-2525. Organized day trips offered January-March in MD, VA, or WV.
- Open University of Washington, DC: (202) 966-9606. Offers cross-country ski trips as well as introductory courses.
- Outdoor School: 1050 Knight Lane, Herndon, VA 22070, (703) 471-0171. Offers organized short trips to New Germany State Park and Canaan Valley, WV, and extended trips to Vermont.
- Potomac Appalachian Trail Club has a Ski Touring Section which invites non-members to join them every ski season weekend to carpool to a ski area. Participants at all levels must get their own equipment. PATC Ski Touring Section, 1718 N Street N.W., Washington, DC 20036. Telephone: (202) 638-5306.
- River and Trail Outfitters: Route 2, Valley Road, Knoxville, MD 21758, (301) 834-9950. Tours to Blackwater Falls, WV, and New Germany State Park and Antietam National Battlefield, MD.

MARYLAND

C&O CANAL NATIONAL HISTORICAL PARK
Park extends for 165 miles from Washington, DC, to Cumberland,

MD. Camping allowed. For general park information, telephone: (301) 739-4200 or write the Superintendent, C&O Canal National Historical Park, Box 4, Sharpsburg, MD 21782.

CATOCTIN MOUNTAIN PARK (NATIONAL PARK)
Thurmont, MD 21788
Take Route 15 north out of Frederick to Route 77. Follow Route 77 to the Park entrance. (Within one and a half hours of Washington, DC.) Catoctin Mountain Park and adjacent CUNNINGHAM FALLS STATE PARK have about 25 miles of marked trails. Terrain is hilly and rocky. Food and lodging nearby. (301) 633-9330.

GAMBRILL STATE PARK AND FREDERICK CITY LAND
Frederick, MD 21701
Take 270 to Frederick to Route 40. Follow signs off Route 40. (Close to Washington, DC.) Gambrill is a park adjacent to Frederick and I-70 west. Skiers follow the plowed road through the park (park has no real ski trails) to the ridgetop until Frederick City Watershed property. This area is full of short trails and skiable roads. (301) 473-8360 (snow conditions).

GREEN RIDGE STATE FOREST
Headquarters Office, Flintstone, MD 21530
Take Route 70 to Hancock, MD. Approximately three miles after Hancock exit take Route 40 exit towards Cumberland. Twenty miles after passing Cumberland exit take left on Fifteen Mile Creek Road to office. Difficult terrain. (The C&O towpath crosses through the southern end of the forest.) (301) 478-2991.

NEW GERMANY STATE PARK
Route 2, Box A-63, Grantsville, MD 21536
In the Savage River State Forest, five miles south of Grantsville, MD. Take Route 48 west out of Cumberland to Lower New Germany Road Exit and follow signs to the park. Easy to difficult, 15 miles of trails. Map, shelter, and wax available at the park headquarters. Lodging and food nearby. (301) 895-5453 office; (301) 768-0895 snow information.

SAVAGE RIVER STATE FOREST
Route 2, Box A-63, Grantsville, MD 21536
Take Route 48 west out of Cumberland to Lower New Germany Road. Follow Lower New Germany Road to Big Run State Park. Information and maps available at park. To get to the SAVAGE MOUNTAIN HIKING TRAIL, which is 16 miles of skiable trail along Big Savage Mountain, take Exit 29 off Route 48 (Finzel Exit). Follow Old Frostburg Road south to the first stop. Turn left and go one more mile to the sign for the trail. Several other skiable trails and logging roads in the State Forest. Savage River State Forest: (301) 895-5759; Big Run State Park: (301) 895-5453.

SENECA CREEK STATE PARK
11950 Clopper Road, Gaithersburg, MD 20878
Montgomery County, 20 miles northwest of Washington, DC. Drive south from I-270 near Gaithersburg on Route 124 for one mile to Route 117 (Clopper Road); turn right (west) on Route 117 for two miles to park. Six miles of easy to difficult trails. (301) 924-2127 weekdays.

SWALLOW FALLS AND HERRINGTON MANOR STATE PARKS
Route 5, Box 122, Oakland, MD 21550
These parks are side by side in western Maryland. Take 270 north to Route 70 west to Route 40 west to 48 west to 219 south to Oakland, MD. At the far end of Oakland turn right on Route 20. Follow signs to parks. Swallow Falls offers a variety of long and short trails. Snowmobile trails in Potomac State Forest connect Swallow Falls with Herrington Manor. Herrington Manor has approximately five miles of trails. Herrington Manor: (301) 334-9180.

NEW JERSEY

FAIRVIEW LAKE
Route 5, Box 230, Newton, NJ 07860
Sussex County in northwestern New Jersey. From I-80 take Exit 25 north on Route 206 to Newton, go south on Route 94 toward Blairstown to Route 610, then right (west) on 610 to Route 521 at Stillwater. Turn right (north) on 521 to Route 617 and then left on 617 four miles and follow signs. Twenty miles of easy to difficult trails, rentals, and instruction. Lodging and food available. (201) 383-9282.

PINE BARRENS
Wharton State Forest, Batsto RD 4, Hammonton, NJ 08037
Burlington County, south central New Jersey, 25 miles west of Camden. Drive east from Camden on Route 30 for 26 miles to Hammonton, turn left (east) on Route 542 for eight miles to Wharton State Forest, turn east from Camden on Route 70 for 27 miles to Route 72, turn right (east) on Route 72 for three miles to Lebanon State Forest office on left. Nine and a half miles of easy trails and 91 miles adjacent. Primitive camping available. (609) 726-1191 or (609) 561-0024.

STOKES FOREST
Sussex County, in northwestern New Jersey. Drive south from Port Jervis on Route 6 for six miles to Milford, turn left on Route 206, cross Delaware River, drive for nine miles. About 12 miles of trails also used for snowmobiles. Some camping. (201) 948-3820.

PENNSYLVANIA

APPLE VALLEY
Zionsville, PA 18092
Lehigh County, southeastern Pennsylvania. Drive south on Route 129 from Allentown to Route 100 and south on Route 100. Eight miles of easy to difficult trails. Rentals and instruction available. Lodging within two miles. (215) 966-5525.

BLACK MOSHANNON
Park Office, Rd. 1, Box 183, Philipsburg, PA 16866
Centre County in central Pennsylvania. Drive south from I-80 on Route 220 for seven miles to Unionville and turn right on Route 504 for five miles. Ten miles of easy trails. Rentals, downhill skiing. (814) 342-1101.

CALEDONIA STATE PARK
Fayetteville, PA 17222
Franklin and Adams counties, south central Pennsylvania. From I-81 drive 10 miles east on US 30 to park on left. From Gettysburg drive 15 miles west on US 30 to park on right. Ten miles of trails, moderate to difficult. Lodging and camping nearby. (717) 352-2161.

CODORUS STATE PARK
RD 3, Box 118, Hanover, PA 17331
York County, south central Pennsylvania, 20 miles southwest of York. Drive west on Route 30 from York for six miles; turn left on Route 116 for 15 miles to Hanover; turn left on Route 216 at Hanover and go two miles south. Fifteen miles of trails and 300 acres of open fields and woodlands. (717) 637-2816.

COWAN'S GAP STATE PARK
Fort Loudon, PA 17224
Near Chambersburg, PA, off Route 75 in the Tuscarora Mountains. Easy to difficult, seven and a half miles of trails. Lodging nearby. (717) 485-3948.

DELAWARE WATER GAP NATIONAL RECREATION AREA
Shawnee, PA 18356
Monroe and Northhampton counties in northeastern Pennsylvania, six miles south of Stroudsburg. Drive east from Stroudsburg on I-80 toward Water Gap and south at Exit 53 to Route 611, south on 611 for three miles to park on right at Slateford Farm. Five and a half miles of easy to difficult trails. (717) 421-9127.

GETTYSBURG NATIONAL MILITARY PARK
Gettysburg, PA 17325
Take 270 north to Frederick; follow Route 15 north to the Battlefield.

Food and lodging available nearby. Maps available at the visitors center. (717) 334-1124.

GIFFORD PINCHOT STATE PARK
2200 Rosstown Road, Lewisberry, PA 17339
York County, 15 miles northwest of York. Drive north on I-83 from York to Route 382 (west) (Exit 13) for three miles to Route 177. Turn left into the park. Eight miles of trails, easy to moderate. Rentals and instruction available. (717) 432-5011.

HICKORY RUN STATE PARK
Carbon County, 40 miles north of Allentown. Drive west from Stroudsburg on I-80 for 38 miles to Hickory Run Exit, then east on Route 534 for four miles. Thirteen miles of easy to difficult trails. Rentals, instruction, food, and camping available. Some snowmobile trails. (717) 443-9991.

HIDDEN VALLEY SKI TOURING CENTER
RD 4, Box 243, Somerset, PA 15501
Take the Pennsylvania Turnpike west to Route 31 at Somerset. Follow 31 west to Hidden Valley. Thirty miles of trails. Rentals, instruction, tours, races, food, lodging, and maps available at the area. Trail charge. (814) 443-1900.

KOOSER STATE PARK AND FORBES STATE FOREST
Westmoreland and Somerset counties. Drive west from Somerset (at Exit 10 on Pennsylvania Turnpike) on Route 31 for nine miles. One and a half miles of trails and 20 miles of trails in adjacent Forbes State Forest. Camping available. (814) 445-8673 for Kooser and (412) 238-9533 for Forbes.

LAUREL MOUNTAIN
Take the Pennsylvania Turnpike west from Route 70 to Route 31 at Somerset. Follow to Hidden Valley, Kooser State Park, or Laurel Ridge State Park. Ski trails on the logging roads near Laurel Mountain ski area or on roads starting at the state parks mentioned. Ask directions to trails at Laurel Mountain ski area. (See Laurel Ridge State Park or Hidden Valley entries.)

LAUREL RIDGE STATE PARK
RD 3, Rockwood, PA 15557
Fayette County. Drive south from Somerset (Exit 10 on Pennsylvania Turnpike) for nine miles on Route 281; turn right (west) on Route 653 for seven miles. Twelve miles of easy to difficult trails. Maps available at office (closed on weekends during winter). Shelters available, advance reservations necessary. (412) 455-3744.

LIGONIER MOUNTAIN
Route 30, Box 206, Laughlintown, PA 15655

Westmoreland County. Drive north from Somerset (Exit 10 on Pennsylvania Turnpike) on Route 219 for 12 miles, left (west) on Route 30 for 10 miles. Twenty miles of easy trails, connecting with 30 miles of more difficult trails. Rentals, instruction, food available. (412) 238-6246.

OHIOPYLE STATE PARK
PO Box 105, Ohiopyle, PA 15470
Fayette County, southwestern Pennsylvania. Drive east from Uniontown for 10 miles on Route 40; turn left (north) for seven miles on Route 381 toward Ohiopyle Falls. Twenty-five miles of trails from easy to difficult. Camping and food available. (412) 329-4707.

POCONO MANOR RESORT
Pocono, PA 18349
Monroe County in northeastern Pennsylvania. Drive west from Stroudsburg on I-80 for 13 miles to I-380 (west). Take first exit (Route 940), turn right, and follow sign to Pocono Manor (two miles). Forty miles of groomed and patrolled easy to difficult trails. Rentals, instruction, ski shop, food, and lodging available. (717) 839-7111.

RIDLEY CREEK STATE PARK
East Sycamore Mills Road, Media, PA 19063
Delaware County in southeast Pennsylvania. Drive west from Philadelphia on Route 3 for 16 miles, through Newtown Square, to park. Ten miles of multi-use trails. (215) 566-4800.

SHAWNEE STATE PARK
Bedford County in southwestern Pennsylvania. Drive west from Bedford (Exit 11 on Pennsylvania Turnpike) on Route 30 for five miles to Schellburg; turn left (south) at Schellburg on Route 96 for one mile. Twelve miles of dual skiing and snowmobiling trails. (814) 733-4218.

STONE VALLEY/SHAVERS CREEK ENVIRONMENTAL CENTER
267 Recreation Building, University Park, PA 16802
Huntingdon County in central Pennsylvania. Drive south from State College on Route 26 over Tussey Mountain; turn right on Petersburg Road at foot of mountain and follow signs. Sixteen miles of easy to difficult trails. Rentals and instruction available on weekends. Lodging available. (717) 588-6652.

TAMIMENT RESORT AND COUNTRY CLUB
Tamiment, PA 18371
Monroe County in northeastern Pennsylvania in the Pocono Mountains. Drive east from Stroudsburg on I-80 to Exit 52 north on

Route 209 for thirteen miles to Bushkill; turn left for four miles. Thirty miles of trails and golf course. Rentals, instruction, lodging, food, and downhill skiing available. (717) 588-6652.

TYLER PARK
Route 413 Bypass and Swamp Road, Newtown, PA 18940
Bucks County in southeastern Pennsylvania. Drive north from Philadelphia on I-95 to Newtown exit; go east on Route 322 for four and a half miles to park. Forty miles of multi-use trails. (215) 968-2021.

VIRGINIA

BLUE RIDGE PARKWAY
Take Route I-66 to 29 south to Charlottesville. Take 250 west to Waynesboro to the Blue Ridge Parkway. Parkway extends 469 miles from Waynesboro, VA, to Cherokee, NC. The parkway (except for the short section between Bedford, VA, and Apple Orchard Radar Station) and surrounding areas are excellent for ski touring. Blue Ridge Parkway Headquarters: (703) 258-2850. Mt. Mitchell State Park: (703) 982-6213.

FAIRFAX COUNTY PARKS
3701 Pender Drive, Fairfax, VA 22030
Fairfax County parks feature a variety of cross-country skiing trails near Washington, DC. Rentals in Fairfax. For information on regional parks, telephone: (703) 941-5000, ext. 278.

MANASSAS NATIONAL BATTLEFIELD PARK
From Washington, DC, go west on I-66 to Route 234. Take Route 234 for two miles to the park office. (Thirty-eight miles west of Washington, DC.) Thirty miles of trails. Ski rentals in Fairfax. Lodging and food nearby. (703) 754-7107.

MOUNT ROGERS NATIONAL RECREATION
AREA/JEFFERSON NATIONAL FOREST
Konnarock, VA. Parking at Elk Garden Gap. Mount Rogers has several miles of designated trails, good elevation. Several skiable logging roads in the forest. For maps and information: Mount Rogers National Recreation Area, Route 1, Box 303, Marion, VA 24354. (703) 982-6270.

SHENANDOAH NATIONAL PARK
Luray, VA 22835
Park entrances: Front Royal (northern entrance); Thornton Gap off Route 211 (central entrance); or Route 29 south to Charlottesville to Route 250 west to Rockfish Gap (southern entrance). Ski touring unlimited in the 195,000 acre park. Parts of Skyline Drive are

skiable; excellent touring on park roads. Intermediate to difficult. Camping allowed. Food and lodging nearby. (703) 999-2266 or 999-2229.

WASHINGTON AND OLD DOMINION REGIONAL PARK
1101 Popeshead Road, Fairfax, VA 22030
Northern Virginia. The Washington and Old Dominion Hiking and Biking Trail extends from Lee Highway in Falls Church at I-66 to Purcellville. The 44-mile trail makes great skiing close to Washington, DC. Trail book available. (703) 278-8880.

DISTRICT OF COLUMBIA

ROCK CREEK PARK
5000 Glover Road N.W., Washington, DC 20015
Northwest Washington, DC, between Connecticut and Georgia avenues N.W. Eleven miles of trails and golf course. Additional two miles of park roads closed for cross-country skiing when snow covered. (202) 426-6832, snow conditions: (202) 426-7716.

WEST VIRGINIA

ALPINE LAKE RESORT AND CONFERENCE CENTER
Terra Alta, WV 26764
Northern West Virginia. Approximately nine miles of groomed and foot-packed trails, lodging, restaurants, heated swimming pools. Rentals and instruction. (304) 789-2481.

BLACKWATER NORDIC CENTER
Blackwater Falls State Park, Davis, WV 26260
Fifteen and a half miles of maintained trails, six miles of machine-set track, ice-skating rink, lighted sled run, telemark slope with tow. Instruction, rentals, backcountry guides, food, and lodging. (304) 259-5511 or 259-5216.

CANAAN VALLEY STATE PARK
Tucker County, 11 miles south of Thomas, WV. West from Cumberland, MD, on Route 48 for 31 miles, south on Route 219 through Oakland for 55 miles to Thomas, south on Route 32 from Thomas for 11 miles to park on right six miles. Rentals and instruction, lodging, camping, food, and downhill skiing available. (304) 866-4121 or (800) 225-5982.

CRANBERRY BACKCOUNTRY
District Ranger, Box 110, Richwood, WV 26261
Pocahontas and Webster counties, central West Virginia in Monongahela National Forest, 26 miles east of Summersville. Drive west on I-64 and Route 60 from Lewisburg for 30 miles to Charmco, right (north) on Route 20 for 17 miles to Route 39, and right east for eight miles.

Two trails of seven and 11 miles each, 70 miles of unplowed roads. Nine Adirondack shelters. (304) 846-2695 weekdays.

ELK RIVER TOURING CENTER
Highway 219, Slatyfork, WV 26291
Twenty-five miles of trails, four miles of machine-groomed trails, and a mile of beginner loops which are lighted for night skiing. Food and lodging, instruction, telemark lessons and rentals, backcountry guided tours. (304) 572-3771.

PIPESTEM RESORT STATE PARK
Pipestem, WV 25979
Eastern West Virginia, 16 miles north of Princeton on Route 20 from Pipestem Exit off I-77. Twenty-five deluxe cabins, two lodges. (304) 466-1800.

SPRUCE KNOB/SENECA ROCK
Seneca Rocks, WV 26884
Randolph and Pendleton counties in Monongahela National Forest. Drive west from Petersburg on Route 28 for 22 miles to Seneca Rocks; turn right (north) on Route 33 for six miles to road for Seneca Creek. Sixty miles of trails. (304) 567-2827.

WHITE GRASS SKI TOURING CENTER
Canaan Valley, Davis, WV 26260
Adjacent to Canaan Valley State Park. Three hundred forty miles of maintained trails, twelve and a half miles of machine-groomed trails, backcountry skiing in the Dolly Sods Wilderness area and in Monongahela National Forest. Instruction, rentals, sales, and guided tours available. (304) 866-4114.

▬▬ CUT-YOUR-OWN CHRISTMAS TREE ▬▬

Nothing says "Merry Christmas" better than the fragrance of a fresh Christmas tree, sparkling with lights and glittering with shiny tinsel. It is possible to relive the "good old days" when Grandpa used to lead the children through the woods to pick the biggest, greenest pine tree in the forest. Many farms allow customers to choose their own trees by tagging them, or by actually cutting or digging them. Be sure to know what size tree you want; the height of an in-the-ground tree can be deceptive.

It is important to telephone ahead to the farm (you may wish to try calling in the evening). Stocks are sometimes limited, and the farmer will tell you what species and heights of trees he has available. The mid-Atlantic area has an abundance of Scotch pines; other trees include White and Austrian pines, Douglas and Concolor firs, and Norway, Blue, and White spruce. Be sure to ask if you must bring your own saw or shovel, if the farmer cuts or digs the tree or if the task is up to you, and what facilities there are for preparing your tree for the trip home.

As soon as you arrive at the farm, check in and ask directions to the cutting, digging, or tagging area. Trees are considerably less expensive than in a city-bound lot; they will probably run between $7 and $18.

Once you get your special tree home, follow a few rules to keep it fresh. Keep it in a cool spot as long as possible before bringing it in the house. If it is a cut tree, cut another inch off the main stem and place it in a clean pail of warm water in a shaded spot. Cut another inch off before you bring it into the house. Place it in a stand that can hold water or in a pail of clean sand to which water can be added. If it is a balled tree, be sure to keep the roots moist by placing it in a large tub of water. Check water and replace daily. Then trim your tree with your best ornaments, sit back, and enjoy the best of nature in your home.

The following are farms where you can choose your own tree:

DELAWARE

Eric Tarburton, Box 195, S. Dual Highway, Camden, DE 19934, (302) 697-9110

L. James Tarburton, Box 196, S. Dual Highway, Camden, DE 19934, (302) 697-7214

Jack Egolf, Box 61, Cheswold, DE 19936, (302) 674-4383

Edward E. Hurd, Box 218, Clayton, DE 19938, (302) 653-8028

Howard E. Moore, RD 1, Box 634, Clayton, DE 19938, (302) 653-7701

Clarence Dyer, 32 Lake Lane, Dover, DE 19901, (302) 734-2111

Timothy A. Kaden, 409 Dogwood Avenue, Dover, DE 19901, (301) 674-4052 (home); (302) 678-4820 (work)

Lester Blades, RD 3, Box 777, Felton, DE 19943, (302) 284-9797

Robert A. Poynter, RD 1, Box 205, Felton, DE 19943, (302) 284-4801

Charles H. Roland, RD 2, Box 59, Felton, DE 19943, (302) 284-9859

Ralph Johnson, RD 2, Box 485B, Frederica, DE 19946, (302) 335-4330

Martin Isaacs, RD 2, Box 100, Georgetown, DE 19947, (302) 653-8028

John M. Schwalm, RD 1, Box 188C, Hartly, DE 19953,
    (302) 492-8071
Raymond B. Williams, RD 1, Box 159J, Hartly, DE 19953,
    (302) 492-8018
Paul Dennison, 233 W. Park Place, Newark, DE 19711,
    (302) 738-3068
William Kranz, 616 New London Road, Newark, DE 19711,
    (302) 731-5505
Glen Flemming, Route 3, Box 307, Seaford, DE 19973,
    (302) 674-4383
J. R. Miller, 514 Phillips Street, Seaford, DE 19973,
    (302) 629-4959
R. Cecil Wilson, RD 2, Box 351, Seaford, DE 19973,
    (302) 629-4226 (home); (302) 629-9121, ext. 2451
John E. Clark, Box 2353, Greenway Road, Smyrna, DE 19977
Bill Hickman, RD 2, Box 2347, Smyrna, DE 19977,
    (302) 653-6088
J. Frank Robinson, RD 2, Box 189A, Smyrna, DE 19977,
    (302) 653-5516
Carlton Blendt, Box 277, Townsend, DE 19734,
    (302) 653-9141
George R. Walton, Sr., RD 1, Box 182A, Magnolia, DE 19962,
    (302) 697-1675
Louis N. Pederson, RD 2, Box 7, Middletown, DE 19709,
    (302) 378-8324
Bill Morris, Evergreen East, Box 10564, Wilmington, DE 19850
Mark Lacey, 1800 Marshall Avenue, Wilmington, DE 19808,
    (302) 994-4678

MARYLAND

William H. Tanner, 14300 Bader-Westwood Road, Brandywine, MD,
    (202) 659-7528 (weekday office hours); (301) 579-2238 (weekends)
Foxwood Farm, Dione Road, Denton, MD,
    (301) 479-0614
Elmwood Farm, Mt. Harmony Road, Dunkirk, MD,
    (301) 586-2292
Hutchinson Brothers, Lewistown Road, Easton, MD,
    (301) 820-2062; (301) 820-2093
Piney Mountain Christmas Tree Farm, Piney Mt. Road, Eckhart,
    MD, (301) 689-3883
The Greenery, Hollingsworth Circle, Goldsboro, MD,
    (301) 482-8642; (301) 822- 1929
Linden Springs Farm, Indian Springs Road, Indian Springs, MD,
    (301) 797-9217; (301) 842-3768 (December 10 through 24)
Locksley Tree Farm, Dunstan Lane, Jacksonville, MD,
    (301) 666-2652

Jarrettsville Nurseries, St. Clair Bridge Road, Jarrettsville, MD,
    (301) 838-3966; (301) 557-9630
Clemsonville Christmas Tree Farm, Route 31, Libertytown, MD,
    (301) 775-7371
Thomas Tree Farm, Route 30, Manchester, MD,
    (301) 374-9589; (301) 374-9538
Woodville Forest Tree Farm, Peddicord Road, Mt. Airy, MD,
    (301) 829-1478
Mountain Top Tree Farm, Route 219, Oakland, MD,
    (301) 334-3210
Cider and Ginger Tree Farm, Elmer School Road, Poolesville, MD,
    (301) 349-5693
I. W. Davidson Farm, Emory Church Road, Reistertown, MD,
    (301) 374-2348
Johnson's Farm, Glencoe Road, Sparks, MD,
    (301) 472-2882
Unionville Tree Farm, Woodville Road, Unionville, MD,
    (301) 829-2799; (301) 751-1237
J.C.K. Christmas Tree Farm, Mayberry Road, Westminster, MD,
    (301) 837-2320; (301) 346-7597
Silver Run Tree Farm, E&E Trees, Inc., Route 97, Westminster,
    MD, (301) 751-1237; (301) 829-2799
Hardee Farms, Renner Road, Woodsboro, MD,
    (301) 384-6576; (301) 384-9455 (from Washington, DC, area)

NEW JERSEY

James A. Haines, Main Street, Juliustown, NJ 08042,
    (609) 894-2967
Juliustown Christmas Tree Farm, E. Main Street, Juliustown, NJ
    08042, (609) 890-1990
Indian Acres Tree Farm, Inc., 104 Christopher Mill Road, Medford,
    NJ, (609) 953-0087
Pariso Farm, 404 Skillman Road, Skillman, NJ 08558,
    (609) 466-0947

PENNSYLVANIA

Mr. and Mrs. Albert Troutman, RD 8, Box 339A, Foxanna Drive,
    Carlisle, PA 17013, (717) 766-4213
Smallbrook Farms, 265 Featherbed Lane, Route 322 W., Glen Mills,
    PA 19342, (215) 459-3961

VIRGINIA

Conrad Jones Xmas Tree Farm, Off Route 607, Bent Mountain, VA
    24059, (703) 929-4770

Reynolds Tree Farm, Route 623, Blacksburg, VA 24060,
(703) 552-2292

Wilson Tree Farm, 2010 Linwood Lane N.W., Blacksburg, VA
24060, (703) 552-4135

Larsen Tree Farm, Route 693, Christiansburg, VA 24073,
(703) 382-4668

Chittum Tree Farm, Box 78, Churchville, VA 24421,
(703) 885-1732

Walnut Ridge Farm, Route 1, Box 145, Clear Brook, VA 22624,
(703) 667-9537

Hollywood Tree Farm, Route 1, Box 82, Earlysville, VA 21936,
(804) 973-3624

Loudoun Nursery, Route 1, Box 175A, Hamilton, VA 22068,
(703) 882-3450

Yule Log Christmas Tree Farm, Route 637, Marshall, VA,
(703) 364-2811

Adams Christmas Trees, Route 690, Roanoke, VA 24018,
(703) 774-2740

Dietz Christmas Tree Farms, 5601 Viceroy Court, Springfield, VA
22151, (703) 569-4587

Tim's Christmas Tree Farm, 1993 Oceana Boulevard, Virginia Beach,
VA 23454, (804) 426-2128

Parson Christmas Tree Farm, Box 85, Washington, VA 22747,
(703) 675-3523

Fox Hill Farm, 1330 Hollins Road, Waynesboro, VA 22980,
(703) 942-1356

Danny-Dayle Christmas Tree Plantation, Route 7, Box 259, Winchester,
VA 22601, (703) 662-9026

Pinehill Christmas Tree Farm, Route 2, Box 95A, Winchester, VA
22601, (703) 877-1643

Pinetop Tree Farm, Route 617, Winchester, VA 22601,
(703) 858-3381

Scuttlebutt Christmas Tree Farm, Siler Star Route, Box 307,
Winchester, VA 22601, (703) 888-3442

Lugar's Tree Farm, Route 623, Woodstock, VA,
(703) 971-5473 or (703) 459-4893

The Annual Cut Your Own Christmas Tree Festival takes place
at Ash Lawn, James Monroe's plantation in Charlottesville, every
December, usually the second and third weekends. The plantation
has 535 acres of fields and woods. There is no charge for the trees,
but a donation is requested. Telephone: (804) 293-9539.

WEST VIRGINIA

Posten Tree Farm, Michael Road, Berkeley Springs, WV 25411,
(304) 258-2534

DOG SHOWS

The traditional dog show is a competition according to strict rules among dogs of pure breed which are registered with the American Kennel Club (AKC). The AKC also publishes, monthly, *The American Kennel Gazette* which, among other things, reports on upcoming shows and special events. There are more than 3,500 AKC-affiliated kennel clubs nationwide and approximately 600 in the mid-Atlantic area. They approve more than 2,000 shows annually, between September and June, including all-breed shows, specialties, field and obedience trials. In some areas events are approved for "junior" handlers from ages 10 through 16. Affiliated with the AKC are a number of nationwide Parent Clubs which control standards within an individual breed. Some examples are: Poodle Club of America (Stratford, CT); American Spaniel Club (Windmere, NY); Doberman Pinscher Club of America (Hayward, CA); German Shepherd Dog Club of America (Englewood, NJ); Labrador Retriever Club (Boise, ID); Golden Retriever Club of America (Pomona, CA); American Miniature Schnauzer Club (Vail, AZ); National Beagle Club (Bedminster, NJ); Dachshund Club of America (Mundelein, IL); American Shetland Sheepdog Association (Alpharetta, GA); Collie Club of America (Worcester, MA). Additional information can be obtained from: The American Kennel Club, 51 Madison Avenue, New York, NY 10010. Telephone: (212) 696-8292.

The 4-H sponsors dog shows for young people in two basic classes. The first, "fitting and grooming," or "fitting and showing," is a competition in how well a dog is cared for and prepared for the show. There is no consideration of the dog within a breed nor does it have to be purebred. The second trial, "obedience," is broken down into several categories and is judged on the same basis as the AKC trials, using the same scorecard, although sometimes one or more "junior" classes are scheduled. Many, but not all, states have this program. Information can be obtained from appropriate 4-H leaders and specialists at the state land-grant university (there is one such university in each state). Participation is limited to 4-H members. Any young person between the ages of nine and 19 is eligible to join. The general public is welcome to attend events.

Throughout the country there are numerous dog clubs which have no national affiliation. Local breeders and pet shops can usually provide information about these clubs as well as about local shows. Look under "Kennels" and "Pet Shops" in the Yellow Pages. Pet shows for youngsters are sponsored by local schools, civic clubs, and other organizations.

State travel and tourism offices often publish calendars of events which list some of the major AKC shows.

EXTENSION SERVICE CONTACTS FOR DOG SHOWS

Mr. Jim Arnold, 4-H and Youth (301) 454-5884
2126 Symons Hall, University of Maryland,
College Park, MD 20742

Mr. Roger Barr, Chairman of State Small (201) 646-2981
Animal Committee, 327 Ridgewood Avenue,
Paramus, NJ 07652

Dr. Maurice S. Kramer, State 4-H Leader (814) 865-6551
405 Agricultural Administration Building,
Pennsylvania State University, University Park, PA 16802

Mr. Cecil McBride, Extension Leader, (703) 961-6371
Virginia Polytechnic Institute and State University,
Blacksburg, VA 24061

Mr. Glenn Snyder, Extension Specialist in the (304) 293-3691
4-H Program, 518 Knapp Hall, Downtown Campus,
West Virginia University, Morgantown, WV 26506

Dr. Donald L. Stormer, Assistant Director, (919) 737-2801
Extension State 4-H Leader, North Carolina State University,
PO Box 5157, Raleigh, NC 27650

STATE TRAVEL OFFICES

Delaware Tourism Office (302) 736-4254
99 Kings Highway, PO Box 1401 outside DE (800) 441-8846
Dover, DE 19903 in DE (800) 282-8667

Maryland Office of Tourist Development (301) 974-3517
45 Calvert Street, (800) 331-1750
Annapolis, MD 21401 from DC, 565-0450

New Jersey Division of Travel and Tourism (609) 292-2470
CN-826, Trenton, NJ 08625 (800) 837-7397

North Carolina Department of Commerce (919) 733-4171
Division of Travel and Tourism,
430 N. Salisbury Street, Raleigh, NC 27611

Pennsylvania Division of Travel Marketing (800) 847-4872
453 Forum Building, in Canada (717) 787-5453
Harrisburg, PA 17120

Virginia State Division of Tourism   (804) 786-4484
202 N. Ninth Street, Suite 500, in DC   (202) 293-5350
Richmond, VA 23219

West Virginia Department of Commerce/Travel
West Virginia   (800) 225-5982
State Capitol Building   (304) 348-2286
Charleston, WV 25305

DOWNHILL SKIING

Downhill skiing in the mid-Atlantic region is ideally suited to the beginning, novice, or intermediate skier. The abundance of good areas only hours from the Baltimore-Washington-Richmond area provides plentiful and varied terrain for learning how to ski or for improving your skills. Advanced skiers used to demanding slopes will find several ski centers with sufficiently challenging runs for weekend trips. Large-scale snowmaking and the recent development of well-crafted trails in nearby mountain areas are making skiing more attractive and accessible to the occasional and the avid skier alike.

The increase of new ski areas, added night skiing, and the availability of more equipment stores and ski clubs in Washington, Baltimore, and Richmond are evidence of the sport's increasing popularity. Night skiing is particularly good on the gentler mid-Atlantic slopes and far more popular than in New England, where temperatures drop drastically after the sun goes down.

While most ski areas listed below are small, nearly all provide instruction, rentals, repairs, and eating facilities. Many locations have other outdoor sporting activities available, and some sort of apres ski life on site or nearby. Larger areas offer weekend and longer ski and accommodation packages which rival the better-known ski centers in New England and the West.

Ski clubs offer weekend and longer excursions during the season to local ski areas, to New England, and to the West. Throughout the year they sponsor weekly social gatherings; canoeing, hiking, and other sports outings; and occasional charters to summer resorts in the U.S. and abroad. The major ski clubs are:

- Baltimore Ski Club, (301) 825-SNOW. (This is an answering service. They will take a message and send you literature.)
- Washington Ski Club, (703) 536-8273. (This is a recording of current events; you can also leave a message for

more information.) 5309 Lee Highway, Arlington, VA 22207.

- Richmond Ski Club, (804) 741-3866.
- Virginia Ski Club, (804) 270-7023. Office: PO Box 6284, Richmond, VA 23230. This club is for singles only.

(See the Special Interest Section on Organized Day Trips for additional information on ski club activities.)

MARYLAND

WISP
Oakland, Maryland 21550   (301) 387-5503
Season: Mid-December to early March.
Twelve miles of slopes and trails. Vertical rise 610 feet. Slopes are beginner, intermediate, advanced. Lift capacity 4,000 per hour. Snowmaking. Open all week, night skiing. Rentals, instruction, lodging, and food available. Cross-country skiing available. Three and a half to four hours from Washington and Baltimore, five hours from Richmond.

NEW JERSEY

BELLE MOUNTAIN
Lambertville, New Jersey 08530   (609) 397-0043
Four slopes over 20 acres, vertical rise 190 feet. Lift capacity 1,500 per hour. Snowmaking. Open all week, night skiing. Instruction available. In central New Jersey near Philadelphia.

CAMPGAW MOUNTAIN SKI CENTER
Mahwah, New Jersey 07430   (201) 327-7800
Three slopes, vertical rise 270 feet. Three lifts, night skiing, snowmaking. Food available. Northeastern New Jersey.

CRAIGMEUR SKI AREA
Newfoundland, New Jersey 07435   (201) 697-4500
Six slopes, vertical rise 300 feet. Four tows/lifts, snowmaking, night skiing, lodge, and restaurants. Accommodations nearby. Northeastern New Jersey.

HIDDEN VALLEY
Vernon, New Jersey 07462   (201) 764-6161
Season: December 1 to end of March.
Six trails and slopes, vertical rise 620 feet. Snowmaking. Lift capacity 2,800 per hour. Open all week, night skiing. Instruction, lodging, and food available. Northeastern New Jersey.

SKI MOUNTAIN

Pine Hill, New Jersey 08021   (609) 783-8484

Two slopes, vertical rise 210 feet. Two tows/lifts, snowmaking, and night skiing. Nearby restaurants and accommodations. Near Philadelphia.

VERNON VALLEY/GREAT GORGE

Vernon, New Jersey 07428   (201) 827-2000

SNOWPHONE: (201) 827-3900

Fifty-two slopes, including one with a vertical rise of 1,040 feet. Seventeen tows/lifts, night skiing, cross-country skiing, and snowmaking. Lodge, restaurant, health spa, and accommodations. Northern New Jersey.

PENNSYLVANIA

BLUE KNOB

Claysburg, Pennsylvania 16625   (814) 239-5111

Season: December to mid-March.

Seven miles of trails, 14 slopes. Vertical rise 1,052 feet. Slopes are beginner, intermediate, advanced. Lift capacity 3,000. Snowmaking. Open all week, night skiing. Rentals, repairs, instruction, lodging, and food available. Three and a half hours from Washington.

CHADDS PEAK

Chadds Ford, Pennsylvania 19317   (215) 388-7421

Season: Mid-December to late March.

Beginner to advanced slopes. Longest run 1,000 feet. Night skiing. Instruction, lodging, and food available. Ten miles from Wilmington, Delaware; 28 miles from Philadelphia.

DOE MOUNTAIN

Macungie, Pennsylvania 18062   (215) 682-7109

Season: December 1-March 31.

Open daily. Ten slopes and trails. Vertical drop 500 feet. Longest run 4,500 feet. Lift capacity 4,000. Instruction and ski shop. Night skiing weekdays. Snowmaking. Fifteen miles southwest of Allentown.

HIDDEN VALLEY SKI TOURING CENTER

Somerset, Pennsylvania 15501   (814) 443-6454

(PA) (800) 452-0893

(out of state) (800) 458-0175

Vertical rise 400 feet. Seven slopes, three trails, two and a half miles of trails. Beginner to advanced. Snowmaking 40 percent of area. Night skiing (except Sunday). Instruction, rentals, lodging, and food. One hundred ninety miles from Washington.

LAUREL MOUNTAIN SKI RESORT

Boswell, Pennsylvania 15531   (412) 238-6688

Vertical rise 900 feet. Twelve trails, beginner to intermediate. Snowmaking in 80 percent of area. Open daily. Night skiing 4:30 p.m. to 10:30 p.m. Rentals, repairs, lodging, and food. Two hundred miles from Washington, 220 miles from Baltimore.

MT. AIRY LODGE
Mt. Pocono, Pennsylvania 18344   (717) 839-8811
(800) 441-4410

Vertical rise 240 feet. Ten slopes and trails, beginner to advanced. Instruction, rentals, lodging, and food. Snowmaking facilities.

RICHMOND HILL SKI AREA
Greencastle, Pennsylvania 17225   (717) 369-2673
Vertical rise 125 feet. Very small area. Intermediate. Open weekends only. Instruction, lodging (only a few rooms), food, and rentals. Located on Route 75, four miles north of Route 30 (Fort Loudon).

SEVEN SPRINGS
Champion, Pennsylvania 15622   (814) 352-7777
Season: December 1 to April 1.
Open daily. Night skiing. Vertical rise 850 feet. Seven trails and nine slopes. Mostly intermediate runs. Instruction, rentals, repairs, food, and lodging. Four to five hours from Washington. One hour from Pittsburgh.

SHAWNEE MOUNTAIN
Shawnee-on-Delaware, Pennsylvania 18356   (717) 421-7231
Season: Thanksgiving to March 30.
Open daily. Vertical rise 700 feet. Eight miles of trails (11 trails and slopes). Instruction, rentals, ski shop, lodging, and food. Snowmaking covers 100 percent of area. Four miles outside of Stroudsburg, Pennsylvania.

SKI LIBERTY
Fairfield, Pennsylvania 17320   (717) 642-8282
Season: Thanksgiving to March 15.   (PA) (800) 382-1390
(out of state) (800) 423-0227

Open daily. Night skiing. Vertical rise 600 feet. Fourteen trails. Beginner to advanced (mostly intermediate). Ski rentals and repair, instruction, lodging, and food. Seventy miles from Washington.

SKI ROUNDTOP
Lewisberry, Pennsylvania 17339   (717) 432-9631
Season: November 15 to March 15.   (PA) (800) 382-1390
(out of state) (800) 233-1134

Open daily. Night skiing. Vertical rise 550 feet. Six trails, four slopes. Beginner to advanced (mostly beginner). Rentals, instruction, food, and lodging. Two and a half hours from Washington. One and a half hours from Baltimore.

SPLIT ROCK SKI AREA
Lake Harmony, Pennsylvania 18624   (717) 722-9111
Season: November 25 to March 15.
Open daily. Night skiing. Vertical rise 200 feet. Two slopes, two trails. Instruction, rentals, and food. Snowmaking. Snowmobiling and tobogganing.

SPRING MOUNTAIN SKI AREA
Spring Mountain, Pennsylvania 19478   (215) 287-7900
Season: December 15 to March 15.
Open daily. Night skiing. Vertical rise 455 feet. Two main slopes and trails. Instruction, rentals, and food. Snowmaking. Twenty-eight miles from Philadelphia.

SUGARBUSH MOUNTAIN
Latrobe, Pennsylvania 15650   (412) 238-9655
Season: (approx.) December 1 to April 1.
Open weekends and holidays. Night skiing Tuesday through Sunday nights, 6:30 p.m. to 10:30 p.m. Vertical rise 200 feet. Two slopes, three trails. Instruction, lodging, and food.

TAMIMENT RESORT AND COUNTRY CLUB
Tamiment, Pennsylvania 18371   (717) 588-6652
Season: Late December to mid-March.   (PA) (800) 532-8211
                                  (out of state) (800) 233-8105
Open daily. Vertical rise 125 feet. Two slopes. Instruction, ski shop, lodging, and food. Snowmaking. Located near Bushkill and Route 209.

VIRGINIA

BRYCE MOUNTAIN RESORT
Basye, Virginia 22810   (703) 856-2121
Season: Mid-December through mid-March.
Four slopes. Vertical rise 500 feet. Slopes are beginner, intermediate, advanced. Lift capacity 2,500 per hour. Snowmaking. Open all week, night skiing. Rentals, repairs, instruction, lodging, and food available. Two and a half to three hours from Baltimore/Richmond via I-66.

CASCADE MOUNTAIN RESORT
Fancy Gap, Virginia 24328   (703) 728-3161
Season: Mid-December through March.
Five slopes. Lifts: one tow, one chair. Snowmaking. Open all week, night skiing. Instruction and food available. Area is 90 miles west of Roanoke, near Blue Ridge Parkway.

THE HOMESTEAD SKI AREA
Hot Springs, Virginia 24445   (703) 839-5079

Season: Mid-December through mid-March.
Six slopes and three trails. Vertical rise is 695 feet. Slopes are beginner, intermediate, advanced. Open all week. Rentals, repairs, instructions, lodging, and food available. Four hours from Baltimore/Richmond.

MASSANUTTEN
Harrisonburg, Virginia 22801 (703) 289-9441
Season: Mid-December through mid-March.
Nine slopes. Vertical rise is 795 feet. Trails are beginner, intermediate, advanced. Lift capacity 5,200 per hour. Open all week, night skiing. Rentals, repairs, instruction, lodging, and food available. Two hours from Baltimore/Richmond via I-66.

WINTERGREEN
Wintergreen, Virginia 22958 (804) 325-2200
Season: December 1 through late March.
Ten slopes and 82 acres of skiing terrain. Vertical rise is 1,003 feet. Snowmaking. Beginner, intermediate, advanced slopes. Lift capacity 6,400 per hour. Open all week, night skiing. Rentals, repairs, instructions, lodging, and food available.

WEST VIRGINIA

ALPINE LAKE
Terra Alta, West Virginia 26764 (304) 789-2481
Season: Thanksgiving through March.
Several novice slopes. Vertical rise 450 feet. Lift capacity 450 per hour. Open Friday nights, weekends, and Christmas. Instruction, lodging, and food available.

CANAAN VALLEY SKI AREA
Davis, West Virginia 26260 (304) 866-4121
Season: Mid-December through mid-March.
Six slopes, 14 trails. Slopes are beginner, intermediate, advanced. Lift capacity is 1,200 per hour. Snowmaking. Open all week, night skiing. Rentals, repairs, instruction, lodging, and food available. Four hours from Baltimore/Richmond.

COONSKIN PARK
Charlestown, West Virginia 25414 (304) 345-8000
Season: December through March.
One gently rolling slope. Vertical rise 125 feet. Lift capacity 200 per hour. Open daily, noon to 10 p.m. Rentals, repairs, and food available. Four miles from Charlestown.

OGLEBAY
Wheeling, West Virginia 26003 (304) 242-3000

Season: December through early March.
Forty acres of terrain. Vertical rise 330 feet. Snowmaking. Open all
week, night skiing. Rentals, instruction, and food available.

SILVER CREEK SKI RESORT
Slatyfork, West Virginia 26291   (WV) (800) 523-6329
Season: Mid-December through mid-March.(out of state) (800) 624-2119
Ten slopes, top elevation 4,800 feet, vertical rise 650 feet. Longest
run 4,400 feet. Three lifts. Snowmaking. Rentals, instruction, food,
and lodging available.

SNOWSHOE
Snowshoe, West Virginia 26209   (304) 527-1000
Season: Thanksgiving to Easter.
One hundred fifty acres of slopes and trails; 11 major trails. Vertical
rise 1,598 feet. Lift capacity 5,000 per hour. Snowmaking. Open all
week. Rentals, repairs, instruction, lodging, and food available.

TIMBERLINE FOUR SEASONS RESORT
Canaan Valley, West Virginia 26260   (304) 866-4801
Season: December through March.   (800) 843-1751
Fourteen slopes and trails from beginner to expert. Vertical rise is
1,084. Longest run 10,640 feet. Lift capacity 3,000 per hour.
Snowmaking. Lodging, food, instruction, and rentals.

━━━━━ FLOWER AND GARDEN SHOWS ━━━━━

The central mid-Atlantic states host numerous diverse
flower and garden shows, many of them very imaginatively
planned. Some of the major ones are listed below. Most towns
and cities have garden clubs which have at least one annual
show. Society editors of local newspapers know the times and
places of these events. The national association for virtually
all these clubs is: Garden Clubs of America, 598 Madison
Avenue, New York, NY 10021. Telephone: (212) 753-8287.

An excellent directory compiled by the American Horticultural Society (Mount Vernon, VA 22121) lists thousands of
public and private organizations and programs in North
America, including garden clubs and centers, state horticultural societies, florists associations, government programs,
public gardens and arboreta, cemetery gardens, and zoo
gardens, to name a few of the entry categories (American
Horticultural Society, *North American Horticulture: A Reference Guide*, New York: Charles Scribner's Sons, 448 pages,
$45). It probably is in your local library.

Historical and botanical gardens, as well as arboreta,
plan both annual events and one-of-a-kind festivals. County
Extension Agents (check county government listings or the

Extension Service offices listed in the Dog Shows section) have information about special local and 4-H shows. Two publications list forthcoming shows: *The American Nurseryman* (twice monthly), and *The Florists Review* (weekly), both published at 310 South Michigan Avenue, Suite 302, Chicago, IL 60604. Telephone: (312) 922-8194.

DELAWARE

Delaware Federation of Garden Clubs   (302) 658-1913
Wilmington Garden Center
503 Market Street Mall, Wilmington, DE 19801
   Obtain information on the club-sponsored Delaware Flower Show (time varies, sometimes every 18 months) as well as on other shows as they are scheduled throughout the state.

Eleutherian Mills   (302) 658-2400
(reached by bus from Hagley Museum)
PO Box 3630, Greenville, DE 19807
   Open April through December, 9:30 a.m. to 4:30 p.m. January through March, Monday to Friday (call for tour times); weekends, 9:30 a.m. to 4:30 p.m. Admission charge for Hagley covers the gardens. Displays: Seasonal displays.

Nemours Mansion and Gardens   (302) 651-6912
PO Box 109, Wilmington, DE 19899
   Open May through November, Tuesday through Saturday, 9:00 a.m. to 4:30 p.m.; Sunday, 11:00 a.m. to 3:00 p.m. Displays: Seasonal displays over one-third of a mile of French-style gardens.

Winterthur Museum and Gardens   (302) 656-8591
Wilmington, DE 19735
   Open year round, Tuesday through Saturday, 9:00 a.m. to 5:00 p.m.; Sunday, noon to 5:00 p.m. Admission charge. Events: Winterthur in Autumn (September-October); Yuletide at Winterthur (December); Winterthur in Spring (April-May); Country Fair (July). Tram tour (extra charge) mid-April through mid-November. Wheelchairs available. Tours in sign language, telephone: (302) 428-1411.

MARYLAND

Brookside Gardens   (301) 949-8230
1500 Glenallen Avenue, Wheaton, MD 20902

Open 9:00 a.m. to 5:00 p.m., daily. Closed Christmas. Admission free. Shows: Christmas Show (approximately December 10 to early January); Easter Show (early April to early May); Chrysanthemums (October 30 to November 29).

Ladew Topiary Gardens and House   (301) 557-9466
3535 Jarrettsville Pike, Monkton, MD 21111
Open April through December, Tuesday through Friday, 10:00 a.m. to 4:00 p.m.; Sunday, noon to 5:00 p.m. Admission charge. Shows: Christmas Extravaganza (early December). Special displays: Wild Garden (April); Azaleas, Lilacs (May); Roses (June). Festivities: One-of- a-kind special events such as "Monte Carlo Night."

Landon School   (301) 320-3200
6101 Wilson Lane, Bethesda, MD 20817
Admission free. Shows: Azalea Festival (first week of May).

London Town Publik House and Garden   (301) 956-4900
839 Londontown Road, Edgewater, MD 21037
Open Tuesday through Saturday, 10:00 a.m. to 4:00 p.m.; Sunday, noon to 4:00 p.m. Closed January and February. Admission charge. Shows: Daffodil Show (usually second week of April); Horticulture Show (last Saturday in April).

William Paca House and Garden   (301) 267-6656; (301) 269-0601
1 Martin Street, Annapolis, MD 21401
Open year round, Tuesday to Saturday, 10:00 a.m. to 4:00 p.m.; Sunday, noon to 4:00 p.m. Monday (gardens only), 10:00 a.m. to 4:00 p.m. Admission charge. Special displays: Roses and Mayflowers (mid-May).

NORTH CAROLINA

Biltmore House and Gardens   (704) 274-1776
1 Biltmore Plaza, Asheville, NC 28803
Open daily, 9:00 a.m. to 5:00 p.m. Closed New Year's, Thanksgiving, Christmas. Admission charge. Displays: Tulips (mid-April); Azaleas (first week of May); Roses (end of May to early June); Annual Flowers (July 4 to Labor Day); Chrysanthemums (mid-September to October); Autumn Foliage (late October).

PENNSYLVANIA

Longwood Gardens   (215) 388-6741
Kennett Square, PA 19348
Open daily, 9:00 a.m. to 5:00 p.m. (6:00 p.m., June through August). Admission charge. Shows: Chrysanthemum Festival (early November); Thanksgiving Evening Display (end of November).

Displays: Poinsettia and Christmas Display (mid-December); varying spring and summer displays.

Pennsylvania Horticultural Society   (215) 625-8250
325 Walnut Street, Philadelphia, PA 19106
    Admission charge. Shows: Philadelphia Flower and Garden Show (usually second week of March—considered by many the finest flower show in the country); Harvest Show (usually last weekend in September).

VIRGINIA

The American Horticultural Society   (703) 768-5700
PO Box 0105, Mount Vernon, VA 22121
    Admission charge. Shows: Christmas Show (late November to early December); Spring Garden Festival (third week in May with a rain date the following week); Fall Festival (third week in October).

The Garden Club of Virginia   (804) 644-7776
12 E. Franklin Street, Richmond, VA 23219
    Show: Historic Garden Week in Virginia (April—200 historic gardens participate in this 50-year-old event). An excellent free guidebook to the gardens in the show is put out by the club. A one-dollar contribution to postage is requested.

Orland E. White Arboretum   (703) 837-1758
(University of Virginia), PO Box 175, Boyce, VA 22620
    Open daily, dawn to dusk. Personnel on duty 9:00 a.m. to 1:00 p.m. Admission free. Special displays: Crabapple and Flowering Shrubs (mid-April).

T.J.S. Productions   (703) 569-7141
7668-B Fullerton Road, Springfield, VA 22153
    Admission charge. Show: Washington Flower and Garden Show (March—several acres of landscaped gardens assembled for show).

FLYING

    When you have seen the sites from the ground level and want to get a different perspective on things, why not view them from the air? There are hundreds of flying enthusiasts who spend every weekend diving out of airplanes or hanging from kites. The sections here list chapters of national clubs and associations that can help you take flight.

HANG GLIDING

    If you have ever dreamed of flying like a bird, hang gliding is the nearest you'll come to fulfilling your fantasy. The U.S. Hang Gliding Association (headquarters in California: (213) 390-3065) has clubs in the area, and members will be glad to show you the ropes.

MARYLAND

Maryland Hang Gliding Association, 318 S. High Street, Baltimore, MD 21202, (301) 531-6458

Potomac Highlands Hang Gliding, Shades Lane, Cumberland, MD 21502, (301) 777-7564

NORTH CAROLINA

Ultra Light Pilots Association, 6024 Paw Creek Road, Charlotte, NC 28214, (704) 399-6409

Triangle Hang Gliding Club, 4113 H Cross Creek Court, Raleigh, NC 27607, (919) 471-3798

PENNSYLVANIA

Wind Riders Hang Gliding Club, 631 Lincoln Avenue, Morrisville, PA 19067

Daedalus Hang Gliding Club, RD 1, Saxonburg Boulevard, Saxonburg, PA 16056, (412) 352-2884

Nittany Valley Hang Gliding Club, 1178 Oneida Street, State College, PA 16802, (814) 234-1967

Blue Ridge Hang Gliding Club, RD 3, Tamaqua, PA 18252, (717) 386-5104

VIRGINIA

Capital Hang Glider Association, PO Box 64, Annandale, VA 22003

An inspiring place to learn hang gliding is on the site of the Wright Brothers' first flight at Kitty Hawk, NC. Write: Kitty Hawk Kites, Box 340, Nags Head, NC 27959. Telephone: (919) 441-4124 or (800) 334-4777 (toll free outside North Carolina).

PARACHUTING

Sport parachuting is a favorite pastime throughout the world. If you would like to see what you are getting into before you leap, attend one of the many shows and promotional events held throughout the year. The U.S. Parachute Association affiliated centers sponsor events and teach classes. Area centers are:

PENNSYLVANIA

Southern Cross Sport Parachute Center, Chambersburg Airport, 3506 Airport Road, Chambersburg, PA 17201, (717) 264-1111

United Parachute Center, Route 663/Swamp Pike, Gilbertsville, PA 19525, (215) 323-9667

Maytown Sport Parachute Center, Box 536, Maytown, PA 17550, (717) 653-9980

York Parachute Center, 2625 Grandview Drive, York Haven, PA
17370, (717) 938-4295

VIRGINIA

Buckingham Parachute Center, 110 Monte Vista Avenue,
Charlottesville, VA 22903, (804) 295-1242

Hartwood Paracenter, Route 6, Box 369B, Hartwood, VA 22471,
(703) 752-4784

Quantico Skydivers, USMCB, Box 344, Quantico, VA 23134,
(703) 221-8344

Suffolk Parachute Center, 3707 Virginia Beach Boulevard, Virginia Beach, VA 23452, (804) 569-9445

WEST VIRGINIA

KERA Parachute Center, 1593 1/2 Lee Street, Charleston, WV
25311, (304) 344-0309

SOARING

Soaring, or gliding as it is sometimes called, provides the thrill
and freedom of silent flight. Sailplanes are towed by a powered
airplane to a certain altitude; when they have caught a "thermal" or
a "wave," the rope tow is released and the sailplane is on its own.
The Soaring Society of America (headquarters in California: (213)
390-4447) is the central information source for those interested in
the sport. Its chapters can arrange lessons or just take you up for an
afternoon of flying.

DELAWARE

See "Brandywine Soaring Association" under Pennsylvania listing

MARYLAND

Cumberland Soaring Group, Box 866, Cumberland, MD 21502,
(301) 738-9118

Mid-Atlantic Soaring Association, 4823 Teen Barnes Road,
Frederick, MD 21701, (301) 663-9753

Eastern Shore Soaring Association, Route 8, Box 98, Parker
Road, Salisbury, MD 21801, (301) 742-5332

NEW JERSEY

South Jersey Soaring Society, 489 Weymouth Road, Vineland,
NJ 08360, (609) 935-5474

PENNSYLVANIA

Cloudniners, Inc., PO Box 262, Exton, PA 19341, (215) 687-1500

Brandywine Soaring Association, c/o PO Box 454, Wilmington,
DE 19899, (302) 654-0536

VIRGINIA

National Capital Soaring Association, 1111 Army-Navy Drive, B-612, Arlington, VA 22202, (703) 979-6498

Ridge and Valley Soaring Club, Route VSC, Belvedere Farm, Earlysville, VA, (804) 973-3142

New London Soaring Society, New London Airport, Route 1, Forest, VA 24551, (804) 929-5452 or 525-2988

Soaring Unlimited of Virginia, 7400 White Pine Road, Richmond, VA 23234, (804) 271-0465

Blue Ridge Soaring Society, Inc., PO Box 122, Salem, VA 24153, (703) 389-0769 or 864-5800

Warrenton Soaring Center, PO Box 185, Warrenton, VA 22186, (703) 347-0054

Tidewater Soaring Society, Inc., Route 2, Box 86, Windsor, VA 23487, (804) 595-7963

WEST VIRGINIA

Mountaineer Soaring Association, 2513 Woodland Avenue, S. Charleston, WV 25303, (304) 744-2846

▬▬▬ FRUIT AND VEGETABLE PICKING ▬▬▬

The "pick-your-own" fruits and vegetables phenomenon has developed in the Middle Atlantic states as an alternative marketing strategy for local farmers who have encountered greater labor, shipping, and handling costs, as well as shortages of labor. The "pick-your-own" farmer changes his planting policy by staggering his crop fields. Although he may have added to his insurance and advertising costs, he frees himself from dependence on labor availability and the necessity of shipping to larger markets.

The "pick-your-own" strategy allows the consumer to save on fruit and vegetable costs, at times up to 50 percent off the supermarket prices. But, more than the savings, consumers enjoy the taste of fresh ripened produce and the fun and exercise they get from picking it themselves.

Many farmers run produce stands that sell cider, honey, preserves, and home-baked bread in conjunction with their "pick-your-own" fields. This is a six-month-long activity; vegetables such as asparagus ripen as early as mid-April while pumpkins ripen through October.

Because vegetables and fruits ripen at different times each year, consumers are advised by the farmers to telephone in advance for day-to-day availability of crops and to go early in the day for the best selection. It is wise also to inquire about directions, hours of operation, availability of containers, and whether or not children are allowed in the fields, before setting out to a "pick-your-own" farm.

There are a great many farms in this region. The following partial listing contains farms which offer three or more fruits or vegetables.

The fruit and vegetable code table below is followed by an Approximate Harvest Dates Table. The code will be used throughout this section and Harvest Dates are only approximations for all of the states listed.

Fruits

CODE		DATES	
A	Apples	August 15	to November 5
B	Blackberries	July 5	to August 1
BT	Blackberries (Thornless)	August 1	to September 10
BR	Black Raspberries	June 15	to July 10
RR	Red Raspberries	June 15	to July 10
BI	Blueberries	June 20	to August 1
C	Cider	July 21	to September 20
G	Grapes	August 15	to September 20
N	Nectarines	July 25	to August 25
P	Peaches	July 5	to September 20
Pe	Pears	August 15	to October 15
Pl	Plums	July 15	to September 15
S	Strawberries	May 15	to June 20
SC	Sour Cherries	June 15	to July 15
SwC	Sweet Cherries	June 10	to July 10

Vegetables

CODE		DATES	
1	Asparagus	April 25	to June 15
2	Beans (Green)	June 10	to September 15
3	Beans (Lima)	July 20	to September 1
4	Beans (Pole)	June 24	to August 30
5	Beets	July 4	to September 1
6	Broccoli	July 10	to September 1
7	Cabbage	June 1	to September 15
8	Cantaloupes	July 15	to September 15
9	Carrots	July 10	to September 15
10	Corn (Sweet)	July 4	to September 15
11	Cucumbers	July 1	to September 1
12	Cucumbers (Pickles)	July 1	to August 1
13	Eggplant	July 25	to September 10
14	Gourds	August 15	to October 30
15	Okra	July 15	to August 30
16	Peas (Green)	June 10	to July 1

17	Peas (Blackeye)	July 20	to August 30
18	Peppers	July 25	to September 15
19	Potatoes	July 1	to September 30
20	Potatoes (Sweet)	September 5	to December 15
21	Pumpkins	September 10	to November 30
22	Spinach (Sp.-Fall)	May 1-30	to October 1-30
23	Squash (Summer)	June 25	to September 1
24	Squash (Winter)	August 1	to September 30
25	Tomatoes	July 4	to September 15
26	Turnips	August 15	to November 1
27	Watermelon	August 1	to October 1
28	Watermelon (Sugar Babies)	July 21	to October 1
29	Cauliflower	August 15	to November 1
30	Onion	June 25	to July 31

Some farms have not provided complete lists of their produce. Where the term "complete selection" is used it means that farm has a selection of eight to 10 vegetables. Fruits, on the other hand, are always given by their letter code.

(The farms listed were compiled by the state agriculture departments and are not endorsements by *Weekender's Guide to the Four Seasons*.)

DELAWARE

NEW CASTLE COUNTY

Baker Farms
RD 1, Box 86
Middletown, DE 19709
(302) 378-9000
Complete Selection

KENT COUNTY

Fifer Farms
RD 1, Box 109
Magnolia, DE 19962
(302) 248-9200
A, P, Pe, N, 11, 10, 25

Stanley Rolle, Jr.
RD 3, Box 267
Dover, DE 19901
(302) 734-2352 or 678-8141
S, 7, 29, 6, 19

Spader Produce Farm
RD 1, Box 166K
Smyrna, DE 19977
(302) 653-5162
Complete Selection

SUSSEX COUNTY

Cod Creek Produce
RD 3
Laurel, DE 19956
(302) 875-5317
   16, 3, 2, 10, 30, 25, 18

Isaacs' Family Farm
Route 113
Georgetown, DE 19947
(302) 856-7245
   S, Complete Selection

Nassau Orchard Market
Nassau, DE 19969
(302) 645-8808
   A, N, P, Pl, BR, RR, S,
   Complete Selection

Donna and William A. O'Day
Route 3, Box 293
Seaford, DE 19973
(302) 629-7854
   S, P, Complete Selection

Pen-Ar Farms
RD 1, Box 234
Milford, DE 19963
(302) 422-7491
   S, 16, 10, 3, 25, 23, 24, 11,
   19, 18

Leon Tyndall
Laurel, DE 19956
(302) 875-7666
   S, 16, 3, 25, 18, 27

Warner Enterprises, Inc.
RD 2, Box 73A
Milford, DE 19963
(302) 422-9506
   Complete Selection

MARYLAND

ALLEGANY COUNTY
Stegmairer Orchards, Inc.
RFD 9, Box 355
Cumberland, MD 21502
(301) 722-5266
   Complete Selection

ANNE ARUNDEL COUNTY
Pumphrey's Homegrown Veg.
10 Route 3 S.
Millersville, MD 21108
(301) 987-0669
   16, 2, 3, 17, 18, 15

BALTIMORE COUNTY
Armacost Farms Orchards
16926 Gorsuch Mill Road
Upperco, MD 21155
(301) 239-3440
   A, 2, 25, 21, 19

Arrowhead
S. Offutt Road
Randallstown, MD 21133
(301) 922-5465
   S, P, BT

Huber's PYO Farm
12010 Philadelphia Road
Bradshaw, MD 21021
(301) 679-1941; 679-1948;
679-4098
   S, Complete Selection

Moore's Orchard
5242 E. Joppa Road
Perry Hall, MD 21128
(301) 256-5982
   A, P, 2

Rutkowski & Taylor Farm
11211 Raphel Road
Upper Falls, MD 21156
(301) 592-9785; 592-8764
   Complete Selection

CALVERT COUNTY
Josef and Donann Seidel
Box 233A
Huntingtown, MD 20639
(301) 535-2128
   G, BT, RR

CARROLL COUNTY
Baugher Enterprises, Inc.
1236 Baugher Road
Westminster, MD 21157
(301) 848-5541
   SwC, SC, BR, RR, 2, 16

Black Rock Orchard
Route 2, Box 33
Lineboro, MD 21088
(301) 374-9719
   SC, A, P, Pl

Blue Ridge Farm
2307 Uniontown Road
Westminster, MD 21157
(301) 548-343
   S, 2, 8, 16

CECIL COUNTY
Conowingo Orchard
Box 312
Conowingo, MD 21918
(301) 378-2441
   P, A, B

CHARLES COUNTY
Murray's Farm
Route 232, Box 277
Bryantown, MD 20617
(301) 645-5429
   S, RR, BR

FREDERICK COUNTY
Catoctin Mt. Orchard
15307 Kelbaugh Road
Thurmont, MD 21788
(301) 271-2737
   S, P, BR, SC, SwC, B

Gateway Orchard
15038 Kelbaugh Road
Thurmont, MD 21788
(301) 271-2322
   2, 25, 26

Glade Link Farm
9332 Links Bridge Road
Walkersville, MD 21793
(301) 898-7131
   S, 6, 21, 29

Pryor's Orchard
13841 Pryor Road
Thurmont, MD 21788
(301) 271-2693
   SC, A, P, Pe, Pl, N,
   SwC, 8, 21

Thanksgiving Farm Produce
2102 Pleasant View Road
Adamstown, MD 21710
(301) 874-5654; 977-2466
   2, 3, 16

HARFORD COUNTY

Jones Produce Farm Market
2100 Philadelphia Road
Edgewood, MD 21040
(301) 676-3709
   S, 16, 2, 3

Lohr's U-Pick-M Farm
3212 Snake Lane
Churchville, MD 21028
(301) 836-2783
   S, P, 2, 10, 18, 21, 25

Mt. Pleasant Orchard, Inc.
1620 Chapel Road
Havre de Grace, MD 21078
(301) 939-2222
   A, P, S, 2, 16, 22, 26, Kale

HOWARD COUNTY

Larriland Farm
Route 94
Florence, MD 21765
(301) 442-2605; (202) 854-6110
  S, RR, P, BT, A, Complete
  Selection

Sewell's Orchard
6233 Oakland Mills Road
Columbia, MD 21045
(301) 730-5959; 730-5500
  S, A, B, 21

Sharp Farm Produce
3779 Sharp Road
Glenwood, MD 21738
(301) 489-4630; 489-4175
  8, 10, 18, 25

KENT COUNTY

Vonnie's Market
Route 213, Box 34
Kennedyville, MD 21645
(301) 778-5300
  S, 7, 16, 18, 25

MONTGOMERY COUNTY

Butler's Orchard
22200 Davis Mill Road
Germantown, MD 20767
(301) 972-3299
  S, BT, 2, 16, 21, 25

Homestead Farm
15600 Sugarland Road
Poolesville, MD 20837
(301) 977-3761
  S, BT, RR, BR, 2, 16, 21, 25

The Innstead Farm
18020 Edwards Ferry Road
Poolesville, MD 20837
(301) 972-7248; 972-8091
  S, BR, B, 10, 16, 21, Snow
  Peas

Sunset View Farms
PO Box 78
Route 107, Martinsburg Road
Poolesville, MD 20837
(301) 972-8445
  S, Complete Selection

Thompson's Farm Produce
14722 New Hampshire Avenue
Silver Spring, MD 20904
(301) 384-9177
  Complete Selection

PRINCE GEORGE'S COUNTY

Cherry Hill Produce
12300 Gallahan Road
Clinton, MD 20735
(301) 292-4642
  S, Complete Selection

Johnson Family Farm
17000 Swanson Road
Upper Marlboro, MD 20870
(301) 627-8316
  S, BT, RR, 2

Kerby's Market
8407 Indian Head Highway
Oxon Hill, MD 20022
(301) 567-4375
  S, Complete Selection

Miller's Farm
Box 649
Clinton, MD 20735
(301) 297-5878
  S, BT, Complete Selection

E. A. Parker & Sons
12720 Parker Lane
Clinton, MD 20735
(301) 292-3940
  S, BT, RR, BR, Complete
  Selection

Ticer Farm Produce
8211 Oxon Hill Road
Oxon Hill, MD 20022
(301) 839-5295
  Complete Selection

ST. MARY'S COUNTY

Moore's Market
Box 186
Great Mills, MD 20634
(301) 994-1134
  S, 2, 3, 16, 18, 25, 26

Thompson's Orchard
PO Box 8
Great Mills, MD 20634
(301) 994-0219
  2, 3, 16

WASHINGTON COUNTY

Lewis Fruit Stand and Farm
Market
Route 64
Cavetown, MD 21720
(301) 824-2811
  S, 2, 16, 21, 25

NEW JERSEY

ATLANTIC COUNTY

Albert Butterhof
55 White Horse Pike
Egg Harbor, NJ 08215
(609) 965-4696
  S, 18, 2, 25, 23

The Fraleigh Farm
56 Clarktown Road
Mays Landing, NJ 08330
(609) 625-0492
  S, RR, 2, 16, 25

John Kertz Farm
266 S. Frankfurt Avenue
Egg Harbor, NJ 08215
(609) 965-2756
  17, 3, 15, 16, 2, 25

Liepe Brothers Inc.
Cologne Avenue
Cologne, NJ 08213
(609) 965-2886
  Complete Selection

Arthur Roesch Farm
626 W. Deurer Street
Leipzig and Deurer Street
Egg Harbor, NJ 08215
(609) 965-6326
  3, 2, 10, 25

BURLINGTON COUNTY

Four-Winds Farm
Medford Lakes Road
Route 532 (*half-mile east of Route 206*)
Tabernacle, NJ 08088
(609) 268-9113
  Bl, RR, S

Haines and O'Neal, Inc.
Carranza Road
Tabernacle, NJ 08088
(609) 268-0484
  Complete Selection

Larchmont Farms
Route 537 (Marne Highway)
Masonville, NJ 08054
(609) 235-0484
  A, B, P, S

Lengyen Farm
108 Old York Road
Crosswicks, NJ 08515
(609) 298-3068
  3, 2, 16, 10, 25

Helen and Bob Major's
Farm and Greenhouses
Paulson Road (*one mile off Route 528*), Jacobstown
Wrightstown PO, NJ 08562
(609) 758-2193
  S, RR, 2, 4, 16

Robson Farm and Green House
178A Monmouth Road (Route
537)
Wrightstown, NJ 08562
(609) 758-2566; 758-2577
   S, RR, B, 3, 16, 15, 2,
   and others

Rolling Acres
Ellisdale Road
Crosswicks, NJ 08515
(609) 298-3342
   1, 8, 16, 10, 25

Strawberry Hill Farm
Corner of Ellisdale and Waln
roads
Trenton RD 2
Chesterfield, NJ 08620
(609) 298-0823
   A, P, S

Vita-Green Farm
Marne Highway, RD 2
Mount Laurel, NJ 08054
(609) 235-4536
   S, 6, 3, 16, 2, 25

Workman's Farm
Moorestown-Centerton Road
Mount Laurel, NJ 08054
(609) 235-4126
   S, 16, 2

CAMDEN COUNTY

The Market Basket-Dobbs
Farms
711 White Horse Road
Voorhees, NJ 08043
(609) 783-1727
   S, 5, 7, 22, 25

CUMBERLAND COUNTY

Bosco Farms
E. Weymouth Road
Vineland, NJ 08360
(609) 697-3473
   S, 27, 18, 2, 22, 25

Perlstein Farms
Big Oak and Parvins Mill Road
Bridgeton, NJ 08302
(609) 455-6899
   Complete Selection

Rottkamp Farms
780 Shiloh Pike
Bridgeton, NJ 08302
(609) 451-2359
   Complete Selection

GLOUCESTER COUNTY

Cali Farms
Asbury Station Road
Repaupo, NJ 08066
(609) 467-0568
   S, 13, 3, 2, 25

Delsea Orchards Farm Market
Hurffville Cross Keys Road
and Fries Mill Road
Washington Township, NJ
(609) 728-0457
   S, 2, 3, 16, 25

Duffield Farm Market
Chapel Heights and Greentree
roads
Sewell, NJ 08080
(609) 589-7090
   S, 16, 2

Mood's Farm Market
Route 77
Mullica Hill, NJ 08062
(609) 478-2500
   A, Bl, SwC, G, N, Pe, Pl,
   RR, 2

Patane's Farm
100 Democrat Road (Route
295, Exit B)
Gibbstown, NJ 08027
(609) 423-2726
   Complete Selection

MERCER COUNTY

Grover Farm
348 Village Road E., RR 1
(*near Dutch Neck*)
Trenton, NJ 08648
(609) 799-1195
  S, 16, 19, 10

Lee Turkey Farm
Hickory Corner Road
Hightstown, NJ 08520
(609) 448-0629
  A, SC, N, P, S, Pe, 16,
  21, 25

Lenco Farms
Kuser Road and Route 130
Robbinsville, NJ 08691
(609) 587-7905
  S, 21, 2, 10, 25, 29

MONMOUTH COUNTY

Battleview Orchards
RD 1, Wemrock Road
Freehold, NJ 07728
(201) 462-0756
  S, A, P, 21

The Berry Farm
Route 34
Colts Neck, NJ 07722
(201) 583-0707
  RR, B, BR

Casola Farms
Route 520
Holmdel, NJ 07733
(201) 946-8885; 946-4281
  3, 15, 2, 25

Crest Fruit Farm
RD 5, Thompson Grove Road
Freehold, NJ 07728
(201) 462-5669
  A, P, Pl

OCEAN COUNTY

DeWolf's Farm
Colliers Mill Road (*off
Route 539*)
New Egypt, NJ 08533
(609) 758-2424
  S, B, RR, BR, P, 2, 3, 25

Hallock's U-Pick Farm
Fischer Road (*near
Route 528*)
New Egypt, NJ 08533
(609) 758-8847
  S, 11, 3, 16, 18, 19, 2, 25

SALEM COUNTY

Bradway's Farm Market
Jericho Road, RD 2
Salem, NJ 08079
(609) 935-5698
  S, 16, 2, 25

NORTH CAROLINA

Martin Farm Orchard &
Vineyard
PO Box 26
Knott's Island, NC 27950
(919) 429-3564, 429-3542

PENNSYLVANIA

ADAMS COUNTY

Bear Mountain Orchards
RD 1
Aspers, PA 17304
(717) 677-8713
  SwC, S, BR

Wayne Heberlig
RD 3, Route 30
Gettysburg, PA 17325
(717) 334-7911
  BT, BR, G, S, 1, 2, 16

Hollabaugh Bros. Fruit Farm
RD 1
Biglerville, PA 17307
(717) 677-8412
  P, Pe, A

Quaker Valley Orchards
RD 1, Quaker Valley Road
Biglerville, PA 17307
(717) 677-7351
  SwC, SC, P, A, Pe

Round Barn Orchards, Inc.
RD 2
Biglerville, PA 17307
(717) 334-446
  A, 16, 2, 3, S

BEDFORD COUNTY

Cuppett Brothers Farm
RD 2
New Paris, PA 15554
(814) 733-4644
  A, SwC, SC

BERKS COUNTY

Manbeck's Orchards
RD, Box 1560
Bethel, PA 19507
(717) 933-4541
  SC, SwC, P, A

Ontelaunee Orchard & Farm
Market
Route 61
Leesport, PA 19533
(215) 926-2929
  S, Bl, A, SC, RR

Shanesville Orchards
RD 3, Route 73
Boyertown, PA 19512
(215) 367-8496
  A, P, Pe, Pl

BUCKS COUNTY

Fairview Farms
Pineville Road
Pineville, PA 18946
(215) 598-3257
  2, 3, 4, 16, 17

Harris Farm Market
RD 1
Milan, PA 18831
(717) 883-4893
  Complete Selection

Paul Valley Farm Market
Easton Road
Warrington, PA 18976
(215) 343-1285
  8, 13, 25

Styer Orchards
Woodbourne Road
RD 1, Box 250
Langhorne, PA 19047
(215) 757-7646
  S, SC, SwC, P

CHESTER COUNTY

Hawthorne Farm
Box 107, RD 7
Coatesville, PA 19320
(215) 383-5494
  S, 21, 26

Highland Orchards, Inc.
1000 Thorndale Road
West Chester, PA 19380
(215) 269-3494
    S, P, SC, SwC, A

CUMBERLAND COUNTY

Ashcombe Vegetable Farm
RD 10, Box 10
Mechanicsburg, PA 17055
(717) 766-7611
    S, Bl, RR

Iron Mountain Orchard
36 Timber Lane
New Cumberland, PA 17070
(717) 774-1407
    SwC, SC, P, Pl

Musser Farm Market
RD 1, Box 340
Carlisle, PA 17013
(717) 766-2367
    S, 2, 3, 4, 17, 16

Toigo Orchards & Cider Mill
RD 2
Shippensburg, PA 17257
(717) 532-4655
    S, A, P, 10, 2

FRANKLIN COUNTY

John denHartog Orchard
Route 1
Fayetteville, PA 17222
(717) 264-7397
    S, A, RR

Pope's Orchards
9669 Mt. Brook Road
St. Thomas, PA 17252
(717) 328-2348
160 Loudon Road
Mercersburg, PA 17236
    SC, P, A

Starliper Orchard
Route 1
Mercersburg, PA 17236
(717) 328-3491
    P, A, SC, SwC, Pl

Twinbrook Orchards
Route 3, Box 284
Smithsburg, MD 21783
(717) 762-1796
    A, P, SwC, 10

LANCASTER COUNTY

Groff's Orchard
Route 1, Street Road
Kirkwood, PA 17536
    S, G, Complete Selection

Herr Fruit Farms
RD 2
Lancaster, PA 17603
(717) 285-5976
    A, S, SwC, SC, P

Manor Hills Orchard
Box 86, RD 2
Seitz Road
Columbia, PA 17512
(717) 285-4346
    S, SwC, SC, G

Wolgemuth Fruit Market
RD 2, Box 2900
Mt. Joy, PA 17552
(717) 653-5661
    SwC, SC, A

LEBANON COUNTY

Frey's Farm Market
1875 Colebrook Road
Lebanon, PA 17042
(717) 272-6342
    S, 16, 2, 3, 26

LEHIGH COUNTY

Hausman Fruit Farm
RD 2, Box 562
Coopersburg, PA 18036
(215) 967-2440
S, P, A, Pe, 10

MONTGOMERY COUNTY

Appleville Orchards
133 Cressman Road
Telford, PA 18969
(215) 723-6516
S, P, N, A

SOMERSET COUNTY

Maple Lane Berry Farm
RD 2, Box 11
Rockwood, PA 15557
(814) 926-2537
S, 2, 16, 17, 6

YORK COUNTY

Barton's Fruit Farm
RD 1, Box 46
Stewartstown, PA 17363
(717) 993-2494
S, A, SwC, P, Pl, N, RR

Blevins Fruit Farm, Inc.
RD 1
Stewartstown, PA 17363
(717) 993-2885
A, S, P, SwC, SC, 2, 3, 4,
16, 17

The Farmer's Daughter
350 W. Railroad Avenue
Shrewsbury, PA 17361
(717) 235-3309
2, 3, 4, 16, 17, 25, 10

Fremor Orchards
RD 2, Windsor Road
Red Lion, PA 17356
(717) 755-1851
S, SwC, SC, A, Pl, Pe

Lerew's Farm Market, Inc.
RD 2
Dillsburg, PA 17019
(717) 432-5925
SwC, SC, P

Maple Lawn Farms
Route 1
New Park, PA 17347
(717) 382-4878
Bl, P, A, Pl

Raab Fruit Farms
RD 2, Box 119
Dallastown, PA 17313
(717) 244-7157
Complete Selection

Red Rooster Farm
RD 1, Box 48
Stewartstown, PA 17363
(717) 993-2464
16, 17, 2, 3

Rinehart Orchards
RD 3
Dillsburg, PA 17019
(717) 766-8352
P, Pe, A, S, Pl

Sleepy Hollow Farm
RD 2
Delta, PA 17314
(717) 456-5172
S, 10, 21, 1, 22, 25

Susquehanna Orchards, Inc.
RD 1, Orchard Road
Delta, PA 17314
(717) 456-5115
SC, SwC, P, A

VIRGINIA

BEDFORD COUNTY

The Produce Patch
Route 1, Box 776
Forest, VA 24551
(703) 586-4242 or
(804) 528-0269
Complete Selection

CAMPBELL COUNTY

Red Acres Farm
Route 1, Box 19-A
Concord, VA 24538
(804) 993-2344
2, 3, 23, 24

CHARLOTTE COUNTY

Hilltop Farm
PO Box 146
Appomattox, VA 24522
(804) 248-6748
Complete Selection

CHESAPEAKE

Vanco Farm
734 Clearfield Avenue
Chesapeake, VA 23320
(804) 547-1433
S, Complete Selection

CHESTERFIELD COUNTY

Kelmarbi Farm
4400 Kelmarbi Road
Colonial Heights, VA 23834
(804) 526-4369
Complete Selection

CRAIG COUNTY

Mountain Grove
Route 1, Box 147-F
New Castle, VA 24127
(703) 544-7285
Complete Selection

CULPEPER COUNTY

Moormont Orchard
Route 1, Box 464
Rapidan, VA 22733
1-800-572-2262 (VA toll free),
(703) 425-9657 (DC & MD), (703)
672- 2730 (Rapidan area)
G, P, A

Rapidan Berry Gardens
PO Box 55
Rapidan, VA 22733
(703) 672-4235 or
(toll free) (800) 552-2379
Complete Selection

DINWIDDIE COUNTY

Bains' Produce Patch
Route 2, Box 81
Dinwiddie, VA 23841
(804) 478-5732
S, 2, 4, 7, 25, 10

Elmwood Farm
Route 6, Box 40
Petersburg, VA 23803
(804) 733-5255
Complete Selection

Glen Evans
General Delivery
Carson, VA 23830
(804) 246-4581; 458-3436
10, 8, 27, 6, 29

Jarratt's Produce
Route 1, Box 90
Petersburg, VA 23805
(804) 732-1193
Complete Selection

Raymond C. Mann
Route 1, Box 39
Church Road, VA 23833
(804) 265-5665
Complete Selection

Mayhew's Garage
Route 1, Box 61
Church Road, VA 23833
(804) 265-5747
  2, 4, 25, 16

Woodland
Route 1, Box 47-A
Ford, VA 23850
(804) 265-8638
  2, 11, 5, 25, 10

FAIRFAX COUNTY

Potomac Vegetable Farms
9627 Leesburg Pike
Vienna, VA 22180
(703) 759-2119
  Complete Selection

FAUQUIER COUNTY

Hartland Orchard
Markham, VA 22643
(703) 364-2316
  A, P, N, SC

Manor Lane Farm of
Warrenton
Route 2, Box 103
Warrenton, VA 22186
(703) 347-4883 (May- October) or
(703) 347-7267
  S, 24, 21, 10

FREDERICK COUNTY

Raspberry Ridge Farms
Route 1, Box 273
Winchester, VA 22601
(703) 662-4552
  16, 2, 25

HANOVER COUNTY

Ashland Berry Farm
Route 2, Box 156
Beaverdam, VA 23015
(804) 798-3371
  Complete Selection

Cedarline Farm
Route 1, Box 52-D
Hanover, VA 23069
(804) 746-3390
  2, 4, 19, 10, 8, 27

Kruger's Orchard
Route 6, Box 238
Mechanicsville, VA 23111
(804) 779-3812
  P, 2, 8, 10

ISLE OF WIGHT COUNTY

Sutton A. Burroughs
Route 1, Box 855
Windsor, VA 23487
(804) 242-6641
  Complete Selection

Stringwood Farm and Nursery
Box 242, Route 1
Carrsville, VA 23315
(804) 562-5734
  S, 2, 4, 16

KING WILLIAM COUNTY

Bell Acre Farm
Box 504
King William, VA 23086
(804) 769-3491; 769-3449
  S, B, 1, 5, 16, 24, 23, 3

LOUDOUN COUNTY

Chantilly Farm Market
Route 2, Box 238-B
Leesburg, VA 22075
(703) 777-8527
  S, 16, 21

Cochran's Vegetable Farm
PO Box 3
Lincoln, VA 22078
(703) 338-7248; 338-7002
  S, Complete Selection

High Hill Orchards
Route 1, Box 14
Round Hill, VA 22141
(703) 338-7997; and metro area
471-1448 (to toll free/ dial
direct)
   S, Complete Selection

Wheatland Vegetable Farms
Route 1, Box 78
Purcellville, VA 22132
(703) 882-3996
   S, Complete Selection

MONTGOMERY COUNTY

O'Dell's Crow's Nest Farm
Route 2, Box 356-A
Blacksburg, VA 24060
(703) 552-4195
   S, P, 1, 6, 2, 4, 25, 10,
   27, 8, 29, 21

ORANGE COUNTY

Double "B" Farm, Inc.
Box 154-C
Rhoadesville, VA 22542
(703) 854-4550 or
1-800-572-2261 toll free
(seasonal)
   S, 16, 2, 4, 6, 25, 18, 23, 21

ROCKINGHAM COUNTY

Gentle Giant Farm
Route 1, Box 170-E
Port Republic, VA 24471
(703) 234-8827
   S, RR, BT, 16, 6, 19

SHENANDOAH COUNTY

Walters' Fruit Farm
Route 2, Box 186
Edinburg, VA 22824
(703) 984-8482
   S, SC, Pl

SPOTSYLVANIA COUNTY

Belvedere Plantation
Star Route Twt, Box 125
Fredericksburg, VA 22401
(703) 371-8494 or 690- 4949
toll free (no. VA & DC)
   S, BT, 6, 29, 16, Snow Peas

Rick and Van's
Route 4, Box 95-B
Fredericksburg, VA 22401
(703) 775-7890
   S, Complete Selection

VIRGINIA BEACH

Bay Breeze Farms
1100 McClanan Lane
Virginia Beach, VA 23456
(804) 721-3288
   16, 2, 10, 4

HORSE EVENTS

   There are many opportunities for the weekend pleasure-seeker to attend horse shows and races throughout the mid-Atlantic area. In contrast to thoroughbred flat and harness races at commercial tracks, hunt club, steeplechase, and polo events also provide a chance for picnicking or "tailgating." (Tailgating refers to the use of the tailgate of a station wagon from which to observe events and to picnic.)

Steeplechase racing, sometimes called point-to-point racing, is a race over hurdles made of brush, timber, stone walls, or water obstacles. Generally the course covers two to four miles over open country. Records of the sport date back to Xenophon (431-355 B.C.). The name is derived from the use of church steeples as landmarks on a course.

Horse shows are held throughout the area covered by the *Weekender's Guide to the Four Seasons* and range from the prestigious Washington (DC) International to 4-H pony shows. The shows have organized programs of exhibitions, demonstrations, and competitions of various types and breeds of horses and riding skills. The show divisions include hunter, jumper, saddle horses, pony (Shetland, Welsh, etc.), Appaloosa, cutting horses, quarter horses, and many others. The equitation events are a test of the rider's skill in controlling the horse. Dressage is a ring event where the horses are trained to execute intricate movements, such as changing gaits, pivoting, and moving laterally. Dressage is one of the three combined events that make up the Olympic equestrian competition. The other two events are cross-country and jumping. Hunters and jumpers are required to jump obstacles either in the ring or the open, and the test of the horse is to complete the course in the fastest time without knocking down obstacles, disobeying the rider, or falling. The jumper course and requirements are similar to the hunter's, except that the jumper has higher and wider obstacles to clear. The American Horse Shows Association sets standards for competition, licenses, judges, and stewards, and presents annual awards.

A fairly new event in the mid-Atlantic area is the carriage or driving competition. In this event, horses pull carriages or carts over a course and are judged on their performance and skill in avoiding obstacles.

A representative sampling of the many equestrian events that the public can enjoy is listed below.

Grand National, Butler, MD, Western Run Valley. Two steeplechase races and one flat race. April.

My Lady's Manor Hunt Race Meet, Monkton, MD, St James Church. Point-to-point steeplechase over timber fences. April.

Harrisburg Horse Show, Grantville, PA, Penn National Race Course. More than 100 classes of hunters and jumpers. Late April. (717) 697-2936.

Maryland Hunt Cup Race, Glyndon, MD, Worthington Valley. World's most difficult timber steeplechase race. (Winner eligible for English Grand National competition.) Last Saturday in April.

Fairfax Hunt Steeplechase Races, Leesburg, VA, Belmont Plantation. Six sanctioned races, including timber and brush races. Third weekend in April; third Saturday after Labor Day. (703) 532-2257.

Frederick Horse and Pony Club Show, Ijamsville, MD, Ijamsville Pony Club Grounds. Junior, hunter, and English equitation classes. Late April. (301) 831-7048.

Loudoun Hunt Spring Point-to-Point Races, Leesburg, VA, Oatlands. Steeplechase races. Late April. (703) 777-3174.

Virginia Gold Cup, Warrenton, VA. Point-to-point steeplechase race. First Saturday in May. (703) 347-2612.

Winterthur Point-to-Point Steeplechase, Winterthur, DE, Winterthur Museum Grounds. Five steeplechase races and horse-drawn carriage parade. First Sunday in May. (302) 656-8591 ext. 392.

Preakness Stakes, Baltimore, MD, Pimlico Race Course. Second race in Triple Crown of thoroughbred racing. Mid-May.

Fair Hill Steeplechase Race, Fair Hill, MD, Fair Hill Fairgrounds. Steeplechase race, pari-mutuel wagering, picnicking. One race in late May; one late October. (301) 398-6565.

Yearling Show, Maryland Horse Breeders Association, Timonium, MD, Timonium Fairgrounds. Yearling show of Maryland-bred thoroughbreds. Third week in May. (301) 252-2100.

My Lady's Manor Driving Club Show, Monkton, MD, St. James Church Show Grounds. Carriage competition for single and multiple ponies and horses, ring and cross-country obstacle course, antique carriages. June.

Burdette Tomlin Hospital Horse Show, Clermont, NJ, Meadow Creek Farm (Cape May area). Benefit show, includes hunters, jumpers, western, and ponies. June. (609) 235-5623.

Upperville Colt and Horse Show, Upperville, VA, Upperville Horse Show Grounds. Oldest horse show in U.S. Hunters, jumpers, juniors. First week in June. (703) 554-8400.

Loudoun Pony and Junior Show, Leesburg, VA, Glenwood Park. Four-day amateur children's show. Mid-June.

St. Mary's Riding Club Driving Show, Leonardtown, MD. Driving competition for ponies and horses, cross-country obstacle course. Late June. (301) 475-8595.

Maple Shade Farm Show, Grantville, PA, Penn National Race Course. More than 50 classes of hunters, jumpers, English, pleasure, road hack, and others. July. (717) 469-0321.

Mid-Atlantic Welsh Pony and Junior Show, Middleburg, VA, Foxcroft School. Mid-July. (703) 567-4248.

Delaware State Fair, Harrington, DE, Harrington Fairgrounds. Four-day event, competition and show. Last week in July. (302) 398-3269.

Howard County Fair, West Friendship, MD, Howard County Fairgrounds. Arabians, ponies, Appaloosas, hunters, quarter horses. Third full week in August. (301) 371-6670.

Nut Temple Arab Mount Horse Show, Wilmington, DE, Carousel Farms. Competition in 39 classes of all types of horses, includes hack, hunter, sidesaddle events. Mid-August. (302) 571-7748.

West Virginia State Fair, Lewisburg, WV, State Fairgrounds. Six-day event with 71 classes, including western, plantation, three- and five-gaited, harness, and walking horses. Third week of August. (304) 645-1090.

Maryland State Fair, Timonium, MD, Timonium Fairgrounds. Hunters, quarter horses, ponies. Late August. (301) 877-7374.

Ludwig's Corner Horse Show, Chestertown, PA, Ludwig's Corner Horse Show Grounds. Two-day fair, includes hunter, jumper, and carriage competition. Labor Day weekend. (609) 235-5623.

Splendor in Horses Show, Ocean City, MD, Francis Scott Key Motel. Four-day competition of hunters, jumpers, pleasure, and western. Weekend after Labor Day. (301) 272-1727.

Potomac Valley Dressage Association Horse Show, Upper Marlboro, MD, Prince George's Equestrian Center. Dressage events and crafts show. Early September. (301) 952-4740.

Carriage Drive to the Great Frederick Fair, Frederick, MD, Carriage Museum Society. Carriages with horse teams, competition. Late September. (301) 694-1650.

Morven Park Fall Race Meet, Leesburg, VA, Morven Park. Steeplechase races—five brush and one flat race. First Saturday in October. (703) 777-2414.

Virginia Fall Race Meet, Middleburg, VA, Glenwood Park. Steeplechase races over brush and timber fences and a flat course. Early October. (703) 347-2612.

Atlantic Shore Memorial Hospital Show, Smithville, NJ, Mattix Run. Benefit show, includes jumpers, carriages, western, and hunters. Early October. (609) 235-5623.

Tri-County Open Dressage, Wilmington, DE, Bellevue State Park. Dressage events, including events for handicapped riders. Early October. (302) 798-2207.

Morven Park Carriage Drive, Leesburg, VA, Morven Park. Competition in antique carriages, driven in conjunction with Carriage Museum. Mid-October. (703) 777-2414.

American Championship Rodeo Finals, Salisbury, MD, Wicomico Civic Center. Mid-October. (301) 742-3201.

Patapsco Valley 25-Mile Competitive Trail Ride, Marriottsville, MD, Patapsco State Park. League of Maryland Horsemen competition. Mid-October. (301) 484-1793, 825-6400.

Washington International Horse Show, Largo, MD, Capital Centre. More than 800 horses from all 50 states and foreign nations compete. Concession booths sell everything from horse-related gift items to antiques. Last week in October. (301) 840-0281.

Washington International Race, Laurel, MD, Laurel Race Course. Thoroughbred race, with horses from U.S. and other nations. Early November. (301) 840-0281.

Carriage Parade, Frederick, MD, Rose Hill Manor. A parade of antique carriages. Early November. (301) 663-8687.

For further information on local clubs and associations, contact:

American Horse Shows Assn., New York, NY 10022, (212) 972-2472.

International Side-Saddle Organization, Mt. Holly, NJ 08060, (609) 261-1777.

National Steeplechase and Hunt Assn., Elmont, NY 11003, (516) 437-6666.

United States Combined Training Assn., South Hamilton, MA 01982, (617) 468-7133.

U.S. Dressage Federation, Lincoln, NE 68501, (402) 474-7632.

▄▄▄▄▄▄▄ HUNTING AND FISHING ▄▄▄▄▄▄▄

Despite the traffic jams, high-rise apartment buildings, and crowds that seem to fill the lives of people living on the mid-Atlantic eastern shores, there is a great bounty of open lands, forests, rushing rivers, and clear lakes all with enough fish and game to delight any sportsman or woman. In this region the angler can pit his skills against saltwater fish or freshwater fish. The small game populations provide the hunter with rabbit, raccoon, opossum, and many other small mammals. White-tailed deer and bear will challenge even the experienced hunter's ability. Quail, grouse, dove, and waterfowl thrive in this region and can be hunted in almost all the areas open to the sport.

The Game and Fish Departments of each state have pamphlets and information that can be obtained free of charge. Useful local information can usually be obtained at any local sporting goods store.

DELAWARE

The state of Delaware hosts large concentrations of wintering waterfowl, especially Canada geese. The white-tailed deer herd is healthy and provides hours of pleasure for the big-game hunter. For the small-game enthusiast, quail, squirrel, cottontail, woodcock, and raccoon provide excellent hunting throughout the state.

Delaware Bay is alive with sea trout and bluefish, while the lower bays provide small blues, flounder, tang, and rockfish. For the freshwater angler, the state offers over 30 state-owned millponds stocked with panfish, pickerel, and bass.

For further information concerning facilities, state regulations, seasons, limits, and directions to designated areas, contact:

Division of Fish and Wildlife
PO Box 1401
Dover, DE 19901
(302) 736-4431

MARYLAND

Hunting in Maryland ranges from the delta regions of the Eastern Shore through the panhandle of central Maryland to the mountains of western Maryland. The list begins with white-tailed deer and sika deer; the white-tails are distributed abundantly throughout the state.

Few areas of the Atlantic Flyway can match Maryland's nearly 4,000 miles of tidal marshlands, most of which are considered prime duck and goose hunting territory. Some of the finest Canada goose hunting can be found on Maryland's Eastern Shore. In addition, bird hunters will find bobwhite quail from the Eastern Shore to the foothills of western Maryland, where ruffed grouse take over the hunter's interest. Central and southern Maryland host ring-neck pheasants, cottontail rabbits, and squirrels.

Maryland's Public Hunting Lands program, involving thousands of acres, encompasses the full spectrum of hunting opportunities. The list is swelled by annual migrations of mourning dove, king rail, clapper, sora and Virginia rail, woodcock, and snipe.

Mountain lake... reservoir... the Chesapeake Bay... wide river... tidal and marshy creeks... the Atlantic Ocean. That's Maryland fishing. Rockfish (striped bass), the state's official fish, are found in the tidal area of the Chesapeake Bay. Favorite methods are trolling, bottom fishing, casting surface plugs or bucktails, or by drifting live eels, peelers, or shrimp. The Chesapeake and its tributaries are home for white perch, bluefish, weakfish (grey trout) and, in lesser numbers, speckled trout. In fact, more than 200 species of fish frequent the Bay during a year. Flounder can be caught in Tangier Sound. Among the big battlers in the Bay are channel bass (red drum) and black drum.

For the bluewater angler, white marlin, blue marlin, dolphin, wahoo, and big bluefish are daily fare for the cruisers running off Ocean City. Ocean fishing doesn't end on boats. Surf fishermen land bluefish, weakfish, channel bass, and kingfish at Assateague Island.

Freshwater anglers like Garrett County's huge Deep Creek Lake for exciting smallmouth bass fishing. The smallmouth join a good resident population of largemouth bass and walleye.

Contact:

Fishing
Tidewater Administration
Department of Natural Resources,
Tawes State Office Building
Annapolis, MD 21401
(301) 269-3765

Hunting
Department of Natural Resources,
Park and Wildlife Service,
Tawes State Office Building
Annapolis, MD 21401
(301) 269-3195

NEW JERSEY

The southern counties of New Jersey offer a wide variety of hunting opportunities. This state's wildlife resources include deer and bear and small game such as turkey, rabbit, and squirrel, and waterfowl such as Canada and snow geese.

The New Jersey coast has provided big game fish for anglers since 1920, while sport-fishing trips to submarine canyons 70 to 90 miles offshore began in the mid-1950s. Yellowfin, bigeye, albacore tuna, and white and blue marlin inhabit these waters in abundance. Inland, there are more than 2,000 acres of warmwater lakes and ponds and more than 100 miles of rivers and streams where trout and other warmwater species are available.

For further information concerning facilities, state regulations, seasons, limits, and directions to designated areas, contact:

Division of Fish, Game and Wildlife
363 Pennington Avenue (Mail: CN 400)
Trenton, NJ 08625
(609) 292-9410 (ask for Information and Education Division)

Hunting in New Jersey can also be done on private property, state and national forests, and other public properties under certain circumstances; inquire from the state office or county or local authorities.

NORTH CAROLINA

The variety and excellence of North Carolina's sport fishing, both salt- and freshwater, is unmatched in the eastern United States. The Outer Banks region contains five sounds (Currituck, Albemarle, Pamlico, Core, and Bogue) and four inlets (Oregon,

Hatteras, Ocracoke, and Beaufort) that provide excellent inland and offshore fishing. Due to this region's close proximity to the Gulf Stream (12 miles), there is year-round fishing. Offshore fishing is usually done from specialized sport-fishing cruisers equipped with twin engines, ship to shore radios, and other nautical accoutrements. These cruisers are manned by a captain and mate(s), many of whom developed big game fishing off the North Carolina coast. On an offshore fishing expedition, you can catch reef fish, sailfish, dolphin, blue marlin, and white marlin. The inlets provide another source of saltwater fishing. From trolling charters you can catch channel bass, bluefish, tarpon, trout, cobia, and several other species.

For further information on offshore and inland fishing, contact:

North Carolina Wildlife Resources Commission
Archdale Building, 512 N. Salisbury Street
Raleigh, NC 27611
(919) 733-3391

North Carolina Travel and Tourism Division
430 N. Salisbury Street
Raleigh, NC 27611
(919) 733-4171; (800) 847-4862

Though eastern North Carolina is known primarily for its fishing, there are some hunting opportunities available. Hunting in North Carolina is highly regulated; thus anyone interested in exploring hunting grounds should seek information from the County Attorney's Office, the Licenses Division, or the Law Enforcement Division (for seasons and locations) at:

North Carolina Wildlife Resources Commission
512 N. Salisbury Street
Archdale Building
Raleigh, NC 27611

Licenses Division: (919) 733-7896
Law Enforcement Division: (919) 733-7191

For hunting on federal lands, state regulations and license requirements also apply. For specific information to these coastal federal areas, contact:

Bodie Island (waterfowl): Superintendent, Cape Hatteras National Seashore, Route 1, PO Box 675, Manteo, NC 27954, (919) 473-2111
Camp Lejeune: Base Maintenance Officer, c/o Natural Resources, Camp Lejeune, NC 28542, (919) 451-5226
Cherry Point Marine Base, Havelock, NC

Dismal Swamp National Wildlife Refuge, PO Box 349, Suffolk, VA 23434

Mackay Island National Wildlife Refuge, Suite 218, 287 Pembroke Office Park, Virginia Beach, VA 23462

Mattamuskeet National Wildlife Refuge: Route 1, Box N-2, Swanquarter, NC 27885, (919) 926-4021

Pungo Refuge (deer): Pungo National Wildlife Refuge, PO Box 267, Plymouth, NC 27962, (919) 793-2143

PENNSYLVANIA

South central and southeastern Pennsylvania offer a wide variety of hunting for both big and small game.

The 11-county south central region, known for its rugged game-filled ridges, is abundant with deer, squirrel, grouse, dove, quail, woodchuck, and pheasant. Waterfowl can also be found throughout much of the area.

The 12-county area of southeastern Pennsylvania has excellent farm game hunting. This part of the state supports nearly one-third of the state hunting licenses with its abundant population of deer, ducks, geese, doves, squirrels, and rabbits. The Middle Creek Wildlife Management Area, located in this region, is one of Pennsylvania's finest facilities for waterfowl hunting and fishing. The lakes, rivers, and streams of this region provide anglers with plenty of varied fishing excitement.

Some waters of Pennsylvania are designated "fly fishing only open to youth and handicapped," or "catch and release" only. Always check the rules governing the area where you intend to fish or hunt. For further information and specific details concerning licensing, facilities, state regulations, seasons, limits, and directions to designated areas, contact:

Pennsylvania Game Commission
License Division
PO Box 1567
Harrisburg, PA 17120
(717) 787-6286

VIRGINIA

Sometimes running furiously, other times meandering quietly through the silent Civil War battlefields are some of Virginia's best known and most loved fishing waters. From the Back Bay of Virginia Beach to Lee County Lake, the angler can pit his ability against the smallmouth bass, blue marlin, channel cat, or any one of 35 species of freshwater fish or 32 species of saltwater fish.

This state is also blessed with a variety of terrain which offers an excellent selection of mammals. One mammal unique to this state is the opossum. Whether it is white-tailed deer or mink the hunter is after, Virginia has it. For further information concerning licensing, facilities, hunting seasons, and regulations, contact:

> Virginia Game and Inland Fisheries Commission
> PO Box 11104
> Richmond, VA 23230
> (804) 257-1000

Private Corporation Lands

The following corporations provide hunting for the public. In all, some 700,000 acres of land have been made available at some expense to the corporations.

Chesapeake Corporation of Virginia. West Point, VA 23181. A 2,700-acre tract in Bedford and Campbell counties plus 2,300 acres in Nelson County posted with Game Commission Cooperative Hunting Area signs. No permit required. About 190,000 acres in other counties, much of which is open to those who obtain a $5 permit. Lands are posted. Maps sent free on request.

Continental Forest Industries. PO Box 1041, Hopewell, VA 23860. Approximately 300,000 acres of land throughout the state. Individual permits are $8 each and cover the general season only. Applications should be made about the first of October. Company boundary lines are well marked. A state map is available for $2.

Union Camp Corporation. Franklin, VA 23851. Sixteen thousand acres in Brunswick County near Edgerton, south of Route 58— several tracts. Managed on a cooperative basis by Game Commission. No permit required. Posted. Maps available.

Champion International Corporation. Halifax Timber Division, PO Box 309, Roanoke Rapids, NC 27870. Thirty-four thousand acres. Cost of permit is $2 for company land in an individual county and $5 for company land statewide. Location maps are not available.

Glatfelter Pulp Wood Company. PO Box 868, Fredericksburg, VA 22401. Annual individual permit is available for $7.

Weyerhaeuser Company. Plymouth, NC 27962. More than 11,000 acres. Most open to public hunting without permit. No tract identification or maps.

Appalachian Power Company. PO Box 2021, Roanoke, VA 24022. A 6,000-acre Smith Mountain tract in Bedford and Pittsylvania counties managed on cooperative basis by Game Commission. No permit required. Maps available from Regional Planning Commission, PO Box 456, Chatham, VA 24531. Additional 1,300 acres in other counties open to hunting without permit unless posted otherwise. No maps or descriptions.

Lester Properties. Forestland Division, Box 4784, Martinsville, VA 24112. Twenty thousand acres in Henry, Franklin, Pittsylvania, and Halifax counties. No maps. Free permit on request with name, address, hunting license number, and self-addressed stamped envelope.

Owens-Illinois Company. Big Island, VA 24526. Thirty-five thousand acres in Botetourt and Rockbridge counties. Posted with Game Commission Cooperative Hunting Area signs. No permit required. No maps.

Westvaco. Virginia Woodlands, Route 3, Box WV, Appomattox, VA 24522. Thirty-six hundred acres of public hunting area. Posted. Westvaco permit not necessary. Maps available. Seventy thousand acres in 18 piedmont counties open to permit hunting. Applicants should submit $5 permit fee, hunting license number, and self-addressed stamped envelope. Maps available for most counties.

WEST VIRGINIA

West Virginia's streams and lakes host all of the best freshwater fish including bass, trout, pike, walleye, bluegill, and catfish. The eastern region of the state is a fisherman's delight. The once nearly extinct trout population now thrives. Today six hatcheries stock the ponds and streams throughout the state with beautiful specimens of rainbow, golden, and brown trout. Some waters are designated "Flyfishing Only" or "Catch and Release Only"; please be sure to check all regulations governing the area where you intend to fish.

Large populations of rabbits, woodchucks, migratory and nonmigratory birds, and deer inhabit the eastern portion of West Virginia. Only the eastern region permits hunting of black bear and turkey. For further information, contact:

West Virginia Department of Natural Resources
Division of Wildlife Resources
Charleston, WV 25305
(304) 348-2771

■ INDUSTRIAL TOURS ■

If you have ever wanted to see firsthand the marathon activity of a seaport, or watch lead and sand be transformed into translucent hand-blown crystal, here is your chance. Both adults and children can get a closer look at how the products they use are manufactured and distributed, as well as the diversity of jobs in industry and public services.

The companies listed below offer tours of their facilities under widely differing conditions. For safety reasons, pets are virtually always forbidden. Children must be at least six in most cases, and sometimes older. Unless a plant specifies that walk-ins are welcome, an appointment (often a week or two in advance) is required. Groups of more than 10 should always reserve in advance. Individuals are sometimes able to join existing groups.

Abbreviations are used to indicate the kinds of visitors that the listed plants are equipped to handle. These are: S—school groups; G—groups from the general public; I—individuals or small family groups (either alone or as additions to existing groups); A—appointment required; W—walk-ins are welcome.

DELAWARE

Air Products & Chemicals (extracts nitrogen and oxygen from atmosphere), Route 9, Delaware City, DE 19706
Contact: Plant Manager   (302) 834-4504   (S,G,A)

Dayett Mills, Route 72, Old Baltimore Pike, Newark, DE 19702
Contact: President   (302) 731-1500   (S,G,I,A)

Delaware Division of Fish and Wildlife (fisheries and hatcheries information), PO Box 1401, Dover, DE 19901   (302) 736-4431

The News-Journal Company, 831 Orange Street, Box 1111, Wilmington, DE 19899
Contact: NIE Coordinator   (302) 573-2007   (S,G,A)

Port of Wilmington, Box 1191, Wilmington, DE 19899
Contact: Receptionist   (302) 571-4600   (S,G,I,A)

Summit Aviation (general airport and flight school), Flight School, N. Route 896, Middletown, DE 19709
Contact: Flight School Director   (302) 834-5400, ext. 42   (S,G,A)

Texaco Refining & Marketing (oil), Route 72, Delaware City, DE 19706
Contact: Public Relations Assistant   (302) 834-6000   (S,G,A)

MARYLAND

Black & Decker (tools), 626 Hanover Pike, Hempstead, MD 21074
Contact: Training Manager, Personnel Dept. (301) 374-4400 (S,G,A)

General Motors Assembly Plant, Box 148, 9122 Broenig Highway, Baltimore, MD 21203
Contact: Tour Coordinator   (301) 955-9508   (S,G,A)

Joseph E. Seagram & Son Distillery, 5001 Washington Boulevard, Relay, MD 21227 (or, PO Box 208, Baltimore, MD 21203)
Contact: Personnel Dept.   (301) 247-1000, ext. 300   (S,G,A)

Maryland Center for Public Broadcasting, Bonita Avenue, Owings Mills, MD 21117
Contact: Coordinator of Volunteer Services (301) 337-4264 (S,G,A)

Maryland Hatcheries and Warm Water Division, Millington, MD 21651   (301) 928-3643

Maryland Tidewater Administration, Tidal Fisheries, 580 Taylor Avenue, Annapolis, MD 21401   (301) 269-3558

NASA Goddard Visitor Center and Museum (space), Greenbelt Road, Greenbelt, MD 20771
Contact: Visitor Center   (301) 344-8981   (S,G,A)

Serta Mattress Co., Division of A.W. Industries, 8415 Ardmore Road, Landover, MD 20785
Contact: Director of Personnel   (301) 322-1000   (S,G,A)

NEW JERSEY

General Motors—Linden Assembly Plant, 1016 W. Edgar Road, Linden, NJ 07036
Contact: Supervisor of Training   (S,A)

Pequest Trout Hatchery and Natural Resources Education Center, Box 389, RR#1, Pequest Road, Oxford, NJ 07863   (S,G,I,A)

Public Service Electric and Gas (PSEG) (utility), PO Box 570, Community Affairs Dept., T10C, Newark, NJ 07101
(201) 430-5862   (S,G,A)

U.S. Coast Guard Training Center, Cape May, NJ 08204
Contact: Public Affairs Officer   (609) 884-8451, ext. 211   (S,G,I,A)

U.S. Coast Guard Station Great Egg, XPO, North Point Road, Ocean City, NJ 08226
Contact: Officer in Charge   (609) 399-0119 (S,G,I,A)

NORTH CAROLINA

North Carolina Inland Fisheries Division (fisheries and hatcheries information), Archdale Building, Room 458, 512 N. Salisbury Street, Raleigh, NC 27611   (919) 733-3633

PENNSYLVANIA

Bombergers Lebanon Bologna, Inc., RD 1, Box 940, Lebanon, PA 17041
Contact: Agnes Bender   (717) 273-6794   (I,G,W)

The Daniel Weaver Company (bologna factory), 15th Avenue and Weavertwon Road, PO Box 525, Lebanon, PA 17042
(717) 274-6100   (S,G,I,W,A for groups)

Dispatch Publishing Company, 15 E. Philadelphia Street, York, PA 17401
Contact: Mike Rossi   (717) 854-1575   (I,G,S,A)

General Telephone Company, 31 S. Beaver Street, York, PA 17401
Contact: Phelps A. Forrest   (717) 846-7878   (I,G,A)

Hershey's Chocolate World, Park Boulevard, Hershey, PA 17033
(717) 534-4913   (W)

Kountry Kraft Kitchens, S. Sheridan Street, Newmanstown, PA 17073
Contact: Dale Hurst   (215) 589-4575   (I,G,W)

Kutztown Bologna Company, 689 Kutztown Road, Myerstown, PA 17067   (800) 822-2063 (in PA); (717) 933-5626
                                        (S,G,I,W,A for groups)

Lyon Metal Products, 500 Windsor Street, York, PA 17403
(800) 433-8488   (I,G,A)

Michter's Distillery, Michter's and Distillery roads, Box 387, Schaefferstown,   PA 17088   (717) 949-6521   (I,G,W,A for groups)

Moravian Pottery and Tile Works, Route 313, Swamp Road, Doylestown, PA 18901
Contact: Charles Yeske   (215) 345-6722   (W,G,I)

Pennsylvania Commonwealth Fish Commission (fisheries and hatcheries information), PO Box 1673, Harrisburg, PA 17105
                                          (717) 787-2579

P. H. Glatfelter Company, Main Street, Spring Grove, PA 17362
Contact: Glenn Markle   (717) 225-4711   (I,G,A)

Philadelphia Water Department (three plants), Philadelphia, PA.
Contact: Water Commissioner's Office   (215) 686-3803   (S,G,I,A)

Seltzer Lebanon Bologna Company, 230 N. College Avenue, Palmyra, PA 17078   (717) 838-6336   (S,G,I,W)

VIRGINIA

Anheuser-Busch Brewery, Route 60, Williamsburg, VA 23185
Contact: Hospitality Center   (804) 253-3600   (I,G,W)

Cashuan Arabian Farms (horse raising and breeding), 2352 Princess Anne Road, Virginia Beach, VA 23456
Contact: Mrs. Cravins   (804) 340-3535   (A)

Chesapeake Corporation of Virginia (paper manufacturer), Highway 30, West Point, VA 23181
Contact: P.R. Assistant   (804) 843-5372   (I,G,A)

Franklin Equipment Company (metal equipment), Council and Carver Roads, Franklin, VA 23851.
Contact: Industrial Relations Manager   (804) 562-6111   (A,I,G)

J. P. Stevens and Company, Inc. (fabric plant), Vaughan Street, South Boston, VA 24592
Contact: George Whitted   (804) 572-2921   (A,I,G)

Norfolk Naval Base, 9809 Hampton Boulevard, Norfolk, VA 23511
Contact: Public Affairs Office   (804) 444-4071 or 444-7955
Admission charge   (I,G,W)

Philip Morris U.S.A. (cigarettes, tobacco), 3601 Commerce Road, outside Richmond, VA 23261
Contact: Public Relations Dept.   (804) 274-2000
                                    (I,G,W,A [for groups])

Portsmouth Marine Terminals, Inc. (marine operations), 2000 Seaboard Avenue, Portsmouth, VA 23704
Contact: Bill Keown   (804) 440-7000   (G,I,A)

Virginia Game and Inland Fisheries (fisheries and hatcheries information), PO Box 11104, Richmond, VA 23230   (804) 257-1000

Virginia Trout Company, Inc. (hatchery), Route 220 N., Monterey, VA 24465   (703) 468-2280   (I,G,W)

WSLS-TV, Third Street and Church Avenue S.W., Roanoke, VA 24009
Contact: Jim Dickey   (703) 981-9110   (I,G,A)

WEST VIRGINIA

Beckley Exhibition Mine (coal), PO Drawer AJ, Beckley, WV 25801.
Contact: Director of Recreation (304) 255-6386 (May 1 to Sept. 30)
(304) 252-8671, ext. 38 (Oct. 1 to April 30)
(S,G,A,W [summer only])

West Virginia Cold Water Fish Management (Director's Office—
fisheries and hatcheries information), PO Box 67, Elkins, WV 26241
(304) 636-1767

JOUSTING

Jousting, the official sport of Maryland, is still practiced
and tournaments are held in Maryland, Virginia, and West
Virginia. The competition is a test of skill on the part of the
rider, who must spear rings ranging from 1½", 1", ¾", ½"
to ¼" in size, and a test of speed for the horse. Competitors
range from teenagers to women 60 years of age.

The tournament held at Natural Chimneys, VA, is the
oldest continuously held sporting event in the United States.
This event has been held annually since 1821 and attracts
about 80 competitors. The National Championship Joust is
held on the Washington, DC Monument Grounds in October.

The following is a list of jousting tournaments held
annually.

MARYLAND

Clear Spring, Divelbiss Farm	late May
Worton Park, Kent County	early July
Chestertown	mid-July
Petersville Farmers Woods	3rd Sunday in July
Barnesville, Montgomery County	last Saturday in July
Smallwood Dutch Picnic	1st Saturday in August
Cordova, St. Joseph's Church	1st Wednesday in August
Queen Anne Fire Company	1st Sunday in August
Mechanicsville, Volunteer Fire Co.	mid-August
Port Republic, Calvert County	late August
Ridgely	586-0565, late August
Oxon Hill, Tucker Road Community Center	mid-September
St. Michael's	mid-September
Easton Airport, Eastern Shore Championship	last Sunday in September
St. Margaret's State Championship	1st Saturday in October

VIRGINIA

Hall of Fame Joust, Mt. Solon	3rd Saturday in June
Milboro Springs, Big Bend Tournament	July
Natural Chimneys, Mt. Solon	mid-August
Clifford, State Championship	late September
Millers Tavern, Essex County	mid-October

WEST VIRGINIA

Mathias	next to last weekend in July
Poultry Festival, Moorefield	last weekend in July
Heritage Weekend, Moorefield	last weekend in September
West Virginia Championship Forest Festival, Elkins	early October

For further information contact:

Maryland Jousting Association	(301) 676-4039
Natural Chimneys Regional Park, VA	(703) 350-2510
South Valley Jousting Association, WV	(304) 538-6535
	(304) 538-6037

▬▬ ORGANIZED DAY AND WEEKEND TRIPS ▬▬

Organized trips can take you places you might not otherwise visit and in ways you might not ordinarily travel, and where there are costs, they are often lower than you might pay on your own. Traveling with a group is a good way to meet people who share some of your interests, and it affords security, assistance, and a group spirit that can add a positive and relaxed atmosphere to an outing. Whether you want to go away for an afternoon, a weekend, or longer, you can find dozens of planned trips with a minimum of effort to suit your sporting, educational, social, or cultural tastes.

Clubs and societies are excellent sources for planned trips, and some are even free. Membership may be required, but some activities are open to non-members for an additional fee.

The following entries are good places to start looking for trips that may interest you. Commercial ventures, including cruises, bus tours, and outfitters, are many in number and are easily found in the Yellow Pages and your area newspapers. Many more organized day and weekend outings, such as biking and skiing, are available through the clubs and associations described elsewhere in *Weekender's Guide to the Four Seasons*. For more possibilities, look under the Special Interest Sections for your favorite activities and in the geographical sections describing the communities you would like to tour.

MEMBERSHIP CLUB ORGANIZED TRIPS

The **Richmond Ski Club,** with about 1,000 members, is open to families and singles. It usually offers four western and European ski trips, four New England trips, and six to 10 local area trips. In addition, the club has social events, tennis, canoe trips, happy hours monthly, and an annual wine and cheese party. Members receive a monthly newsletter. Write: PO Box 1048, Richmond, VA 23208. Telephone: (804) 741-3866 evenings and weekends.

The **Ski Club of Washington, DC,** with more than 6,000 members, has year-round activities. In addition to local and New England ski trips, they organize flight trips to the western states, Canada, and Europe. A sampling of the club's other activities include: sailing excursions, a Bavarian Festival, weekly volleyball, tennis, racquetball, soccer, softball, social parties, annual picnics, Saturday strolls, theater, hikes, soaring, whitewater rafting, sports classes, and instruction. Members receive a monthly newsletter. Write: 5309 Lee Highway, Arlington, VA 22207. Telephone: (703) 536-TAPE for current upcoming activities, (703) 532-7776 for information about membership.

The **Smithsonian Institution** sponsors various outings throughout the year to sites of historic and cultural interest. There are walking tours in Washington and in the immediate outlying vicinity, and longer excursions of a full day or overnight to locations in Pennsylvania, Delaware, Virginia, and New York. Examples of their tours include: the West Virginia homes of members of George Washington's family; Longwood Gardens in Pennsylvania; exploring old and new Baltimore. The tours are set up two months in advance and are open to both the general public and to members of the Smithsonian's Resident Associate Program. For information on the trips and also membership in the Resident Associate Program, write: Smithsonian Resident Associate Program, Smithsonian Institution, Washington, DC 20560 and request a copy of the newsletter. Telephone: (202) 357-3030.

The **Virginia Ski Club** is strictly a single person's club. A sample of its year-round activities include an annual golf tournament, a night at the Atlantic City casinos, weekends of Chesapeake Bay sailing and whitewater rafting, and skiing in Vermont and Colorado as well as in the mid-Atlantic region. Every year there is a trip to a resort in such locations as Hawaii and the Caribbean. Members receive a monthly newsletter. Write: Virginia Ski Club, PO Box 6284, Richmond, VA 23230. Telephone: (804) 270-7023.

CANOE TRIPS

The **Maryland Forest, Park and Wildlife Service** offers canoe trips from June through October. They vary in length from one to three days. Participants must be able to swim and no one under 12 will be accepted. For information and reservations, write: Department of Natural Resources, Maryland Forest, Park and Wildlife Service, Tawes State Office Building, Annapolis, MD 21401. Telephone: (301) 974-3771.

These Maryland outfitters offer a wide variety of guided canoe trips. Contact them for complete schedules and prices.

Pocomoke River Canoe Company. Snow Hill, MD 21863, (301) 632-3971.

River and Trail Outfitters. Route 2, Valley Road, Box 246, Knoxville, MD 21758, (301) 695-5177.

Harpers Ferry River Riders, Inc. PO Box 267, Knoxville, MD 21758, (301) 834-8051.

Patuxent River Park. RR Box 3380, Upper Marlboro, MD 20772, (301) 627-6074.

CRUISES

Cruises around the Chesapeake Bay and the Inland Waterway are available by commercial boats. Some cruises are all-day outings, others an hour or less. Depending on the company, the boats may operate all year long or only from May through September. Here is a sampling of what is available:

Smith Island from Crisfield, MD: Memorial Day through September 30, one day round trip. Telephone: Captain Alan Tyler (301) 425-2771

Patuxent River from Solomons, MD: End of May through end of October, one-hour and three-hour cruises. Telephone: Calvert Marine Museum (301) 326-3719.

Annapolis Harbor tour: 40-minute narrated tour of historic harbor includes Naval Academy, Severn River, and Chesapeake Bay Bridge. Leaves from City Dock, Annapolis, MD. Telephone: (301) 268-7600.

Chesapeake Bay and St. Michaels tour: Memorial Day through Labor Day. Seven hours on the Bay. Leaves from City Dock, Annapolis. Write: Chesapeake Marine Tours, Inc., PO Box 3323, Annapolis, MD 21403, (301) 268-7600.

Miles River tour: 90 minutes of sailing past historic landmarks dating back to the 18th century. Leaves St. Michaels, MD. Telephone: (301) 822-6201.

Baltimore Harbor tour: May through October, 90-minute narrated tour includes Federal Hill and Ft. McHenry. Telephone: (301) 727-3113.

Oxford-Bellevue Ferry: Across the Tred Avon River, MD, America's oldest established ferry service (c. 1683) takes 20 minutes. May to Labor Day. Write: Oxford, MD 21654. Telephone: (301) 226-5408.

Smith Island from Reedville, VA: May through September,

one-and-a-half-hour cruises halfway across the Bay to this remote Maryland island. For cruise and meal reservations, telephone: Island and Bay Cruises, Inc. (804) 453-3430.

Historic Chesapeake Maryland and Virginia Cruise: Seven-day cruises available during May and June include Yorktown and Williamsburg, VA, Solomons Island, St. Michaels, Crisfield, and Oxford, MD. Telephone: (800) 243-6755.

Inland Waterway Cruise from Newport News, VA: All-day cruise down Inland Waterway almost to North Carolina, including Norfolk Naval Base. Food and entertainment provided. April through October. Telephone: Wharton's Wharf Harbor Cruises (804) 245-1533 or 877-6114.

Tangier Island, VA, from Crisfield, MD: Memorial Day through October, half-day cruises to Tangier Island chartered by Captain John Smith. Write: Captain Rudy Thomas, Tangier Island, VA 23440. Telephone: (301) 968-2338. Passenger ferries also leave from the Crisfield city dock. Telephone: (301) 425-2631.

Potomac River Cruises of varied lengths and destinations are available through the Washington Boat Lines, Inc. Trips include Mt. Vernon and Alexandria, evening dance cruises on weekends. Leave from Pier #4, Sixth and Water streets S.W., Washington, DC, or Torpedo Factory Dock, Cameron and Union streets, Alexandria, VA. Telephone: (202) 554-8000.

Mystic Whaler Windjammer Cruises from Annapolis, MD: May through October, one- to five-day Chesapeake Bay cruises aboard a two-masted, gaffed-rigged sailing ship with auxiliary diesel engines. Passengers may relax or help the crew set sails or handle lines. Write: 7 Holmes Street, Mystic, CT 06355. Telephone: (800) 243-0416 or (203) 536-4218.

Jamestown Island Cruise from Newport News, VA: All-day cruise down the James River, passing by the Idle Fleet, a collection of more than 150 ships anchored in the James River past Jamestown. At Jamestown Island, replicas of the ships used by the first English-speaking settlers can be seen, as well as the original settlement at Jamestown. Food and entertainment provided. April through October. Telephone: Wharton's Wharf Harbor Cruises (804) 245-1533 or 877-6114.

Rappahannock River Cruise from Tappahannock, VA: All-day cruise up the Rappahannock to Ingleside Plantation Vineyards for winery tour, wine tasting, and lunch. The cruise continues to Saunder's Wharf, the last remaining steamboat wharf on the river. While there, visitors also tour Wheatlands and its gardens. May through October. Telephone: Rappahannock River Cruises (804) 333-4656.

HIKING

Appalachian Trail Clubs. The Appalachian Trail is a 2,075-mile stretch covering 14 states from Maine to Georgia. More than 60 clubs help maintain the trail with patrols and caretaker programs. The following are clubs which participate in the Appalachian Trail program and are within 200 miles of Baltimore, Washington, and Richmond. Additional information may be obtained from the Appalachian Trail Conference, PO Box 807, Harpers Ferry, WV, 25425-0807. Telephone: (304) 535-6331.

DELAWARE
Brandywine Valley Outing Club, M. J. Brinton, President, Box 7033, Wilmington, DE 19810

MARYLAND
Maryland A.T. Club, Kent Roberts, President, 252 Frederick Street, Hagerstown, MD 21740

Mountain Club of Maryland, Terri Wetzel-Eckard, President, 4809 Roland Avenue, Apt. 2-B, Baltimore, MD 21210

PENNSYLVANIA
AMC-Delaware Valley Chapter, Katherine C. Cox, Chairman, 476 Kerr Lane, Springfield, PA 19064

Batona Hiking Club, Oreste Unti, President, 600 E. Phil-Ellena Street, Philadelphia, PA 19119

Blue Mountain Eagle Climbing Club, Robert A. Fisher, President, 2118 Fairview Avenue, Reading, PA 19606

Keystone Trails Association, David L. Raphael, President, 230 E. Hartswick Avenue, State College, PA 16801

Springfield Trail Club, Mrs. Mary Lou Zimmerman, President, 43 S. Malin Road, Broomall, PA 19008

Susquehanna A.T. Club, Robert H. Keck, President, 67 W. Caracas Avenue, Hershey, PA 17033

York Hiking Club, R. Ronald Gray, President, 89 W. Main Street, Dallastown, PA 17313

VIRGINIA
Mount Rogers A.T. Club, David Thomas, President, Route 7, Box 248, Abingdon, VA 24210

Natural Bridge A.T. Club, Edwin R. Page, President, 2316 Glencove Place, Lynchburg, VA 24503

Old Dominion A.T. Club, Lynne Overman, President, PO Box 25283, Richmond, VA 23260

Roanoke A.T. Club, Mary F. Stewart, President, 4551 Nelms Lane N.E., Roanoke, VA 24019

Tidewater A.T. Club, Reese R. Lukei, Jr., President, PO Box 8246, Norfolk, VA 23503

Virginia Tech Outing Club, John Wise, President, PO Box 459, Blacksburg, VA 24060

Virginia Trails Association, 13 W. Maple, Alexandria, VA 22301

WASHINGTON, DC
Potomac Appalachian Trail Club, Bill Hutchinson, President,
1718 N Street N.W., Washington, DC 20036

WEST VIRGINIA
Appalachian Trail Conference, Box 236, Harpers Ferry, WV
25425
West Virginia Scenic Trails Association, PO Box 4042, Charleston,
WV 25304

The **Mountain Club of Maryland** has an extensive schedule of
hiking trips; weekend and weekday hike opportunities are available
every week and backpacking trips are scheduled every month. Rock
climbing, canoeing, rafting, and other activities are also offered
periodically. Member of the Appalachian Trail Conference. Contact
Terri Wetzel-Eckhard, 4809 Roland, 2-B, Baltimore, MD 21210,
(301) 377-6266.

The **Virginia Tech Outing Club**, which is mainly, but not solely,
comprised of college students, offers hiking, backpacking, canoeing,
kayaking, skiing, rock climbing, and caving. Member of the Appalachian Trail Conference. Write: PO Box 459, Blacksburg, VA 24060.

The **American Hiking Society** is a national membership organization of clubs and individuals who are interested in protecting foot
trails. It sponsors seminars on such subjects as nature photography,
backpacking, and how to interest friends in hiking. It runs a trail
maintenance program for volunteers. It works with the U.S. Forest
Service, providing names of volunteers who can travel to U.S.
forests throughout the country in order to clear trails for one- and
two-week periods. For information, write: American Hiking Society,
1701 18th Street N.W., Washington, DC 20009. Telephone: (202)
234-4610.

The **Capitol Hiking Club** offers one-day hikes throughout the
year, concentrating on state parks and areas such as the Shenandoah
and the C&O Canal. Telephone: Debbie Kramer (703) 360-6554 or
Judith Van Lunen (202) 434-8518.

The **Center Hiking Club** sponsors various outdoor recreational
activities year round: hiking, backpacking (up to 40-mile trips),
cross-country skiing, canoeing, swimming, picnicking, and auto tours.
Open to everyone, including families. Trips range from Philadelphia
to North Carolina and western Maryland. Emphasis is on combining
fun and fresh air in a relaxed atmosphere. Hikes are posted in the
Washington Post Weekend Section. Write: Erna Sternheim, Center
Hiking Club, 780 Fairview Avenue, #506, Takoma Park, MD 20912.
Telephone: (301) 891-2369.

The **Sierra Club** offers hiking and other outings. Telephone
"Dial-A-Hike" (202) 547-2326 for information on current hikes in the

Washington, DC, area. For more information, write: Sierra Club, 2200 Greenery Lane, Apt. 201, Silver Spring, MD 20906.

POLO

Polo is becoming an increasingly popular sport throughout the country, and Virginia, Maryland, and eastern Pennsylvania provide excellent opportunities to sample the game at high quality levels. Polo is an exciting sport, and fast, competitive, colorful, and dangerous. You need only to see one game to appreciate the thrill of eight horses thundering across three football fields in pursuit of a baseball-sized object that can soar at 70 m.p.h.

Polo is also an excellent family outing event. Most games allow tailgating (picnicking from a station wagon) along the sidelines and there is usually plenty to watch even when the game is not going on: the bustle of grooms, riders, ponies and spectators, private parties, dogs and a menagerie of tents, pick-up trucks and horse trailers vying for space and adding flavor to the setting.

Bring your binoculars to better follow the game and your own refreshments for warm summer days. It is a good idea to call ahead for exact time and directions if you have never been to a particular site before.

The speed and rapid changes of position of the players appear to make the game more complex than it actually is to the observer. The rules are easy to master, and knowing them will of course enhance the pleasure of watching. Playing polo is a challenge since you need to learn to ride first. Still, you need not own your own horse or have a polo-playing buddy to get started. The Potomac Polo Club in Potomac, MD, offers a full curriculum of lessons for every level of rider and player. Potomac Polo Club, 5101 Wisconsin Avenue N.W., Washington, DC 20016, (301) 972-7241; (202) 362-0840; (301) 983-1555.

The sport's national organization is the U.S. Polo Association, which can supply interested persons with more information (1301 W. 22nd Street, Oak Brook, IL 60521, (312) 654-1631). Many of the following clubs belong to the USPA's Eastern Circuit:

Brandywine Polo Club   (215) 268-8692
101 East Street Road, Kennett Square, PA 19348   444-3300
    Field located at corner of Newark and Polo roads. Games Sundays at 3:00 p.m. (alternate with Mallet Hill Polo Club). Admission charge.

Chukker Valley Farms Polo Club   No phone
RFD 1, Gilbertsville, PA 19525
    Field located in Gilbertsville, PA.

Farmington Hunt Club   (804) 295-0547
    Field located on Garth Road, Charlottesville, VA. Games May,
June, July; Fridays at 7:30 p.m. Admission charge.

Mallet Hill Polo Club, Contact: Brandywine Polo Club (see above)
    Field at corner of Forest Manor and Ewing roads, Cochransville,
PA. Games Sundays at 3:00 p.m. (alternate with Brandywine Polo
Club). Admission free.

Middleburg Polo Club   (703) 554-8116
    Field located off Route 50 west of Middleburg, VA. Games
Sundays; times vary. Admission charge.

National Capital Polo Association   (202) 362-3095 (Jack Sted)
(Lincoln Mall Polo Club)   (202) 426-6841 (National Park Service)
    Field located west of Tidal Basin between Independence Ave-
nue and Ohio Drive N.W., Washington, DC. Games Sundays at 3:00
p.m.

Potomac Polo Club   (301) 983-1555
10250 River Road, Potomac, MD 20854
    Field located at Hughes and River roads, Potomac, MD. Games
Sundays, usually at 4:00 p.m but times vary. Shows and entertainment frequently precede games. High-goal invitational tournaments
played several times during season.

Rappahannock Polo Club   (703) 937-4177
Castleton, VA 22716

University of Virginia Polo Club   (703) 554-8116
    Field located in Charlottesville, VA. Games Fridays at 9:00 p.m.
and Sunday afternoons. Admission charge.

RAILROADS

    Railfans at this end of the country have a lot going for
them. Because many American railroads were begun in the
East, there are many opportunities locally to see restored
engines, passenger cars, and other railway memorabilia displays. Some museums offer rides on restored trains. Prices
vary depending on the distance traveled; some trains go only
a few miles, others travel 50 miles or more. You will also find
that there are hundreds of other railfans in this area who
have organized club meetings and frequent excursions on
vintage trains.

DELAWARE

The **Wilmington and Western Steam Railroad**, in
Greenbank at the junction of Routes 2 and 41, has regularly
scheduled trips to nearby towns. The train runs on weekends
year round, and there is also an open house at the Marshallton
engine terminal the last weekend in April. Other special
excursions are arranged throughout the year. Telephone:
(302) 998-1930.

The **New Castle and Frenchtown Railroad** ticket office
is at Battery Park in New Castle. This was one of America's
oldest railroads. A section of track is nearby.

MARYLAND

The **Brunswick Museum and Art Gallery** in Brunswick,
two miles off Route 340 southwest of Frederick, is the home
of the Brunswick Model Railroad Club and Sidetrack Gift
Shop. The museum has an extensive collection of old trains,
including a circa 1925 wooden caboose. Open April through
December, Saturday, 10:00 a.m. to 4:00 p.m., and Sunday,
1:00 to 4:00 p.m. Nominal adult admission charge. Each
August the museum has a Railroad Weekend, and every
October it sponsors the Brunswick Weekend-Brunswick Railroad Days. Telephone: (301) 834-7100.

The **Ellicott City B&O Railroad Station Museum**, at
the corner of Main Street and Maryland Avenue, is America's
oldest remaining station. It offers a tour of the 1831 stone
building, a sight and sound show, and a 45-foot model of the
railroad in the Patapsco Valley from Baltimore to Ellicott
City as it was in the 1870s. Open January through March,
Saturday, 11:00 a.m. to 4:00 p.m.; Sunday, noon to 5:00 p.m.;
April through December, Wednesday through Saturday, from
11:00 a.m. to 4:00 p.m.; Sunday, noon to 5:00 p.m. Admission
charge. Telephone: (301) 461-1944.

The **National Capital Trolley Museum** in Wheaton displays a collection of passenger and work cars. There is a
visitors center, and you can take a ride on an old train. Open
weekends, Memorial Day, July 4, and Labor Day, noon to 5:00
p.m. During July and August, also open on Wednesday, noon
to 4:00 p.m. Admission free. Telephone: (301) 384-9797.

The **Western Maryland Railway Historical Society Museum**, on North Main Street in Union Bridge, has restored
trains as well as railroad memorabilia, photos, and artifacts.
Open April through December, Wednesday to Saturday, 11:00
a.m. to 4:00 p.m.; Sunday, noon to 5:00 p.m. January through
March, Saturday, 11:00 a.m. to 4:00 p.m.; Sunday, noon to

Railroads   439

5:00 p.m. Closed major holidays. Admission free. Telephone: (301) 868-5849.

Throughout the area there are a number of railroad bridges. Near Savage Mill in Savage, MD, is an iron Bollman truss bridge, the only one of its type remaining in the world. In Elkridge, MD, over the Thomas Viaduct, is a railroad bridge built between 1833 and 1835.

The railroad station in Point of Rocks, Frederick County, is still used by **Chessie System**; it is a prime example of the small-town railroad depots that served the country in the late 1800s.

Maryland Midland Railway in Westminster offers scenic four- to six-hour trips departing from Westminster and Union Bridge, traveling to and from High Field, MD. June through October. Telephone: (301) 775-7718.

PENNSYLVANIA

You can take a ride through the picturesque Aughwick Valley in an authentic steam train. The **East Broad Top Railroad** is a National Historic Landmark, on Route 522 in Orbisonia. Open daily, July and August, 11:00 a.m. to 4:00 p.m.; June, September, and October, Saturday and Sunday, 11:00 a.m. to 4:00 p.m. Telephone: (814) 447-3011.

Other rides are offered by the **Gettysburg Railroad Company** on North Washington Street in Gettysburg. Sixteen-mile round trips run June through October, Saturday and Sunday. Longer trips of 50 miles are by reservation only. Telephone: (717) 334-6932.

The **Strasburg Rail Road** and the state-owned **Railroad Museum of Pennsylvania** have such extensive collections that four of their coaches were used to film the movie *Hello Dolly*. You can take nine-mile runs on restored late-1800 railroad cars. Train rides daily, May through October; weekends only during the winter months. Museum open Monday through Saturday, 10:00 a.m. to 5:00 p.m.; Sunday, 11:00 a.m. to 5:00 p.m. Closed Election Day, Thanksgiving, Christmas, and New Year's. Adult admission charge; children under 12, free. Telephone: (717) 687-8628.

VIRGINIA

The **Virginia Museum of Transportation** in Roanoke has seven steam engines and one of the largest model train layouts in the Southeast. Open year round, Monday through Saturday, 10:00 a.m. to 5:00 p.m.; Sunday, noon to 5:00 p.m. Closed New Year's, Thanksgiving, and Christmas. Admission charge. Telephone: (703) 342-5670.

The **W&OD Railroad Regional Trail** is a uniquely shaped recreation facility, 42 miles long by 100 feet wide. Partially completed, it follows the old roadbed of the Washington and Old Dominion Railroad from the Potomac River almost to the Blue Ridge Mountains. There are bike and bridle paths along much of the trail. Old railroad stations are still standing along the trail in Vienna, Dunn Loring, East Falls Church, and Sunset Hills. Enter the trail anywhere along its 42 miles; a map is available by telephoning (703) 278-8880. Admission free. Open daily, dawn to dusk.

WEST VIRGINIA

The historic C&O station in Cass burned to the ground in 1975, but a replica has been faithfully executed on the same spot. The **Cass Railroad** offers excursions through the Monongahela National Forest to Whittaker (two and a half hours round trip) and Bald Knob (four and a half hours round trip). The company also sponsors "Railfan Weekends" in the spring and special fall color schedules during the first three weeks of October. Also in Cass, the History Museum has displays of railroad memorabilia and old photos. Regularly scheduled trips are from Memorial Day to Labor Day, Tuesday through Sunday; September and October, Saturday and Sunday. No reservations. Telephone: (304) 456-4300; toll-free in West Virginia, (800) 225-5982.

Two national railroad clubs have chapters in the area: **National Railway Historical Society** and the **Railroad Enthusiasts, Inc.** Membership as well as participation on trips are open to the general public. If you love old trains, you will find plenty of camaraderie here, as well as opportunities to learn. There are often chances to help repair old engines and cars. One RRE chapter, for example, is restoring a 1923 Pullman with the hopes of using it for excursions. Chapters in this area are:

NATIONAL RAILWAY HISTORICAL SOCIETY

Delaware
   Wilmington: Box 1261, Wilmington, DE 19899

Maryland
   Baltimore: 2107 N. Charles, Baltimore, MD 21218
   Potomac: Box 235, Kensington, MD 20795
   Western Maryland: Route 1, Box 75P, LaVale, MD 21502

New Jersey
  Jersey Central: Box 700, Clark, NJ 07066
  West Jersey: Box 101, Oaklyn, NJ 08107

North Carolina
  East Carolina: Caboose 5228, Farmville, NC 27828

Pennsylvania
  Bucktail: 127 Parkway Road, St. Mary's, PA 15857
  Central Pennsylvania: Route 2, Box 370, Lewisburg, PA 17837
  Cumberland Valley: 132 N. Sixth, Chambersburg, PA 17201
  Harrisburg: Box 3423, Shiremanstown, PA 17011
  Hawk Mountain: Box 372, Allentown, PA 18105
  Horseshoe Curve: Box 1361, Altoona, PA 16603
  Lancaster: 342 W. Fritz Avenue, Quarrysville, PA 17566
  Lehigh Valley: Route 1, Box 110, Stroudsburg, PA 18360
  Philadelphia: Box 7302, Philadelphia, PA 13101
  Pottstown: 808 James Street, Sinking Spring, PA 19608

Virginia
  Blue Ridge: 122 Berkshire Place, Lynchburg, VA 24502
  Old Dominion: Box 8583, Richmond, VA 23226
  Rivanna: Box 6321, Charlottesville, VA 22906
  Roanoke: Box 13222, Roanoke, VA 24032
  Tidewater: Box 7185 (Midtown Station), Portsmouth, VA 23707
  Winchester: Box 282, Winchester, VA 22601

West Virginia
  Collis P. Huntington: 1221 Anne Street, Huntington, WV 25703
  Pocahontas: 1604 Jefferson Street, Bluefield, WV 24701

RRE DIVISIONS

Chesapeake: Box 548, Laurel, MD 20810
Old Dominion: Box 307, Vienna, VA 22180

Far from being in competition with each other, NRHS and RRE chapters often work together to sponsor trips on old trains. One excursion on the Royal Hudson Limited, a vintage 1937 steam locomotive, took 20th-century passengers from Alexandria to Charlottesville, VA. Other trips operate to Harrisburg, Warrenton, and Keysville, VA, to Oakdale, TN, and to Strasburg, PA, where participants also ride the antique wooden passenger cars at the Railroad Museum of Pennsylvania.

If you book passage on such an excursion, come prepared with picnic baskets stocked with goodies to munch on, and—

if you are a real railfan—a tape recorder to capture the unique "tweet-tweet-choo-choo" of the particular engine pulling your train. (Veterans claim there is a subtle difference between each engine's sound.) Most of all, remember that getting there is half the fun. All aboooaard!!

ROCK CLIMBING

Although rock climbing is a popular sport in the mid-Atlantic area, it is not well organized as far as clubs and membership organizations go. On any given weekend year round, you can find dozens of enthusiasts climbing mountains and cliffs throughout the area, but few will belong to clubs.

There are, however, many general outdoor groups which sponsor organized trips as well as lessons at all levels, including beginners. Equipment shops also have frequent on-site activities as well as films and talks by area experts. Lessons are frequently given by both individual rock climbers and schools; make sure your instructor and his or her organization is qualified and has taken necessary liability and insurance precautions.

Most clubs, schools, and shops are in metropolitan areas because that is where enthusiasts live. Members or students then carpool or bus to sites. Popular spots in this area are Great Falls, MD; Old Rag Mountain, VA; and (especially for ice climbing) Shenandoah National Park, VA; Carderock and Rocks State Park, MD; and Seneca Rocks, WV (one of the best spots in the entire mid-Atlantic region).

CLUBS

Appalachian Mountain Club   (215) 328-2799
Delaware Valley Chapter, c/o 476 Kerr Lane,
Springfield, PA 19064
      (Covers Pennsylvania, Delaware, and New Jersey; AMC does
      not have chapters in other mid-Atlantic states)

Buck Ridge Ski Club   (215) 242-0714
c/o 302 Brighton Terrace, Holmes, PA 19043

Pittsburgh Boondockers Hiking Club   (412) 731-2844
c/o 553 Midland Street, Pittsburgh, PA 15221

Potomac Appalachian Trail Club   (301) 587-5062
Mountaineering Section, 1718 N Street N.W.,
Washington, DC 20036

INSTRUCTION

Open University of Washington   (202) 966-9606
3333 Connecticut Avenue N.W., Washington, DC 20008

Jesse Reynolds,* The Outdoor School, Inc.   (703) 471-0171
1050 Knight Lane, Herndon, VA 22070

Steven Schneider,*
Northcountry Mountaineering, Inc.   (301) 327-8194
1602 Shakespeare Street,
Historic Fells Point (Baltimore), MD 21231

Seneca Rocks Climbing School   (304) 567-2600
Gendarme Shop
Box 53, Seneca Rocks, WV 26884

Transmontane Outfitters   (304) 259-5117
Route 32, Main Street, Davis, WV 26260

*Certified by American Professional Mountain Guides Association

SAILING

Mid-Atlantic residents are fortunate to be living near many excellent large and somewhat sheltered bays, sounds, and major rivers. The best way to enjoy them is not by gazing longingly from ashore, but by experiencing the power of the bounding main under sail. There are literally hundreds of marinas, charter companies, sailboat rental places, and schools waiting to help you set sail. Rather than list vast numbers of these organizations, this section is necessarily limited to sailing schools and other commercial establishments offering instruction. Whether you are just starting out or you want to polish your skills, you are sure to find a school or class to meet your needs.

Ask a few questions before you sign on at a particular school. Find out if you will get "hands on" experience on the water, or if your learning is confined to classrooms. If you do go on the water, ask what the ratio of passengers to crew will be, and how many people will be aboard. You want to try out your new skills, but you won't get a chance if the boat is packed with other students. Make sure the instructor does not hog the helm and that he or she rotates students through each crew job so that you get a chance to be skipper, cockpit crew, and foredeck crew during the course.

In addition to the selection of commercial schools and

establishments listed below, you can also take excellent courses in basic sailing and boating skills from your local Coast Guard Auxiliary flotilla or Red Cross chapter.

DELAWARE

Lisa's Sailboat (at Waterfront Restaurant), McKinley Street-on-the-Bay, Dewey Beach, DE 19971, (302) 277-9292

Rehoboth Bay Sailing Association, Highway One, Dewey Beach, DE 19971, (302) 227-9723

MARYLAND

Annapolis Sailing School, 601 Sixth Street, Box 3334, Annapolis, MD 21403, (301) 267-7205, (800) 638-9192 (toll free), 261-1947 (toll free from Washington, DC)

Capital Sailing Academy, Fort Washington Marina, Fort Washington, MD 20744, (301) 299-2227

Chesapeake Sailing School, 7074 Bembe Beach Road, Port Annapolis, MD 21403, (301) 269-1594, 261-2810 (toll free from Washington, DC)

Havre de Grace Sailing School, 724 Water Street, Havre de Grace, MD 21078, (301) 939-0363

Sailing School of Baltimore, 1700 Bowsleys Quarter Road, Middle River, MD 21220, (301) 335-7555

Severn Sailing Association, PO Box 1463, Annapolis, MD 21403, (301) 269-6744.

NEW JERSEY

Corinthian Yacht Club, Delaware Avenue, Cape May, NJ 08204, (609) 884-8000

VIRGINIA

BOAT/U.S., 880 S. Pickett Street, Alexandria, VA 22340, (703) 823-9555

Mariners Sailing School, Belle Haven Marina, Alexandria, VA 22307, (703) 768-0018

Old Dominion University, Hampton Boulevard, Norfolk, VA 23508, (804) 440-3000

Washington Sailing Marina, PO Box 1038, Alexandria, VA 22313, (703) 548-0001

■■■■■ VINEYARDS ■■■■■

by David Pursglove

One of the more interesting day trips from Washington, Baltimore, and Richmond nowadays is a visit to a working vineyard and winery, or a "winery tour" that can take you to five or six wineries on a weekend.

American colonists made wine of sorts in Virginia and Maryland, and in the years before Prohibition there was a sizeable "wine industry." Some statistics led to the impression that Virginia, for instance, was one of the country's largest wine-producing states. However, much of that wine was made from grapes brought by rail from California; much was not even made in Virginia, but was California's cheapest tank-car wine bottled in Virginia. A little wine, usually rather poor, was made in Virginia from grapes grown in Virginia. Those grapes often were scuppernongs, a thick-skinned, musky fruit which is the source of several cultivated grapes.

Now, a growing and correctly termed wine industry has developed in the mid-Atlantic region, and the trained viticulturalists (grape growers) and viniculturists (wine makers) are making good wine from the right grapes. Before you begin a tour of the wineries—where you will taste the wines as part of the tour, or, in several instances, chat in the homes of the families who own the smallest wineries—you will want to understand the wines. They will usually be quite different from the wines you are accustomed to from Europe and California and even different from the ones you may have tasted from New York. The vineyard and winery owners will hope you approach their wines for what they are—wines of the mid-Atlantic made from the grapes that make the best area wines—and not compare and rate them against wines from other regions and from other grapes.

In America, wines are made from two kinds of grapes—and from yet a third kind developed especially for eastern North America. California wines, because of the state's climate, soil, and freedom from certain plant diseases, are produced from the same grapes used in Europe. These are the traditional "wine grapes" such as the chardonnay that yields white Burgundy, pinot noir that produces red Burgundy, cabernet sauvignon that makes up the largest portion of fine Bordeaux reds, riesling that results in the best German wines, and many other names familiar on California bottles and common in Europe, such as gamay, barbera, sauvignon blanc, gewurztraminer, etc. Those grapes grow in the eastern U.S. only with difficulty, although some of the vineyards in Maryland and Virginia do produce small quantities of good wine from them.

The grapes that were native to eastern North America when the first settlers arrived and some that were later developed from them are basically "table grapes," or eating grapes, and do not, as a rule, produce good wine. They may be "wild" or "foxy" in flavor, a bit bubblegumish, perhaps acidic or too fruity or "grapey." Some people like wines from the native grapes and their eastern descendents, but most people prefer the wines from Euro-Californian (vinifera) grapes. Some eastern grapes you may encounter are the most popular table grape, concord, whose wine (usually sweet and red, although occasionally dry and white) is enjoyed by millions and disliked by other millions; ives; cataba (which is now being handled better by some wineries that are making an acceptable, yet still very much "eastern," wine from it); niagara; and scuppernong, which is an acquired taste, and most wine drinkers have not acquired it. The chief virtue of these grapes, other than their often fine table qualities, is that they grow easily in our climate and resist diseases indigenous to our part of the country, including root louse, mildew, and various rots.

One of our worst diseases, phylloxera, a root louse, was inadvertently carried to Europe around the middle of the 19th century and nearly wiped out Europe's vineyards. Grape hybridizers, especially in France, attempted crossings of European fine-wine grapes with native American grapes that were resistant to the disease. They were partly successful and many "French-American hybrids" were planted. But greater success was achieved by grafting European wine grapes to American grape rootstock, and most of the hybrids have been pulled out of European vineyards.

But, in this country, wine-grape growers pursued the art of hybridizing and crossed the already successful French-American varieties even further with more American and more French in order to develop grapes that would withstand the rigors of growing here, but which would give us the fine wines of European and California grapes.

A pioneer hybridizer was an editor of the *Baltimore Sun* and protege of H. L. Mencken, Philip Wagner of Riderwood, on the northern edge of Baltimore at what is now the Beltway. To prove his efforts, Wagner and his wife Jocelyn built a small winery that they named Boordy. (Wagner, whenever asked what the name meant, said, "It's simply a great place name of the future.") The wines were different from any available here before the time of Boordy Vineyards. They were far superior to wines made from native grapes, yet not—in the opinion of longtime wine drinkers—up to the standards of Europe or California. Today, most wine enthusiasts taste them, and all the other hybrid wines now produced around here, as their own kind of wine and forego the comparison against Euro-Californian wines. But Philip and Jocelyn Wagner, with their Boordy Vineyards, put this part of the country in the business of making good table wines. Boordy was a small place and the Wagners very private people. Getting to take a tour of Boordy was a major event. In 1980, the Wagners sold Boordy to the DeFord family, who had been longtime grape suppliers and were closely associated with the winery. Young Rob DeFord had studied wine making professionally. The DeFords moved the winery, although the Wagners maintain the original experimental grape nursery.

MARYLAND

Basignani Winery, Ltd., 15722 Falls Road, Sparks, MD 21152, (301) 472-4718. In Baltimore County.

Berrywine Plantations Winery and Linganore Wine Cellars, 13601 Glissans Mill Road, Mount Airy, MD 21771, (301) 662-8687. Best known for peach, plum, strawberry, and other "fruit wines," but also produces some hybrid wine under its "Plantation" label.

Boordy Vineyards, 12820 Long Green Pike, Hydes, MD 21082, (301) 592-5015. In Baltimore County north of the Beltway from Exit 29. Concentration is still on hybrids. A cult has developed around a red labeled as from the "Cedar Point" vineyard on the Eastern Shore.

Byrd Vineyards, Church Hill Road, Myersville, MD 21773, (301) 293-1110. Between Frederick and Hagerstown. They specialize in wines from vinifera wine grapes (Euro-Californians) with some hybrids, and have supplanted Boordy as the largest and commercially most important winery in Maryland. Chardonnay and sauvignon blanc and the hybrid seyval blanc are among the best.

Catoctin Vineyards, 805 Greenbridge Road, Brookville, MD 20729, (301) 774-2310. In Montgomery County near Brighton Dam. This large, very modern winery specializes in hybrids and sells grapes to home wine makers.

Elk Run Vineyards, Inc., 15113 Liberty Road, Mount Airy, MD 21771, (301) 775-2513. In Frederick County. Produces both the "Liberty Tavern" and "Elk Run Vineyards" labels.

La Felicetta Vineyard and Wine Cellars, 3026 Whiteford Road, Pylesville, MD 21132, (301) 836-7605 or 836-1860. In Harford County.

The Loew Vineyards, 14001 Liberty Road (Route 26), Mount Airy, MD 21771, (301) 460-5728. In Frederick County, five miles west of Route 27.

Montbray Vineyards, 818 Silver Run Valley Road, Westminster, MD 21157, (301) 346-7878. This small winery between Westminster and Gettysburg is the home of Hamilton

Mowbray and, as such, may now be Maryland's most important center for winery research and education. Both hybrid and vinifera grapes are used.

Whitemarsh Cellars, 2810 Hoffman Mill Road, Hampstead, MD 21074, (301) 848-4488. Located in Carroll County, Whitemarsh produces wine under the "Aspen Run" label.

Woodhall Vineyards and Wine Cellars, Inc., 15115 Wheeler Lane, Sparks, MD (301) 771-4664. In Baltimore County.

Ziem Vineyards, Route 63, Downsville, MD 21733, (301) 223-8352. Near Fairplay, a few miles south of Hagerstown. This may be the state's smallest winery. Concentration is on hybrids, although a few wines are produced from native grapes. The hybrid Chancellor is considered one of the area's best reds.

PENNSYLVANIA

Adams County Winery, RD 1, Orrtanna, PA 17353, (717) 334-4631. Five miles west of Gettysburg.

Allegro Vineyards, RD 2, Box 64, Brogue, PA 17309, (717) 927-9148.

Blue Ridge Winery, 1101 Pine Road, Carlisle, PA 17013, (717) 486-5030.

Brandywine Vineyards and Winery, Box A, Kemblesville, PA 19347, (215) 255-4171.

Bucks County Vineyard and Winery, Route 202, RD 1, New Hope, PA 18938, (800) 362-0309 or (800) 523-2510 (in Pennsylvania).

Calvaresi Winery, 832 Thorn Street, Reading, PA 19601, (215) 373-7821.

Chadds Ford Winery, Route 1, Box 229, Chadds Ford, PA 19317, (215) 388-6221.

Conestoga Vineyards, 415 S. Queen Street, Lancaster, PA 17603, (717) 393-0141.

Country Creek Vineyards and Winery, 133 Cressman Road, Telford, PA 18969, (215) 723-6516.

Fox Meadow Farm, Chester Springs, PA 19425, (215) 827-7898.

Lancaster County Winery, Rawlinsville Road, RD 1, Willow Street, PA 17584, (717) 464-3555.

Mount Hope Estate and Winery, Box 685, Cornwall, PA 17016, (717) 665-7021.

Naylor Wine Cellars, RD 3, Stewartstown, PA 17363, (717) 993-2431.

Neri Wine Cellars, 373 Bridgetown Pike, Langhorne, PA 19047, (215) 355-9952.

Nissley Vineyards, Route 1, Bainbridge, PA 17502, (717) 426-3514.

Quarry Hill Winery, RD 2, Box 168, Shippensburg, PA 17257, (717) 776-3411.

Stephen Bahn Winery, RD 1, Box 758, Goram Road, Brogue, PA 17309, (717) 927-9051.

Tucquan Vineyard, RD 2, Holtwood, PA 17532, (717) 284-2221.

York Springs Vineyard and Winery, RD 1, Box 194, York Springs, PA 17372, (717) 528-8490.

VIRGINIA

NORTHERN VIRGINIA

Farfelu Vineyard, Flint Hill, VA 22627, (703) 364-2930. On Route 647 in the Blue Ridge foothills about four miles east of Flint Hill, this is one of the smallest wineries in the state and perhaps the oldest of the new generation. Hybrids simply labeled "red" and "white" vary in quality from year to year, but have won regional awards several times.

Linden Vineyards, Route 1, Box 96, Linden, VA 22642, (703) 364-1997. Near Skyline Drive in Fauquier County, this vineyard offers a dramatic mountain view and historic varieties of apple wine.

Locust Hill Vineyard, Box 1, Rectortown, VA 22140, (703) 364-1138. This small winery produces red, white, and chardonnay wines.

Meredyth Vineyards, Box 347, Middleburg, VA 22117, (703) 687-6277. About three miles south of Middleburg, this is the largest and most sophisticated of the older wineries in Virginia's wine industry. Since the winery closely resembles in scale and equipment the wineries of Europe and California, this is a good place to begin learning the basics. Hybrids and Euro-California vinifera grapes are used.

Naked Mountain Vineyard, Box 131, Markham, VA 22643, (703) 364-1609. This beautiful vineyard is east of Front Royal. It has a shaded picnic area.

Oasis Vineyard, Route 635, Hume, VA 22639, (703) 635-7627 or 635-3103. East of Front Royal.

Piedmont Vineyards and Winery, Route 626 S., Box 286, Middleburg, VA 22117, (703) 687-5528. About a mile south of Middleburg, this is one of the state's larger and important wineries. Several white Euro-California vinifera wines have achieved critical acclaim.

Swedenburg Winery, Middleburg, VA 22117, (703) 687-5219. In Loudoun County on historic Valley View Farm (ca. 1762).

Willowcroft Farm Vineyards, Route 2, Box 174-A, Leesburg, VA 22075, (703) 777-8161. The winery at Willowcroft is in a rustic barn overlooking the Blue Ridge Mountains.

EASTERN VIRGINIA

Accomack Vineyards, Box 38, Painter, VA 23420, (804) 442-2110. This is the only farm winery on the Eastern Shore.

Ingleside Plantation Vineyards, Box 1083, Oak Grove, VA 22443, (804) 224-8687. Located about 30 miles east of Fredericksburg. A Germanic riesling and a Bourdeaux-like cabernet sauvignon with small amounts of merlot and cabernet franc have drawn favorable notice.

Williamsburg Winery, Ltd., 2638 Lake Powell Road, Williamsburg, VA 23185, (804) 229-0999. The winery is located on a 300-acre farm five minutes from Colonial Williamsburg.

CENTRAL VIRGINIA

Autumn Hill Vineyards, Route 1, Box 199C, Stanardsville, VA 22973, (804) 985-3081. In Greene County.

Barboursville Vineyards, RFD 1, Box 136, Barboursville, VA 22923, (703) 832-3824. In Orange County about 15 miles northeast of Charlottesville, this large operation is the project of one of Italy's largest wine families, Zonin, and part of its interest is in carrying out Thomas Jefferson's plan for a Virginia wine industry based on Italian grapes. Other grapes are also used.

Burnley Vineyards, Route 1, Box 122, Barboursville, VA 22923, (703) 832-2828 or 832-3874. North of Charlottesville.

Chermont Winery, Route 1, Box 59, Esmont, VA 22937, (804) 286-2211 or 286-2639. In Albemarle County.

Dominion Wine Cellars, 1 Winery Avenue, Box 1057, Culpeper, VA 22701, (703) 825-8772. Owned by the Virginia Winery Cooperative.

Misty Mountain Winery, SR 2, Box 458, Madison, VA 22727, (703) 923-4738. In Madison County; specializes in French-style vinifera wines.

MontDomaine Cellars, Route 6, Box 188A, Charlottesville, VA 22901, (804) 971-8947. The largest winery in the area, MontDomaine features a 20,000-gallon underground winery.

Mountain Cove Vineyards, Route 1, Box 135, Lovingston, VA 22949, (804) 263-5392. About 30 miles south of Charlottesville toward Lynchburg.

Oakencroft Vineyard and Winery, Route 5, Charlottesville, VA 22901, (804) 296-4188 or 295-9870.

Prince Michel Vineyards, SR 4, Box 77, Leon, VA

22725, (703) 547-3707. Features a 150,000-gallon winery with a museum, gift shop, and tasting room.

Rapidan River Vineyards, Route 4, Box 199, Culpeper, VA 22701, (703) 399-1855. About 15 miles south of Culpeper, the vineyard produces some of the state's better German-style rieslings.

Rebec Vineyards, Route 3, Box 185, Amherst, VA 24521, (804) 946-5168. This estate is listed in the Historic American Buildings Survey at the Library of Congress.

Riverside Winery, Route 635, Riverside, Rapidan, VA 22733, (703) 672-4673. In Orange County.

Rose Bower Vineyard and Winery, Route 686, Box 126, Hampden Sydney, VA 23943, (804) 223-8209. South of Farmville, between Richmond and Lynchburg.

Rose River Vineyards, Route 2, Box 186, Syria, VA 22743, (703) 923-4591. The vineyard features hiking trails and picnic sites.

Simeon Vineyard, Ltd., RFD 9, Box 293, Charlottesville, VA 22901, (804) 977-0800 or 977-3502. In Madison County.

Stonewall Vineyard, Ltd., Route 2, Box 107A, Concord, VA 24538, (804) 993-2158. In Appomattox County.

SHENANDOAH VALLEY

Deer Meadow Vineyard, Mountain Falls Route, Box 127-C, Winchester, VA 22601, (703) 877-1919. This small winery welcomes picnickers.

Guilford Ridge, Route 5, Box 148, Luray, VA 22835, (703) 778-3853. Produces estate-bottled "Page Valley" wines.

Shenandoah Vineyards, Route 2, Box 323, Edinburg, VA 22824, (703) 984-8699. Near Woodstock between Winchester and Harrisonburg.

Tri-Mountain Winery and Vineyards, Box 391, Middletown, VA 22645, (703) 869-3030 or 869-3571.

Winchester Winery, Mountain Falls Route, Box 188, Winchester, VA 22601, (703) 877-1275. Visitors can view the cellars and the art gallery of Raymond F. Smith.

SOUTHWEST VIRGINIA

Chateau Morrisette Winery, Box 766, Meadows of Dan, VA 24120, (703) 593-2865. Chateau Morrisette has a 25,000-gallon winery constructed of native stones and timber.

Chateau Naturel Vineyard, Route 4, Box 1535, Rocky Mount, VA 24151, (703) 483-0758. In Franklin County.

WEST VIRGINIA

Robert F. Pliska and Company Winery, 101 Piterra Place, Purgitsville, WV 26852, (304) 289-3493. This 160-acre Hampshire County winery produces several popular wines, including "Mountain Mama" apple wine.

West-Whitehall Winery, Route 1, Box 247A, Keyser, WV 26726, (304) 788-3066. This Potomac Highland winery has won gold medals for its dry seyval blanc wine.

Points to remember:

(1) In the case of most small wineries, the winery may also be the proprietor's home and the manners for visiting a home should be observed. (2) Most wineries in Maryland charge a small tour fee. (3) Addresses listed are mailing addresses and the vineyard or winery may not be quite at the town listed. Call ahead for directions and days and hours for visits. (4) Some wineries offer picnic and children's playground facilities. It is hoped persons using those facilities will pay a tour fee or buy some wine. (5) For further information send a stamped, self-addressed business-size envelope to:

Maryland Dept. of Agriculture, 50 Harry S. Truman Parkway, Annapolis, MD 21401 (Request Wineries List)

Maryland Grape Growers Assn., Box HH, Burkittsville, MD 21718

Dept. of Agriculture and Consumer Services, Division of Markets, Box 1163, Richmond, VA 23209

Virginia Wineries Assn., Box 527, Richmond, VA 23204

Pennsylvania Wine Country, Dept. SLA, 416 Forum Building, Harrisburg, PA 17120

David Pursglove is a syndicated wine columnist for newspapers and magazines, editor of "Wine Review for the Trade," and president of *Wine Industry News.* He is the wine reviewer for WGMS Radio AM & FM in Washington, DC.

■■■ WHITEWATER RAFTING ■■■

The call of white water has become stronger in recent years and thousands of area residents now exchange their business suits for bathing suits (or wet suits) on weekends. Whitewater rafting is truly a sport suitable for all ages and degrees of skill. This area is blessed with rafting opportunities ranging from mild, family outings to rapids equaling those of the famed Colorado. All that is required to enjoy the sport is an ability to swim moderately well (you will always be wearing a life jacket) and a taste for outdoor adventure.

Spring, summer, and fall are all good times for whitewater rafting. The months of April and May usually provide the most exciting trips because the melting spring snow causes the rivers to swell and makes the rapids more challenging; fall is delightful with its colorful autumn foliage lining the banks; and a good trip in summer, with the hot sun beating down and the cool, clear water beckoning, is hard to beat. The price of most guided trips includes the rental of all rafting equipment (raft, paddle, life jacket), guide services, and transportation at the end of the trip back to the meeting point. Lunch is usually (but not always) included. Reservations are necessary, and should be made well in advance for large groups or for popular weekends.

Rafting is a sport in which everyone is expected to do his or her share of the paddling. On some trips, especially the more difficult ones, there will be a guide in every raft to direct the group's efforts. On easier trips, the guides may be in kayaks, or in only the first and last rafts, in which case each raft selects a leader to navigate a course down the river.

While most people drive to the various rivers where there is whitewater rafting, there are groups and organizations which sponsor trips and sometimes arrange transportation. One such organization is the American Rivers Conservation Council, which offers a variety of rafting trips on local rivers and can also provide information on outfitters as well as on trips in the West. ARCC's address is 323 Pennsylvania Avenue S.E., Washington, DC 20003. Telephone: (202) 547-6900. Other groups that organize raft trips include local ski clubs and county recreation departments. The sports calendar in the weekend section of your local newspaper is a good source of information on such trips. Another alternative is to make individual contact with private outfitters and join a scheduled trip. A list of outfitters follows for each river in the area. As most rafting trips start early in the morning and are some distance from Baltimore-Washington-Richmond, a listing of accommodations is also given below. For a complete listing of eastern rafting outfitters, write the Eastern Professional River Outfitters Association (EPRO), Route 1, Ocoee, TN 37361.

MARYLAND

THE POTOMAC RIVER, through the Mather Gorge, runs wild and free for several miles below Great Falls. This spectacular wilderness area, located just minutes from downtown Washington, offers a wonderful one-day raft trip suitable for beginners. The river is enjoyable year round, but is more exciting in the early spring or after heavy rains. This river has been known to be dangerous, however, so some parts should only be attempted by experienced rafters.

PENNSYLVANIA

THE YOUGHIOGHENY RIVER, in southwestern Pennsylvania, flows through beautiful Ohiopyle State Park. The river provides an intermediate trip chockfull of exciting rapids, gorgeous scenery, and inviting places to swim. Advanced boaters can rent their own rafts. The Youghiogheny is runnable all year, and is approximately four hours from Washington or Baltimore and six hours from Richmond.

Where to Stay
    Bill and Adeline's Guest House, Ohiopyle, (412) 329-4968
    The Fall Inn, Ohiopyle, (412) 329-4973
    Green Acres Motel, Route 40, Farmington, (412) 329-5664
    Hidden Valley Resort, Somerset, (814) 445-6014
    Holiday Inn, Route 40 West, Uniontown, (412) 437-2816
    Laurel Highlands Motor Lodge, Donegal, (412) 593-7222
    Ohiopyle Youth Hostel, Ohiopyle, (412) 329-4476

THE LEHIGH RIVER, in the Poconos of eastern Pennsylvania, provides a raft run through a wild, rugged mountain gorge. The best times to raft are the spring and fall, although certain portions of the river can be run all summer. Continuous, easily navigated rapids give beginners and intermediates plenty of excitement. The Lehigh is a five-hour drive from the Washington area and approximately four hours from Baltimore.

Where to Stay
    Country Place Motel, Route 903, Jim Thorpe, (717) 325-2214
    Holiday Inn-Pocono-Lake Harmony, White Haven, (717) 443-8471
    Howard Johnson, White Haven, (717) 443-8461
    Tudor Inn, Routes 115 and 903, Blakeslee, (717) 649-2950

VIRGINIA

Richmond's historic **JAMES RIVER** offers an unusual trip which begins in a beautiful wilderness setting and ends up beneath towering buildings in the heart of the city. Although the pace is relaxed, excitement builds to a crescendo as paddlers encounter the thrilling Falls of Richmond. The trip is suitable for beginners and intermediates.

WEST VIRGINIA

THE SHENANDOAH RIVER, near Harpers Ferry, provides a beautiful setting for a half-day, beginner raft trip. Spectacular views of the surrounding Blue Ridge Mountains alternate with glimpses of historic churches, bridges, and other structures. The rafting season is April through October. The Shenandoah is a little more than an hour from Washington or Baltimore and approximately two and a half hours from Richmond.

Where to Stay
>   Cliffside Motor Inn, (304) 535-6307
>   Hillside Motel, (301) 834-8144
>   Hilltop House, (304) 535-6321
>   Kiwanis AYH Hostel, (301) 834-7625

THE DRY FORK, near Davis, WV, is a tiny mountain river only runnable in the early spring. The raft trip features rapid after rapid in a fairyland of cascading waterfalls, sheer rock cliffs, and lush pockets of farmland. It is suitable for beginners and intermediates. The river is approximately four and a half hours from Washington and five hours from Baltimore or Richmond.

Where to Stay
>   Best Western Alpine Lodge, Davis, (304) 259-5245
>   Canaan Valley State Park Lodge, Davis, (304) 866-4121/(800)
>   624-8632
>   Mirror Lake Resort, Route 32, Canaan Valley, (304) 866-4216
>   Transmontane Outfitters Bunk House, Davis, (304) 259-5117

THE CHEAT RIVER, at Albright, WV, is one of the most scenic and challenging rivers in the area. It contains more than 20 major rapids in less than 12 miles, and is a good trip for intermediate and advanced rafters. It is usually runnable in rafts until early June. In the dry summer months, it can be paddled in one-person inflatables. The drive from Washington or Baltimore is approximately four hours; about six hours from Richmond.

Where to Stay
>   Heldreth Motel, Kingwood, (304) 329-1145
>   Holiday Inn of Morgantown, Morgantown, (304) 599-1680
>   Kingwood Inn, Kingwood, (304) 329-2793
>   Kingwood Motel, Kingwood, (304) 329-0405
>   Lakeview Inn, Route 5, Morgantown, (304) 292-6311/(800) 624-8300
>   Ramada Inn, Morgantown, (304) 296-3431

THE NEW RIVER, in southern West Virginia, is approximately seven hours from Washington and five and a half hours from Richmond, but the trip is definitely worth it. Known as the "Grand Canyon of the East," the New offers big, roller-coaster rapids in a breathtaking mountain setting. The New is raftable year round, and is suitable for intermediate and advanced paddlers.

Where to Stay
    Bankers Club Hotel, Thurmond, (304) 469-9161
    Best Western Motor Lodge, Beckley, (304) 252-0671
    Chuckwagon Motel, Route 16 N., Fayetteville, (304) 469-3364
    Coast-to-Coast Motel, Ansted, (304) 658-5100
    Hawks Nest State Park Lodge, Route 60, Ansted, (304) 658-5212
    Holiday Inn, Beckley, (304) 255-1511
    Lake Service Motel, Summersville, (304) 872-3011
    Mountain State Motel, Summersville, (304) 872-2701
    Oxford Inn, Summersville, (304) 872-2811
    Oylers Motel, Oak Hill, (304) 469-9631
    Shirleys Motel, Route 60, Hico, (304) 658-5654

THE GAULEY RIVER, a tributary of the New, is probably the most challenging rafting river on the East Coast. It should only be attempted by rafters who have experienced such rivers as the Cheat or the New. Because of an upstream dam, paddlers can only be sure of good water levels in September and October, when the Army Corps of Engineers schedules releases in order to lower the level of the reservoir. The Gauley is six to seven hours from Washington and approximately five and a half hours from Richmond.

Where to Stay
    (See the New River above.)

OUTFITTER	RIVER	TELEPHONE
American Canadian Expeditions	Cheat Gauley, New	(304) 469-2651
American Whitewater Tours, Inc.	Cheat, Gauley, New	(304) 454-2475
Appalachian Wildwaters, Inc.	Cheat, Gauley, New	(800) 624-8060 (304) 454-2475
Blue Ridge Outfitters	Shenandoah	(304) 725-3444
Cheat River Outfitters, Inc.	Cheat, N. Fork of S. Branch of Potomac	(304) 329-2024
Class VI River Runners, Inc.	Gauley, New	(304) 574-0704
Drift-A-Bit	Gauley, New	(304) 574-3282
Gauley Expeditions, Inc.	Gauley, New	(304) 574-3679 (800) 472-7238
Mountain River Tours, Inc.	Cheat, Gauley, New	(304) 658-5817 (800) 822-1386

New River Adventures	Gauley, New	(304) 574-3008
New River Scenic White-	Gauley, New	(304) 466-2288
water Tours, Inc.		(800) 292-0880
North American River	Cheat, Gauley, New	(304) 658-5276
Runners, Inc.		
Passages to Adventure,	Cheat, Gauley, New	(304) 574-1037
Inc.		
Precision Rafting	Potomac, Youghiogheny	(301) 746-5290
Expeditions		
River and Trail Outfitters	Shenandoah	(301) 695-5177
The Rivermen	Gauley, New	(304) 574-0515
		(800) 422-7238
Rivers, Inc.	Cheat, Gauley, New	(304) 574-3834
Rough Run Outfitters	Cheat	(304) 457-1260
Songer Enterprises, Inc.	Cheat, Gauley, New	(304) 658-4207
Transmontane Outfitters,	Cheat, Dry Fork	(304) 259-5117
Ltd.		
West Virginia River	Gauley, New	(304) 658-5241
Adventures		
West Virginia Whitewater	Gauley, New	(304) 574-0871
The Whitewater Classic	Potomac, Youghiogheny	(301) 387-4644
Whitewater Information,	Gauley, New	(304) 465-0855
Ltd. (800) 782-7238		
Whole Earth Rafting, Inc.	Gauley, New	(304) 255-6563
Wildwater Expeditions	Cheat, Gauley, New	(304) 469-2551
Unlimited Inc.		(800) 782-7238
Youghiogheny Out-	Youghiogheny (raft	(412) 329-4549
	fitters rentals)	

▬▬▬ WINDSURFING (BOARDSAILING) ▬▬▬

Most people's idea of boardsailing is a grueling afternoon attempting to keep a sail and board upright, spending as much time in the water as out. Truthfully, that will probably describe your first hour or two at the sport, but experts practically guarantee you will be sailing along in no time at all. "Boardsailing" is the generic name for the sport, although you will occasionally hear it referred to as "windsurfing" (Windsurfer is a brand name of a sailboard).

The only piece of equipment you'll need to join the fun is a sailboard, a contraption invented in California in the mid-1960s. The flat board has a universal joint allowing the mast and sail to turn in all directions. The idea is to stand on the board, hold onto a bar across the sail, and keep the whole thing upright while trying to catch the wind.

Sailboards sell for between $600 and $1,000, but you can rent them for about $7 an hour. Depending on local regulations, you may need to be certified to rent. The certification process entails a two-day, six-hour course during which students learn how to rig and de-rig their sailboards, plus sailing tactics and emergency procedures. There are a number of certifying organizations, although local chapters may be few and far between because the sport is so new. The major groups are Boardsailing USA (PO Box 7124, Winterhaven, FL 33880, (813) 324-4378) and U.S. Board Sailing Association (PO Box 206, Oyster Bay, NY 11771, (516) 922-1289).

In addition, most sailboard manufacturers such as Windsurfer and Mistral have their own national and international clubs with local "fleets" that offer lessons and sponsor races and regattas. To participate in their events (except for lessons), you must own their brand of sailboard. There are more than 160 manufacturers around the country, so the list of fleets is too numerous to mention. Any sailboard dealer, however, can direct you to fleets in your area.

Some of the best boardsailing locations on the East Coast are along North Carolina's Outer Banks. Other popular spots are Pohick Bay (Virginia) and Sandy Point State Park (Maryland).

The following is a selection of instructors in the area and some of the many outfitters who rent sailboards:

MARYLAND
> Sailing, Etc., 5307 Coastal Highway, Ocean City, MD 21842
> Windsurfing Unlimited, 7123 Fairfax Road, Bethesda, MD 20814, (301) 951-0705

NEW JERSEY
> Thomas Marine Sailing Center, Route 73, Berlin, NJ 08009, (609) 768-0707
> Water Sports, Inc., 3100 Long Beach Boulevard, Brant Beach, NJ 08008, (609) 494-2727

NORTH CAROLINA
> Bayside Watersports, 158 Bypass Road, Nags Head, NC 27959, (919) 441-4270
> Kitty Hawk Sports, PO Box 340, Nags Head, NC 27959, (919) 441-6247 or (800) 334-4777

PENNSYLVANIA
> Ski Station, 107 McAllister Alley, State College, PA 16801, (814) 237-2655
> Wildwear, Ltd., 46 S. Pershing Avenue, York, PA 17401, (717) 843-9526

VIRGINIA
> Sea and Ski Sports, 1017 Laskin Road, Virginia Beach, VA 23451, (804) 428-5477

CALENDAR OF EVENTS

This section is a partial listing; events were selected to appeal to a wide range of interests. A few are outside the 200-mile range established for *Weekender's Guide to the Four Seasons* because they are unique or especially popular.

Many of the annual events listed here have been held for dozens of years, and in some cases hundreds of years. The actual dates may vary from year to year, so be sure to contact the state, county, or city tourist office before you plan any trip.

Delaware Tourism Office
99 Kings Highway, PO Box 1401
Dover, DE 19903

(800) 282-8667
(toll free within DE)
(800) 441-8846
(toll free outside DE)

Maryland Office of Tourist Development
45 Calvert Street
Annapolis, MD 21401

(800) 331-1750
(301) 974-3517

New Jersey Division of Travel and Tourism
CN-826
Trenton, NJ 08625

(800) 837-7397

North Carolina Division of Travel and Tourism
430 N. Salisbury Street
Raleigh, NC 27611

(919) 733-4171

Pennsylvania Division of Travel Marketing
453 Forum Building
Harrisburg, PA 17120

(800) 847-4872
(toll free)
(717) 787-5453
(in Canada)

Virginia State Division of Tourism
202 N. Ninth Street, Suite 500
Richmond, VA 23219

(804) 786-4484
(202) 293-5350
(in Washington, DC)

West Virginia Department of Commerce/
Travel West Virginia

(800) 225-5982
(toll free out of state)

State Capitol Building   (304) 348-2286
Charleston, WV 25305

JANUARY

Early

Cherryville, NC, New Year's Shooting (traditional New Year's
greeting celebration)

Harrisburg, PA, Farm Show
Philadelphia, PA, Mummers' New Year's Day Parade

Middle

Baltimore, MD, Chinese New Year Festival

Fredericksburg, VA, Religious Freedom Day
Stratford, VA, Stratford Hall Plantation, Open House
Davis, WV, Cross-Country Ski Workshops and Tournaments

Late

Alexandria, VA, Birthday Celebration of Robert E. Lee and
"Lighthorse Harry" Lee
Lexington, VA, Stonewall Jackson Birthday Celebration
Roanoke, VA, Shrine Circus
Williamsburg, VA, Annual Williamsburg Antiques Forum

Davis, WV, Alpine Citizens 10 Kilometer Cross-Country Ski
Race
Martinsburg, WV, Cabin Fever Doubles Tennis Tournament
Snowshoe, WV, Grand Marnier Ski Club Challenge

FEBRUARY

Early

Punxsutawney, PA, Ground Hog Day

Beckley, WV, Annual Raleigh County Powerlifting Cham-
pionships
Berkeley Springs, WV, Mountain Heritage Weekend
Davis, WV, Sno Cross at Canaan Valley

Middle

Frederick, MD, Mardi Gras
Ocean City, MD, Mardi Gras

Valley Forge, PA, Annual Washington's Birthday Celebration

Alexandria, VA, George Washington Birthday Eve Celebration
Alexandria, VA, Revolutionary War Encampment
Fredericksburg, VA, George Washington Birthday Party in
the Home of Washington's Mother
Richmond, VA, Annual Wildfowl Carving and Art Exhibit
Williamsburg, VA, Washington's Birthday Weekend

Late

Alexandria, VA, Mount Vernon Classic

Davis, WV, Seniors on Skis (Blackwater Falls State Park)
Morgantown, WV, Annual Winter Music Festival

MARCH

Early

Mount Vernon, VA, Annual Woodlawn Plantation Needlework Exhibit

Davis, WV, Alpine Winter Festival
Martinsburg, WV, Men's 55 Doubles Tennis Tournament

Middle

McHenry, MD, Winterfest
Thurmont, MD, Maple Syrup Demonstrations (Cunningham
Falls State Park)

Morristown, NJ, Revolutionary War Encampment

Philadelphia, PA, Pennsylvania Horticultural Society Spring
Show

Alexandria, VA, Living History Weekend at Lee Corner
Chase City, VA, Easter Sunrise Service
Fredericksburg, VA, Annual Fine Art Show
Fredericksburg, VA, Mardi Gras
Highland County, VA, Maple Festival
Lorton, VA, Kite Festival at Gunston Hall Plantation

Elkins, WV, Eastern Regional Science Fair

Late

Potomac, MD, Annual Doll Festival
St. Mary's City, MD, Maryland Day Celebration

Louisburg, NC, Annual Folk Festival

Great Falls, VA, Flapjack Day

Bluefield, WV, World Championship Rodeo
Davis, WV, "Spring Thing" Athletic Competition
Pipley, WV, Annual Birthday Celebration
Wheeling, WV, Annual Obbay Institute Antique Show

APRIL

Early

Rehoboth, DE, Easter Parade
Wilmington, DE, Cherry Blossom Festival

Atlantic City, NJ, Atlantic City Arts Festival

Alexandria, VA, George Washington's Visit to Boyhood Home
   of Robert E. Lee
Blacksburg, VA, Annual Brush Mountain Arts & Crafts Fair
Fredericksburg, VA, Annual State Frisbee Tournament
Gloucester, VA, Garden Club of Gloucester Daffodil Show
Grundy, VA, Kiwanis River Raft Race
Natural Bridge, VA, Annual Easter Sunrise Service
Norfolk, VA, Annual Conference on Scottish Studies
Petersburg, VA, Civil War Surrender Route Bus Trip to
   Appomattox
Richmond, VA, Annual Colonial Muster
Williamsburg, VA, Easter Weekend

Berkeley Springs, WV, Easter Celebration (Cacapon Resort
   State Park)
Cairo, WV, Easter Sunday Sunrise Service & Easter Egg
   Hunt
Davis, WV, Easter Holiday Memories (Canaan Valley State
   Park)

Middle

Edgewater, MD, London Town Publik House and Garden
   Daffodil Show

Murfreesboro, NC, Historic Murfreesboro Heritage Festival

Meyersdale, PA, Pennsylvania Maple Festival

Alexandria, VA, Annual Cherry Blossom Invitational
Charlottesville, VA, Annual Dogwood Festival
Fredericksburg, VA, Annual All-Breed Dog Show and Obe-
   dience Trial

Great Falls, VA, Colvin Run Mill Park—Blacksmithing Days
Norfolk, VA, International Azalea Festival
Richmond, VA, Virginia State Horse Show
Vinton, VA, Vinton Folklife Festival

Morgantown, WV, Annual Antique Special Interest Car Show

Late

Baltimore, MD, Maryland Kite Festival
Edgewater, MD, Horticulture Day
Frederick, MD, Catoctones Annual Show
Hagerstown, MD, Spring Arts Festival
Huntingtown, MD, Southern Maryland Celtic Festival

Washington, PA, National Pike Festival

Alexandria, VA, Annual Azalea Festival of the Arts
Alexandria, VA, Spring Candlelight Tour
Charlottesville, VA, Champagne and Candlelight Tour
Charlottesville, VA, Spring Meeting of the Foxfield Races
Fredericksburg, VA, Anniversary of the Battle of Chancellorsville
Front Royal, VA, Virginia Championship Canoe Races
Norfolk, VA, Annual British Isles Festival
Petersburg, VA, Annual Poplar Lawn Art Festival
Richmond and Statewide, VA, Historic Garden Week in Virginia
Roanoke, VA, Annual Spring Festival
Roanoke, VA, Annual Wildflower Pilgrimage
Roanoke, VA, Garden Club Weekend
Williamsburg, VA, Garden Week in Williamsburg
Winchester, VA, Annual Shenandoah Apple Blossom Festival (through early May)

Cass, WV, Spring Weekend
Mullens, WV, Dogwood Festival
Shepherdstown, WV, Annual House and Garden Tour

MAY

Early

Dover, DE, Old Dover Days
Wilmington, DE, Wilmington Garden Day
Winterhaven, DE, Point-to-Point Horse Race

Baltimore, MD, Cylburn Market Days
Baltimore, MD, Preakness Festival Balloon Race
Baltimore, MD, "Pride" of Baltimore Festival

Denton, MD, George Martinak Day (Martinak State Park)
Ellicott City, MD, Spring Festival
Laurel, MD, Montpelier Spring Festival
Rockville, MD, National Capital Area Scottish s-6estival
Towson, MD, Towsontown Spring Festival
West Friendship, MD, Maryland Sheep and Wool Festival

Rocky Mount, NC, Annual Outdoor Art Show

Brandywine, PA, "Treasures of the Brandywine" annual tour
of historic sites
Gettysburg, PA, Apple Blossom Festival

Alexandria, VA, Craft Fair at Woodlawn
Charlottesville, VA, Annual Kite Day at Ash Lawn
Chincoteaque, VA, Annual Seafood Festival (first weekend)
Culpeper, VA, Street Festival (first weekend)
Farmville, VA, Heart of Virginia Festival
Hurley, VA, Knox Creek Mountain Festival
Leesburg, VA, Annual Art Exhibition of the Loudoun Sketch
Club
New Market, VA, Annual Reenactment of the Battle of New
Market
Richmond, VA, Westover Hills Azalea Festival and Parade
Virginia Beach, VA, Tidewater Scottish Festival and Clan
Gathering

Bluefield, WV, Area State Band Festival
Harpers Ferry, WV, Annual Blue Ridge Quilt Show

Middle

Wilmington, DE, Polish Festival

Annapolis, MD, William Paca House and Garden Show
Baltimore, MD, Preakness Stakes Thoroughbred Race
Cheverly, MD, Cheverly Day
Glen Echo, MD, Glen Echo Park, The Chautauqua Season
Begins (until end of September)
McHenry, MD, Garrett County Arts Festival
Mitchellville, MD, Italian Spring Festival
Prince Frederick, MD, Cavalier Days (Fair of the 1780s)

Nags Head, NC, Annual Gliding Spectacular
Windsor, NC, Springtime on the Plantation
Winston-Salem, NC, Annual Rose Show

Chantilly, VA, Sully Plantation Daily Life
Charlottesville, VA, Annual Barracks Road Art Show
Crozet, VA, Crozet Arts & Crafts Festival
Fredericksburg, VA, Beach Music Festival

Fredericksburg, VA, Market Square Fair
Harrisonburg, VA, Virginia Poultry Festival
Jamestown, VA, Jamestown Day
Stuart, VA, Gospel Music Festival
Upperville, VA, Annual Stable Tour
Virginia Beach, VA, Annual Music Festival
Williamsburg, VA, Prelude to Independence Celebration
    (through July 4)

Davis, WV, Annual Wildflower Pilgrimage
Shepherdstown, WV, Mayfest

Late

Dewey Beach, DE, Mid-Atlantic Spring Arts and Crafts
    Festival
Wilmington, DE, Greek Festival
Wilmington, DE, Memorial Day Observance

Annapolis, MD, U.S. Naval Academy Commissioning Week
Bowie, MD, Memorial Day Parade
Cambridge, MD, Antique Aircraft Fly-In
Chestertown, MD, Chestertown Tea Party Festival
Frederick, MD, Family Festival Day
Timonium, MD, Sugarloaf Spring Crafts Festival

Devon, PA, Devon Horse Show and County Fair
Gettysburg, PA, Memorial Day Parade

Arlington, VA, Memorial Day Service At Arlington Cemetery
Fredericksburg, VA, May Mardi-Gras
Fredericksburg, VA, Memorial Day Ceremonies
Manassas, VA, Manassas Fun Day
Middletown, VA, Belle Grove Plantation, Dulcimer Gathering
Roanoke, VA, Festival-on-the-River (Wasenq Park)
Shenandoah, VA, Shenandoah Spring Festival
Staunton, VA, Annual Outdoor Art Show

Belmont, WV, Annual Quilt Show and Sale

JUNE

Early

Wilmington, DE, Greek and Italian Festivals
Bel Air, MD, Deer Creek Fiddlers Convention and Contest
Bowie, MD, Bowie Fest
Cumberland, MD, Heritage Days (second weekend)
Frederick, MD, The Frederick Craft Fair
Glen Echo, MD, Glen Echo Park, Washington Folk Festival

Laurel, MD, Civil War Encampment and Battle
Mt. Airy, MD, Springtime Wine Festival

Cape May, NJ, Foot Race
Cape May, NJ, Old Fashioned Strawberry Festival

Eden, NC, Annual Bluegrass Fiddlers Convention
Manteo, NC, Annual Dare Days
Mount Airy, NC, Annual Bluegrass and Old Time Fiddlers
    Convention

Gettysburg, PA, Annual Observances of Battle of Gettysburg
Philadelphia, PA, Freedom Festival

Fredericksburg, VA, Fredericksburg's Annual Art Festival
Fredericksburg, VA, The Great Rappahannock River White
    Water Canoe Race
Middletown, VA, Belle Grove Annual Needlework Exhibit
Nokesville, VA, Nokesville Day
Roanoke, VA, Festival-In-The-Park

Purgitsville, WV, Annual Old Music Weekend
Union, WV, Farmers' Day

Middle

Delaware City, DE, Annual Polish Day
Wilmington, DE, Annual Crafts Fair, Delaware Art Museum

Annapolis, MD, Annapolis Arts Festival
Cumberland, MD, Heritage Days
Easton, MD, Delmarva Chicken Festival
Mountain Lake Park, MD, Garrett County Seafood Festival

Cape May, NJ, Senior Citizens Craft Show
Wharton State Forest, NJ, Historic Crafts Festival

Durham, NC, American Dance Festival
Hatteras, NC, Annual Invitational Blue Marlin Tournament
Washington, NC, Annual Summer Festival

Brandywine Valley, PA, Delco Scottish Games and County
    Fair

Colonial Beach, VA, Annual Potomac River Festival
Crewe, VA, Chicken Festival
Lorton, VA, Gunston Hall Arts & Crafts Celebration
Mt. Solon, VA, National Hall of Fame Jousting Tournament

Bluefield, WV, Blue Gray Horseman's Association Horse
    Show

Charles Town, WV, Annual Mountain Heritage Arts & Crafts
Festival

Late

Delaware City, DE, Delaware City Days

Grantsville, MD, Grantsville Days (last Friday and Saturday
of June)
Pocomoke City, MD, Pocomoke Cypress Festival

Cape May, NJ, Classic Hobie Cat Regatta
Stanhope, NJ, Kool Jazz Festival, Waterloo Village

Linville, NC, Annual "Singing On The Mountain" (Grandfather Mountain)

Richboro, PA, Annual State Craft Fair

Alexandria, VA, Waterfront Festival
Front Royal, VA, Virginia Wineries Festival
Hampton, VA, Hampton Institute, Kool Jazz Festival
Radford, VA, "Pike Day"
Salem, VA, Annual Roanoke Valley Horse Show
Virginia Beach, VA, Annual Boardwalk Art Show

Hillsboro, WV, Pearl S. Buck Annual Birthday Celebration

JULY

Early

Dover, DE, July 4th Celebration
Rehoboth, DE, July 4th Celebration
Wilmington, DE, July 4th Jubilee

Grantsville, MD, Penn Alps Summerfest and Quilt Show
Largo, MD, Prince George's Community College Music Pro-
gram (every Thursday evening July-August)
St. Mary's City, MD, St. Mary's City Summer Festival
(through mid-August)
Cape May, NJ, Kiwanis Pancake Day

Winston-Salem, NC, Traditional Torchlight Procession, Old
Salem

Kempton Berks County, PA, Bavarian Summer Festival
Kutztown, PA, Kutztown Folk Festival
Philadelphia, PA, Independence Day Celebration and Free-
dom Week

Alexandria, VA, Custis-Fitzhugh Wedding Re-enactment
Charlottesville, VA, Annual Independence Day Celebration

Charlottesville, VA, Ash Lawn Summer Festival and Crafts Day (through August)
Charlottesville, VA, Annual Naturalization Ceremony
Chase City, VA, Freedom Day Celebration
Fairfax, VA, Fourth of July Celebration
Fredericksburg, VA, Fredericksburg Heritage Festival
Great Falls, VA, Colvin Run Mill Park—4th of July Celebration
New Market, VA, 19th Century Craft Days
Reston, VA, Annual Fireworks Display
Richmond, VA, Maymont—Old Time Fourth of July
Roanoke, VA, Miss Virginia Pageant
Staunton, VA, Happy Birthday USA

Athens, WV, Annual John Henry Folk Festival
Fayetteville, WV, July Jamboree

Middle

Clinton, MD, Civil War Encampment at Surratt House
Friendsville, MD, Annual Friendsville Fiddler's Contest
Lilypons, MD, Lotus Blossom Festival
North East, MD, North East Water Festival

Cape May, NJ, Marlin Tournament
Cape May, NJ, Promenade Art Show

Elizabeth City, NC, Pasquotank River Yacht Club Regatta
Linville, NC, Grandfather Mountain Highland Games and Gathering of Scottish Clans
Southern Pines, NC, Annual Black Cultural Arts Festival

Belle Grove, Middletown, VA, Annual Shenandoah Valley Farm Craft Days
Chippokes Plantation, Surry County, VA, Pork, Peanut and Pine Festival
Colonial Beach, VA, Annual Chicken Bar-B-Q
Mount Vernon, VA, Annual Music, Candlelight and Champagne, Woodlawn Plantation
Washington's Birthplace, VA, Encampment of the First Virginia Regiment

Late

Harrington, DE, Delaware State Fair
Rehoboth, DE, Combined Horse Show

Baltimore, MD, Hog Calling Contest
Big Pool, MD, Military Field Days

Cape May, NJ, Decoy and Woodcarving Show
Ocean City, NJ, Art Center Bake-off and Sale
Ocean City, NJ, Auction at Historical Museum

Abingdon, VA, The VA Highlands Festival
Alexandria, VA, Annual Virginia Scottish Games
Chincoteaque Island, VA, Pony Round-up (last two weeks)
Fredericksburg, VA, Annual Black Arts Festival
Orkey Springs, VA, Shenandoah Valley Music Festival
Stuarts Draft, VA, Annual Raft Race, Shenandoah Acres

AUGUST

Early

Brunswick, MD, Brunswick-Potomac River Festival
Cordova, MD, Old Saint Joseph's Jousting Tournament

Atlantic City, NJ, Art Show
Cape May, NJ, Baby Parade
Cape May, NJ, Queen Maysea Coronation
Ocean City, NJ, Boardwalk Art Show

Hershey, PA, Pennsylvania Dutch Days

Alexandria, VA, Annual Civil War Reenactment of the Battle of Ft. Stevens
Alexandria, VA, Annual Tavern Days
Orange, VA, Annual Orange Street Festival (first Saturday)
Statewide, VA, County Fairs held throughout the month

Middle

Rehoboth, DE, Annual Outdoor Fine Arts Show

Nanjemoy, MD, Old Durham Church Festival

Cape May, NJ, Peach Festival
Cape May, NJ, Tennis Ball

Winston-Salem, NC, Annual Piedmont/Triad Country Music Championships
Coatesville, PA, Annual Old Fiddler's Picnic at Hibernia Park
East Greenville, PA, Annual Goschenhoppen Folk Festival
Lancaster County, PA, Annual Old Threshermans Reunion

Colonial Beach, VA, Annual Boardwalk Art & Craft Show
Galax, VA, Old Fiddler's Convention
Leesburg, VA, August Court Days
Portsmouth, VA, Portsmouth Chamber Annual Seafood Festival
Roanoke, VA, Roanoke Valley Fair
Stuarts Draft, VA, Annual Sand Castle Contest

Richwood, WV, Cherry River Festival

Late

Wilmington, DE, City Fest

Cumberland, MD, C&O Canal Boat Festival
Port Republic, MD, Calvert County Jousting Tournament
Williamsport, MD, Williamsport C&O Canal Days

Cape May, NJ, Annual Clamshell Pitchup Tournament
Cape May, NJ, Jersey Cape Shell Club Show and Sale
Stone Harbor, NJ, Carver's show

Bethlehem, PA, Musikfest
Philadelphia, PA, Annual Folk Festival

Bristol, VA, Bristol International Raceway, Busch 500 Race
Crozet, VA, Albemarle County Fair
Middleburg, VA, Annual Wine Festival
Monterey, VA, Highland County Fair
Mt. Solon, VA, Annual Jousting Tournament

Augusta, WV, Hampshire County Fair
Beckley, WV, Appalachian Arts and Crafts Festival
Charles Town, WV, Jefferson County Fair
Elkins, WV, Augusta Festival
Lewisburg, WV, State Fair of West Virginia
Petersburg, WV, Tri-County Cooperative Fair

SEPTEMBER

Early

Arden, DE, Annual Arden Fair
Wilmington, DE, Brandywine Arts Festival

Columbia, MD, Maryland Renaissance Festival (weekends
    through September 30)
Crisfield, MD, National Hard Crab Derby and Fair
Deal Island, MD, Labor Day Skipjack Races
Greenbelt, MD, Greenbelt Labor Day Festival
Lilypons, MD, Koi Festival at the Lilypons Water Gardens

Chapel Hill, NC, North Carolina Botanical Garden Annual
    Open House

Brandywine Battlefield State Historical Park, PA, Reenactment
    of Battle of Brandywine
Chadds Ford, PA, Pennsylvania Crafts Fair Day
York, PA, York Interstate Fair

Belle Grove, Middletown, VA, Draft Horse Days
Richmond, VA, International Festival

Grafton, WV, WV Railroad Heritage Festival
Hamlin, WV, Lincoln County Tobacco Fair

Middle

Baltimore, MD, Defenders Day
Burkittsville, MD (Gathland State Park), Civil War Days
Chestertown, MD, Candlelight Walking Tour of Chestertown
Cumberland, MD, Jaycee Seafood Festival and Annual
    Motorama
Jefferson, MD, Civil War Days at Gathland State Park
Lexington Park, MD, Air Expo Open House and Air Show at
    the Naval Air Test Center
Towson, MD, Hampton Colonial Farm Day
Upper Marlboro, MD, St. Barnabas Church Crab Feast

Seaside Heights, NJ, Mardi Gras Boardwalk
Wharton State Forest, NJ, Historic Arts Festival

Linville, NC, Annual Masters of Hang Gliding Championships

Chadds Ford, PA, Chadds Ford Days (Traditional County
    Fair)
St. Helena, Montgomery County, PA, Annual Horse Show
    and County Fair

Chase City, VA, Bluegrass Festival
Edinburg, VA, Annual Shenandoah Vineyards Harvest Festival
Edinburg, VA, Edinburg Ole' Time Festival
Grundy, VA, Kid's Day
Lorton, VA, The Annual Gunston Hall Car Show
Richlands, VA, Richlands Coal Show
Richmond, VA, Annual Civil War Re-enactment
Winchester, VA, Apple Harvest Arts & Crafts Festival

Davis, WV, Annual Milk & Honey 10K Run
Franklin, WV, Treasure Mountain Festival
Harpers Ferry, WV, Harpers Ferry Annual Civil War Show
Shepherdstown, WV, Shepherdstown Harvest Fair and
    Octoberfest
Snowshoe, WV, Snowshoe Resort Bicycle Race

Late

Germantown, MD, Indian Summer Celebration
Havre de Grace, MD, Fall Food Festival at Steppingstone
    Museum

New Market, MD, New Market Days
Ocean City, MD, Sunfest
Snow Hill, MD, Fall Festival at Furnacetown
Westminister, MD, Westminister Fall Fest

Atlantic City, NJ, Miss America Pageant

Beaufort, NC, Annual Traditional Wooden Boat Show

Elverson, Chester County, PA, Annual Harvest Festival
Mount Hope, Lancaster County, PA, Renaissance Faire

Chilhowie, VA, Chilhowie Community Apple Festival
Emporia, VA, Annual Peanut Festival
Great Falls, VA, Colvin Run Mill Park—Lumberjack Day
Norfolk, VA, Annual Elizabeth River Blues Festival
Richmond, VA, State Fair of Virginia (through first week in
    October)
Salem, VA, Annual Art in the Alley
Virginia Beach, VA, Annual VA Beach Neptune Festival

Charles Town, WV, Annual Fall Mountain Heritage Arts &
    Crafts Festival
Kingwood, WV, Preston County Buckwheat Festival

OCTOBER

Early

Bethany-Fenwick Island, DE, Annual Surf Fishing Tournament
Bethel, DE, Heritage Day

Brandywine, MD, Southern Maryland Farm Festival and
    Craft Fair
Columbia, MD, Maryland State Championship Joust
Frederick, MD, Annual Ethnic Festival
Frederick, MD, Oktoberfest
Frederick, MD, Rose Hill Manor Fall Festival
Gaithersburg, MD, Oktoberfest
Grantsville, MD, Springs Folk Festival
Oakland, MD, Annual Garrett County Autumn Glory Festival
Ocean City, MD, Ocean City Convention Hall Sat. Night Big
    Band Dances (through April)
Village of Springs, MD, Springs Folk Festival

Nags Head, NC, Annual Nags Head Surf Fishing Tournament
Outer Banks, NC, Annual North Carolina Waterfowl Weekend
Outer Banks, NC, Annual Outer Banks Marsh and Sea Fest
Raleigh, NC, Oktoberfest
Spring Hope, NC, National Pumpkin Festival

Gettysburg, PA, Annual Apple Harvest Festival
Harrisburg, PA, Pennsylvania National Horse Show

Charlottesville, VA, Bacchanalian Feast & Monticello Wine
   Festival
Charlottesville, VA, Court Days in Old Charlottesville
Clifford, VA, Sorghum Festival
Cobham (Historic Castle Hill), VA, Annual Castle Hill An-
   tique Show
Danville, VA, Danville Harvest Jubilee
Fairfax, VA, Annual Fall Street Festival
Fairfax, VA, Fall Festival
Front Royal, VA, Festival of Leaves
Luray, VA, Page County Heritage Festival
Madison Heights, VA, Amherst County Apple Harvest Arts
   and Crafts Festival
Newbern, VA, Newbern Fall Festival
Petersburg, VA, Petersburg Nostalgiafest
Roanoke, VA, Harvest Festival and Fiddlers Convention
Strasburg, VA, Octoberfest
Waterford, VA, Waterford Homes Tour and Craft Exhibit
Waynesboro, VA, Fall Foliage Festival

Berkeley Springs, WV, Apple Butter Festival
Burlington, WV, Old Fashioned Apple Harvest Festival
Elkins, WV, Mountain State Forest Festival

Middle

Fair Hill, MD, Apple Butter Festival
Leonardtown, MD, St. Mary's County Oyster Festival &
   National Oyster Shucking Championships
Mt. Airy, MD, Berrywine Plantations, October Wine Festival
Princess Anne, MD, Olde Princess Anne Days
Solomons, MD, Patuxent River Appreciation Days
Westminster, MD, Fall Harvest Days

Cape May, NJ, Victorian Weekend

Raleigh, NC, North Carolina State Fair

Aldie, VA, Aldie Harvest Festival
Chantilly, VA, Sully Plantation—Harvest Days
Charlottesville, VA, Annual Kruger Farms Apple Classic
   Bicycle Race
Fredericksburg, VA, Annual Creative Stitchery Exhibit
Fredericksburg, VA, Octoberfest
Richmond, VA, Annual National Tobacco Festival
Roanoke, VA, Annual Attic Fair
Yorktown, VA, Yorktown Day

Late

Dover, DE, Delaware Agricultural Museum Fall Harvest Festival

Annapolis, MD, Heritage Weekend
Bethesda, MD, Halloween Happening
Sandy Point State Park, MD, Maryland's Chesapeake Appreciation Days

Chester County, PA, Annual Chester County Day
York, PA, Annual Halloween Parade

Great Falls, VA, Colvin Run Mill Park, All Hallows Eve

Davis, WV, Canaan Valley Autumn Fling for Persons Over 50 Years Old
Martinsburg, WV, Mountain State Apple Harvest Festival
Mathias, WV, West Virginia Turkey Festival
Shepherdstown, WV, Halloween Party

NOVEMBER

Early

Baltimore, MD, Athenian Agora XI Greek Festival
Baltimore, MD, Shrine Circus

Newport, NC, Annual Mill Creek Oyster Festival

Kennett Square, PA, Chrysanthemum Festival at Longwood Gardens
Berkeley Plantation, VA, Virginia Thanksgiving Festival
Cobham, VA, Castle Hill—Annual Quilt Show
Fredericksburg, VA, Annual Kenmore Needlework Exhibit
Roanoke, VA, Annual Holiday House
Urbana, VA, Oyster Festival (first weekend)
Williambsurg, VA, Public Times and Fair

Middle

Easton, MD, Waterfowl Festival
Gaithersburg, MD, Sugarloaf Autumn Crafts Festival

Greenville, NC, Southern Flue-Cured Tobacco Festival

Gettysburg, PA, Annual Celebration of Lincoln's Gettysburg Address

Alexandria, VA, Commemoration of George Washington's Visit

Arlington, VA, Veteran's Day Service At Arlington Cemetery

Late

Annapolis, MD, Christmas Parade
Baltimore, MD, Maryland All American Square Dance Festival
Ocean City, MD, Turkeytime Bluegrass Festival

Kennett Square, PA, Thanksgiving Evening Conservatory, Longwood Gardens
Philadelphia, PA, Thanksgiving Day Parade

Charlottesville, VA, Annual Barracks Road Christmas Parade
Charlottesville, VA, Thanksgiving Hunt Weekend
Mt. Vernon, VA, Christmas Flower Show
Roanoke, VA, Christmas Fantasyland (through December 24)

Snowshoe, WV, Ski Season Opening

DECEMBER

Early

Odessa, DE, Christmas in Odessa

Annapolis, MD, "State House by Candlelight"
Ellicott City, MD, Ellicott City Open House
Monkton, MD, Christmas Show At Ladew Topiary Gardens and House
St. Mary's City, MD, Madrigal Dinners Medieval Feast
Vansville, MD, Vansville Yule Log Festival

Alexandria, VA, Annual Scottish Christmas Walk
Alexandria, VA, Old Town Christmas Candlelight Tour
Charlottesville, VA, Annual Christmas Candlelight Carol Sing
Fredericksburg, VA, Christmas Candlelight Weekend
Lexington, VA, Jackson House Victorian Candlelight Tours
Luray, VA, Christmas In Luray
Mount Vernon, VA, Carols By Candlelight At Woodlawn Plantation
Roanoke, VA, Annual Christmas Parade
Salem, VA, Annual Salem Christmas Parade
Vinton, VA, Annual Christmas Parade

Bolivar, WV, West Virginia Country Christmas
Harpers Ferry, WV, Annual Old Tyme Christmas

Middle

Annapolis, MD, Candlelight Pub Crawl
Edgewater, MD, Christmas Candlelight Tour
Gaithersburg, MD, Sugarloaf Winter Crafts Festival
Wheaton, MD, Brookside Gardens Christmas Show

Bath, Edenton, Halifax, Hope Plantation, Murfreesboro,
    Somerset Place, Tarboro, NC, Christmas Tours
Kitty Hawk, NC, Annual Anniversary Celebration of First
    Flight by the Wright Brothers

Brookneal, VA, Christmas By Candlelight
Chantilly, VA, Sully Plantation—Candlelight Tours at Sully
Charlottesville, VA, Annual Yuletide Traditions (through
    end of December)
Fredericksburg, VA, Anniversary of the Battle of Fred-
    ericksburg
Lynchburg, VA, Diamond Hill Christmas Candlelight Tour
Roanoke, VA, Annual Singing Christmas Tree
Stratford, VA, Stratford's Special Christmas Celebration

Late

Baltimore, MD, New Year's Eve Celebration

Cape May, NJ, Christmas House Tour

Washington Crossing, PA, Re-enactment of Washington Cross-
    ing the Delaware

Alexandria, VA, Hogmanay (Scottish New Year's Eve)
Charlottesville, VA, Annual Merrie Olde England Christmas
    Festival
Staunton, VA, Open House on Woodrow Wilson's Birthday

HOTLINES

The Hotline section is a random selection of information sources that may trigger ideas on great ways to spend an afternoon, a day, or weekend, if other suggestions don't inspire you. Some of the hotlines are recordings of current events; others are direct home or office numbers where you can inquire about area or club activities. Be aware, therefore, that some numbers won't answer on weekends. Those numbers with asterisks (*) are tape recordings of general information. (Please note that extended-calling-area phone numbers allow metropolitan residents to call outlying areas without being charged for long distance. Therefore, if you get a recording asking you to recheck the number you have dialed, it could mean that you don't need to use the area code.) In addition, the (800) area code numbers are toll free.

Alexandria, VA, Tourist Council	(703) 838-4200
Allegany County, MD, Parks	(301) 759-6440
Allegany County, MD, Tourism	(301) 777-5905
Annapolis, MD, Sailing School	(800) 638-9192
Annapolis, MD, Tourism	(301) 263-7940
Anne Arundel County, MD, Community Affairs	(301) 224-1122
Baltimore County Office of Tourism	(301) 494-3648
Baltimore Ski Club	(301) 825-7669
Bicycling in DC area	(202) 439-2453*
Bicycling in Maryland	(301) 333-1663*
Boating information in Maryland	(301) 267-7740
Brandywine Valley, PA, Information	(215) 431-6365
	(215) 565-3679
Bucks County Historical-Tourist Commission	(215) 345-4552
Busch Gardens, VA	(804) 253-3350
Cape May, NJ, Chamber of Commerce	(609) 884-5508
Cape May, NJ, Welcome Center	(609) 884-3323

Carroll County, MD, Tourism	(301) 848-4500
Charles County, MD, Parks & Recreation	(301) 934-9305
Charles County, MD, Tourism	(301) 645-0580
Charlottesville, VA, Visitors Bureau	(804) 293-6789
Chincoteague, VA, Chamber of Commerce	(804) 336-6161
Cloisters Children's Museum	(301) 823-2550
Delaware Tourism Office (DE)	(800) 282-8667
(out of state)	(800) 441-8846
Dial-a-Phenomenon (Smithsonian Institution)	(202) 357-2000

> Tape of movements of planets, constellations, stars, and comets for stargazers in the mid-Atlantic area

Dorchester County, MD, Tourism	(301) 228-3234
Dover, DE, Visitor Center	(302) 737-4059
Fairfax County, VA, Park Authority	(703) 941-5000
Fairfax County, VA, Tourism	(703) 790-0600
Frederick County, MD, Tourism and Parks	(301) 663-8687
Fredericksburg, VA, Visitor Center	(703) 373-1776
Gaithersburg, MD, Community Center	(301) 258-6366
Garrett County, MD, Tourism	(301) 334-1948
Gettysburg, PA, Travel Council	(717) 334-6274
Hampton, VA, Visitors Center	(804) 727-6108
"Hatfields & McCoys" outdoor drama (WV)	(800) 642-2766
at Grandview State Park, WV	(304) 253-8313
Hersheypark, PA (current activities)	(717) 534-3900
(group rates)	(717) 534-3916
(Hersheypark Arena)	(717) 534-3911
Howard County, MD, Parks	(301) 992-2483
Howard County, MD, Tourism	(301) 730-7817
Jefferson County, WV, Chamber of Commerce	(304) 725-5514
Kings Dominion, VA (VA)	(800) 552-9912
(out of state)	(800) 876-5561
Lexington, VA, Visitors Center	(703) 463-3777
Loudoun County, VA, Tourism	(703) 777-0519
Maryland Information for the Handicapped	(301) 383-6523

Maryland Parks activities & campsite availability	(301) 768-0895
Maryland State Parks cabin rentals	(301) 974-3771
Maryland Tourism (MD)	(800) 331-1750
	(DC) 565-0450
(TTY for deaf)	(301) 269-2609
Maryland, Tourism Council of the Upper Chesapeake	(301) 758-2300
Montgomery County, MD, Parks	(301) 468-4022*
	(301) 495-2525
Montgomery County, MD, Tourism	(301) 588-8687
Mystic Whaler Chesapeake Bay cruises	(800) 243-0416
New Jersey Audubon birdwatching	(201) 766-2661*
New Jersey Div. of Travel and Tourism	(800) 837-7397
Norfolk, VA, Visitors Bureau	(804) 441-5266
Outer Banks, NC, Chamber of Commerce	(919) 441-8144
Pennsylvania State Parks	(717) 787-8800
Pennsylvania State Travel	(800) 847-4872
Petersburg, VA, Information	(804) 733-2400
Potomac Appalachian Trail Club	(202) 638-5306*
Potomac Highlands (WV) Convention and Visitors Bureau	(304) 636-8400
Prince George's, MD, Parks	(301) 699-2414*
Prince George's, MD, Tourism	(301) 927-0700
Queen Anne's County, MD, Tourism	(301) 758-0322
Richmond Ski Club	(804) 741-3866
Rockville, MD, Recreation Dept.	(301) 424-8000 x330
Shenandoah Valley, VA, Information	(703) 740-3132
Ski Club of Washington, DC	(703) 536-8273*
Smithsonian Institution—Resident Associate Program	(202) 357-3030
Southern Delaware Tourism	(800) 345-4444
	(302) 422-3301
Takoma Park, MD, Recreation	(301) 270-4048
Talbot County, MD, Chamber of Commerce	(301) 822-4606
University of Maryland activities	(301) 454-3311

Virginia Beach, VA, Information	(800) 446-8038
	(804) 425-7511
Virginia Peninsula Tourism Council	(outside VA) (800) 237-5606
	(Newport News) (800) 558-1818
Virginia Ski Club	(804) 270-7023
Virginia State Division of Tourism	(804) 786-4484
	(DC) (202) 293-5350
Virginia State Parks, Campsite Reservations	(804) 786-1712
Washington County, MD, Tourism and Recreation	(301) 791-3130
	(301) 797-8800*
Weather	
Baltimore	(301) 936-1212*
DC & vicinity	(202) 936-1212*
Eastern Cities	(301) 899-3244*
Richmond	(804) 268-1212*
Tides, conditions of rivers in mid-Atlantic states, Chesapeake Bay, Baltimore Harbor	(301) 899-3210*
West Virginia, New River Travel Council	(304) 252-2244
West Virginia Parks & Forest Reservations and Information	(800) 225-5982
West Virginia Tourism	(800) 225-5982
	(304) 348-2286
Wicomico County, MD, Tourism	(301) 749-8687*
Wild World	(301) 249-1500
Williamsburg Accommodations	(out of state) (800) 446-9244
	(VA) (800) 582-8977
Williamsburg, VA, Visitor Center	(804) 229-1000
Wilmington, DE, Tourism	(800) 422-1181
Winchester-Frederick County, VA, Visitor Center	(703) 662-4118
Wise County, VA, Tourism	(703) 679-0961
Wisp, MD, Ski Conditions	(301) 387-5503*
	(Baltimore) 768-0895*
Worcester County, MD, Tourism	(301) 289-8181

INFORMATION SOURCES INDEX

Throughout the pages of the *Weekender's Guide* you will find dozens of tourist councils, information centers, chambers of commerce, and visitors centers whose purpose it is to help you plan a memorable weekend. Contact them in advance (consult pages listed below for exact address and telephone number), and they will happily supply you with maps, brochures, and lodging and restaurant information.